Monographs in Visual Communications

Property of :-
Robin Ezra

Springer

Berlin
Heidelberg
New York
Barcelona
Budapest
Hong Kong
London
Milan
Paris
Santa Clara
Singapore
Tokyo

Les Piegl
Wayne Tiller

The *NURBS* Book

Second Edition
with 334 Figures in 578 Parts

Springer

Prof. Dr. Les Piegl
University of South Florida
Department of Computer Science and Engineering
Fowler Avenue, ENG 118
Tampa, FL 33620-5399, USA

Dr. Wayne Tiller
GeomWare, Inc.
3036 Ridgetop Road
Tyler, TX 75703-8906, USA

ISBN 3-540-61545-8 2nd ed. Springer-Verlag Berlin Heidelberg New York
ISBN 3-540-55069-0 1st ed. Springer-Verlag Berlin Heidelberg New York

Cip data applied for
Die Deutsche Bibliothek - CIP-Einheitsaufnahme
Piegl, Les: The NURBS book / Les Piegl ; Wayne Tiller. - 2. ed. -
Berlin ; Heidelberg ; New York ; Barcelona ; Budapest ; Hong Kong ; London ;
Milan ; Paris ; Tokyo : Springer, 1997
(Monographs in visual communications)
ISBN 3-540-61545-8
NE: Tiller, Wayne

Printed in Germany

Cover design: Design & Production, Heidelberg
Typesetting: Nancy A. Rogers, NAR Assoc., Annapolis, MD, using $\TeX$
SPIN:10569543 33/3020-5 4 3 2 1 - Printed on acid-free paper

To the memory of my mother Anna, and to my father János

L.P.

To my grandmother, Fern Melrose Bost, and to the memories of my grandparents, James Raney Bost, Pearl Weeks Tiller, and Albert Carroll Tiller

W.T.

FOREWORD

Until recently B-spline curves and surfaces (NURBS) were principally of interest to the computer aided design community, where they have become the standard for curve and surface description. Today we are seeing expanded use of NURBS in modeling objects for the visual arts, including the film and entertainment industries, art, and sculpture. NURBS are now also being used for modeling scenes for virtual reality applications. These applications are expected to increase. Consequently, it is quite appropriate for *The NURBS Book* to be part of the *Monographs in Visual Communication* Series.

B-spline curves and surfaces have been an enduring element throughout my professional life. The first edition of *Mathematical Elements for Computer Graphics*, published in 1972, was the first computer aided design/interactive computer graphics textbook to contain material on B-splines. That material was obtained through the good graces of Bill Gordon and Louie Knapp while they were at Syracuse University. A paper of mine, presented during the Summer of 1977 at a Society of Naval Architects and Marine Engineers meeting on computer aided ship surface design, was arguably the first to examine the use of B-spline curves for ship design.

For many, B-splines, rational B-splines, and NURBS have been a bit mysterious. Consequently, for the last several years a thorough, detailed, clearly written, and easily understood book on B-splines and rational B-splines has been needed. Thus, it was with considerable anticipation that I awaited Les Piegl and Wayne Tiller's book. I was not disappointed: They have elegantly and fully satisfied that need with *The NURBS Book*. In developing the material for the book, they draw from their considerable academic and industrial experience with NURBS to present this rather complex subject in a straightforward manner: Their presentation style is clear and detailed. The necessary mathematics is presented with considerable attention to detail and more than adequate rigor. The algorithms (many of which are in C-like pseudocode) are well thought out and meticulously prepared. In the interests of accuracy, each and every illustration in the book was computer generated – a monumental task. They have created a book of lasting value.

B-spline curves and surfaces grew out of the pioneering work of Pierre Bézier in the early 1970s. Perhaps one can consider B-spline curves and surfaces the children of Bézier curves and surfaces, and nonuniform rational B-splines, or NURBS, the grandchildren. The timing is about right; they have certainly come of age.

Finally, it is only appropriate to acknowledge my pleasure in working with both Les Piegl and Wayne Tiller to bring this project to fruition.

David F. Rogers
Series Editor
Monographs in Visual Communication

PREFACE

Non-Uniform **R**ational **B**-**S**plines, commonly referred to as **NURBS**, have become the de facto industry standard for the representation, design, and data exchange of geometric information processed by computers. Many national and international standards, e.g., IGES, STEP, and PHIGS, recognize NURBS as powerful tools for geometric design. The enormous success behind NURBS is largely due to the fact that

- NURBS provide a unified mathematical basis for representing both analytic shapes, such as conic sections and quadric surfaces, as well as free-form entities, such as car bodies and ship hulls;
- designing with NURBS is intuitive; almost every tool and algorithm has an easy-to-understand geometric interpretation;
- NURBS algorithms are fast and numerically stable;
- NURBS curves and surfaces are invariant under common geometric transformations, such as translation, rotation, parallel and perspective projections;
- NURBS are generalizations of nonrational B-splines and rational and nonrational Bézier curves and surfaces.

The excellent mathematical and algorithmic properties, combined with successful industrial applications, have contributed to the enormous popularity of NURBS. NURBS play a role in the CAD/CAM/CAE world similar to that of the English language in science and business: "Want to talk business? Learn to talk NURBS".

The purpose of this book is basically twofold: to fill a large gap in the literature that has existed since the early seventies, and to provide a comprehensive reference on all aspects of NURBS. The literature on NURBS is sparse and scattered, and the available papers deal mainly with the mathematics of splines, which is fairly complex and requires a detailed understanding of spline theory. This book is aimed at the average engineer who has a solid background in elementary college mathematics and computing. No doctoral degree is required to understand the concepts and to implement the literally hundreds of algorithms that are introduced.

During the four years of writing this book, we have

- surveyed the available literature and presented important results;
- continued our research on NURBS and included the latest developments; in fact, about half of the book contains new material developed in the last few years;
- developed a comprehensive NURBS library, called *Nlib V1.0, V2.0*. This library is the result of over 20 man-years of experience in NURBS research and development, and it combines new and well-tried software practices applied in previous systems that we designed;

- tested every single formula and algorithm, and presented graphical illustrations precisely computed using the routines of *Nlib*. **This book does not contain any hand-drawn figures; each figure is precisely computed and hence is accurate**.

We are pleased to present all of the accomplishments to the reader: (1) the book as a comprehensive reference, (2) *Nlib* source code (to order please see page 639 of this volume), and (3) the illustrations to instructors who adopt the book to teach a course on NURBS. In order for the reader to appreciate the enormous amount of work that went into this reference book, we present some data. To generate the graphical illustrations and to build *Nlib*, we wrote exactly (not counting the hundreds of test programs)

- **1,524** programs, that required
- **15,001,600** bytes of storage, which is roughly equivalent to
- **350,000** lines of code.

It was no picnic!

Some years ago a few researchers joked about NURBS, saying that the acronym really stands for **N**obody **U**nderstands **R**ational **B**-**S**plines. We admit that our colleagues were right. In the last four years, we were largely influenced by this interpretation and tried to present the material in the book in an intuitive manner. We hope that this helps change the acronym NURBS to EURBS, that is, **E**verybody **U**nderstands **R**ational **B**-**S**plines. We welcome the reader's opinion on our job and suggestions on possible improvements.

It is our pleasure to acknowledge the help and support of many people and organizations. First and foremost, we are grateful to our spouses, Karen Piegl and LaVella Tiller, for their patience, support, and love. We owe special thanks to Nancy Rogers of NAR Associates for the beautiful typesetting job, and David Rogers for the editorial and technical discussions that led to many improvements in the manuscript. We also thank Jim Oliver and Tim Strotman for the many suggestions and technical correspondence that helped shape this book into its current form. Tiller also thanks the many past and present colleagues in industry who over the years contributed inspiring discussions, valuable insights, support, and collegial companionship: They know who they are. Piegl's research was supported in part by the National Science Foundation under grant CCR-9217768 awarded to the University of South Florida, and by various grants from the Florida High Technology and Industry Council.

March 1995

Les Piegl
Wayne Tiller

It is less than a year since the first printing of *The NURBS Book*. Due to its popularity, Springer-Verlag decided to publish a soft cover edition of the book. Apart from being significantly more affordable, the second printing corrects a number of errors; redesigns Algorithm `A3.5` to eliminate the use of a local array; and fixes minor bugs in the knot insertion algorithms, `A5.1` and `A5.3`, as well the degree elevation algorithm, `A5.9`. Apart from these corrections, this printing is identical to the first printing.

July 1996

Les Piegl
Wayne Tiller

CONTENTS

Chapter Five ' Fundamental Geometric Algorithms

Chapter Six Advanced Geometric Algorithms

Chapter Seven Conics and Circles

Chapter Eight Construction of Common Surfaces

Chapter Nine Curve and Surface Fitting

CHAPTER

ONE

Curve and Surface Basics

1.1 Implicit and Parametric Forms

The two most common methods of representing curves and surfaces in geometric modeling are implicit equations and parametric functions.

The implicit equation of a curve lying in the xy plane has the form $f(x,y) = 0$. This equation describes an implicit relationship between the x and y coordinates of the points lying on the curve. For a given curve the equation is unique up to a multiplicative constant. An example is the circle of unit radius centered at the origin, specified by the equation $f(x,y) = x^2 + y^2 - 1 = 0$ (Figure 1.1).

In parametric form, each of the coordinates of a point on the curve is represented separately as an explicit function of an independent parameter

$$\mathbf{C}(u) = \big(x(u), y(u)\big) \qquad a \le u \le b$$

Thus, $\mathbf{C}(u)$ is a vector-valued function of the independent variable, u. Although the interval $[a,b]$ is arbitrary, it is usually normalized to $[0,1]$. The first quadrant of the circle shown in Figure 1.1 is defined by the parametric functions

$$\begin{aligned} x(u) &= \cos(u) \\ y(u) &= \sin(u) \qquad 0 \le u \le \frac{\pi}{2} \end{aligned} \tag{1.1}$$

Setting $t = \tan(u/2)$, one can derive the alternate representation

$$\begin{aligned} x(t) &= \frac{1-t^2}{1+t^2} \\ y(t) &= \frac{2t}{1+t^2} \qquad 0 \le t \le 1 \end{aligned} \tag{1.2}$$

Thus, the parametric representation of a curve is not unique.

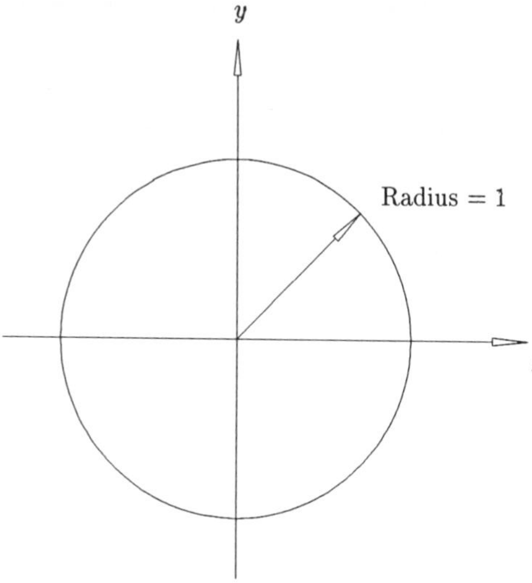

Figure 1.1. A circle of radius 1, centered at the origin.

It is instructive to think of $\mathbf{C}(u) = \big(x(u), y(u)\big)$ as the path traced out by a particle as a function of time; u is the time variable, and $[a,b]$ is the time interval. The first and second derivatives of $\mathbf{C}(u)$ are the velocity and acceleration of the particle, respectively. Differentiating Eqs. (1.1) and (1.2) once yields the velocity functions

$$\mathbf{C}'(u) = \big(x'(u), y'(u)\big) = \big(-\sin(u), \cos(u)\big)$$

$$\mathbf{C}'(t) = \big(x'(t), y'(t)\big) = \left(\frac{-4t}{(1+t^2)^2}, \frac{2(1-t^2)}{(1+t^2)^2}\right)$$

Notice that the magnitude of the velocity vector, $\mathbf{C}'(u)$, is a constant

$$|\mathbf{C}'(u)| = \sqrt{\sin^2(u) + \cos^2(u)} = 1$$

i.e., the direction of the particle is changing with time, but its speed is constant. This is referred to as a *uniform parameterization*. Substituting $t = 0$ and $t = 1$ into $\mathbf{C}'(t)$ yields $\mathbf{C}'(0) = (0,2)$ and $\mathbf{C}'(1) = (-1,0)$, i.e., the particle's starting speed is twice its ending speed (Figure 1.2).

A surface is defined by an implicit equation of the form $f(x,y,z) = 0$. An example is the sphere of unit radius centered at the origin, shown in Figure 1.3 and specified by the equation $x^2 + y^2 + z^2 - 1 = 0$. A parametric representation (not unique) of the same sphere is given by $\mathbf{S}(u,v) = \big(x(u,v), y(u,v), z(u,v)\big)$, where

$$\begin{aligned} x(u,v) &= \sin(u)\cos(v) \\ y(u,v) &= \sin(u)\sin(v) \\ z(u,v) &= \cos(u) \qquad 0 \le u \le \pi, \; 0 \le v \le 2\pi \end{aligned} \tag{1.3}$$

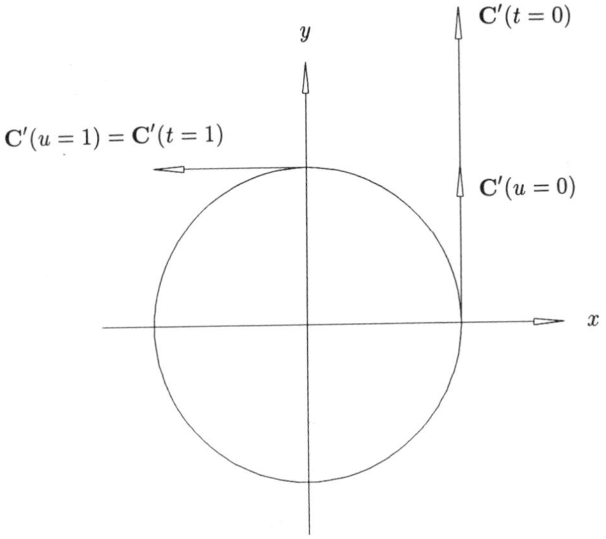

Figure 1.2. Velocity vectors $\mathbf{C}'(u)$ and $\mathbf{C}'(t)$ at $u, t = 0$, and 1.

Notice that two parameters are required to define a surface. Holding u fixed and varying v generates the latitudinal lines of the sphere; holding v fixed and varying u generates the longitudinal lines.

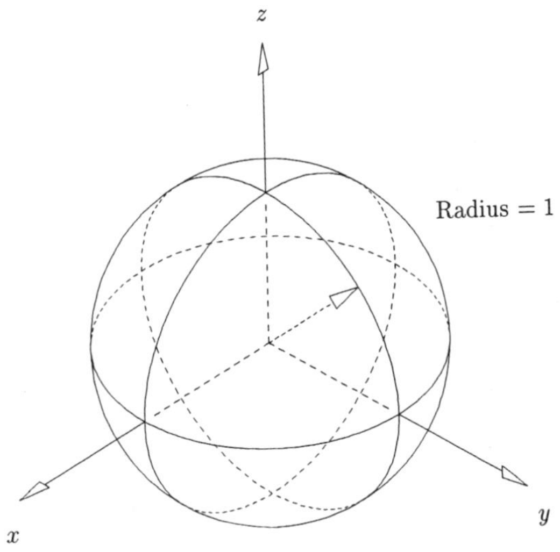

Figure 1.3. A sphere of radius 1, centered at the origin.

Denote the partial derivatives of $\mathbf{S}(u,v)$ by $\mathbf{S}_u(u,v) = (x_u(u,v), y_u(u,v), z_u(u,v))$ and $\mathbf{S}_v(u,v) = (x_v(u,v), y_v(u,v), z_v(u,v))$, i.e., the velocities along latitudinal and longitudinal lines. At any point on the surface where the vector cross product $\mathbf{S}_u \times \mathbf{S}_v$ does not vanish, the unit normal vector, $\mathbf{N}$, is given by (Figure 1.4)

$$\mathbf{N} = \frac{\mathbf{S}_u \times \mathbf{S}_v}{|\mathbf{S}_u \times \mathbf{S}_v|} \tag{1.4}$$

The existence of a normal vector at a point, and the corresponding tangent plane, is a geometric property of the surface independent of the parameterization. Different parameterizations give different partial derivatives, but Eq. (1.4) always yields $\mathbf{N}$ provided the denominator does not vanish. From Eq. (1.3) it can be seen that for all v, $0 \le v \le 2\pi$, $\mathbf{S}_v(0,v) = \mathbf{S}_v(\pi,v) = 0$, that is, $\mathbf{S}_v$ vanishes at the north and south poles of the sphere. Clearly, normal vectors do exist at the two poles, but under this parameterization Eq. (1.4) cannot be used to compute them.

Of the implicit and parametric forms, it is difficult to maintain that one is always more appropriate than the other. Both have their advantages and disadvantages. Successful geometric modeling is done using both techniques. A comparison of the two methods follows:

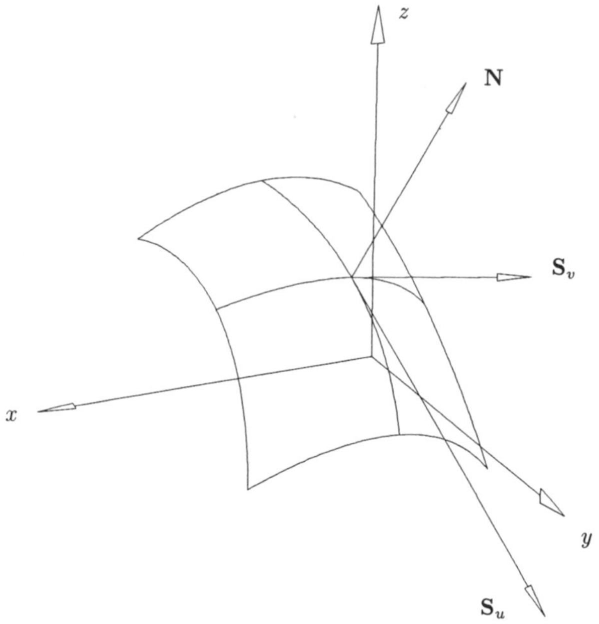

Figure 1.4. Partial derivative and unit normal vectors of $\mathbf{S}(u,v)$.

- By adding a z coordinate, the parametric method is easily extended to represent arbitrary curves in three-dimensional space, $\mathbf{C}(u) = \big(x(u), y(u), z(u)\big)$; the implicit form only specifies curves in the xy (or xz or yz) plane;
- It is cumbersome to represent bounded curve segments (or surface patches) with the implicit form. However, boundedness is built into the parametric form through the bounds on the parameter interval. On the other hand, unbounded geometry (e.g., a simple straight line given by $f(x, y) = ax + by + c = 0$) is difficult to implement using parametric geometry;
- Parametric curves possess a natural direction of traversal $\big($from $\mathbf{C}(a)$ to $\mathbf{C}(b)$ if $a \le u \le b\big)$; implicit curves do not. Hence, it is easy to generate ordered sequences of points along a parametric curve. A similar statement holds for generating meshes of points on surfaces;
- The parametric form is more natural for designing and representing shape in a computer. The coefficients of many parametric functions, e.g., Bézier and B-spline, possess considerable geometric significance. This translates into intuitive design methods and numerically stable algorithms with a distinctly geometric flavor;
- The complexity of many geometric operations and manipulations depends greatly on the method of representation. Two classic examples are:
  - compute a point on a curve or surface – difficult in the implicit form;
  - given a point, determine if it is on the curve or surface – difficult in the parametric form;
- In the parametric form, one must sometimes deal with parametric anomalies which are unrelated to true geometry. An example of this is the unit sphere (see Eq.[1.3]). The poles are parametric critical points which are algorithmically difficult, but geometrically the poles are no different than any other point on the sphere.

We are concerned almost exclusively with parametric forms in the remainder of this book. More details on implicit and parameteric forms can be found in standard texts $\big($[Faux81; Mort85; Hoff89; Beac91]$\big)$.

1.2 Power Basis Form of a Curve

Clearly, by allowing the coordinate functions $x(u)$, $y(u)$, and $z(u)$ to be arbitrary, we obtain a great variety of curves. However, there are trade-offs when implementing a geometric modeling system. The ideal situation is to restrict ourselves to a class of functions which

- are capable of precisely representing all the curves the users of the system need;
- are easily, efficiently, and accurately processed in a computer, in particular:
  - the computation of points and derivatives on the curves is efficient;

   - numerical processing of the functions is relatively insensitive to floating point round-off error;
   - the functions require little memory for storage;
- are simple and mathematically well understood.

A widely used class of functions is the polynomials. Although they satisfy the last two criteria in this list, there are a number of important curve (and surface) types which cannot be precisely represented using polynomials; these curves must be approximated in systems using polynomials. In this section and the next, we study two common methods of expressing polynomial functions, power basis and Bézier. Although mathematically equivalent, we will see that the Bézier method is far better suited to representing and manipulating shape in a computer.

An nth-degree power basis curve is given by

$$\mathbf{C}(u) = \bigl(x(u), y(u), z(u)\bigr) = \sum_{i=0}^{n} \mathbf{a}_i u^i \qquad 0 \le u \le 1 \tag{1.5}$$

The $\mathbf{a}_i = (x_i, y_i, z_i)$ are vectors, hence

$$x(u) = \sum_{i=0}^{n} x_i u^i \quad y(u) = \sum_{i=0}^{n} y_i u^i \quad z(u) = \sum_{i=0}^{n} z_i u^i$$

In matrix form Eq. (1.5) is

$$\mathbf{C}(u) = [\mathbf{a}_0 \quad \mathbf{a}_1 \quad \cdots \quad \mathbf{a}_n] \begin{bmatrix} 1 \\ u \\ \vdots \\ u^n \end{bmatrix} = [\mathbf{a}_i]^T [u^i] \tag{1.6}$$

(We write a row vector as the transpose of a column vector.)

Differentiating Eq. (1.5) yields

$$\mathbf{a}_i = \frac{\mathbf{C}^{(i)}(u)|_{u=0}}{i!}$$

where $\mathbf{C}^{(i)}(u)|_{u=0}$ is the ith derivative of $\mathbf{C}(u)$ at $u = 0$. The $n+1$ functions, $\{u^i\}$, are called the basis (or blending) functions, and the $\{\mathbf{a}_i\}$ the coefficients of the power basis representation.

Given u_0, the point $\mathbf{C}(u_0)$ on a power basis curve is most efficiently computed using Horner's method

- for degree $= 1 :\ \mathbf{C}(u_0) = \mathbf{a}_1 u_0 + \mathbf{a}_0$
- degree $= 2 :\ \mathbf{C}(u_0) = (\mathbf{a}_2 u_0 + \mathbf{a}_1)\, u_0 + \mathbf{a}_0$
- $\vdots$
- degree $=$ n $:\ \mathbf{C}(u_0) = \bigl((\cdots(\mathbf{a}_n u_0 + \mathbf{a}_{n-1})\, u_0 + \mathbf{a}_{n-2}\bigr)\, u_0 + \cdots + \mathbf{a}_0$

The general algorithm is

```
ALGORITHM A1.1
  Horner1(a,n,u0,C)
    { /*  Compute point on power basis curve.  */
      /*  Input:  a,n,u0  */
      /*  Output: C  */
    C = a[n];
    for (i=n-1; i>=0; i--)
      C = C*u0 + a[i];
    }
```

Examples

Ex1.1 $n = 1$. $\mathbf{C}(u) = \mathbf{a}_0 + \mathbf{a}_1 u$, $0 \le u \le 1$, is a straight line segment between the points $\mathbf{a}_0$ and $\mathbf{a}_0 + \mathbf{a}_1$ (Figure 1.5). The constant $\mathbf{C}'(u) = \mathbf{a}_1$ gives the direction of the line.

Ex1.2 $n = 2$. In general, $\mathbf{C}(u) = \mathbf{a}_0 + \mathbf{a}_1 u + \mathbf{a}_2 u^2$, $0 \le u \le 1$, is a parabolic arc between the points $\mathbf{a}_0$ and $\mathbf{a}_0 + \mathbf{a}_1 + \mathbf{a}_2$ (Figure 1.6). This is shown by

1. transforming $\mathbf{C}(u)$ into the xy plane ($\mathbf{C}(u)$ does lie in a unique plane);
2. setting $x = x_0 + x_1 u + x_2 u^2$ and $y = y_0 + y_1 u + y_2 u^2$, and then eliminating u and u^2 from these equations to obtain a second-degree implicit equation in x and y;
3. observing that the form of the implicit equation is that of a parabola.

Notice that the acceleration vector, $\mathbf{C}''(u) = 2\mathbf{a}_2$, is a constant. There are two special (degenerate) cases of interest, both occurring when the vector $\mathbf{a}_2$ is parallel to the initial tangent vector, $\mathbf{a}_1$ (when $x_1 y_2 = x_2 y_1$). In this case, the tangent vector does not turn, i.e., we get a straight line. The vector $\mathbf{a}_2$ can point in the same direction as $\mathbf{a}_1$ (Figure 1.7a), or in the opposite direction (Figure 1.7b). In Figure 1.7b, $\mathbf{a}_1 + 2\mathbf{a}_2 u_0 = 0$ for some $0 \le u_0 \le 1$ (velocity goes to zero, the particle stops), and a portion of the line segment is retraced in the opposite direction.

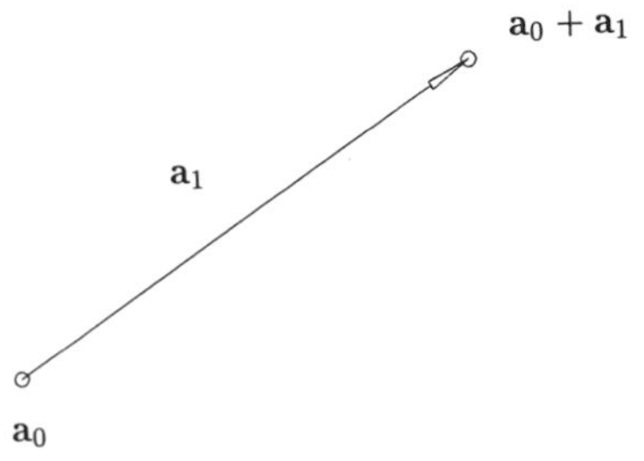

Figure 1.5. Straight line segment, $\mathbf{C}(u) = \mathbf{a}_0 + \mathbf{a}_1 u$.

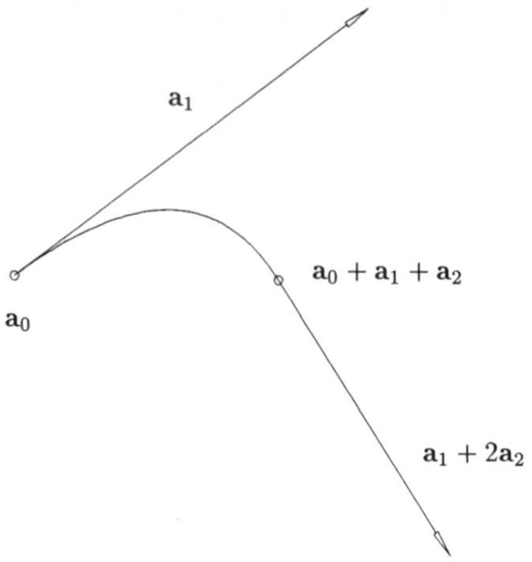

Figure 1.6. Parabolic arc, $\mathbf{C}(u) = \mathbf{a}_0 + \mathbf{a}_1 u + \mathbf{a}_2 u^2$.

Ex1.3 $n = 3$. The cubic, $\mathbf{C}(u) = \mathbf{a}_0 + \mathbf{a}_1 u + \mathbf{a}_2 u^2 + \mathbf{a}_3 u^3$, is a very general curve; it can be a truly *twisted* three-dimensional curve, not lying in a single plane (Figure 1.8a); it can have an inflection point (Figure 1.8b); a cusp (Figure 1.8c); or a loop (Figure 1.8d). A twisted curve results if $\mathbf{a}_0, \mathbf{a}_1, \mathbf{a}_2, \mathbf{a}_3$ do not lie in a unique plane. An inflection point on a planar curve is defined as a point where the curve is smooth (no cusp) and the tangent line at that point passes through the curve. This implies a change in the turning direction of the curve. At an inflection point, either $\mathbf{C}''(u) = 0$, or $\mathbf{C}'(u) \parallel \mathbf{C}''(u)$. A necessary (but not sufficient) condition for a cusp at $u = u_0$ is $\mathbf{C}'(u_0) = 0$ (velocity zero). Conditions for a loop to occur are also known (see [Ferg66, 67, 69, 93; Forr70, 80; Wang81; Ston89; Su89]).

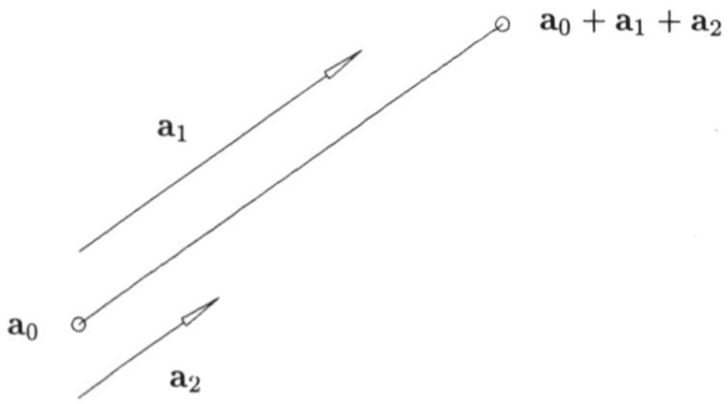

(a)

Figure 1.7. $\mathbf{a}_1$ and $\mathbf{a}_2$ parallel. (a) Same direction; (b) opposite directions.

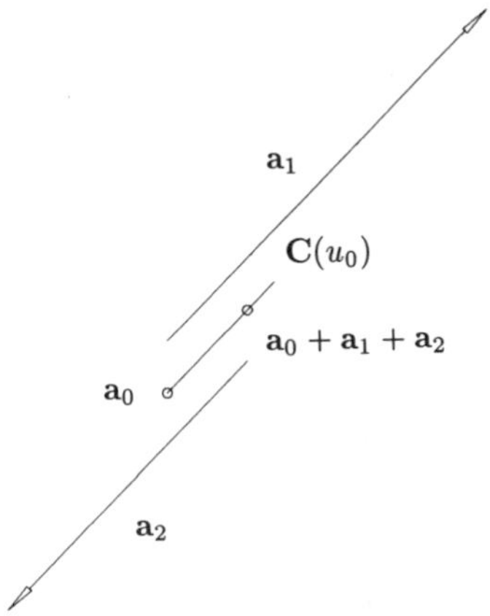

(b)

Figure 1.7. (*Continued.*)

1.3 Bézier Curves

Next we study another parametric polynomial curve, the Bézier curve. Since they both use polynomials for their coordinate functions, the power basis and Bézier forms are mathematically equivalent; i.e., any curve that can be represented in one form can also be represented in the other form. However, the Bézier method is superior to the power basis form for geometric modeling. Our presentation of Bézier curves is rather informal; for a more rigorous and complete treatment the reader should consult other references [Forr72; Bezi72, 86; Gord74a; Chan81; Fari93; Yama88; Hosc93; Roge90].

The power basis form has the following disadvantages:

- it is unnatural for interactive shape design; the coefficients $\{\mathbf{a}_i\}$ convey very little geometric insight about the shape of the curve. Furthermore, a designer typically wants to specify end conditions at both ends of the curve, not just at the starting point;
- algorithms for processing power basis polynomials have an algebraic rather than a geometric flavor (e.g., Horner's method);
- numerically, it is a rather poor form; e.g., Horner's method is prone to round-off error if the coefficients vary greatly in magnitude (see [Faro87, 88; Dani89]).

The Bézier method remedies these shortcomings.

An nth-degree Bézier curve is defined by

$$\mathbf{C}(u) = \sum_{i=0}^{n} B_{i,n}(u)\mathbf{P}_i \qquad 0 \le u \le 1 \tag{1.7}$$

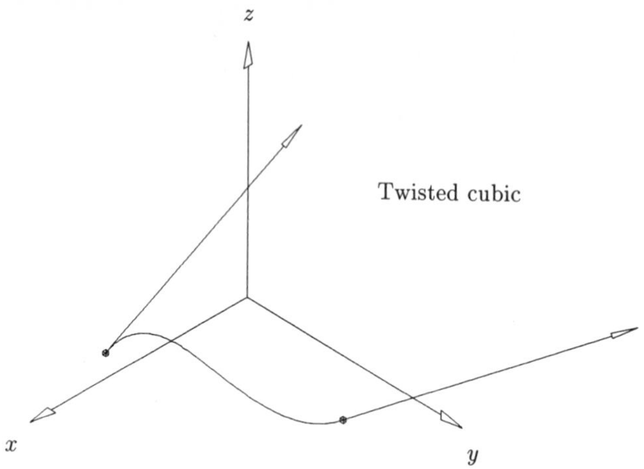

(a)

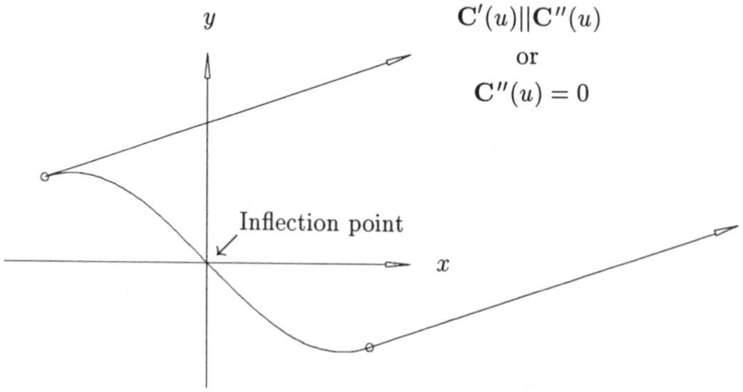

(b)

Figure 1.8. Cubic curves. (a) Three-dimensional twisted; (b) inflection point; (c) cusp; (d) loop.

The basis (blending) functions, $\{B_{i,n}(u)\}$, are the classical nth-degree Bernstein polynomials ([Bern12; Lore86]) given by

$$B_{i,n}(u) = \frac{n!}{i!(n-i)!}\, u^i\,(1-u)^{n-i} \tag{1.8}$$

The geometric coefficients of this form, $\{\mathbf{P}_i\}$, are called *control points*. Notice that the definition, Eq. (1.7), requires that $u \in [0,1]$.

Examples

`Ex1.4` $n = 1$. From Eq. (1.8) we have $B_{0,1}(u) = 1 - u$ and $B_{1,1}(u) = u$; and Eq. (1.7) takes the form $\mathbf{C}(u) = (1-u)\,\mathbf{P}_0 + u\mathbf{P}_1$. This is a straight line segment from $\mathbf{P}_0$ to $\mathbf{P}_1$ (see Figure 1.9).

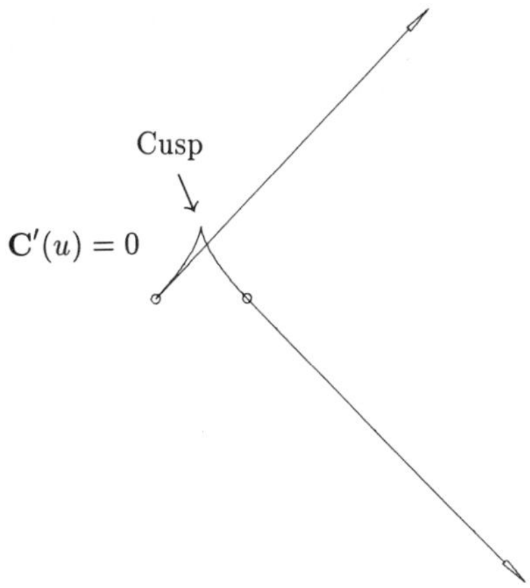

(c)

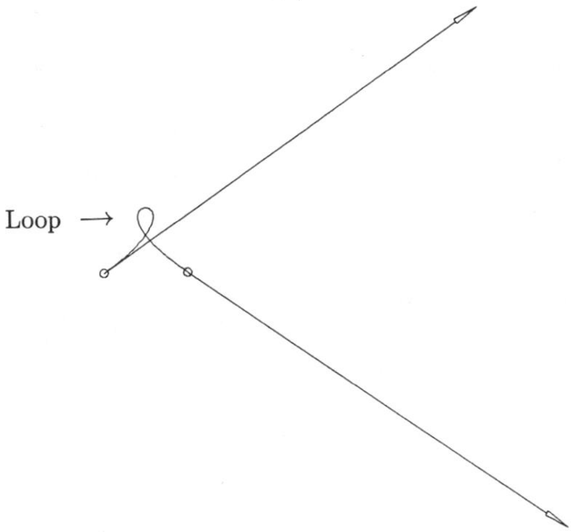

(d)

Figure 1.8. (*Continued.*)

Ex1.5 $n = 2$. From Eqs. (1.7) and (1.8) we have $\mathbf{C}(u) = (1-u)^2\,\mathbf{P}_0 + 2u(1-u)\,\mathbf{P}_1 + u^2\,\mathbf{P}_2$. This is a parabolic arc from $\mathbf{P}_0$ to $\mathbf{P}_2$ (see Figure 1.10). Notice that

- the polygon formed by $\{\mathbf{P}_0, \mathbf{P}_1, \mathbf{P}_2\}$, called the *control polygon*, approximates the shape of the curve rather nicely;
- $\mathbf{P}_0 = \mathbf{C}(0)$ and $\mathbf{P}_2 = \mathbf{C}(1)$;
- the tangent directions to the curve at its endpoints are parallel to $\mathbf{P}_1 - \mathbf{P}_0$ and $\mathbf{P}_2 - \mathbf{P}_1$ (this is derived later);
- the curve is contained in the triangle formed by $\mathbf{P}_0\,\mathbf{P}_1\,\mathbf{P}_2$.

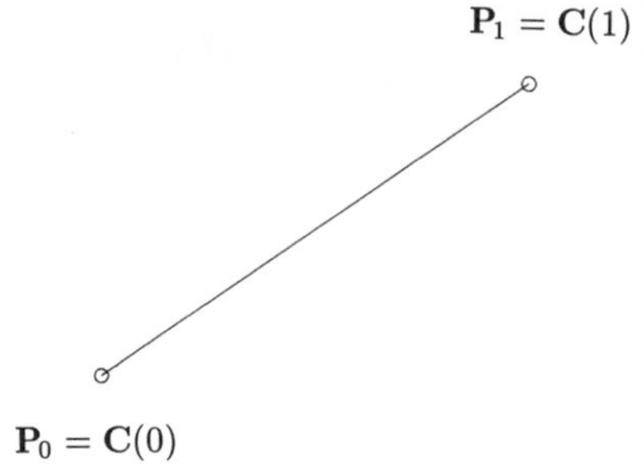

Figure 1.9. A first-degree Bézier curve.

Ex1.6 $n = 3$. We have $\mathbf{C}(u) = (1-u)^3\,\mathbf{P}_0 + 3u(1-u)^2\,\mathbf{P}_1 + 3u^2(1-u)\,\mathbf{P}_2 + u^3\,\mathbf{P}_3$. Examples of cubic Bézier curves are shown in Figures 1.11a to 1.11f. Notice that

- the control polygons approximate the shapes of the curves;
- $\mathbf{P}_0 = \mathbf{C}(0)$ and $\mathbf{P}_3 = \mathbf{C}(1)$;
- the endpoint tangent directions are parallel to $\mathbf{P}_1 - \mathbf{P}_0$ and $\mathbf{P}_3 - \mathbf{P}_2$;
- convex hull property: the curves are contained in the convex hulls of their defining control points (Figure 1.11c);
- variation diminishing property: no straight line intersects a curve more times than it intersects the curve's control polygon (for a three-dimensional Bézier curve, replace the words 'straight line' with the

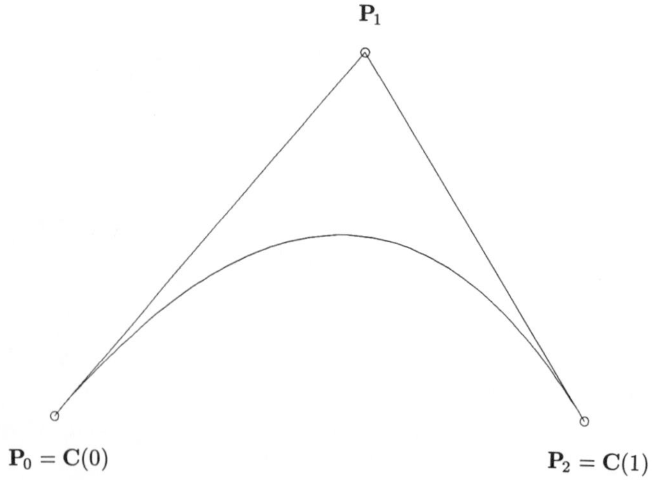

Figure 1.10. A second-degree Bézier curve.

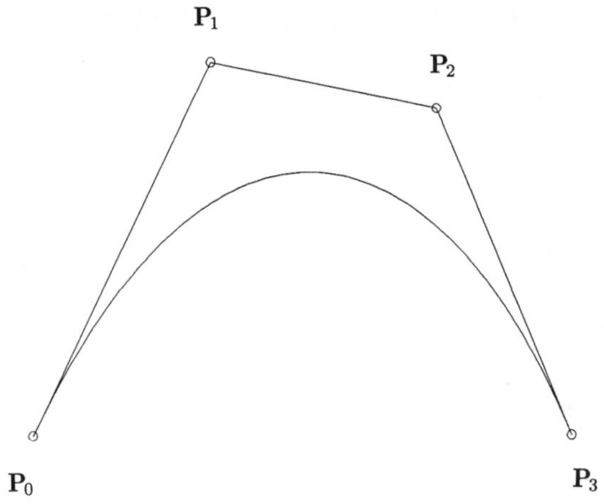

(a)

Figure 1.11. Cubic Bézier curves.

word 'plane'). This expresses the property that a Bézier curve follows its control polygon rather closely and does not wiggle more than its control polygon (Figure 1.11f);

- initially (at $u = 0$) the curve is turning in the same direction as $\mathbf{P}_0\mathbf{P}_1\mathbf{P}_2$. At $u = 1$ it is turning in the direction $\mathbf{P}_1\mathbf{P}_2\mathbf{P}_3$;
- a loop in the control polygon may or may not imply a loop in the curve. The transition between Figure 1.11e and Figure 1.11f is a curve with a cusp.

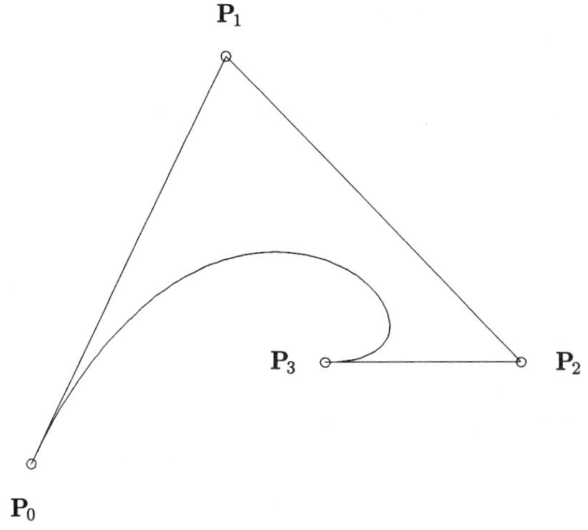

(b)

Figure 1.11. (*Continued.*)

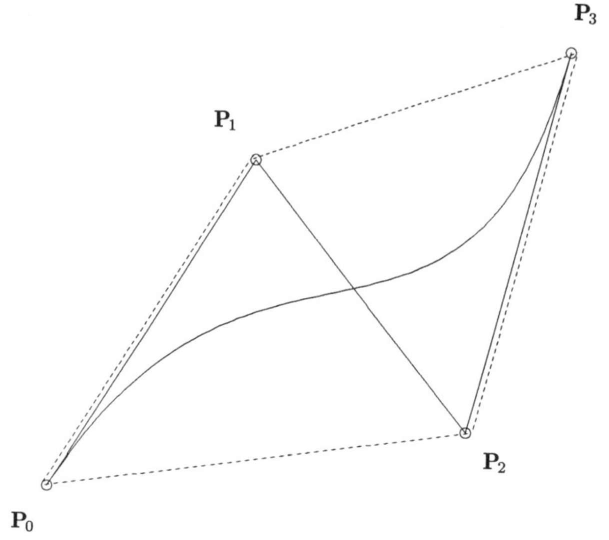

(c)

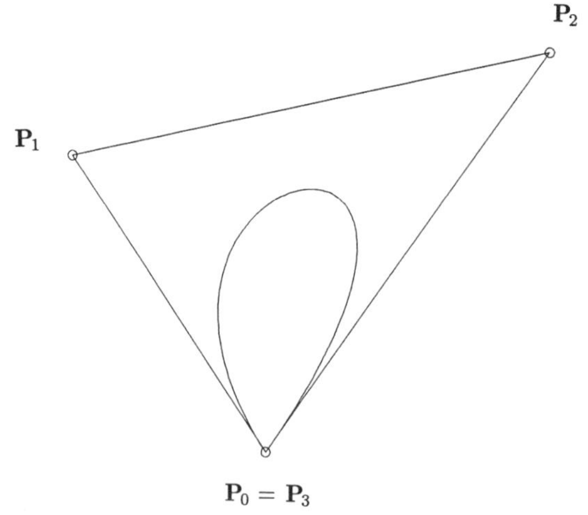

(d)

Figure 1.11. (*Continued.*)

Ex1.7 $n = 6$. Figure 1.12 shows a sixth-degree, closed Bézier curve. The curve is smooth at $\mathbf{C}(0)\ \big(= \mathbf{C}(1)\big)$ because $\mathbf{P}_1 - \mathbf{P}_0$ is parallel to $\mathbf{P}_6 - \mathbf{P}_5$. By smooth we mean that the tangent vectors at $u = 0$ and $u = 1$ have the same direction.

In addition to the previously mentioned properties, Bézier curves are invariant under the usual transformations such as rotations, translations, and scalings;

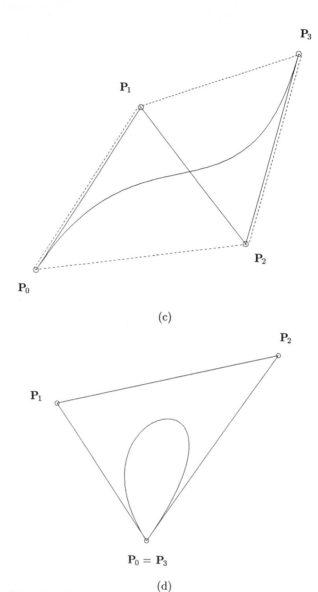

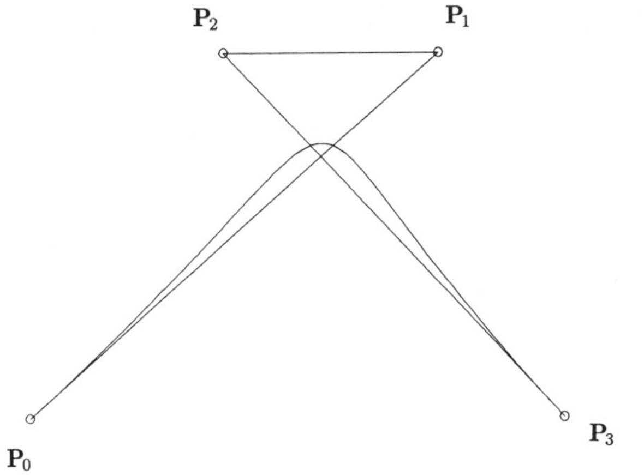

(e)

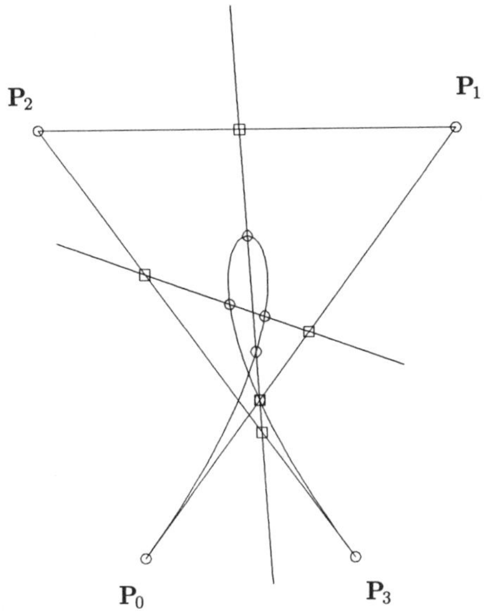

(f)

Figure 1.11. (*Continued.*)

that is, one applies the transformation to the curve by applying it to the control polygon. We present this concept more rigorously in Chapter 3 for B-spline curves (of which Bézier curves are a special case).

In any curve (or surface) representation scheme, the choice of basis functions determines the geometric characteristics of the scheme. Figures 1.13a–d show the basis functions $\{B_{i,n}(u)\}$ for $n = 1, 2, 3, 9$. These functions have these properties:

P1.1 nonnegativity: $B_{i,n}(u) \geq 0$ for all i, n and $0 \leq u \leq 1$;

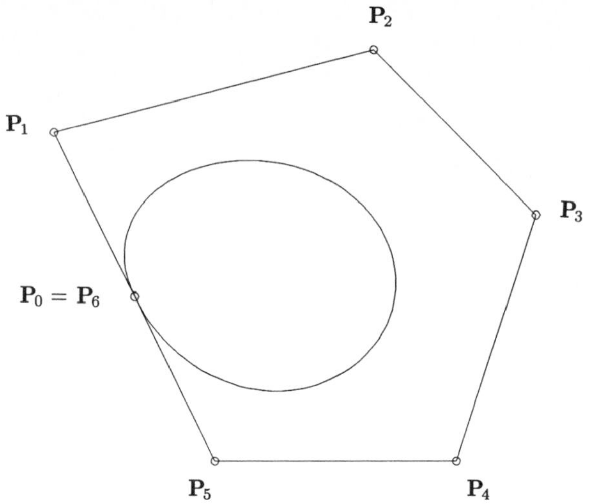

Figure 1.12. A smooth, closed, sixth-degree Bézier curve.

P1.2 partition of unity: $\sum_{i=0}^{n} B_{i,n}(u) = 1$ for all $0 \leq u \leq 1$;

P1.3 $B_{0,n}(0) = B_{n,n}(1) = 1$;

P1.4 $B_{i,n}(u)$ attains exactly one maximum on the interval $[0, 1]$, that is, at $u = i/n$;

P1.5 symmetry: for any n, the set of polynomials $\{B_{i,n}(u)\}$ is symmetric with respect to $u = 1/2$;

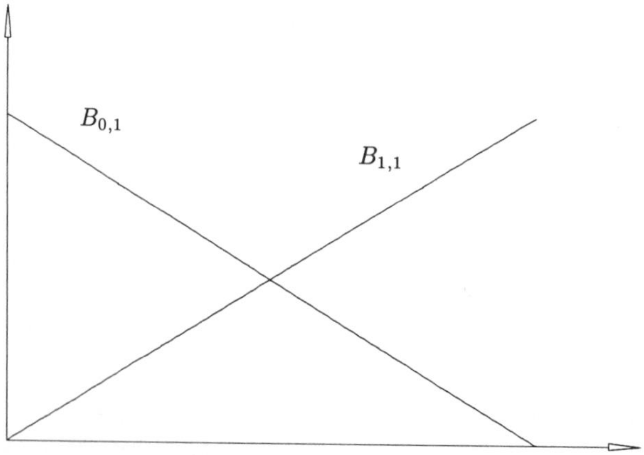

(a)

Figure 1.13. The Bernstein polynomials for (a) $n = 1$; (*b*) n = 2; (c) $n = 3$; (*d*) n = 9.

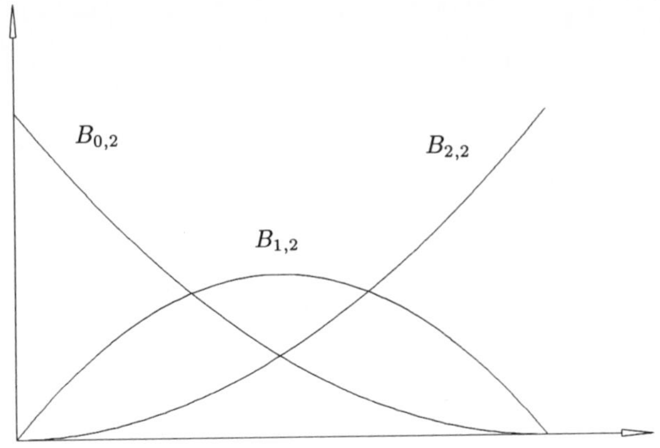

(b)

Figure 1.13. (*Continued.*)

P1.6 recursive definition: $B_{i,n}(u) = (1-u)B_{i,n-1}(u) + uB_{i-1,n-1}(u)$ (see Figure 1.14); we define $B_{i,n}(u) \equiv 0$ if $i < 0$ or $i > n$;

P1.7 derivatives:

$$B'_{i,n}(u) = \frac{dB_{i,n}(u)}{du} = n\big(B_{i-1,n-1}(u) - B_{i,n-1}(u)\big)$$

with $$B_{-1,n-1}(u) \equiv B_{n,n-1}(u) \equiv 0$$

Figure 1.15a shows the definition of $B'_{2,5}$, and Figure 1.15b illustrates all the cubic derivative functions.

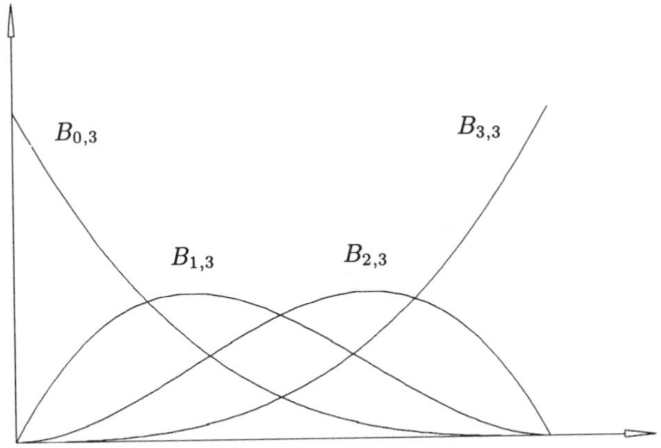

(c)

Figure 1.13. (*Continued.*)

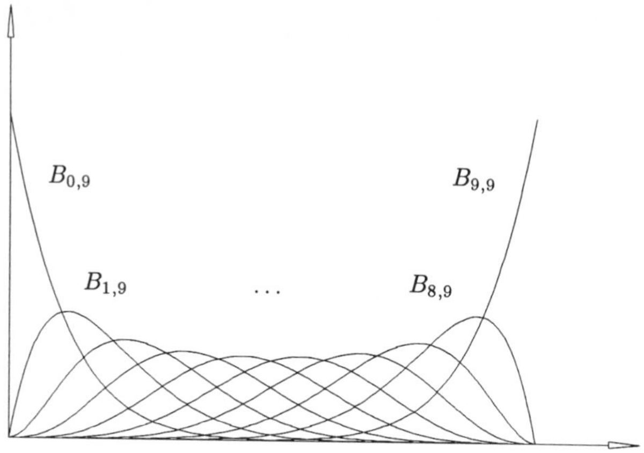

(d)

Figure 1.13. (*Continued.*)

From Eq. (1.8) we have $B_{0,0}(u) = 1$. Using property P1.6, the linear and quadratic Bernstein polynomials are

$$B_{0,1}(u) = (1-u)B_{0,0}(u) + uB_{-1,0}(u) = 1-u$$

$$B_{1,1}(u) = (1-u)B_{1,0}(u) + uB_{0,0}(u) = u$$

$$B_{0,2}(u) = (1-u)B_{0,1}(u) + uB_{-1,1}(u) = (1-u)^2$$

$$B_{1,2}(u) = (1-u)B_{1,1}(u) + uB_{0,1}(u) = (1-u)u + u(1-u) = 2u(1-u)$$

$$B_{2,2}(u) = (1-u)B_{2,1}(u) + uB_{1,1}(u) = u^2$$

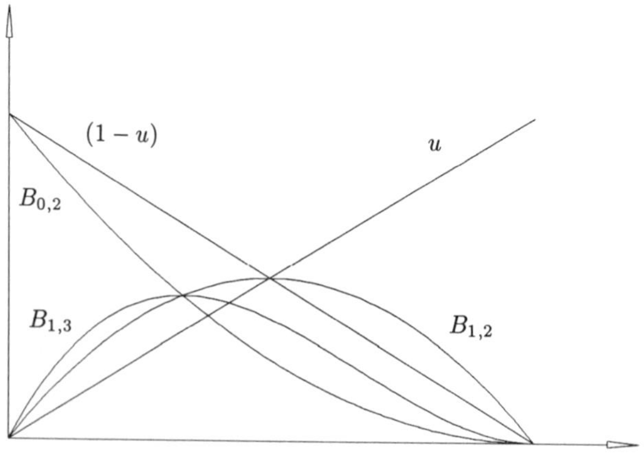

Figure 1.14. The recursive definition of the Bernstein polynomial, $B_{1,3}(u)$.

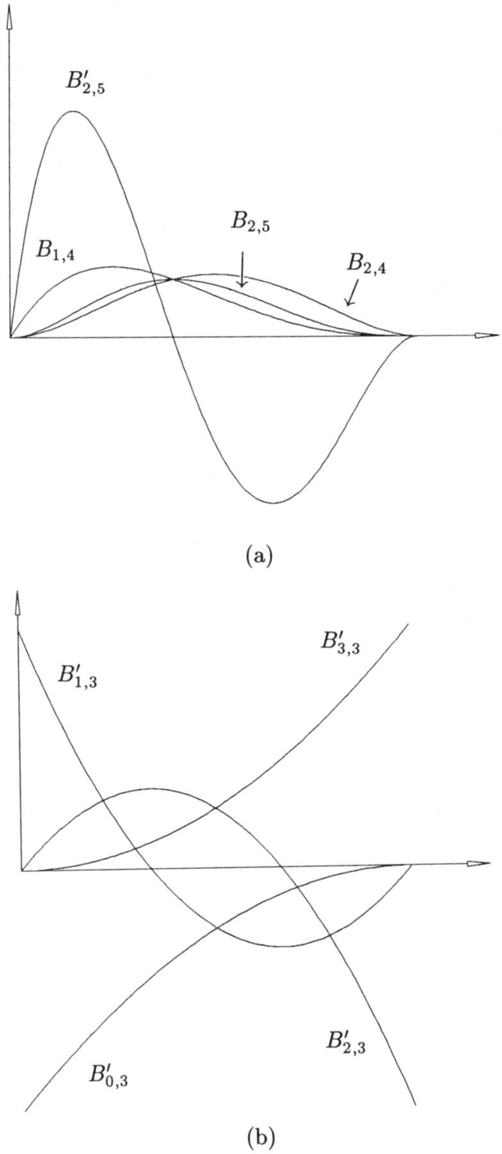

Figure 1.15. Derivatives. (a) The derivative $B'_{2,5}(u)$ in terms of $B_{1,4}(u)$ and $B_{2,4}(u)$; (b) the derivatives of the four cubic Bernstein polynomials, $B'_{0,3}(u)$; $B'_{1,3}(u)$; $B'_{2,3}(u)$; $B'_{3,3}(u)$.

Property `P1.6` yields simple algorithms to compute values of the Bernstein polynomials at fixed values of u. Algorithm `A1.2` computes the value $B_{i,n}(u)$ for fixed u. The computation of $B_{1,3}$ is depicted in Table 1.1.

```
ALGORITHM A1.2
  Bernstein(i,n,u,B)
    { /*  Compute the value of a Bernstein polynomial.  */
      /*  Input:  i,n,u  */
      /*  Output: B  */
    for (j=0; j<=n; j++)  /* compute the columns */
      temp[j] = 0.0;        /* of Table 1.1 */
    temp[n-i] = 1.0;      /* in a temporary array */
    u1 = 1.0-u;
    for (k=1; k<=n; k++)
      for (j=n; j>=k; j--)
        temp[j] = u1*temp[j] + u*temp[j-1];
    B = temp[n];
    }
```

Algorithm A1.3 computes the $n+1$ nth-degree Bernstein polynomials which are nonzero at fixed u. It avoids unnecessary computation of zero terms. The algorithm is depicted in Table 1.2 for the cubic case.

```
ALGORITHM A1.3
  AllBernstein(n,u,B)
```

Table 1.1. The computation of $B_{1,3}$.

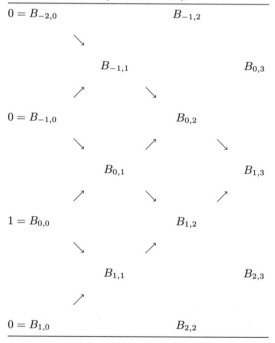

$0 = B_{-2,0}$				$B_{-1,2}$		
	$\searrow$					
		$B_{-1,1}$				$B_{0,3}$
	$\nearrow$		$\searrow$			
$0 = B_{-1,0}$				$B_{0,2}$		
	$\searrow$		$\nearrow$		$\searrow$	
		$B_{0,1}$				$B_{1,3}$
	$\nearrow$		$\searrow$		$\nearrow$	
$1 = B_{0,0}$				$B_{1,2}$		
	$\searrow$		$\nearrow$			
		$B_{1,1}$				$B_{2,3}$
	$\nearrow$					
$0 = B_{1,0}$				$B_{2,2}$		

Table 1.2. Computation of all the cubic Bernstein polynomials.

		$B_{-1,1}$				$B_{0,3}$
					$\nearrow$	
$B_{-1,0}$				$B_{0,2}$		
			$\nearrow$		$\searrow$	
		$B_{0,1}$				$B_{1,3}$
	$\nearrow$		$\searrow$		$\nearrow$	
$1 = B_{0,0}$				$B_{1,2}$		
	$\searrow$		$\nearrow$		$\searrow$	
		$B_{1,1}$				$B_{2,3}$
			$\searrow$		$\nearrow$	
$B_{1,0}$				$B_{2,2}$		
					$\searrow$	
		$B_{2,1}$				$B_{3,3}$

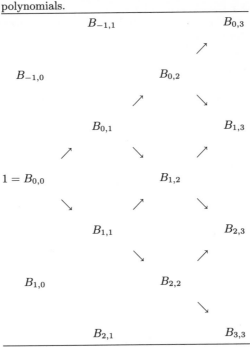

```
{ /* Compute all nth-degree Bernstein polynomials.  */
  /* Input:  n,u  */
  /* Output: B (an array, B[0],...,B[n])  */
B[0] = 1.0;
u1 = 1.0-u;
for (j=1; j<=n; j++)
  {
  saved = 0.0;
  for (k=0; k<j; k++)
    {
    temp = B[k];
    B[k] = saved+u1*temp;
    saved = u*temp;
    }
  B[j] = saved;
  }
}
```

Algorithm `A1.4` combines `A1.3` and Eq. (1.7) to compute the point on an nth-degree Bézier curve at a fixed u value.

```
ALGORITHM A1.4
  PointOnBezierCurve(P,n,u,C)
    { /*  Compute point on Bezier curve.  */
      /*  Input:  P,n,u  */
      /*  Output: C (a point)  */
    AllBernstein(n,u,B)   /* B is a local array */
    C = 0.0;
    for (k=0; k<=n; k++)   C = C + B[k]*P[k];
    }
```

Using property P1.7, it is easy to derive the general expression for the derivative of a Bézier curve

$$
\begin{aligned}
\mathbf{C}'(u) &= \frac{d\left(\sum_{i=0}^{n} B_{i,n}(u)\,\mathbf{P}_i\right)}{du} = \sum_{i=0}^{n} B'_{i,n}(u)\,\mathbf{P}_i \\
&= \sum_{i=0}^{n} n\big(B_{i-1,n-1}(u) - B_{i,n-1}(u)\big)\,\mathbf{P}_i \\
&= n\sum_{i=0}^{n-1} B_{i,n-1}(u)(\mathbf{P}_{i+1} - \mathbf{P}_i)
\end{aligned}
\tag{1.9}
$$

From Eq. (1.9) we easily obtain formulas for the end derivatives of a Bézier curve, e.g.

$$
\begin{aligned}
\mathbf{C}'(0) &= n(\mathbf{P}_1 - \mathbf{P}_0) & \mathbf{C}''(0) &= n(n-1)(\mathbf{P}_0 - 2\mathbf{P}_1 + \mathbf{P}_2) \\
\mathbf{C}'(1) &= n(\mathbf{P}_n - \mathbf{P}_{n-1}) & \mathbf{C}''(1) &= n(n-1)(\mathbf{P}_n - 2\mathbf{P}_{n-1} + \mathbf{P}_{n-2})
\end{aligned}
\tag{1.10}
$$

Notice from Eqs. (1.9) and (1.10) that

- the derivative of an nth-degree Bézier curve is an $(n-1)$th-degree Bézier curve;
- the expressions for the end derivatives at $u = 0$ and $u = 1$ are symmetric (due, of course, to the symmetry of the basis functions);
- the kth derivative at an endpoint depends (in a geometrically very intuitive manner) solely on the $k+1$ control points at that end.

Let $n = 2$ and $\mathbf{C}(u) = \sum_{i=0}^{2} B_{i,2}(u)\,\mathbf{P}_i$. Then

$$
\begin{aligned}
\mathbf{C}(u) &= (1-u)^2\,\mathbf{P}_0 + 2u(1-u)\,\mathbf{P}_1 + u^2\,\mathbf{P}_2 \\
&= (1-u)\big(\underbrace{(1-u)\,\mathbf{P}_0 + u\,\mathbf{P}_1}_{\text{linear}}\big) + u\big(\underbrace{(1-u)\,\mathbf{P}_1 + u\mathbf{P}_2}_{\text{linear}}\big)
\end{aligned}
$$

Thus, $\mathbf{C}(u)$ is obtained as the linear interpolation of two first-degree Bézier curves; in particular, any point on $\mathbf{C}(u)$ is obtained by three linear interpolations.

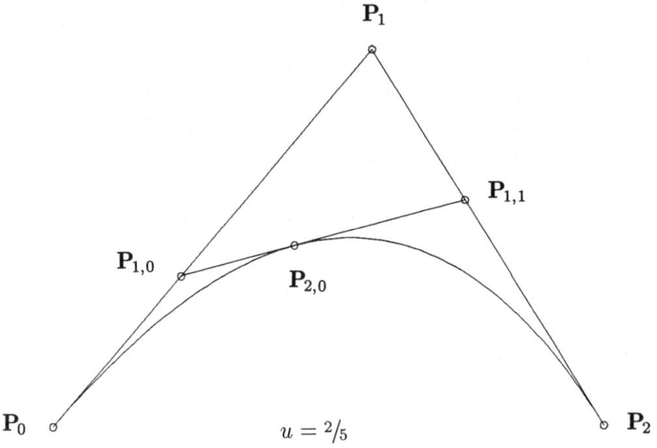

Figure 1.16. Obtaining a point on a quadratic Bézier curve by repeated linear interpolation at $u_0 = 2/5$.

Assuming a fixed $u = u_0$ and letting $\mathbf{P}_{1,0} = (1 - u_0)\,\mathbf{P}_0 + u_0\,\mathbf{P}_1$, $\mathbf{P}_{1,1} = (1 - u_0)\,\mathbf{P}_1 + u_0\,\mathbf{P}_2$, and $\mathbf{P}_{2,0} = (1 - u_0)\,\mathbf{P}_{1,0} + u_0\,\mathbf{P}_{1,1}$, it follows that $\mathbf{C}(u_0) = \mathbf{P}_{2,0}$. The situation is depicted in Figure 1.16, and the cubic case is shown in Figure 1.17.

Denoting a general nth-degree Bézier curve by $\mathbf{C}_n(\mathbf{P}_0, \ldots, \mathbf{P}_n)$, we have

$$\mathbf{C}_n(\mathbf{P}_0, \ldots, \mathbf{P}_n) = (1 - u)\mathbf{C}_{n-1}(\mathbf{P}_0, \ldots, \mathbf{P}_{n-1}) + u\mathbf{C}_{n-1}(\mathbf{P}_1, \ldots, \mathbf{P}_n) \tag{1.11}$$

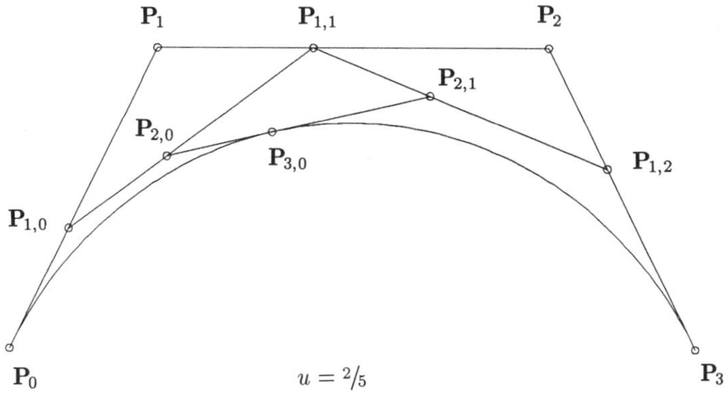

Figure 1.17. A point on a cubic Bézier curve by repeated linear interpolation at $u_0 = 2/5$.

This follows from the recursive definition of the basis functions (see `P1.6`). Fixing $u = u_0$ and denoting $\mathbf{P}_i$ by $\mathbf{P}_{0,i}$, Eq. (1.11) yields a recursive algorithm for computing the point $\mathbf{C}(u_0) = \mathbf{P}_{n,0}(u_0)$ on an nth-degree Bézier curve, i.e.

$$\mathbf{P}_{k,i}(u_0) = (1-u_0)\,\mathbf{P}_{k-1,i}(u_0) + u_0\,\mathbf{P}_{k-1,i+1}(u_0) \quad \text{for} \begin{cases} k = 1,\ldots,n \\ i = 0,\ldots,n-k \end{cases} \tag{1.12}$$

Equation (1.12) is called the *deCasteljau Algorithm* (see [Boeh84; deCa86, 93]). It is a corner cutting process (see Figures 1.16 and 1.17) which yields the triangular table of points shown in Table 1.3.

```
ALGORITHM A1.5
  deCasteljau1(P,n,u,C)
    { /* Compute point on a Bézier curve */
      /* using deCasteljau  */
      /* Input:  P,n,u  */
      /* Output: C (a point)  */
    for (i=0; i<=n; i++)    /* Use local array so we do not */
      Q[i] = P[i];          /* destroy control points */
    for (k=1; k<=n; k++)
      for (i=0; i<=n-k; i++)
        Q[i] = (1.0-u)*Q[i] + u*Q[i+1];
    C = Q[0];
    }
```

We conclude this section with a comparison of the Bézier and power basis methods. Clearly, the Bézier form is the more geometric of the two. Equation (1.10), together with the convex hull and variation diminishing properties, makes

Table 1.3. Points generated by the deCasteljau algorithm.

$\mathbf{P}_0$							
	$\mathbf{P}_{1,0}$						
$\mathbf{P}_1$		$\mathbf{P}_{2,0}$					
	$\mathbf{P}_{1,1}$						
$\mathbf{P}_2$		$\vdots$					
$\vdots$	$\vdots$	$\vdots$		$\mathbf{P}_{n-1,0}$			
$\vdots$	$\vdots$	$\vdots$	$\cdots$		$\mathbf{P}_{n,0}$	$=$	$\mathbf{C}(u_0)$
$\vdots$	$\vdots$	$\vdots$		$\mathbf{P}_{n-1,1}$			
$\mathbf{P}_{n-2}$		$\vdots$					
	$\mathbf{P}_{1,n-2}$						
$\mathbf{P}_{n-1}$		$\mathbf{P}_{2,n-2}$					
	$\mathbf{P}_{1,n-1}$						
$\mathbf{P}_n$							

Bézier curves more suitable for interactive curve design. The control points give the designer a more intuitive handle on curve shape than do the power basis coefficients. Furthermore, the deCasteljau algorithm is less prone to round-off error than Horner's algorithm. This is intuitively clear when one considers that the deCasteljau algorithm is simply repeated linear interpolation between points, all of which lie in the vicinity of the curve. The only disadvantage of the Bézier form is that point evaluation is less efficient (see Algorithms `A1.1`, `A1.4`, and `A1.5`, and Exercise 1.13 later in the chapter).

1.4 Rational Bézier Curves

Next we introduce the concepts of rational curves and homogeneous coordinates. To illustrate these concepts we give a brief introduction to rational Bézier curves. These curves are special cases of rational B-spline curves and as such are treated more completely and rigorously in subsequent chapters.

Although polynomials offer many advantages, there exist a number of important curve and surface types which cannot be represented precisely using polynomials, e.g., circles, ellipses, hyperbolas, cylinders, cones, spheres, etc. As an example, we give a proof that the unit circle in the xy plane, centered at the origin, cannot be represented using polynomial coordinate functions. To the contrary, let us assume that

$$x(u) = a_0 + a_1 u + \cdots + a_n u^n$$
$$y(u) = b_0 + b_1 u + \cdots + b_n u^n$$

Then $x^2 + y^2 - 1 = 0$ implies that

$$\begin{aligned} 0 &= (a_0 + a_1 u + \cdots + a_n u^n)^2 + (b_0 + b_1 u + \cdots + b_n u^n)^2 - 1 \\ &= (a_0^2 + b_0^2 - 1) + 2(a_0 a_1 + b_0 b_1)u + (a_1^2 + 2a_0 a_2 + b_1^2 + 2b_0 b_2)u^2 \\ &\quad + \cdots + (a_{n-1}^2 + 2a_{n-2}a_n + b_{n-1}^2 + 2b_{n-2}b_n)u^{2n-2} \\ &\quad + 2(a_n a_{n-1} + b_n b_{n-1})u^{2n-1} + (a_n^2 + b_n^2)u^{2n} \end{aligned}$$

This equation must hold for all u, which implies that all coefficients are zero. Starting with the highest degree and working down, we show in n steps that all $a_i = 0$ and $b_i = 0$ for $1 \le i \le n$.

Step

1. $a_n^2 + b_n^2 = 0$ implies $a_n = b_n = 0$.
2. $a_{n-1}^2 + 2a_{n-2}a_n + b_{n-1}^2 + 2b_{n-2}b_n = 0$ and Step 1 imply that $a_{n-1}^2 + b_{n-1}^2 = 0$ which implies that $a_{n-1} = b_{n-1} = 0$.

$\vdots$

n. $a_1^2 + 2a_0a_2 + b_1^2 + 2b_0b_2 = 0$ and Step $n-1$ imply that $a_1^2 + b_1^2 = 0$, which implies that $a_1 = b_1 = 0$.

Thus, $x(u) = a_0$ and $y(u) = b_0$, which is an obvious contradiction.

It is known from classical mathematics that all the conic curves, including the circle, can be represented using *rational functions*, which are defined as the ratio of two polynomials. In fact, they are represented with rational functions of the form

$$x(u) = \frac{X(u)}{W(u)} \qquad y(u) = \frac{Y(u)}{W(u)} \tag{1.13}$$

where $X(u)$, $Y(u)$, and $W(u)$ are polynomials, that is, each of the coordinate functions has the same denominator.

Examples

Ex1.8 Circle of radius 1, centered at the origin

$$x(u) = \frac{1-u^2}{1+u^2} \qquad y(u) = \frac{2u}{1+u^2}$$

Ex1.9 Ellipse, centered at the origin; the y-axis is the major axis, the x-axis is the minor axis, and the major and minor radii are 2 and 1, respectively

$$x(u) = \frac{1-u^2}{1+u^2} \qquad y(u) = \frac{4u}{1+u^2}$$

Ex1.10 Hyperbola, center at $\mathbf{P} = (0, 4/3)$; the y-axis is the transverse axis

$$x(u) = \frac{-1+2u}{1+2u-2u^2} \qquad y(u) = \frac{4u(1-u)}{1+2u-2u^2}$$

The lower branch $\big($with vertex at $\mathbf{P} = (0, 2/3)\big)$ is traced out for

$$u \in \left(\frac{1-\sqrt{3}}{2}, \frac{1+\sqrt{3}}{2}\right)$$

Ex1.11 Parabola, vertex at the origin; the y-axis is the axis of symmetry

$$x(u) = u \qquad y(u) = u^2$$

Notice that the parabola does not require rational functions. The reader should sketch these functions. For the circle equations it is easy to see that for any u, $\big(x(u), y(u)\big)$ lies on the unit circle centered at the origin

$$\big(x(u)\big)^2 + \big(y(u)\big)^2 = \left(\frac{1-u^2}{1+u^2}\right)^2 + \left(\frac{2u}{1+u^2}\right)^2$$

$$= \frac{1-2u^2+u^4+4u^2}{(1+u^2)^2} = \frac{(1+u^2)^2}{(1+u^2)^2} = 1$$

Define an nth-degree *rational Bézier curve* by (see [Forr68; Pieg86; Fari83, 89])

$$\mathbf{C}(u) = \frac{\sum_{i=0}^{n} B_{i,n}(u) w_i \mathbf{P}_i}{\sum_{i=0}^{n} B_{i,n}(u) w_i} \qquad 0 \le u \le 1 \tag{1.14}$$

The $\mathbf{P}_i = (x_i, y_i, z_i)$ and $B_{i,n}(u)$ are as before; the w_i are scalars, called the *weights*. Thus, $W(u) = \sum_{i=0}^{n} B_{i,n}(u) w_i$ is the common denominator function. Except where explicitly stated otherwise, we assume that $w_i > 0$ for all i. This ensures that $W(u) > 0$ for all $u \in [0,1]$. We write

$$\mathbf{C}(u) = \sum_{i=0}^{n} R_{i,n}(u) \mathbf{P}_i \qquad 0 \le u \le 1 \tag{1.15}$$

where
$$R_{i,n}(u) = \frac{B_{i,n}(u) w_i}{\sum_{j=0}^{n} B_{j,n}(u) w_j}$$

The $R_{i,n}(u)$ are the rational basis functions for this curve form. Figure 1.18a shows an example of cubic basis functions, and Figure 1.18b a corresponding cubic rational Bézier curve.

The $R_{i,n}(u)$ have properties which can be easily derived from Eq. (1.15) and the corresponding properties of the $B_{i,n}(u)$:

P1.8 nonnegativity: $R_{i,n}(u) \ge 0$ for all i, n and $0 \le u \le 1$;

P1.9 partition of unity: $\sum_{i=0}^{n} R_{i,n}(u) = 1$ for all $0 \le u \le 1$;

P1.10 $R_{0,n}(0) = R_{n,n}(1) = 1$;

P1.11 $R_{i,n}(u)$ attains exactly one maximum on the interval $[0,1]$;

P1.12 if $w_i = 1$ for all i, then $R_{i,n}(u) = B_{i,n}(u)$ for all i; i.e., the $B_{i,n}(u)$ are a special case of the $R_{i,n}(u)$.

These yield the following geometric properties of rational Bézier curves:

P1.13 convex hull property: the curves are contained in the convex hulls of their defining control points (the $\mathbf{P}_i$);

P1.14 transformation invariance: rotations, translations, and scalings are applied to the curve by applying them to the control points;

P1.15 variation diminishing property: same as for polynomial Bézier curves (see previous section);

P1.16 endpoint interpolation: $\mathbf{C}(0) = \mathbf{P}_0$ and $\mathbf{C}(1) = \mathbf{P}_n$;

P1.17 the kth derivative at $u = 0$ ($u = 1$) depends on the first (last) $k+1$ control points and weights; in particular, $\mathbf{C}'(0)$ and $\mathbf{C}'(1)$ are parallel to $\mathbf{P}_1 - \mathbf{P}_0$ and $\mathbf{P}_n - \mathbf{P}_{n-1}$, respectively;

P1.18 polynomial Bézier curves are a special case of rational Bézier curves.

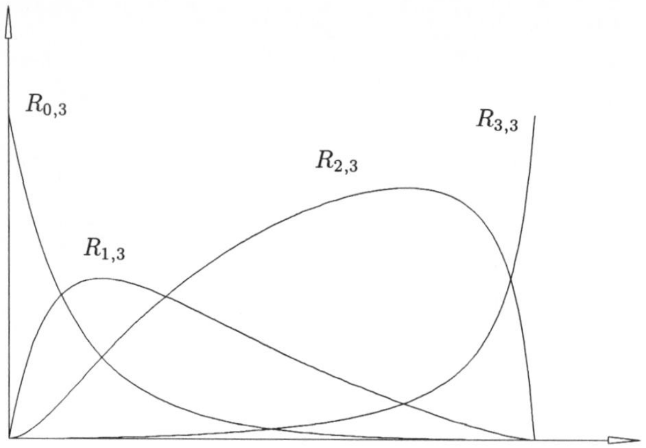

(a)

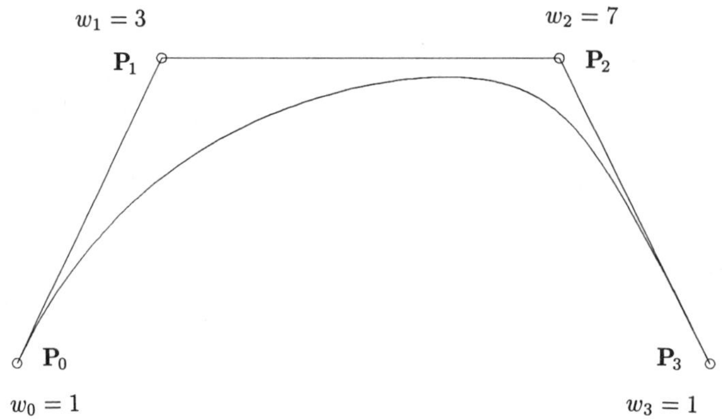

(b)

Figure 1.18. Rational cubic. (a) Basis functions; (b) Bézier curve.

Example

`Ex1.12` Let us consider the rational Bézier circular arc.

$$\mathbf{C}(u) = \big(x(u), y(u)\big) = \left(\frac{1-u^2}{1+u^2}, \frac{2u}{1+u^2}\right) \qquad 0 \le u \le 1$$

represents one quadrant of the unit circle, as shown in Figure 1.19a. We now derive the quadratic rational Bézier representation of this circular arc. Clearly, from `P1.16` and `P1.17`, $\mathbf{P}_0 = (1,0)$, $\mathbf{P}_1 = (1,1)$, and $\mathbf{P}_2 = (0,1)$. For the weights we have

$$W(u) = 1 + u^2 = \sum_{i=0}^{2} B_{i,2}(u) w_i = (1-u)^2 w_0 + 2u(1-u)w_1 + u^2 w_2$$

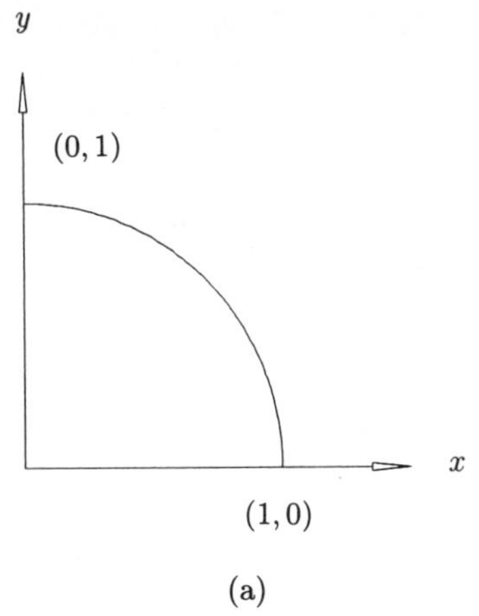

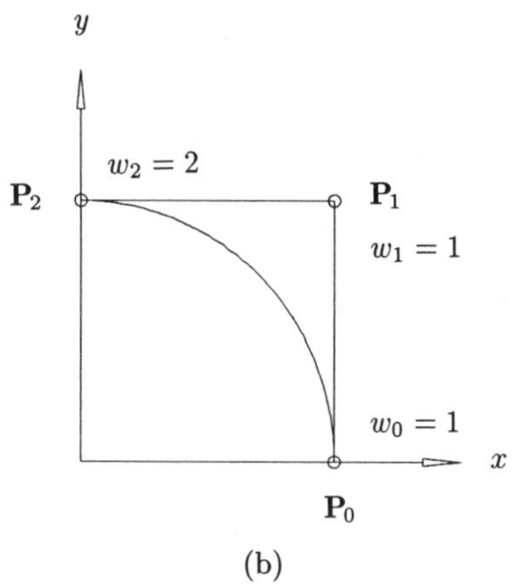

Figure 1.19. Representation of the unit circle. (a) $x(u) = {}^{(1-u^2)}/(1+u^2)$ and $y(u) = {}^{(2u)}/(1+u^2)$ for one quadrant; (b) the Bézier representation corresponding to Figure 1.19a ($w_0 = 1$, $w_1 = 1$, $w_2 = 2$).

> Substituting $u = 0$ yields $w_0 = 1$, and $u = 1$ yields $w_2 = 2$. Finally, substituting $u = 1/2$ yields $5/4 = 1/4 w_0 + 1/2 w_1 + 1/4 w_2$, and using $w_0 = 1$ and $w_2 = 2$ yields $w_1 = 1$ (see Figure 1.19b).

Rational curves with coordinate functions in the form of Eq. (1.13) (one common denominator) have an elegant geometric interpretation which yields efficient processing and compact data storage. The idea is to use *homogeneous coordinates* to represent a rational curve in n-dimensional space as a polynomial curve in $(n+1)$-dimensional space (see [Robe65; Ries81; Patt85]). Let us start with a point in three-dimensional Euclidean space, $\mathbf{P} = (x, y, z)$. Then $\mathbf{P}$ is written as $\mathbf{P}^w = (wx, wy, wz, w) = (X, Y, Z, W)$ in four-dimensional space, $w \neq 0$. Now

$\mathbf{P}$ is obtained from $\mathbf{P}^w$ by dividing all coordinates by the fourth coordinate, W, i.e., by mapping $\mathbf{P}^w$ from the origin to the hyperplane $W = 1$ (see Figure 1.20 for the two-dimensional case, $\mathbf{P} = (x, y)$). This mapping, denoted by H, is a perspective map with center at the origin

$$\mathbf{P} = H\{\mathbf{P}^w\} = H\{(X, Y, Z, W)\} = \begin{cases} \left(\dfrac{X}{W}, \dfrac{Y}{W}, \dfrac{Z}{W}\right) & \text{if } W \neq 0 \\ \text{direction } (X, Y, Z) & \text{if } W = 0 \end{cases} \tag{1.16}$$

Notice that for arbitrary x, y, z, w_1, w_2, where $w_1 \neq w_2$

$$\begin{aligned} H\{\mathbf{P}^{w_1}\} &= H\{(w_1x, w_1y, w_1z, w_1)\} = (x, y, z) \\ &= H\{(w_2x, w_2y, w_2z, w_2)\} = H\{\mathbf{P}^{w_2}\} \end{aligned}$$

Now for a given set of control points, $\{\mathbf{P}_i\}$, and weights, $\{w_i\}$, construct the weighted control points, $\mathbf{P}_i^w = (w_ix_i, w_iy_i, w_iz_i, w_i)$. Then define the *nonrational* (polynomial) Bézier curve in four-dimensional space

$$\mathbf{C}^w(u) = \sum_{i=0}^{n} B_{i,n}(u)\, \mathbf{P}_i^w \tag{1.17}$$

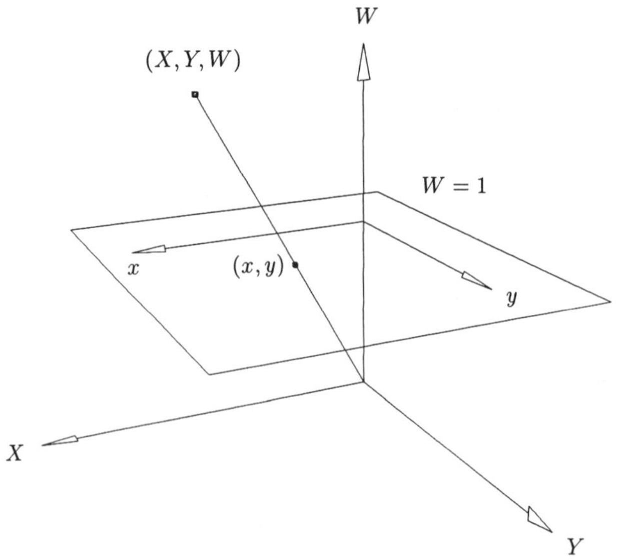

Figure 1.20. A representation of Euclidean points in homogeneous form.

Then, applying the perspective map, H, to $\mathbf{C}^w(u)$ yields the corresponding rational Bézier curve of Eq. (1.14) (see Figure 1.21), that is, writing out the coordinate functions of Eq. (1.17), we get

$$X(u) = \sum_{i=0}^{n} B_{i,n}(u) w_i x_i \qquad Y(u) = \sum_{i=0}^{n} B_{i,n}(u) w_i y_i$$

$$Z(u) = \sum_{i=0}^{n} B_{i,n}(u) w_i z_i \qquad W(u) = \sum_{i=0}^{n} B_{i,n}(u) w_i$$

Locating the curve in three-dimensional space yields

$$x(u) = \frac{X(u)}{W(u)} = \frac{\sum_{i=0}^{n} B_{i,n}(u) w_i x_i}{\sum_{i=0}^{n} B_{i,n}(u) w_i}$$

$$y(u) = \frac{Y(u)}{W(u)} = \frac{\sum_{i=0}^{n} B_{i,n}(u) w_i y_i}{\sum_{i=0}^{n} B_{i,n}(u) w_i}$$

$$z(u) = \frac{Z(u)}{W(u)} = \frac{\sum_{i=0}^{n} B_{i,n}(u) w_i z_i}{\sum_{i=0}^{n} B_{i,n}(u) w_i}$$

Using vector notation, we get

$$\mathbf{C}(u) = (x(u), y(u), z(u)) = \frac{\sum_{i=0}^{n} B_{i,n}(u) w_i (x_i, y_i, z_i)}{\sum_{i=0}^{n} B_{i,n}(u) w_i}$$

$$= \frac{\sum_{i=0}^{n} B_{i,n}(u) w_i \mathbf{P}_i}{\sum_{i=0}^{n} B_{i,n}(u) w_i} \tag{1.18}$$

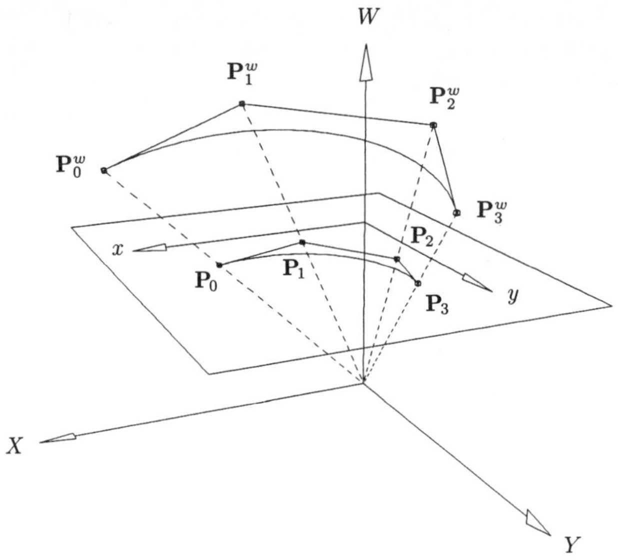

Figure 1.21. A geometric construction of a rational Bézier curve.

For algorithms in this book we primarily use the form given by Eq. (1.17), and an analogous form for rational B-spline curves. Thus, nonrational forms are processed in four-dimensional space, and the results are located in three-dimensional space using the map H. We refer interchangeably to either $\mathbf{C}^w(u)$ or $\mathbf{C}(u)$ as the rational Bézier (or B-spline) curve, although strictly speaking, $\mathbf{C}^w(u)$ is not a rational curve.

Examples

Ex1.13 Let us return to the circular arc of Figure 1.19b. We have $\mathbf{P}_0 = (1,0)$, $\mathbf{P}_1 = (1,1)$, $\mathbf{P}_2 = (0,1)$, and $w_0 = 1$, $w_1 = 1$, $w_2 = 2$. Hence, for Eq. (1.17) the three-dimensional control points are $\mathbf{P}_0^w = (1,0,1)$, $\mathbf{P}_1^w = (1,1,1)$, and $\mathbf{P}_2^w = (0,2,2)$. Then $\mathbf{C}^w(u) = (1-u)^2\,\mathbf{P}_0^w + 2u(1-u)\,\mathbf{P}_1^w + u^2\,\mathbf{P}_2^w$ is a parabolic arc (nonrational), which projects onto a circular arc on the $W = 1$ plane (see Figure 1.22).

Let u_0 be fixed. Since $\mathbf{C}^w(u)$ is a polynomial Bézier curve, we use the deCasteljau algorithm to compute $\mathbf{C}^w(u_0)$; subsequently, $\mathbf{C}(u_0) = H\{\mathbf{C}^w(u_0)\}$. Thus, we apply Eq. (1.12) to the $\mathbf{P}_i^w$

$$\mathbf{P}_{k,i}^w(u_0) = (1-u_0)\,\mathbf{P}_{k-1,i}^w + u_0\,\mathbf{P}_{k-1,i+1}^w \quad \text{for} \quad \begin{cases} k = 1,\ldots,n \\ i = 0,\ldots,n-k \end{cases} \tag{1.19}$$

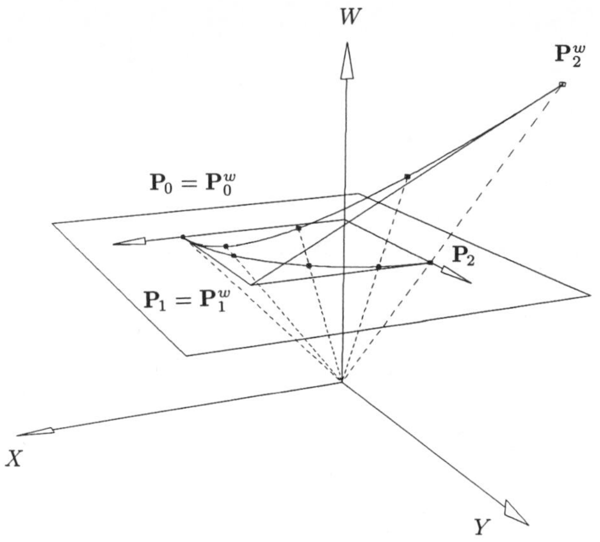

Figure 1.22. A homogeneous representation of a circular arc.

Ex1.14 Let us apply Eq. (1.19) to compute the point at $u = 1/2$ on the rational Bézier circular arc of Example 1.13. The arc is given by $\mathbf{C}^w(u) = (1-u)^2\,\mathbf{P}_0^w + 2u(1-u)\,\mathbf{P}_1^w + u^2\,\mathbf{P}_2^w$, where $\mathbf{P}_0^w = (1,0,1)$, $\mathbf{P}_1^w = (1,1,1)$, $\mathbf{P}_2^w = (0,2,2)$. The triangular set of generated points is shown in Table 1.4. Then $\mathbf{C}(1/2) = H\{\mathbf{C}^w(1/2)\} = H\{(3/4, 1, 5/4)\} = (3/5, 4/5)$.

Now let us compute the point using the other representations we have developed. Let

$$\mathbf{C}(u) = \left(\frac{(1-u^2)}{(1+u^2)}, \frac{(2u)}{(1+u^2)}\right)$$

Table 1.4. Generation of the point $\mathbf{C}^w(1/2)$ on the circular arc.

$(1,0,1)$				
	$\left(1, \frac{1}{2}, 1\right)$			
$(1,1,1)$		$\left(\frac{3}{4}, 1, \frac{5}{4}\right)$	$=$	$\mathbf{C}^w\left(\frac{1}{2}\right)$
	$\left(\frac{1}{2}, \frac{3}{2}, \frac{3}{2}\right)$			
$(0,2,2)$				

Then
$$\mathbf{C}\left(\frac{1}{2}\right) = \left(\frac{1-\left(\frac{1}{2}\right)^2}{1+\left(\frac{1}{2}\right)^2}, \frac{2\left(\frac{1}{2}\right)}{1+\left(\frac{1}{2}\right)^2}\right) = \left(\frac{3}{5}, \frac{4}{5}\right)$$

Using Eq. (1.17)

$$\mathbf{C}^w\left(\frac{1}{2}\right) = \sum_{i=0}^{2} B_{i,2}\left(\frac{1}{2}\right)\mathbf{P}_i^w =$$
$$= \left(1-\left(\frac{1}{2}\right)\right)^2 (1,0,1) + 2\left(\frac{1}{2}\right)\left(1-\left(\frac{1}{2}\right)\right)(1,1,1)$$
$$+ \left(\frac{1}{2}\right)^2 (0,2,2)$$
$$= \frac{1}{4}(1,0,1) + \frac{1}{2}(1,1,1) + \frac{1}{4}(0,2,2) = \left(\frac{3}{4}, 1, \frac{5}{4}\right)$$

Projecting yields $(3/5, 4/5)$. Equations (1.18) and (1.15) yield the same result.

Finally, we note that $\mathbf{C}(1/2) = (3/5, 4/5)$ is not the midpoint of the circular arc in the first quadrant; i.e., the parameterization is not uniform (see Section 1.1). The point $(3/5, 4/5)$ is more than half the arc length from the starting point. This is intuitively correct, since by differentiating $\mathbf{C}(u)$ one can see that the starting speed is twice the end speed.

1.5 Tensor Product Surfaces

The curve $\mathbf{C}(u)$ is a vector-valued function of one parameter. It is a mapping (deformation) of a straight line segment into Euclidean three-dimensional space. A surface is a vector-valued function of two parameters, u and v, and represents a mapping of a region, $\mathcal{R}$, of the uv plane into Euclidean three-dimensional space. Thus it has the form $\mathbf{S}(u,v) = \big(x(u,v), y(u,v), z(u,v)\big)$, $(u,v) \in \mathcal{R}$. There are many schemes for representing surfaces (see [Hosc93; Pieg89a, 93] and the many references cited in [Pieg89a]). They differ in the coordinate functions used and the type of region $\mathcal{R}$. Probably the simplest method, and the one most widely used in geometric modeling applications, is the *tensor product* scheme. This is the method we use in the remainder of this book.

The tensor product method is basically a bidirectional curve scheme. It uses basis functions and geometric coefficients. The basis functions are bivariate functions of u and v, which are constructed as products of univariate basis functions.

The geometric coefficients are arranged (topologically) in a bidirectional, $n \times m$ net. Thus, a tensor product surface has the form

$$\mathbf{S}(u,v) = \big(x(u,v), y(u,v), z(u,v)\big) = \sum_{i=0}^{n} \sum_{j=0}^{m} f_i(u) g_j(v) \mathbf{b}_{i,j} \tag{1.20}$$

where
$$\begin{cases} \mathbf{b}_{i,j} = (x_{i,j}, y_{i,j}, z_{i,j}) \\ 0 \le u,\ v \le 1 \end{cases}$$

Note that the (u,v) domain of this mapping is a square (a rectangle, in general). Note also that $\mathbf{S}(u,v)$ has a matrix form

$$\mathbf{S}(u,v) = [\, f_i(u)\,]^T \, [\, \mathbf{b}_{i,j}\,] \, [\, g_j(v)\,]$$

where $[\, f_i(u)\,]^T$ is a $(1) \times (n+1)$ row vector, $[\, g_j(v)\,]$ is a $(m+1) \times (1)$ column vector, and $[\, \mathbf{b}_{i,j}\,]$ is a $(n+1) \times (m+1)$ matrix of three-dimensional points.

As an example we consider the power basis surface

$$\mathbf{S}(u,v) = \sum_{i=0}^{n} \sum_{j=0}^{m} \mathbf{a}_{i,j} u^i v^j = [\, u^i\,]^T \, [\, \mathbf{a}_{i,j}\,] \, [\, v^j\,] \qquad \begin{cases} \mathbf{a}_{i,j} = (x_{i,j}, y_{i,j}, z_{i,j}) \\ 0 \le u,\ v \le 1 \end{cases} \tag{1.21}$$

We have $f_i(u) = u^i$ and $g_j(v) = v^j$, and the basis functions are the products, $\{u^i v^j\}$. If we fix $u = u_0$, then

$$\mathbf{C}_{u_0}(v) = \mathbf{S}(u_0, v) = \sum_{j=0}^{m} \left(\sum_{i=0}^{n} \mathbf{a}_{i,j}\, u_0^i \right) v^j = \sum_{j=0}^{m} \mathbf{b}_j(u_0)\, v^j \tag{1.22}$$

where
$$\mathbf{b}_j(u_0) = \sum_{i=0}^{n} \mathbf{a}_{i,j}\, u_0^i$$

is a power basis curve lying on the surface, $\mathbf{S}(u,v)$. Similarly, $\mathbf{C}_{v_0}(u)$ is a power basis curve lying on $\mathbf{S}(u,v)$; and the curves $\mathbf{C}_{u_0}(v)$ and $\mathbf{C}_{v_0}(u)$ intersect at the surface point, $\mathbf{S}(u_0, v_0)$. These curves are called *isoparametric curves* (or *isocurves*). $\mathbf{C}_{u_0}(v)$ is called a *v curve*, $\mathbf{C}_{v_0}(u)$ a *u curve* (see Figure 1.23).

Equation (1.21) can be written as

$$\begin{aligned}
\mathbf{S}(u,v) = {} & \underbrace{\{\mathbf{a}_{0,0} + \mathbf{a}_{0,1} v + \mathbf{a}_{0,2} v^2 + \cdots + \mathbf{a}_{0,m} v^m\}}_{\mathbf{b}_0} \\
& + u \underbrace{\{\mathbf{a}_{1,0} + \mathbf{a}_{1,1} v + \mathbf{a}_{1,2} v^2 + \cdots + \mathbf{a}_{1,m} v^m\}}_{\mathbf{b}_1} \\
& + u^2 \underbrace{\{\mathbf{a}_{2,0} + \mathbf{a}_{2,1} v + \mathbf{a}_{2,2} v^2 + \cdots + \mathbf{a}_{2,m} v^m\}}_{\mathbf{b}_2} \\
& \vdots \\
& + u^n \underbrace{\{\mathbf{a}_{n,0} + \mathbf{a}_{n,1} v + \mathbf{a}_{n,2} v^2 + \cdots + \mathbf{a}_{n,m} v^m\}}_{\mathbf{b}_n} \\
= {} & \mathbf{b}_0 + \mathbf{b}_1 u + \mathbf{b}_2 u^2 + \cdots + \mathbf{b}_n u^n
\end{aligned}$$

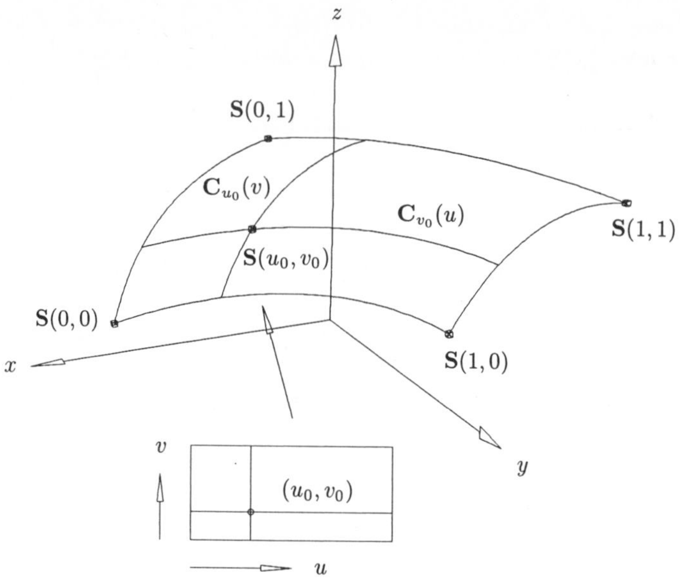

Figure 1.23. A tensor product surface showing isoparametric curves.

The terms in the braces are simple polynomials that can be evaluated by the Horner Algorithm (A1.1), yielding $\mathbf{b}_0, \mathbf{b}_1, \ldots, \mathbf{b}_n$. Using the **b**s and reapplying the algorithm, we obtain the point on the surface. Thus we have Algorithm A1.6.

```
ALGORITHM A1.6
  Horner2(a,n,m,u0,v0,S)
    { /*  Compute point on a power basis surface.  */
      /*  Input:  a,n,m,u0,v0  */
      /*  Output: S  */
    for (i=0; i<=n; i++)
      Horner1(a[i][],m,v0,b[i]); /* a[i][] is the ith row */
    Horner1(b,n,u0,S);
    }
```

Algorithm A1.6 is typical of the algorithms for tensor product surfaces. They can usually be obtained by extending from the curve algorithms, often by processing the n (or m) rows of coefficients (as curves) in one direction, then processing one or more rows in the other direction.

Differentiating Eq. (1.21), we obtain

$$\mathbf{S}_u(u,v) = \sum_{i=1}^{n}\sum_{j=0}^{m} i\,\mathbf{a}_{i,j}\,u^{i-1}v^j \qquad \mathbf{S}_v(u,v) = \sum_{i=0}^{n}\sum_{j=1}^{m} j\,\mathbf{a}_{i,j}\,u^i v^{j-1}$$

Notice that for fixed (u_0,v_0), $\mathbf{S}_u(u_0,v_0) = \mathbf{C}'_{v_0}(u_0)$ and $\mathbf{S}_v(u_0,v_0) = \mathbf{C}'_{u_0}(v_0)$. The normal vector, $\mathbf{N}$, is computed using Eq. (1.4).

Nonrational Bézier surfaces are obtained by taking a bidirectional net of control points and products of the univariate Bernstein polynomials

$$\mathbf{S}(u,v) = \sum_{i=0}^{n}\sum_{j=0}^{m} B_{i,n}(u)B_{j,m}(v)\,\mathbf{P}_{i,j} \qquad 0 \le u,v \le 1 \tag{1.23}$$

The basis function $B_{0,2}(u)B_{1,3}(v)$ is shown in Figure 1.24a, and Figure 1.24b shows a quadratic $\times$ cubic Bézier surface.

For fixed $u = u_0$

$$\begin{aligned}\mathbf{C}_{u_0}(v) = \mathbf{S}(u_0,v) &= \sum_{i=0}^{n}\sum_{j=0}^{m} B_{i,n}(u_0)B_{j,m}(v)\,\mathbf{P}_{i,j} \\ &= \sum_{j=0}^{m} B_{j,m}(v)\left(\sum_{i=0}^{n} B_{i,n}(u_0)\,\mathbf{P}_{i,j}\right) \\ &= \sum_{j=0}^{m} B_{j,m}(v)\,\mathbf{Q}_j(u_0)\end{aligned} \tag{1.24}$$

where $\quad \mathbf{Q}_j(u_0) = \sum_{i=0}^{n} B_{i,n}(u_0)\,\mathbf{P}_{i,j} \qquad j = 0,\ldots,m$

is a Bézier curve lying on the surface. Analogously, $\mathbf{C}_{v_0}(u) = \sum_{i=0}^{n} B_{i,n}(u)\,\mathbf{Q}_i(v_0)$ is a Bézier u isocurve lying on the surface.

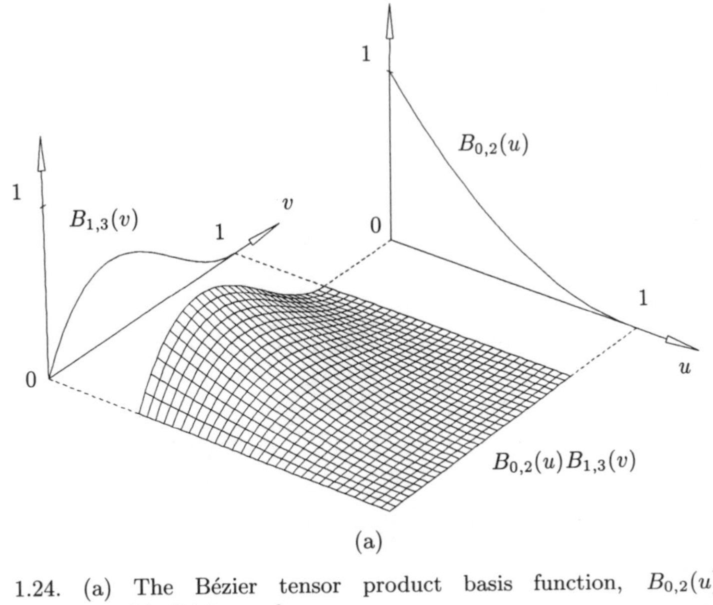

(a)

Figure 1.24. (a) The Bézier tensor product basis function, $B_{0,2}(u)B_{1,3}(v)$; (b) a quadratic $\times$ cubic Bézier surface.

As is the case for curves, because of their excellent properties Bézier surfaces are better suited for geometric modeling applications than power basis surfaces. In particular,

- nonnegativity: $B_{i,n}(u)B_{j,m}(v) \geq 0$ for all i, j, u, v;
- partition of unity: $\sum_{i=0}^{n} \sum_{j=0}^{m} B_{i,n}(u)B_{j,m}(v) = 1$ for all u and v;
- $\mathbf{S}(u, v)$ is contained in the convex hull of its control points;
- transformation invariance;
- the surface interpolates the four corner control points;
- when triangulated, the control net forms a planar polyhedral approximation to the surface.

It is interesting to note that there is no known variation diminishing property for Bézier surfaces (see [Prau92]).

The deCasteljau algorithm (`A1.5`) is also easily extended to compute points on a Bézier surface. Refer to Eq. (1.24) and Figure 1.25. Let (u_0, v_0) be fixed. For fixed j_0, $\mathbf{Q}_{j_0}(u_0) = \sum_{i=0}^{n} B_{i,n}(u_0)\mathbf{P}_{i,j_0}$ is the point obtained by applying the deCasteljau algorithm to the j_0 row of control points, i.e., to $\{\mathbf{P}_{i,j_0}\}$, $i = 0, \ldots, n$. Therefore, applying the deCasteljau Algorithm $(m+1)$ times yields $\mathbf{C}_{u_0}(v)$; and applying it once more to $\mathbf{C}_{u_0}(v)$ at $v = v_0$ yields $\mathbf{C}_{u_0}(v_0) = \mathbf{S}(u_0, v_0)$. This process requires

$$\frac{n(n+1)(m+1)}{2} + \frac{m(m+1)}{2} \tag{1.25}$$

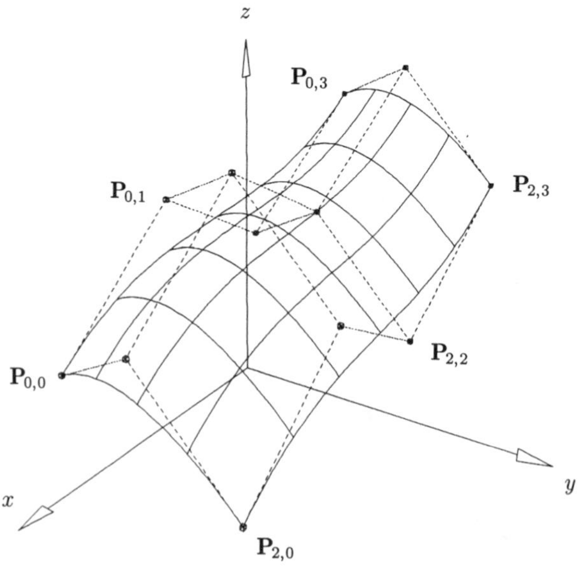

(b)

Figure 1.24. (*Continued.*)

linear interpolations (see Exercise 1.21). By symmetry, we can compute $\mathbf{C}_{v_0}(u)$ first ($n+1$ applications of deCasteljau) and then compute $\mathbf{C}_{v_0}(u_0) = \mathbf{S}(u_0, v_0)$. This requires

$$\frac{m(m+1)(n+1)}{2} + \frac{n(n+1)}{2} \tag{1.26}$$

linear interpolations. Thus, if $n > m$ compute $\mathbf{C}_{v_0}(u)$ first, then $\mathbf{C}_{v_0}(u_0)$; otherwise, compute $\mathbf{C}_{u_0}(v)$ first, then $\mathbf{C}_{u_0}(v_0)$.

```
ALGORITHM A1.7
  deCasteljau2(P,n,m,u0,v0,S)
    { /*  Compute a point on a Bézier surface */
      /*  by the deCasteljau.  */
      /*  Input:  P,n,m,u0,v0  */
      /*  Output: S
    if (n <= m)
      {
      for (j=0; j<=m; j++) /* P[j][] is jth row */
        deCasteljau1(P[j][],n,u0,Q[j]);
      deCasteljau1(Q,m,v0,S);
      }
    else
      {
      for (i=0; i<=n; i++)
```

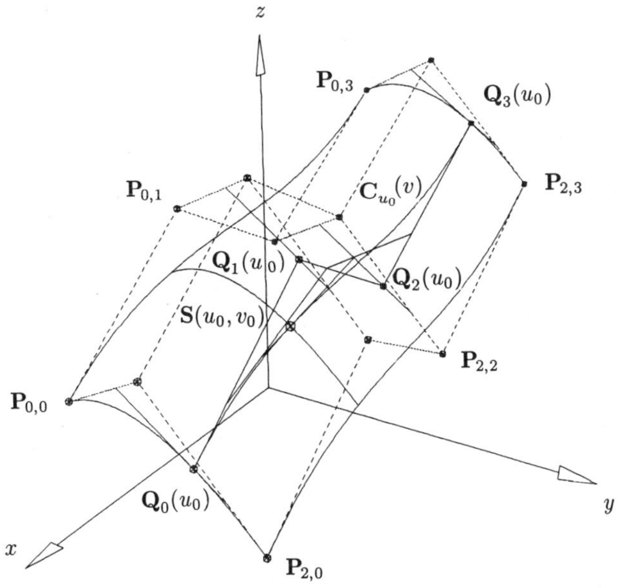

Figure 1.25. The deCasteljau algorithm for a Bézier surface.

```
      deCasteljau1(P[][i],m,v0,Q[i]);
    deCasteljau1(Q,n,u0,S);
    }
}
```

We define a *rational Bézier surface* to be the perspective projection of a four-dimensional polynomial Bézier surface (see [Pieg86; Fari89])

$$\mathbf{S}^w(u,v) = \sum_{i=0}^{n}\sum_{j=0}^{m} B_{i,n}(u)B_{j,m}(v)\,\mathbf{P}^w_{i,j} \tag{1.27}$$

and

$$\mathbf{S}(u,v) = H\{\mathbf{S}^w(u,v)\} = \frac{\sum_{i=0}^{n}\sum_{j=0}^{m} B_{i,n}(u)B_{j,m}(v)w_{i,j}\,\mathbf{P}_{i,j}}{\sum_{i=0}^{n}\sum_{j=0}^{m} B_{i,n}(u)B_{j,m}(v)w_{i,j}}$$

$$= \sum_{i=0}^{n}\sum_{j=0}^{m} R_{i,j}(u,v)\,\mathbf{P}_{i,j} \tag{1.28}$$

where

$$R_{i,j}(u,v) = \frac{B_{i,n}(u)B_{j,m}(v)w_{i,j}}{\sum_{r=0}^{n}\sum_{s=0}^{m} B_{r,n}(u)B_{s,m}(v)w_{r,s}}$$

Notice that the $R_{i,j}(u,v)$ are rational functions, but they are not products of other basis functions. Hence, $\mathbf{S}(u,v)$ is not a tensor product surface, but $\mathbf{S}^w(u,v)$ is. As with curves, we generally work with Eq. (1.27) and project the results. Figure 1.26a shows a rational basis function, and Figure 1.26b depicts a quadratic × cubic rational Bézier surface. Compare these figures with Figures 1.24a and 1.24b.

Assuming $w_{i,j} > 0$ for all i and j, the properties listed previously for nonrational Bézier surfaces (and the product functions $B_{i,n}(u)B_{j,m}(v)$) extend naturally to rational Bézier surfaces. Furthermore, if $w_{i,j} = 1$ for all i and j, then $R_{i,j}(u,v) = B_{i,n}(u)B_{j,m}(v)$, and the corresponding surface is nonrational.

Example

`Ex1.15` Let us construct a cylindrical surface patch. From Section 1.4 we know that

$$\mathbf{C}^w(u) = \sum_{i=0}^{2} B_{i,2}(u)\,\mathbf{P}^w_i$$

for $\{\mathbf{P}^w_i\} = \{(0,1,0,1), (0,1,1,1), (0,0,2,2)\}$, is a circular arc in the yz plane. Using translation (`P1.14`, Section 1.4)

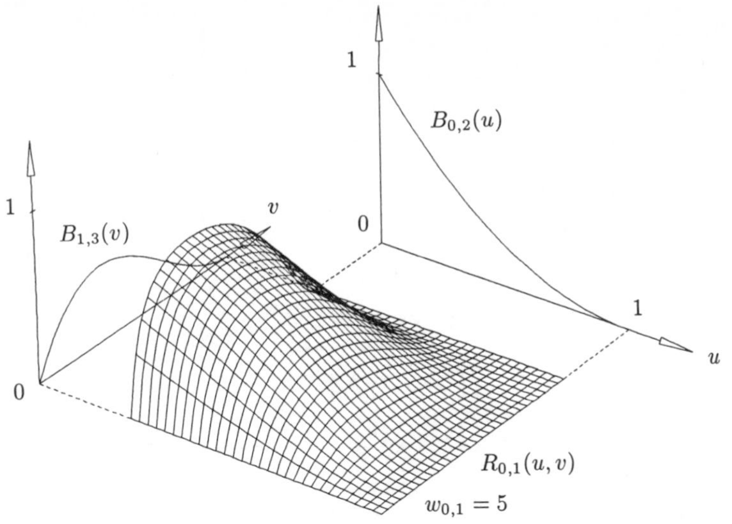

(a)

Figure 1.26. (a) The rational basis function $R_{0,1}(u,v)$ (with $w_{0,1} = 5$ and all other weights equal to one); (b) a quadratic × cubic rational Bézier surface.

$$\mathbf{C}_0^w(u) = \sum_{i=0}^{2} B_{i,2}(u)\mathbf{P}_{i,0}^w \quad \text{and} \quad \mathbf{C}_1^w(u) = \sum_{i=0}^{2} B_{i,2}(u)\mathbf{P}_{i,1}^w$$

where $$\{\mathbf{P}_{i,0}^w\} = \{(1,1,0,1),(1,1,1,1),(2,0,2,2)\}$$

and $$\{\mathbf{P}_{i,1}^w\} = \{(-1,1,0,1),(-1,1,1,1),(-2,0,2,2)\}$$

are circular arcs in the $x = 1$ and $x = -1$ planes, respectively (see Figure 1.27). A linear interpolation between $\mathbf{C}_0^w$ and $\mathbf{C}_1^w$ yields a cylindrical surface, i.e.

$$\mathbf{S}^w(u,v) = \sum_{i=0}^{2}\sum_{j=0}^{1} B_{i,2}(u)B_{j,1}(v)\mathbf{P}_{i,j}^w$$

For fixed $u = u_0$, $\mathbf{C}_{u_0}^w(v) = \sum_{j=0}^{1} B_{j,1}(v)\mathbf{Q}_j^w(u_0)$ is a straight line segment from $\mathbf{C}_0^w(u_0)$ to $\mathbf{C}_1^w(u_0)$ parallel to the x-axis. For fixed $v = v_0$, $\mathbf{C}_{v_0}^w = \mathbf{S}^w(u,v_0) = \sum_{i=0}^{2} B_{i,2}(u)\mathbf{Q}_i^w(v_0)$ is a circular arc in the plane $x = (1-v_0)(1) + v_0(-1) = 1 - 2v_0$. Now let us compute the point $\mathbf{S}(1/2, 1/2)$, using Algorithm A1.7. Note that $n > m$. First obtain $\mathbf{C}_{v_0=1/2}^w(u)$

$$\begin{matrix} (1,1,0,1) & \\ & (0,1,0,1) = \mathbf{Q}_0^w(v_0) \\ (-1,1,0,1) & \end{matrix}$$

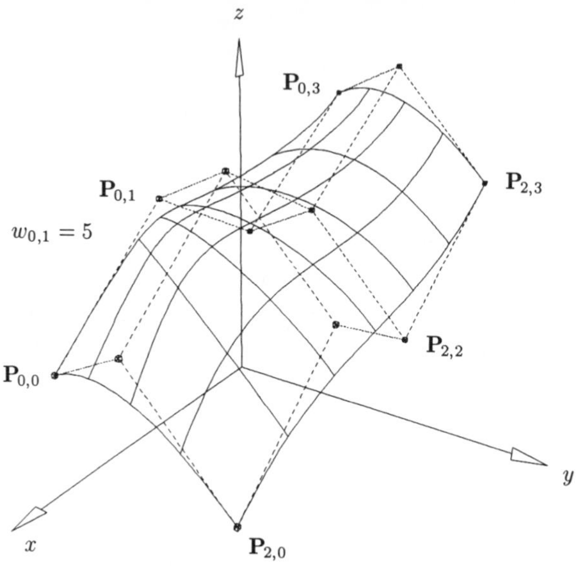

(b)

Figure 1.26. (b) (*Continued.*)

$$\begin{array}{ll} (1,1,1,1) & \\ & (0,1,1,1) = \mathbf{Q}_1^w(v_0) \\ (-1,1,1,1) & \end{array}$$

$$\begin{array}{ll} (2,0,2,2) & \\ & (0,0,2,2) = \mathbf{Q}_2^w(v_0) \\ (-2,0,2,2) & \end{array}$$

Now $\mathbf{C}^w_{v_0=1/2}(u) = \sum_{i=0}^{2} B_{i,2}(u)\,\mathbf{Q}_i^w(v_0)$ is the circular arc in the yz plane. Then

$$\begin{array}{lll} (0,1,0,1) & & \\ & \left(0,1,\frac{1}{2},1\right) & \\ (0,1,1,1) & & \left(0,\frac{3}{4},1,\frac{5}{4}\right) = \mathbf{S}^w\left(\frac{1}{2},\frac{1}{2}\right) \\ & \left(0,\frac{1}{2},\frac{3}{2},\frac{3}{2}\right) & \\ (0,0,2,2) & & \end{array}$$

And projecting yields

$$\mathbf{S}\left(\frac{1}{2},\frac{1}{2}\right) = H\left\{\left(0,\frac{3}{4},1,\frac{5}{4}\right)\right\} = \left(0,\frac{3}{5},\frac{4}{5}\right)$$

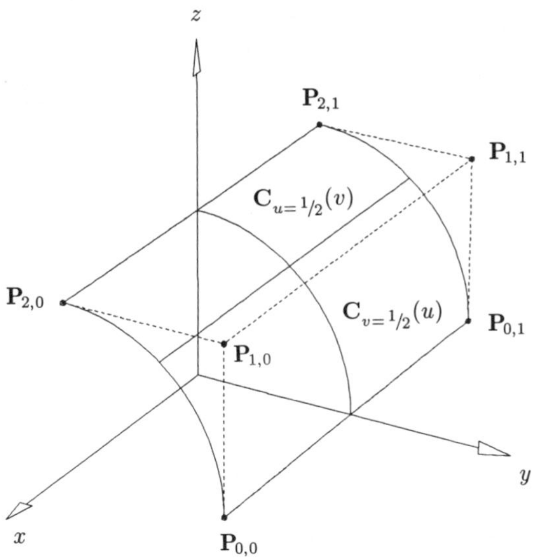

Figure 1.27. A cylindrical surface patch as a rational Bézier surface.

EXERCISES

1.1. Consider the two parametric representations of the circular arc given by Eqs. (1.1) and (1.2). Using Eq. (1.1), compute the curve point at $u = \pi/4$ and, using Eq. (1.2), the point at $t = 1/2$. Explain the results.

1.2. Compute the acceleration vector, $\mathbf{C}''(u)$, for Eq. (1.1). Explain the result.

1.3. Using trigonometric functions, give a parametric definition of the bounded surface of

- a right circular cone, with apex at the origin and axis of symmetry along the z-axis;
- the cone is opening upward, and is bounded above at $z = 2$ by the circle with radius $= 1$.

Modify Eq. (1.2) to get another representation of the same cone. Compute the first partial derivatives, $\mathbf{S}_u$ and $\mathbf{S}_v$, of the trigonometric representation. What are the values of these derivatives at the apex of the cone?

1.4. Consider the parabolic arc $\mathbf{C}(u) = (x(u), y(u)) = (-1 - u + 2u^2, -2u + u^2)$, $0 \le u \le 1$. Sketch this curve. The curve is rotated and translated by applying the transformations to the functions $x(u)$ and $y(u)$. Apply the two transformations

(1) 90° rotation about the origin. The rotation matrix (applied from the left) is

$$\begin{bmatrix} 0 & -1 \\ 1 & 0 \end{bmatrix}$$

(2) translation with the vector $(-1, -1)$.

The implicit equation of the underlying parabola is $x^2 - 4xy + 4y^2 - 4x - y - 5 = 0$. Sketch this curve. Apply the previous rotation and translation to this equation. Hint: let $\bar{x}, \bar{y}$ be the transformed coordinates. Find expressions $x = f(\bar{x}, \bar{y})$ and $y = g(\bar{x}, \bar{y})$ and substitute these into the implicit equation to obtain the implicit equation of the transformed parabola.

1.5. Determine formulas for the number of additions and multiplications necessary to compute a point on an nth-degree three-dimensional power basis curve.

1.6. Construct a cubic power basis curve with a loop. Hint: think about what endpoints and end derivatives, $\mathbf{C}'(0)$ and $\mathbf{C}'(1)$, are necessary.

1.7. Construct a cubic power basis curve with a cusp. Hint: think about $\mathbf{C}'(u)$ and $\mathbf{C}''(u)$. Sketch what $x'(u)$, $y'(u)$, $x''(u)$, and $y''(u)$ need to look like as functions of u. Determine a suitable $\mathbf{C}''(u)$, and then integrate to obtain $\mathbf{C}'(u)$ and $\mathbf{C}(u)$.

1.8. Construct a cubic power basis curve with an inflection point.

1.9. Let $\mathbf{C}(u) = (x(u), y(u)) = (1 + u - 2u^2 + u^3, 1 - 2u + u^3)$, $-1 \leq u \leq 1$. Let $u = 2v - 1$. Derive the curve $\mathbf{C}(v)$ by substituting $2v - 1$ for u in $\mathbf{C}(u)$. What degree is the curve $\mathbf{C}(v)$? Compute $\mathbf{C}(u)$ for $u = -1, 0, 1$. Compute $\mathbf{C}(v)$ for $v = 0, 1/2, 1$. What can you say about the curves $\mathbf{C}(u)$ and $\mathbf{C}(v)$? $\mathbf{C}(v)$ is called a *reparameterization* of $\mathbf{C}(u)$.

1.10. Check the property `P1.7` of the Bernstein polynomials for the cases $n = 2$ and $n = 3$.

1.11. It is sometimes necessary to reverse a curve, i.e., given $\mathbf{C}_1(u)$, $0 \leq u \leq 1$, produce $\mathbf{C}_2(v)$, $0 \leq v \leq 1$, such that the two curves are the same geometrically, but $\mathbf{C}_1(0) = \mathbf{C}_2(1)$ and $\mathbf{C}_1(1) = \mathbf{C}_2(0)$. How would you do this using the Bézier form? The power basis form?

1.12. Consider the xy planar cubic Bézier curve given by the control points $\mathbf{P}_0 = (0, 6)$, $\mathbf{P}_1 = (3, 6)$, $\mathbf{P}_2 = (6, 3)$, $\mathbf{P}_3 = (6, 0)$. Compute the point $\mathbf{C}(1/3)$ using the deCasteljau algorithm. Compute the same point by using Eqs. (1.7) and (1.8) directly, i.e., evaluate the basis functions at $u = 1/3$ and multiply by the appropriate control points.

1.13. Determine formulas for the number of additions and multiplications necessary to compute a point on an nth-degree three-dimensional Bézier curve using the deCasteljau algorithm, `A1.5`, and algorithm `A1.4`. Compare the results with Exercise 1.5 (the Horner algorithm).

1.14. For given n, row vector $[B_{0,n}(u), \ldots, B_{n,n}(u)]$ can be written as $[1, u, \ldots, u^n]M$, where M is an $(n+1) \times (n+1)$ matrix. Thus, a Bézier curve can be written in matrix form, $\mathbf{C}(u) = [u^i]^T M [\mathbf{P}_i]$. Compute the matrices M for $n = 1, 2, 3$. Notice that setting $[\mathbf{a}_i] = M[\mathbf{P}_i]$ yields the conversion of a Bézier curve to power basis form. Assuming $0 \leq u \leq 1$, $[\mathbf{P}_i] = M^{-1}[\mathbf{a}_i]$ gives the conversion from power basis to Bézier form.

1.15. Compare this with Exercise 1.9. It is also possible to define a Bézier curve on a parameter interval other than $[0, 1]$. This is equivalent to reparameterizing a Bézier curve. Let

$$\mathbf{C}(u) = \sum_{i=0}^{n} B_{i,n}(u)\mathbf{P}_i \qquad u \in [0, 1]$$

Let $v \in [a, b]$. Then $u = (v - a)/(b - a)$. Substitute this equation into Eq. (1.8) and derive this expression for the reparameterized curve

$$\mathbf{C}(v) = \frac{1}{(b-a)^n} \sum_{i=0}^{n} \frac{n!}{i!(n-i)!} (v-a)^i (b-v)^{n-i} \, \mathbf{P}_i$$

It is interesting to note that the control points do not change, only the basis functions. Reparameterization of the power basis form changes the geometric coefficients but not the basis functions.

1.16. Consider the circle

$$\mathbf{C}(u) = \left(\frac{1-u^2}{1+u^2}, \frac{2u}{1+u^2} \right)$$

Determine which ranges of the parameter u yield which quadrants of the circle. Do these equations yield the entire circle? What can you say about the parameterization?

1.17. Consider the following rational cubic Bézier curve in the xy plane: $\mathbf{P}_0 = (0,6)$, $\mathbf{P}_1 = (3,6)$, $\mathbf{P}_2 = (6,3)$, $\mathbf{P}_3 = (6,0)$, $w_0 = 4$, $w_1 = 1$, $w_2 = 1$, $w_3 = 4$. Compute the point $\mathbf{C}(2/3)$ by expanding the deCasteljau table.

1.18. What characteristic is it of the rational functions we are using that allows us to use the homogeneous coordinate representation? Why is this representation advantageous?

1.19. Find the rational Bézier representation of the circular arc in the second quadrant, i.e., determine the $\mathbf{P}_i$ and w_i. Hint: use symmetry and check your result by showing that $(x(u))^2 + (y(u))^2 = 1$ for all $u \in [0,1]$.

1.20. The circular arc in the first quadrant is also given by the equation

$$\mathbf{C}(u) = \left(\frac{1+(\sqrt{2}-2)u+(1-\sqrt{2})u^2}{1+(\sqrt{2}-2)u+(2-\sqrt{2})u^2}, \frac{\frac{\sqrt{2}}{2}u\left((\sqrt{2}-2)u+2\right)}{1+(\sqrt{2}-2)u+(2-\sqrt{2})u^2} \right)$$

Determine the rational Bézier representation corresponding to these equations. Hint: the $\mathbf{P}_i$ must be the same as before – $(1,0)$, $(1,1)$, $(0,1)$; Why? Compute the weights w_i by equating polynomials and substituting $u = 0, 1/2, 1$, as done previously. Compute the point $\mathbf{C}(1/2)$, using any method. What is interesting about $\mathbf{C}(1/2)$?

1.21. Derive Eqs. (1.25) and (1.26). Hint: use the formula $1+2+\cdots+n = n(n+1)/2$.

1.22. For the cylindrical surface example (**Ex1.15**) compute the control points $\mathbf{Q}_j^w(u_0)$ for the isocurve $\mathbf{C}^w_{u_0=1/3}(v)$.

1.23. Let $n = 3$ and $m = 2$. Consider the nonrational Bézier surface defined by the control net

$$\{\mathbf{P}_{i,0}\} = \{(0,0,0),(3,0,3),(6,0,3),(9,0,0)\}$$

$$\{\mathbf{P}_{i,1}\} = \{(0,2,2),(3,2,5),(6,2,5),(9,2,2)\}$$

$$\{\mathbf{P}_{i,2}\} = \{(0,4,0),(3,4,3),(6,4,3),(9,4,0)\}$$

a. sketch this surface;

b. use the deCasteljau algorithm to compute the surface point $\mathbf{S}(1/3, 1/2)$;

c. fix $u_0 = 1/2$ and extract the Bézier representation (control points) of the curve $\mathbf{C}_{u_0=1/2}(v)$.

1.24. Let

$$\mathbf{S}(u,v) = \sum_{i=0}^{n}\sum_{j=0}^{m} B_{i,n}(u)B_{j,m}(v)\,\mathbf{P}_{i,j}$$

and assume that $\mathbf{P}_{0,0} = \mathbf{P}_{1,0} = \cdots = \mathbf{P}_{n,0}$. How does this affect $\mathbf{S}(u,v)$, the derivatives $\mathbf{S}_u(u,v)$ and $\mathbf{S}_v(u,v)$, and the curves $\mathbf{C}_{v_0}(u)$? Assume that $\mathbf{P}_{i,0} = (1,0,0)$ for $i = 0,1,2$ in Example Ex1.15, with $w_{0,0} = 1$, $w_{1,0} = 1$, and $w_{2,0} = 2$. What type of surface do you get?

1.25. The prerequisite for this problem is Exercise 1.14. The rational Bézier surface (Eq. [1.27]) has a matrix form

$$\mathbf{S}^w(u,v) = [\,B_{i,n}(u)\,]^T\,[\,\mathbf{P}^w_{i,j}\,]\,[\,B_{j,m}(v)\,] = [\,u^i\,]^T\,M_n\,[\,\mathbf{P}^w_{i,j}\,]\,M^T_m\,[\,v^j\,]$$

where $[\,u^i\,]^T$ and $[\,v^j\,]$ are vectors, M_n is an $(n+1)\times(n+1)$ matrix, M^T_m is a $(m+1)\times(m+1)$ matrix, and $[\,\mathbf{P}^w_{i,j}\,]$ is an $(n+1)\times(m+1)$ matrix of four-dimensional points. Write this form down explicitly for the cylindrical surface example, Ex1.15. Using this matrix form, compute the point $\mathbf{S}^w(1/2, 1/2)$, and then project to obtain $\mathbf{S}(1/2, 1/2)$. There is no direct matrix form for $\mathbf{S}(u,v)$; why not?

CHAPTER

TWO

B-Spline Basis Functions

2.1 Introduction

Curves consisting of just one polynomial or rational segment are often inadequate. Their shortcomings are:

- a high degree is required in order to satisfy a large number of constraints; e.g., $(n-1)$-degree is needed to pass a polynomial Bézier curve through n data points. However, high degree curves are inefficient to process and are numerically unstable;
- a high degree is required to accurately fit some complex shapes;
- single-segment curves (surfaces) are not well-suited to interactive shape design; although Bézier curves can be shaped by means of their control points (and weights), the control is not sufficiently local.

The solution is to use curves (surfaces) which are *piecewise polynomial*, or *piecewise rational*. Figure 2.1 shows a curve, $\mathbf{C}(u)$, consisting of m $(=3)$ nth-degree polynomial *segments*. $\mathbf{C}(u)$ is defined on $u \in [0,1]$. The parameter values $u_0 = 0 < u_1 < u_2 < u_3 = 1$ are called *breakpoints*. They map into the endpoints of the three polynomial segments. We denote the segments by $\mathbf{C}_i(u)$, $1 \le i \le m$. The segments are constructed so that they join with some level of continuity (not necessarily the same at every breakpoint). Let $\mathbf{C}_i^{(j)}$ denote the jth derivative of $\mathbf{C}_i$. $\mathbf{C}(u)$ is said to be C^k continuous at the breakpoint u_i if $\mathbf{C}_i^{(j)}(u_i) = \mathbf{C}_{i+1}^{(j)}(u_i)$ for all $0 \le j \le k$.

Any of the standard polynomial forms can be used to represent $\mathbf{C}_i(u)$. Figure 2.2 shows the curve of Figure 2.1 with the three segments in cubic Bézier form. $\mathbf{P}_i^j$ denotes the ith control point of the jth segment.

If the degree equals three and the breakpoints $U = \{u_0, u_1, u_2, u_3\}$ remain fixed, and if we allow the twelve control points, $\mathbf{P}_i^j$, to vary arbitrarily, we obtain the vector space, $\mathcal{V}$, consisting of all piecewise cubic polynomial curves

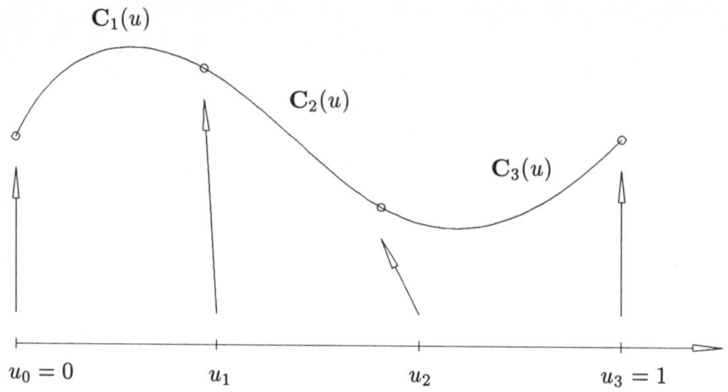

Figure 2.1. A piecewise cubic polynomial curve with three segments.

on U. $\mathcal{V}$ has dimension twelve, and a curve in $\mathcal{V}$ may be discontinuous at u_1 or u_2. Now suppose we specify (as in Figure 2.2) that $\mathbf{P}_3^1 = \mathbf{P}_0^2$ and $\mathbf{P}_3^2 = \mathbf{P}_0^3$. This gives rise to $\mathcal{V}^0$, the vector space of all piecewise cubic polynomial curves on U which are at least C^0 continuous everywhere. $\mathcal{V}^0$ has dimension ten, and $\mathcal{V}^0 \subset \mathcal{V}$.

Imposing C^1 continuity is a bit more involved. Let us consider $u = u_1$. Assume that $\mathbf{P}_3^1 = \mathbf{P}_0^2$. Let

$$v = \frac{u - u_0}{u_1 - u_0} \quad \text{and} \quad w = \frac{u - u_1}{u_2 - u_1}$$

be local parameters on the intervals $[u_0, u_1]$ and $[u_1, u_2]$, respectively. Then $0 \le v,\, w \le 1$. C^1 continuity at u_1 implies

$$\frac{1}{u_1 - u_0}\, \mathbf{C}_1^{(1)}(v = 1) = \mathbf{C}_1^{(1)}(u_1) = \mathbf{C}_2^{(1)}(u_1) = \frac{1}{u_2 - u_1}\, \mathbf{C}_2^{(1)}(w = 0)$$

and from Eq. (1.10) it follows that

$$\frac{3}{u_1 - u_0}(\mathbf{P}_3^1 - \mathbf{P}_2^1) = \frac{3}{u_2 - u_1}(\mathbf{P}_1^2 - \mathbf{P}_0^2)$$

Thus

$$\mathbf{P}_3^1 = \frac{(u_2 - u_1)\mathbf{P}_2^1 + (u_1 - u_0)\mathbf{P}_1^2}{u_2 - u_0} \qquad (2.1)$$

Equation (2.1) says that $\mathbf{P}_3^1$ and $\mathbf{P}_3^2$ can be written in terms of $\mathbf{P}_2^1, \mathbf{P}_1^2$ and $\mathbf{P}_2^2, \mathbf{P}_1^3$, respectively. Hence, $\mathcal{V}^1$, the vector space of all C^1 continuous piecewise cubic polynomial curves on U, has dimension eight, and $\mathcal{V}^1 \subset \mathcal{V}^0 \subset \mathcal{V}$.

This makes it clear that storing and manipulating the individual polynomial segments of a piecewise polynomial curve is not the ideal method for handling

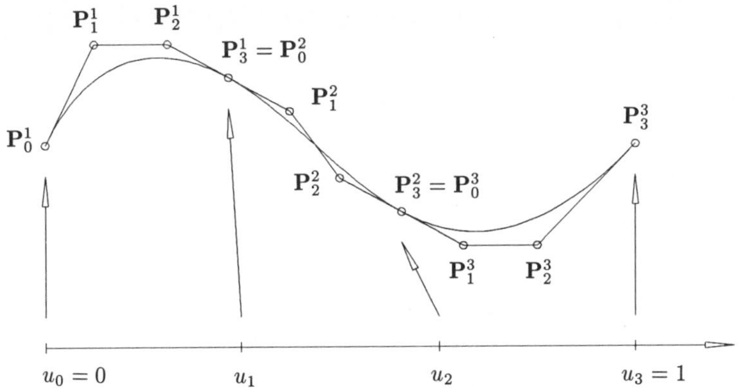

Figure 2.2. The curve of Figure 2.1 shown with the polynomial segments represented in Bézier form.

such curves. First, redundant data must be stored: twelve coefficients, where only eight are required for C^1 continuous cubic curves, and only six for C^2 continuous cubic curves. Second, for the Bézier form the continuity of $\mathbf{C}(u)$ depends on the positions of the control points, hence there is little flexibility in positioning control points while maintaining continuity. If a designer wants C^1 continuity and is satisfied with the segments $\mathbf{C}_1(u)$ and $\mathbf{C}_3(u)$, but wants to modify the shape of $\mathbf{C}_2(u)$, he is out of luck: none of $\mathbf{C}_2(u)$'s control points can be modified. Third, determining the continuity of a curve requires computation (such as Eq. [2.1]).

We want a curve representation of the form

$$\mathbf{C}(u) = \sum_{i=0}^{n} f_i(u)\,\mathbf{P}_i \tag{2.2}$$

where the $\mathbf{P}_i$ are *control points*, and the $\{f_i(u),\ i = 0, \ldots, n\}$ are *piecewise polynomial functions* forming a basis for the vector space of all piecewise polynomial functions of the desired degree and continuity (for a fixed breakpoint sequence, $U = \{u_i\}$, $0 \le i \le m$). Note that continuity is determined by the basis functions, hence the control points can be modified without altering the curve's continuity. Furthermore, the $\{f_i\}$ should have the 'usual' nice analytic properties, e.g. those listed in Section 1.3. This ensures that the curves defined by Eq. (2.2) have nice geometric properties similar to Bézier curves, e.g., convex hull, variation diminishing, transformation invariance. Another important property that we seek in our basis functions is that of *local support*; this implies that each $f_i(u)$ is nonzero only on a limited number of subintervals, not the entire domain, $[u_0, u_m]$. Since $\mathbf{P}_i$ is multiplied by $f_i(u)$, moving $\mathbf{P}_i$ affects curve shape only on the subintervals where $f_i(u)$ is nonzero.

Finally, given appropriate piecewise polynomial basis functions, we can construct piecewise rational curves

$$\mathbf{C}^w(u) = \sum_{i=0}^{n} f_i(u)\,\mathbf{P}_i^w \tag{2.3}$$

and nonrational and rational tensor product surfaces

$$\mathbf{S}(u,v) = \sum_{i=0}^{n}\sum_{j=0}^{m} f_i(u)g_j(v)\,\mathbf{P}_{i,j}$$

$$\mathbf{S}^w(u,v) = \sum_{i=0}^{n}\sum_{j=0}^{m} f_i(u)g_j(v)\,\mathbf{P}_{i,j}^w \tag{2.4}$$

For the remainder of this chapter we study the so-called B-spline basis functions. In Chapters 3 and 4 we combine these functions with three-dimensional and four-dimensional control points to obtain nonrational and rational curves and surfaces, respectively.

2.2 Definition and Properties of B-spline Basis Functions

There are a number of ways to define the B-spline basis functions and to prove their important properties, e.g., by divided differences of truncated power functions [Curr47; Scho46], by blossoming [Rams87], and by a recurrence formula due to deBoor, Cox, and Mansfield [Cox72; DeBo72, 78]. We use the recurrence formula, since it is the most useful for computer implementation.

Let $U = \{u_0, \ldots, u_m\}$ be a nondecreasing sequence of real numbers, i.e., $u_i \le u_{i+1}$, $i = 0, \ldots, m-1$. The u_i are called *knots*, and U is the *knot vector*. The ith B-spline basis function of p-degree (*order* $p+1$), denoted by $N_{i,p}(u)$, is defined as

$$N_{i,0}(u) = \begin{cases} 1 & \text{if } u_i \le u < u_{i+1} \\ 0 & \text{otherwise} \end{cases}$$

$$N_{i,p}(u) = \frac{u - u_i}{u_{i+p} - u_i} N_{i,p-1}(u) + \frac{u_{i+p+1} - u}{u_{i+p+1} - u_{i+1}} N_{i+1,p-1}(u) \tag{2.5}$$

Note that

- $N_{i,0}(u)$ is a step function, equal to zero everywhere except on the half-open interval $u \in [u_i, u_{i+1})$;
- for $p > 0$, $N_{i,p}(u)$ is a linear combination of two $(p-1)$-degree basis functions (Figure 2.3);

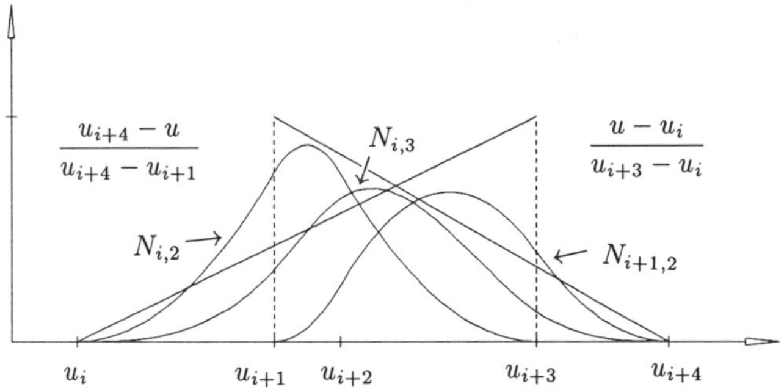

Figure 2.3. The recursive definition of B-spline basis functions.

- computation of a set of basis functions requires specification of a knot vector, U, and the degree, p;
- Equation (2.5) can yield the quotient $0/0$ (see examples later); we define this quotient to be zero;
- the $N_{i,p}(u)$ are piecewise polynomials, defined on the entire real line; generally only the interval $[u_0, u_m]$ is of interest;
- the half-open interval, $[u_i, u_{i+1})$, is called the *ith knot span*; it can have zero length, since knots need not be distinct;
- the computation of the pth-degree functions generates a truncated triangular table

$$
\begin{array}{cccc}
N_{0,0} & & & \\
& N_{0,1} & & \\
N_{1,0} & & N_{0,2} & \\
& N_{1,1} & & N_{0,3} \\
N_{2,0} & & N_{1,2} & \\
& N_{2,1} & & N_{1,3} \\
N_{3,0} & & N_{2,2} & \vdots \\
& N_{3,1} & \vdots & \\
N_{4,0} & \vdots & & \\
\vdots & & &
\end{array}
$$

For brevity we often write $N_{i,p}$ instead of $N_{i,p}(u)$.

A word about terminology. In Section 2.1 we used the term breakpoint and required $u_i < u_{i+1}$ for all i. In the remainder of this book we use the term knot and assume $u_i \le u_{i+1}$. The breakpoints correspond to the set of *distinct* knot values, and the knot spans of nonzero length define the individual polynomial segments. Hence, we use the word knot with two different meanings: a distinct value (breakpoint) in the set U, and an element of the set U (there can exist additional knots in U having the same value). It should be clear from the context which meaning is intended.

Examples

Ex2.1 Let $U = \{u_0 = 0, u_1 = 0, u_2 = 0, u_3 = 1, u_4 = 1, u_5 = 1\}$ and $p = 2$. We now compute the B-spline basis functions of degrees 0, 1, and 2

$$N_{0,0} = N_{1,0} = 0 \qquad -\infty < u < \infty$$

$$N_{2,0} = \begin{cases} 1 & 0 \le u < 1 \\ 0 & \text{otherwise} \end{cases}$$

$$N_{3,0} = N_{4,0} = 0 \qquad -\infty < u < \infty$$

$$N_{0,1} = \frac{u-0}{0-0}N_{0,0} + \frac{0-u}{0-0}N_{1,0} = 0 \qquad -\infty < u < \infty$$

$$N_{1,1} = \frac{u-0}{0-0}N_{1,0} + \frac{1-u}{1-0}N_{2,0} = \begin{cases} 1-u & 0 \le u < 1 \\ 0 & \text{otherwise} \end{cases}$$

$$N_{2,1} = \frac{u-0}{1-0}N_{2,0} + \frac{1-u}{1-1}N_{3,0} = \begin{cases} u & 0 \le u < 1 \\ 0 & \text{otherwise} \end{cases}$$

$$N_{3,1} = \frac{u-1}{1-1}N_{3,0} + \frac{1-u}{1-1}N_{4,0} = 0 \qquad -\infty < u < \infty$$

$$N_{0,2} = \frac{u-0}{0-0}N_{0,1} + \frac{1-u}{1-0}N_{1,1} = \begin{cases} (1-u)^2 & 0 \le u < 1 \\ 0 & \text{otherwise} \end{cases}$$

$$N_{1,2} = \frac{u-0}{1-0}N_{1,1} + \frac{1-u}{1-0}N_{2,1} = \begin{cases} 2u(1-u) & 0 \le u < 1 \\ 0 & \text{otherwise} \end{cases}$$

$$N_{2,2} = \frac{u-0}{1-0}N_{2,1} + \frac{1-u}{1-1}N_{3,1} = \begin{cases} u^2 & 0 \le u < 1 \\ 0 & \text{otherwise} \end{cases}$$

Note that the $N_{i,2}$, restricted to the interval $u \in [0,1]$, are the quadratic Bernstein polynomials (Section 1.3 and Figure 1.13b). For this reason, the B-spline representation with a knot vector of the form

$$U = \{\underbrace{0,\ldots,0}_{p+1},\underbrace{1,\ldots,1}_{p+1}\}$$

is a generalization of the Bézier representation.

Ex2.2 Let $U = \{u_0 = 0, u_1 = 0, u_2 = 0, u_3 = 1, u_4 = 2, u_5 = 3, u_6 = 4, u_7 = 4, u_8 = 5, u_9 = 5, u_{10} = 5\}$ and $p = 2$. The zeroth-, first-, and second-degree basis functions are computed here. The ones not identically zero are shown in Figures 2.4, 2.5, and 2.6, respectively

$$N_{0,0} = N_{1,0} = 0 \quad \text{for} \quad -\infty < u < \infty$$

$$N_{2,0} = \begin{cases} 1 & 0 \le u < 1 \\ 0 & \text{otherwise} \end{cases}$$

$$N_{3,0} = \begin{cases} 1 & 1 \le u < 2 \\ 0 & \text{otherwise} \end{cases}$$

$$N_{4,0} = \begin{cases} 1 & 2 \le u < 3 \\ 0 & \text{otherwise} \end{cases}$$

$$N_{5,0} = \begin{cases} 1 & 3 \le u < 4 \\ 0 & \text{otherwise} \end{cases}$$

$$N_{6,0} = 0 \quad \text{for} \quad -\infty < u < \infty$$

$$N_{7,0} = \begin{cases} 1 & 4 \le u < 5 \\ 0 & \text{otherwise} \end{cases}$$

$$N_{8,0} = N_{9,0} = 0 \quad \text{for} \quad -\infty < u < \infty$$

$$N_{0,1} = \frac{u-0}{0-0} N_{0,0} + \frac{0-u}{0-0} N_{1,0} = 0 \qquad -\infty < u < \infty$$

$$N_{1,1} = \frac{u-0}{0-0} N_{1,0} + \frac{1-u}{1-0} N_{2,0} = \begin{cases} 1-u & 0 \le u < 1 \\ 0 & \text{otherwise} \end{cases}$$

$$N_{2,1} = \frac{u-0}{1-0} N_{2,0} + \frac{2-u}{2-1} N_{3,0} = \begin{cases} u & 0 \le u < 1 \\ 2-u & 1 \le u < 2 \\ 0 & \text{otherwise} \end{cases}$$

$$N_{3,1} = \frac{u-1}{2-1} N_{3,0} + \frac{3-u}{3-2} N_{4,0} = \begin{cases} u-1 & 1 \le u < 2 \\ 3-u & 2 \le u < 3 \\ 0 & \text{otherwise} \end{cases}$$

$$N_{4,1} = \frac{u-2}{3-2} N_{4,0} + \frac{4-u}{4-3} N_{5,0} = \begin{cases} u-2 & 2 \le u < 3 \\ 4-u & 3 \le u < 4 \\ 0 & \text{otherwise} \end{cases}$$

$$N_{5,1} = \frac{u-3}{4-3} N_{5,0} + \frac{4-u}{4-4} N_{6,0} = \begin{cases} u-3 & 3 \le u < 4 \\ 0 & \text{otherwise} \end{cases}$$

$$N_{6,1} = \frac{u-4}{4-4} N_{6,0} + \frac{5-u}{5-4} N_{7,0} = \begin{cases} 5-u & 4 \le u < 5 \\ 0 & \text{otherwise} \end{cases}$$

$$N_{7,1} = \frac{u-4}{5-4} N_{7,0} + \frac{5-u}{5-5} N_{8,0} = \begin{cases} u-4 & 4 \le u < 5 \\ 0 & \text{otherwise} \end{cases}$$

$$N_{8,1} = \frac{u-5}{5-5} N_{8,0} + \frac{5-u}{5-5} N_{9,0} = 0 \qquad -\infty < u < \infty$$

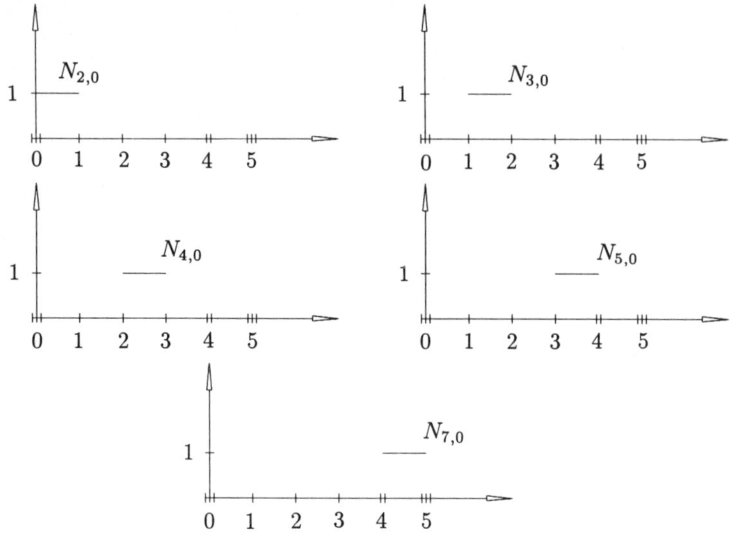

Figure 2.4. The nonzero zeroth-degree basis functions, $U = \{0,0,0,1,2,3,4,4,5,5,5\}$.

All of the following $N_{i,2}$ are zero everywhere except on the specified intervals, that is

$$N_{0,2} = \frac{u-0}{0-0}N_{0,1} + \frac{1-u}{1-0}N_{1,1} = (1-u)^2 \qquad 0 \le u < 1$$

$$N_{1,2} = \frac{u-0}{1-0}N_{1,1} + \frac{2-u}{2-0}N_{2,1} = \begin{cases} 2u - {}^3\!/_2 u^2 & 0 \le u < 1 \\ {}^1\!/_2(2-u)^2 & 1 \le u < 2 \end{cases}$$

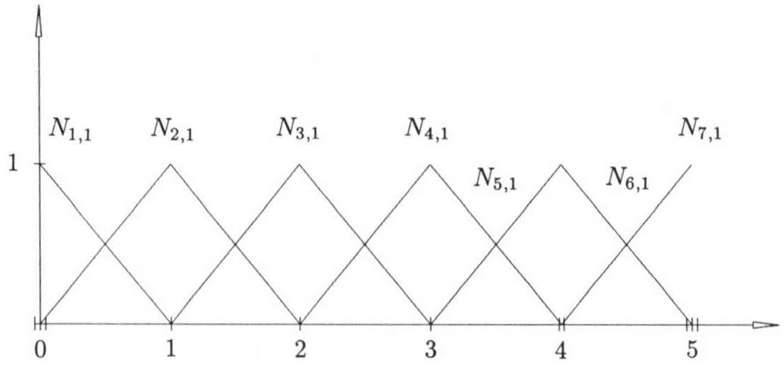

Figure 2.5. The nonzero first-degree basis functions, $U = \{0,0,0,1,2,3,4,4,5,5,5\}$.

$$N_{2,2} = \frac{u-0}{2-0}N_{2,1} + \frac{3-u}{3-1}N_{3,1} = \begin{cases} 1/2u^2 & 0 \le u < 1 \\ -3/2 + 3u - u^2 & 1 \le u < 2 \\ 1/2(3-u)^2 & 2 \le u < 3 \end{cases}$$

$$N_{3,2} = \frac{u-1}{3-1}N_{3,1} + \frac{4-u}{4-2}N_{4,1} = \begin{cases} 1/2(u-1)^2 & 1 \le u < 2 \\ -11/2 + 5u - u^2 & 2 \le u < 3 \\ 1/2(4-u)^2 & 3 \le u < 4 \end{cases}$$

$$N_{4,2} = \frac{u-2}{4-2}N_{4,1} + \frac{4-u}{4-3}N_{5,1} = \begin{cases} 1/2(u-2)^2 & 2 \le u < 3 \\ -16 + 10u - 3/2u^2 & 3 \le u < 4 \end{cases}$$

$$N_{5,2} = \frac{u-3}{4-3}N_{5,1} + \frac{5-u}{5-4}N_{6,1} = \begin{cases} (u-3)^2 & 3 \le u < 4 \\ (5-u)^2 & 4 \le u < 5 \end{cases}$$

$$N_{6,2} = \frac{u-4}{5-4}N_{6,1} + \frac{5-u}{5-4}N_{7,1} = 2(u-4)(5-u) \qquad 4 \le u < 5$$

$$N_{7,2} = \frac{u-4}{5-4}N_{7,1} + \frac{5-u}{5-5}N_{8,1} = (u-4)^2 \qquad 4 \le u < 5$$

We now list a number of important properties of the B-spline basis functions. As we see in the next chapter, it is these properties which determine the many desirable geometric characteristics in B-spline curves and surfaces. Assume degree p and a knot vector $U = \{u_0, \ldots, u_m\}$.

P2.1 $N_{i,p}(u) = 0$ if u is outside the interval $[u_i, u_{i+p+1})$ (local support property). This is illustrated by the triangular scheme shown here. Notice

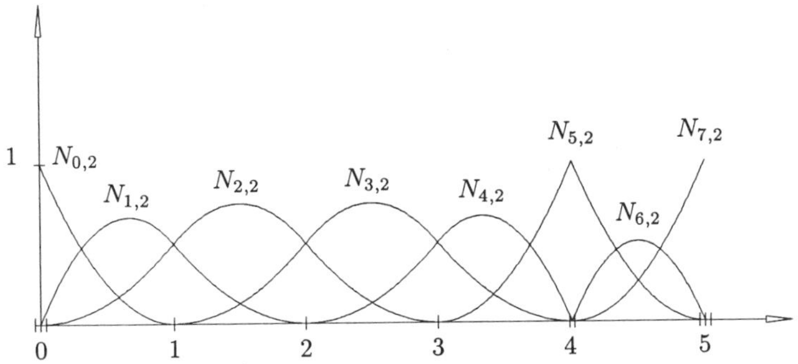

Figure 2.6. The nonzero second-degree basis functions, $U = \{0,0,0,1,2,3,4,4,5,5,5\}$.

that $N_{1,3}$ is a combination of $N_{1,0}$, $N_{2,0}$, $N_{3,0}$, and $N_{4,0}$. Thus, $N_{1,3}$ is nonzero only for $u \in [u_1, u_5)$

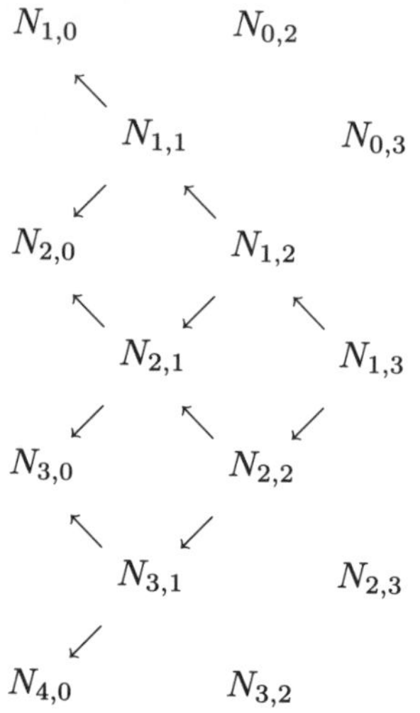

P2.2 In any given knot span, $[u_j, u_{j+1})$, at most $p+1$ of the $N_{i,p}$ are nonzero, namely the functions $N_{j-p,p}, \ldots, N_{j,p}$. On $[u_3, u_4)$ the only nonzero zeroth-degree function is $N_{3,0}$. Hence, the only cubic functions not zero on $[u_3, u_4)$ are $N_{0,3}, \ldots, N_{3,3}$. This property is illustrated here

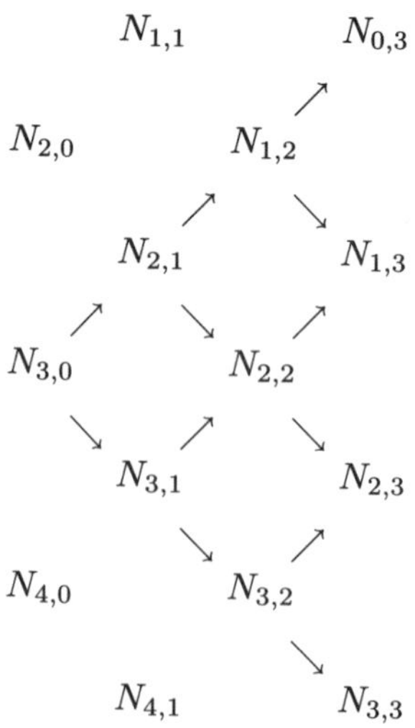

P2.3 $N_{i,p}(u) \geq 0$ for all i, p, and u (nonnegativity). This is proven by induction on p. It is clearly true for $p = 0$; assume it is true for $p-1$, $p \geq 0$, with i and u arbitrary. By definition

$$N_{i,p}(u) = \frac{u - u_i}{u_{i+p} - u_i} N_{i,p-1}(u) + \frac{u_{i+p+1} - u}{u_{i+p+1} - u_{i+1}} N_{i+1,p-1}(u) \tag{2.6}$$

By P2.1, $N_{i,p-1}(u) = 0$ if $u \notin [u_i, u_{i+p})$. But $u \in [u_i, u_{i+p})$ implies

$$\frac{u - u_i}{u_{i+p} - u_i}$$

is nonnegative. By assumption, $N_{i,p-1}(u)$ is nonnegative, and thus the first term of Eq. (2.6) is nonnegative. The same is true for the second term, and hence the $N_{i,p}(u)$ are nonnegative;

P2.4 For an arbitrary knot span, $[u_i, u_{i+1})$, $\sum_{j=i-p}^{i} N_{j,p}(u) = 1$ for all $u \in [u_i, u_{i+1})$ (partition of unity). To prove this, consider

$$\sum_{j=i-p}^{i} N_{j,p}(u) = \sum_{j=i-p}^{i} \frac{u - u_j}{u_{j+p} - u_j} N_{j,p-1}(u) + \sum_{j=i-p}^{i} \frac{u_{j+p+1} - u}{u_{j+p+1} - u_{j+1}} N_{j+1,p-1}(u)$$

Changing the summation variable in the second sum from $i-p$ to $i-p+1$, and considering that $N_{i-p,p-1}(u) = N_{i+1,p-1}(u) = 0$, we have

$$\sum_{j=i-p}^{i} N_{j,p}(u) = \sum_{j=i-p+1}^{i} \left[\frac{u - u_j}{u_{j+p} - u_j} + \frac{u_{j+p} - u}{u_{j+p} - u_j} \right] N_{j,p-1}(u) = \sum_{j=i-p+1}^{i} N_{j,p-1}(u)$$

Applying the same concept recursively yields

$$\sum_{j=i-p}^{i} N_{j,p}(u) = \sum_{j=i-p+1}^{i} N_{j,p-1}(u) = \sum_{j=i-p+2}^{i} N_{j,p-2}(u) = \cdots = \sum_{j=i}^{i} N_{j,0}(u) = 1$$

P2.5 All derivatives of $N_{i,p}(u)$ exist in the interior of a knot span (where it is a polynomial, see Figure 2.7). At a knot $N_{i,p}(u)$ is $p-k$ times continuously differentiable, where k is the multiplicity of the knot. Hence, increasing

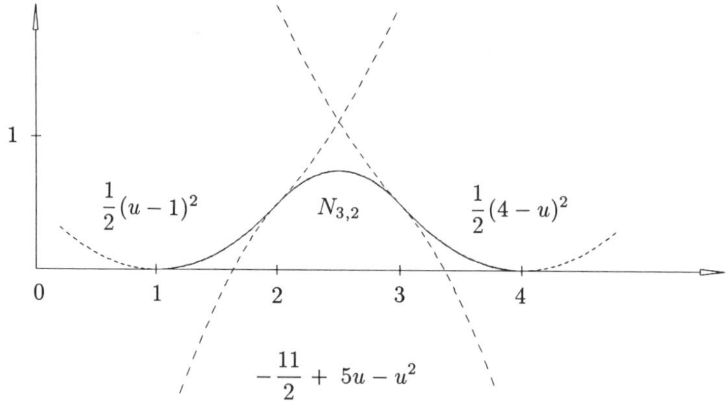

Figure 2.7. The decomposition of $N_{3,2}$ into its polynomial pieces (parabolas).

degree increases continuity, and increasing knot multiplicity decreases continuity;

P2.6 Except for the case $p = 0$, $N_{i,p}(u)$ attains exactly one maximum value.

It is important to understand the effect of multiple knots. Consider the functions $N_{0,2}$, $N_{1,2}$, $N_{2,2}$, $N_{5,2}$, and $N_{6,2}$ of Figure 2.6. Recalling that $U = \{0,0,0,1,2,3,4,4,5,5,5\}$, from Eq. (2.5) and P2.1, we see that these functions are computed on the following knot spans and are zero outside these spans

$$\begin{aligned} N_{0,2} &: \{0,0,0,1\} \\ N_{1,2} &: \{0,0,1,2\} \\ N_{2,2} &: \{0,1,2,3\} \\ N_{5,2} &: \{3,4,4,5\} \\ N_{6,2} &: \{4,4,5,5\} \end{aligned}$$

Now the word 'multiplicity' is understood in two different ways:

- the multiplicity of a knot in the knot vector;
- the multiplicity of a knot with respect to a specific basis function.

For example, $u = 0$ has multiplicity three in the previous knot vector U. But with respect to the functions $N_{0,2}$, $N_{1,2}$, $N_{2,2}$, and $N_{5,2}$, $u = 0$ is a knot of multiplicity 3, 2, 1, and 0, respectively. From P2.5, the continuity of these functions at $u = 0$ is $N_{0,2}$ discontinuous; $N_{1,2}$ C^0 continuous; $N_{2,2}$ C^1 continuous; and $N_{5,2}$ totally unaffected ($N_{5,2}$ and all its derivatives are zero at $u = 0$, from both sides). $N_{1,2}$ 'sees' $u = 0$ as a double knot, hence it is C^0 continuous. $N_{2,2}$ 'sees' all its knots with multiplicity 1, thus it is C^1 continuous everywhere. Clearly, another effect of multiple knots (as seen by the functions) is to reduce the number of 'apparent' intervals on which a function is nonzero; e.g., $N_{6,2}$ is nonzero only on $u \in [4,5)$, and it is only C^0 continuous at $u = 4$ and $u = 5$.

2.3 Derivatives of B-spline Basis Functions

The derivative of a basis function is given by

$$N'_{i,p} = \frac{p}{u_{i+p} - u_i} N_{i,p-1}(u) - \frac{p}{u_{i+p+1} - u_{i+1}} N_{i+1,p-1}(u) \tag{2.7}$$

(See Figure 2.8 for a graphical illustration.) We prove this by induction on p. For $p = 1$, $N_{i,p-1}$ and $N_{i+1,p-1}$ are either 0 or 1, and thus $N'_{i,p}$ is either

$$\frac{1}{u_{i+1} - u_i} \quad \text{or} \quad -\frac{1}{u_{i+2} - u_{i+1}}$$

(see Figure 2.5). Now assume that Eq. (2.7) is true for $p - 1$, $p > 1$. Using the product rule, $(fg)' = f'g + fg'$, to differentiate the basis function

$$N_{i,p}(u) = \frac{u - u_i}{u_{i+p} - u_i} N_{i,p-1}(u) + \frac{u_{i+p+1} - u}{u_{i+p+1} - u_{i+1}} N_{i+1,p-1}(u)$$

yields

$$N'_{i,p} = \frac{1}{u_{i+p} - u_i} N_{i,p-1} + \frac{u - u_i}{u_{i+p} - u_i} N'_{i,p-1} - \frac{1}{u_{i+p+1} - u_{i+1}} N_{i+1,p-1} + \frac{u_{i+p+1} - u}{u_{i+p+1} - u_{i+1}} N'_{i+1,p-1} \tag{2.8}$$

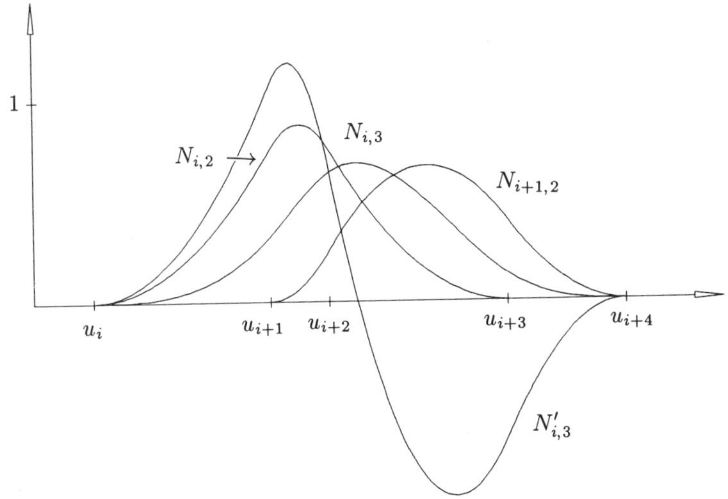

Figure 2.8. The recursive definition of B-spline derivatives.

Substituting Eq. (2.7) into Eq. (2.8) for $N'_{i,p-1}$ and $N'_{i+1,p-1}$ yields

$$
\begin{aligned}
N'_{i,p} = {} & \frac{1}{u_{i+p}-u_i} N_{i,p-1} - \frac{1}{u_{i+p+1}-u_{i+1}} N_{i+1,p-1} \\
& + \frac{u-u_i}{u_{i+p}-u_i}\left(\frac{p-1}{u_{i+p-1}-u_i} N_{i,p-2} - \frac{p-1}{u_{i+p}-u_{i+1}} N_{i+1,p-2}\right) \\
& + \frac{u_{i+p+1}-u}{u_{i+p+1}-u_{i+1}}\left(\frac{p-1}{u_{i+p}-u_{i+1}} N_{i+1,p-2} - \frac{p-1}{u_{i+p+1}-u_{i+2}} N_{i+2,p-2}\right) \\
= {} & \frac{1}{u_{i+p}-u_i} N_{i,p-1} - \frac{1}{u_{i+p+1}-u_{i+1}} N_{i+1,p-1} \\
& + \frac{p-1}{u_{i+p}-u_i}\,\frac{u-u_i}{u_{i+p-1}-u_i} N_{i,p-2} \\
& + \frac{p-1}{u_{i+p}-u_{i+1}}\left(\frac{u_{i+p+1}-u}{u_{i+p+1}-u_{i+1}} - \frac{u-u_i}{u_{i+p}-u_i}\right) N_{i+1,p-2} \\
& - \frac{p-1}{u_{i+p+1}-u_{i+1}}\,\frac{u_{i+p+1}-u}{u_{i+p+1}-u_{i+2}} N_{i+2,p-2}
\end{aligned}
$$

Noting that

$$
\begin{aligned}
\frac{u_{i+p+1}-u}{u_{i+p+1}-u_{i+1}} - \frac{u-u_i}{u_{i+p}-u_i} &= -1 + \frac{u_{i+p+1}-u}{u_{i+p+1}-u_{i+1}} + 1 - \frac{u-u_i}{u_{i+p}-u_i} \\
&= -\frac{u_{i+p+1}-u_{i+1}}{u_{i+p+1}-u_{i+1}} + \frac{u_{i+p+1}-u}{u_{i+p+1}-u_{i+1}} \\
&\quad + \frac{u_{i+p}-u_i}{u_{i+p}-u_i} - \frac{u-u_i}{u_{i+p}-u_i} \\
&= \frac{u_{i+p}-u}{u_{i+p}-u_i} - \frac{u-u_{i+1}}{u_{i+p+1}-u_{i+1}}
\end{aligned}
$$

we obtain

$$
\begin{aligned}
N'_{i,p} = {} & \frac{1}{u_{i+p}-u_i} N_{i,p-1} - \frac{1}{u_{i+p+1}-u_{i+1}} N_{i+1,p-1} \\
& + \frac{p-1}{u_{i+p}-u_i}\left(\frac{u-u_i}{u_{i+p-1}-u_i} N_{i,p-2} + \frac{u_{i+p}-u}{u_{i+p}-u_{i+1}} N_{i+1,p-2}\right) \\
& - \frac{p-1}{u_{i+p+1}-u_{i+1}}\left(\frac{u-u_{i+1}}{u_{i+p}-u_{i+1}} N_{i+1,p-2} + \frac{u_{i+p+1}-u}{u_{i+p+1}-u_{i+2}} N_{i+2,p-2}\right)
\end{aligned}
$$

By the Cox-deBoor formula (Eq. [2.5]), the expressions in the parentheses can be replaced by $N_{i,p-1}$ and $N_{i+1,p-1}$, respectively. It follows that

$$\begin{aligned} N'_{i,p} &= \frac{1}{u_{i+p}-u_i} N_{i,p-1} - \frac{1}{u_{i+p+1}-u_{i+1}} N_{i+1,p-1} \\ &\quad + \frac{p-1}{u_{i+p}-u_i} N_{i,p-1} - \frac{p-1}{u_{i+p+1}-u_{i+1}} N_{i+1,p-1} \\ &= \frac{p}{u_{i+p}-u_i} N_{i,p-1} - \frac{p}{u_{i+p+1}-u_{i+1}} N_{i+1,p-1} \end{aligned}$$

This completes the proof.

Now let $N^{(k)}_{i,p}$ denote the kth derivative of $N_{i,p}(u)$. Repeated differentiation of Eq. (2.7) produces the general formula

$$N^{(k)}_{i,p}(u) = p\left(\frac{N^{(k-1)}_{i,p-1}}{u_{i+p}-u_i} - \frac{N^{(k-1)}_{i+1,p-1}}{u_{i+p+1}-u_{i+1}}\right) \tag{2.9}$$

Equation (2.10) is another generalization of Eq. (2.7). It computes the kth derivative of $N_{i,p}(u)$ in terms of the functions $N_{i,p-k}, \ldots, N_{i+k,p-k}$

$$N^{(k)}_{i,p} = \frac{p!}{(p-k)!}\sum_{j=0}^{k} a_{k,j} N_{i+j,p-k} \tag{2.10}$$

with

$$\begin{aligned} a_{0,0} &= 1 \\ a_{k,0} &= \frac{a_{k-1,0}}{u_{i+p-k+1}-u_i} \\ a_{k,j} &= \frac{a_{k-1,j}-a_{k-1,j-1}}{u_{i+p+j-k+1}-u_{i+j}} \qquad j=1,\ldots,k-1 \\ a_{k,k} &= \frac{-a_{k-1,k-1}}{u_{i+p+1}-u_{i+k}} \end{aligned}$$

Remarks on Eq. (2.10):

- k should not exceed p (all higher derivatives are zero);
- the denominators involving knot differences can become zero; the quotient is defined to be zero in this case (see Example `Ex2.4` and Algorithm `A2.3` in Section 2.5).

We omit a proof of Eq. (2.10) but verify that it holds for $k = 1, 2$. By definition

$$a_{1,0} = \frac{1}{u_{i+p}-u_i} \qquad a_{1,1} = -\frac{1}{u_{i+p+1}-u_{i+1}}$$

and

$$N^{(1)}_{i,p} = 2(a_{1,0}\, N_{i,p-1} + a_{1,1}\, N_{i+1,p-1})$$

Comparing this with Eq. (2.7) proves the case for $k = 1$; now let $k = 2$. Differentiating Eq. (2.7) yields

$$
\begin{aligned}
N_{i,p}^{(2)} &= \frac{p}{u_{i+p} - u_i} N_{i,p-1}^{(1)} - \frac{p}{u_{i+p+1} - u_{i+1}} N_{i+1,p-1}^{(1)} \\
&= \frac{p}{u_{i+p} - u_i} \left(\frac{p-1}{u_{i+p-1} - u_i} N_{i,p-2} - \frac{p-1}{u_{i+p} - u_{i+1}} N_{i+1,p-2} \right) \\
&\quad - \frac{p}{u_{i+p+1} - u_{i+1}} \left(\frac{p-1}{u_{i+p} - u_{i+1}} N_{i+1,p-2} - \frac{p-1}{u_{i+p+1} - u_{i+2}} N_{i+2,p-2} \right) \\
&= p(p-1) \left[\frac{a_{1,0}}{u_{i+p-1} - u_i} N_{i,p-2} \right. \\
&\quad - \frac{1}{u_{i+p} - u_{i+1}} \left(\frac{1}{u_{i+p} - u_i} + \frac{1}{u_{i+p+1} - u_{i+1}} \right) N_{i+1,p-2} \\
&\quad \left. + \frac{a_{1,1}}{u_{i+p+1} - u_{i+2}} N_{i+2,p-2} \right] \\
&= p(p-1) \left(a_{2,0}\, N_{i,p-2} + \frac{a_{1,1} - a_{1,0}}{u_{i+p} - u_{i+1}} N_{i+1,p-2} + a_{2,2}\, N_{i+2,p-2} \right)
\end{aligned}
$$

Noting that $k = 2$ and

$$
a_{2,1} = \frac{a_{1,1} - a_{1,0}}{u_{i+p} - u_{i+1}}
$$

it follows that

$$
N_{i,p}^{(2)}(u) = 2 \sum_{j=0}^{2} a_{2,j} N_{i+j,p-2}(u)
$$

For completeness, we give an additional formula for computing derivatives of the B-spline basis functions (see [Butt76])

$$
N_{i,p}^{(k)} = \frac{p}{p-k} \left(\frac{u - u_i}{u_{i+p} - u_i} N_{i,p-1}^{(k)} + \frac{u_{i+p+1} - u}{u_{i+p+1} - u_{i+1}} N_{i+1,p-1}^{(k)} \right) \qquad k = 0, \ldots, p-1 \tag{2.11}
$$

Equation (2.11) gives the kth derivative of $N_{i,p}(u)$ in terms of the kth derivative of $N_{i,p-1}$ and $N_{i+1,p-1}$.

Figures 2.9b and 2.10b show the derivatives corresponding to the basis functions in Figures 2.9a and 2.10a. Figure 2.11 shows all the nonzero derivatives of $N_{i,3}$. Note the effect of multiple knots in Figure 2.10b; $N'_{6,3}$ has a jump at the triple knot.

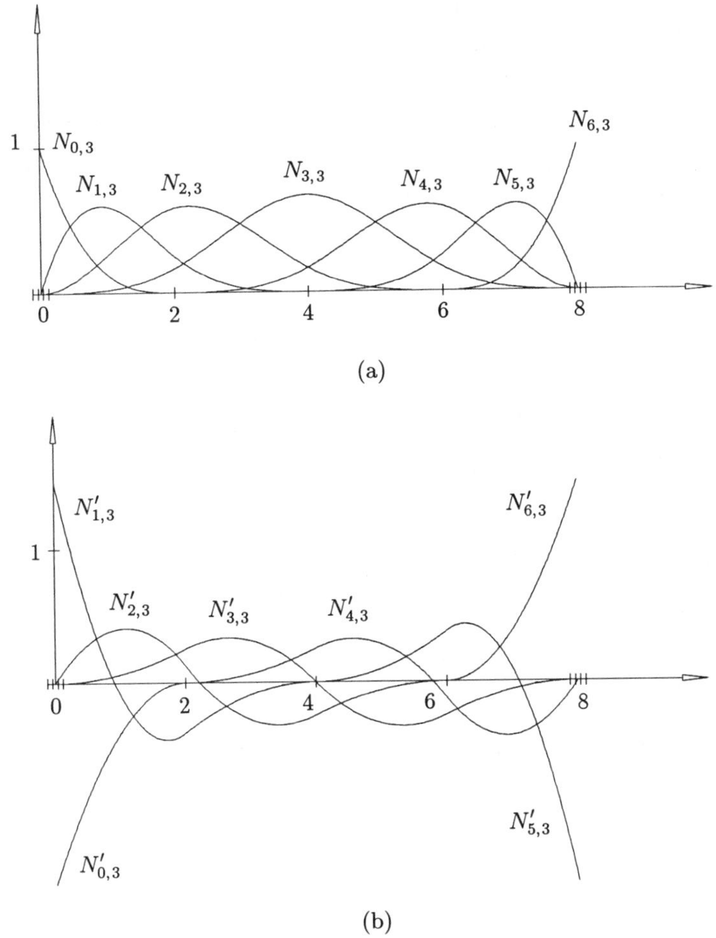

Figure 2.9. (a) Cubic basis functions; (b) derivatives corresponding to the basis functions in Figure 2.9a.

2.4 Further Properties of the Basis Functions

Let $\{u_j\}$, $0 \le j \le k$, be a strictly increasing set of breakpoints. The set of all piecewise polynomial functions of degree p on $\{u_j\}$ which are C^{r_j} continuous at $u = u_j$ forms a vector space, $\mathcal{V}$ $(-1 \le r_j \le p)$. If no continuity constraints are imposed ($r_j = -1$ for all j), then the dimension of $\mathcal{V}$ (denoted $\dim(\mathcal{V})$) is equal to $k(p+1)$. Each continuity constraint decreases the dimension by one, thus

$$\dim(\mathcal{V}) = k(p+1) - \sum_{j=0}^{k} (r_j + 1) \tag{2.12}$$

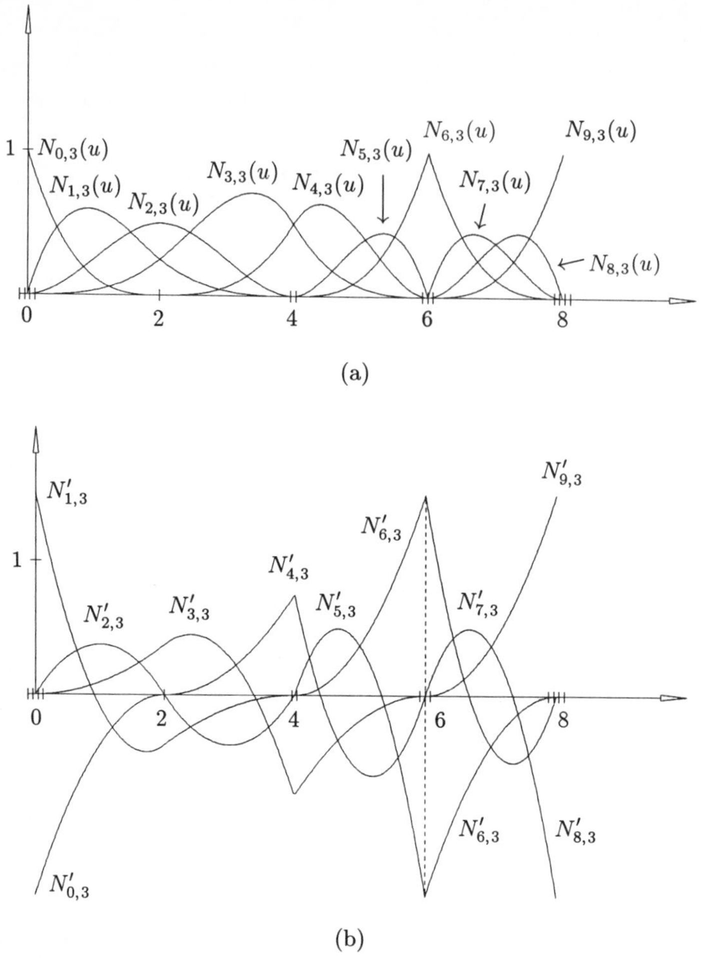

Figure 2.10. (a) Cubic basis functions showing single, double, and triple knots; (b) derivatives of the functions in Figure 2.10a.

By Property P2.5, we obtain the B-spline basis functions of p-degree with knots at the $\{u_j\}$, and with the desired continuity, by setting the appropriate knot multiplicities, s_j, where $s_j = p - r_j$. Hence, we use a knot vector of the form

$$U = \{\underbrace{u_0, \ldots, u_0}_{s_0}, \underbrace{u_1, \ldots, u_1}_{s_1}, \ldots, \underbrace{u_k, \ldots, u_k}_{s_k}\}$$

Now set

$$m = \left(\sum_{j=0}^{k} s_j\right) - 1$$

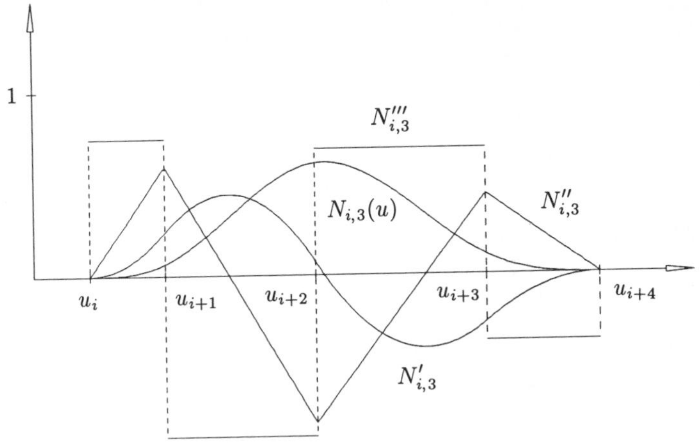

Figure 2.11. $N_{i,3}$ and all its nonzero derivatives.

Then clearly, there are m zeroth-degree functions, $N_{i,0}$, $m-1$ first degree functions, $N_{i,1}$, and in general, $m-p$ pth-degree functions, $N_{i,p}$, which have the desired continuity, $r_j = p - s_j$. Hence the $N_{i,p}$ are contained in $\mathcal{V}$. Substituting $s_j = p - r_j$ into Eq. (2.12) yields

$$\begin{aligned}
\dim(\mathcal{V}) &= k(p+1) - \sum_{j=0}^{k} (p - s_j + 1) \\
&= k(p+1) - (k+1)p + \sum_{j=0}^{k} s_j - (k+1) \\
&= -p - 1 + \sum_{j=0}^{k} s_j \\
&= m - p
\end{aligned}$$

Thus, the number of pth-degree B-spline basis functions on U is equal to $\dim(\mathcal{V})$. We now justify the term 'basis' functions by showing that the $N_{i,p}$ are linearly independent, i.e., they form a basis for the vector space, $\mathcal{V}$. The proof is by induction on p. Clearly, the zeroth-degree functions are linearly independent. Assume the $(p-1)$th-degree functions are linearly independent for $p > 0$. Set $n = m - p - 1$, and assume that

$$\sum_{i=0}^{n} \alpha_i N_{i,p}(u) = 0 \quad \text{for all } u$$

Using Eq. (2.7) we obtain

$$0 = \left(\sum_{i=0}^{n} \alpha_i N_{i,p}\right)' = \sum_{i=0}^{n} \alpha_i N'_{i,p}$$

$$= p\sum_{i=0}^{n} \alpha_i \left(\frac{N_{i,p-1}}{u_{i+p} - u_i} - \frac{N_{i+1,p-1}}{u_{i+p+1} - u_{i+1}}\right)$$

which implies that

$$0 = \sum_{i=0}^{n} \alpha_i \frac{N_{i,p-1}}{u_{i+p} - u_i} - \sum_{i=0}^{n} \alpha_i \frac{N_{i+1,p-1}}{u_{i+p+1} - u_{i+1}}$$

Now noting that $N_{0,p-1} = N_{n+1,p-1} = 0$, and changing the summation variable in the second term, we have

$$0 = \sum_{i=1}^{n} \frac{\alpha_i - \alpha_{i-1}}{u_{i+p} - u_i} N_{i,p-1}$$

which implies $\alpha_i - \alpha_{i-1} = 0$ for all i (by assumption), which in turn implies $\alpha_i = 0$ for all i. This completes the proof.

We turn our attention now to knot vectors. Clearly, once the degree is fixed the knot vector completely determines the functions $N_{i,p}(u)$. There are several types of knot vectors, and unfortunately terminology varies in the literature. In this book we consider only *nonperiodic* (or *clamped* or *open*) knot vectors, which have the form

$$U = \{\underbrace{a, \ldots, a}_{p+1}, u_{p+1}, \ldots, u_{m-p-1}, \underbrace{b, \ldots, b}_{p+1}\} \tag{2.13}$$

that is, the first and last knots have multiplicity $p+1$. For nonperiodic knot vectors we have two additional properties of the basis functions:

P2.7 A knot vector of the form

$$U = \{\underbrace{0, \ldots, 0}_{p+1}, \underbrace{1, \ldots, 1}_{p+1}\}$$

yields the Bernstein polynomials of degree p (see Example Ex2.1 in Section 2.2);

P2.8 Let $m+1$ be the number of knots. Then there are $n+1$ basis functions, where $n = m - p - 1$; $N_{0,p}(a) = 1$ and $N_{n,p}(b) = 1$. For example, $N_{0,p}(a) = 1$ follows from the fact that $N_{0,0}, \ldots, N_{p-1,0} = 0$, since this implies that $N_{0,p}(a) = N_{p,0}(a) = 1$. From P2.4 it follows that $N_{i,p}(a) = 0$ for $i \neq 0$, and $N_{i,p}(b) = 0$ for $i \neq n$.

For the remainder of this book, all knot vectors are understood to be nonperiodic. We define a knot vector $U = \{u_0, \ldots, u_m\}$ to be *uniform* if all interior knots are equally spaced, i.e., if there exists a real number, d, such that $d = u_{i+1} - u_i$ for all $p \leq i \leq m-p-1$; otherwise it is *nonuniform*. The knot vector of Example

Ex2.2, Section 2.2 is nonuniform because of the double knot at $u = 4$. Figure 2.9a shows a set of uniform cubic basis functions, and Figures 2.10a and 2.12 show nonuniform cubic basis functions.

2.5 Computational Algorithms

In this section we develop algorithms to compute values of the basis functions and their derivatives. Let $U = \{u_0, \ldots, u_m\}$ be a knot vector of the form in Eq. (2.13), and assume we are interested in the basis functions of degree p. Furthermore, assume u is fixed, and $u \in [u_i, u_{i+1})$. We develop five algorithms that compute:

- the knot span index, i;
- $N_{i-p,p}(u), \ldots, N_{i,p}(u)$ (based on Eq. [2.5]);
- $N^{(k)}_{i-p,p}(u), \ldots, N^{(k)}_{i,p}(u)$ for $k = 0, \ldots, p$; for $k > p$ the derivatives are zero (this algorithm is based on Eq. [2.10]);
- a single basis function, $N_{j,p}(u)$, where $0 \leq j \leq m - p - 1$;
- the derivatives of a single basis function, $N^{(k)}_{j,p}(u)$, where $0 \leq j \leq m-p-1$ and $k = 0,\ldots, p$ (based on Eq. [2.9]).

We present the two algorithms which compute $p + 1$ functions before the two which compute only one, because they are the most important and actually are somewhat simpler.

From P2.2 and the assumption that $u \in [u_i, u_{i+1})$, it follows that we can focus our attention on the functions $N_{i-p,p}, \ldots, N_{i,p}$ and their derivatives; all other functions are identically zero, and it is wasteful to actually compute them. Hence, the first step in evaluation is to determine the knot span in which u lies. Either a linear or a binary search of the knot vector can be used; we present here a binary

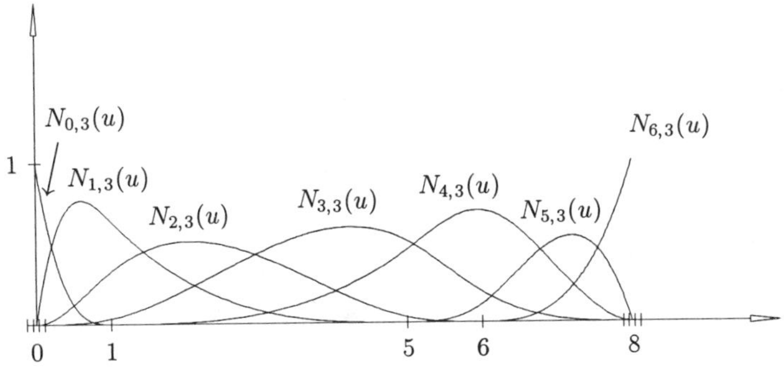

Figure 2.12. Nonuniform cubic basis functions defined on $U = \{0, 0, 0, 0,1, 5, 6,8, 8, 8, 8\}$.

search. Since we are using intervals of the form $u \in [u_i, u_{i+1})$, a subtle problem in the evaluation of the basis functions is the special case $u = u_m$. It is best to handle this at the lowest level by setting the span index to n $(= m - p - 1)$. Hence, in this case $u \in (u_{m-p-1}, u_{m-p}]$. FindSpan is an integer function which returns the span index.

```
ALGORITHM A2.1
  int  FindSpan(n,p,u,U)
    { /*  Determine the knot span index  */
      /*  Input:  n,p,u,U  */
      /*  Return: the knot span index  */
    if (u == U[n+1])  return(n);     /* Special case */
    low = p;   high = n+1;    /* Do binary search */
    mid =(low+high)/2;
    while (u < U[mid] || u >= U[mid+1])
      {
      if (u < U[mid])    high = mid;
        else             low = mid;
      mid = (low+high)/2;
      {
    return(mid);
    }
```

Now we tackle the second algorithm. Assuming u is in the ith span, computation of the nonzero functions results in an inverted triangular scheme

$$\begin{array}{cccc} & & & N_{i-p,p} \\ & N_{i-1,1} & & \\ N_{i,0} & & \cdots & \vdots \\ & N_{i,1} & & \\ & & & N_{i,p} \end{array}$$

Example

Ex2.3 Let $p = 2$, $U = \{0,0,0,1,2,3,4,4,5,5,5\}$, and $u = 5/2$ (see Figure 2.6). Then $i = 4$, since $u \in [u_4, u_5)$. Thus, we compute

$$\begin{array}{ccc} & & N_{2,2}(5/2) \\ & N_{3,1}(5/2) & \\ N_{4,0}(5/2) & & N_{3,2}(5/2) \\ & N_{4,1}(5/2) & \\ & & N_{4,2}(5/2) \end{array}$$

Substituting $u = 5/2$ into Eq. (2.5) (the reader should do this) yields

$$N_{4,0}\left(\frac{5}{2}\right) = 1$$

$$N_{3,1}\left(\frac{5}{2}\right) = \frac{1}{2} \qquad N_{4,1}\left(\frac{5}{2}\right) = \frac{1}{2}$$

$$N_{2,2}\left(\frac{5}{2}\right) = \frac{1}{8} \qquad N_{3,2}\left(\frac{5}{2}\right) = \frac{6}{8} \quad N_{4,2}\left(\frac{5}{2}\right) = \frac{1}{8}$$

Notice that for fixed degree the functions sum to 1 (P2.4).

It will be clear to the reader who carried out the substitutions in this example that there is a great deal of redundant computation inherent in Eq. (2.5). For example, writing out the second-degree functions in general terms, we have

$$N_{i-2,2}(u) = \frac{u - u_{i-2}}{u_i - u_{i-2}} N_{i-2,1}(u) + \frac{u_{i+1} - u}{u_{i+1} - u_{i-1}} N_{i-1,1}(u) \tag{2.14}$$

$$N_{i-1,2}(u) = \frac{u - u_{i-1}}{u_{i+1} - u_{i-1}} N_{i-1,1}(u) + \frac{u_{i+2} - u}{u_{i+2} - u_i} N_{i,1}(u) \tag{2.15}$$

$$N_{i,2}(u) = \frac{u - u_i}{u_{i+2} - u_i} N_{i,1}(u) + \frac{u_{i+3} - u}{u_{i+3} - u_{i+1}} N_{i+1,1}(u) \tag{2.16}$$

Note that

- the first term of Eq. (2.14) and the last term of Eq. (2.16) are not computed, since $N_{i-2,1}(u) = N_{i+1,1}(u) = 0$;
- the expression

$$\frac{N_{i-1,1}(u)}{u_{i+1} - u_{i-1}}$$

  which appears in the second term of Eq. (2.14) appears in the first term of Eq. (2.15); a similar statement holds for the second term of Eq. (2.15) and the first term of Eq. (2.16).

We introduce the notation

$$\text{left}\ [j] = u - u_{i+1-j} \qquad \text{right}\ [j] = u_{i+j} - u$$

Equations (2.14)–(2.16) are then

$$N_{i-2,2}(u) = \frac{\text{left [3]}}{\text{right [0] + left [3]}} N_{i-2,1}(u) + \frac{\text{right [1]}}{\text{right [1] + left [2]}} N_{i-1,1}(u)$$

$$N_{i-1,2}(u) = \frac{\text{left [2]}}{\text{right [1]} + \text{left [2]}} N_{i-1,1}(u) + \frac{\text{right [2]}}{\text{right [2]} + \text{left [1]}} N_{i,1}(u)$$

$$N_{i,2}(u) = \frac{\text{left [1]}}{\text{right [2]} + \text{left [1]}} N_{i,1}(u) + \frac{\text{right [3]}}{\text{right [3]} + \text{left [0]}} N_{i+1,1}(u)$$

Based on these observations, Algorithm `A2.2` computes all the nonvanishing basis functions and stores them in the array `N[0],...,N[p]`.

```
ALGORITHM A2.2
  BasisFuns(i,u,p,U,N)
    { /*  Compute the nonvanishing basis functions  */
      /*  Input:  i,u,p,U  */
      /*  Output: N  */
    N[0]=1.0;
    for (j=1; j<=p; j++)
      {
      left[j] = u-U[i+1-j];
      right[j] = U[i+j]-u;
      saved = 0.0;
      for (r=0; r<j; r++)
        {
        temp = N[r]/(right[r+1]+left[j-r]);
        N[r] = saved+right[r+1]*temp;
        saved = left[j-r]*temp;
        }
      N[j] = saved;
      }
    }
```

We remark that Algorithm `A2.2` is not only efficient, but it also guarantees that there will be no division by zero, which can occur with a direct application of Eq. (2.5).

Now to the third algorithm; in particular, we want to compute all $N_{r,p}^{(k)}(u)$, for $i - p \leq r \leq i$ and $0 \leq k \leq n$, where $n \leq p$. Inspection of Eq. (2.10) reveals that the basic ingredients are:

- the inverted triangle of nonzero basis functions computed in Algorithm `A2.2`;
- differences of knots (the sums: `right[r+1]+left[j-r]`), also computed in Algorithm `A2.2`;
- differences of the $a_{k,j}$; note that the $a_{k,j}$ depend on the $a_{k-1,j}$ but not the $a_{s,j}$, for $s < k - 1$.

Viewed as a two-dimensional array of dimension $(p + 1) \times (p + 1)$, the basis functions fit into the upper triangle (including the diagonal), and the knot differences fit into the lower triangle, that is

$N_{i,0}(u)$	$N_{i-1,1}(u)$	$N_{i-2,2}(u)$
$u_{i+1} - u_i$	$N_{i,1}(u)$	$N_{i-1,2}(u)$
$u_{i+1} - u_{i-1}$	$u_{i+2} - u_i$	$N_{i,2}(u)$

Example

Ex2.4 Let $p = 2$, $U = \{0,0,0,1,2,3,4,4,5,5,5\}$, and $u = {}^5\!/\!_2$. Then $u \in [u_4, u_5)$, and the array becomes

$N_{4,0}\left(\frac{5}{2}\right) = 1$	$N_{3,1}\left(\frac{5}{2}\right) = \frac{1}{2}$	$N_{2,2}\left(\frac{5}{2}\right) = \frac{1}{8}$
$u_5 - u_4 = 1$	$N_{4,1}\left(\frac{5}{2}\right) = \frac{1}{2}$	$N_{3,2}\left(\frac{5}{2}\right) = \frac{6}{8}$
$u_5 - u_3 = 2$	$u_6 - u_4 = 2$	$N_{4,2}\left(\frac{5}{2}\right) = \frac{1}{8}$

Now compute $N_{4,2}^{(1)}({}^5\!/\!_2)$ and $N_{4,2}^{(2)}({}^5\!/\!_2)$; with $i = 4$ in Eq. (2.10), we have

$$a_{1,0} = \frac{1}{u_6 - u_4} = \frac{1}{2}$$

$$a_{1,1} = -\frac{1}{u_7 - u_5} = -1$$

$$a_{2,0} = \frac{a_{1,0}}{u_5 - u_4} = \frac{1}{2}$$

$$a_{2,1} = \frac{a_{1,1} - a_{1,0}}{u_6 - u_5} = \frac{-1 - \frac{1}{2}}{4 - 3} = -\frac{3}{2}$$

$$a_{2,2} = -\frac{a_{1,1}}{u_7 - u_6} = \frac{1}{4 - 4} = \frac{1}{0}$$

$$N_{4,2}^{(1)} = 2\left[a_{1,0} N_{4,1}\left(\frac{5}{2}\right) + a_{1,1} N_{5,1}\left(\frac{5}{2}\right)\right]$$

and

$$N_{4,2}^{(2)} = 2\left[a_{2,0} N_{4,0}\left(\frac{5}{2}\right) + a_{2,1} N_{5,0}\left(\frac{5}{2}\right) + a_{2,2} N_{6,0}\left(\frac{5}{2}\right)\right]$$

Now $a_{1,1}$, $a_{2,1}$, and $a_{2,2}$ all use knot differences which are not in the array, but they are multiplied respectively by $N_{5,1}({}^5\!/\!_2)$, $N_{5,0}({}^5\!/\!_2)$, and

$N_{6,0}(5/2)$, which are also not in the array. These terms are defined to be zero, and we are left with

$$N_{4,2}^{(1)} = 2a_{1,0}N_{4,1}\left(\frac{5}{2}\right) = \frac{1}{2}$$

$$N_{4,2}^{(2)} = 2a_{2,0}N_{4,0}\left(\frac{5}{2}\right) = 1$$

To check these values, recall from Section 2.2 that $N_{4,2}(u) = 1/2(u-2)^2$ on $u \in [2,3)$. The computation of $N_{3,2}^{(1)}(5/2)$, $N_{3,2}^{(2)}(5/2)$, $N_{2,2}^{(1)}(5/2)$, and $N_{2,2}^{(2)}(5/2)$ is analogous.

Based on these observations (and Ex2.4), it is not difficult to develop Algorithm A2.3, which computes the nonzero basis functions and their derivatives, up to and including the nth derivative ($n \le p$). Output is in the two-dimensional array, ders. ders[k][j] is the kth derivative of the function $N_{i-p+j,p}$, where $0 \le k \le n$ and $0 \le j \le p$. Two local arrays are used:

- ndu[p+1][p+1], to store the basis functions and knot differences;
- a[2][p+1], to store (in an alternating fashion) the two most recently computed rows $a_{k,j}$ and $a_{k-1,j}$.

The algorithm avoids division by zero and/or the use of terms not in the array ndu[][].

```
ALGORITHM A2.3
  DersBasisFuns(i,u,p,n,U,ders)
    { /*  Compute nonzero basis functions and their  */
      /*  derivatives.  First section is A2.2 modified  */
      /*  to store functions and knot differences.  */
      /*  Input:  i,u,p,n,U  */
      /*  Output: ders  */
    ndu[0][0]=1.0;
    for (j=1; j<=p; j++)
      {
      left[j] = u-U[i+1-j];
      right[j] = U[i+j]-u;
      saved = 0.0;
      for (r=0; r<j; r++)
        {                                    /* Lower triangle */
        ndu[j][r] = right[r+1]+left[j-r];
        temp = ndu[r][j-1]/ndu[j][r];
                                             /* Upper triangle */
        ndu[r][j] = saved+right[r+1]*temp;
        saved = left[j-r]*temp;
        }
      ndu[j][j] = saved;
```

```
  }
for (j=0; j<=p; j++)   /* Load the basis functions */
  ders[0][j] = ndu[j][p];
/* This section computes the derivatives (Eq. [2.9]) */
for (r=0; r<=p; r++)   /* Loop over function index */
  {
  s1=0;   s2=1;   /* Alternate rows in array a */
  a[0][0] = 1.0;
  /* Loop to compute kth derivative */
  for (k=1; k<=n; k++)
    {
    d = 0.0;
    rk = r-k;    pk = p-k;
    if (r >= k)
      {
      a[s2][0] = a[s1][0]/ndu[pk+1][rk];
      d = a[s2][0]*ndu[rk][pk];
      }
    if (rk >= -1)   j1 = 1;
      else          j1 = -rk;
    if (r-1 <= pk)   j2 = k-1;
      else           j2 = p-r;
    for (j=j1; j<=j2; j++)
      {
      a[s2][j] = (a[s1][j]-a[s1][j-1])/ndu[pk+1][rk+j];
      d += a[s2][j]*ndu[rk+j][pk];
      }
    if (r <= pk)
      {
      a[s2][k] = -a[s1][k-1]/ndu[pk+1][r];
      d += a[s2][k]*ndu[r][pk];
      }
    ders[k][r] = d;
    j=s1;   s1=s2;   s2=j;   /* Switch rows */
    }
  }
/* Multiply through by the correct factors */
/* (Eq. [2.9]) */
r = p;
for (k=1; k<=n; k++)
  {
  for (j=0; j<=p; j++)   ders[k][j] *= r;
  r *= (p-k);
  }
}
```

We turn our attention now to the last two algorithms, namely computing a single basis function, $N_{i,p}(u)$, or the derivatives, $N_{i,p}^{(k)}(u)$, of a single basis function. The solutions to these problems result in triangular tables of the form

$$\begin{array}{cccc}
N_{i,0} & & & \\
& N_{i,1} & & \\
N_{i+1,0} & & N_{i,2} & \\
\vdots & & \cdots & N_{i,p} \\
N_{i+p-1,0} & & N_{i+p-2,2} & \\
& N_{i+p-1,1} & & \\
N_{i+p,0} & & &
\end{array}$$

Example

Ex2.5 Let $p = 2$, $U = \{0,0,0,1,2,3,4,4,5,5,5\}$, and $u = {}^5\!/\!_2$. The computation of $N_{3,2}({}^5\!/\!_2)$ yields

$$\begin{array}{ccc}
N_{3,0}({}^5\!/\!_2) = 0 & & \\
& N_{3,1}({}^5\!/\!_2) = \frac{1}{2} & \\
N_{4,0}({}^5\!/\!_2) = 1 & & N_{3,2}({}^5\!/\!_2) = \frac{6}{8} \\
& N_{4,1}({}^5\!/\!_2) = \frac{1}{2} & \\
N_{5,0}({}^5\!/\!_2) = 0 & &
\end{array}$$

$N_{4,2}({}^5\!/\!_2)$ is obtained from

$$\begin{array}{ccc}
N_{4,0}({}^5\!/\!_2) = 1 & & \\
& N_{4,1}({}^5\!/\!_2) = \frac{1}{2} & \\
N_{5,0}({}^5\!/\!_2) = 0 & & N_{4,2}({}^5\!/\!_2) = \frac{1}{8} \\
& N_{5,1}({}^5\!/\!_2) = 0 & \\
N_{6,0}({}^5\!/\!_2) = 0 & &
\end{array}$$

Notice that the position and relative number of nonzero entries in the table depend on p and on the position of the 1 in the first column. Algorithm A2.4 computes only the nonzero entries. The value $N_{i,p}(u)$ is returned in Nip; m is the high index of U ($m+1$ knots). The algorithm is similar to Algorithm A2.2 in its use of the variables temp and saved.

```
ALGORITHM A2.4
  OneBasisFun(p,m,U,i,u,Nip)
    { /*  Compute the basis function Nip  */
      /*  Input:  p,m,U,i,u  */
      /*  Output: Nip  */
```

```
if ((i == 0 && u == U[0]) ||      /* Special */
    (i == m-p-1 && u == U[m]))    /*  cases  */
  {
  Nip = 1.0;    return;
  }
if (u < U[i] || u >= U[i+p+1])    /* Local property */
  {
  Nip = 0.0;    return;
  }
for (j=0; j<=p; j++) /* Initialize zeroth-degree functs */
  if (u >= U[i+j] && u < U[i+j+1])  N[j] = 1.0;
    else             N[j] = 0.0;
for (k=1; k<=p; k++)  /* Compute triangular table */
  {
  if (N[0] == 0.0)  saved = 0.0;
    else        saved = ((u-U[i])*N[0])/(U[i+k]-U[i]);
  for (j=0; j<p-k+1; j++)
    {
    Uleft = U[i+j+1];
    Uright = U[i+j+k+1];
    if (N[j+1] == 0.0)
      {
      N[j] = saved;   saved = 0.0;
      }
      else
      {
      temp = N[j+1]/(Uright-Uleft);
      N[j] = saved+(Uright-u)*temp;
      saved = (u-Uleft)*temp;
      }
    }
  }
Nip = N[0];
}
```

Now for fixed i, the computation of the derivatives, $N_{i,p}^{(k)}(u)$, for $k = 0, \ldots, n$, $n \le p$, uses Eq. (2.9). For example, if $p = 3$ and $n = 3$, then

$$N_{i,3}^{(1)} = 3\left(\frac{N_{i,2}}{u_{i+3} - u_i} - \frac{N_{i+1,2}}{u_{i+4} - u_{i+1}}\right)$$

$$N_{i,3}^{(2)} = 3\left(\frac{N_{i,2}^{(1)}}{u_{i+3} - u_i} - \frac{N_{i+1,2}^{(1)}}{u_{i+4} - u_{i+1}}\right)$$

$$N_{i,3}^{(3)} = 3\left(\frac{N_{i,2}^{(2)}}{u_{i+3} - u_i} - \frac{N_{i+1,2}^{(2)}}{u_{i+4} - u_{i+1}}\right)$$

Using triangular tables, we must compute

$k = 0$:

$$\begin{array}{cccc}
N_{i,0} & & & \\
 & N_{i,1} & & \\
N_{i+1,0} & & N_{i,2} & \\
 & N_{i+1,1} & & N_{i,3} \\
N_{i+2,0} & & N_{i+1,2} & \\
 & N_{i+2,1} & & \\
N_{i+3,0} & & &
\end{array}$$

$k = 1$:

$$\begin{array}{cc}
N_{i,2} & \\
 & N_{i,3}^{(1)} \\
N_{i+1,2} &
\end{array}$$

$k = 2$:

$$\begin{array}{ccc}
N_{i,1} & & \\
 & N_{i,2}^{(1)} & \\
N_{i+1,1} & & N_{i,3}^{(2)} \\
 & N_{i+1,2}^{(1)} & \\
N_{i+2,1} & &
\end{array}$$

$k = 3$:

$$\begin{array}{cccc}
N_{i,0} & & & \\
 & N_{i,1}^{(1)} & & \\
N_{i+1,0} & & N_{i,2}^{(2)} & \\
 & N_{i+1,1}^{(1)} & & N_{i,3}^{(3)} \\
N_{i+2,0} & & N_{i+1,2}^{(2)} & \\
 & N_{i+2,1}^{(1)} & & \\
N_{i+3,0} & & &
\end{array}$$

In words, the algorithm is:

1. compute and store the entire triangular table corresponding to $k = 0$;
2. to get the kth derivative, load the column of the table which contains the functions of degree $p - k$, and compute the remaining portion of the triangle.

Algorithm `A2.5` computes $N_{i,p}^{(k)}(u)$ for $k = 0, \ldots, n$, $n \le p$. The kth derivative is returned in `ders[k]`.

```
ALGORITHM A2.5
  DersOneBasisFun(p,m,U,i,u,n,ders)
    { /*  Compute derivatives of basis function Nip  */
```

```
  /*  Input:  p,m,U,i,u,n  */
  /*  Output: ders  */
if (u < U[i] || u >= U[i+p+1])   /* Local property */
  {
  for (k=0; k<=n; k++)  ders[k] = 0.0;
  return;
  }
for (j=0; j<=p; j++)  /* Initialize zeroth-degree functs */
  if (u >= U[i+j] && u < U[i+j+1])  N[j][0] = 1.0;
    else                    N[j][0] = 0.0;
for (k=1; k<=p; k++)   /* Compute full triangular table */
  {
  if (N[0][k-1] == 0.0)  saved = 0.0;
    else    saved = ((u-U[i])*N[0][k-1])/(U[i+k]-U[i]);
  for (j=0; j<p-k+1; j++)
    {
    Uleft = U[i+j+1];
    Uright = U[i+j+k+1];
    if (N[j+1][k-1] == 0.0)
      {
      N[j][k] = saved;   saved = 0.0;
      }
      else
      {
      temp = N[j+1][k-1]/(Uright-Uleft);
      N[j][k] = saved+(Uright-u)*temp;
      saved = (u-Uleft)*temp;
      }
    }
  }
ders[0] = N[0][p];   /* The function value */
for (k=1; k<=n; k++)   /* Compute the derivatives */
  {
  for (j=0; j<=k; j++)   /* Load appropriate column */
    ND[j] = N[j][p-k];
  for (jj=1; jj<=k; jj++)   /* Compute table of width k */
    {
    if (ND[0] == 0.0)  saved = 0.0;
      else     saved = ND[0]/(U[i+p-k+jj]-U[i]);
    for (j=0; j<k-jj+1; j++)
      {
      Uleft = U[i+j+1];
      Uright = U[i+j+p+jj+1];
      if (ND[j+1] == 0.0)
        {
```

```
                ND[j] = (p-k+jj)*saved;    saved = 0.0;
                }
                else
                {
                temp = ND[j+1]/(Uright-Uleft);
                ND[j] = (p-k+jj)*(saved-temp);
                saved = temp;
                }
            }
        }
    ders[k] = ND[0];    /* kth derivative */
    }
}
```

Finally, note that Algorithms **A2.3** and **A2.5** compute derivatives from the right if u is a knot. However, Eqs. (2.5), (2.9), (2.10), and others in this chapter could have been defined using intervals of the form $u \in (u_i, u_{i+1}]$. This would not change Algorithms **A2.2** through **A2.5**. In other words, derivatives from the left can be found by simply having the span-finding algorithm use intervals of the form $(u_i, u_{i+1}]$, instead of $[u_i, u_{i+1})$. In the preceding example, with $p = 2$ and $U = \{0, 0, 0, 1, 2, 3, 4, 4, 5, 5, 5\}$, if $u = 2$ then span $i = 3$ yields derivatives from the left, and $i = 4$ yields derivatives from the right.

Exercises

2.1. Consider the linear and quadratic functions computed earlier and shown in Figures 2.5 and 2.6. Substitute $u = 5/2$ into the polynomial equations to obtain $N_{3,1}(5/2)$, $N_{4,1}(5/2)$, $N_{2,2}(5/2)$, $N_{3,2}(5/2)$, and $N_{4,2}(5/2)$. What do you notice about the sum of the two linear, and the sum of the three quadratic functions?

2.2. Consider the quadratic functions of Figure 2.6. Using the polynomial expressions for $N_{3,2}(u)$, evaluate the function and its first and second derivatives at $u = 2$ from both the left and right. Observe the continuity. Does Property **P2.5** hold? Do the same with $N_{4,2}(u)$ at $u = 4$.

2.3. Let $U = \{0, 0, 0, 0, 1, 2, 3, 4, 4, 5, 5, 5, 5\}$. How does this change the degree 0, 1, and 2 functions of Figures 2.4–2.6? Compute and sketch the nine cubic basis functions associated with U.

2.4. Consider the function $N_{2,2}(u)$ of Figure 2.5, $N_{2,2}(u) = 1/2u^2$ on $[0, 1)$, $-3/2 + 3u - u^2$ on $[1, 2)$ and $1/2(3 - u)^2$ on $[2, 3)$. Use Eq. (2.10) to obtain the expressions for the first and second derivatives of $N_{2,2}(u)$.

2.5. Again consider $N_{2,2}(u)$ of Figure 2.5. Obtain the first derivatives of $N_{2,1}$ and $N_{3,1}$ by differentiating the polynomial expressions directly. Then use these, together with Eq. (2.11), to obtain $N'_{2,2}$.

2.6. Again let $p = 2$, $u = 5/2$, and $U = \{0, 0, 0, 1, 2, 3, 4, 4, 5, 5, 5\}$. Trace through Algorithm **A2.2** by hand to find the values of the three nonzero basis functions. Trace through Algorithm **A2.3** to find the first and second derivatives of the basis functions.

2.7. Use the same p and U as in Exercise 2.6, with $u = 2$. Trace through Algorithm `A2.3` with $n = 1$, once with $i = 3$, and once with $i = 4$. Then differentiate the appropriate polynomial expressions for the $N_{j,2}$ given in Section 2.2, and evaluate the derivatives from the left and right at $u = 2$. Compare the results with what you obtained from Algorithm `A2.3`.

2.8. Using the same p and U as in Exercise 2.6, let $u = 4$. Trace through Algorithms `A2.2` and `A2.3` to convince yourself there are no problems with double knots.

2.9. With the same p and U as in Exercise 2.6, let $u = 5/2$. Trace through Algorithm `A2.5` and compute the derivatives $N_{4,2}^{(k)}(5/2)$ for $k = 0, 1, 2$.

CHAPTER

THREE

B-spline Curves and Surfaces

3.1 Introduction

In this chapter we define nonrational B-spline curves and surfaces, study their properties, and derive expressions for their derivatives. For brevity we drop the word nonrational for the remainder of this chapter. The primary goal is to acquire an intuitive understanding of B-spline curves and surfaces, and to that end the reader should carefully study the many examples and figures given in this chapter. We also give algorithms for computing points and derivatives on B-spline curves and surfaces. The use of B-splines to define curves and surfaces for computer-aided geometric design was first proposed by Gordon and Riesenfeld [Gord74b; Ries73]. B-spline techniques are now covered in many books on curves and surfaces – see [DeBo78; Mort85; Bart87; Fari93; Yama88; Hosc93; Su89; Roge90; Beac91].

3.2 The Definition and Properties of B-spline Curves

A *pth-degree B-spline curve* is defined by

$$\mathbf{C}(u) = \sum_{i=0}^{n} N_{i,p}(u)\,\mathbf{P}_i \qquad a \le u \le b \tag{3.1}$$

where the $\{\mathbf{P}_i\}$ are the *control points*, and the $\{N_{i,p}(u)\}$ are the pth-degree B-spline basis functions (Eq. [2.5]) defined on the nonperiodic (and nonuniform) knot vector

$$U = \{\underbrace{a,\ldots,a}_{p+1}, u_{p+1},\ldots,u_{m-p-1},\underbrace{b,\ldots,b}_{p+1}\}$$

($m+1$ knots). Unless stated otherwise, we assume that $a = 0$ and $b = 1$. The polygon formed by the $\{\mathbf{P}_i\}$ is called the *control polygon*. Examples of B-spline curves (in some cases together with their corresponding basis functions) are shown in Figures 3.1–3.14.

Three steps are required to compute a point on a B-spline curve at a fixed u value:

1. find the knot span in which u lies (Algorithm `A2.1`);
2. compute the nonzero basis functions (Algorithm `A2.2`);
3. multiply the values of the nonzero basis functions with the corresponding control points.

Consider Example `Ex2.3` of Section 2.5, with $U = \{0,0,0,1,2,3,4,4,5,5,5\}$, $u = 5/2$, and $p = 2$. Then $u \in [u_4, u_5)$, and

$$N_{2,2}\left(\frac{5}{2}\right) = \frac{1}{8} \qquad N_{3,2}\left(\frac{5}{2}\right) = \frac{6}{8} \qquad N_{4,2}\left(\frac{5}{2}\right) = \frac{1}{8}$$

Multiplying with the control points yields

$$\mathbf{C}\left(\frac{5}{2}\right) = \frac{1}{8}\mathbf{P}_2 + \frac{6}{8}\mathbf{P}_3 + \frac{1}{8}\mathbf{P}_4$$

The algorithm follows.

```
ALGORITHM A3.1:
  CurvePoint(n,p,U,P,u,C)
    { /*  Compute curve point  */
      /*  Input:  n,p,U,P,u  */
      /*  Output: C  */
    span = FindSpan(n,p,u,U);
    BasisFuns(span,u,p,U,N);
    C = 0.0;
    for (i=0; i<=p; i++)
      C = C + N[i]*P[span-p+i];
    }
```

We now list a number of properties of B-spline curves. These properties follow from those given in Chapter 2 for the functions $N_{i,p}(u)$. Let $\mathbf{C}(u)$ be defined by Eq. (3.1).

`P3.1` If $n = p$ and $U = \{0,\ldots,0,1,\ldots,1\}$, then $\mathbf{C}(u)$ is a Bézier curve (Figure 3.1);

`P3.2` $\mathbf{C}(u)$ is a piecewise polynomial curve (since the $N_{i,p}(u)$ are piecewise polynomials); the degree, p, number of control points, $n+1$, and number of knots, $m+1$, are related by

$$m = n + p + 1 \tag{3.2}$$

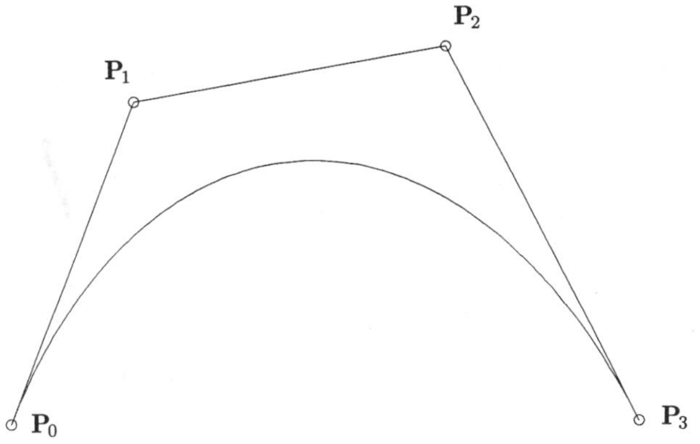

Figure 3.1. A cubic B-spline curve on $U = \{0,0,0,0,1,1,1,1\}$, i.e., a cubic Bézier curve.

(see Section 2.4). Figures 3.2 and 3.3 show basis functions and sections of the B-spline curves corresponding to the individual knot spans; in both figures the alternating solid/dashed segments correspond to the different polynomials (knot spans) defining the curve.

P3.3 Endpoint interpolation: $\mathbf{C}(0) = \mathbf{P}_0$ and $\mathbf{C}(1) = \mathbf{P}_n$;

P3.4 Affine invariance: an affine transformation is applied to the curve by applying it to the control points. Let $\mathbf{r}$ be a point in $\mathcal{E}^3$ (three-dimensional Euclidean space). An *affine transformation*, denoted by Φ, maps $\mathcal{E}^3$ into $\mathcal{E}^3$ and has the form

$$\Phi(\mathbf{r}) = A\mathbf{r} + \mathbf{v}$$

where A is a 3×3 matrix and $\mathbf{v}$ is a vector. Affine transformations include translations, rotations, scalings, and shears. The affine invariance property for B-spline curves follows from the partition of unity property of the $N_{i,p}(u)$. Thus, let $\mathbf{r} = \sum \alpha_i \mathbf{p}_i$, where $\mathbf{p}_i \in \mathcal{E}^3$ and $\sum \alpha_i = 1$. Then

$$\begin{aligned}\Phi(\mathbf{r}) &= \Phi\left(\sum \alpha_i \mathbf{p}_i\right) = A\left(\sum \alpha_i \mathbf{p}_i\right) + \mathbf{v} = \sum \alpha_i A\mathbf{p}_i + \sum \alpha_i \mathbf{v} \\ &= \sum \alpha_i (A\mathbf{p}_i + \mathbf{v}) = \sum \alpha_i \Phi(\mathbf{p}_i)\end{aligned}$$

P3.5 Strong convex hull property: the curve is contained in the convex hull of its control polygon; in fact, if $u \in [u_i, u_{i+1})$, $p \le i < m - p - 1$, then $\mathbf{C}(u)$ is in the convex hull of the control points $\mathbf{P}_{i-p}, \ldots, \mathbf{P}_i$ (Figures 3.4, 3.5, and 3.6). This follows from the nonnegativity and partition of unity properties of the $N_{i,p}(u)$ (Properties P2.3 and P2.4), and the property that $N_{j,p}(u) = 0$ for $j < i - p$ and $j > i$ when $u \in [u_i, u_{i+1})$ (Property P2.2). Figure 3.6 shows how to construct a quadratic curve containing a straight line segment. Since $\mathbf{P}_2$, $\mathbf{P}_3$, and $\mathbf{P}_4$ are colinear, the strong

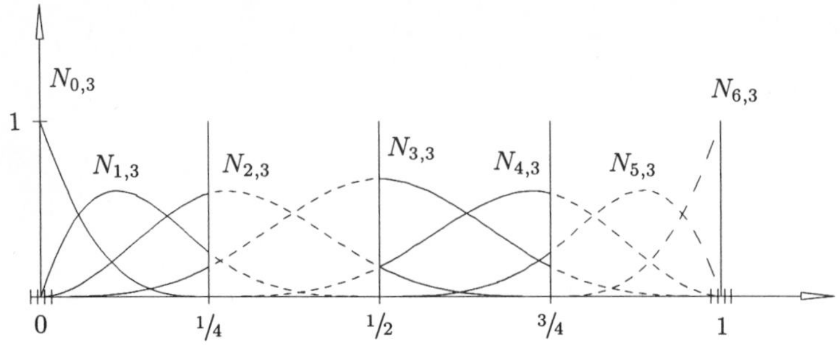

(a)

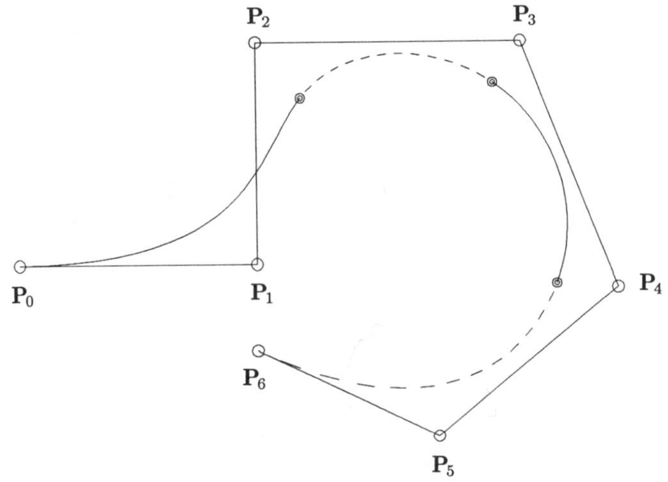

(b)

Figure 3.2. (a) Cubic basis functions $U = \{0, 0, 0, 0, 1/4, 1/2, 3/4, 1, 1, 1, 1\}$; (b) a cubic curve using the basis functions of Figure 3.2a.

convex hull property forces the curve to be a straight line segment from $\mathbf{C}(2/5)$ to $\mathbf{C}(3/5)$;

P3.6 Local modification scheme: moving $\mathbf{P}_i$ changes $\mathbf{C}(u)$ only in the interval $[u_i, u_{i+p+1})$ (Figure 3.7). This follows from the fact that $N_{i,p}(u) = 0$ for $u \notin [u_i, u_{i+p+1})$ (Property P2.1).

P3.7 The control polygon represents a piecewise linear approximation to the curve; this approximation is improved by knot insertion or degree elevation (see Chapter 5). As a general rule, the lower the degree, the closer a B-spline curve follows its control polygon (see Figures 3.8 and 3.9). The curves of Figure 3.9 are defined using the same six control points, and the knot vectors

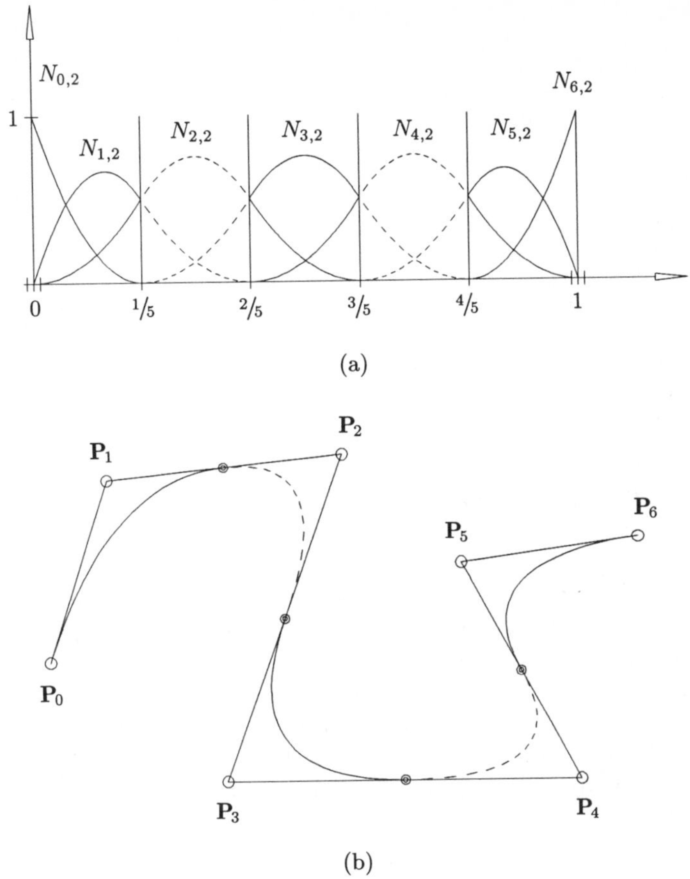

Figure 3.3. (a) Quadratic basis functions on $U = \{0, 0, 0, {}^1\!/_5, {}^2\!/_5, {}^3\!/_5, {}^4\!/_5, 1, 1, 1\}$; (b) a quadratic curve using the basis functions of Figure 3.3a.

$$p = 1 : U = \left\{0, 0, \frac{1}{5}, \frac{2}{5}, \frac{3}{5}, \frac{4}{5}, 1, 1\right\}$$

$$p = 2 : U = \left\{0, 0, 0, \frac{1}{4}, \frac{1}{2}, \frac{3}{4}, 1, 1, 1\right\}$$

$$p = 3 : U = \left\{0, 0, 0, 0, \frac{1}{3}, \frac{2}{3}, 1, 1, 1, 1\right\}$$

$$p = 4 : U = \left\{0, 0, 0, 0, 0, \frac{1}{2}, 1, 1, 1, 1, 1\right\}$$

$$p = 5 : U = \{0, 0, 0, 0, 0, 0, 1, 1, 1, 1, 1, 1\}$$

The reason for this phenomenon is intuitive: the lower the degree, the fewer the control points that are contributing to the computation of

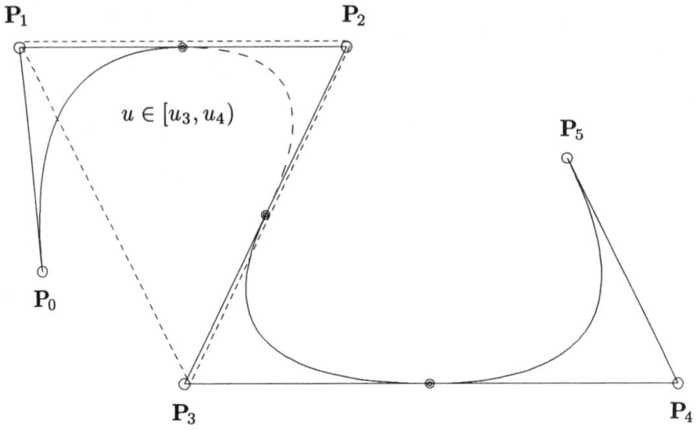

Figure 3.4. The strong convex hull property for a quadratic B-spline curve; for $u \in [u_i, u_{i+1})$, $\mathbf{C}(u)$ is in the triangle $\mathbf{P}_{i-2}\mathbf{P}_{i-1}\mathbf{P}_i$.

$\mathbf{C}(u_0)$ for any given u_0. The extreme case is $p = 1$, for which every point $\mathbf{C}(u)$ is just a linear interpolation between two control points. In this case, the curve *is* the control polygon;

P3.8 Moving along the curve from $u = 0$ to $u = 1$, the $N_{i,p}(u)$ functions act like switches; as u moves past a knot, one $N_{i,p}(u)$ (and hence the corresponding $\mathbf{P}_i$) switches off, and the next one switches on (Figures 3.2 and 3.3).

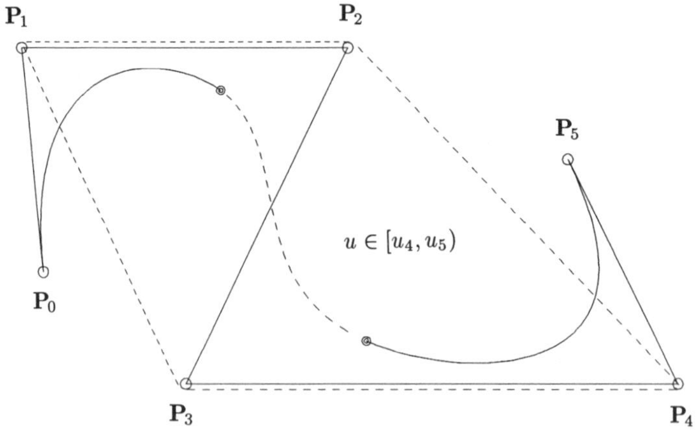

Figure 3.5. The strong convex hull property for a cubic B-spline curve; for $u \in [u_i, u_{i+1})$, $\mathbf{C}(u)$ is in the quadrilateral $\mathbf{P}_{i-3}\mathbf{P}_{i-2}\mathbf{P}_{i-1}\mathbf{P}_i$.

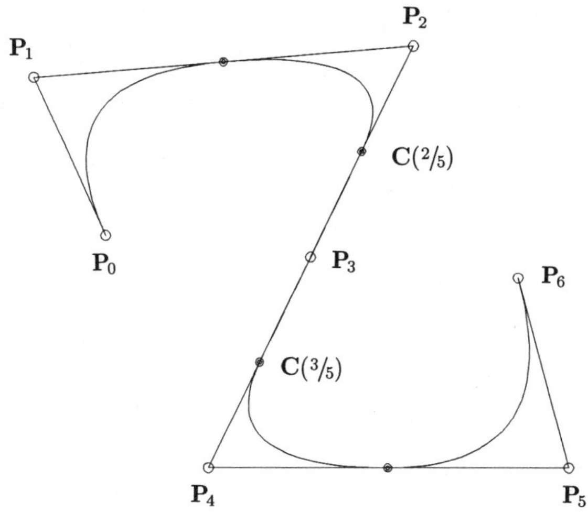

Figure 3.6. A quadratic B-spline curve on $U = \{0, 0, 0, {}^1\!/_5, {}^2\!/_5, {}^3\!/_5, {}^4\!/_5, 1, 1, 1\}$. The curve is a straight line between $\mathbf{C}({}^2\!/_5)$ and $\mathbf{C}({}^3\!/_5)$.

P3.9 Variation diminishing property: no plane has more intersections with the curve than with the control polygon (replace the word plane with line, for two-dimensional curves) – see [Lane83] for proof;

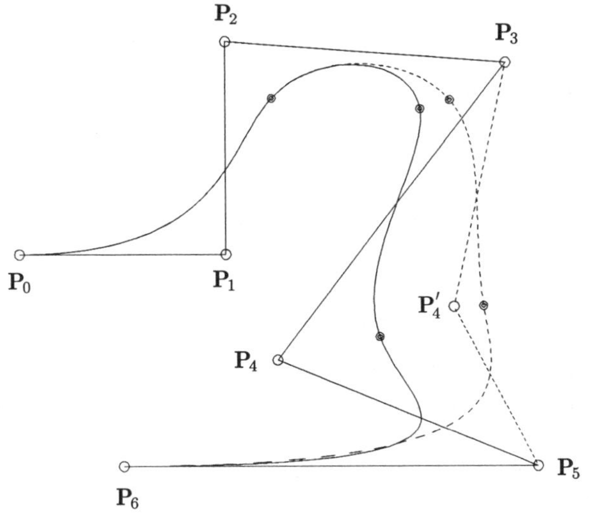

Figure 3.7. A cubic curve on $U = \{0, 0, 0, 0, {}^1\!/_4, {}^1\!/_2, {}^3\!/_4, 1, 1, 1, 1\}$; moving $\mathbf{P}_4$ (to $\mathbf{P}'_4$) changes the curve in the interval $[{}^1\!/_4, 1)$.

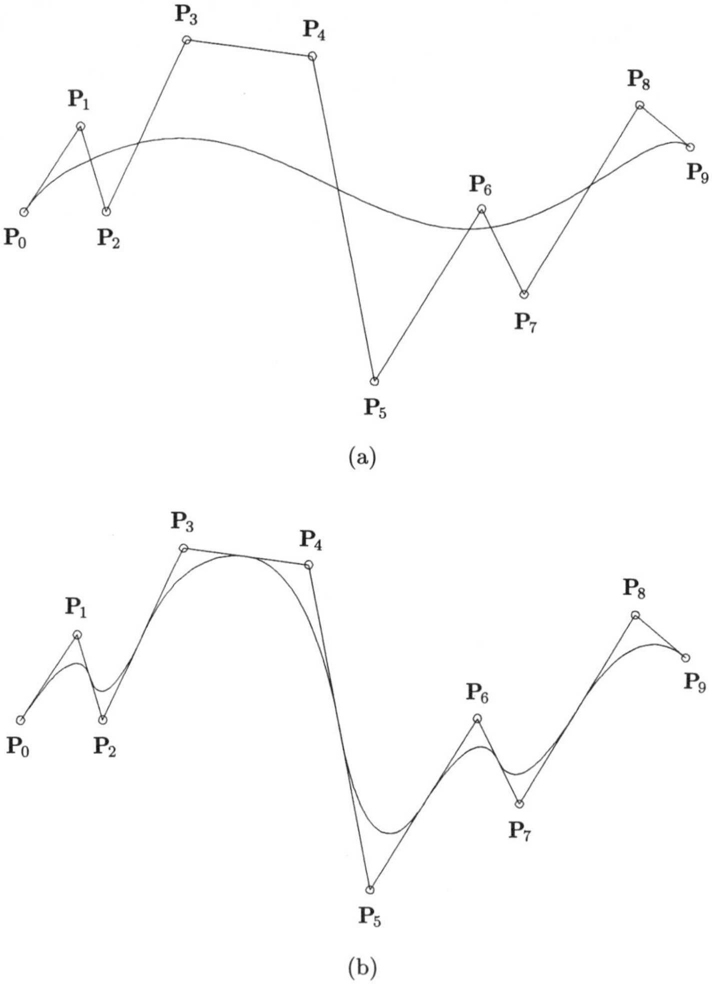

Figure 3.8. B-spline curves. (a) A ninth-degree Bézier curve on the knot vector $U = \{0,0,0,0,0,0,0,0,0,0,1,1,1,1,1,1,1,1,1,1\}$; (b) a quadratic curve using the same control polygon defined on $U = \{0,0,0,\ ^1\!/_8,\ ^2\!/_8,\ ^3\!/_8,\ ^4\!/_8,\ ^5\!/_8,\ ^6\!/_8,\ ^7\!/_8,1,1,1\}$.

P3.10 The continuity and differentiability of $\mathbf{C}(u)$ follow from that of the $N_{i,p}(u)$ (since $\mathbf{C}(u)$ is just a linear combination of the $N_{i,p}(u)$). Thus, $\mathbf{C}(u)$ is infinitely differentiable in the interior of knot intervals, and it is at least $p-k$ times continuously differentiable at a knot of multiplicity k. Figure 3.10 shows a quadratic curve ($p = 2$). The curve is $\mathbf{C}^1$ continuous (the first derivative is continuous but the second is not) at all interior knots of multiplicity 1. At the double knot, $u = {}^4\!/_5$, $\mathbf{C}(u)$ is only $\mathbf{C}^0$ continuous, thus there is a cusp (a visual discontinuity). Figure 3.11 shows a

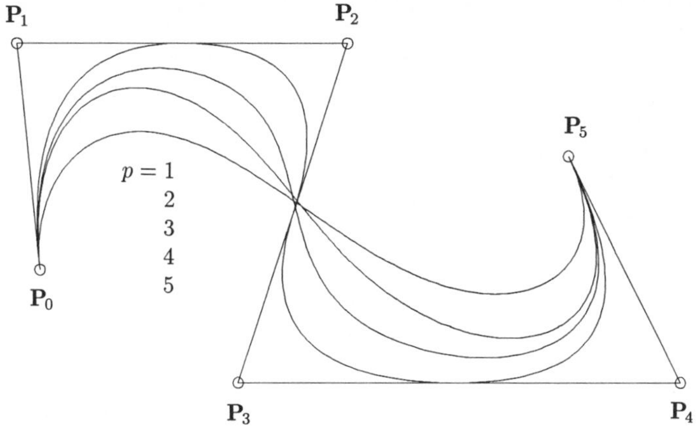

Figure 3.9. B-spline curves of different degree, using the same control polygon.

quadratic curve defined on the same knot vector. Hence, the two curves use the same basis functions, $N_{i,p}(u)$, for their definitions. But the curve of Figure 3.11 is $\mathbf{C}^1$ continuous at $u = 4/5$; this is not obvious but can be seen using the derivative expression given in Section 3.3. This is simply a consequence of the fact that discontinuous functions can sometimes be combined in such a way that the result is continuous. Notice that $\mathbf{P}_4$, $\mathbf{P}_5$, and $\mathbf{P}_6$ are colinear, and length$(\mathbf{P}_4\mathbf{P}_5)$ = length$(\mathbf{P}_5\mathbf{P}_6)$. Figure 3.12 shows a cubic curve which is $\mathbf{C}^2$ continuous at $u = 1/4$ and $u = 1/2$, but only $\mathbf{C}^1$ continuous at the double knot $u = 3/4$. The eye detects discontinuities in the second derivative but probably not in third and higher derivatives. Thus, cubics are generally adequate for visual purposes.

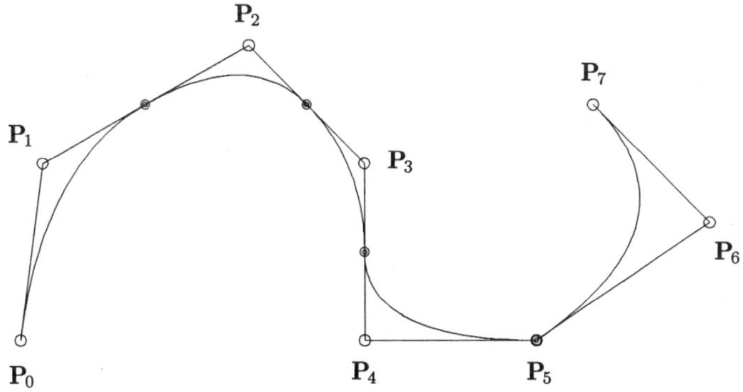

Figure 3.10. A quadratic curve on $U = \{0, 0, 0, 1/5, 2/5, 3/5, 4/5, 4/5, 1, 1, 1\}$ with a cusp at $u = 4/5$.

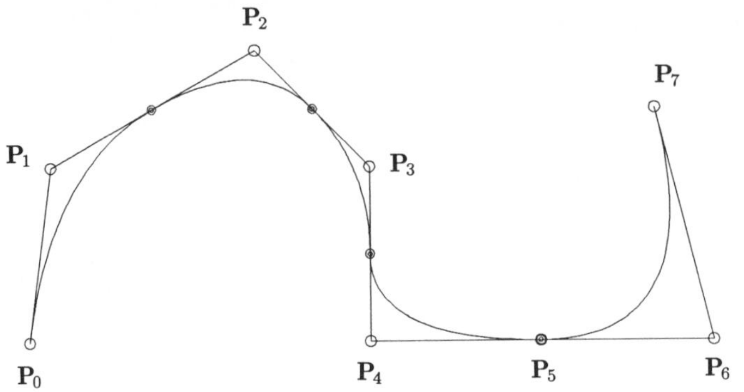

Figure 3.11. A quadratic curve on $U = \{0,0,0,{}^1\!/_5,{}^2\!/_5,{}^3\!/_5,{}^4\!/_5,{}^4\!/_5,1,1,1\}$; the first derivative is continuous at $u = {}^4\!/_5$.

P3.11 It is possible (and sometimes useful) to use multiple (coincident) control points. Figure 3.13 shows a quadratic curve with a double control point, $\mathbf{P}_2 = \mathbf{P}_3$. The interesting portion of this curve lies between $\mathbf{C}({}^1\!/_4)$ and $\mathbf{C}({}^3\!/_4)$. Indeed, $\mathbf{C}({}^1\!/_2) = \mathbf{P}_2 = \mathbf{P}_3$, and the curve segments between $\mathbf{C}({}^1\!/_4)$ and $\mathbf{C}({}^1\!/_2)$, and $\mathbf{C}({}^1\!/_2)$ and $\mathbf{C}({}^3\!/_4)$, are straight lines. This follows from Property P3.5, e.g., $\mathbf{C}(u)$ is in the convex hull of $\mathbf{P}_1\mathbf{P}_2\mathbf{P}_3$ (a line) if $u \in [{}^1\!/_4, {}^1\!/_2)$. Furthermore, since the knot $u = {}^1\!/_2$ has multiplicity $= 1$, the curve must be $\mathbf{C}^1$ continuous there, even though it has a cusp (visual discontinuity). This is a result of the magnitude of the first derivative vector going to zero (continuously) at $u = {}^1\!/_2$. In the next section we see that the derivative at $u = {}^1\!/_2$ is proportional to the difference, $\mathbf{P}_3 - \mathbf{P}_2$. Figures 3.14a and 3.14b are cubic examples using the same

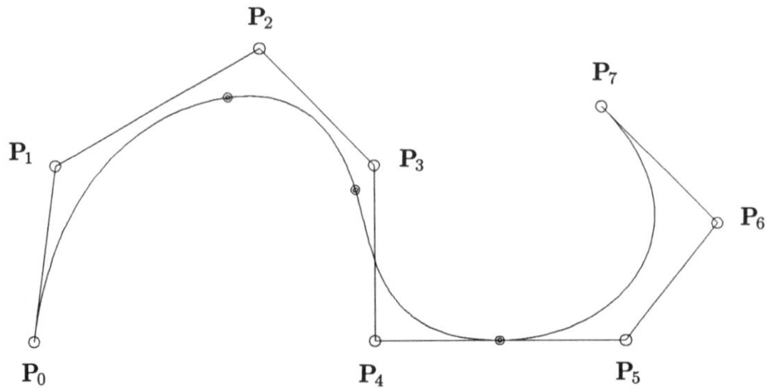

Figure 3.12. A cubic curve on $U = \{0,0,0,0,{}^1\!/_4,{}^1\!/_2,{}^3\!/_4,{}^3\!/_4,1,1,1,1\}$, $\mathbf{C}^2$ continuous at $u = {}^1\!/_4$ and $u = {}^1\!/_2$, and $\mathbf{C}^1$ continuous at $u = {}^3\!/_4$.

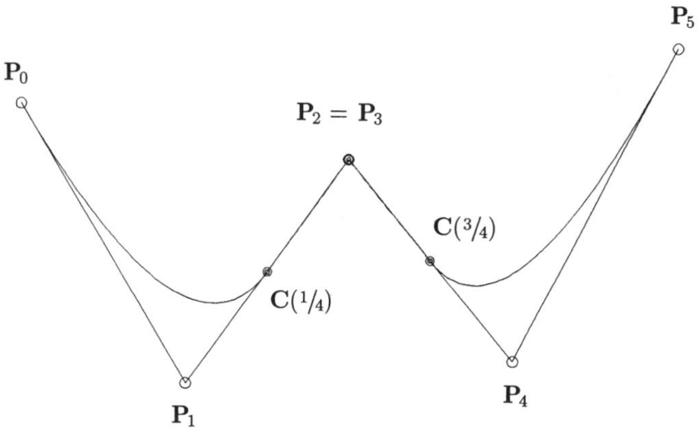

Figure 3.13. A quadratic curve on $U = \{0, 0, 0, 1/4, 1/2, 3/4, 1, 1, 1\}$; $\mathbf{P}_2 = \mathbf{P}_3$ is a double control point.

control polygon, including the double control point, $\mathbf{P}_2 = \mathbf{P}_3$, but with different knot vectors.

3.3 The Derivatives of a B-spline Curve

Let $\mathbf{C}^{(k)}(u)$ denote the kth derivative of $\mathbf{C}(u)$. If u is fixed, we can obtain $\mathbf{C}^{(k)}(u)$ by computing the kth derivatives of the basis functions (see Eqs. [2.7], [2.9], and [2.10] and Algorithm A2.3). In particular

$$\mathbf{C}^{(k)}(u) = \sum_{i=0}^{n} N_{i,p}^{(k)}(u)\,\mathbf{P}_i \tag{3.3}$$

Consider the example of Section 2.5, with $p = 2$, $U = \{0, 0, 0, 1, 2, 3, 4, 4, 5, 5, 5\}$, and $u = 5/2$. From Eq. (2.7) we have

$$N'_{2,2}\left(\frac{5}{2}\right) = 0 - \frac{2}{3-1}\frac{1}{2} = -\frac{1}{2}$$

$$N'_{3,2}\left(\frac{5}{2}\right) = \frac{2}{3-1}\frac{1}{2} - \frac{2}{4-2}\frac{1}{2} = 0$$

$$N'_{4,2}\left(\frac{5}{2}\right) = \frac{2}{4-2}\frac{1}{2} - 0 = \frac{1}{2}$$

It follows that

$$\mathbf{C}'\left(\frac{5}{2}\right) = -\frac{1}{2}\mathbf{P}_2 + \frac{1}{2}\mathbf{P}_4$$

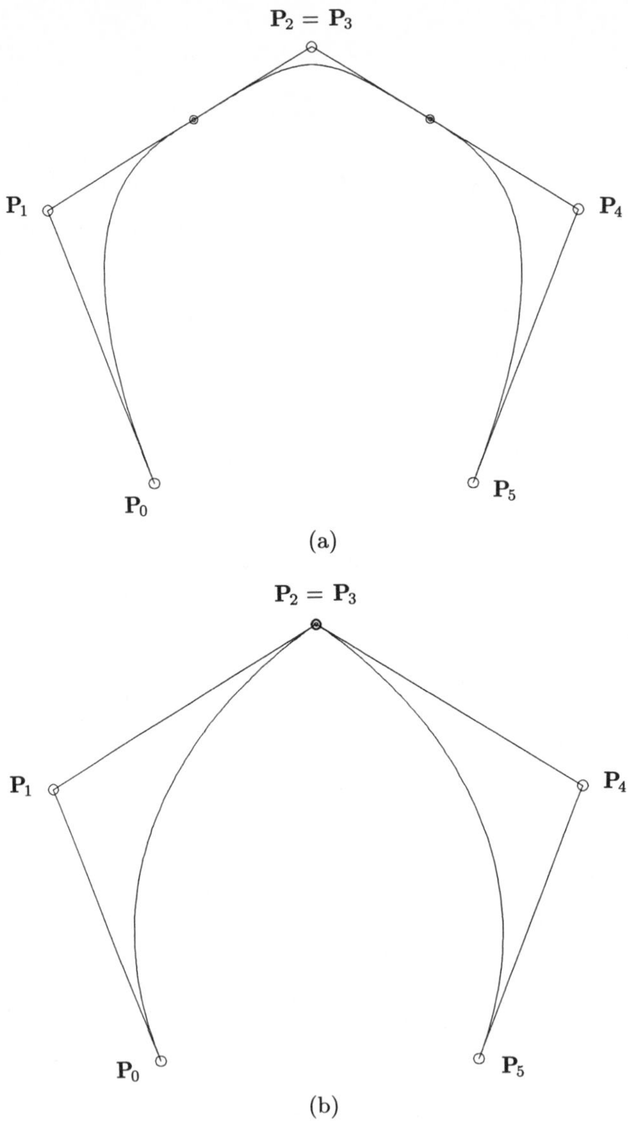

Figure 3.14. Cubic curves with double control point $\mathbf{P}_2 = \mathbf{P}_3$. (a) $U = \{0,0,0,0,\,^1\!/_4,\,^3\!/_4,\,1,1,1,1\}$; (b) $U = \{0,0,0,0,\,^1\!/_2,\,^1\!/_2,1,1,1,1\}$.

An algorithm to compute the point on a B-spline curve and all derivatives up to and including the dth at a fixed u value follows. We allow $d > p$, although the derivatives are 0 in this case (for nonrational curves); these derivatives are necessary for rational curves. Input to the algorithm is `u,d`, and the B-spline curve, defined (throughout the remainder of this book) by `n` : the number of control points is $n+1$;

`p` : the degree of the curve;

`U` : the knots;

`P` : the control points.

Output is the array `CK[]`, where `CK[k]` is the kth derivative, $0 \le k \le d$. We use Algorithms `A2.1` and `A2.3`. A local array, `nders[][]`, is used to store the derivatives of the basis functions.

```
ALGORITHM A3.2:
  CurveDerivsAlg1(n,p,U,P,u,d,CK)
    { /*  Compute curve derivatives  */
      /*  Input:  n,p,U,P,u,d  */
      /*  Output: CK  */
    du = min(d,p);
    for (k=p+1; k<=d; k++)   CK[k] = 0.0;
    span = FindSpan(n,p,u,U);
    DersBasisFuns(span,u,p,du,U,nders);
    for (k=0; k<=du; k++)
      {
      CK[k] = 0.0;
      for (j=0; j<=p; j++)
        CK[k] = CK[k] + nders[k][j]*P[span-p+j];
      }
    }
```

Now instead of fixing u, we want to formally differentiate the pth-degree B-spline curve,

$$\mathbf{C}(u) = \sum_{i=0}^{n} N_{i,p}(u)\,\mathbf{P}_i$$

defined on the knot vector

$$U = \{\underbrace{0,\ldots,0}_{p+1}, u_{p+1},\ldots,u_{m-p-1},\underbrace{1,\ldots,1}_{p+1}\}$$

From Eqs. (3.3) and (2.7) we obtain

$$\begin{aligned}
\mathbf{C}'(u) &= \sum_{i=0}^{n} N'_{i,p}(u)\,\mathbf{P}_i \\
&= \sum_{i=0}^{n} \left(\frac{p}{u_{i+p}-u_i} N_{i,p-1}(u) - \frac{p}{u_{i+p+1}-u_{i+1}} N_{i+1,p-1}(u) \right) \mathbf{P}_i \\
&= \left(p \sum_{i=-1}^{n-1} N_{i+1,p-1}(u) \frac{\mathbf{P}_{i+1}}{u_{i+p+1}-u_{i+1}} \right)
\end{aligned}$$

$$- \left(p \sum_{i=0}^{n} N_{i+1,p-1}(u) \frac{\mathbf{P}_i}{u_{i+p+1} - u_{i+1}} \right)$$

$$= p \frac{N_{0,p-1}(u)\,\mathbf{P}_0}{u_p - u_0} + p \sum_{i=0}^{n-1} N_{i+1,p-1}(u) \frac{(\mathbf{P}_{i+1} - \mathbf{P}_i)}{u_{i+p+1} - u_{i+1}} - p \frac{N_{n+1,p-1}(u)\,\mathbf{P}_n}{u_{n+p+1} - u_{n+1}}$$

The first and last terms evaluate to $0/0$, which is 0 by definition. Thus

$$\mathbf{C}'(u) = p \sum_{i=0}^{n-1} N_{i+1,p-1}(u) \frac{(\mathbf{P}_{i+1} - \mathbf{P}_i)}{u_{i+p+1} - u_{i+1}} = \sum_{i=0}^{n-1} N_{i+1,p-1}(u)\,\mathbf{Q}_i$$

where

$$\mathbf{Q}_i = p \frac{\mathbf{P}_{i+1} - \mathbf{P}_i}{u_{i+p+1} - u_{i+1}} \tag{3.4}$$

Now let U' be the knot vector obtained by dropping the first and last knots from U, i.e.

$$U' = \{\underbrace{0, \ldots, 0}_{p}, u_{p+1}, \ldots, u_{m-p-1}, \underbrace{1, \ldots, 1}_{p}\} \tag{3.5}$$

(U' has $m-1$ knots). Then it is easy to check that the function $N_{i+1,p-1}(u)$, computed on U, is equal to $N_{i,p-1}(u)$ computed on U'. Thus

$$\mathbf{C}'(u) = \sum_{i=0}^{n-1} N_{i,p-1}(u)\,\mathbf{Q}_i \tag{3.6}$$

where the $\mathbf{Q}_i$ are defined by Eq. (3.4), and the $N_{i,p-1}(u)$ are computed on U'. Hence, $\mathbf{C}'(u)$ is a $(p-1)$th-degree B-spline curve.

Examples

`Ex3.1` Let $\mathbf{C}(u) = \sum_{i=0}^{4} N_{i,2}(u)\,\mathbf{P}_i$ be a quadratic curve defined on

$$U = \{0, 0, 0, 2/5, 3/5, 1, 1, 1\}$$

Then $U' = \{0, 0, 2/5, 3/5, 1, 1\}$ and $\mathbf{C}'(u) = \sum_{i=0}^{3} N_{i,1}(u)\,\mathbf{Q}_i$, where

$$\mathbf{Q}_0 = \frac{2(\mathbf{P}_1 - \mathbf{P}_0)}{\frac{2}{5} - 0} = 5(\mathbf{P}_1 - \mathbf{P}_0)$$

$$\mathbf{Q}_1 = \frac{2(\mathbf{P}_2 - \mathbf{P}_1)}{\frac{3}{5} - 0} = \frac{10}{3}(\mathbf{P}_2 - \mathbf{P}_1)$$

$$\mathbf{Q}_2 = \frac{2(\mathbf{P}_3 - \mathbf{P}_2)}{1 - \frac{2}{5}} = \frac{10}{3}(\mathbf{P}_3 - \mathbf{P}_2)$$

$$\mathbf{Q}_3 = \frac{2(\mathbf{P}_4 - \mathbf{P}_3)}{1 - \frac{3}{5}} = 5(\mathbf{P}_4 - \mathbf{P}_3)$$

$\mathbf{C}(u)$ and $\mathbf{C}'(u)$ are shown in Figures 3.15a and 3.15b, respectively.

Ex3.2 Let $\mathbf{C}(u) = \sum_{i=0}^{6} N_{i,3}(u)\,\mathbf{P}_i$ be a cubic curve defined on

$$U = \{0,0,0,0,{}^2\!/\!_5,{}^3\!/\!_5,{}^3\!/\!_5,1,1,1,1\}$$

Then $U' = \{0,0,0,{}^2\!/\!_5,{}^3\!/\!_5,{}^3\!/\!_5,1,1,1\}$ and $\mathbf{C}'(u) = \sum_{i=0}^{5} N_{i,2}(u)\,\mathbf{Q}_i$,

where

$$\mathbf{Q}_0 = \frac{3(\mathbf{P}_1 - \mathbf{P}_0)}{\frac{1}{3} - 0} = 9(\mathbf{P}_1 - \mathbf{P}_0)$$

$$\mathbf{Q}_1 = \frac{3(\mathbf{P}_2 - \mathbf{P}_1)}{\frac{2}{3} - 0} = \frac{9}{2}(\mathbf{P}_2 - \mathbf{P}_1)$$

$$\mathbf{Q}_2 = \frac{3(\mathbf{P}_3 - \mathbf{P}_2)}{\frac{2}{3} - 0} = \frac{9}{2}(\mathbf{P}_3 - \mathbf{P}_2)$$

$$\mathbf{Q}_3 = \frac{3(\mathbf{P}_4 - \mathbf{P}_3)}{1 - \frac{1}{3}} = \frac{9}{2}(\mathbf{P}_4 - \mathbf{P}_3)$$

$$\mathbf{Q}_4 = \frac{3(\mathbf{P}_5 - \mathbf{P}_4)}{1 - \frac{2}{3}} = 9(\mathbf{P}_5 - \mathbf{P}_4)$$

$$\mathbf{Q}_5 = \frac{3(\mathbf{P}_6 - \mathbf{P}_5)}{1 - \frac{2}{3}} = 9(\mathbf{P}_6 - \mathbf{P}_5)$$

$\mathbf{C}(u)$ and $\mathbf{C}'(u)$ are shown in Figures 3.16a and 3.16b, respectively. Notice that $\mathbf{C}'(u)$ is a quadratic curve with a cusp at the double knot $u = {}^3\!/\!_5$.

Ex3.3 Recalling that a pth-degree Bézier curve is a B-spline curve on $U = \{0,\ldots,0,1,\ldots,1\}$ (no interior knots), Eq. (3.4) reduces to $\mathbf{Q}_i = p(\mathbf{P}_{i+1} - \mathbf{P}_i)$ for $0 \le i \le n-1$. Since $n = p$ and $N_{i,p-1}(u) = B_{i,n-1}(u)$, the Bernstein polynomials, Eq. (3.6) is equivalent to Eq. (1.9).

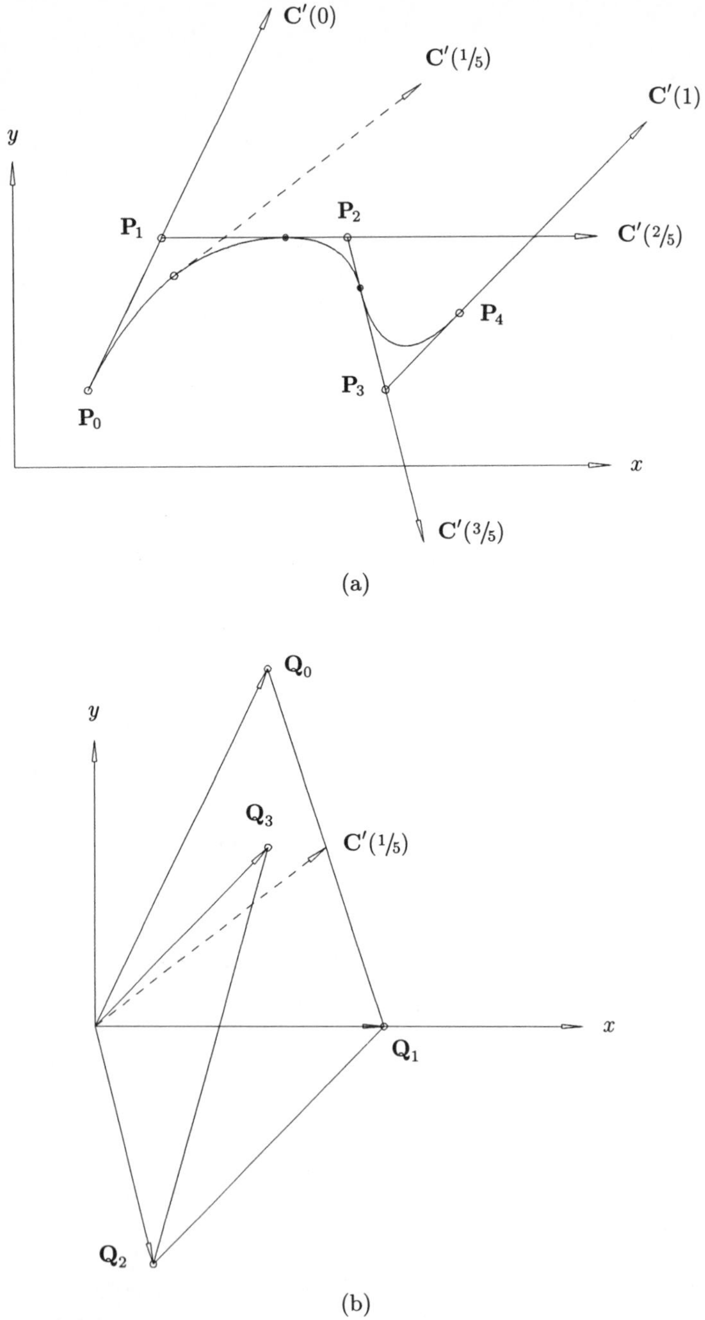

Figure 3.15. (a) A quadratic curve on $U = \{0, 0, 0, {}^2/_5, {}^3/_5, 1, 1, 1\}$; (b) the derivative of the curve is a first-degree B-spline curve on $U' = \{0, 0, {}^2/_5, {}^3/_5, 1, 1\}$.

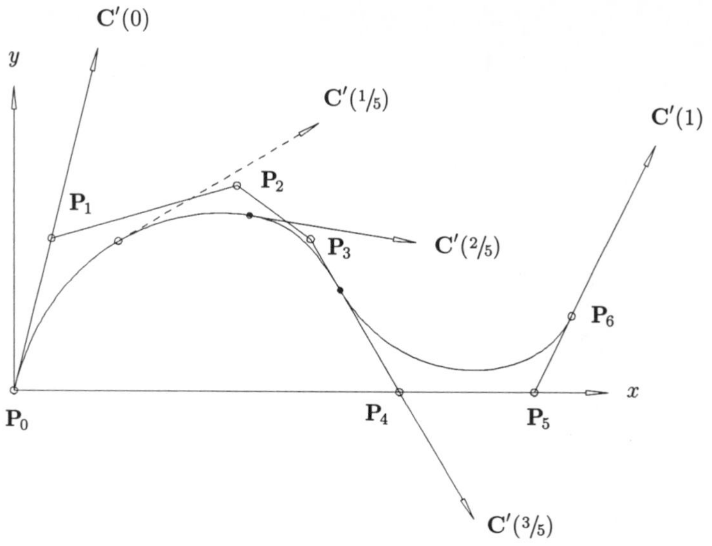

(a)

Figure 3.16. (a) A cubic curve on $U = \{0,0,0,0,\,^2\!/_5,\,^3\!/_5,\,^3\!/_5,1,1,1,1\}$; (b) the quadratic derivative curve on $U' = \{0,0,0,\,^2\!/_5,\,^3\!/_5,\,^3\!/_5,1,1,1\}$.

The first derivatives at the endpoints of a B-spline curve are given by

$$\mathbf{C}'(0) = \mathbf{Q}_0 = \frac{p}{u_{p+1}}(\mathbf{P}_1 - \mathbf{P}_0)$$

$$\mathbf{C}'(1) = \mathbf{Q}_{n-1} = \frac{p}{1-u_{m-p-1}}(\mathbf{P}_n - \mathbf{P}_{n-1}) \tag{3.7}$$

(see Examples Ex3.1 and Ex3.2, and Figures 3.15(a) and (b) and Figures 3.16 (a) and (b)). Note that in Figures 3.15b and 3.16b the derivative vectors and control point differences are scaled down for better visualization, by $^1\!/_2$ and by $^1\!/_3$, respectively.

Since $\mathbf{C}'(u)$ is a B-spline curve, we apply Eqs. (3.4) through (3.6) recursively to obtain higher derivatives. Letting $\mathbf{P}_i^{(0)} = \mathbf{P}_i$, we write

$$\mathbf{C}(u) = \mathbf{C}^{(0)}(u) = \sum_{i=0}^{n} N_{i,p}(u)\,\mathbf{P}_i^{(0)}$$

Then

$$\mathbf{C}^{(k)}(u) = \sum_{i=0}^{n-k} N_{i,p-k}(u)\,\mathbf{P}_i^{(k)} \tag{3.8}$$

with

$$\mathbf{P}_i^{(k)} = \begin{cases} \mathbf{P}_i & k = 0 \\ \dfrac{p-k+1}{u_{i+p+1}-u_{i+k}}\left(\mathbf{P}_{i+1}^{(k-1)} - \mathbf{P}_i^{(k-1)}\right) & k > 0 \end{cases}$$

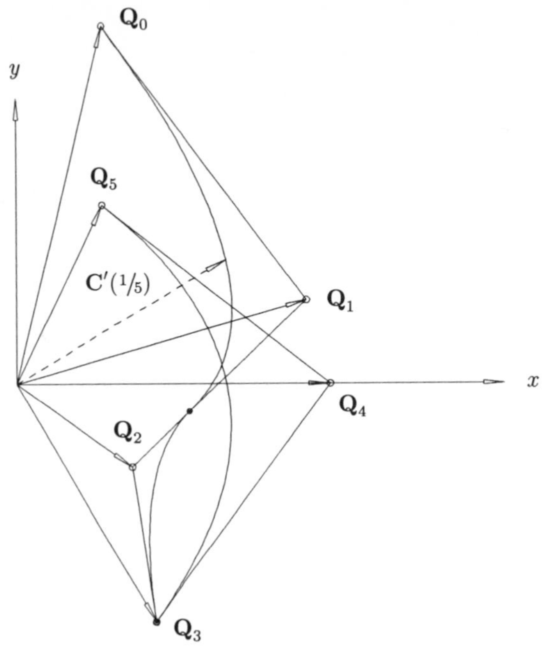

(b)

Figure 3.16. (*Continued.*)

and
$$U^{(k)} = \{\underbrace{0,\ldots,0}_{p-k+1}, u_{p+1},\ldots,u_{m-p-1},\underbrace{1,\ldots,1}_{p-k+1}\}$$

Algorithm A3.3 is a nonrecursive implementation of Eq. (3.8). It computes the control points of all derivative curves up to and including the dth derivative ($d \le p$). On output, PK[k][i] is the ith control point of the kth derivative curve, where $0 \le k \le d$ and $r_1 \le i \le r_2 - k$. If $r_1 = 0$ and $r_2 = n$, all control points are computed.

```
ALGORITHM A3.3
  CurveDerivCpts(n,p,U,P,d,r1,r2,PK)
    { /*  Compute control points of curve derivatives  */
      /*  Input:  n,p,U,P,d,r1,r2  */
      /*  Output: PK  */
    r = r2-r1;
    for (i=0; i<=r; i++)
      PK[0][i] = P[r1+i];
    for (k=1; k<=d; k++)
      {
      tmp = p-k+1;
```

```
      for (i=0; i<=r-k; i++)
        PK[k][i] = tmp*(PK[k-1][i+1]-PK[k-1][i])/
            (U[r1+i+p+1]-U[r1+i+k]);
      }
  }
```

Using Eq. (3.8), we compute the second derivative at the endpoint, $u = 0$, of a B-spline curve ($p > 1$)

$$\mathbf{C}^{(2)}(0) = \mathbf{P}_0^{(2)} = \frac{p-2+1}{u_{p+1}-u_2}\left(\mathbf{P}_1^{(1)} - \mathbf{P}_0^{(1)}\right)$$

$$= \frac{p-1}{u_{p+1}-u_2}\left[\frac{p}{u_{p+2}-u_2}\left(\mathbf{P}_2^{(0)} - \mathbf{P}_1^{(0)}\right) - \frac{p}{u_{p+1}-u_1}\left(\mathbf{P}_1^{(0)} - \mathbf{P}_0^{(0)}\right)\right]$$

From $u_1 = u_2 = 0$ it follows that

$$\mathbf{C}^{(2)}(0) = \frac{p(p-1)}{u_{p+1}}\left[\frac{\mathbf{P}_0}{u_{p+1}} - \frac{(u_{p+1}+u_{p+2})\mathbf{P}_1}{u_{p+1}u_{p+2}} + \frac{\mathbf{P}_2}{u_{p+2}}\right] \tag{3.9}$$

Analogously,

$$\mathbf{C}^{(2)}(1) = \frac{p(p-1)}{1-u_{m-p-1}} \times$$

$$\left[\frac{\mathbf{P}_n}{1-u_{m-p-1}} - \frac{(2-u_{m-p-1}-u_{m-p-2})\mathbf{P}_{n-1}}{(1-u_{m-p-1})(1-u_{m-p-2})} + \frac{\mathbf{P}_{n-2}}{1-u_{m-p-2}}\right] \tag{3.10}$$

Notice that for Bézier curves these equations reduce to the corresponding expressions of Eq. (1.10). Figure 3.17 shows the quadratic curve of Figure 3.15a with the vectors $\mathbf{C}^{(2)}(0)$ and $\mathbf{C}^{(2)}(1)$. $\mathbf{C}^{(2)}(u)$ is a piecewise zeroth-degree curve, i.e., it is a constant (but different) vector on each of the three intervals $[0, 2/5)$, $[2/5, 3/5)$, and $[3/5, 1]$.

We close this section with another algorithm to compute the point on a B-spline curve and all derivatives up to and including the dth derivative at a fixed u value (compare with Algorithm `A3.2`). The algorithm is based on Eq. (3.8) and Algorithm `A3.3`. We assume a routine, `AllBasisFuns`, which is a simple modification of `BasisFuns` (Algorithm `A2.2`), to return all nonzero basis functions of all degrees from 0 up to p. In particular, `N[j][i]` is the value of the ith-degree basis function, $N_{\text{span}-i+j,\,i}(u)$, where $0 \le i \le p$ and $0 \le j \le i$.

```
ALGORITHM A3.4
  CurveDerivsAlg2(n,p,U,P,u,d,CK)
    { /* Compute curve derivatives */
      /* Input: n,p,U,P,u,d */
      /* Output: CK */
    du = min(d,p);
```

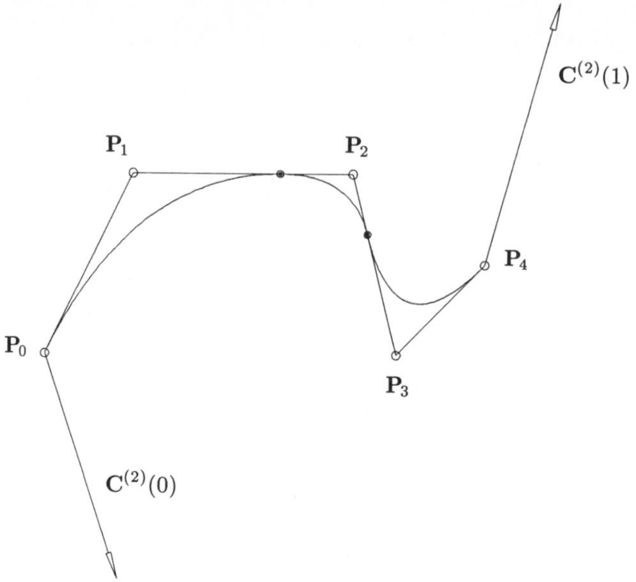

Figure 3.17. The second derivatives at the endpoints of the curve of Figure 3.15a.

```
for (k=p+1; k<=d; k++)    CK[k] = 0.0;
span = FindSpan(n,p,u,U);
AllBasisFuns(span,u,p,U,N);
CurveDerivCpts(n,p,U,P,du,span-p,span,PK);
for (k=0; k<=du; k++)
  {
  CK[k] = 0.0;
  for (j=0; j<=p-k; j++)
    CK[k] = CK[k] + N[j][p-k]*PK[k][j];
  }
}
```

Figure 3.18 shows a cubic curve with first, second, and third derivatives computed at $u = 2/5$. (The derivatives are scaled down by $2/5$.)

3.4 Definition and Properties of B-spline Surfaces

A B-spline surface is obtained by taking a bidirectional net of control points, two knot vectors, and the products of the univariate B-spline functions

$$\mathbf{S}(u,v) = \sum_{i=0}^{n} \sum_{j=0}^{m} N_{i,p}(u) N_{j,q}(v) \mathbf{P}_{i,j} \tag{3.11}$$

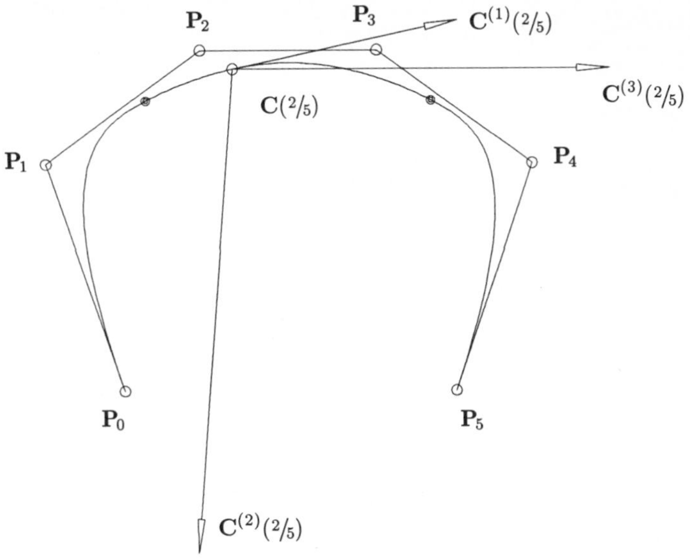

Figure 3.18. A cubic curve on $U = \{0,0,0,0,\,^1\!/\!_4,\,^3\!/\!_4,1,1,1,1\}$ with first, second, and third derivatives computed at $u = {}^2\!/\!_5$.

with

$$U = \{\underbrace{0,\ldots,0}_{p+1}, u_{p+1},\ldots,u_{r-p-1},\underbrace{1,\ldots,1}_{p+1}\}$$

$$V = \{\underbrace{0,\ldots,0}_{q+1}, v_{q+1},\ldots,v_{s-q-1},\underbrace{1,\ldots,1}_{q+1}\}$$

U has $r+1$ knots, and V has $s+1$. Equation (3.2) takes the form

$$r = n + p + 1 \quad \text{and} \quad s = m + q + 1 \tag{3.12}$$

Let U and $\{N_{i,3}(u)\}$ be the knot vector and cubic basis functions of Figure 3.2a, and $\{N_{j,2}(v)\}$ the quadratic basis functions defined on $V = \{0,0,0,\,^1\!/\!_5,\,^2\!/\!_5,\,^3\!/\!_5,\,^3\!/\!_5,\,^4\!/\!_5,1,1,1\}$. Figures 3.19a and 3.19b show the tensor product basis functions $N_{4,3}(u)N_{4,2}(v)$ and $N_{4,3}(u)N_{2,2}(v)$, respectively. Figures 3.20–3.25 show examples of B-spline surfaces.

Five steps are required to compute a point on a B-spline surface at fixed (u,v) parameter values:

1. find the knot span in which u lies, say $u \in [u_i, u_{i+1})$ (Algorithm A2.1);
2. compute the nonzero basis functions $N_{i-p,p}(u),\ldots,N_{i,p}(u)$ (A2.2);
3. find the knot span in which v lies, say $v \in [v_j, v_{j+1})$ (A2.1);
4. compute the nonzero basis functions $N_{j-q,q}(v),\ldots,N_{j,q}(v)$ (A2.2);

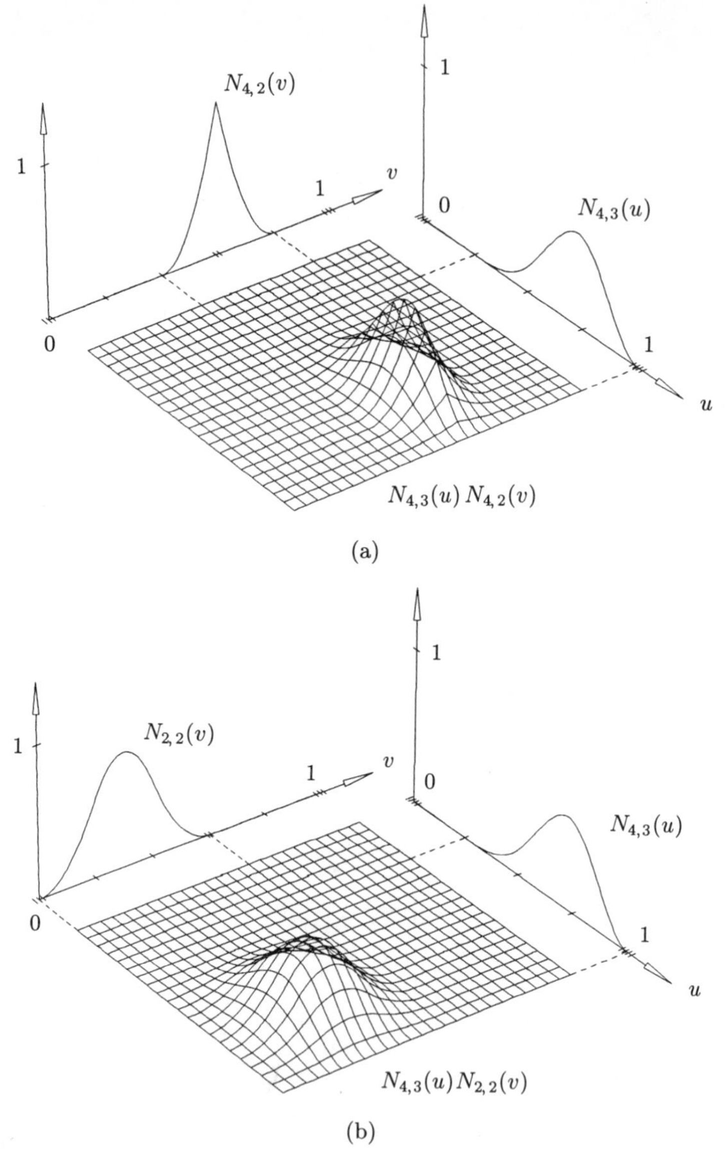

Figure 3.19. Cubic × quadratic basis functions. (a) $N_{4,3}(u)N_{4,2}(v)$; (b) $N_{4,3}(u)N_{2,2}(v)$; $U = \{0,0,0,0,\, ^1\!/_4,\, ^1\!/_2,\, ^3\!/_4, 1,1,1,1\}$ and $V = \{0,0,0,\, ^1\!/_5,\, ^2\!/_5,\, ^3\!/_5,\, ^3\!/_5,\, ^4\!/_5, 1,1,1\}$.

5. multiply the values of the nonzero basis functions with the corresponding control points.

The last step takes the form

$$\mathbf{S}(u,v) = [\,N_{k,p}(u)\,]^T\,[\mathbf{P}_{k,l}\,]\,[\,N_{l,q}(v)\,] \qquad i-p \le k \le i, \;\; j-q \le l \le j \quad (3.13)$$

Note that $[N_{k,p}(u)]^T$ is a $1\times(p+1)$ row vector of scalars, $[\mathbf{P}_{k,l}]$ is a $(p+1)\times(q+1)$ matrix of control points, and $[N_{l,q}(v)]$ is a $(q+1)\times 1$ column vector of scalars.

Example

Ex3.4 Let $p = q = 2$ and $\sum_{i=0}^{4} \sum_{j=0}^{5} N_{i,2}(u)N_{j,2}(v)\mathbf{P}_{i,j}$, with

$$U = \{0,0,0,{}^2\!/_5,{}^3\!/_5,1,1,1\}$$

$$V = \{0,0,0,{}^1\!/_5,{}^1\!/_2,{}^4\!/_5,1,1,1\}$$

Compute $\mathbf{S}({}^1\!/_5,{}^3\!/_5)$. Then ${}^1\!/_5 \in [u_2,u_3)$ and ${}^3\!/_5 \in [v_4,v_5)$, and

$$\mathbf{S}\left(\frac{1}{5},\frac{3}{5}\right) = \left[N_{0,2}\left(\frac{1}{5}\right) \quad N_{1,2}\left(\frac{1}{5}\right) \quad N_{2,2}\left(\frac{1}{5}\right)\right] \times$$

$$\begin{bmatrix} \mathbf{P}_{0,2} & \mathbf{P}_{0,3} & \mathbf{P}_{0,4} \\ \mathbf{P}_{1,2} & \mathbf{P}_{1,3} & \mathbf{P}_{1,4} \\ \mathbf{P}_{2,2} & \mathbf{P}_{2,3} & \mathbf{P}_{2,4} \end{bmatrix} \begin{bmatrix} N_{2,2}\left(\frac{3}{5}\right) \\ N_{3,2}\left(\frac{3}{5}\right) \\ N_{4,2}\left(\frac{3}{5}\right) \end{bmatrix}$$

Algorithm A3.5 computes the point on a B-spline surface at fixed (u,v) values. For efficiency, it uses a local array, **temp[]**, to store the vector/matrix product, $[N_{k,p}(u)]^T\,[\mathbf{P}_{k,l}]$. The resulting vector of points (in **temp[]**) is then multiplied with the vector $[N_{l,q}(v)]$.

```
ALGORITHM A3.5
  SurfacePoint(n,p,U,m,q,V,P,u,v,S)
    { /*  Compute surface point  */
      /*  Input:  n,p,U,m,q,V,P,u,v  */
      /*  Output: S  */
    uspan = FindSpan(n,p,u,U);
    BasisFuns(uspan,u,p,U,Nu);
    vspan = FindSpan(m,q,v,V);
    BasisFuns(vspan,v,q,V,Nv);
    uind = uspan-p;
    S = 0.0;
    for (l=0; l<=q; l++)
      {
      temp = 0.0;
      vind = vspan-q+l;
      for (k=0; k<=p; k++)
        temp = temp + Nu[k]*P[uind+k][vind];
      S = S + Nv[l]*temp;
      }
    }
```

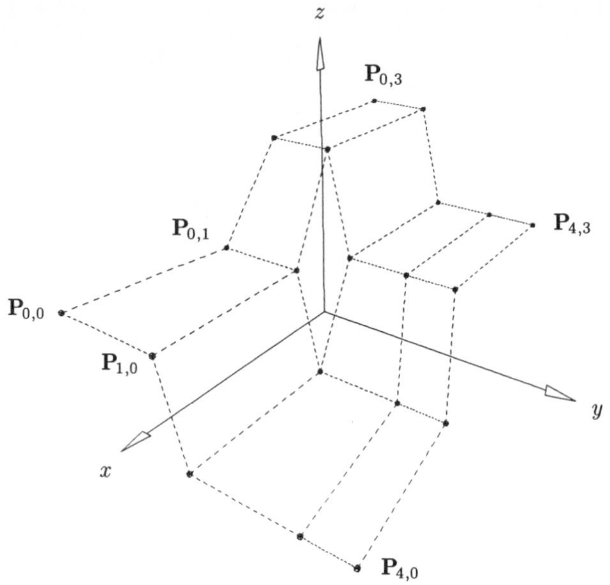

(a)

Figure 3.20. A B-spline surface. (a) The control net; (b) the surface.

The properties of the tensor product basis functions follow from the corresponding properties of the univariate basis functions listed in Chapter 2.

P3.12 Nonnegativity: $N_{i,p}(u)N_{j,q}(v) \geq 0$ for all i, j, p, q, u, v;

P3.13 Partition of unity: $\sum_{i=0}^{n} \sum_{j=0}^{m} N_{i,p}(u)N_{j,q}(v) = 1$ for all $(u,v) \in [0,1] \times [0,1]$;

P3.14 If $n = p$, $m = q$, $U = \{0,\ldots,0,1,\ldots,1\}$, and $V = \{0,\ldots,0,1,\ldots,1\}$, then $N_{i,p}(u)N_{j,q}(v) = B_{i,n}(u)B_{j,m}(v)$ for all i, j; that is, products of B-spline functions degenerate to products of Bernstein polynomials;

P3.15 $N_{i,p}(u)N_{j,q}(v) = 0$ if (u,v) is outside the rectangle $[u_i, u_{i+p+1}) \times [v_j, v_{j+q+1})$ (see Figures 3.19a and 3.19b);

P3.16 In any given rectangle, $[u_{i_0}, u_{i_0+1}) \times [v_{j_0}, v_{j_0+1})$, at most $(p+1)(q+1)$ basis functions are nonzero, in particular the $N_{i,p}(u)N_{j,q}(v)$ for $i_0 - p \leq i \leq i_0$ and $j_0 - q \leq j \leq j_0$;

P3.17 If $p > 0$ and $q > 0$, then $N_{i,p}(u)N_{j,q}(v)$ attains exactly one maximum value (see Figures 3.19a and 3.19b);

P3.18 Interior to the rectangles formed by the u and v knot lines, where the function is a bivariate polynomial, all partial derivatives of $N_{i,p}(u)$ $N_{j,q}(v)$ exist; at a u knot (v knot) it is $p - k$ ($q - k$) times differentiable in the u (v) direction, where k is the multiplicity of the knot. In

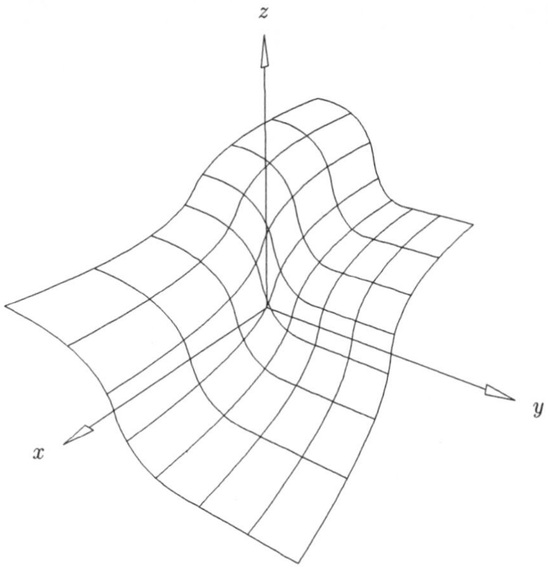

(b)

Figure 3.20. (*Continued.*)

Figure 3.19a the first partial derivative of $N_{4,3}(u)N_{4,2}(v)$ with respect to v is discontinuous along the knot line $v = 3/5$ where $N_{4,2}(v)$ has a cusp. The second partial derivative with respect to u is everywhere continuous, because $N_{4,3}(u)$ is $\mathbf{C}^2$ continuous.

B-spline surfaces have the following properties:

P3.19 If $n = p$, $m = q$, $U = \{0,\ldots,0,1,\ldots,1\}$, and $V = \{0,\ldots,0,1,\ldots,1\}$, then $\mathbf{S}(u,v)$ is a Bézier surface; this follows from P3.14;

P3.20 The surface interpolates the four corner control points: $\mathbf{S}(0,0) = \mathbf{P}_{0,0}$, $\mathbf{S}(1,0) = \mathbf{P}_{n,0}$, $\mathbf{S}(0,1) = \mathbf{P}_{0,m}$, and $\mathbf{S}(1,1) = \mathbf{P}_{n,m}$ (see Figures 3.20 through 3.25); this follows from P3.13 and the identity

$$\begin{aligned} N_{0,p}(0)N_{0,q}(0) &= N_{n,p}(1)N_{0,q}(0) = N_{0,p}(0)N_{m,q}(1) \\ &= N_{n,p}(1)N_{m,q}(1) = 1 \end{aligned}$$

P3.21 Affine invariance: an affine transformation is applied to the surface by applying it to the control points; this follows from P3.13;

P3.22 Strong convex hull property: if $(u,v) \in [u_{i_0}, u_{i_0+1}) \times [v_{j_0}, v_{j_0+1})$, then $\mathbf{S}(u,v)$ is in the convex hull of the control points $\mathbf{P}_{i,j}$, $i_0 - p \le i \le i_0$ and $j_0 - q \le j \le j_0$ (see Figures 3.21); this follows from P3.12, P3.13, and P3.16;

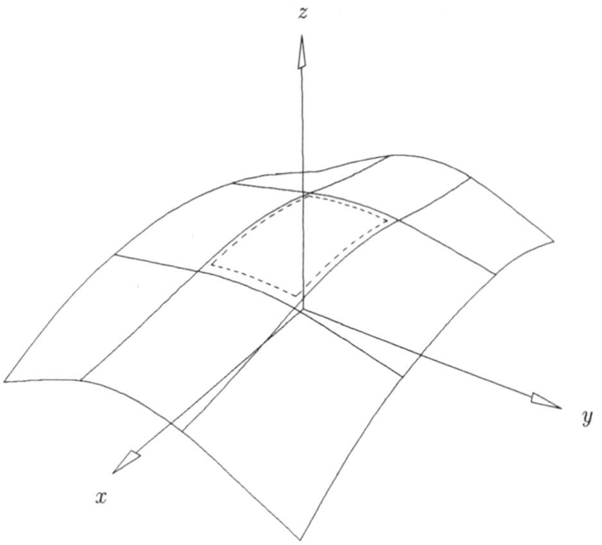

(a)

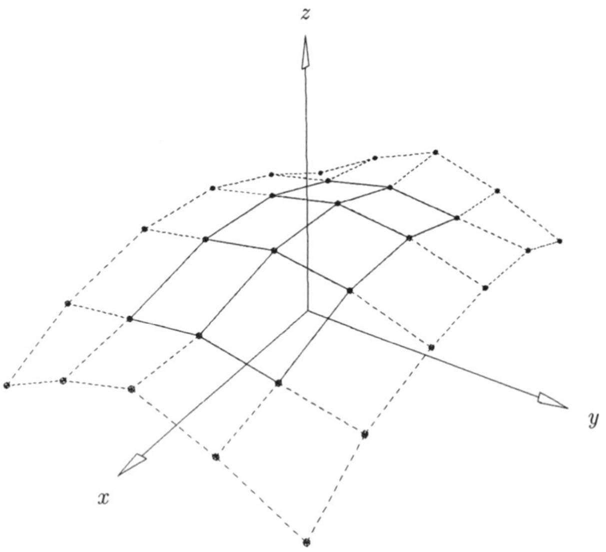

(b)

Figure 3.21. (a) A cubic×quadratic B-spline surface; (b) the strong convex hull property.

P3.23 If triangulated, the control net forms a piecewise planar approximation to the surface; as is the case for curves, the lower the degree the better the approximation (see Figures 3.22a and 3.22b);

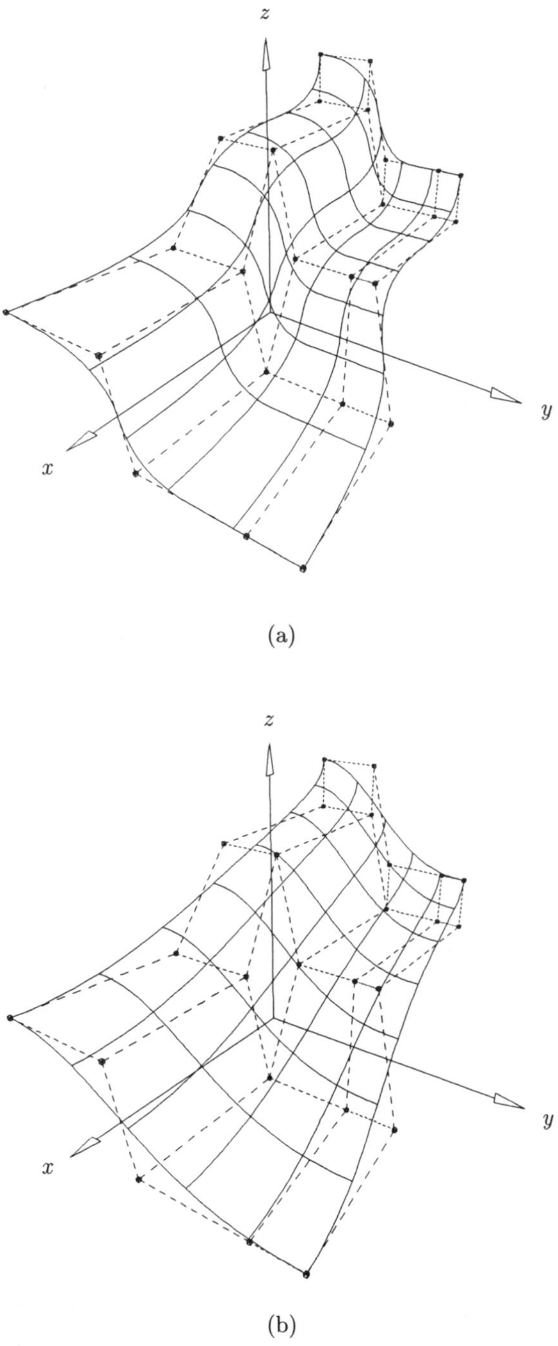

Figure 3.22. (a) A biquadratic surface; (b) a biquartic surface ($p = q = 4$) using the same control points as in Figure 3.22a.

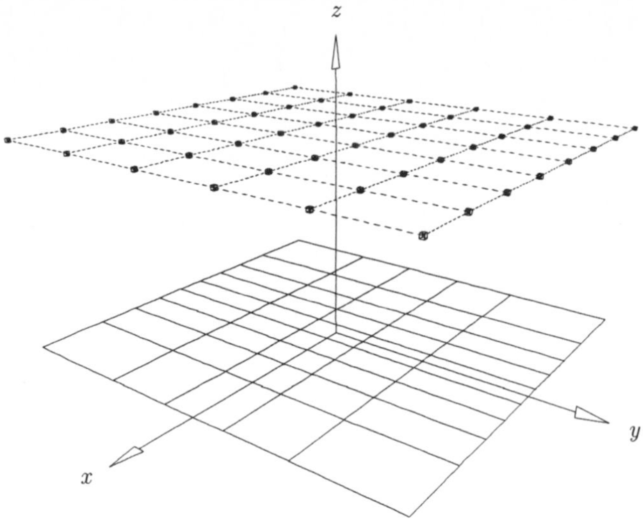

(a)

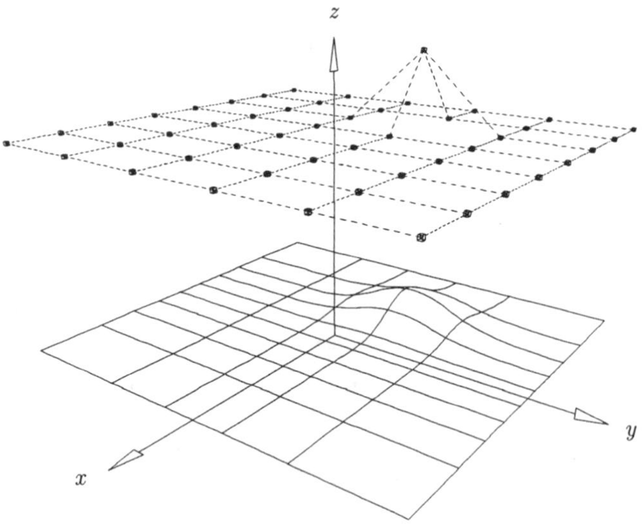

(b)

Figure 3.23. (a) A planar quadratic × cubic surface, $U = \{0,0,0,{}^1\!/_4,{}^1\!/_2,{}^3\!/_4,1,1,1\}$ and $V = \{0,0,0,0,{}^1\!/_5,{}^2\!/_5,{}^3\!/_5,{}^4\!/_5,1,1,1,1\}$; (b) $\mathbf{P}_{3,5}$ is moved, affecting surface shape only in the rectangle $[{}^1\!/_4,1) \times [{}^2\!/_5,1)$.

P3.24 Local modification scheme: if $\mathbf{P}_{i,j}$ is moved it affects the surface only in the rectangle $[u_i, u_{i+p+1}) \times [v_j, v_{j+q+1})$; this follows from P3.15. Now consider Figures 3.23a and 3.23b: the initial surface is flat because all the control points lie in a common plane (P3.22); the control net is offset from the surface for better visualization. When $\mathbf{P}_{3,5}$ is moved it affects the surface shape only in the rectangle $[1/4, 1) \times [2/5, 1)$;

P3.25 The continuity and differentiability of $\mathbf{S}(u,v)$ follows from that of the basis functions. In particular, $\mathbf{S}(u,v)$ is $p-k$ $(q-k)$ times differentiable in the u (v) direction at a u (v) knot of multiplicity k. Figure 3.24 shows a quadratic $\times$ cubic surface defined on the knot vectors $U = \{0,0,0,1/2,1/2,1,1,1\}$ and $V = \{0,0,0,0,1/2,1,1,1,1\}$. Notice the crease in the surface, corresponding to the knot line $u = 1/2$. Of course, as is the case for curves, it is possible to position the control points in such a way that they cancel the discontinuities in the basis functions. By using multiply coincident control points, visual discontinuities can be created where there are no corresponding discontinuities in the basis functions; Figure 3.25 shows such a surface, which is bicubic with no multiple knots. Hence, the second partial derivatives are everywhere continuous. The crease is due to the multiple control points.

We remark here that there is no known variation diminishing property for B-spline surfaces (see [Prau92]).

Isoparametric curves on $\mathbf{S}(u,v)$ are obtained in a manner analogous to that for Bézier surfaces. Fix $u = u_0$

$$\mathbf{C}_{u_0}(v) = \mathbf{S}(u_0, v) = \sum_{i=0}^{n}\sum_{j=0}^{m} N_{i,p}(u_0)N_{j,q}(v)\mathbf{P}_{i,j}$$

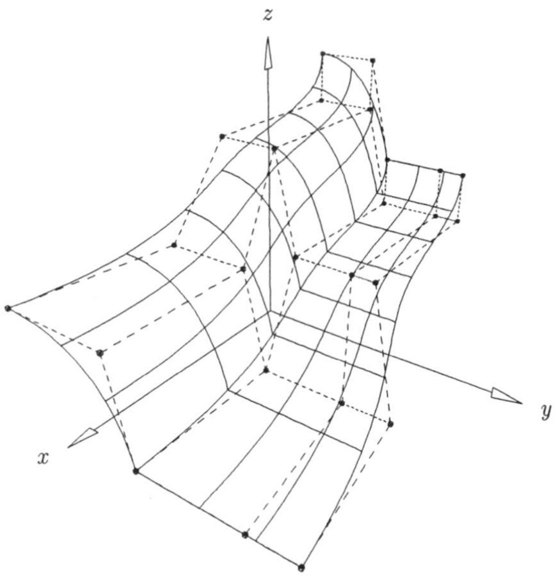

Figure 3.24. A quadratic $\times$ cubic surface with crease, $U = \{0,0,0,1/2,1/2,1,1,1\}$ and $V = \{0,0,0,0,1/2,1,1,1,1\}$.

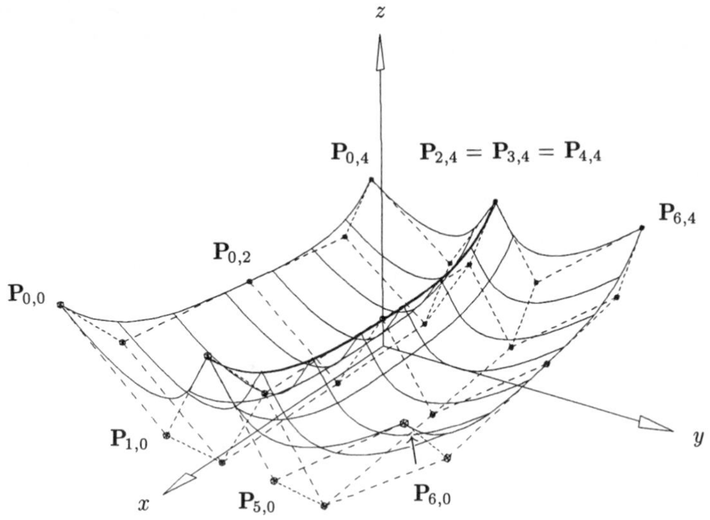

Figure 3.25. A bicubic surface with crease, $U = \{0,0,0,0,{}^1\!/_4,{}^1\!/_2,{}^3\!/_4,1,1,1,1\}$ and $V = \{0,0,0,0,{}^1\!/_2,1,1,1,1\}$; $\mathbf{P}_{2,j} = \mathbf{P}_{3,j} = \mathbf{P}_{4,j}$ for $0 \le j \le 4$.

$$= \sum_{j=0}^{m} N_{j,q}(v) \left(\sum_{i=0}^{n} N_{i,p}(u_0) \mathbf{P}_{i,j} \right) = \sum_{j=0}^{m} N_{j,q}(v)\, \mathbf{Q}_j(u_0) \tag{3.14}$$

where
$$\mathbf{Q}_j(u_0) = \sum_{i=0}^{n} N_{i,p}(u_0) \mathbf{P}_{i,j}$$

Analogously
$$\mathbf{C}_{v_0}(u) = \sum_{i=0}^{n} N_{i,p}(u)\, \mathbf{Q}_i(v_0)$$

where
$$\mathbf{Q}_i(v_0) = \sum_{j=0}^{m} N_{j,q}(v_0) \mathbf{P}_{i,j} \tag{3.15}$$

is a u isocurve on $\mathbf{S}(u,v)$. $\mathbf{C}_{u_0}(v)$ is a qth-degree B-spline curve on V, and $\mathbf{C}_{v_0}(u)$ is a pth-degree B-spline curve on U. The point $\mathbf{S}(u_0, v_0)$ is at the intersection of $\mathbf{C}_{u_0}(v)$ and $\mathbf{C}_{v_0}(u)$. All lines shown on the surfaces of Figures 3.20–3.25 are isolines.

3.5 Derivatives of a B-spline Surface

Let (u,v) be fixed. Generally, one is interested in computing all partial derivatives of $\mathbf{S}(u,v)$ up to and including order d, that is

$$\frac{\partial^{k+l}}{\partial^k u\, \partial^l v} \mathbf{S}(u,v) \qquad 0 \le k+l \le d \tag{3.16}$$

As for curves, we obtain these derivatives by computing derivatives of the basis functions (see Eqs. [2.9] and[2.10], and Algorithm A2.3). In particular

$$\frac{\partial^{k+l}}{\partial^k u\, \partial^l v}\mathbf{S}(u,v) = \sum_{i=0}^{n}\sum_{j=0}^{m} N_{i,p}^{(k)}\, N_{j,q}^{(l)}\, \mathbf{P}_{i,j} \tag{3.17}$$

Algorithm A3.6 computes the point on a B-spline surface and all partial derivatives up to and including order d ($d > p, q$ is allowed). Analogous to Algorithm A3.5, this is a five-step process, with the last step being vector/matrix/vector multiplications of the form

$$\frac{\partial^{k+l}}{\partial^k u\, \partial^l v}\mathbf{S}(u,v) = \left[\, N_{r,p}^{(k)}(u)\,\right]^T \left[\mathbf{P}_{r,s}\,\right]\left[\, N_{s,q}^{(l)}(v)\,\right]$$

$$0 \le k+l \le d \quad uspan - p \le r \le uspan$$
$$vspan - q \le s \le vspan \tag{3.18}$$

Output is the array SKL[][], where SKL[k][l] is the derivative of $\mathbf{S}(u,v)$ with respect to u k times, and v l times. For fixed k, $0 \le k \le d$, local array temp[] stores the vector/matrix product, $\left[\, {N_{r,p}}^{(k)}(u)\,\right]^T \left[\mathbf{P}_{r,s}\,\right]$, while it is being multiplied with the $\left[\, {N_{s,q}}^{(l)}(v)\,\right]$, for $0 \le l \le d-k$. Arrays Nu[][] and Nv[][] are used to store the derivatives of the basis functions.

```
ALGORITHM A3.6
  SurfaceDerivsAlg1(n,p,U,m,q,V,P,u,v,d,SKL)
    { /*  Compute surface derivatives  */
      /*  Input:  n,p,U,m,q,V,P,u,v,d  */
      /*  Output: SKL  */
    du = min(d,p);
    for (k=p+1; k<=d; k++)
      for (l=0; l<=d-k; l++)    SKL[k][l] = 0.0;
    dv = min(d,q);
    for (l=q+1; l<=d; l++)
      for (k=0; k<=d-l; k++)    SKL[k][l] = 0.0;
    uspan = FindSpan(n,p,u,U);
    DersBasisFuns(uspan,u,p,du,U,Nu);
    vspan = FindSpan(m,q,v,V);
    DersBasisFuns(vspan,v,q,dv,V,Nv);
    for (k=0; k<=du; k++)
      {
      for (s=0; s<=q; s++)
        {
        temp[s] = 0.0;
        for (r=0; r<=p; r++)
          temp[s] = temp[s] + Nu[k][r]*P[uspan-p+r][vspan-q+s];
        }
```

```
        dd = min(d-k,dv);
        for (l=0; l<=dd; l++)
          {
          SKL[k][l] = 0.0;
          for (s=0; s<=q; s++)
            SKL[k][l] = SKL[k][l] + Nv[l][s]*temp[s];
          }
        }
      }
```

Figure 3.26 shows a bicubic surface and its first and second partial derivatives. Note that the derivatives are scaled down by $1/2$ for better visualization.

Let us formally differentiate $\mathbf{S}(u,v)$. With respect to u we have

$$\mathbf{S}_u(u,v) = \frac{\partial}{\partial u}\mathbf{S}(u,v) = \sum_{j=0}^{m} N_{j,q}(v)\left(\frac{\partial}{\partial u}\sum_{i=0}^{n} N_{i,p}(u)\mathbf{P}_{i,j}\right) \qquad (3.19)$$

$$= \sum_{j=0}^{m} N_{j,q}(v)\left(\frac{\partial}{\partial u}\mathbf{C}_j(u)\right)$$

where $$\mathbf{C}_j(u) = \sum_{i=0}^{n} N_{i,p}(u)\mathbf{P}_{i,j} \qquad j=0,\ldots,m$$

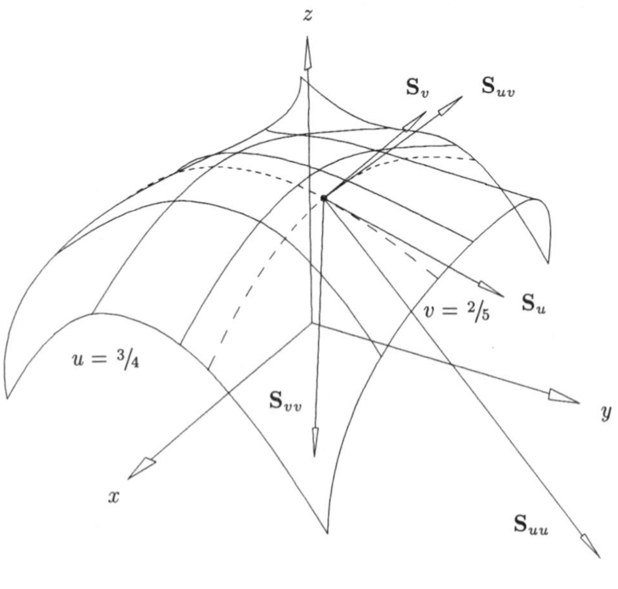

Figure 3.26. A bicubic surface defined on $U = V = \{0,0,0,0,1/2,1,1,1,1\}$ and its first and second partial derivatives computed at $u = 3/4$ and $v = 2/5$.

are B-spline curves. Applying Eq. (3.6) to each of the $\mathbf{C}_j(u)$ and substituting into Eq. (3.19), we obtain

$$\mathbf{S}_u(u,v) = \sum_{i=0}^{n-1}\sum_{j=0}^{m} N_{i,p-1}(u)N_{j,q}(v)\,\mathbf{P}_{i,j}^{(1,0)} \tag{3.20}$$

where
$$\mathbf{P}_{i,j}^{(1,0)} = p\,\frac{\mathbf{P}_{i+1,j} - \mathbf{P}_{i,j}}{u_{i+p+1} - u_{i+1}} \qquad \text{(see Eq. [3.4])}$$

$$U^{(1)} = \{\underbrace{0,\ldots,0}_{p}, u_{p+1},\ldots,u_{r-p-1},\underbrace{1,\ldots,1}_{p}\}$$

$$V^{(0)} = V$$

Analogously
$$\mathbf{S}_v(u,v) = \sum_{i=0}^{n}\sum_{j=0}^{m-1} N_{i,p}(u)N_{j,q-1}(v)\,\mathbf{P}_{i,j}^{(0,1)} \tag{3.21}$$

where
$$\mathbf{P}_{i,j}^{(0,1)} = q\,\frac{\mathbf{P}_{i,j+1} - \mathbf{P}_{i,j}}{v_{j+q+1} - v_{j+1}}$$

$$U^{(0)} = U$$

$$V^{(1)} = \{\underbrace{0,\ldots,0}_{q}, v_{q+1},\ldots,v_{s-q-1},\underbrace{1,\ldots,1}_{q}\}$$

Applying first Eq. (3.20), then Eq. (3.21) yields

$$\mathbf{S}_{uv}(u,v) = \sum_{i=0}^{n-1}\sum_{j=0}^{m-1} N_{i,p-1}(u)N_{j,q-1}(v)\,\mathbf{P}_{i,j}^{(1,1)} \tag{3.22}$$

where
$$\mathbf{P}_{i,j}^{(1,1)} = q\,\frac{\mathbf{P}_{i,j+1}^{(1,0)} - \mathbf{P}_{i,j}^{(1,0)}}{v_{j+q+1} - v_{j+1}}$$

and $U^{(1)}$ and $V^{(1)}$ are as defined previously.

In general

$$\frac{\partial^{k+l}}{\partial^k u\,\partial^l v}\mathbf{S}(u,v) = \sum_{i=0}^{n-k}\sum_{j=0}^{m-l} N_{i,p-k}(u)N_{j,q-l}(v)\,\mathbf{P}_{i,j}^{(k,l)} \tag{3.23}$$

where
$$\mathbf{P}_{i,j}^{(k,l)} = (q-l+1)\,\frac{\mathbf{P}_{i,j+1}^{(k,l-1)} - \mathbf{P}_{i,j}^{(k,l-1)}}{v_{j+q+1} - v_{j+l}}$$

Using Eqs. (3.20)–(3.23), we derive useful formulas for corner derivatives. For example, at the corner $(u,v) = (0,0)$, we have

$$\begin{aligned}
\mathbf{S}_u(0,0) = \mathbf{P}_{0,0}^{(1,0)} &= \frac{p}{u_{p+1}}(\mathbf{P}_{1,0} - \mathbf{P}_{0,0}) \\
\mathbf{S}_v(0,0) = \mathbf{P}_{0,0}^{(0,1)} &= \frac{q}{v_{q+1}}(\mathbf{P}_{0,1} - \mathbf{P}_{0,0}) \\
\mathbf{S}_{uv}(0,0) = \mathbf{P}_{0,0}^{(1,1)} &= \frac{q}{v_{q+1}}\left(\mathbf{P}_{0,1}^{(1,0)} - \mathbf{P}_{0,0}^{(1,0)}\right) \\
&= \frac{pq}{u_{p+1}v_{q+1}}(\mathbf{P}_{1,1} - \mathbf{P}_{0,1} - \mathbf{P}_{1,0} + \mathbf{P}_{0,0})
\end{aligned} \tag{3.24}$$

Now let $u_0 = 0$ and $v_0 = 0$. From the properties of the basis functions, it is easy to see that the isocurves $\mathbf{C}_{u_0}(v)$ and $\mathbf{C}_{v_0}(u)$ are given by

$$\mathbf{C}_{u_0}(v) = \sum_{j=0}^{m} N_{j,q}(v)\mathbf{P}_{0,j} \qquad \mathbf{C}_{v_0}(u) = \sum_{i=0}^{n} N_{i,p}(u)\mathbf{P}_{i,0}$$

From Eq. (3.7) it follows that

$$\mathbf{S}_u(0,0) = \mathbf{C}'_{v_0}(0) \qquad \mathbf{S}_v(0,0) = \mathbf{C}'_{u_0}(0)$$

Algorithm A3.7 computes all (or optionally some) of the control points, $\mathbf{P}_{i,j}^{(k,l)}$, of the derivative surfaces up to order d $(0 \le k+l \le d)$. The algorithm is based on Eq. (3.23) and Algorithm A3.3. Output is the array, PKL[][][][], where PKL[k][l][i][j] is the i,jth control point of the surface, differentiated k times with respect to u and l times with respect to v.

```
ALGORITHM A3.7
  SurfaceDerivCpts(n,p,U,m,q,V,P,d,r1,r2,s1,s2,PKL)
    { /*  Compute control points of derivative surfaces  */
      /*  Input:  n,p,U,m,q,V,P,d,r1,r2,s1,s2  */
      /*  Output: PKL  */
    du = min(d,p);     dv = min(d,q);
    r = r2-r1;     s = s2-s1;
    for (j=s1; j<=s2; j++)
      {
      CurveDerivCpts(n,p,U,&P[][j],du,r1,r2,temp);
      for (k=0; k<=du; k++)
        for (i=0; i<=r-k; i++)
          PKL[k][0][i][j-s1] = temp[k][i];
      }
    for (k=0; k<du; k++)
      for (i=0; i<=r-k; i++)
        {
```

```
      dd = min(d-k,dv);
      CurveDerivCpts(m,q,&V[s1],&PKL[k][0][i][],dd,0,s,temp);
      for (l=1; l<=dd; l++)
        for (j=0; j<=s-l; j++)
          PKL[k][l][i][j] = temp[l][j];
      }
  }
```

Algorithm A3.8 computes the point on a B-spline surface and all partial derivatives up to and including order d, at fixed parameters (u, v) (compare with Algorithm A3.6). $d > p, q$ is allowed. On output, SKL[k][l] is the derivative of $\mathbf{S}(u, v)$ k times with respect to u and l times with respect to v.

```
ALGORITHM A3.8:
  SurfaceDerivsAlg2(n,p,U,m,q,V,P,u,v,d,SKL)
    { /* Compute surface derivatives */
      /* Input: n,p,U,m,q,V,P,u,v,d */
      /* Output: SKL */
    du = min(d,p);
    for (k=p+1; k<=d; k++)
      for (l=0; l<=d-k; l++)   SKL[k][l] = 0.0;
    dv = min(d,q);
    for (l=q+1; l<=d; l++)
      for (k=0; k<=d-l; k++)   SKL[k][l] = 0.0;
    uspan = FindSpan(n,p,u,U);
    AllBasisFuns(uspan,u,p,U,Nu);
    vspan = FindSpan(m,q,v,V);
    AllBasisFuns(vspan,v,q,V,Nv);
    SurfaceDerivCpts(n,p,U,m,q,V,P,d,uspan-p,uspan,
                                         vspan-q,vspan,PKL);
    for (k=0; k<=du; k++)
      {
      dd = min(d-k,dv);
      for (l=0; l<=dd; l++)
        {
        SKL[k][l] = 0.0;
        for (i=0; i<=q-l; i++)
          {
          tmp = 0.0;
          for (j=0; j<=p-k; j++)
            tmp = tmp + Nu[j][p-k]*PKL[k][l][j][i];
          SKL[k][l] = SKL[k][l] + Nv[i][q-l]*tmp;
          }
        }
      }
    }
```

EXERCISES

3.1. Why do quadratic curves touch their control polygons at knots?

3.2. If a quadratic curve has an inflection point, it must be at a knot (see the figures). Why?

3.3. Construct a $\mathbf{C}^2$ continuous cubic curve with a cusp.

3.4. Let a cubic curve be defined by $\mathbf{C}(u) = \sum_{i=0}^{7} N_{i,3}(u)\mathbf{P}_i$ and the knot vector $U = \{0,0,0,0, 1/4, 1/4, 2/3, 3/4, 1,1,1,1\}$.

a. Assume some arbitrary locations for the $\mathbf{P}_i$ and sketch the curve.

b. Where is the point $\mathbf{C}(1/4)$?

c. If $\mathbf{P}_2$ is moved, on what subinterval of $[0,1]$ is $\mathbf{C}(u)$ affected? If $\mathbf{P}_5$ is moved, what subinterval is affected?

d. Which control points are affecting curve shape on the interval $u \in [1/4, 2/3)$? On the interval $u \in [2/3, 3/4)$?

3.5. Let $\mathbf{C}(u) = \sum_{i=0}^{3} N_{i,2}(u)\mathbf{P}_i$, where $U = \{0,0,0, 1/2, 1,1,1\}$ and $\mathbf{P}_0 = (-1,0)$, $\mathbf{P}_1 = (-1,1)$, $\mathbf{P}_2 = (1,1)$, and $\mathbf{P}_3 = (1,0)$. Sketch $\mathbf{C}(u)$. Compute $\mathbf{C}'(u)$, i.e., its control points and knot vector. Sketch $\mathbf{C}'(u)$.

3.6. For the cubic curve of Figure 3.16a, assume the control points $\{\mathbf{P}_i\} = \{(0,0), (1,2), (3,4), (5,2), (5,0), (8,0), (9,3)\}$. Sketch the curve. Using Eq. (3.8), compute the second derivative curve, $\mathbf{C}^{(2)}(u)$. Sketch $\mathbf{C}^{(2)}(u)$. Let $\mathbf{P}_0^{(2)}$ and $\mathbf{P}_4^{(2)}$ be the first and last control points of $\mathbf{C}^{(2)}(u)$, i.e., $\mathbf{P}_0^{(2)} = \mathbf{C}^{(2)}(0)$ and $\mathbf{P}_4^{(2)} = \mathbf{C}^{(2)}(1)$. Compute $\mathbf{C}^{(2)}(0)$ and $\mathbf{C}^{(2)}(1)$ using Eqs. (3.9) and (3.10).

3.7. A crease in a surface can be created using either multiple knots or multiple control points (see Figures 3.24 and 3.25). Which would you use if you wanted a crease running less than the full length of the surface? Construct and sketch such an example.

3.8. Consider the B-spline surface $\mathbf{S}(u,v) = \sum_{i=0}^{3}\sum_{j=0}^{2} N_{i,2}(u)N_{j,2}(v)\mathbf{P}_{i,j}$

where
$$U = \{0,0,0, 1/2, 1,1,1\}$$
$$V = \{0,0,0,1,1,1\}$$

and
$$\mathbf{P}_{0,0} = (0,0,0) \quad \mathbf{P}_{1,0} = (3,0,3) \quad \mathbf{P}_{2,0} = (6,0,3) \quad \mathbf{P}_{3,0} = (9,0,0)$$
$$\mathbf{P}_{0,1} = (0,2,2) \quad \mathbf{P}_{1,1} = (3,2,5) \quad \mathbf{P}_{2,1} = (6,2,5) \quad \mathbf{P}_{3,1} = (9,2,2)$$
$$\mathbf{P}_{0,2} = (0,4,0) \quad \mathbf{P}_{1,2} = (3,4,3) \quad \mathbf{P}_{2,2} = (6,4,3) \quad \mathbf{P}_{3,2} = (9,4,0)$$

Compute $\mathbf{S}(3/10, 6/10)$ by evaluating the nonzero B-spline basis functions and multiplying these by the appropriate control points.

3.9. Derive the expressions for $\mathbf{S}_u(u,v)$, $\mathbf{S}_v(u,v)$, and $\mathbf{S}_{uv}(u,v)$ at the three corners, $(u,v) = (0,1)$, $(1,0)$, and $(1,1)$ (see Eq. [3.24]).

3.10. Let $\mathbf{S}(u,v)$ be as in Exercise 3.8. Sketch this surface. Using Eqs. (3.20) and (3.21), compute the surfaces $\mathbf{S}_u(u,v)$ and $\mathbf{S}_v(u,v)$. Sketch these two surfaces. Using Eq. (3.22) and the expressions derived in Exercise 3.9, compute the mixed partial derivative, $\mathbf{S}_{uv}(u,v)$, at each of the four corners of the surface. What is the geometric significance of these four vectors?

CHAPTER

FOUR

Rational B-spline Curves and Surfaces

4.1 Introduction

In this chapter we combine the concepts of Sections 1.4 and 1.5 of Chapter 1 and those of Chapter 3 to obtain **N**on**U**niform **R**ational **B**-**S**pline (NURBS) curves and surfaces. We present definitions and general properties and derive formulas and algorithms for the derivatives of NURBS curves and surfaces in terms of their nonrational counterparts. The earliest published works on NURBS are [Vers75; Till83]. A more recent survey can be found in [Pieg91a].

4.2 Definition and Properties of NURBS Curves

A pth-degree NURBS curve is defined by

$$\mathbf{C}(u) = \frac{\sum_{i=0}^{n} N_{i,p}(u) w_i \mathbf{P}_i}{\sum_{i=0}^{n} N_{i,p}(u) w_i} \qquad a \le u \le b \tag{4.1}$$

where the $\{\mathbf{P}_i\}$ are the *control points* (forming a *control polygon*), the $\{w_i\}$ are the *weights*, and the $\{N_{i,p}(u)\}$ are the pth-degree B-spline basis functions defined on the nonperiodic (and nonuniform) knot vector

$$U = \{\underbrace{a, \ldots, a}_{p+1}, u_{p+1}, \ldots, u_{m-p-1}, \underbrace{b, \ldots, b}_{p+1}\}$$

Unless otherwise stated, we assume that $a = 0$, $b = 1$, and $w_i > 0$ for all i. Setting

$$R_{i,p}(u) = \frac{N_{i,p}(u)w_i}{\sum_{j=0}^{n} N_{j,p}(u)w_j} \tag{4.2}$$

allows us to rewrite Eq. (4.1) in the form

$$\mathbf{C}(u) = \sum_{i=0}^{n} R_{i,p}(u)\,\mathbf{P}_i \tag{4.3}$$

The $\{R_{i,p}(u)\}$ are the *rational basis functions*; they are piecewise rational functions on $u \in [0,1]$.

The $R_{i,p}(u)$ have the following properties derived from Eq. (4.2) and the corresponding properties of the $N_{i,p}(u)$:

P4.1 Nonnegativity: $R_{i,p}(u) \geq 0$ for all i, p, and $u \in [0,1]$;

P4.2 Partition of unity: $\sum_{i=0}^{n} R_{i,p}(u) = 1$ for all $u \in [0,1]$;

P4.3 $R_{0,p}(0) = R_{n,p}(1) = 1$;

P4.4 For $p > 0$, all $R_{i,p}(u)$ attain exactly one maximum on the interval $u \in [0,1]$;

P4.5 Local support: $R_{i,p}(u) = 0$ for $u \notin [u_i, u_{i+p+1})$. Furthermore, in any given knot span, at most $p+1$ of the $R_{i,p}(u)$ are nonzero (in general, $R_{i-p,p}(u), \ldots, R_{i,p}(u)$ are nonzero in $[u_i, u_{i+1})$);

P4.6 All derivatives of $R_{i,p}(u)$ exist in the interior of a knot span, where it is a rational function with nonzero denominator. At a knot, $R_{i,p}(u)$ is $p-k$ times continuously differentiable, where k is the multiplicity of the knot;

P4.7 If $w_i = 1$ for all i, then $R_{i,p}(u) = N_{i,p}(u)$ for all i; i.e., the $N_{i,p}(u)$ are special cases of the $R_{i,p}(u)$. In fact, for any $a \neq 0$, if $w_i = a$ for all i then $R_{i,p}(u) = N_{i,p}(u)$ for all i.

Properties P4.1–P4.7 yield the following important geometric characteristics of NURBS curves:

P4.8 $\mathbf{C}(0) = \mathbf{P}_0$ and $\mathbf{C}(1) = \mathbf{P}_n$; this follows from P4.3;

P4.9 Affine invariance: an affine transformation is applied to the curve by applying it to the control points (see P3.4, Section 3.1); NURBS curves are also invariant under perspective projections ([Lee87; Pieg91a]), a fact which is important in computer graphics;

P4.10 Strong convex hull property: if $u \in [u_i, u_{i+1})$, then $\mathbf{C}(u)$ lies within the convex hull of the control points $\mathbf{P}_{i-p}, \ldots, \mathbf{P}_i$ (see Figure 4.1, where $\mathbf{C}(u)$ for $u \in [1/4, 1/2)$ (dashed segment) is contained in the convex hull

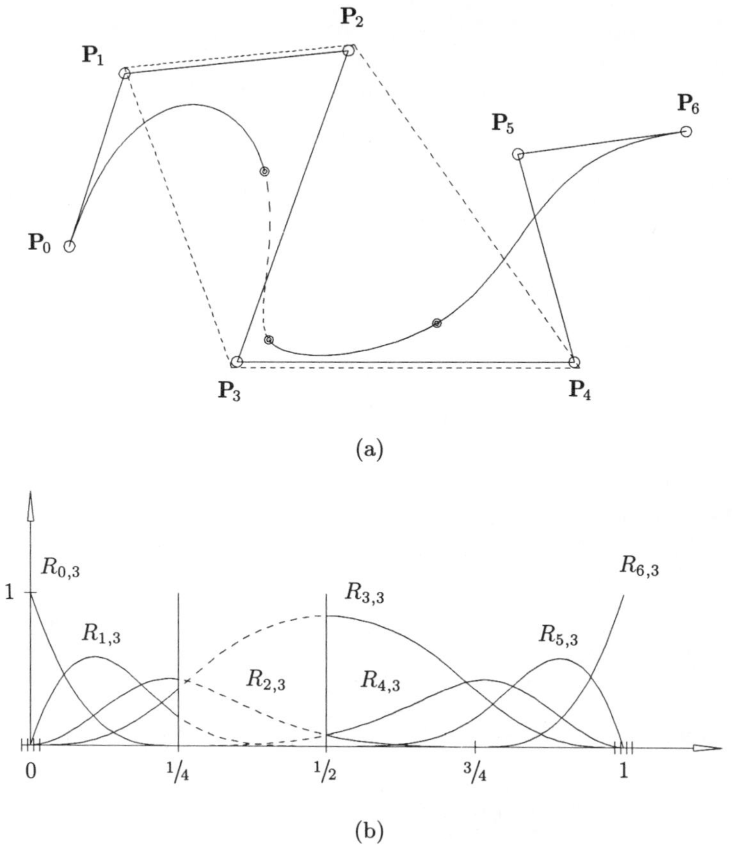

Figure 4.1. $U = \{0,0,0,0,1/4,1/2,3/4,1,1,1,1\}$ and $\{w_0,\ldots,w_6\} = \{1,1,1,3,1,1,1\}$. (a) A cubic NURBS curve; (b) associated basis functions.

of $\{\mathbf{P}_1, \mathbf{P}_2, \mathbf{P}_3, \mathbf{P}_4\}$, the dashed area); this follows from P4.1, P4.2, and P4.5;

P4.11 $\mathbf{C}(u)$ is infinitely differentiable on the interior of knot spans and is $p-k$ times differentiable at a knot of multiplicity k;

P4.12 Variation diminishing property: no plane has more intersections with the curve than with the control polygon (replace the word 'plane', with 'line' for two-dimensional curves);

P4.13 A NURBS curve with no interior knots is a rational Bézier curve, since the $N_{i,p}(u)$ reduce to the $B_{i,n}(u)$; compare Eqs. (4.2) and (4.3) with Eq. (1.15). This, together with P4.7, implies that NURBS curves contain nonrational B-spline and rational and nonrational Bézier curves as special cases;

P4.14 Local approximation: if the control point $\mathbf{P}_i$ is moved, or the weight w_i is changed, it affects only that portion of the curve on the interval $u \in [u_i, u_{i+p+1})$; this follows from P4.5.

Property P4.14 is very important for interactive shape design. Using NURBS curves, we can utilize both control point movement and weight modification to attain local shape control. Figures 4.2–4.6 show the effects of modifying a single weight. Qualitatively the effect is: Assume $u \in [u_i, u_{i+p+1})$; then if w_i increases (decreases), the point $\mathbf{C}(u)$ moves closer to (farther from) $\mathbf{P}_i$, and hence the curve is pulled toward (pushed away from) $\mathbf{P}_i$. Furthermore, the movement of $\mathbf{C}(u)$ for fixed u is along a straight line (Figure 4.6). In Figure 4.6, u is fixed and w_3 is changing. Let

$$\mathbf{B} = \mathbf{C}(u; w_3 = 0) \tag{4.4}$$

$$\mathbf{N} = \mathbf{C}(u; w_3 = 1)$$

Then the straight line defined by $\mathbf{B}$ and $\mathbf{N}$ passes through $\mathbf{P}_3$, and for arbitrary $0 < w_3 < \infty$, $\mathbf{B}_3 = \mathbf{C}(u; w_3)$ lies on this line segment between $\mathbf{B}$ and $\mathbf{P}_3$. We return to this topic in a later chapter.

As is the case for rational Bézier curves, homogeneous coordinates offer an efficient method of representing NURBS curves. Let H be the perspective map given by Eq. (1.16). For a given set of control points, $\{\mathbf{P}_i\}$, and weights, $\{w_i\}$, construct the weighted control points, $\mathbf{P}_i^w = (w_i x_i, w_i y_i, w_i z_i, w_i)$. Then define the nonrational (piecewise polynomial) B-spline curve in four-dimensional space as

$$\mathbf{C}^w(u) = \sum_{i=0}^{n} N_{i,p}(u)\mathbf{P}_i^w \tag{4.5}$$

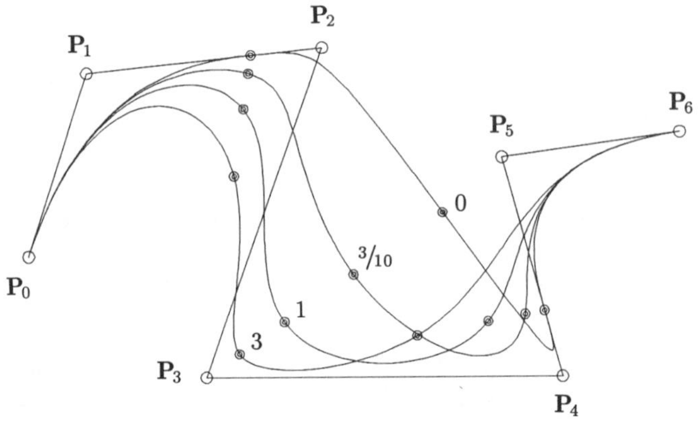

Figure 4.2. Rational cubic B-spline curves, with w_3 varying.

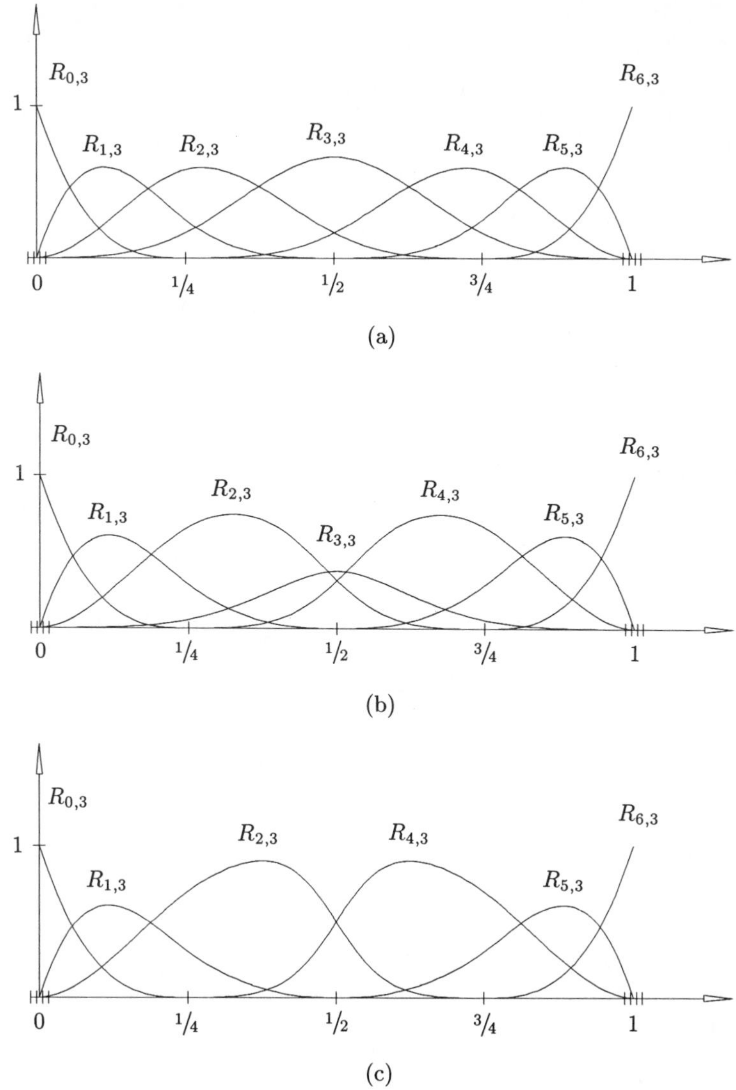

Figure 4.3. The cubic basis functions for the curves of Figure 4.2. (a) $w_3 = 1$; (b) $w_3 = 3/10$; (c) $w_3 = 0$.

Applying the perspective map, H, to $\mathbf{C}^w(u)$ yields the corresponding rational B-spline curve (piecewise rational in three-dimensional space)

$$\mathbf{C}(u) = H\{\mathbf{C}^w(u)\} = H\left\{\sum_{i=0}^{n} N_{i,p}(u)\,\mathbf{P}_i^w\right\}$$

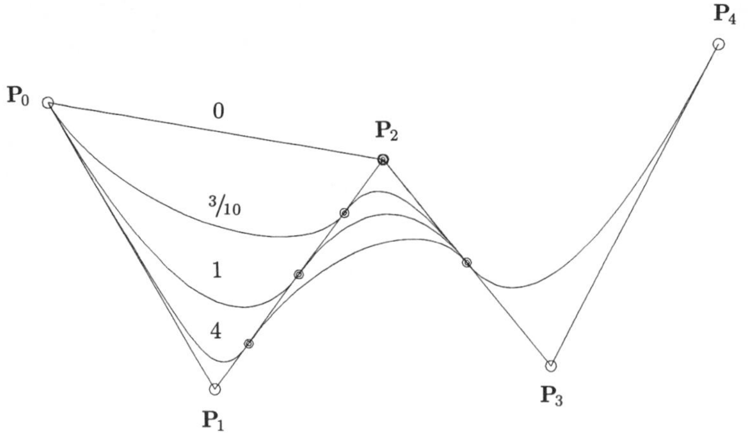

Figure 4.4. Rational quadratic curves, with w_1 varying.

$$= \frac{\sum_{i=0}^{n} N_{i,p}(u) w_i \mathbf{P}_i}{\sum_{i=0}^{n} N_{i,p}(u) w_i} = \sum_{i=0}^{n} R_{i,p}(u) \mathbf{P}_i$$

We refer interchangeably to either $\mathbf{C}^w(u)$ or $\mathbf{C}(u)$ as the NURBS curve, although strictly speaking, $\mathbf{C}^w(u)$ is not a rational curve.

Example

Ex4.1 Let $U = \{0,0,0,1,2,3,3,3\}$, $\{w_0,\ldots,w_4\} = \{1,4,1,1,1\}$, $\{\mathbf{P}_0,\ldots,\mathbf{P}_4\} = \{(0,0),(1,1),(3,2),(4,1),\ (5,-1)\}$. We compute the point on the rational B-spline curve at $u = 1$. Now u is in the knot span $[u_3, u_4)$, and

$$N_{3,0}(1) = 1$$

$$N_{2,1}(1) = \frac{2-1}{2-1}\, N_{3,0}(1) = 1$$

$$N_{3,1}(1) = \frac{1-1}{2-1}\, N_{3,0}(1) = 0$$

$$N_{1,2}(1) = \frac{2-1}{2-0}\, N_{2,1}(1) = \frac{1}{2}$$

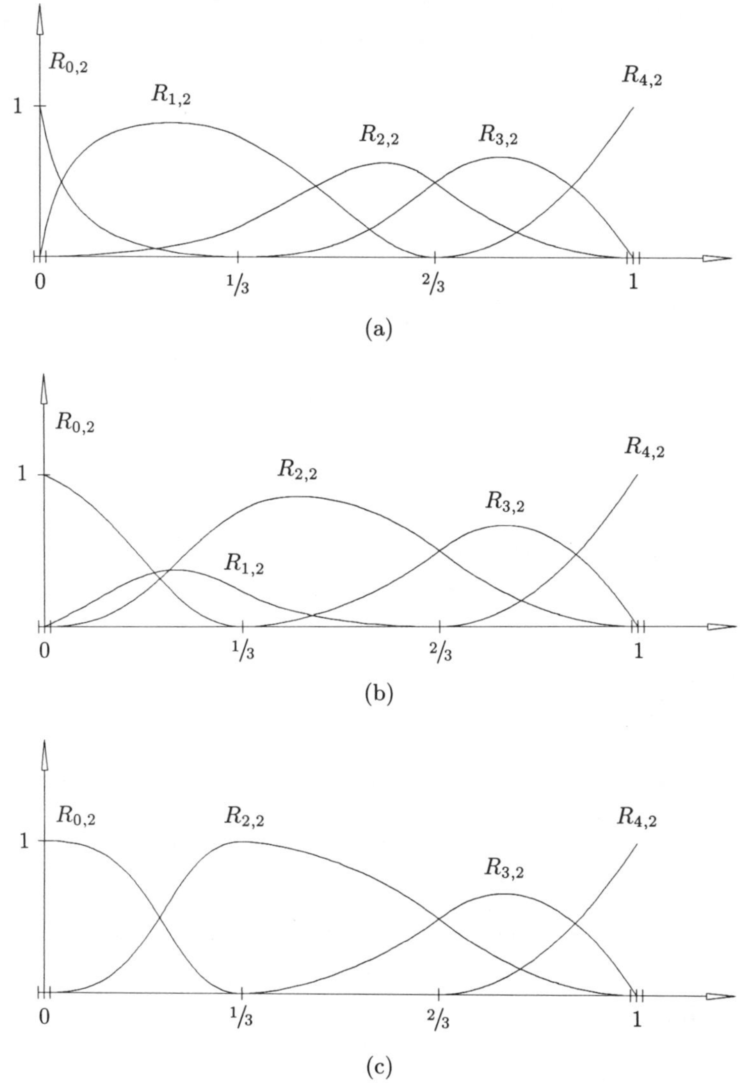

Figure 4.5. The quadratic basis functions for the curves of Figure 4.4. (a) $w_1 = 4$; (b) $w_1 = {}^{3}/_{10}$; (c) $w_1 = 0$.

$$N_{2,2}(1) = \frac{1-0}{2-0}\, N_{2,1}(1) = \frac{1}{2}$$

$$N_{3,2}(1) = 0$$

Hence

$$\mathbf{C}^w(1) = \frac{1}{2}\mathbf{P}_1^w + \frac{1}{2}\mathbf{P}_2^w = \frac{1}{2}(4,4,4) + \frac{1}{2}(3,2,1) = \left(\frac{7}{2}, 3, \frac{5}{2}\right)$$

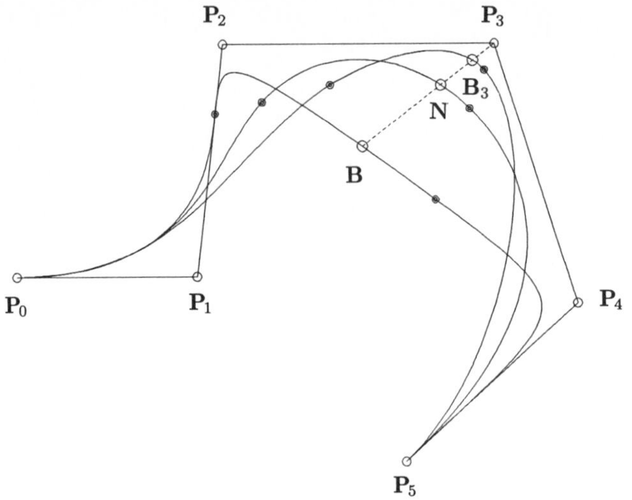

Figure 4.6. Modification of the weight w_3.

Projecting yields

$$\mathbf{C}(1) = \left(\frac{7}{5}, \frac{6}{5}\right)$$

Algorithm A4.1 computes the point on a rational B-spline curve at a fixed u value. It is based on Eq. (4.5), i.e., it assumes weighted control points in the array Pw (as do all algorithms in the remainder of this book, unless otherwise stated). Hence, Pw[i] contains $\mathbf{P}_i = (w_i x_i, w_i y_i, w_i z_i, w_i)$. Cw denotes the four-dimensional point on $\mathbf{C}^w(u)$, and C the three-dimensional point on $\mathbf{C}(u)$ (the output). For the remainder of the book we use the notation C = Cw/w to denote projection.

```
ALGORITHM A4.1
  CurvePoint(n,p,U,Pw,u,C)
    { /*  Compute point on rational B-spline curve  */
      /*  Input:  n,p,U,Pw,u  */
      /*  Output: C  */
    span = FindSpan(n,p,u,U);
    BasisFuns(span,u,p,U,N);
    Cw = 0.0;
    for (j=0; j<=p; j++)
      Cw = Cw + N[j]*Pw[span-p+j];
    C = Cw/w;    /*  Divide by weight  */
    }
```

4.3 Derivatives of a NURBS Curve

Derivatives of rational functions are complicated, involving denominators to high powers. In Section 3.3 we developed formulas and algorithms to compute the derivatives of nonrational B-spline curves. Those formulas and algorithms apply, of course, to $\mathbf{C}^w(u)$, since it is a nonrational curve in four-dimensional space. In this section we develop formulas that express the derivatives of $\mathbf{C}(u)$ in terms of the derivatives of $\mathbf{C}^w(u)$.

Let

$$\mathbf{C}(u) = \frac{w(u)\mathbf{C}(u)}{w(u)} = \frac{\mathbf{A}(u)}{w(u)}$$

where $\mathbf{A}(u)$ is the vector-valued function whose coordinates are the first three coordinates of $\mathbf{C}^w(u)$ ($\mathbf{A}(u)$ is the numerator of Eq. [4.1]). Then

$$\mathbf{C}'(u) = \frac{w(u)\mathbf{A}'(u) - w'(u)\mathbf{A}(u)}{w(u)^2}$$

$$= \frac{w(u)\mathbf{A}'(u) - w'(u)w(u)\mathbf{C}(u)}{w(u)^2} = \frac{\mathbf{A}'(u) - w'(u)\mathbf{C}(u)}{w(u)} \tag{4.7}$$

Since $\mathbf{A}(u)$ and $w(u)$ represent the coordinates of $\mathbf{C}^w(u)$, we obtain their first derivatives using Eqs. (3.4)–(3.6). We compute higher order derivatives by differentiating $\mathbf{A}(u)$ using Leibnitz' rule

$$\mathbf{A}^{(k)}(u) = \big(w(u)\mathbf{C}(u)\big)^{(k)} = \sum_{i=0}^{k} \binom{k}{i} w^{(i)}(u)\mathbf{C}^{(k-i)}(u)$$

$$= w(u)\mathbf{C}^{(k)}(u) + \sum_{i=1}^{k} \binom{k}{i} w^{(i)}(u)\mathbf{C}^{(k-i)}(u)$$

from which we obtain

$$\mathbf{C}^{(k)}(u) = \frac{\mathbf{A}^{(k)}(u) - \displaystyle\sum_{i=1}^{k} \binom{k}{i} w^{(i)}(u)\mathbf{C}^{(k-i)}(u)}{w(u)} \tag{4.8}$$

Equation (4.8) gives the kth derivative of $\mathbf{C}(u)$ in terms of the kth derivative of $\mathbf{A}(u)$, and the first through $(k-1)$th derivatives of $\mathbf{C}(u)$ and $w(u)$. The derivatives $\mathbf{A}^{(k)}(u)$ and $w^{(i)}(u)$ are obtained using either Eq. (3.3) and Algorithm `A3.2` or Eq. (3.8) and Algorithm `A3.4`.

Let us derive expressions for the first derivatives of a NURBS curve at its endpoints $(u = 0, u = 1)$. From Eq. (3.7) we have

$$\mathbf{A}'(0) = \frac{p}{u_{p+1}}(w_1\mathbf{P}_1 - w_0\mathbf{P}_0) \qquad w'(0) = \frac{p}{u_{p+1}}(w_1 - w_0)$$

and from Eq. (4.7)

$$\mathbf{C}'(0) = \frac{\frac{p}{u_{p+1}}(w_1\mathbf{P}_1 - w_0\mathbf{P}_0) - \frac{p}{u_{p+1}}(w_1 - w_0)\mathbf{P}_0}{w_0}$$

from which follows

$$\mathbf{C}'(0) = \frac{p}{u_{p+1}}\frac{w_1}{w_0}(\mathbf{P}_1 - \mathbf{P}_0) \tag{4.9}$$

Analogously
$$\mathbf{C}'(1) = \frac{p}{1-u_{m-p-1}}\frac{w_{n-1}}{w_n}(\mathbf{P}_n - \mathbf{P}_{n-1}) \tag{4.10}$$

Example

Ex4.2 Consider the quadratic rational Bézier circular arc given in Section 1.4 (Figure 1.19b). This is a NURBS curve on the knot vector $U = \{0,0,0,1,1,1\}$, with $\{\mathbf{P}_i\} = \{(1,0),(1,1),(0,1)\}$ and $\{w_i\} = \{1,1,2\}$. From Eqs. (4.9) and (4.10) we have

$$\mathbf{C}'(0) = \frac{2}{1}\frac{1}{1}(\mathbf{P}_1 - \mathbf{P}_0) = (0,2)$$

$$\mathbf{C}'(1) = \frac{2}{1-0}\frac{1}{2}(\mathbf{P}_2 - \mathbf{P}_1) = (-1,0)$$

From Eq. (4.8)

$$\mathbf{C}''(0) = \frac{\mathbf{A}''(0) - 2w'(0)\mathbf{C}'(0) - w''(0)\mathbf{C}(0)}{w_0}$$

From Eq. (3.9) or Eq. (1.10)

$$\mathbf{A}''(0) = 2(w_0\mathbf{P}_0 - 2w_1\mathbf{P}_1 + w_2\mathbf{P}_2)$$

and
$$w''(0) = 2(w_0 - 2w_1 + w_2)$$

From $w'(0) = 2(w_1 - w_0)$ it follows that

$$\mathbf{C}''(0) = \frac{2}{w_0}[w_0\mathbf{P}_0 - 2w_1\mathbf{P}_1 + w_2\mathbf{P}_2 - 4(w_1 - w_0)(\mathbf{P}_1 - \mathbf{P}_0)$$

$$-(w_0 - 2w_1 + w_2)\mathbf{P}_0]$$

$$= 2(\mathbf{P}_0 - 2\mathbf{P}_1 + 2\mathbf{P}_2 - \mathbf{P}_0) = 4(\mathbf{P}_2 - \mathbf{P}_1) = (-4,0)$$

The computation of $\mathbf{C}''(1)$ is left as an exercise.

Now assume that u is fixed, and that the zeroth through the dth derivatives of $\mathbf{A}(u)$ and $w(u)$ have been computed and loaded into the arrays `Aders` and `wders`, respectively, i.e., $\mathbf{C}^w(u)$ has been differentiated and its coordinates separated off into `Aders` and `wders`. Algorithm `A4.2` computes the point, $\mathbf{C}(u)$, and the derivatives, $\mathbf{C}^{(k)}(u)$, $1 \le k \le d$. The curve point is returned in `CK[0]` and the kth derivative is returned in `CK[k]`. The array `Bin[][]` contains the precomputed binomial coefficients (`Bin[k][i]` is $\binom{k}{i}$).

```
ALGORITHM A4.2
  RatCurveDerivs(Aders,wders,d,CK)
    { /*  Compute C(u) derivatives from Cw(u) derivatives  */
      /*  Input:  Aders,wders,d  */
      /*  Output: CK  */
    for (k=0; k<=d; k++)
      {
      v = Aders[k];
      for (i=1; i<=k; i++)
        v = v - Bin[k][i]*wders[i]*CK[k-i];
      CK[k] = v/wders[0];
      }
    }
```

Figure 4.7 shows the first, second, and third derivatives of a cubic NURBS curve. The derivative vectors are scaled down by 0.4, 0.08, and 0.03, respectively.

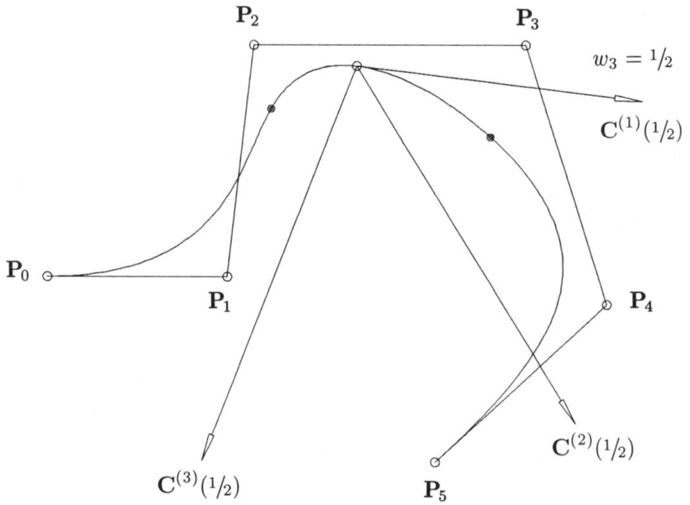

Figure 4.7. First, second, and third derivatives of a cubic NURBS curve computed at $u = 1/2$, with $w_3 = 1/2$ and $w_i = 1, i \neq 3$.

4.4 Definition and Properties of NURBS Surfaces

A NURBS surface of degree p in the u direction and degree q in the v direction is a bivariate vector-valued piecewise rational function of the form

$$\mathbf{S}(u,v) = \frac{\sum_{i=0}^{n}\sum_{j=0}^{m} N_{i,p}(u)N_{j,q}(v)w_{i,j}\,\mathbf{P}_{i,j}}{\sum_{i=0}^{n}\sum_{j=0}^{m} N_{i,p}(u)N_{j,q}(v)w_{i,j}} \qquad 0 \le u,v \le 1 \tag{4.11}$$

The $\{\mathbf{P}_{i,j}\}$ form a bidirectional control net, the $\{w_{i,j}\}$ are the weights, and the $\{N_{i,p}(u)\}$ and $\{N_{j,q}(v)\}$ are the nonrational B-spline basis functions defined on the knot vectors

$$U = \{\underbrace{0,\ldots,0}_{p+1}, u_{p+1},\ldots,u_{r-p-1},\underbrace{1,\ldots,1}_{p+1}\}$$

$$V = \{\underbrace{0,\ldots,0}_{q+1}, v_{q+1},\ldots,v_{s-q-1},\underbrace{1,\ldots,1}_{q+1}\}$$

where $r = n+p+1$ and $s = m+q+1$.

Introducing the piecewise rational basis functions

$$R_{i,j}(u,v) = \frac{N_{i,p}(u)N_{j,q}(v)w_{i,j}}{\sum_{k=0}^{n}\sum_{l=0}^{m} N_{k,p}(u)N_{l,q}(v)\,w_{k,l}} \tag{4.12}$$

the surface Eq. (4.11) can be written as

$$\mathbf{S}(u,v) = \sum_{i=0}^{n}\sum_{j=0}^{m} R_{i,j}(u,v)\,\mathbf{P}_{i,j} \tag{4.13}$$

Figures 4.8 and 4.9 show examples of NURBS surfaces.

The important properties of the functions $R_{i,j}(u,v)$ are roughly the same as those given in Section 3.4 for the nonrational basis functions, $N_{i,p}(u)\,N_{j,q}(v)$. We summarize them here.

P4.15 Nonnegativity: $R_{i,j}(u,v) \ge 0$ for all i, j, u, and v;

P4.16 Partition of unity: $\sum_{i=0}^{n}\sum_{j=0}^{m} R_{i,j}(u,v) = 1$ for all $(u,v) \in [0,1]\times[0,1]$;

P4.17 Local support: $R_{i,j}(u,v) = 0$ if (u,v) is outside the rectangle given by $[u_i,u_{i+p+1}) \times [v_j,v_{j+q+1})$;

P4.18 In any given rectangle of the form $[u_{i_0},u_{i_0+1}) \times [v_{j_0},v_{j_0+1})$, at most $(p+1)(q+1)$ basis functions are nonzero, in particular the $R_{i,j}(u,v)$ for $i_0-p \le i \le i_0$ and $j_0-q \le j \le j_0$ are nonzero;

P4.19 Extrema: if $p>0$ and $q>0$, then $R_{i,j}(u,v)$ attains exactly one maximum value;

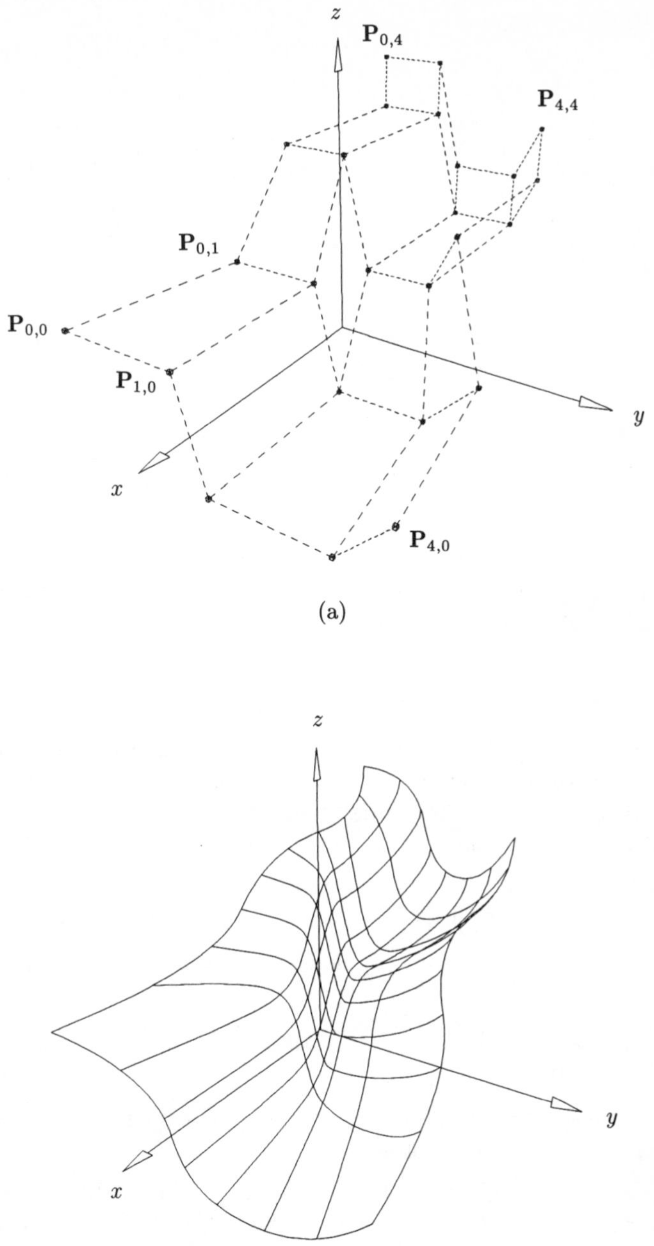

(a)

(b)

Figure 4.8. Control net and biquadratic NURBS surface, $w_{1,1} = w_{1,2} = w_{2,1} = w_{2,2} = 10$, with the rest of the weights 1. $U = V = \{0, 0, 0, {}^{1}\!/_{3}, {}^{2}\!/_{3}, 1, 1, 1\}$. (a) Control net; (b) biquadratic NURBS surface.

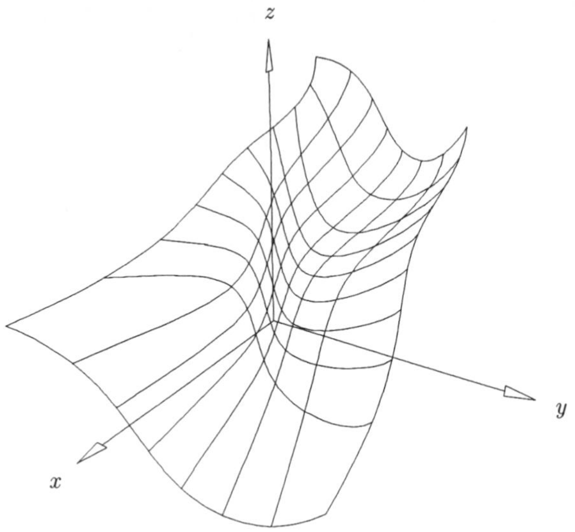

Figure 4.9. Bicubic NURBS surface defined by the control net in Figure 4.8a, with $U = V = \{0,0,0,0,1/2,1,1,1,1\}$ and with the same weights as in Figures 4.8.

P4.20 $R_{0,0}(0,0) = R_{n,0}(1,0) = R_{0,m}(0,1) = R_{n,m}(1,1) = 1$;

P4.21 Differentiability: interior to the rectangles formed by the u and v knot lines, all partial derivatives of $R_{i,j}(u,v)$ exist. At a u knot (v knot) it is $p-k$ ($q-k$) times differentiable in the u (v) direction, where k is the multiplicity of the knot;

P4.22 If all $w_{i,j} = a$ for $0 \le i \le n$, $0 \le j \le m$, and $a \ne 0$, then $R_{i,j}(u,v) = N_{i,p}(u)N_{j,q}(v)$ for all i,j.

Properties P4.15–P4.22 yield the following important geometric properties of NURBS surfaces:

P4.23 Corner point interpolation: $\mathbf{S}(0,0) = \mathbf{P}_{0,0}$, $\mathbf{S}(1,0) = \mathbf{P}_{n,0}$, $\mathbf{S}(0,1) = \mathbf{P}_{0,m}$, and $\mathbf{S}(1,1) = \mathbf{P}_{n,m}$;

P4.24 Affine invariance: an affine transformation is applied to the surface by applying it to the control points;

P4.25 Strong convex hull property: assume $w_{i,j} \ge 0$ for all i,j. If $(u,v) \in [u_{i_0}, u_{i_0+1}) \times [v_{j_0}, v_{j_0+1})$, then $\mathbf{S}(u,v)$ is in the convex hull of the control points $\mathbf{P}_{i,j}$, $i_0 - p \le i \le i_0$ and $j_0 - q \le j \le j_0$;

P4.26 Local modification: if $\mathbf{P}_{i,j}$ is moved, or $w_{i,j}$ is changed, it affects the surface shape only in the rectangle $[u_i, u_{i+p+1}) \times [v_j, v_{j+q+1})$;

P4.27 Nonrational B-spline and Bézier and rational Bézier surfaces are special cases of NURBS surfaces;

P4.28 Differentiability: $\mathbf{S}(u,v)$ is $p-k$ $(q-k)$ times differentiable with respect to u (v) at a u knot (v knot) of multiplicity k.

We remark that there is no known variation diminishing property for NURBS surfaces (see [Prau92]).

We can use both control point movement and weight modification to locally change the shape of NURBS surfaces. Figures 4.10 and 4.11 show the effects on the basis function $R_{i,j}(u,v)$ and the surface shape when a single weight, $w_{i,j}$, is modified. Compare these figures with Figures 3.19b and 3.20a,b. Qualitatively, the effect on the surface is: Assume $(u,v) \in [u_i, u_{i+p+1}) \times [v_j, v_{j+q+1})$; then if $w_{i,j}$ increases (decreases), the point $\mathbf{S}(u,v)$ moves closer to (farther from) $\mathbf{P}_{i,j}$, and hence the surface is pulled toward (pushed away from) $\mathbf{P}_{i,j}$. As is the case for curves, the movement of $\mathbf{S}(u,v)$ is along a straight line. In Figure 4.12 (u,v) are fixed and $w_{2,2}$ is changing. Let

$$\mathbf{S} = \mathbf{S}(u,v; w_{2,2}=0)$$
$$\mathbf{M} = \mathbf{S}(u,v; w_{2,2}=1) \qquad (4.14)$$

Then the straight line defined by $\mathbf{S}$ and $\mathbf{M}$ passes through $\mathbf{P}_{2,2}$, and for arbitrary $w_{2,2}$, $0 < w_{2,2} < \infty$, $\mathbf{S}_{2,2} = \mathbf{S}(u,v;w_{2,2})$ lies on this line segment between $\mathbf{S}$ and $\mathbf{P}_{2,2}$.

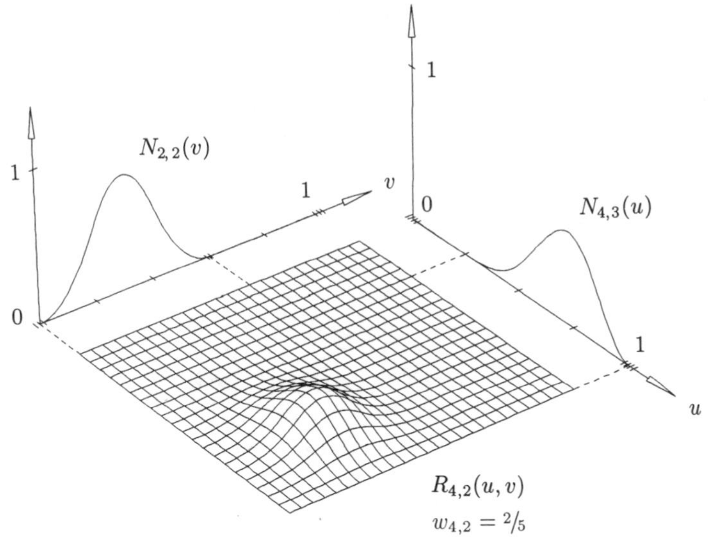

(a)

Figure 4.10. The basis function $R_{4,2,}(u,v)$, with $U = \{0,0,0,0,{}^1\!/_4,{}^1\!/_2,{}^3\!/_4,1,1,1,1\}$ and $V = \{0,0,0,{}^1\!/_5,{}^2\!/_5,{}^3\!/_5,{}^3\!/_5,{}^4\!/_5,1,1,1\}$. $w_{i,j} = 1$ for all $(i,j) \neq (4,2)$. (a) $w_{4,2} = {}^2\!/_5$; (b) $w_{4,2} = 6$.

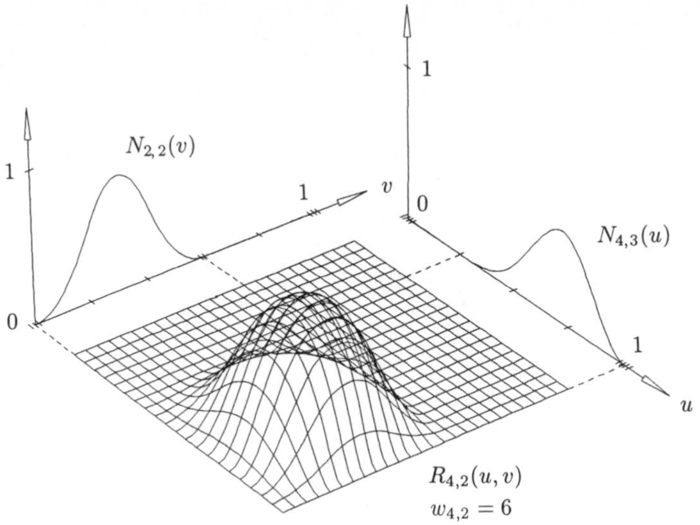

(b)

Figure 4.10. (*Continued.*)

It is convenient to represent a NURBS surface using homogeneous coordinates, that is

$$\mathbf{S}^w(u,v) = \sum_{i=0}^{n} \sum_{j=0}^{m} N_{i,p}(u) N_{j,q}(v) \mathbf{P}^w_{i,j} \tag{4.15}$$

where $\mathbf{P}^w_{i,j} = (w_{i,j}x_{i,j}, w_{i,j}y_{i,j}, w_{i,j}z_{i,j}, w_{i,j})$. Then $\mathbf{S}(u,v) = H\{\mathbf{S}^w(u,v)\}$. We refer interchangeably to either $\mathbf{S}^w(u,v)$ or $\mathbf{S}(u,v)$ as the NURBS surface. Strictly speaking, $\mathbf{S}^w(u,v)$ is a tensor product, piecewise polynomial surface in four-dimensional space. $\mathbf{S}(u,v)$ is a piecewise rational surface in three-dimensional space; it is not a tensor product surface, since the $R_{i,j}(u,v)$ are not products of univariate basis functions.

Example

Ex4.3 Let $\mathbf{S}^w(u,v) = \sum_{i=0}^{7} \sum_{j=0}^{4} N_{i,2}(u) N_{j,2}(v)$, with

$$U = \{0,0,0,1,2,3,4,4,5,5,5\}$$

and

$$V = \{0,0,0,1,2,3,3,3\}$$

Let us evaluate the surface at $(u,v) = (5/2, 1)$. Then $u \in [u_4, u_5)$ and $v \in [v_3, v_4)$, and from Sections 3.2 and 4.2 we know that

$$N_{2,2}\left(\frac{5}{2}\right) = \frac{1}{8} \quad N_{3,2}\left(\frac{5}{2}\right) = \frac{6}{8} \quad N_{4,2}\left(\frac{5}{2}\right) = \frac{1}{8}$$

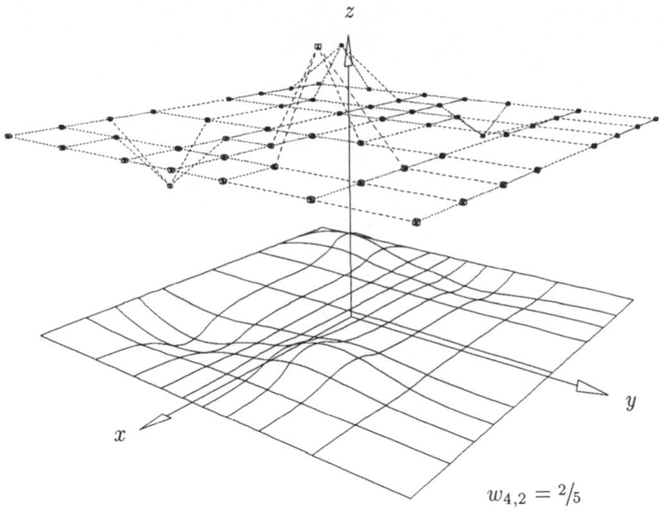

(a)

Figure 4.11. Cubic × quadratic surfaces corresponding to Figure 4.10, with the control net offset for better visualization. (a) $w_{4,2} = 2/5$; (b) $w_{4,2} = 6$.

and
$$N_{1,2}(1) = \frac{1}{2} \quad N_{2,2}(1) = \frac{1}{2} \quad N_{3,2}(1) = 0$$

Now assume that

$$[\,\mathbf{P}^w_{i,j}\,] = \begin{bmatrix} (0,2,4,1) & (0,6,4,2) & (0,2,0,1) \\ (4,6,8,2) & (12,24,12,6) & (4,6,0,2) \\ (4,2,4,1) & (8,6,4,2) & (4,2,0,1) \end{bmatrix}$$
$$i = 2,3,4; \quad j = 1,2,3$$

Then

$$\mathbf{S}^w\left(\frac{5}{2},1\right) = \begin{bmatrix} \frac{1}{8} & \frac{6}{8} & \frac{1}{8} \end{bmatrix} \times$$
$$\begin{bmatrix} (0,2,4,1) & (0,6,4,2) & (0,2,0,1) \\ (4,6,8,2) & (12,24,12,6) & (4,6,0,2) \\ (4,2,4,1) & (8,6,4,2) & (4,2,0,1) \end{bmatrix} \begin{bmatrix} \frac{1}{2} \\ \frac{1}{2} \\ 0 \end{bmatrix}$$
$$= \left(\frac{54}{8}, \frac{98}{8}, \frac{68}{8}, \frac{27}{8}\right)$$

Projecting yields

$$\mathbf{S}\left(\frac{5}{2},1\right) = \left(2, \frac{98}{27}, \frac{68}{27}\right)$$

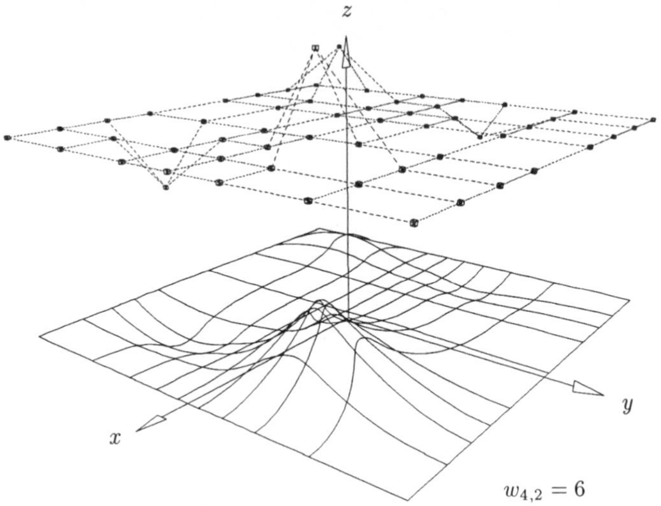

(b)

Figure 4.11. (*Continued.*)

Algorithm A3.5 can be adapted to compute a point on a rational B-spline surface by simply allowing the array P to contain weighted control points (use Pw), accumulating the four-dimensional surface point in Sw and inserting the line S = Sw/w at the end of the algorithm.

```
ALGORITHM A4.3
  SurfacePoint(n,p,U,m,q,V,Pw,u,v,S)
    { /* Compute point on rational B-spline surface */
      /* Input: n,p,U,m,q,V,Pw,u,v */
      /* Output: S */
    uspan = FindSpan(n,p,u,U);
    BasisFuns(uspan,u,p,U,Nu);
    vspan = FindSpan(m,q,v,V);
    BasisFuns(vspan,v,q,V,Nv);
    for (l=0; l<=q; l++)
      {
      temp[l] = 0.0;
      for (k=0; k<=p; k++)
        temp[l] = temp[l] + Nu[k]*Pw[uspan-p+k][vspan-q+l];
      }
    Sw = 0.0;
    for (l=0; l<=q; l++)
      Sw = Sw + Nv[l]*temp[l];
    S = Sw/w;
    }
```

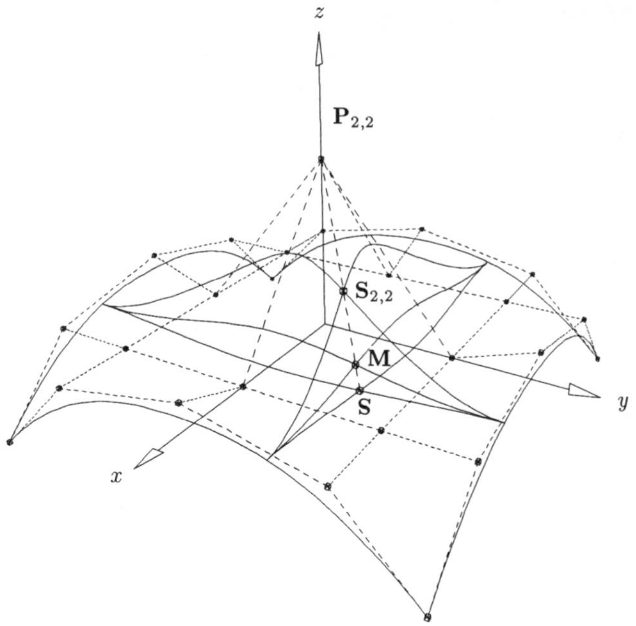

Figure 4.12. Modification of the weight $w_{2,2}$.

By applying Eqs. (3.14) and (3.15), we obtain isoparametric curves on a NURBS surface. First, fix $u = u_0$

$$\begin{aligned}\mathbf{C}^w_{u_0}(v) = \mathbf{S}^w(u_0, v) &= \sum_{i=0}^{n}\sum_{j=0}^{m} N_{i,p}(u_0)N_{j,q}(v)\,\mathbf{P}^w_{i,j} \\ &= \sum_{j=0}^{m} N_{j,q}(v)\left(\sum_{i=0}^{n} N_{i,p}(u_0)\,\mathbf{P}^w_{i,j}\right) \\ &= \sum_{j=0}^{m} N_{j,q}(v)\,\mathbf{Q}^w_j(u_0)\end{aligned} \tag{4.16}$$

where
$$\mathbf{Q}^w_j(u_0) = \sum_{i=0}^{n} N_{i,p}(u_0)\,\mathbf{P}^w_{i,j}$$

Analogously
$$\mathbf{C}^w_{v_0}(u) = \sum_{i=0}^{n} N_{i,p}(u)\,\mathbf{Q}^w_i(v_0) \tag{4.17}$$

where
$$\mathbf{Q}^w_i(v_0) = \sum_{j=0}^{m} N_{j,q}(v_0)\,\mathbf{P}^w_{i,j}$$

$\mathbf{C}^w_{u_0}(v)$ ($\mathbf{C}^w_{v_0}(u)$) is a qth- (pth)-degree NURBS curve on the knot vector V (U). The point $\mathbf{S}^w(u_0, v_0)$ lies at the intersection of $\mathbf{C}^w_{u_0}(v)$ and $\mathbf{C}^w_{v_0}(u)$. Projecting yields

$$\mathbf{C}_{u_0}(v) = H\{\mathbf{C}^w_{u_0}(v)\} = H\{\mathbf{S}^w(u_0, v)\} = \mathbf{S}(u_0, v)$$

$$\mathbf{C}_{v_0}(u) = H\{\mathbf{C}^w_{v_0}(u)\} = H\{\mathbf{S}^w(u, v_0)\} = \mathbf{S}(u, v_0) \tag{4.18}$$

4.5 Derivatives of a NURBS Surface

The derivatives of $\mathbf{S}^w(u,v)$ are computed using Eqs. (3.17)–(3.24). We now derive formulas for the derivatives of $\mathbf{S}(u,v)$ in terms of those of $\mathbf{S}^w(u,v)$. Let

$$\mathbf{S}(u,v) = \frac{w(u,v)\mathbf{S}(u,v)}{w(u,v)} = \frac{\mathbf{A}(u,v)}{w(u,v)}$$

where $\mathbf{A}(u,v)$ is the numerator of $\mathbf{S}(u,v)$ (Eq. [4.11]). Then

$$\mathbf{S}_\alpha(u,v) = \frac{\mathbf{A}_\alpha(u,v) - w_\alpha(u,v)\mathbf{S}(u,v)}{w(u,v)} \tag{4.19}$$

where α denotes either u or v.

In general

$$\mathbf{A}^{(k,l)} = \left[(w\mathbf{S})^k\right]^l = \left(\sum_{i=0}^{k}\binom{k}{i} w^{(i,0)}\mathbf{S}^{(k-i,0)}\right)^l$$

$$= \sum_{i=0}^{k}\binom{k}{i}\sum_{j=0}^{l}\binom{l}{j} w^{(i,j)}\mathbf{S}^{(k-i,l-j)}$$

$$= w^{(0,0)}\mathbf{S}^{(k,l)} + \sum_{i=1}^{k}\binom{k}{i} w^{(i,0)}\mathbf{S}^{(k-i,l)} + \sum_{j=1}^{l}\binom{l}{j} w^{(0,j)}\mathbf{S}^{(k,l-j)}$$

$$+ \sum_{i=1}^{k}\binom{k}{i}\sum_{j=1}^{l}\binom{l}{j} w^{(i,j)}\mathbf{S}^{(k-i,l-j)}$$

and it follows that

$$\mathbf{S}^{(k,l)} = \frac{1}{w}\left(\mathbf{A}^{(k,l)} - \sum_{i=1}^{k}\binom{k}{i} w^{(i,0)}\mathbf{S}^{(k-i,l)}\right.$$

$$\left. - \sum_{j=1}^{l}\binom{l}{j} w^{(0,j)}\mathbf{S}^{(k,l-j)} - \sum_{i=1}^{k}\binom{k}{i}\sum_{j=1}^{l}\binom{l}{j} w^{(i,j)}\mathbf{S}^{(k-i,l-j)}\right) \tag{4.20}$$

From Eq. (4.20) we obtain

$$\mathbf{S}_{uv} = \frac{\mathbf{A}_{uv} - w_{uv}\mathbf{S} - w_u\mathbf{S}_v - w_v\mathbf{S}_u}{w} \tag{4.21}$$

$$\mathbf{S}_{uu} = \frac{\mathbf{A}_{uu} - 2w_u\mathbf{S}_u - w_{uu}\mathbf{S}}{w} \tag{4.22}$$

$$\mathbf{S}_{vv} = \frac{\mathbf{A}_{vv} - 2w_v\mathbf{S}_v - w_{vv}\mathbf{S}}{w} \tag{4.23}$$

From Eqs. (3.24), (4.19), and (4.20)

$$\mathbf{S}_u(0,0) = \frac{p}{u_{p+1}} \frac{w_{1,0}}{w_{0,0}} (\mathbf{P}_{1,0} - \mathbf{P}_{0,0}) \tag{4.24}$$

$$\mathbf{S}_v(0,0) = \frac{q}{v_{q+1}} \frac{w_{0,1}}{w_{0,0}} (\mathbf{P}_{0,1} - \mathbf{P}_{0,0}) \tag{4.25}$$

$$\mathbf{S}_{uv}(0,0) = \frac{pq}{w_{0,0}u_{p+1}v_{q+1}} \left(w_{1,1}\mathbf{P}_{1,1} - \frac{w_{1,0}w_{0,1}}{w_{0,0}} (\mathbf{P}_{1,0} + \mathbf{P}_{0,1}) + \left(\frac{2w_{1,0}w_{0,1}}{w_{0,0}} - w_{1,1} \right) \mathbf{P}_{0,0} \right) \tag{4.26}$$

Figure 4.13 shows the first- and second-order partial derivatives of a NURBS surface. The first partials are scaled down by $1/2$, and the second partials are scaled down by $1/3$.

Now assume that (u, v) is fixed, and that all derivatives $\mathbf{A}^{(k,l)}$, $w^{(k,l)}$ for $k, l \geq 0$ and $0 \leq k + l \leq d$, have been computed and loaded into the arrays `Aders` and `wders`, respectively. Algorithm `A4.4` computes the point $\mathbf{S}(u, v)$ and the derivatives $\mathbf{S}^{(k,l)}(u, v)$, $0 \leq k + l \leq d$. `Bin[][]` contains the precomputed binomial coefficients.

```
ALGORITHM A4.4
  RatSurfaceDerivs(Aders,wders,d,SKL)
    { /* Compute S(u,v) derivatives  */
      /* from Sw(u,v) derivatives  */
      /* Input:  Aders,wders,d  */
      /* Output: SKL  */
    for (k=0; k<=d; k++)
      for (l=0; l<=d-k; l++)
        {
        v = Aders[k][l];
        for (j=1; j<=l; j++)
          v = v - Bin[l][j]*wders[0][j]*SKL[k][l-j];
```

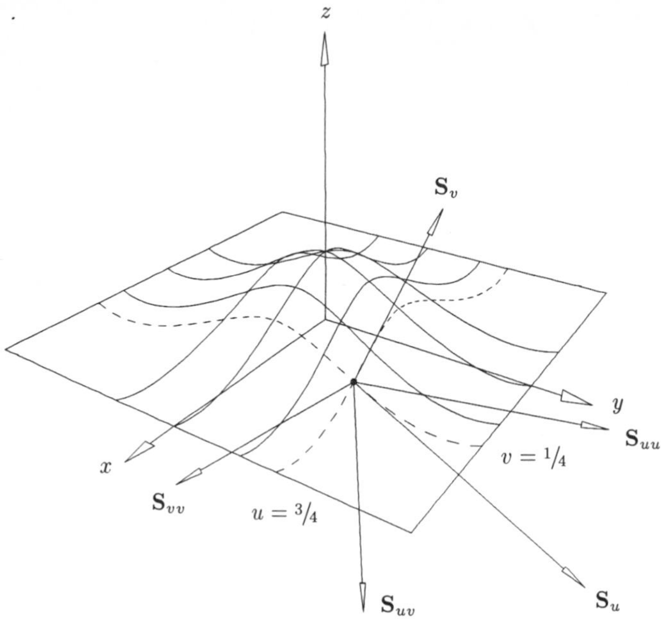

Figure 4.13. The first- and second-order partial derivatives of a bicubic NURBS surface computed at $u = 3/4$ and $v = 1/4$.

```
        for (i=1; i<=k; i++)
          {
          v = v - Bin[k][i]*wders[i][0]*SKL[k-i][l];
          v2 = 0.0;
          for (j=1; j<=l; j++)
            v2 = v2 + Bin[l][j]*wders[i][j]*SKL[k-i][l-j];
          v = v - Bin[k][i]*v2;
          }
        SKL[k][l] = v/wders[0][0];
        }
    }
```

Exercises

4.1. Let $U = \{0, 0, 0, 1/3, 2/3, 1, 1, 1\}$ and $\{w_0, \ldots, w_4\}=\{1, 4, 1, 1, 1\}$. Using the Cox-deBoor recurrence formula (Eq. [2.5]) and Eq. (4.2), compute the five quadratic rational functions, $R_{i,2}(u)$, $0 \le i \le 4$. The graphs of these functions are shown in Figure 4.5a. Assume $\{\mathbf{P}_0, \ldots, \mathbf{P}_4\} = \{(0,0), (1,1), (3,2), (4,1), (5,-1)\}$ are control points in the xy plane. Compute the rational coordinate functions $x(u)$ and $y(u)$ representing $\mathbf{C}(u)$ in the interval $u \in [1/3, 2/3)$.

4.2. Refer to Example Ex4.2 for a quadratic rational Bézier circular arc; compute $\mathbf{C}''(1)$.

4.3. Let $\mathbf{C}^w(u) = \sum_{i=0}^{1} N_{i,1}(u)\mathbf{P}_i^w$ be a line segment in the xy plane, where $\mathbf{P}_0 = (0,1)$, $\mathbf{P}_1 = (2,0)$, $w_0 = 1$, $w_1 = 3$, and $U = \{0,0,1,1\}$. Derive the rational functions representing the x and y coordinates of this line segment, i.e., $x(u)$ and $y(u)$, where $\mathbf{C}(u) = (x(u), y(u))$. Compute $\mathbf{C}'(0)$ using Eq. (4.9) and $\mathbf{C}''(0)$ using Eqs. (4.8) and (3.9). Then set $w_1 = 1$ and recompute $x(u)$, $y(u)$, $\mathbf{C}'(0)$, and $\mathbf{C}''(0)$.

4.4. Let $\mathbf{S}^w(u,v) = \sum_{i=0}^{1} \sum_{j=0}^{1} N_{i,1}(u)N_{j,1}(v)\mathbf{P}_{i,j}^w$, where $\{\mathbf{P}_{0,0}, \mathbf{P}_{1,0}, \mathbf{P}_{0,1}, \mathbf{P}_{1,1}\} = \{(0,0,1), (0,1,3), (2,1,1), (2,0,3)\}$, $\{w_{0,0}, w_{1,0}, w_{0,1}, w_{1,1}\} = \{2,1,1,1\}$, and $U = V = \{0,0,1,1\}$. Derive the four rational basis functions, $R_{i,j}(u,v)$, $0 \le i,j \le 1$, and the rational coordinate functions $x(u,v)$, $y(u,v)$, and $z(u,v)$ of the surface $\mathbf{S}(u,v)$.

4.5. From $\mathbf{S}^w(u,v)$ in Exercise 4.4 derive the two rational isoparametric curves $\mathbf{C}_{u0}^w(v)$ and $\mathbf{C}_{v0}^w(u)$, for $u_0 = 1/3$ and $v_0 = 1/2$. Then evaluate the curves $\mathbf{C}_{u_0}(v)$ and $\mathbf{C}_{v_0}(u)$ at $v = 1/2$ and $u = 1/3$, respectively. Check your results by substituting $(u,v) = (1/3, 1/2)$ into the rational coordinate functions obtained in Exercise 4.4.

4.6. Let $\mathbf{S}^w(u,v) = \sum_{i=0}^{1} \sum_{j=0}^{1} N_{i,1}(u)N_{j,1}(v)\mathbf{P}_{i,j}^w$ be the surface given in Exercise 4.4. Since $N_{0,1}(1/2) = N_{1,1}(1/2) = 1/2$, it follows that

$$\mathbf{S}^w\left(\frac{1}{2},\frac{1}{2}\right) = \frac{1}{4}\left(\mathbf{P}_{0,0}^w + \mathbf{P}_{0,1}^w + \mathbf{P}_{1,0}^w + \mathbf{P}_{1,1}^w\right) = \left(1,\frac{1}{2},\frac{9}{4},\frac{5}{4}\right)$$

Compute $\mathbf{S}_u(1/2, 1/2)$, $\mathbf{S}_v(1/2, 1/2)$, $\mathbf{S}_{uv}(1/2, 1/2)$, $\mathbf{S}_{uu}(1/2, 1/2)$.

CHAPTER

FIVE

Fundamental Geometric Algorithms

5.1 Introduction

In this chapter we present five tools which are fundamental in the implementation of B-spline curves and surfaces; these are knot insertion, knot refinement, knot removal, degree elevation, and degree reduction. We devote a section to each topic, and the layout of each section is roughly:

- a statement of the problem (for curves);
- a list of applications;
- clarification of the problem and solution approaches (curves);
- a list of references where more rigorous derivations and proofs can be found;
- the solution formulas (curves);
- worked examples (curves);
- computer algorithms;
- examples of applications;
- the solution for surfaces, and outlines of the surface algorithms.

5.2 Knot Insertion

Let $\mathbf{C}^w(u) = \sum_{i=0}^{n} N_{i,p}(u)\mathbf{P}_i^w$ be a NURBS curve defined on $U = \{u_0, \ldots, u_m\}$. Let $\bar{u} \in [u_k, u_{k+1})$, and insert $\bar{u}$ into U to form the new knot vector $\bar{U} = \{\bar{u}_0 = u_0, \ldots, \bar{u}_k = u_k, \bar{u}_{k+1} = \bar{u}, \bar{u}_{k+2} = u_{k+1}, \ldots, \bar{u}_{m+1} = u_m\}$. If $\mathcal{V}_U$ and $\mathcal{V}_{\bar{U}}$ denote the vector spaces of curves defined on U and $\bar{U}$, respectively, then clearly $\mathcal{V}_U \subset \mathcal{V}_{\bar{U}}$ (and $\dim(\mathcal{V}_{\bar{U}}) = \dim(\mathcal{V}_U) + 1$); thus $\mathbf{C}^w(u)$ has a representation on $\bar{U}$ of the form

$$\mathbf{C}^w(u) = \sum_{i=0}^{n+1} \bar{N}_{i,p}(u)\,\mathbf{Q}_i^w \tag{5.1}$$

where the $\{\bar{N}_{i,p}(u)\}$ are the pth-degree basis functions on $\bar{U}$. The term *knot insertion* generally refers to the process of determining the $\{\mathbf{Q}_i^w\}$ in Eq. (5.1). It is important to note that knot insertion is really just a change of vector space basis; the curve is not changed, either geometrically or parametrically.

Although not immediately obvious, knot insertion is one of the most important of all B-spline algorithms. Some of its uses are:

- evaluating points and derivatives on curves and surfaces;
- subdividing curves and surfaces;
- adding control points in order to increase flexibility in shape control (interactive design).

Now the $\{\mathbf{Q}_i^w\}$ in Eq. (5.1) can be obtained by setting up and solving a system of linear equations. If we set

$$\sum_{i=0}^{n} N_{i,p}(u)\,\mathbf{P}_i^w = \sum_{i=0}^{n+1} \bar{N}_{i,p}(u)\,\mathbf{Q}_i^w \tag{5.2}$$

then by substituting $n+2$ suitable values of u into Eq. (5.2) we obtain a nonsingular, banded system of $n+2$ linear equations in the $n+2$ unknowns, $\mathbf{Q}_i^w$. However, there is a more efficient solution. Property P2.2 and $\bar{u} \in [u_k, u_{k+1})$ imply that

$$\sum_{i=k-p}^{k} N_{i,p}(u)\,\mathbf{P}_i^w = \sum_{i=k-p}^{k+1} \bar{N}_{i,p}(u)\,\mathbf{Q}_i^w \tag{5.3}$$

for all $u \in [u_k, u_{k+1})$, and

$$\begin{aligned} N_{i,p}(u) &= \bar{N}_{i,p}(u) \qquad && i = 0, \ldots, k-p-1 \\ N_{i,p}(u) &= \bar{N}_{i+1,p}(u) \qquad && i = k+1, \ldots, n \end{aligned} \tag{5.4}$$

Equations (5.3) and (5.4), together with the linear independence of the basis functions (Section 2.4), imply that

$$\begin{aligned} \mathbf{P}_i^w &= \mathbf{Q}_i^w \qquad && i = 0, \ldots, k-p-1 \\ \mathbf{P}_i^w &= \mathbf{Q}_{i+1}^w \qquad && i = k+1, \ldots, n \end{aligned} \tag{5.5}$$

Now consider the $N_{i,p}(u)$ for $i = k-p, \ldots, k$. They can be expressed in terms of the $\bar{N}_{i,p}(u)$ when $i = k-p, \ldots, k+1$, by

$$N_{i,p}(u) = \frac{\bar{u} - \bar{u}_i}{\bar{u}_{i+p+1} - \bar{u}_i}\,\bar{N}_{i,p}(u) + \frac{\bar{u}_{i+p+2} - \bar{u}}{\bar{u}_{i+p+2} - \bar{u}_{i+1}}\,\bar{N}_{i+1,p}(u) \tag{5.6}$$

Equation (5.6) is proven by induction on p (and using Eq. [2.5]), but we omit the proof here as it is quite messy. Proofs using divided differences are found in [DeBo78; Boeh80; Lee83].

For brevity we now write $\bar{N}_i$ for $\bar{N}_{i,p}(u)$. Substituting Eq. (5.6) into Eq. (5.3) yields

$$\begin{aligned}
&\left(\frac{\bar{u}-\bar{u}_{k-p}}{\bar{u}_{k+1}-\bar{u}_{k-p}}\,\bar{N}_{k-p}+\frac{\bar{u}_{k+2}-\bar{u}}{\bar{u}_{k+2}-\bar{u}_{k-p+1}}\,\bar{N}_{k-p+1}\right)\mathbf{P}^w_{k-p}\\
&\qquad+\left(\frac{\bar{u}-\bar{u}_{k-p+1}}{\bar{u}_{k+2}-\bar{u}_{k-p+1}}\,\bar{N}_{k-p+1}+\frac{\bar{u}_{k+3}-\bar{u}}{\bar{u}_{k+3}-\bar{u}_{k-p+2}}\,\bar{N}_{k-p+2}\right)\mathbf{P}^w_{k-p+1}\\
&\qquad\qquad\vdots\\
&\qquad+\left(\frac{\bar{u}-\bar{u}_{k}}{\bar{u}_{k+p+1}-\bar{u}_{k}}\,\bar{N}_{k}+\frac{\bar{u}_{k+p+2}-\bar{u}}{\bar{u}_{k+p+2}-\bar{u}_{k+1}}\,\bar{N}_{k+1}\right)\mathbf{P}^w_{k}\\
&\quad=\bar{N}_{k-p}\mathbf{Q}^w_{k-p}+\cdots+\bar{N}_{k+1}\mathbf{Q}^w_{k+1}
\end{aligned}$$

By equating coefficients and using the knot vector U in place of $\bar{U}$, we obtain

$$\begin{aligned}
0=\ &\bar{N}_{k-p}\left(\mathbf{Q}^w_{k-p}-\mathbf{P}^w_{k-p}\right)\\
&+\bar{N}_{k-p+1}\left(\mathbf{Q}^w_{k-p+1}-\frac{\bar{u}-u_{k-p+1}}{u_{k+1}-u_{k-p+1}}\mathbf{P}^w_{k-p+1}-\frac{u_{k+1}-\bar{u}}{u_{k+1}-u_{k-p+1}}\mathbf{P}^w_{k-p}\right)\\
&\qquad\vdots\\
&+\bar{N}_{k}\left(\mathbf{Q}^w_{k}-\frac{\bar{u}-u_{k}}{u_{k+p}-u_{k}}\mathbf{P}^w_{k}-\frac{u_{k+p}-\bar{u}}{u_{k+p}-u_{k}}\mathbf{P}^w_{k-1}\right)+\bar{N}_{k+1}\left(\mathbf{Q}^w_{k+1}-\mathbf{P}^w_{k}\right)
\end{aligned}\tag{5.7}$$

For $i=k-p+1,\ldots,k$, we set

$$\alpha_i=\frac{\bar{u}-u_i}{u_{i+p}-u_i}\tag{5.8}$$

and note that

$$1-\alpha_i=\frac{u_{i+p}-\bar{u}}{u_{i+p}-u_i}\tag{5.9}$$

Using the linear independence of the basis functions, and substituting Eqs. (5.8) and (5.9) into Eq. (5.7), yields

$$\begin{aligned}
&\mathbf{Q}^w_{k-p}=\mathbf{P}^w_{k-p}\\
&\mathbf{Q}^w_{i}=\alpha_i\mathbf{P}^w_{i}+(1-\alpha_i)\mathbf{P}^w_{i-1}\qquad k-p+1\le i\le k\\
&\mathbf{Q}^w_{k+1}=\mathbf{P}^w_{k}
\end{aligned}\tag{5.10}$$

Finally, by combining Eqs. (5.5) and (5.10) we obtain the formula for computing all the new control points, $\mathbf{Q}^w_i$, of Eq. (5.1), that is

$$\mathbf{Q}^w_{i}=\alpha_i\mathbf{P}^w_{i}+(1-\alpha_i)\mathbf{P}^w_{i-1}\tag{5.11}$$

where
$$\alpha_i = \begin{cases} 1 & i \le k-p \\ \dfrac{\bar{u}-u_i}{u_{i+p}-u_i} & k-p+1 \le i \le k \\ 0 & i \ge k+1 \end{cases}$$

Equation (5.11) says that only p new control points must be computed. For brevity we use $\mathbf{P}$ instead of $\mathbf{P}^w$ in examples `Ex5.1` – `Ex5.4`.

Examples

`Ex5.1` Let $p = 3$ and $U = \{0,0,0,0,1,2,3,4,5,5,5,5\}$. The control points are $\mathbf{P}_0, \ldots, \mathbf{P}_7$. We insert $\bar{u} = 5/2$. Then $\bar{u} \in [u_5, u_6)$ and $k = 5$. Thus, $\mathbf{Q}_0 = \mathbf{P}_0, \ldots, \mathbf{Q}_2 = \mathbf{P}_2$ and $\mathbf{Q}_6 = \mathbf{P}_5, \ldots, \mathbf{Q}_8 = \mathbf{P}_7$. Applying Eq. (5.11) we find that

$$\alpha_3 = \frac{\frac{5}{2}-0}{3-0} = \frac{5}{6} \implies \mathbf{Q}_3 = \frac{5}{6}\mathbf{P}_3 + \frac{1}{6}\mathbf{P}_2$$

$$\alpha_4 = \frac{\frac{5}{2}-1}{4-1} = \frac{1}{2} \implies \mathbf{Q}_4 = \frac{1}{2}\mathbf{P}_4 + \frac{1}{2}\mathbf{P}_3$$

$$\alpha_5 = \frac{\frac{5}{2}-2}{5-2} = \frac{1}{6} \implies \mathbf{Q}_5 = \frac{1}{6}\mathbf{P}_5 + \frac{5}{6}\mathbf{P}_4$$

Figure 5.1a shows the control polygon before and after the insertion, and Figure 5.1b shows the basis functions before and after the insertion. The bottom part of Figure 5.1a shows the ratios used to subdivide the polygon legs.

`Ex5.2` Use the same curve as in `Ex5.1`, that is, $p = 3$, $U = \{0,0,0,0,1,2,3,4,5,5,5,5\}$, and $\mathbf{P}_0, \ldots, \mathbf{P}_7$. This time we insert a knot which is already in the knot vector, namely $\bar{u} = 2$. Then $\bar{u} \in [u_5, u_6)$, $k = 5$, and again we compute $\mathbf{Q}_3$, $\mathbf{Q}_4$, and $\mathbf{Q}_5$

$$\alpha_3 = \frac{2-0}{3-0} = \frac{2}{3} \implies \mathbf{Q}_3 = \frac{2}{3}\mathbf{P}_3 + \frac{1}{3}\mathbf{P}_2$$

$$\alpha_4 = \frac{2-1}{4-1} = \frac{1}{3} \implies \mathbf{Q}_4 = \frac{1}{3}\mathbf{P}_4 + \frac{2}{3}\mathbf{P}_3$$

$$\alpha_5 = \frac{2-2}{5-2} = 0 \implies \mathbf{Q}_5 = \mathbf{P}_4$$

The control polygons and basis functions, before and after knot insertion, are shown in Figures 5.2a and 5.2b. From Eq. (5.6) one can verify

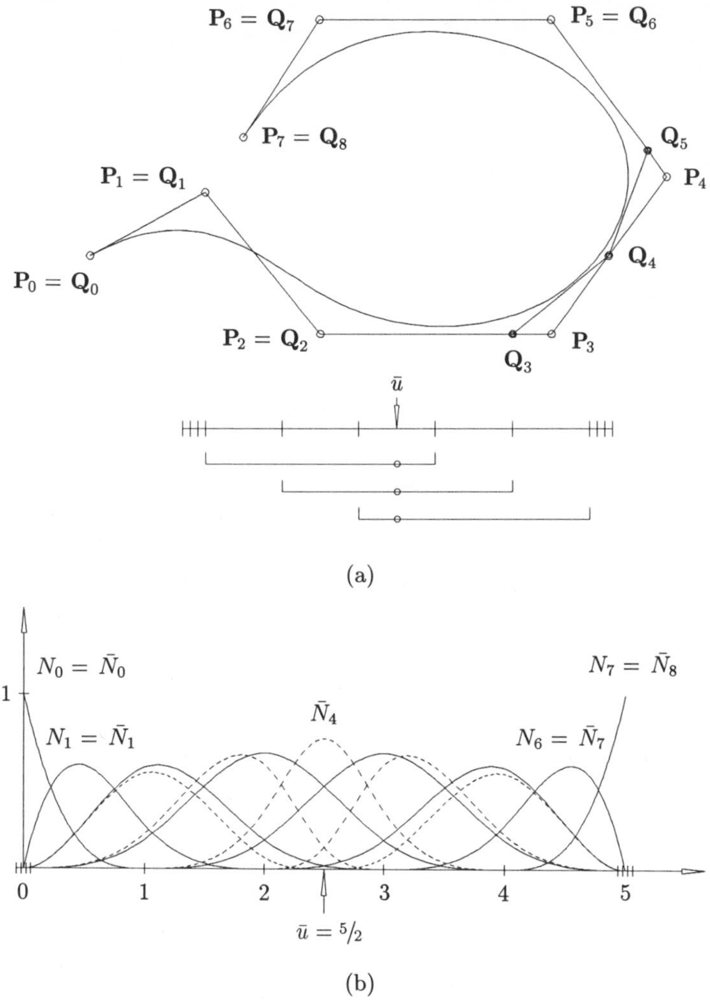

Figure 5.1. Knot insertion into a cubic curve. (a) The control polygon after inserting $u = {}^5\!/_2$ into the knot vector $\{0,0,0,0,1,2,3,4,5,5,5,5\}$; (b) the original (solid) and the new (dashed) basis functions before and after knot insertion.

that $N_5 = \bar{N}_6$. As we did previously, observe the subdivision of the legs obtained by mapping the appropriate scales shown in the bottom of Figure 5.2a.

Clearly, knot insertion is similar to the deCasteljau algorithm for Bézier curves, and in fact they are equivalent for a curve with no interior knots, i.e., a Bézier curve. However, a glance at Example `Ex5.1` and Figure 5.1a shows that the linear interpolation is not the same on each of the p legs of the control polygon. Indeed, in the example, $\alpha_3 = {}^5\!/_6$, $\alpha_4 = {}^1\!/_2$, and $\alpha_5 = {}^1\!/_6$. Based on the previous

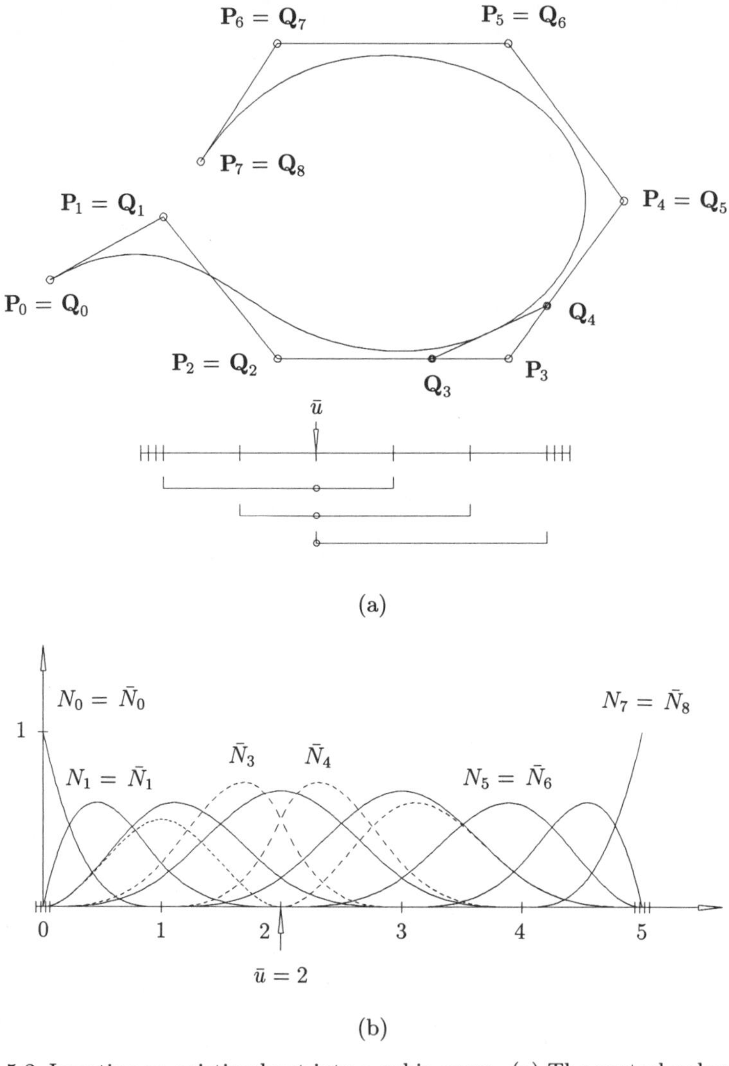

Figure 5.2. Inserting an existing knot into a cubic curve. (a) The control polygon after inserting $u = 2$ into $\{0,0,0,0,1,2,3,4,5,5,5,5\}$; (b) the original (solid) and the new (dashed) basis functions before and after knot insertion.

examples, we arrive at the general result: For $i = 1,\ldots,n$ let L_i denote the ith-leg of the control polygon

$$L_i = \mathbf{P}^w_{i-1}\mathbf{P}^w_i \qquad \text{and} \qquad d_i = \text{length}\ (L_i) = \mid \mathbf{P}^w_i - \mathbf{P}^w_{i-1} \mid$$

We emphasize that d_i is measured in four-dimensional (homogeneous) space, i.e.

$$d_i = \sqrt{(w_i x_i)^2 + (w_i y_i)^2 + (w_i z_i)^2 + (w_i)^2}$$

With each leg L_i, we associate the knots u_{i+j}, $j = 0, \ldots, p$. Refer to Figures 5.3a and 5.3b and Figures 5.1a and 5.2a. For fixed i let λ_i^j, $j = 0, \ldots, p-1$, denote the length of the knot span $[u_{i+j}, u_{i+j+1})$ relative to $[u_i, u_{i+p})$

$$\lambda_i^j = \frac{u_{i+j+1} - u_{i+j}}{u_{i+p} - u_i} \qquad j = 0, \ldots, p-1 \tag{5.12}$$

Then L_i is partitioned into segments L_i^j, whose lengths are

$$d_i^j = \lambda_i^j d_i \tag{5.13}$$

respectively. Notice that λ_i^j, and hence d_i^j, can be zero. For example, $d_1^0 = d_1^1 = 0$ and $d_1^2 = d_1$ in Example `Ex5.1`; thus, there is only one segment on the first leg.

Now Figures 5.3a and 5.3b and Eq. (5.13) show how the polygon legs are subdivided, and Figures 5.1a and 5.2a show how polygon corners are cut in the knot insertion process. In particular, if $\bar{u} \in [u_k, u_{k+1})$ is a knot of multiplicity s, $0 \le s \le p-1$, then the corners with control points $\mathbf{P}_{k-p+1}, \ldots, \mathbf{P}_{k-s-1}$ are cut, and the following $p-s$ new control points are generated on the indicated segments

$$\mathbf{Q}_{k-j}^w \in L_{k-j}^j \qquad j = p-1, \ldots, s \tag{5.14}$$

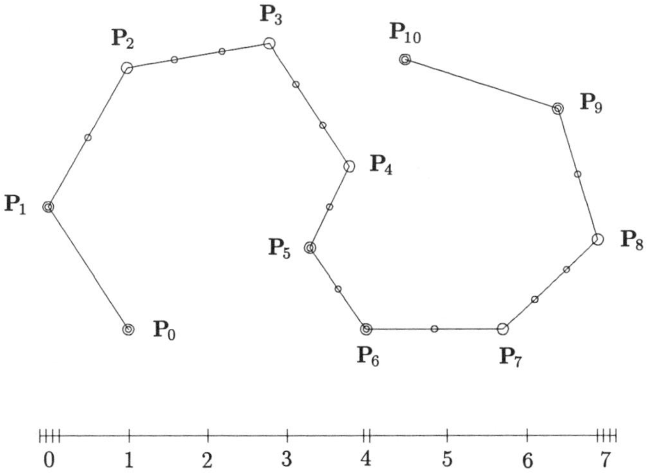

(a)

Figure 5.3. The control polygon and its partitioning by its knot vector. (a) Partitioning of the entire polygon by the knot vector $\{0,0,0,0,1,2,3,4,4,5,6,7,7,7,7\}$; (b) partitioning of the polygon side $\mathbf{P}_2\mathbf{P}_3$ by the knot span $[u_3, u_6]$.

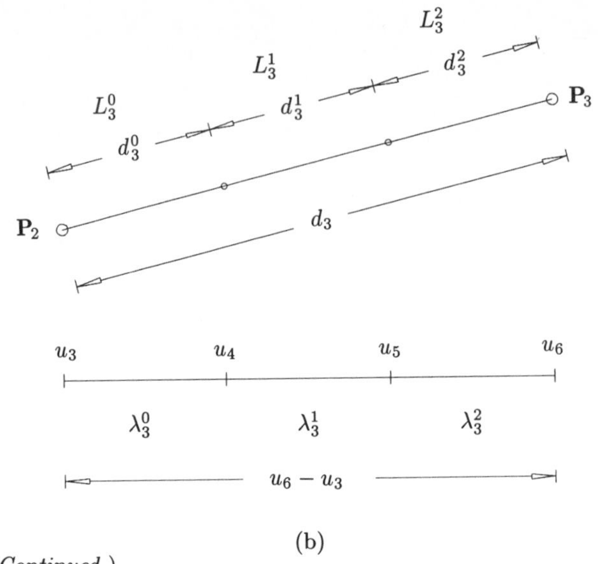

Figure 5.3. (*Continued.*)

Examples

Ex5.3 Let us check Eqs. (5.12)–(5.14) in Example Ex5.1. We have $k = 5$ and $s = 0$. By Eq. (5.14)

$$\mathbf{Q}_3 \in L_3^2 \qquad \mathbf{Q}_4 \in L_4^1 \qquad \mathbf{Q}_5 \in L_5^0$$

Furthermore

$$\lambda_3^2 = \frac{u_6 - u_5}{u_6 - u_3} = \frac{3-2}{3-0} = \frac{1}{3}$$

$$\lambda_4^1 = \frac{u_6 - u_5}{u_7 - u_4} = \frac{3-2}{4-1} = \frac{1}{3}$$

$$\lambda_5^0 = \frac{u_6 - u_5}{u_8 - u_5} = \frac{3-2}{5-2} = \frac{1}{3}$$

(This is not surprising, since the knots are equally spaced). Recalling that $\alpha_3 = 5/6$, $\alpha_4 = 1/2$, and $\alpha_5 = 1/6$, we see that $\mathbf{Q}_3$, $\mathbf{Q}_4$, and $\mathbf{Q}_5$ are located at the midpoints of their segments, L_3^2, L_4^1, and L_5^0. This follows from the fact that $\bar{u} = 5/2$ is halfway between $u_5 = 2$ and $u_6 = 3$.

Ex5.4 For Example Ex5.2, $k = 5$ and $s = 1$. By Eq. (5.14)

$$\mathbf{Q}_3 \in L_3^2 \qquad \mathbf{Q}_4 \in L_4^1$$

We still have $\lambda_3^2 = \lambda_4^1 = 1/3$. Now $\alpha_3 = 2/3$ and $\alpha_4 = 1/3$, which imply that $\mathbf{Q}_3$ and $\mathbf{Q}_4$ are located at the starting points of their segments, L_3^2

and L_4^1, respectively. This follows from the fact that $\bar{u} = 2$ lies at the start of the knot span, $[u_5, u_6)$.

Figure 5.4 shows the partitioning of the same control polygon as in Figure 5.3a but with the nonuniform knot vector $U = \{0,0,0,0,1,1.5,2.3,3.9,4.3,5,6.5, 7,7,7,7\}$.

As we shall see later, it is often necessary to insert a knot multiple times. Equation (5.11) can be generalized to handle this. Suppose $\bar{u} \in [u_k, u_{k+1})$ initially has multiplicity s, and suppose it is to be inserted r times, where $r + s \le p$ (it generally makes no practical sense to have interior knot multiplicities greater than p). Denote the ith new control point in the rth insertion step by $\mathbf{Q}^w_{i,r}$ (with $\mathbf{Q}^w_{i,0} = \mathbf{P}^w_i$). Then $\mathbf{Q}^w_{i,r}$ is

$$\mathbf{Q}^w_{i,r} = \alpha_{i,r}\,\mathbf{Q}^w_{i,r-1} + (1 - \alpha_{i,r})\,\mathbf{Q}^w_{i-1,r-1} \tag{5.15}$$

where
$$\alpha_{i,r} = \begin{cases} 1 & i \le k - p + r - 1 \\ \dfrac{\bar{u} - u_i}{u_{i+p-r+1} - u_i} & k - p + r \le i \le k - s \\ 0 & i \ge k - s + 1 \end{cases}$$

If $s = 0$ and $r = p$, then Eq. (5.15) generates a triangular table of control points (see Table 5.1, and see Figure 5.5 with $p = 3$). The outer control points

$$\mathbf{Q}^w_{k-p+1,1},\ \mathbf{Q}^w_{k-p+2,2}, \ldots,\ \mathbf{Q}^w_{k,p}, \ldots,\ \mathbf{Q}^w_{k,2},\ \mathbf{Q}^w_{k,1}$$

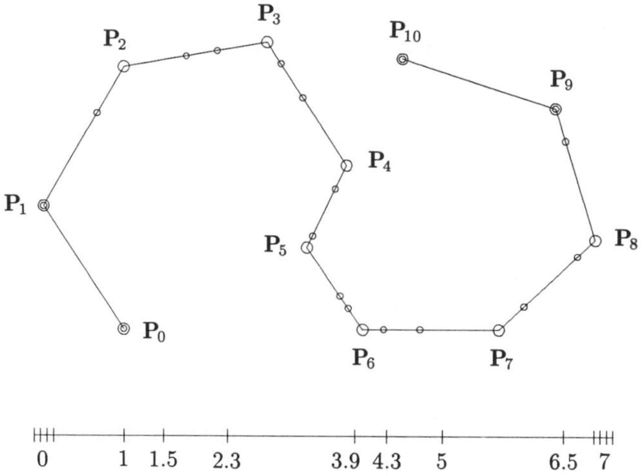

Figure 5.4. Nonuniform partitioning of the control polygon in Figure 5.3a defined by the knot vector $\{0,0,0,0,1,1.5,2.3,3.9,4.3,5,6.5,7,7,7,7\}$.

Table 5.1. Control points generated by Eq. (5.15).

$\mathbf{Q}^w_{k-p+1,1}$			
	$\mathbf{Q}^w_{k-p+2,2}$		
$\mathbf{Q}^w_{k-p+2,1}$			
$\vdots$	$\vdots$	$\cdots$	$\mathbf{Q}^w_{k,p}$
$\mathbf{Q}^w_{k-1,1}$			
	$\mathbf{Q}^w_{k,2}$		
$\mathbf{Q}^w_{k,1}$			

are kept, and the inner ones are discarded. In general, the table is less than full if $s > 0$ and/or $r + s < p$. But in any case, the final control points are obtained by traversing the resulting table in a clockwise fashion, starting at the top of the first column generated. The number of new control points in the last column is $p-(s+r)+1$. In all other columns, two new points are kept (top and bottom); thus, the total number of new (keeper) control points is

$$p - s + r - 1 \tag{5.16}$$

These new control points replace

$$p - s - 1 \tag{5.17}$$

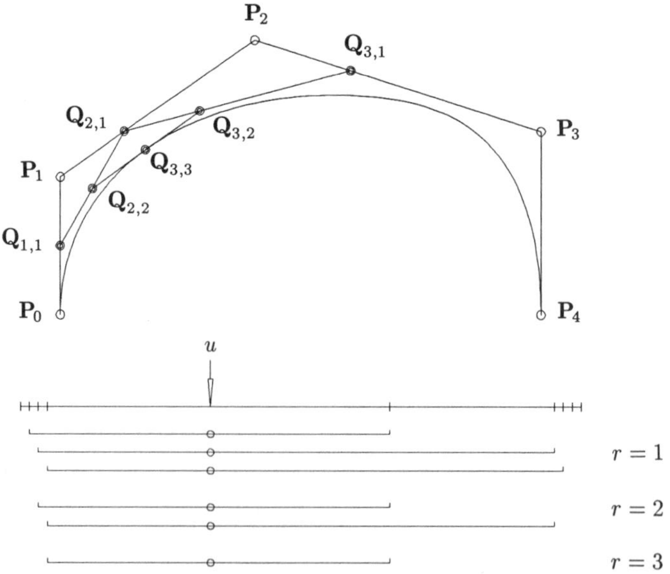

Figure 5.5. Knot insertion into a cubic curve three times. The curve is defined on $\{0, 0, 0, 0, 2, 3, 3, 3, 3\}$.

old ones, starting at the index

$$k - p + 1 \tag{5.18}$$

Algorithm A5.1 implements Eq. (5.15). It computes the new curve corresponding to the insertion of $\bar{u}$ into $[u_k, u_{k+1})$ r times, where it is assumed that $r + s \leq p$. Rw[] is a local array of length $p + 1$. UP[] and UQ[] are the knot vectors before and after knot insertion, respectively.

```
ALGORITHM A5.1
  CurveKnotIns(np,p,UP,Pw,u,k,s,r,nq,UQ,Qw)
    { /*  Compute new curve from knot insertion  */
      /*  Input:  np,p,UP,Pw,u,k,s,r  */
      /*  Output: nq,UQ,Qw  */
    mp = np+p+1;
    nq = np+r;
      /*  Load new knot vector */
    for(i=0; i<=k; i++)  UQ[i] = UP[i];
    for(i=1; i<=r; i++)  UQ[k+i] = u;
    for(i=k+1; i<=mp; i++)  UQ[i+r] = UP[i];
      /*  Save unaltered control points */
    for(i=0; i<=k-p; i++)  Qw[i] = Pw[i];
    for(i=k-s; i<=np; i++)  Qw[i+r] = Pw[i];
    for(i=0; i<=p-s; i++)  Rw[i] = Pw[k-p+i];
    for(j=1; j<=r; j++)   /* Insert the knot r times */
      {
      L = k-p+j;
      for(i=0; i<=p-j-s; i++)
        {
        alpha = (u-UP[L+i])/(UP[i+k+1]-UP[L+i]);
        Rw[i] = alpha*Rw[i+1] + (1.0-alpha)*Rw[i];
        }
      Qw[L] = Rw[0];
      Qw[k+r-j-s] = Rw[p-j-s];
      }
    for(i=L+1; i<k-s; i++)  /* Load remaining control points */
      Qw[i] = Rw[i-L];
    }
```

We now consider three applications of knot insertion, curve splitting (or subdivision), the evaluation of points and derivatives, and insertion in order to obtain an additional control point for interactive shape design. Refer to Figure 5.5. The original curve, $\mathbf{C}(u)$, is a cubic defined by $U = \{0,0,0,0,2,3,3,3,3\}$ and $\mathbf{P}_0, \ldots, \mathbf{P}_4$. $\bar{u} = 1$ is now inserted three times. Figures 5.6a and 5.6b show the basis functions before and after insertion. The process *splits* the curve. The sets of control points $\{\mathbf{P}_0, \mathbf{Q}_{1,1}, \mathbf{Q}_{2,2}, \mathbf{Q}_{3,3}\}$ and $\{\mathbf{Q}_{3,3}, \mathbf{Q}_{3,2}, \mathbf{Q}_{3,1}, \mathbf{P}_3, \mathbf{P}_4\}$ define cubic B-spline curves, $\mathbf{C}_l(u)$ and $\mathbf{C}_r(u)$, on the knot vectors $U_l = \{0,0,0,0,1,1,$

1, 1} and $U_r = \{1,1,1,1,2,3,3,3,3\}$, respectively. Furthermore, $\mathbf{C}_l(u)$ is $\mathbf{C}(u)$ restricted to the domain $u \in [0,1]$, and $\mathbf{C}_r(u)$ is $\mathbf{C}(u)$ restricted to $u \in [1,3]$. Curve splitting, together with the convex hull property (P4.10), forms the basis for "divide and conquer" algorithms using NURBS. Figure 5.7 shows an example of recursive curve splitting: The original curve $\mathbf{C}$ is split at $u = 1/2$, resulting in $\mathbf{C}_1$ and $\mathbf{C}_2$, which are then split at $1/8$ and $3/8$, respectively, yielding $\mathbf{C}_{1,1}$ and $\mathbf{C}_{1,2}$, and $\mathbf{C}_{2,1}$ and $\mathbf{C}_{2,2}$.

Figures 5.5 and 5.6b also show that knot insertion can be used to evaluate points and derivatives on curves. Clearly, $\mathbf{C}(1) = \mathbf{Q}_{3,3}$; furthermore, the derivatives from *both the left and right* can easily be computed using the starting point and endpoint derivative formulas, Eqs. (3.7), (3.9), (3.10), (4.9), and (4.10).

Algorithm `A5.2` computes a point on a curve using knot insertion ("corner cutting"). It assumes a routine, `FindSpanMult`, which finds the knot span, k, and the multiplicity, s.

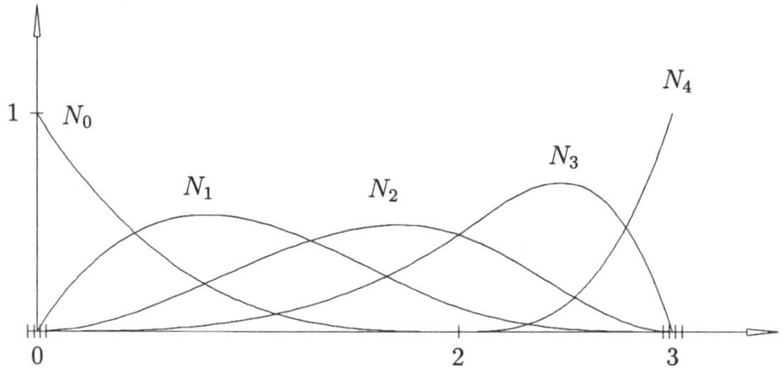

(a)

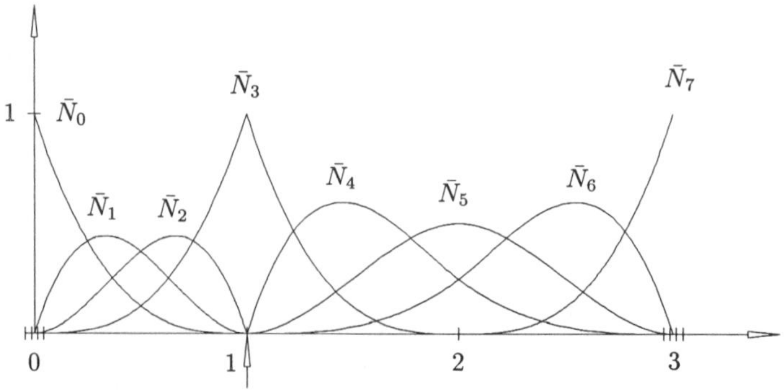

(b)

Figure 5.6. Basis functions corresponding to Figure 5.5. (a) Before knot insertion; (b) after knot insertion.

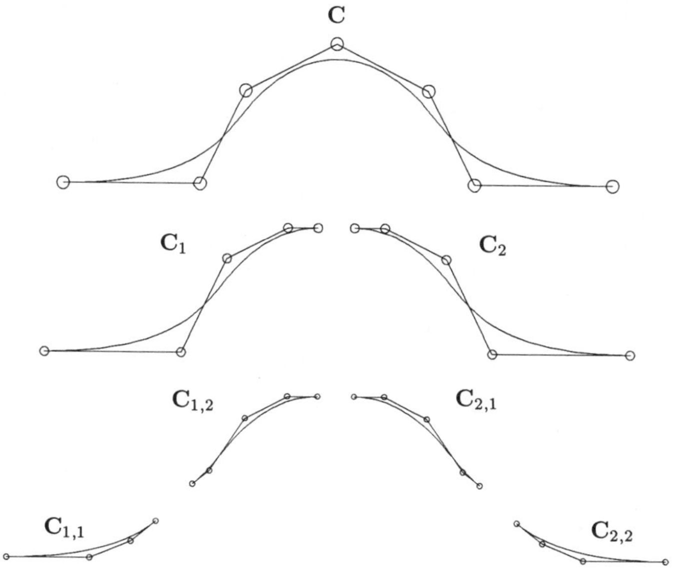

Figure 5.7. Splitting a cubic curve defined on $\{0,0,0,0,\,^1\!/_4,\,^1\!/_2,\,^3\!/_4,1,1,1,1\}$.

```
ALGORITHM A5.2
  CurvePntByCornerCut(n,p,U,Pw,u,C)
    { /*  Compute point on rational B-spline curve  */
      /*  Input:  n,p,U,Pw,u  */
      /*  Output: C  */
    if (u == U[0])  /* Endpoints are special cases */
      {
      C = Pw[0]/w;   return;
      }
    if (u == U[n+p+1])
      {
      C = Pw[n]/w;   return;
      }
    FindSpanMult(n,p,u,U,&k,&s);   /* General case */
    r = p-s;
    for (i=0; i<=r; i++)   Rw[i] = Pw[k-p+i];
    for (j=1; j<=r; j++)
      for (i=0; i<=r-j; i++)
        {
        alfa = (u-U[k-p+j+i])/(U[i+k+1]-U[k-p+j+i]);
        Rw[i] = alfa*Rw[i+1] + (1.0-alfa)*Rw[i];
```

```
      }
   C = Rw[0]/w;
   }
```

The third application is interactive shape design. As we saw in Chapter 4, curves and surfaces can be shaped by moving control points and/or modifying weights. For modification purposes, a designer might like to have a control point somewhere on the control polygon where one currently does not exist. For example, suppose he picks the point $\mathbf{Q}$ on the three-dimensional polygon leg, $\mathbf{P}_{i-1}\mathbf{P}_i$ (see Figure 5.8). Denote the corresponding four-dimensional point on the leg, $L_i = \mathbf{P}^w_{i-1}\mathbf{P}^w_i$, by $\mathbf{Q}^w$. Then there exists a $\bar{u} \in [u_i, u_{i+p})$ such that a single insertion of $\bar{u}$ causes $\mathbf{Q}^w$ to become a new control point and $\mathbf{Q}$ its projection. This process of determining $\bar{u}$ is called *inverse knot insertion* [Pieg89c]. Now there exists a value s, $0 \le s \le 1$, such that

$$\mathbf{Q}^w = (1-s)\mathbf{P}^w_{i-1} + s\mathbf{P}^w_i$$

which upon projection yields

$$\mathbf{Q} = \frac{(1-s)w_{i-1}\mathbf{P}_{i-1} + sw_i\mathbf{P}_i}{(1-s)w_{i-1} + sw_i} \tag{5.19}$$

It follows that

$$s = \frac{w_{i-1} \mid \mathbf{Q} - \mathbf{P}_{i-1} \mid}{w_{i-1} \mid \mathbf{Q} - \mathbf{P}_{i-1} \mid + w_i \mid \mathbf{P}_i - \mathbf{Q} \mid} \tag{5.20}$$

and thus

$$\bar{u} = u_i + s(u_{i+p} - u_i) \tag{5.21}$$

Knots are inserted into surfaces by simply applying the previous formulas and algorithms to the rows and/or columns of control points. In particular, let $\mathbf{P}^w_{i,j}$,

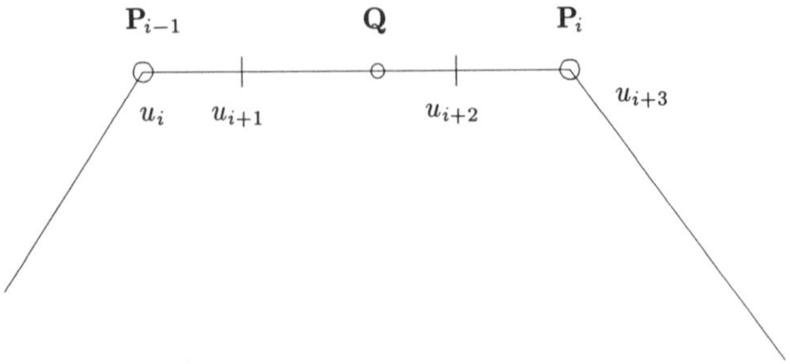

Figure 5.8. Inverse knot insertion for cubic curves; the point $\mathbf{Q}$ lies on the leg $\mathbf{P}_{i-1}\mathbf{P}_i$ partitioned by the knots u_i, u_{i+1}, u_{i+2}, and u_{i+3}.

$0 \le i \le n$, $0 \le j \le m$, be the control points of a NURBS surface; call i the row index and j the column index. Then $\bar{u}$ is added to the knot vector U by doing a $\bar{u}$ knot insertion on each of the $m+1$ columns of control points. The resulting control net is $\mathbf{Q}^w_{i,j}$, $0 \le i \le n+1$, $0 \le j \le m$. Analogously, $\bar{v}$ must be inserted on each of the $n+1$ rows of control points. The resulting control net is $\mathbf{Q}^w_{i,j}$, $0 \le i \le n$, $0 \le j \le m+1$. Figure 5.9 shows a cubic $\times$ quadratic surface on $U = \{0,0,0,0,1,1,1,1\}$ and $V = \{0,0,0,{}^1\!/_2,1,1,1\}$. Figures 5.10a and 5.10b show insertion of the knots $\bar{u} = {}^4\!/_{10}$ and $\bar{v} = {}^7\!/_{10}$, respectively, and Figure 5.10c shows the insertion of both knots. We point out that a surface knot insertion algorithm should not merely consist of a loop in which Algorithm `A5.1` is called $m+1$ (or $n+1$) times. The computation of the alphas (`alpha` in `A5.1`) does not depend on the control points. Hence, they should be computed only once and stored in a local array before entering the loop which executes the $m+1$ or $n+1$ knot insertions. Algorithm `A5.3` is such an algorithm.

```
ALGORITHM A5.3
  SurfaceKnotIns(np,p,UP,mp,q,VP,Pw,dir,uv,k,s,r,nq,UQ,mq,VQ,Qw)
    {  /*  Surface knot insertion  */
       /*  Input:  np,p,UP,mp,q,VP,Pw,dir,uv,k,s,r  */
       /*  Output: nq,UQ,mq,VQ,Qw  */
    if (dir == U_DIRECTION)
```

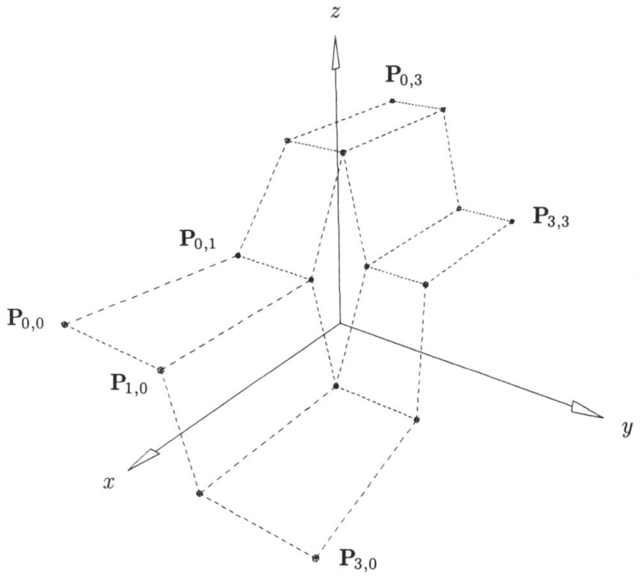

Figure 5.9. The control net of a (cubic $\times$ quadratic) surface defined on the knot vectors $U = \{0,0,0,0,1,1,1,1\}$ and $V = \{0,0,0,{}^1\!/_2,1,1,1\}$.

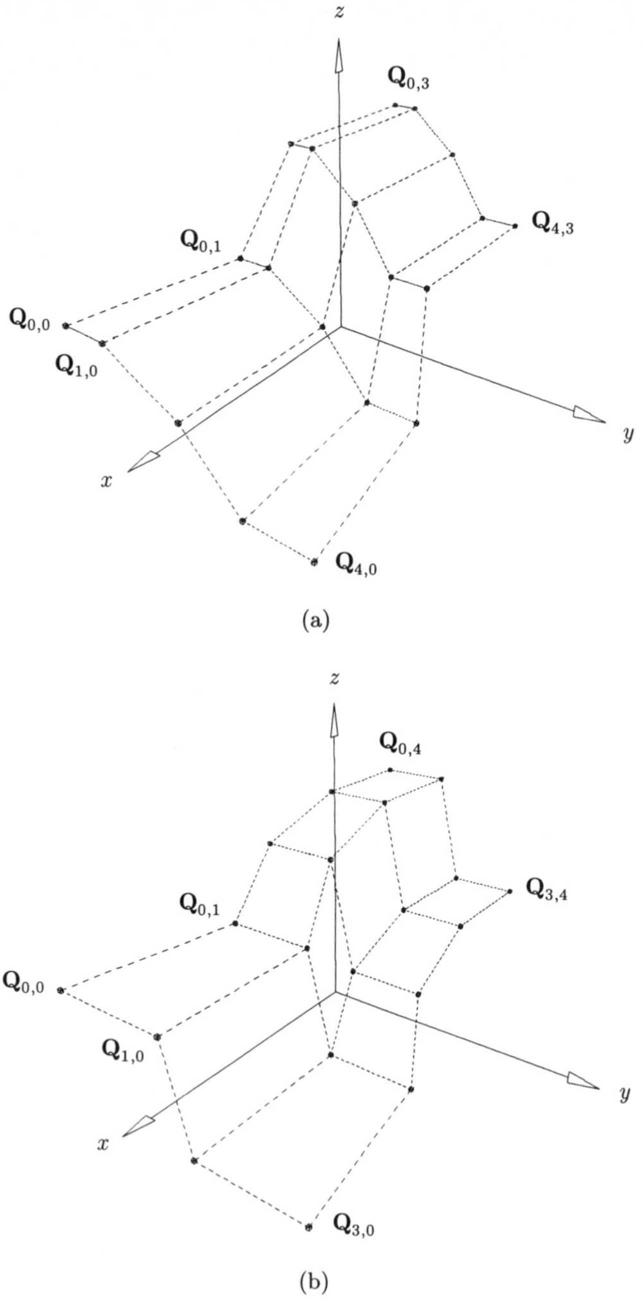

Figure 5.10. Knot insertion into the surface in Figure 5.9. (a) Inserting $u = 2/5$ one time in the u direction; (b) inserting $v = 7/10$ one time in the v direction; (c) inserting both knots at the same time.

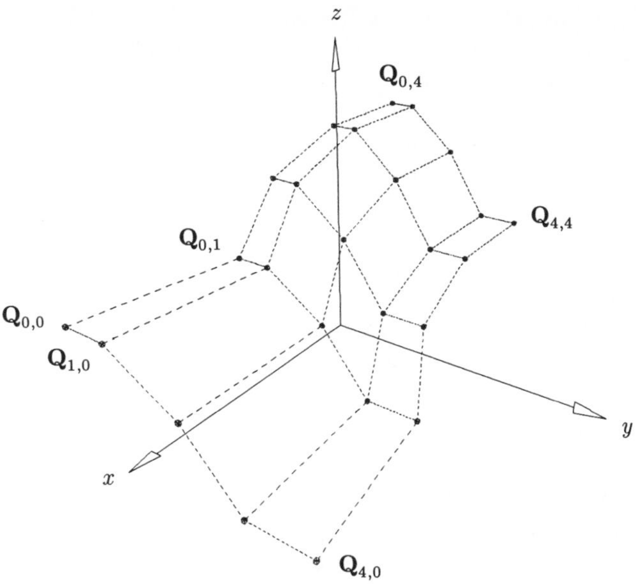

(c)

Figure 5.10. (*Continued.*)

```
{
load u-vector as in A5.1
copy v-vector into VQ
    /* Save the alphas */
for (j=1; j<=r; j++)
  {
  L = k-p+j;
  for (i=0; i<=p-j-s; i++)
    alpha[i][j] = (uv-UP[L+i])/(UP[i+k+1]-UP[L+i]);
  }
for (row=0; row<=mp; row++)    /* For each row do */
  {
        /* Save unaltered control points */
  for (i=0; i<=k-p; i++)    Qw[i][row] = Pw[i][row];
  for (i=k-s; i<=np; i++)    Qw[i+r][row] = Pw[i][row];
        /* Load auxiliary control points.  */
  for (i=0; i<=p-s; i++)    Rw[i] = Pw[k-p+i][row];
  for (j=1; j<=r; j++)    /* Insert the knot r times */
    {
    L = k-p+j;
    for (i=0; i<=p-j-s; i++)
```

```
          Rw[i] = alpha[i][j]*Rw[i+1] + (1.0-alpha[i][j])*Rw[i];
        Qw[L][row] = Rw[0];
        Qw[k+r-j-s][row] = Rw[p-j-s];
        }
            /* Load the remaining control points */
      for (i=L+1; i<k-s; i++)   Qw[i][row] = Rw[i-L];
      }
    }
  if (dir == V_DIRECTION)
    {
    Similar code as above with u- and v-directional
      parameters switched.
    }
  }
```

We conclude this section with remarks on surface knot insertion.

- Surface subdivision: Let $\bar{u}$ and $\bar{v}$ be interior parameter values. Inserting$\bar{u}$ p times and $\bar{v}$ q times subdivides the surface into four B-spline (sub-)surfaces. This fact, together with the convex hull property, implies that recursive subdivision is applicable to B-spline surface problems. Figure 5.11 shows a surface to be subdivided. In Figures 5.12–5.14, subdivisions in the u- and v- and in both directions, respectively, are illustrated;

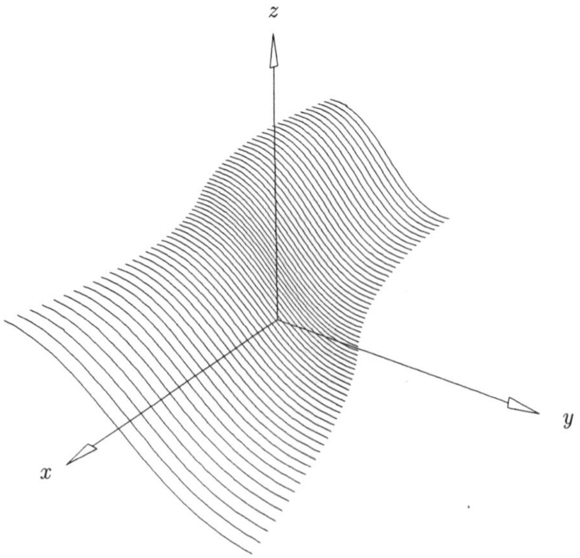

Figure 5.11. A (cubic × quadratic) surface defined as in Figure 5.9.

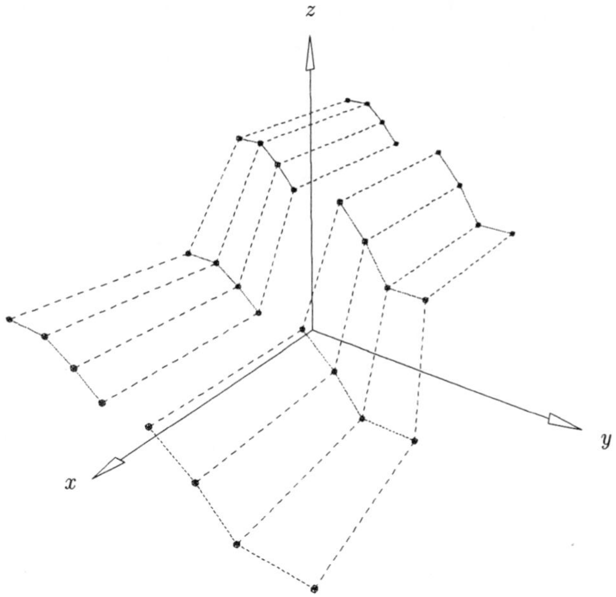

(a)

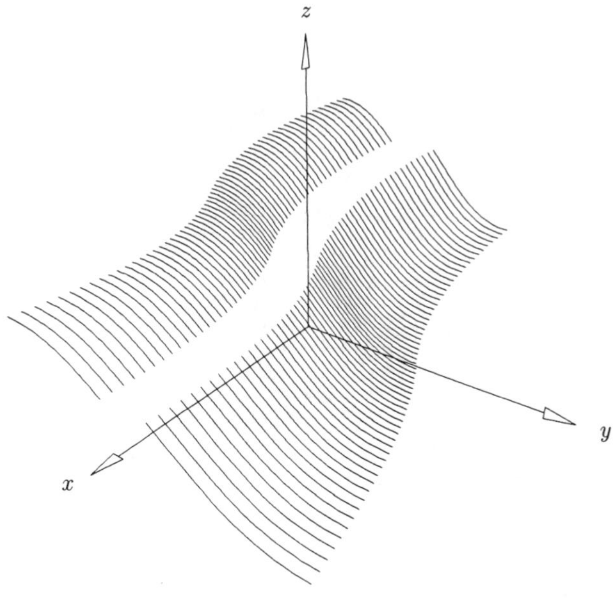

(b)

Figure 5.12. Splitting the surface in Figure 5.11 in the v direction at $u = 2/5$. (a) The control net of the split surface; (b) the split surface.

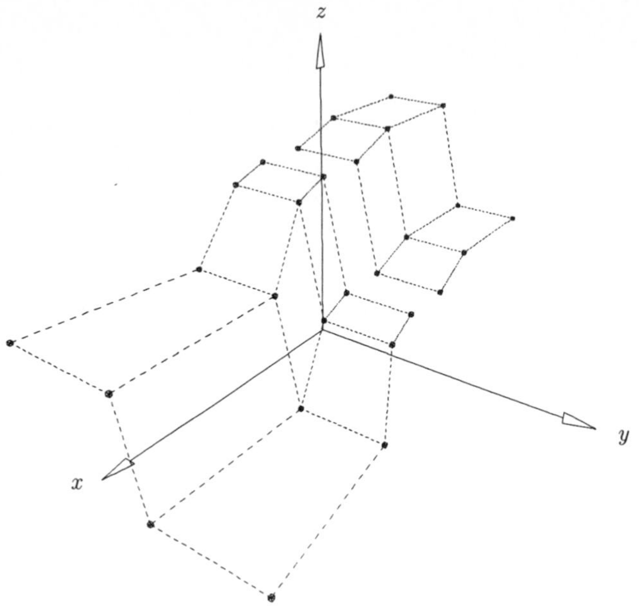

(a)

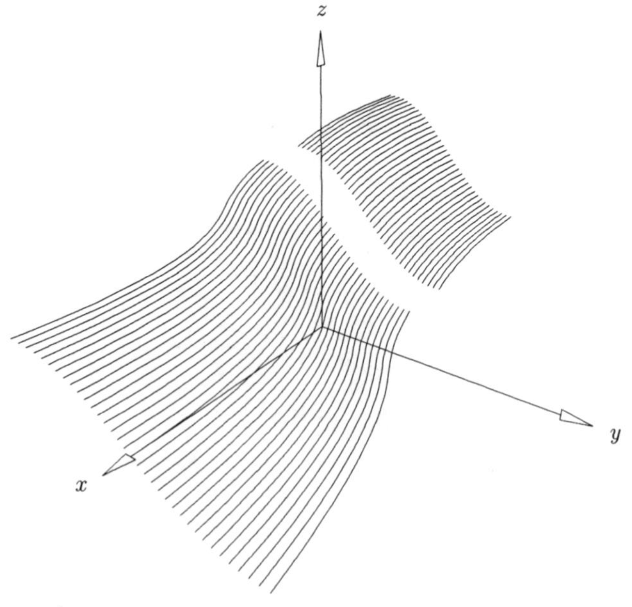

(b)

Figure 5.13. Splitting the surface in Figure 5.11 in the u direction at $v = {}^7\!/_{10}$. (a) The control net of the split surface; (b) the split surface.

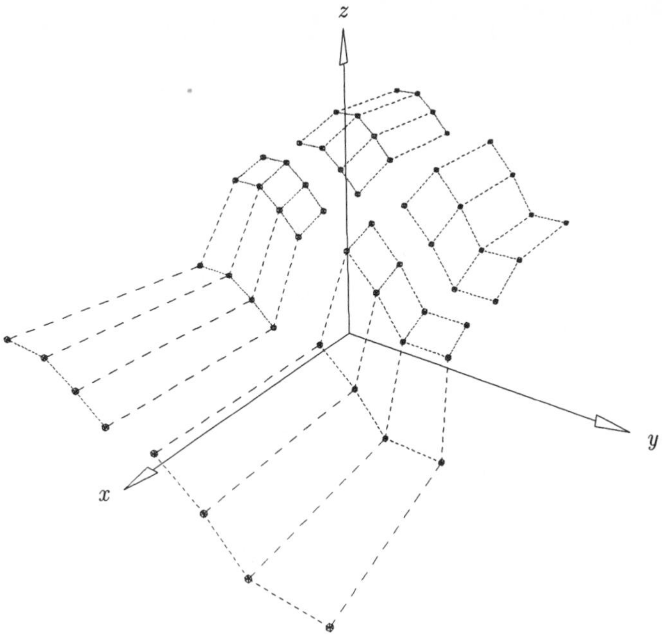

(a)

Figure 5.14. Splitting the surface in Figure 5.11 in both u and v directions at $u = 2/5$ and $v = 7/10$. (a) The control net of the split surface; (b) the split surface.

- Curve extraction: To extract the isoparametric curve, $\mathbf{C}^w_{\bar{u}}(v)$, we must do p $\bar{u}$ knot insertions on each of the $m+1$ columns of control points, i.e., a total of $p(m+1)$ knot insertions; this yields the $\{\mathbf{Q}^w_j(\bar{u})\}$ of Eq. (4.16). Extracting a curve, $\mathbf{C}^w_{\bar{v}}(u)$, requires $q(n+1)$ knot insertions; Figure 5.15 shows an example of this;

- Surface evaluation: Inserting $\bar{u}$ p times and $\bar{v}$ q times causes the surface point, $\mathbf{S}(\bar{u},\bar{v})$, to become a corner control point of the resulting four subsurfaces. A corner cutting algorithm similar to Algorithm A5.2 can be developed. Either $\bar{u}$ or $\bar{v}$ may be inserted first, but as was the case for Bézier surface evaluation using the deCasteljau algorithm, the computational complexity is order-dependent if $p \neq q$ (see Eqs. [1.25] and [1.26]). Hence, we can compute $\mathbf{S}(\bar{u},\bar{v})$ with either

  - $p(q+1)$ $\bar{u}$ knot insertions, plus q $\bar{v}$ knot insertions;
  - $q(p+1)$ $\bar{v}$ knot insertions, plus p $\bar{u}$ knot insertions.

  Using corner point derivative formulas (for example, Eqs. [3.24], [4.24], [4.25], and [4.26]), the partial derivatives and normal vectors from all four directions (left and right for both u and v) are obtained.

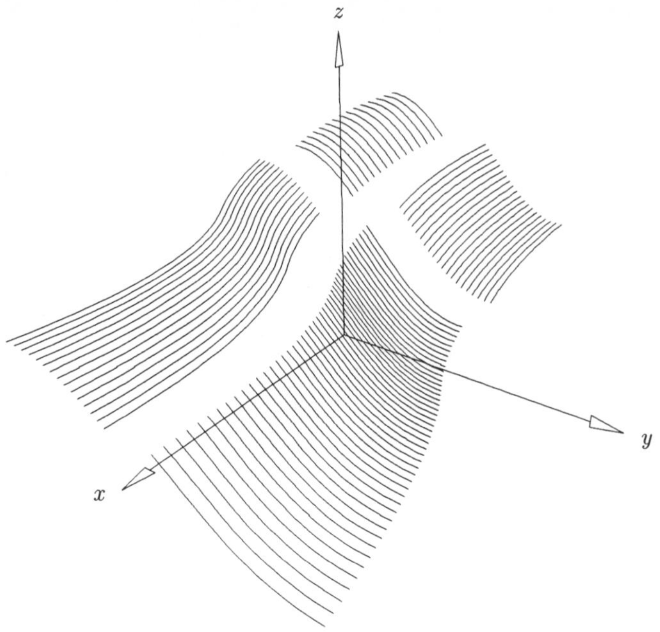

(b)

Figure 5.14. (*Continued.*)

5.3 Knot Refinement

Knot insertion concerned itself with inserting a single knot, possibly multiple times. It is often necessary to insert many knots at once; this is called *knot refinement.* To state the problem, let $\mathbf{C}^w(u) = \sum_{i=0}^{n} N_{i,p}(u)\mathbf{P}_i^w$ be defined on the knot vector $U = \{u_0, \ldots, u_m\}$, and let $X = \{x_0, \ldots, x_r\}$ satisfy $x_i \le x_{i+1}$ and $u_0 < x_i < u_m$ for all i. The elements of X are to be inserted into U, and the corresponding new set of control points, $\{\mathbf{Q}_i^w\}$, $i = 0, \ldots, n+r+1$, is to be computed. New knots, x_i, should be repeated in X with their multiplicities; e.g., if x and y $(x < y)$ are to be inserted with multiplicities 2 and 3, respectively, then $X = \{x, x, y, y, y\}$. Clearly, knot refinement can be accomplished by multiple applications of knot insertion. However, we distinguish the two problems here because there exist more efficient algorithms for knot refinement (see [Cohe80; Boeh85a, 85b; Lych85]).

The applications of knot refinement include:

- decomposition of B-spline curves and surfaces into their constituent (Bézier) polynomial pieces – we elaborate on this later;
- merging of two or more knot vectors in order to obtain a set of curves which are defined on one common knot vector; as we see in subsequent chapters, this is important in constructing certain types of surfaces;

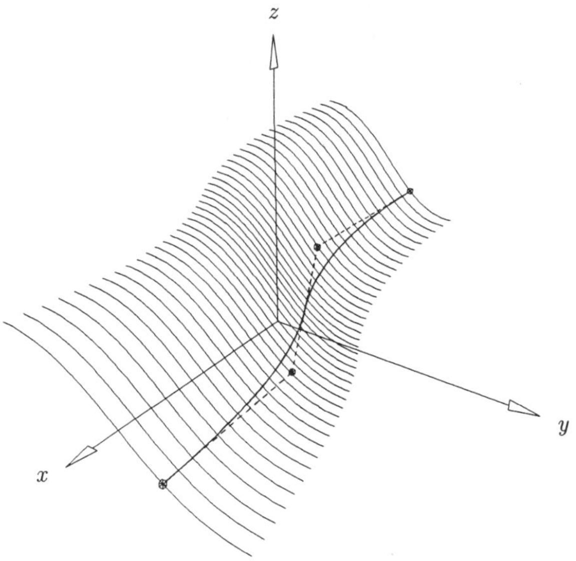

Figure 5.15. Extracting a surface isoparametric curve via knot insertion.

- obtaining polygonal (polyhedral) approximations to curves (surfaces); refining knot vectors brings the control polygon (net) closer to the curve (surface), and in the limit the polygon (net) converges to the curve (surface). A proof of this is found in [Lane80; DeBo87]. Figures 5.16b and 5.16c show one and two midpoint knot refinements applied to the cubic curve of Figure 5.16a (a new knot is inserted at the midpoint of each knot span). Figures 5.17a to 5.17c show three midpoint knot refinements to the surface of Figure 5.9, in the u-, v-, and in both directions, respectively.

We require no additional mathematics to develop an algorithm for knot refinement; it is really just a software problem. The solution steps are:

1. find indices a and b such that $u_a \leq x_i < u_b$ for all i;
2. from Eqs. (5.14) and (5.18) it follows that the control points $\mathbf{P}_0^w, \ldots, \mathbf{P}_{a-p}^w$ and $\mathbf{P}_{b-1}^w \ldots, \mathbf{P}_n^w$ do not change; therefore, copy these to the appropriate $\mathbf{Q}_i^w$ locations, leaving room for the $r+p+b-a-1$ new control points;
3. denote the new knot vector by $\bar{U}$ (U merged with X); copy the knots on either end which do not change;
4. go into a loop and
   4.1. compute the new control points;
   4.2. merge the elements from U and X into $\bar{U}$;

   the loop can work forward (starting at $\mathbf{Q}_{a-p+1}^w$) or backward (starting at $\mathbf{Q}_{b+r-1}^w$).

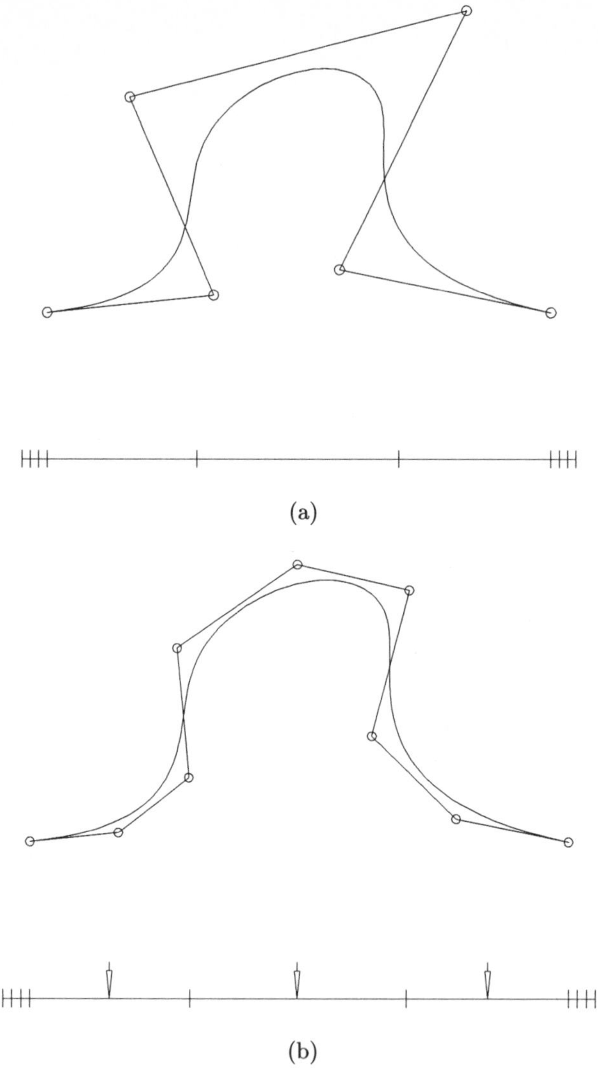

Figure 5.16. Curve refinement. (a) Cubic curve defined on $\{0,0,0,0,{}^{3}\!/_{10},{}^{7}\!/_{10},1,1,1,1\}$; (b) the first midpoint knot refinement; (c) the second midpoint knot refinement.

Algorithm `A5.4` is by Boehm and Prautzsch [Boeh85a]. It works backward and overwrites intermediate control points while inserting a knot. `Ubar` is the new knot vector, $\bar{U}$.

```
ALGORITHM A5.4
  RefineKnotVectCurve(n,p,U,Pw,X,r,Ubar,Qw)
    { /*  Refine curve knot vector  */
      /*  Input:  n,p,U,Pw,X,r  */
```

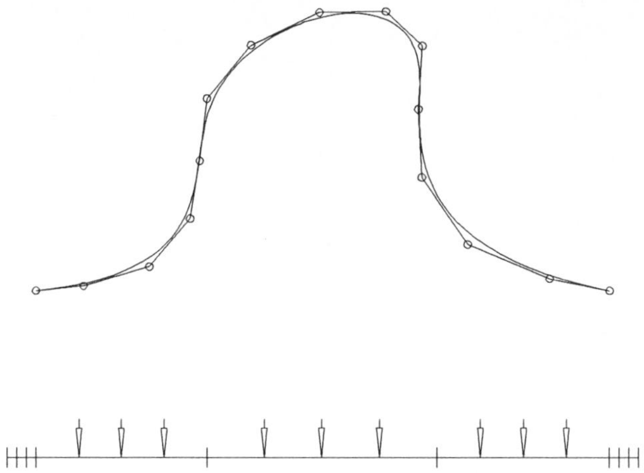

(c)

Figure 5.16. (*Continued.*)

```
   /*  Output: Ubar,Qw  */
m = n+p+1;
a = FindSpan(n,p,X[0],U);    /* Algorithm A2.1 */
b = FindSpan(n,p,X[r],U);
b = b+1;
for (j=0; j<=a-p; j++)   Qw[j] = Pw[j];
for (j=b-1; j<=n; j++)   Qw[j+r+1] = Pw[j];
for (j=0; j<=a; j++)     Ubar[j] = U[j];
for (j=b+p; j<=m; j++)   Ubar[j+r+1] = U[j];
i = b+p-1;     k = b+p+r;
for (j=r; j>=0; j--)
  {
  while (X[j] <= U[i] && i > a)
    {
    Qw[k-p-1] = Pw[i-p-1];
    Ubar[k] = U[i];
    k = k-1;     i = i-1;
    }
  Qw[k-p-1] = Qw[k-p];
  for (l=1; l<=p; l++)
    {
    ind = k-p+l;
    alfa = Ubar[k+l]-X[j];
    if (abs(alfa) == 0.0)
      Qw[ind-1] = Qw[ind];
    else
```

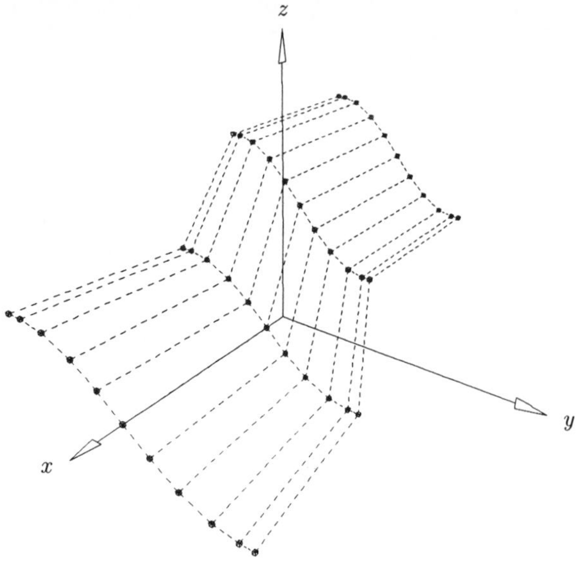

(a)

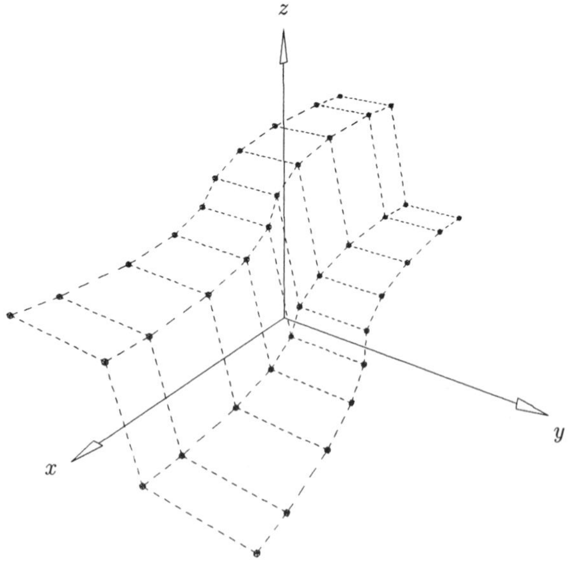

(b)

Figure 5.17. Refining the surface in Figure 5.9. (a) The third midpoint refinement in the u direction; (b) the second midpoint refinement in the v direction; (c) the third refinement in the u direction and second in the v direction.

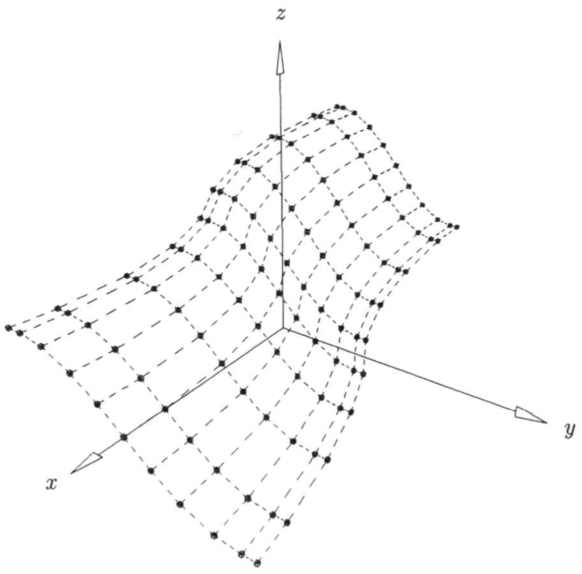

(c)

Figure 5.17. (*Continued.*)

```
          {
          alfa = alfa/(Ubar[k+l]-U[i-p+l]);
          Qw[ind-1] = alfa*Qw[ind-1] + (1.0-alfa)*Qw[ind];
          }
        }
      Ubar[k] = X[j];
      k = k-1;
      }
  }
```

Let $\mathbf{S}^w(u,v) = \sum_{i=0}^{n}\sum_{j=0}^{m} N_{i,p}(u)N_{j,q}(v)\mathbf{P}_{i,j}^w$ be a NURBS surface on U and V. A U knot vector refinement is accomplished by simply applying Algorithm A5.4 to the $m+1$ columns of control points. A V refinement requires $n+1$ applications of Algorithm A5.3. The algorithm can be organized so that redundant operations are eliminated (e.g., the values of the alfas in the last for-loop are the same for each of the $m+1$ columns of control points). A sketch of the algorithm is:

```
ALGORITHM A5.5
  RefineKnotVectSurface(n,p,U,m,q,V,Pw,X,r,dir,Ubar,Vbar,Qw)
    { /*  Refine surface knot vector  */
      /*  Input:  n,p,U,m,q,V,Pw,X,r,dir  */
      /*  Output: Ubar,Vbar,Qw  */
```

```
if (dir == U_DIRECTION)
  {
  find indexes a and b;
  initialize Ubar;
  copy V into Vbar;
            /* Save unaltered ctrl pts */
  for (row=0; row<=m; row++)
    {
    for (k=0; k<=a-p; k++)  Qw[k][row] = Pw[k][row];
    for (k=b-1; k<=n; k++)  Qw[k+r+1][row] = Pw[k][row];
    }
  for (j=r; j>=0; j--)
    {
    while (X[j]<=U[i] && i>a)
      {
      compute Ubar;
      for ( row ...  )  Qw[k-p-1][row] = Pw[i-p-1][row];
      k = k-1;    i = i-1;
      }
    for ( row ...  )   Qw[k-p-1][row] = Qw[k-p][row];
    for (l=1; l<=p; l++)
      {
      ind = k-p+l;
      compute alfa;
      if (abs(alfa) == 0.0)
        for ( row ...  )   Qw[ind-1][row] = Qw[ind][row];
      else
        {
        compute alfa;
        for ( row ...  )
          Qw[ind-1][row] =
             alfa*Qw[ind-1][row]+(1.0-alfa)*Qw[ind][row];
        }
      }
    Ubar[k] = X[j];    k = k-1;
    }
  }
if (dir == V_DIRECTION)
  {
  /* Similar code as above with u and v directional
    parameters switched */
  }
}
```

An important application of knot refinement is the problem of decomposing a NURBS curve into its constituent (four-dimensional) polynomial segments. This is required when converting a NURBS curve to another spline form, e.g., to the IGES Parametric Spline Curve, Entity type 112 [IGE93]. In such a conversion, the first step is to decompose the curve into its piecewise Bézier form. The Bézier control points of the segments are obtained by inserting each interior knot until it has multiplicity p. This is done in two steps:

1. pass through U and build the refinement vector X;
2. call Algorithm `A5.4`.

Figures 5.18a and 5.18b show a cubic curve and its corresponding basis functions; Figures 5.19a and 5.19b show the same curve and its basis functions after decomposition. The control points in Figure 5.19a are the Bézier control points of the curve's segments. Figures 5.20a, 5.20b, 5.21a, and 5.21b show the decomposition of a surface.

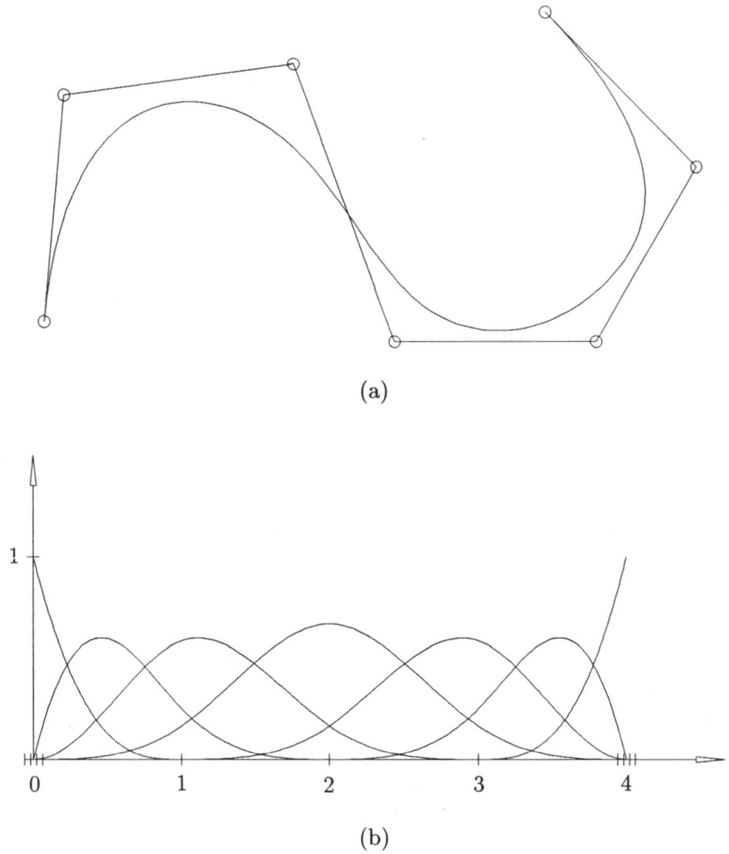

Figure 5.18. A cubic curve. (a) The curve and its control polygon; (b) basis functions defined over $\{0,0,0,0,1,2,3,4,4,4,4\}$.

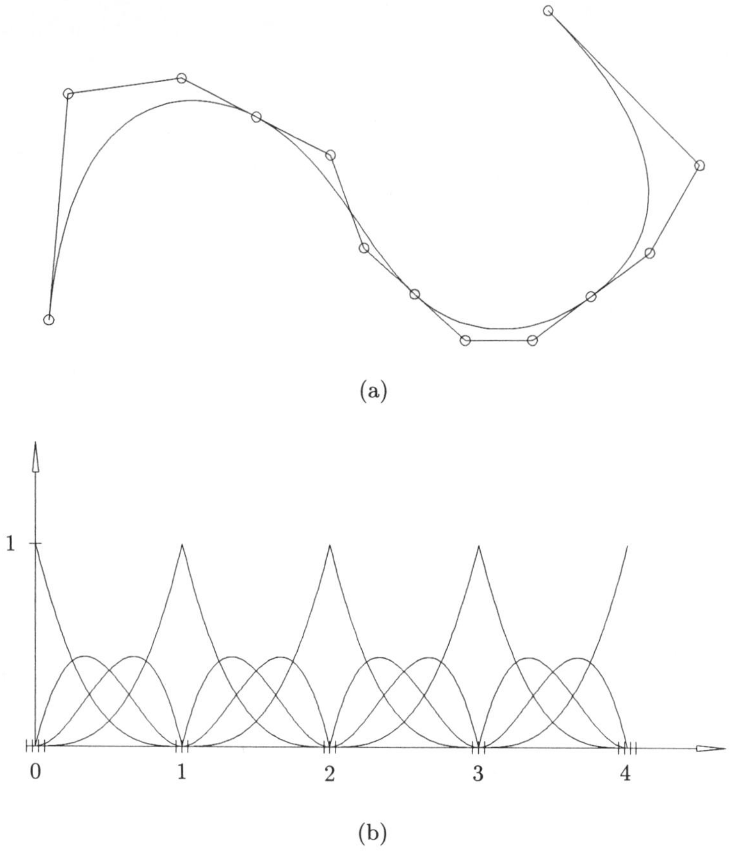

Figure 5.19. Decomposition of the curve in Figure 5.18 into a piecewise Bézier curve via knot refinement. (a) The decomposed curve and its control polygon; (b) basis functions after inserting knots 1, 2, and 3 two times each.

We now give an algorithm which extracts all the Bézier segments of a curve, working from left to right, in an efficient manner. For convenience we drop the w superscipts from control points. Figures 5.22a through 5.22d best explain the algorithm. Let $\mathbf{C}(u) = \sum_{i=0}^{5} N_{i,3}(u)\mathbf{P}_i$ be a cubic curve with two distinct interior knots, and let $\mathbf{Q}_k^j$ be the kth control point of the jth Bézier segment, $k = 0, \ldots, p$ and $j = 0, 1, 2$. Notice in Figures 5.22b and 5.22c that while the rightmost Bézier control points of the zeroth segment, $\mathbf{Q}_2^0$ and $\mathbf{Q}_3^0$, are being computed (via knot insertion), the leftmost Bézier points of the first segment, $\mathbf{Q}_0^1$ and $\mathbf{Q}_1^1$, are also being computed and stored.

Another major reduction in computation, as compared with using general knot refinement, is achieved by examining the computation of the knot insertion alphas (Eq. [5.15]). Assume $[u_a, u_b]$ is the current segment being processed, where a and b are the indices of the rightmost occurrences of knots u_a and u_b.

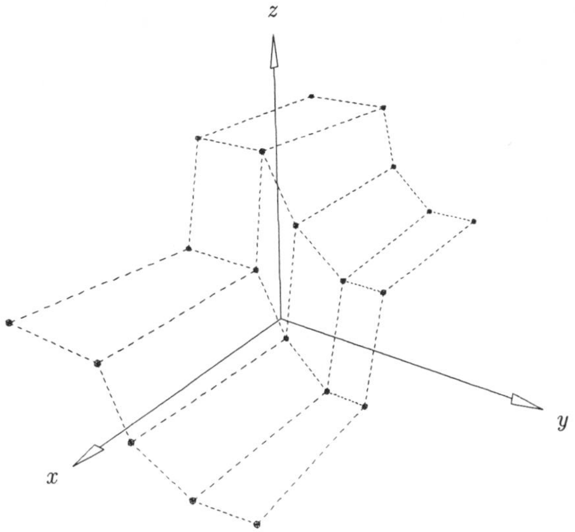

(a)

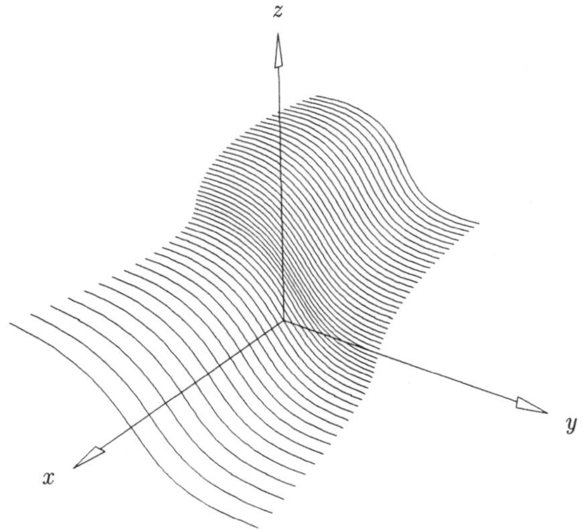

(b)

Figure 5.20. A (cubic × quadratic) surface to be decomposed. (a) The control net; (b) the surface defined over $U = \{0,0,0,0,{}^3\!/_5,1,1,1,1\}$ and $V = \{0,0,0,{}^2\!/_5,1,1,1\}$.

Then, when we start to insert u_b the knot vector has the form (locally)

$$\ldots, \underbrace{u_{a-p+1} = \cdots = u_a}_{p}, \underbrace{u_{b-s+1} = \cdots = u_b}_{s} \tag{5.22}$$

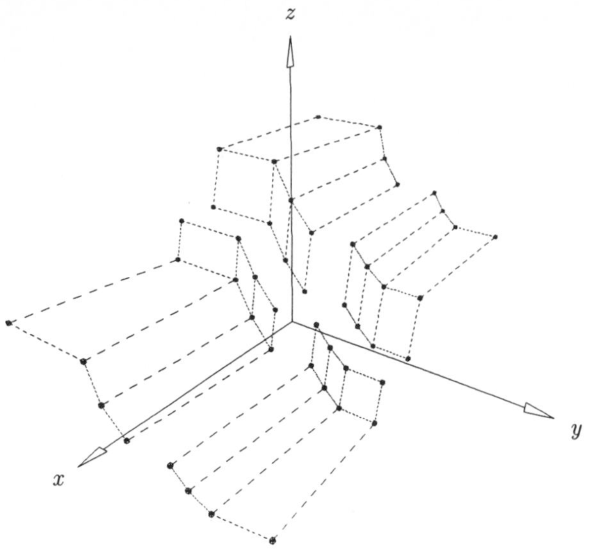

(a)

Figure 5.21. Piecewise Bézier patch decomposition via knot refinement. (a) The control nets; (b) Bézier surface patches.

where s is the original multiplicity of u_b. By Eq. (5.15) the insertion of u_b $p-s$ more times generates the triangular table

$$\begin{array}{llll}
\alpha_{b-p+1,1} & & & \\
 & \alpha_{b-p+2,2} & & \\
\alpha_{b-p+2,1} & & & \\
\vdots & & \cdots & \alpha_{b-s,p-s} \\
\alpha_{b-s-1,1} & & & \\
 & \alpha_{b-s,2} & & \\
\alpha_{b-s,1} & & &
\end{array}$$

Examining Eqs. (5.15) and (5.22) reveals two facts:

- $\alpha_{b-p+i,1} = \alpha_{b-p+i+1,2} = \cdots = \alpha_{b-s,p-s-i+1}$ for $i = 1, \ldots, p-s$; the αs are equal along southeasterly pointing diagonals;
- the numerator in Eq. (5.15) remains the same, namely $u_b - u_a$, for the entire set of $\alpha_{i,j}$s.

To illustrate this, consider the example shown in Figure 5.23. After the first segment is extracted, the knot vector takes the form

$$U = \{0,0,0,0,0,\ ^1\!/_5,\ ^1\!/_5,\ ^1\!/_5,\ ^1\!/_5,\ ^2\!/_5,\ ^3\!/_5,\ ^4\!/_5, 1,1,1,1,1\}$$

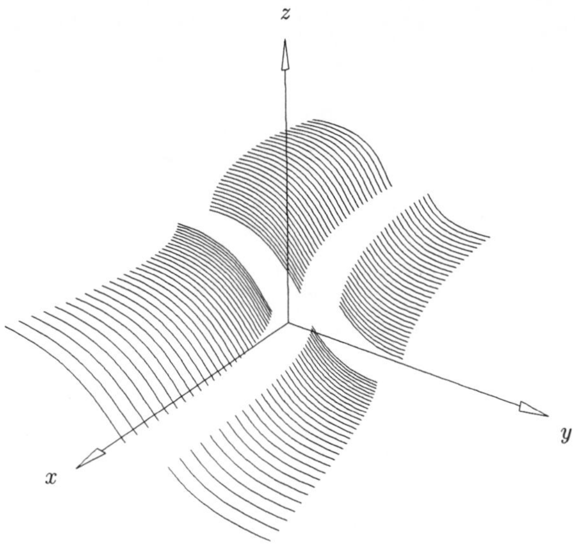

(b)

Figure 5.21. (*Continued.*)

When the second segment is computed, $a = 8$ and $b = 9$, and the following αs are generated

$$r = 1 \qquad\qquad r = 2 \qquad\qquad r = 3$$

$$\alpha_{6,1} = \frac{u_9 - u_6}{u_{10} - u_6} = \frac{0.2}{0.4}$$

$$\alpha_{7,2} = \frac{u_9 - u_7}{u_{10} - u_7} = \frac{0.2}{0.4}$$

$$\alpha_{7,1} = \frac{u_9 - u_7}{u_{11} - u_7} = \frac{0.2}{0.6} \qquad\qquad \alpha_{8,3} = \frac{u_9 - u_8}{u_{10} - u_8} = \frac{0.2}{0.4}$$

$$\alpha_{8,2} = \frac{u_9 - u_8}{u_{11} - u_8} = \frac{0.2}{0.6}$$

$$\alpha_{8,1} = \frac{u_9 - u_8}{u_{12} - u_8} = \frac{0.2}{0.8}$$

Notice that the αs along southeasterly diagonals are ${}^{0.2}/_{0.4}$, ${}^{0.2}/_{0.6}$, and ${}^{0.2}/_{0.8}$, respectively, and that the numerator remains 0.2.

Algorithm `A5.6` decomposes a NURBS curve and returns `nb` Bézier segments. `Qw[j][k]` is the kth control point of the jth segment. The local array `alphas[]` contains the alphas, with their indices shifted to start at 0.

```
ALGORITHM A5.6
  DecomposeCurve(n,p,U,Pw,nb,Qw)
    { /* Decompose curve into Bézier segments */
```

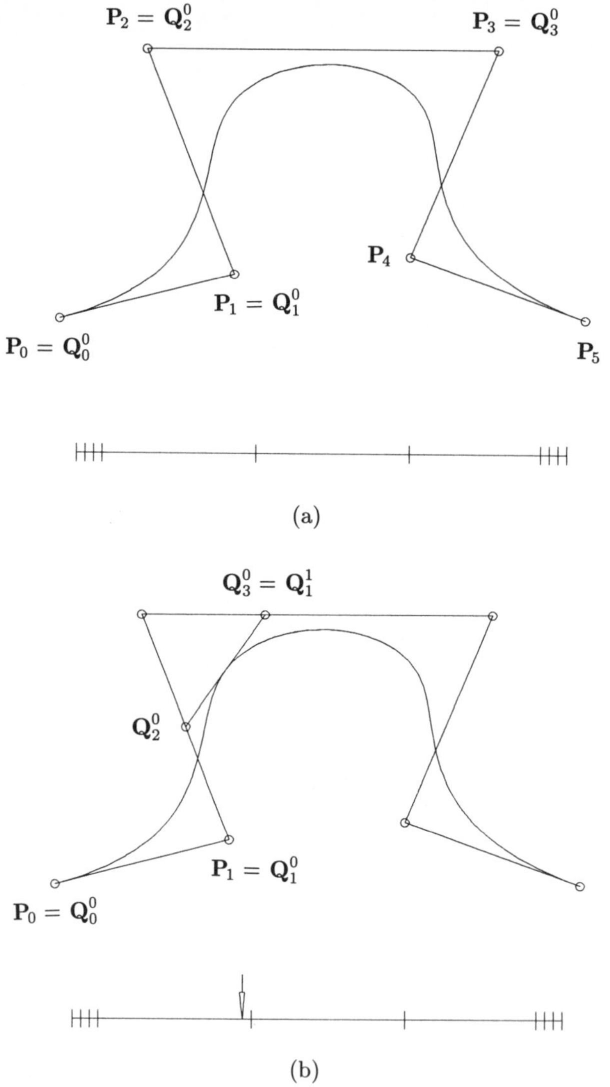

Figure 5.22. On-the-fly curve decomposition. (a) The original cubic curve; (b) first knot inserted; (c) second knot inserted; (d) preparation for the second segment.

```
    /*  Input:  n,p,U,Pw  */
    /*  Output: nb,Qw  */
m = n+p+1;
a = p;
b = p+1;
nb = 0;
for (i=0; i<=p; i++)   Qw[nb][i] = Pw[i];
```

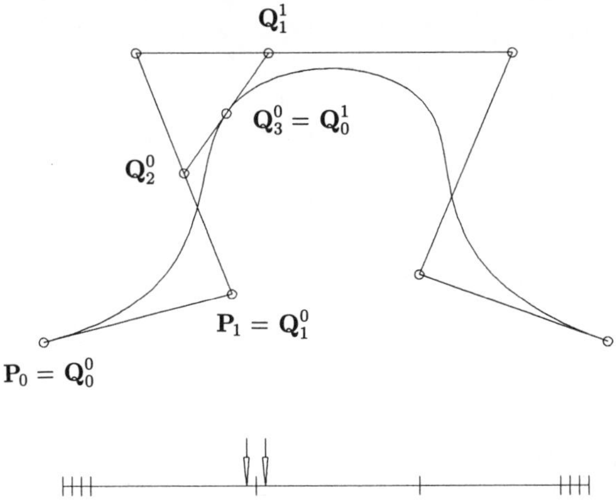

(c)

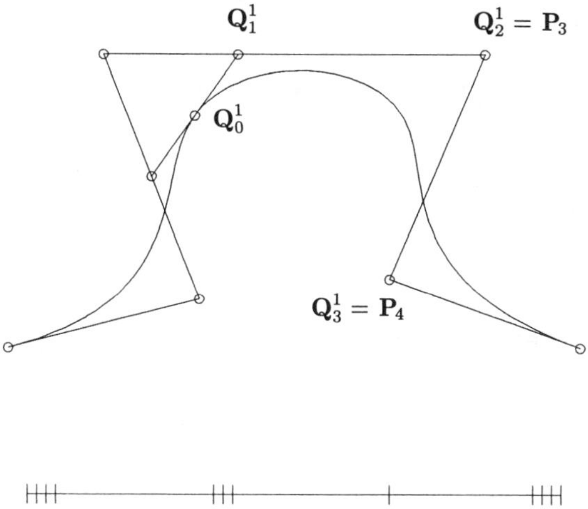

(d)

Figure 5.22. (*Continued.*)

```
while (b < m)
  {
  i = b;
  while (b < m && U[b+1] == U[b])   b++;
  mult = b-i+1;
  if (mult < p)
    {
    numer = U[b]-U[a];   /* Numerator of alpha */
```

```
          /* Compute and store alphas */
        for (j=p; j>mult; j--)
          alphas[j-mult-1] = numer/(U[a+j]-U[a]);
        r = p-mult;   /* Insert knot r times */
        for (j=1; j<=r j++)
          {
          save = r-j;
          s = mult+j;   /* This many new points */
          for (k=p; k>=s; k--)
            {
            alpha = alphas[k-s];
            Qw[nb][k] = alpha*Qw[nb][k] + (1.0-alpha)*Qw[nb][k-1];
            }
          if (b < m)            /* Control point of */
            Qw[nb+1][save] = Qw[nb][p];  /* next segment */
          }
        }
      nb = nb+1;   /* Bézier segment completed */
      if (b < m)
        {   /* Initialize for next segment */
        for (i=p-mult; i<=p; i++)   Qw[nb][i] = Pw[b-p+i];
        a = b;
        b = b+1;
        }
      }
    }
```

Algorithm `A5.6` is an ideal interface between a NURBS system and a system (hardware or software) which displays Bézier curves. With modifications, Algorithm `A5.6` computes the Bézier segments on-the-fly, passes each one down for display, and overwrites each with the next. Nothing is returned. These modifications are:

- remove `nb` and `Qw` from the argument list;
- use local arrays `Qw[]` (length $p+1$) and `NextQw[]` (length $p-1$); `NextQw` is used to store the leftmost control points of the next segment;
- after a segment has been computed (see the comment in the code, `/* Bézier segment completed */`) pass it down for display;
- after displaying a segment, overwrite it with points from `NextQw[]` and `Pw[]`.

An example is shown in Figures 5.24a–5.24c; for more detail see [Pieg91b].

Algorithm `A5.7` shows the organization of a surface decomposition. The routine computes a Bézier strip, i.e., a NURBS surface that is Bézier in one direction and B-spline in the other. The routine must be called twice, once in the u direction to get the Bézier strips, and then the strips must be fed into the routine in the v direction to get the Bézier patches.

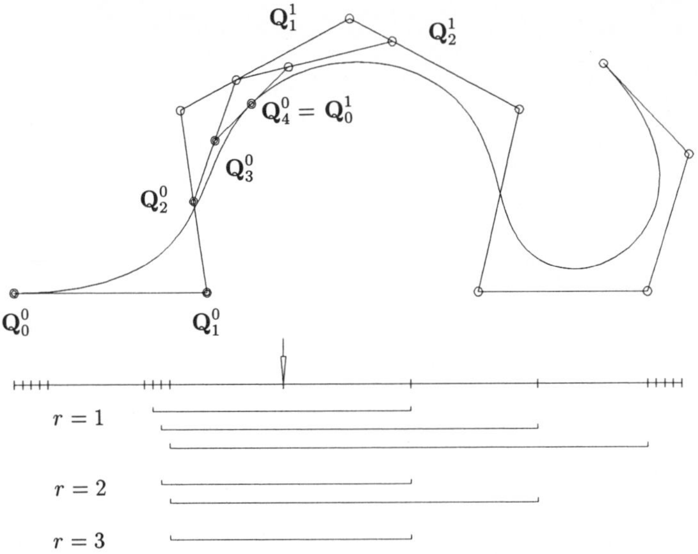

Figure 5.23. Ratios for the alphas used to compute the second Bézier segment of a quartic curve.

```
ALGORITHM A5.7
  DecomposeSurface(n,p,U,m,q,V,Pw,dir,nb,Qw)
    { /* Decompose surface into Bézier patches */
      /* Input:  n,p,U,m,q,V,Pw,dir  */
      /* Output: nb,Qw  */
    if (dir == U_DIRECTION)
```

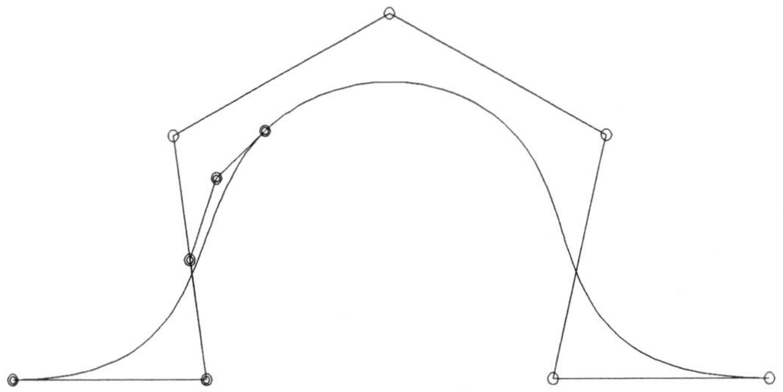

(a)

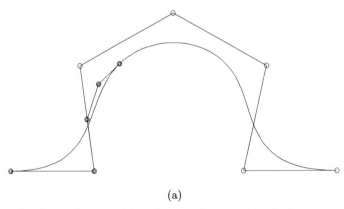

Figure 5.24. On-the-fly decomposition of a quartic curve. (a) The first Bézier segment; (b) the second Bézier segment; (c) the third Bézier segment.

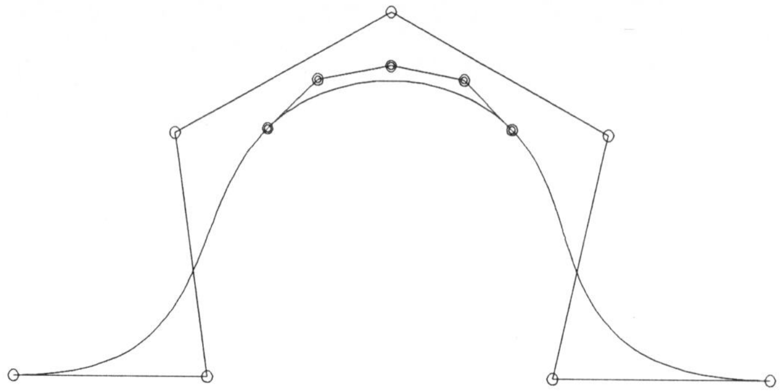

(b)

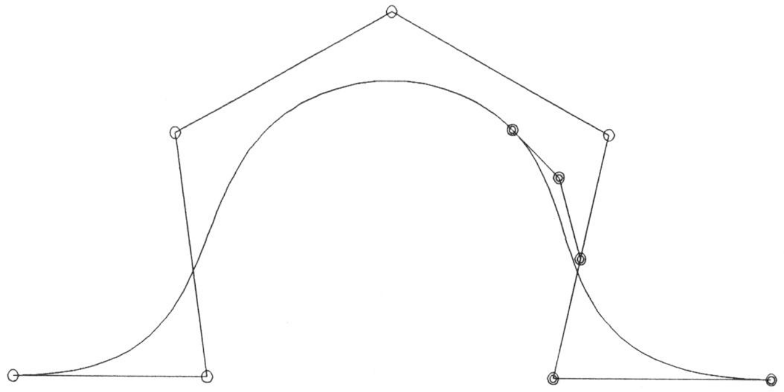

(c)

Figure 5.24. (*Continued.*)

```
{
a=p;    b=p+1;
nb=0;
for (i=0; i<=p; i++)
  for (row=0; row<=m; row++)
    Qw[nb][i][row] = Pw[i][row];
while (b<m)
  {
  get mult;
  if ( mult<p )
    {
    get the numerator and the alfas;
    for (j=1; j<=p-mult; j++)
      {
      save= ...;
      s = ...;
```

```
            for(k=p; k>=s; k--)
              {
              get alfa;
              for ( row ...  )
                Qw[nb][k][row] = alfa*Qw[nb][k][row]
                                   +(1.0-alfa)*Qw[nb][k-1][row];
              }
            if ( b<m )
              for ( row ...  )
                Qw[nb+1][save][row] = Qw[nb][p][row];
            }
          }
        nb=nb+1;
        if ( b<m )
          {
          for (i=p-mult; i<=p; i++)
            for ( row ...  )
              Qw[nb][i][row] = Pw[b-p+i][row];
          a = b;    b = b+1;
          }
        }
      }
    if (dir == V_DIRECTION)
      {
      /* Similar code as above with u- and v-directional
         parameters switched */
      }
    }
```

An example is shown in Figure 5.25.

5.4 Knot Removal

Knot removal is the reverse process of knot insertion. Let

$$\mathbf{C}^w(u) = \sum_{i=0}^{n} N_{i,p}(u)\,\mathbf{P}_i^w \tag{5.23}$$

be defined on U, and let u_r be an interior knot of multiplicity s in U; end knots are not removed. Let U_t denote the knot vector obtained by removing u_r t times from U $(1 \le t \le s)$. We say that u_r is t times *removable* if $\mathbf{C}^w(u)$ has a precise representation of the form

$$\mathbf{C}^w(u) = \sum_{i=0}^{n-t} \bar{N}_{i,p}(u)\,\mathbf{Q}_i^w \tag{5.24}$$

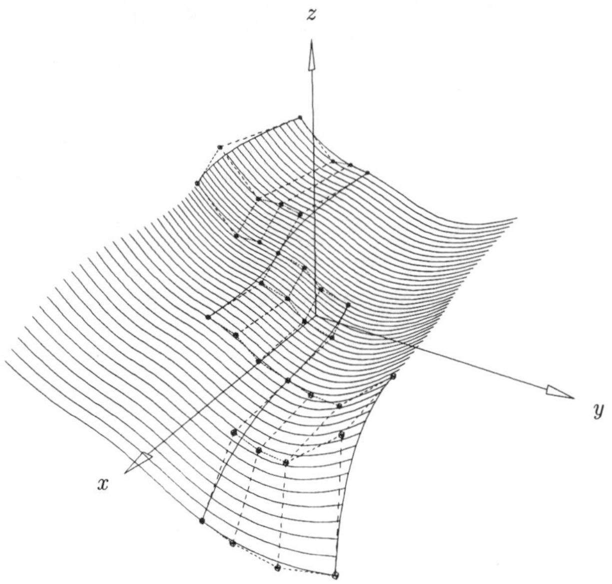

Figure 5.25. Surface decomposition on the fly; three Bézier patches are shown.

where $\bar{N}_{i,p}(u)$ are the basis functions on U_t, that is, Eqs. (5.23) and (5.24) geometrically and parametrically represent the same curve.

From earlier chapters we know that the basis functions $N_{i,p}(u)$ which are nonzero at u_r are only C^{p-s} continuous there. Furthermore, although one does not generally expect more than C^{p-s} continuity of the curve, the control points $\mathbf{P}_i^w$ can lie in positions such that the $(p-s+1)$th (or even higher) derivative is continuous. Hence, the knot u_r is t times removable if and only if the curve $\mathbf{C}^w(u)$ is C^{p-s+t} continuous at $u = u_r$. It is important to note that the continuity must be with respect to $\mathbf{C}^w(u)$, not its projection $\mathbf{C}(u)$ which can be continuous even though $\mathbf{C}^w(u)$ is not.

A knot removal algorithm must do two things:

- determine if a knot is removable and how many times;
- compute the new control points, $\mathbf{Q}_i^w$.

Details can be found in [Till92].

Knot removal is an important utility in several applications:

- The standard method to convert a spline curve or surface represented in power basis form to B-spline form is:
  - convert the segments (patches) to Bézier form;
  - obtain a B-spline representation by piecing the Bézier segments together and using knot vectors in which all interior knots have multiplicity equal to the degree;

- remove as many knots (and hence control points) as the continuity of the spline curve (surface) allows;

- When interactively shaping B-spline curves and surfaces, knots are sometimes added to increase the number of control points which can be modified. When control points are moved, the level of continuity at the knots can change (increase or decrease); hence, after modification is completed knot removal can be invoked in order to obtain the most compact representation of the curve or surface;

- It is sometimes useful to link B-spline curves together to form composite curves. The first step is to make the curves compatible, i.e., of common degree, and the end parameter value of the ith curve is equal to the start parameter of the $(i+1)$th curve. Once this is done, the composition is accomplished by using interior knots of multiplicity equal to the common degree of the curves. Knot removal can then be invoked in order to remove unnecessary knots.

We describe the knot removal process with an example. As usual, the algorithm operates on the four coordinates of the control points, but we drop the w superscript for the sake of notational convenience. Consider the cubic curve of Figure 5.26. Assume the original curve is defined by $\{\mathbf{P}_0^0, \ldots, \mathbf{P}_6^0\}$ and $U = \{u_0, \ldots, u_{10}\}$, where the superscript on the control points denotes the step number in the knot removal process, and the knots are $u_0 = \cdots = u_3 = 0$, $u_4 = u_5 = u_6 = 1$, and $u_7 = \cdots = u_{10} = 2$. Consider removing $u = 1 (= u_6)$.

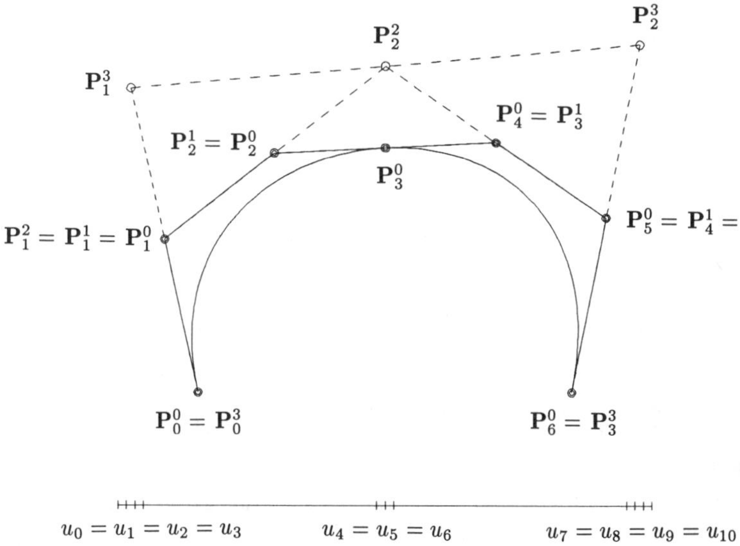

Figure 5.26. Knot removal from a cubic curve with a triple knot.

The first derivative is continuous if and only if

$$\frac{p}{u_6 - u_3}(\mathbf{P}_3^0 - \mathbf{P}_2^0) = \frac{p}{u_7 - u_4}(\mathbf{P}_4^0 - \mathbf{P}_3^0)$$

Setting $u = u_4 = u_6$ and rearranging terms yields

$$\mathbf{P}_3^0 = \frac{u - u_3}{u_7 - u_3}\mathbf{P}_4^0 + \frac{u_7 - u}{u_7 - u_3}\mathbf{P}_2^0$$

Using $\mathbf{P}_2^0 = \mathbf{P}_2^1$ and $\mathbf{P}_4^0 = \mathbf{P}_3^1$ yields

$$\mathbf{P}_3^0 = \alpha_3 \mathbf{P}_3^1 + (1 - \alpha_3)\mathbf{P}_2^1 \qquad \alpha_3 = \frac{u - u_3}{u_7 - u_3} \tag{5.25}$$

Equation (5.25) is just the equation for inserting $u = 1$ into the knot vector having 1 as a double knot (u_7 is u_6 in that knot vector). Furthermore, the second derivative at $u = 1$ is continuous if and only if the knot $u = 1$ can be removed a second time. It can be removed when

$$\begin{aligned} \mathbf{P}_2^1 &= \alpha_2 \mathbf{P}_2^2 + (1 - \alpha_2)\mathbf{P}_1^2 \\ \mathbf{P}_3^1 &= \alpha_3 \mathbf{P}_3^2 + (1 - \alpha_3)\mathbf{P}_2^2 \end{aligned} \tag{5.26}$$

with

$$\alpha_i = \frac{u - u_i}{u_{i+p+2} - u_i} \qquad i = 2, 3$$

Finally, the third derivative is continuous if and only if $u = 1$ can be removed a third time, which implies that

$$\begin{aligned} \mathbf{P}_1^2 &= \alpha_1 \mathbf{P}_1^3 + (1 - \alpha_1)\mathbf{P}_0^3 \\ \mathbf{P}_2^2 &= \alpha_2 \mathbf{P}_2^3 + (1 - \alpha_2)\mathbf{P}_1^3 \\ \mathbf{P}_3^2 &= \alpha_3 \mathbf{P}_3^3 + (1 - \alpha_3)\mathbf{P}_2^3 \end{aligned} \tag{5.27}$$

with

$$\alpha_i = \frac{u - u_i}{u_{i+p+3} - u_i} \qquad i = 1, 2, 3$$

Let $n = p - s + 1$, where s is the multiplicity of the knot to be removed. Then note that

- there are no unknowns in Eq. (5.25), $\mathbf{P}_2^2$ is the only unknown in Eq. (5.26), and $\mathbf{P}_1^3$ and $\mathbf{P}_2^3$ are unknown in Eq. (5.27). Knot removal produces n equations in $n - 1$ unknowns;
- knot removal destroys n control points and replaces them with $n - 1$ new control points.

Let us solve Eqs. (5.25) through (5.27). For Eq. (5.25) we compute the right side of the single equation and check to see if it is equal to $\mathbf{P}_3^0$ (to within a meaningful tolerance). If not equal the knot cannot be removed; if it is equal, then the knot and $\mathbf{P}_3^0$ are removed.

From the two equations in Eq. (5.26) we obtain

$$\mathbf{P}_2^2 = \frac{\mathbf{P}_2^1 - (1-\alpha_2)\mathbf{P}_1^2}{\alpha_2} \qquad \mathbf{P}_2^2 = \frac{\mathbf{P}_3^1 - \alpha_3\mathbf{P}_3^2}{1-\alpha_3}$$

If these two values for $\mathbf{P}_2^2$ are within tolerance, then the knot can be removed and $\mathbf{P}_2^1$ and $\mathbf{P}_3^1$ are replaced by $\mathbf{P}_2^2$.

Solving the first and third equations of Eq. (5.27), we obtain

$$\mathbf{P}_1^3 = \frac{\mathbf{P}_1^2 - (1-\alpha_1)\mathbf{P}_0^3}{\alpha_1} \qquad \mathbf{P}_2^3 = \frac{\mathbf{P}_3^2 - \alpha_3\mathbf{P}_3^3}{1-\alpha_3}$$

Then substitute $\mathbf{P}_1^3$ and $\mathbf{P}_2^3$ into the right side of the second of Eqs. (5.27), and check to see if it is within tolerance of $\mathbf{P}_2^2$. If it is, remove the knot and replace $\mathbf{P}_1^2$, $\mathbf{P}_2^2$, and $\mathbf{P}_3^2$ with $\mathbf{P}_1^3$ and $\mathbf{P}_2^3$.

In general, to solve the system of equations start with the first and last equations and work inward, computing the new control points. If the number of equations is even (as in Eq. [5.26]), then the final new control point is computed twice. The knot can be removed if the two values of the control point are within tolerance. If the number of equations is odd (as in Eqs. [5.25] and [5.27]), then all new control points are computed once, and the last two computed are substituted into the middle equation. If the result is within tolerance of the old control point on the left side of the middle equation, then the knot is removable.

We now give general formulas. Let $u = u_r \neq u_{r+1}$ be a knot of multiplicity s, where $1 \leq s \leq p$. The equations for computing the new control points for one removal of u are

$$\mathbf{P}_i^1 = \frac{\mathbf{P}_i^0 - (1-\alpha_i)\mathbf{P}_{i-1}^1}{\alpha_i} \qquad r-p \leq i \leq \frac{1}{2}(2r-p-s-1)$$

$$\mathbf{P}_j^1 = \frac{\mathbf{P}_j^0 - \alpha_j\mathbf{P}_{j+1}^1}{(1-\alpha_j)} \qquad \frac{1}{2}(2r-p-s+2) \leq j \leq r-s \tag{5.28}$$

with
$$\alpha_k = \frac{u-u_k}{u_{k+p+1}-u_k} \qquad k=i,j$$

The simplest way to program Eq. (5.28) is

$$\begin{aligned}
&i = r-p; \;\; j = r-s; \\
&\text{while } (j-i > 0) \\
&\quad \alpha_i = \cdots \\
&\quad \alpha_j = \cdots \\
&\quad \mathbf{P}_i^1 = \cdots \\
&\quad \mathbf{P}_j^1 = \cdots \\
&\quad i = i+1; \;\; j = j-1;
\end{aligned}$$

Now suppose we want to remove $u = u_r$ multiple times. Each time the knot is removed, s and r are decremented (in Eq. [5.28]) and the superscripts on the control points are incremented. Thus, the equations for removing $u = u_r$ the tth time are

$$\mathbf{P}_i^t = \frac{\mathbf{P}_i^{t-1} - (1-\alpha_i)\,\mathbf{P}_{i-1}^t}{\alpha_i} \qquad r-p-t+1 \le i \le \frac{1}{2}(2r-p-s-t)$$

$$\mathbf{P}_j^t = \frac{\mathbf{P}_j^{t-1} - \alpha_j \mathbf{P}_{j+1}^t}{(1-\alpha_j)} \qquad \frac{1}{2}(2r-p-s+t+1) \le j \le r-s+t-1 \tag{5.29}$$

with

$$\alpha_i = \frac{u-u_i}{u_{i+p+t}-u_i} \qquad \alpha_j = \frac{u-u_{j-t+1}}{u_{j+p+1}-u_{j-t+1}}$$

Assume u is to be removed k times. Equation (5.29) can be programmed as

$first = r-p+1;\;\; last = r-s-1;$
for $t = 1,\ldots,k$
  $first = first - 1;\;\; last = last + 1;$
  $i = first;\;\; j = last;$
  while $(j - i > t - 1)$
    $\alpha_i = \cdots$
    $\alpha_j = \cdots$
    $\mathbf{P}_i^t = \cdots$
    $\mathbf{P}_j^t = \cdots$
    $i = i+1;\;\; j = j-1;$

The factor which complicates the implementation of knot removal is that it is generally unknown in advance whether a knot is removable, and if it is, how many times. The (potentially) new control points must be computed in temporary storage, and it is not known in advance how many knots and control points will be in the output. Algorithm `A5.8` tries to remove the knot $u = u_r$ *num* times, where $1 \le num \le s$. It returns t, the actual number of times the knot is removed, and if $t > 0$ it returns the new knot vector and control points. It computes the new control points in place, overwriting the old ones. Only one local array (`temp`) of size $2p+1$ is required to compute the new control points at each step. If removal fails at step t, the control points from step $t-1$ are still intact. At the end, knots and control points are shifted down to fill the gap left by removal. A minimum number of shifts is done. To check for coincident points, a value, `TOL`, and a function, `Distance4D()`, which computes the distance between the points, are used. If the curve is rational we assume the homogeneous representation; in this case, `Distance4D()` computes the four-dimensional distance. The weights are treated as ordinary coordinates. `TOL` has the meaning [Till92]

- if the curve is nonrational (all $w_i = 1$), then one knot removal results in a curve whose deviation from the original curve is less than TOL, on the entire parameter domain;
- if the curve is rational, then the deviation is everywhere less than

$$\frac{\text{TOL}(1+ |\mathbf{P}|_{\max})}{w_{\min}}$$

where $w_{\min}$ is the minimum weight on the original curve, and $|\mathbf{P}|_{\max}$ is the maximum distance of any three-dimensional point on the original curve from the origin. The convex hull property of B-splines is used to compute bounds for $w_{\min}$ and $|\mathbf{P}|_{\max}$. If the desired bound on deviation is d, then TOL should be set to

$$\text{TOL} = \frac{d\, w_{\min}}{1 + |\mathbf{P}|_{\max}} \tag{5.30}$$

```
ALGORITHM A5.8
RemoveCurveKnot(n,p,U,Pw,u,r,s,num,t)
  { /*  Remove knot u (index r) num times.  */
    /*  Input:  n,p,U,Pw,u,r,s,num  */
    /*  Output: t, new knots & ctrl pts in U & Pw  */
  m = n+p+1;
  ord = p+1;
  fout = (2*r-s-p)/2;  /* First control point out */
  last = r-s;
  first = r-p;
  for (t=0; t<num; t++)
    { /* This loop is Eq.(5.28) */
    off = first-1;  /* Diff in index between temp and P */
    temp[0] = Pw[off];   temp[last+1-off] = Pw[last+1];
    i = first;      j=last;
    ii = 1;     jj = last-off;
    remflag = 0;
    while (j-i > t)
      { /* Compute new control points for one removal step */
      alfi = (u-U[i])/(U[i+ord+t]-U[i]);
      alfj = (u-U[j-t])/(U[j+ord]-U[j-t]);
      temp[ii] = (Pw[i]-(1.0-alfi)*temp[ii-1])/alfi;
      temp[jj] = (Pw[j]-alfj*temp[jj+1])/(1.0-alfj);
      i = i+1;    ii = ii+1;
      j = j-1;    jj = jj-1;
      } /* End of while-loop */
    if (j-i < t)  /* Check if knot removable */
      {
      if (Distance4D(temp[ii-1],temp[jj+1]) <= TOL)
        remflag = 1;
```

```
        }
      else
        {
        alfi = (u-U[i])/(U[i+ord+t]-U[i]);
        if (Distance4D(Pw[i],alfi*temp[ii+t+1]
                              +(1.0-alfi)*temp[ii-1]) <= TOL)
          remflag = 1;
        }
      if (remflag == 0)   /* Cannot remove any more knots */
        break;           /* Get out of for-loop */
      else
        {   /* Successful removal. Save new cont.pts. */
        i = first;   j = last;
        while (j-i > t)
          {
          Pw[i] = temp[i-off];   Pw[j] = temp[j-off];
          i = i+1;    j = j-1;
          }
        }
      first = first-1;     last = last+1;
      } /* End of for-loop */
    if (t == 0)    return;
    for (k=r+1; k<=m; k++) U[k-t] = U[k];  /* Shift knots */
    j = fout;   i=j;   /* Pj thru Pi will be overwritten */
    for (k=1; k<t; k++)
      if (Mod(k,2) == 1)     /* k modulo 2 */
        i = i+1;    else    j = j-1;
    for (k=i+1; k<=n; k++)     /* Shift */
      {  Pw[j] = Pw[k];    j = j+1;  }
    return;
    }
```

Table 5.2 shows how the control point array changes for the cubic curve example given in Figure 5.26. The first row shows the contents before entering the for-loop ($0 \le t < num$). Rows 2–4 show the array (changes only) at the bottom of the for-loop for $t = 0$, $t = 1$, and $t = 2$. An 'X' denotes an unused array element.

We remark that Algorithm `A5.8` can create negative or zero weights. Theoretically this is correct, but it may be undesirable for software reasons. It can be avoided by simply inserting a check after the distance computation, before setting **`remflag`** to 1.

Let $\mathbf{S}^w(u,v) = \sum_{i=0}^{n}\sum_{j=0}^{m} N_{i,p}(u)N_{j,q}(v)\mathbf{P}^w_{i,j}$ be a NURBS surface. A u knot (v knot) is removed from $\mathbf{S}^w(u,v)$ by applying the knot removal algorithm (Algorithm `A5.8`) to the $m+1$ columns ($n+1$ rows) of control points. But the knot can be removed only if the removal is successful for all $m+1$ columns ($n+1$ rows).

Two additional algorithms for knot removal are given in [Till92]. These are:

- given a curve, remove as many knots as possible;

Table 5.2. The control point array for the cubic curve of Figure 5.15.

$\mathbf{P}_0^0$	$\mathbf{P}_1^0$	$\mathbf{P}_2^0$	$\mathbf{P}_3^0$	$\mathbf{P}_4^0$	$\mathbf{P}_5^0$	$\mathbf{P}_6^0$	before loop
			X				$t = 0$
		$\mathbf{P}_2^2$	X	$\mathbf{P}_2^2$			$t = 1$
	$\mathbf{P}_1^3$	X	X	X	$\mathbf{P}_2^3$		$t = 2$

- given a surface, remove as many u knots as possible (v knots are analogous).

Instead of giving details of these algorithms, which are quite involved, we illustrate the effects of curve and surface knot removal through a variety of examples. Figure 5.27a shows a curve with single, double, and triple knots. In Figure 5.27b the single knot, $u = 3/10$, and in Figures 5.27c–5.27e one, two, and three occurrences of the triple knot, $u = 1/2$, respectively, are removed.

Surface knot removal examples are shown in Figures 5.28a–5.28d. Figure 5.28a shows the original surface. In Figure 5.28b the triple knot, $u = 3/10$, is removed three times. In Figure 5.28c the single knot, $v = 1/4$, is removed, and in Figure 5.28d both knots are removed at the same time. In Figures 5.27b–5.27d as well as in Figures 5.28b–5.28d the original curve/surface is shown dashed, whereas the knot removed curves/surfaces are drawn solid.

All removable knots are removed from the curve illustrated in Figure 5.29a. The curves shown in Figures 5.29b–5.29f were computed using the tolerance values 0.007, 0.025, 0.07, 0.6, and 1.2, respectively. These figures illustrate how many and what knots are removable (removed knots are circled and the original polygon and curve are drawn dashed); how to compute the new control

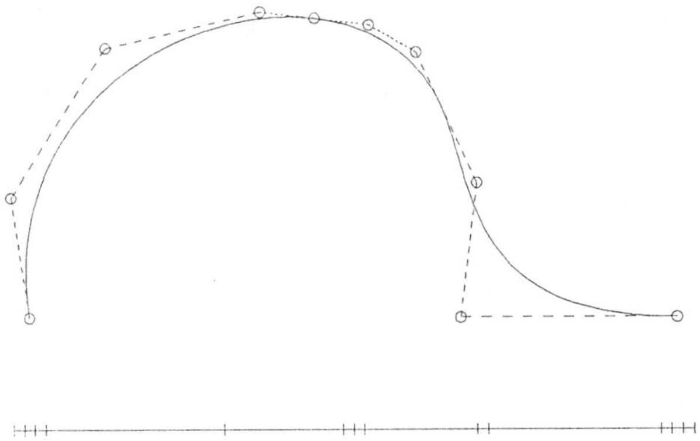

(a)

Figure 5.27. Curve knot removal example. (a) The original cubic curve defined over the knot vector $\{0, 0, 0, 0, 3/10, 1/2, 1/2, 1/2, 7/10, 7/10, 1, 1, 1, 1\}$; (b) removal of $3/10$, one time; (c) removal of $1/2$ one time; (d) removal of $1/2$ two times; (e) removal of $1/2$ three times.

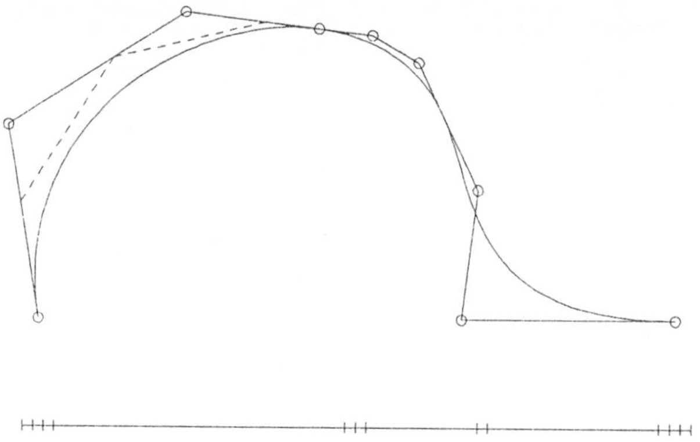

(b)

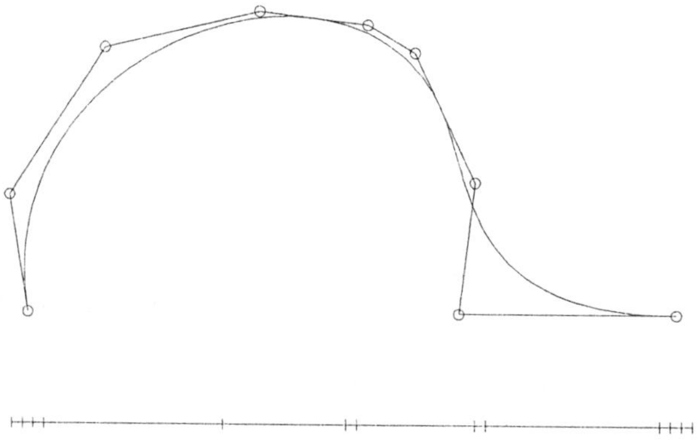

(c)

Figure 5.27. (*Continued.*)

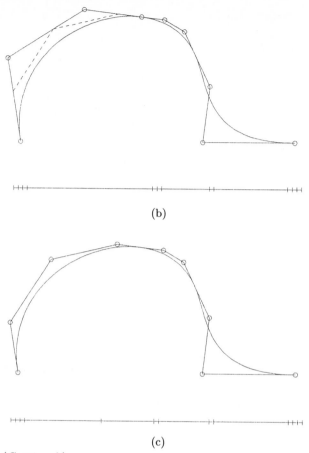

points; and what is the deviation between the original and the knot removed curve. Similar examples are shown for the surfaces in Figures 5.30a and 5.30b through Figures 5.34a and 5.34b. The control net for the original surface is seen in Figure 5.30a. The original surface is shown in Figure 5.30b. Knot removed surfaces are illustrated in Figures 5.31a and 5.31b through Figures 5.34a and 5.34b, using the tolerances 0.05, 0.1, 0.3, and 0.5, respectively.

5.5 Degree Elevation

Let $\mathbf{C}_n(u) = \sum_{i=0}^{n} \mathbf{a}_i u^i$ be an nth-degree polynomial curve. Clearly, we can set $\mathbf{a}_{n+1} = 0$ and write $\mathbf{C}_n(u)$ as an $(n+1)$th-degree curve

$$\mathbf{C}_n(u) = \mathbf{C}_{n+1}(u) = \sum_{i=0}^{n+1} \mathbf{a}_i u^i$$

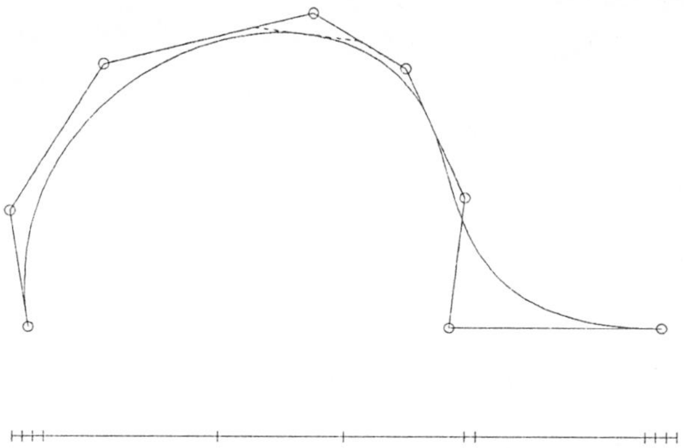

(d)

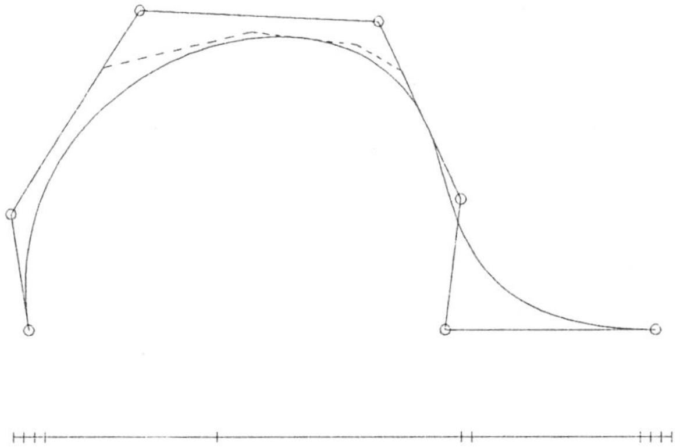

(e)

Figure 5.27. (*Continued.*)

From a vector space point of view, $\mathbf{C}_{n+1}(u)$ is simply $\mathbf{C}_n(u)$ embedded in a higher dimensional space.

Now let $\mathbf{C}_p^w(u) = \sum_{i=0}^{n} N_{i,p}(u)\mathbf{P}_i^w$ be a pth-degree NURBS curve on the knot vector U. Since $\mathbf{C}_p^w(u)$ is a piecewise polynomial curve, it should be possible to elevate its degree to $p+1$, that is, there must exist control points $\mathbf{Q}_i^w$ and a knot vector $\hat{U}$ such that

$$\mathbf{C}_p^w(u) = \mathbf{C}_{p+1}^w(u) = \sum_{i=0}^{\hat{n}} N_{i,p+1}(u)\,\mathbf{Q}_i^w \tag{5.31}$$

$\mathbf{C}_{p+1}^w(u)$ and $\mathbf{C}_p^w(u)$ are the same curve, both geometrically and parametrically. $\mathbf{C}_{p+1}^w(u)$ is simply $\mathbf{C}_p^w(u)$ embedded in a higher dimensional space. *Degree elevation* refers to the process (the algorithm) for computing the unknown $\mathbf{Q}_i^w$ and $\hat{U}$.

The applications of degree elevation include:

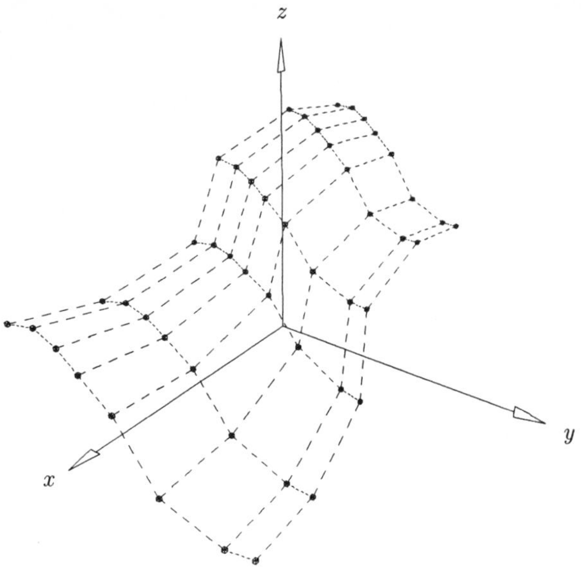

(a)

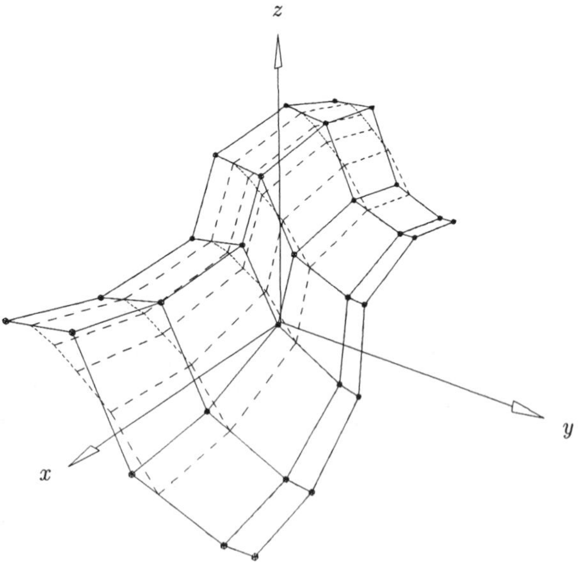

(b)

Figure 5.28. Surface knot removal example. (a) The original (cubic × quadratic) surface defined over $U = \{0,0,0,0,{}^3\!/_{10},{}^3\!/_{10},{}^3\!/_{10},{}^7\!/_{10},1,1,1,1\}$ and $V = \{0,0,0,{}^1\!/_4,{}^1\!/_2,{}^3\!/_4,1,1,1\}$; (b) removal of $u = {}^3\!/_{10}$ three times in the u direction.

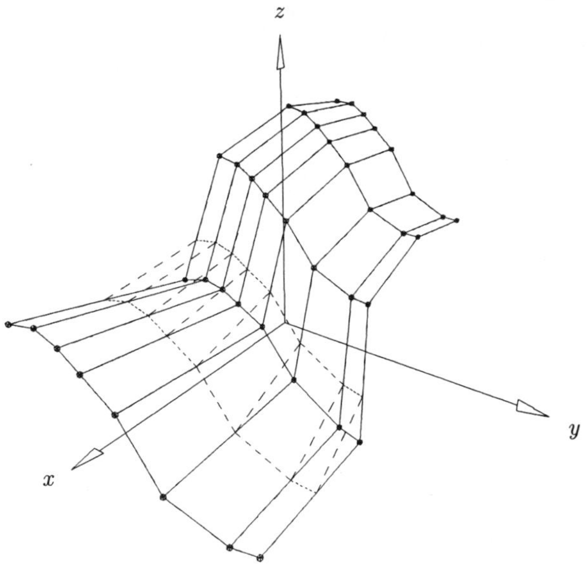

(c)

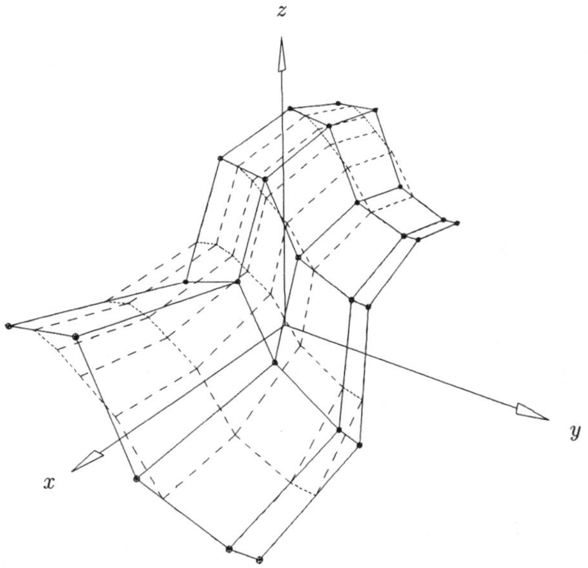

(d)

Figure 5.28. *Continued.* (c) removal of $v = 1/4$ one time in the v direction; (d) removal of the knots in both directions.

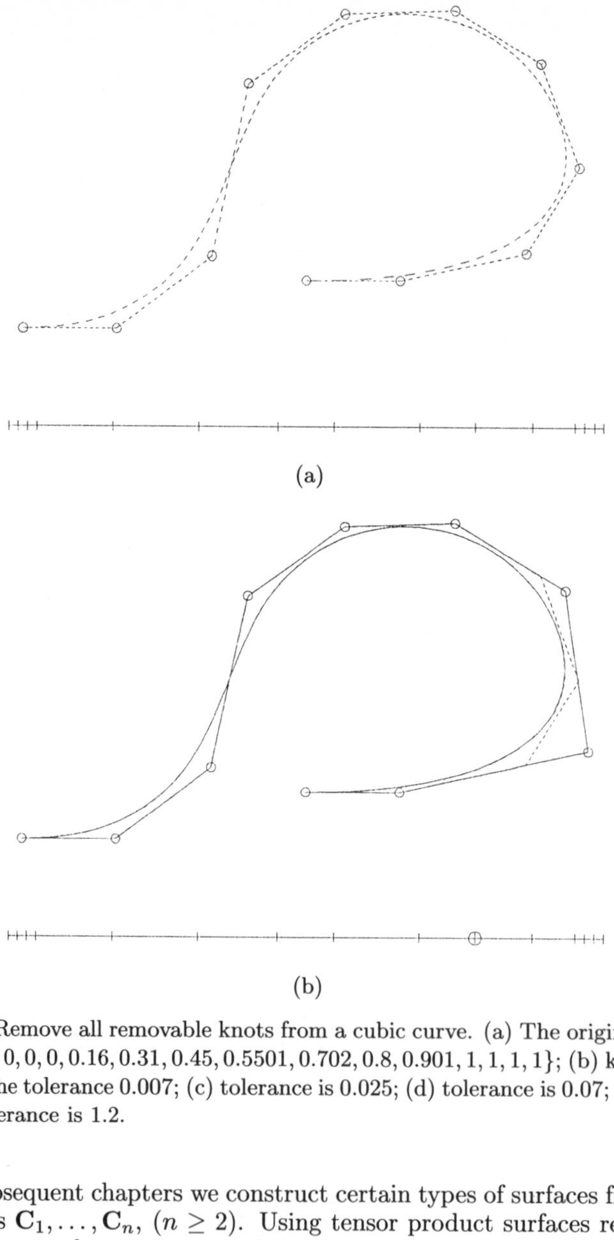

Figure 5.29. Remove all removable knots from a cubic curve. (a) The original curve defined over $\{0,0,0,0,0.16,0.31,0.45,0.5501,0.702,0.8,0.901,1,1,1,1\}$; (b) knot removed curve using the tolerance 0.007; (c) tolerance is 0.025; (d) tolerance is 0.07; (e) tolerance is 0.6; (f) tolerance is 1.2.

- in subsequent chapters we construct certain types of surfaces from a set of curves $\mathbf{C}_1, \ldots, \mathbf{C}_n$, $(n \geq 2)$. Using tensor product surfaces requires that these curves have a common degree, hence the degrees of some curves may require elevation;
- let $\mathbf{C}_1, \ldots, \mathbf{C}_n$, $(n \geq 2)$ be a sequence of NURBS curves with the property that the endpoint of $\mathbf{C}_i$ is coincident with the starting point of $\mathbf{C}_{i+1}$; then the curves can be combined into a single NURBS curve. One step in this process is to elevate the curves to a common degree.

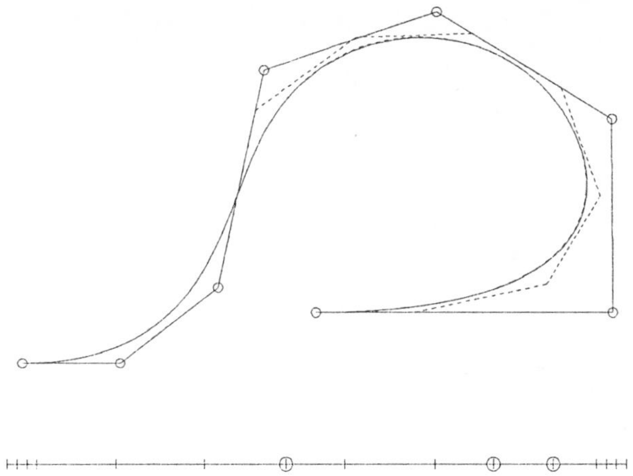

(c)

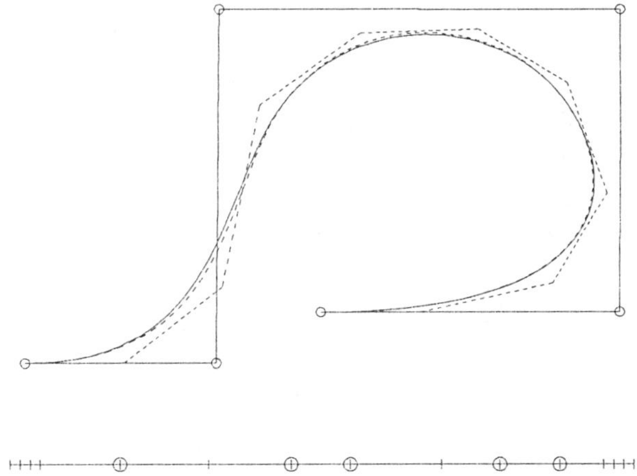

(d)

Figure 5.29. (*Continued.*)

As usual, degree elevation algorithms are applied to $\mathbf{C}_p^w(u)$ in four-dimensional space, not to $\mathbf{C}_p(u)$, and again we drop the w for the remainder of this section.

There are three unknowns in Eq. (5.31), $\hat{n}$, $\hat{U}$, and the $\{\mathbf{Q}_i\}$. To determine $\hat{n}$ and $\hat{U}$ assume that U has the form

$$U = \{u_0, \ldots, u_m\} = \{\underbrace{a, \ldots, a}_{p+1}, \underbrace{u_1, \ldots, u_1}_{m_1}, \ldots, \underbrace{u_s, \ldots, u_s}_{m_s}, \underbrace{b, \ldots, b}_{p+1}\}$$

where $m_1, \ldots, m_s$ denote the multiplicities of the interior knots. Now $\mathbf{C}_p(u)$ is a polynomial curve on each nondegenerate knot span, hence its degree can be elevated to $p+1$ on each such knot span. At a knot of multiplicity m_i, $\mathbf{C}_p(u)$ is C^{p-m_i} continuous. Since the degree elevated curve, $\mathbf{C}_{p+1}(u)$, must have the

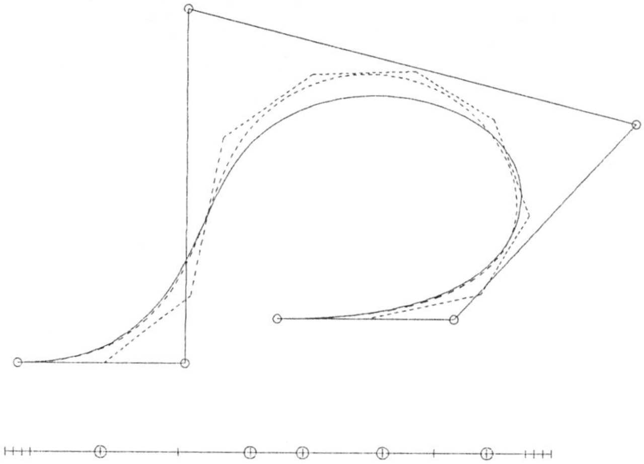

(e)

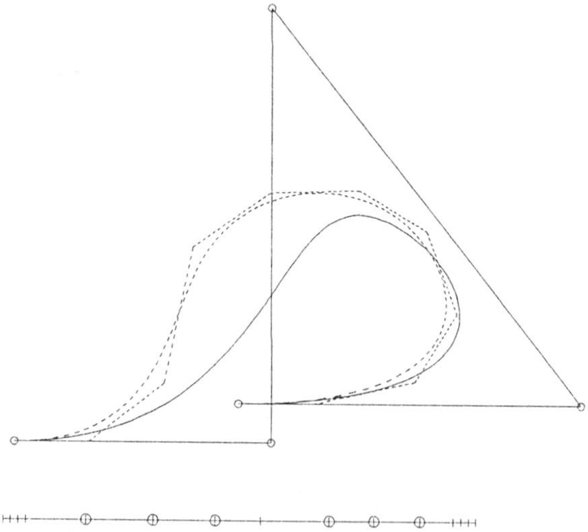

(f)

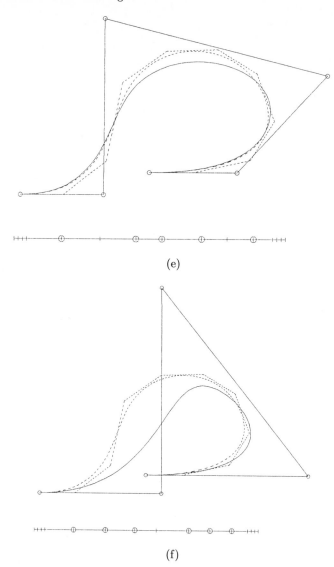

Figure 5.29. (*Continued*.)

same continuity, it follows that the same knot must have multiplicity $m_i + 1$ for $\mathbf{C}_{p+1}(u)$. This yields

$$\hat{n} = n + s + 1 \tag{5.32}$$

and $$\hat{U} = \{u_0, \ldots, u_{\hat{m}}\} = \{\underbrace{a, \ldots, a}_{p+2}, \underbrace{u_1, \ldots, u_1}_{m_1+1}, \ldots, \underbrace{u_s, \ldots, u_s}_{m_{s+1}}, \underbrace{b, \ldots, b}_{p+2}\} \tag{5.33}$$

where $\hat{m} = m + s + 2$.

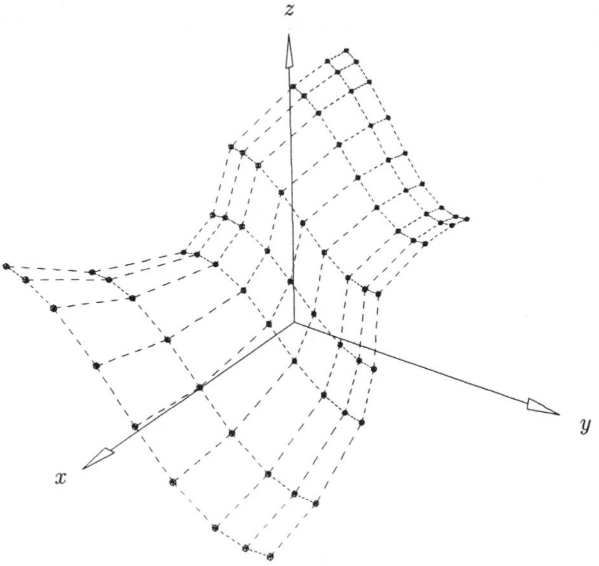

(a)

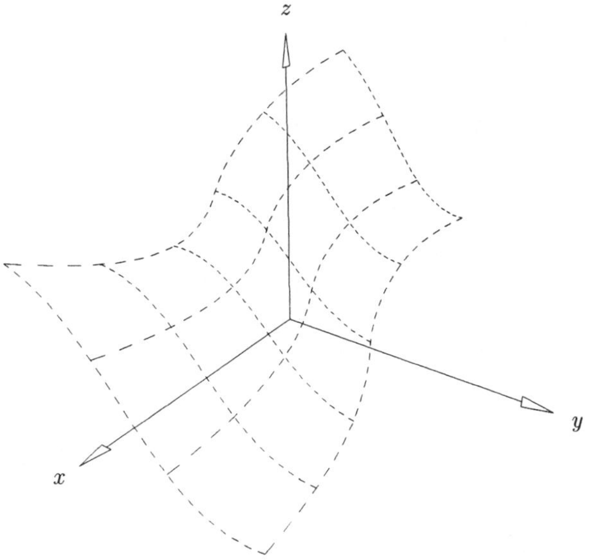

(b)

Figure 5.30. A (cubic $\times$ quadratic) surface for knot removal. (a) The control net; (b) the surface defined over $U = \{0,0,0,0,0.22,0.3,0.52,0.7,0.79,1,1,1,1\}$ and $V = \{0,0,0,0.2,0.42,0.5,\ 0.81,0.9,1,1,1\}$.

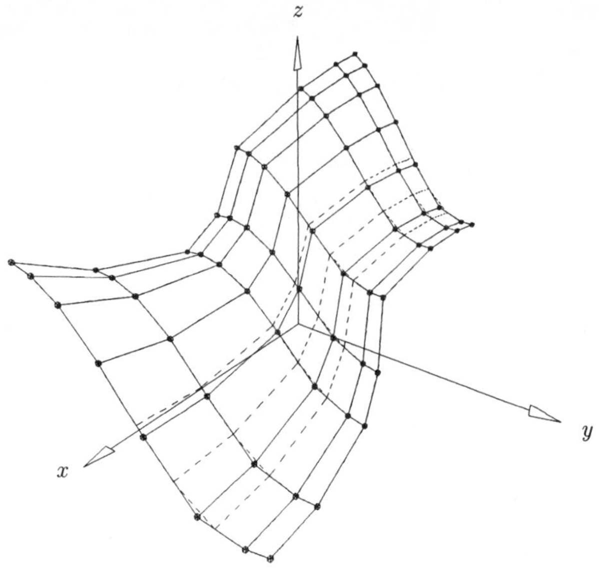

(a)

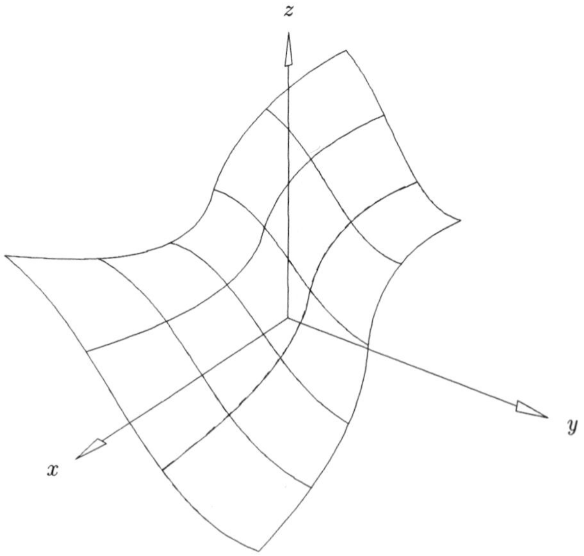

(b)

Figure 5.31. Remove all removable knots in both directions using the tolerance 0.05. (a) The control net of both the original (dashed) and the knot removed surface (solid); (b) isoparametric lines of both surfaces.

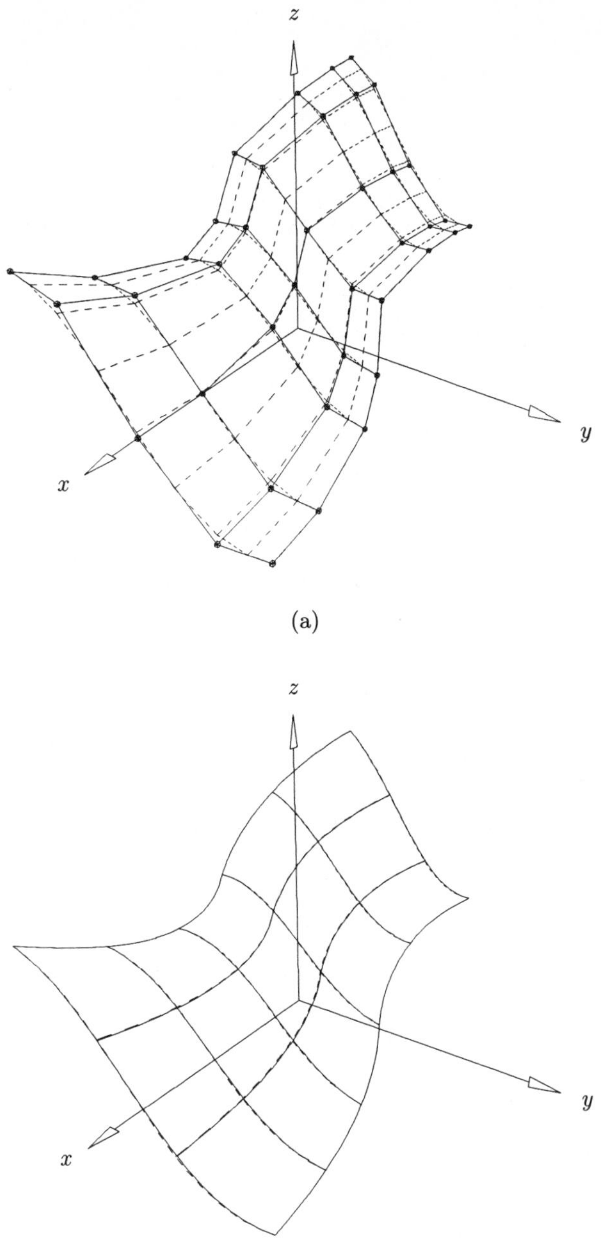

(b)

Figure 5.32. Remove all removable knots in both directions using the tolerance 0.1. (a) The control net of both the original (dashed) and the knot removed surface (solid); (b) isoparametric lines of both surfaces.

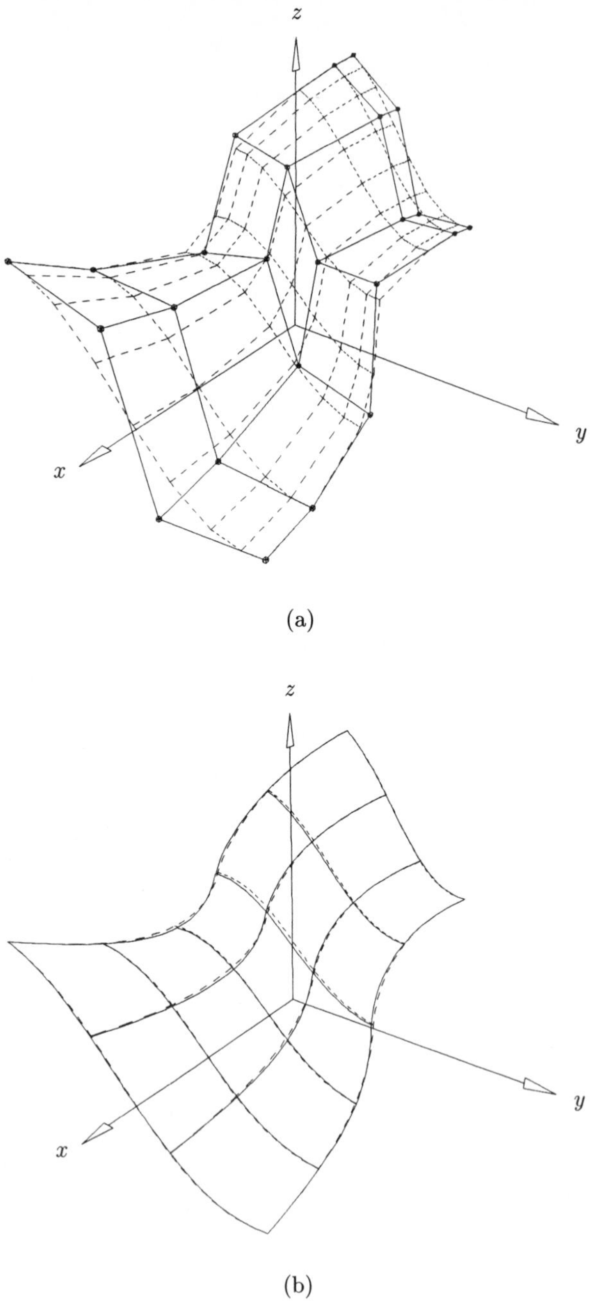

Figure 5.33. Remove all removable knots in both directions using the tolerance 0.3. (a) The control net of both the original (dashed) and the knot removed surface (solid); (b) isoparametric lines of both surfaces.

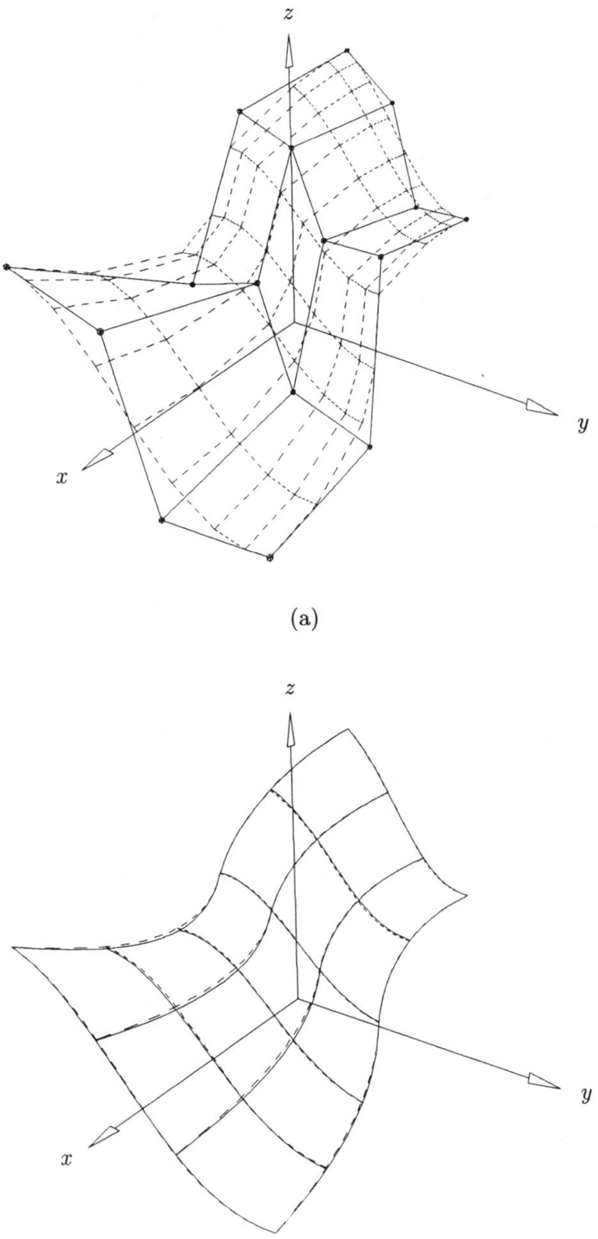

(b)

Figure 5.34. Remove all removable knots in both directions using the tolerance 0.5. (a) The control net of both the original (dashed) and the knot removed surface (solid); (b) isoparametric lines of both surfaces.

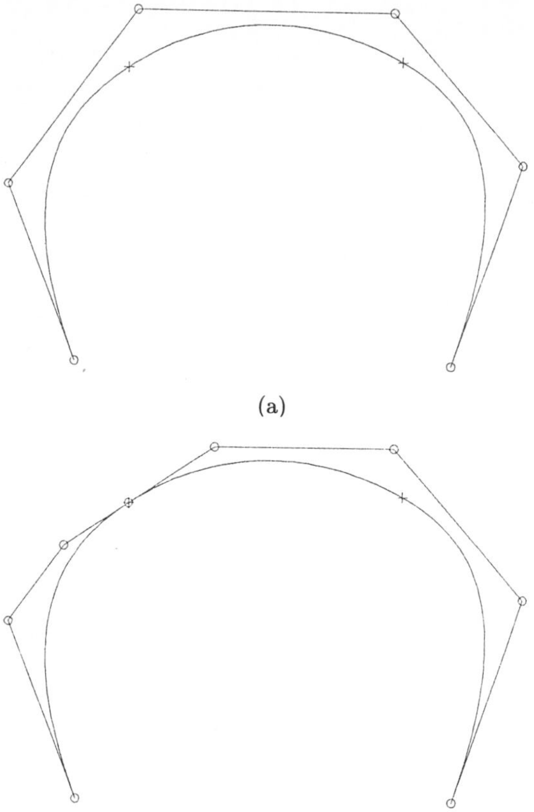

(a)

(b)

Figure 5.35. Degree elevation of a cubic curve defined over $\{0,0,0,0,{}^3\!/_{10},{}^7\!/_{10},1,1,1,1\}$. (a) The original curve; (b) the first Bézier segment obtained via knot insertion.

The only remaining problem is to compute the $\{\mathbf{Q}_i\}$. An obvious but very inefficient method to do this is to solve a system of linear equations. Setting

$$\sum_{i=0}^{\hat{n}} N_{i,p+1}(u)\,\mathbf{Q}_i = \sum_{i=0}^{n} N_{i,p}(u)\,\mathbf{P}_i$$

and evaluating the $N_{i,p}(u)$ and $N_{i,p+1}(u)$ at appropriate $\hat{n}+1$ values yields a banded system of $\hat{n}+1$ linear equations in the unknowns, $\mathbf{Q}_i$.

More efficient but mathematically more complicated methods are given by Prautzsch [Prau84], by Cohen et al. [Cohe85], and by Prautzsch and Piper [Prau91]. The algorithm due to Prautzsch and Piper is the most efficient for the general case, but Cohen et al. also give simple and efficient algorithms for low-degree special cases, such as linear to quadratic, and quadratic to cubic. All these algorithms raise the degree by 1 ($p \rightarrow p+1$).

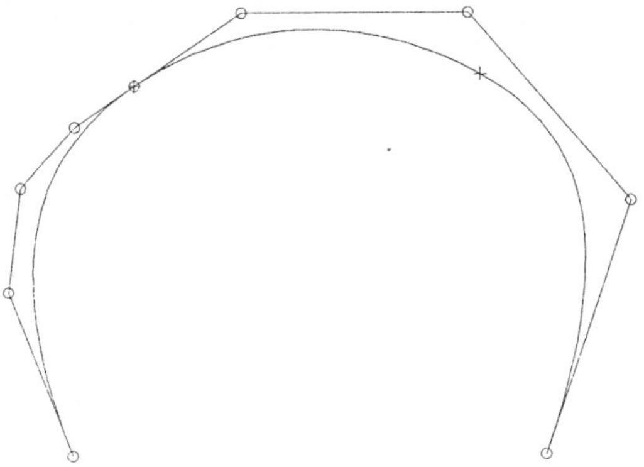

(c)

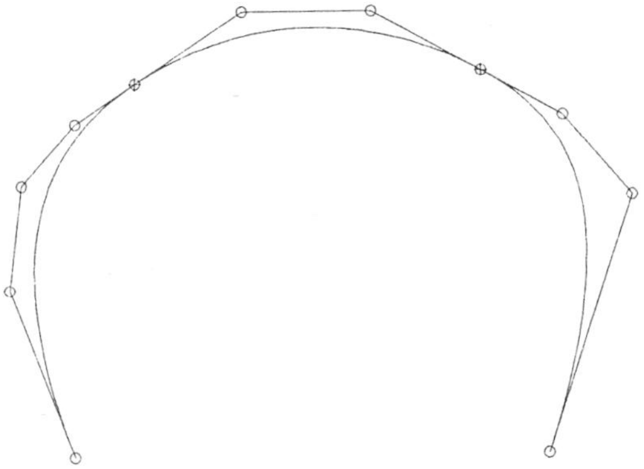

(d)

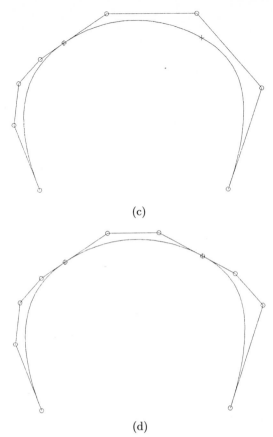

Figure 5.35. *Continued.* (c) the first Bézier segment is degree elevated, (d) the second Bézier segment is computed.

We present another algorithm here which is mathematically simpler, and competitive with that given in [Prau91], particularly in the case where the degree is to be raised by more than 1 (see [Pieg94]). The solution consists of applying three steps, on-the-fly, while moving through the knot vector. The steps are:

1. using the logic of Algorithm A5.6, extract the ith Bézier segment from the curve;
2. degree elevate the ith Bézier segment;
3. remove unnecessary knots separating the $(i-1)$th and ith segments.

Figures 5.35a–5.35h show the progress of the algorithm. The original curve is a cubic with knot vector $U = \{0,0,0,0,u_a,u_b,1,1,1,1\}$. It is elevated to fourth-degree. The figures are explained as:

a. the original curve;

b. u_a is inserted twice, bringing it to multiplicity 3;

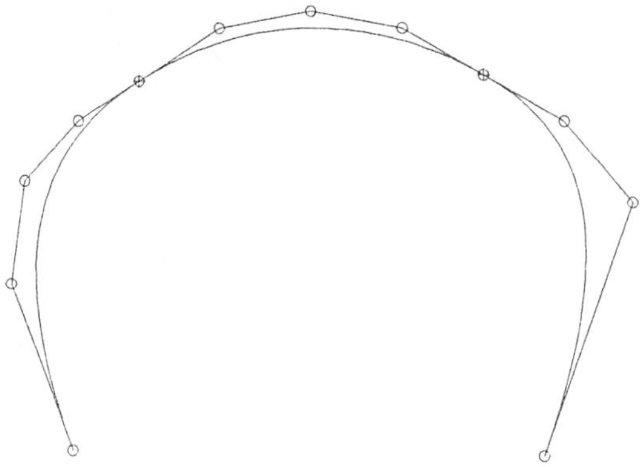

(e)

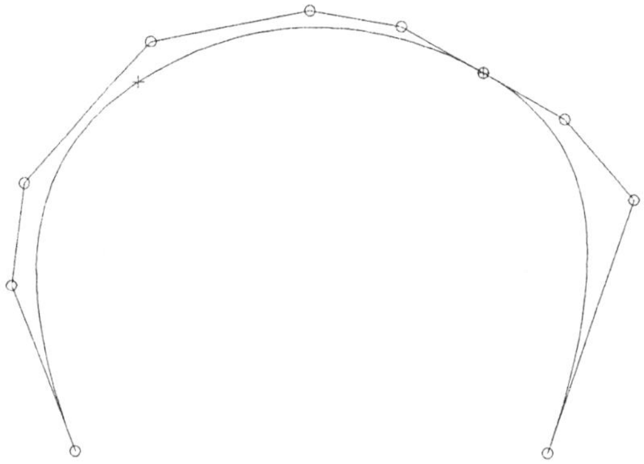

(f)

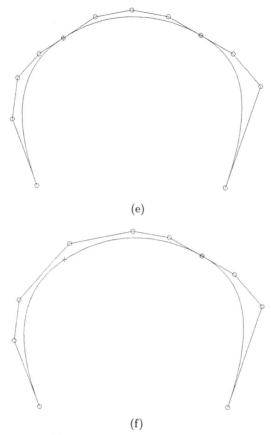

Figure 5.35. *Continued.* (e) the second Bézier segment is degree elevated; (f) two occurrences of the knot $u = {}^{3}\!/_{10}$ are removed.

c. The Bézier segment on $[0, u_a]$ is degree elevated; this replaces the first four control points with five new ones (see subsequent text);
d. u_b is inserted twice to obtain the Bézier segment on $[u_a, u_b]$;
e. the Bézier segment on $[u_a, u_b]$ is degree elevated;
f. two occurrences of the knot u_a are removed;
g. the last segment $[u_b, 1]$ is degree elevated;
h. two occurrences of u_b are removed, yielding the final fourth-degree, C^2 continuous curve.

Step 1 is a straightforward application of Algorithm `A5.6`. It is modified to not return the Bézier segments, but rather to process them on-the-fly.

Step 2 degree elevates a Bézier segment. We present two formulas to do this. The first is the well-known formula (due to Forrest [Forr72]) to elevate from degree p to degree $p + 1$. Let

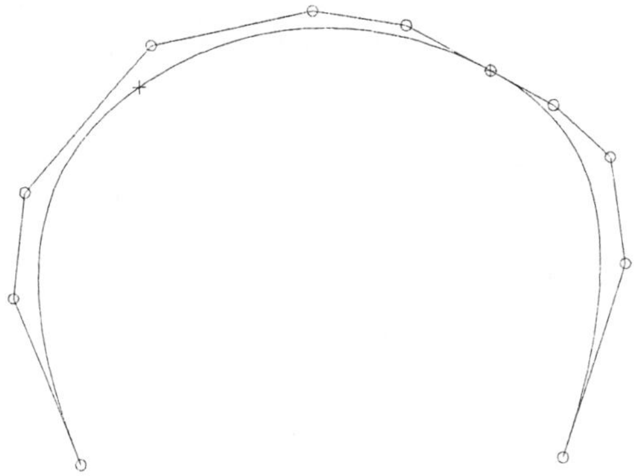

(g)

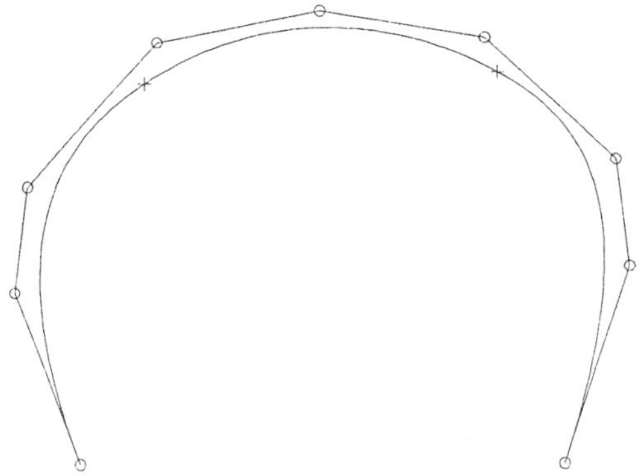

(h)

Figure 5.35. *Continued.* (g) the third Bézier segment is degree elevated; (h) two occurrences of the knot $u = {}^7\!/_{10}$ are removed.

$$\mathbf{C}_p(u) = \sum_{i=0}^{p} B_{i,p}(u)\,\mathbf{P}_i$$

be a pth-degree Bézier curve. Its representation as a $(p+1)$th-degree curve is

$$\mathbf{C}_{p+1}(u) = \sum_{i=0}^{p+1} B_{i,p+1}(u)\,\mathbf{Q}_i \tag{5.34}$$

Setting these equal and multiplying $\mathbf{C}_p(u)$ by $\bigl(u + (1-u)\bigr)$ $(=1)$ yields

$$\sum_{i=0}^{p+1} B_{i,p+1}\,\mathbf{Q}_i = \bigl(u + (1-u)\bigr)\sum_{i=0}^{p} B_{i,p}\,\mathbf{P}_i$$

$$= \sum_{i=0}^{p} \bigl((1-u)\,B_{i,p} + uB_{i,p}\bigr)\,\mathbf{P}_i$$

Using the notation

$$\frac{p!}{i!(p-i)!} = \binom{p}{i}$$

and applying Eq. (1.8), we obtain

$$\sum_{i=0}^{p+1} \binom{p+1}{i} u^i(1-u)^{p+1-i}\mathbf{Q}_i$$

$$= \sum_{i=0}^{p} \binom{p}{i} \left(u^i(1-u)^{p+1-i} + u^{i+1}(1-u)^{p-i}\right) \mathbf{P}_i$$

$$= \sum_{i=0}^{p} \binom{p}{i} u^i(1-u)^{p+1-i}\mathbf{P}_i + \sum_{i=1}^{p+1} \binom{p}{i-1} u^i(1-u)^{p+1-i}\mathbf{P}_{i-1}$$

Equating coefficients of $u^i(1-u)^{p+1-i}$ yields

$$\binom{p+1}{i}\mathbf{Q}_i = \binom{p}{i}\mathbf{P}_i + \binom{p}{i-1}\mathbf{P}_{i-1}$$

From

$$\binom{p}{i} \Big/ \binom{p+1}{i} = \frac{p!i!(p+1-i)!}{i!(p-i)!(p+1)!} = \frac{p+1-i}{p+1} = 1 - \frac{i}{p+1}$$

and

$$\binom{p}{i-1} \Big/ \binom{p+1}{i} = \frac{p!i!(p+1-i)!}{(i-1)!(p+1-i)!(p+1)!} = \frac{i}{p+1}$$

it follows that

$$\mathbf{Q}_i = (1-\alpha_i)\mathbf{P}_i + \alpha_i \mathbf{P}_{i-1} \tag{5.35}$$

where

$$\alpha_i = \frac{i}{p+1} \qquad i = 0, \ldots, p+1$$

Notice that Eq. (5.35) represents a corner cutting process (see Figures 5.35c, 5.35e, and 5.35g). Regarding Eq. (5.35):

- it can be applied recursively to elevate the degree t times ($t \geq 1$);
- its growth rate is $O(t^2)$; if $t > 1$, recursive application of Eq. (5.35) involves some redundant computations;
- the α_is depend only on the degree, not on the particular Bézier segment to which they are applied, thus they can be computed one time and stored in a local array before processing of the segments begins;
- it is a convex combination scheme.

It is possible to degree elevate from p to $p+t$ in one step. Writing out several recursive applications of Eq. (5.35), and cleverly rearranging coefficients, yields

$$\mathbf{P}_i^t = \sum_{j=\max(0,i-t)}^{\min(p,i)} \frac{\binom{p}{j}\binom{t}{i-j}\mathbf{P}_j}{\binom{p+t}{i}} \qquad i = 0, \ldots, p+t \tag{5.36}$$

where $\mathbf{P}_i^t$ denotes the degree elevated control points after t-degree elevations. As an example, consider the case of $p = 2$ and $t = 4$, that is

$$\mathbf{P}_0^4 = \mathbf{P}_0$$

$$\mathbf{P}_1^4 = \frac{4}{6}\mathbf{P}_0 + \frac{2}{6}\mathbf{P}_1$$

$$\mathbf{P}_2^4 = \frac{6}{15}\mathbf{P}_0 + \frac{8}{15}\mathbf{P}_1 + \frac{1}{15}\mathbf{P}_2$$

$$\mathbf{P}_3^4 = \frac{4}{20}\mathbf{P}_0 + \frac{12}{20}\mathbf{P}_1 + \frac{4}{20}\mathbf{P}_2$$

$$\mathbf{P}_4^4 = \frac{1}{15}\mathbf{P}_0 + \frac{8}{15}\mathbf{P}_1 + \frac{6}{15}\mathbf{P}_2$$

$$\mathbf{P}_5^4 = \frac{2}{6}\mathbf{P}_1 + \frac{4}{6}\mathbf{P}_2$$

$$\mathbf{P}_6^4 = \mathbf{P}_2$$

As regards Eq. (5.36):

- its growth rate is $O(t)$, as the width of the scheme is fixed (bounded by $p+1$);
- the coefficients for each $\mathbf{P}_i^t$ sum to one (see example), hence it is a convex combination scheme;
- there are no redundant computations;
- the coefficient matrix is symmetric with respect to the row $^{p+t}/_2$;
- the coefficients depend both on p and t, but not on the particular Bézier segment to which they are applied; hence, they can be computed one time and stored in a local array before processing of the segments begins.

The knot removal of Step 3 is much less expensive than general knot removal as described in the previous section. There are two reasons for this:

- we know how many knots are removable – the number that were inserted;
- the knot vector has a specific structure in the neighborhood of the knot being removed.

As an example of this, Figure 5.36 shows a curve whose degree is being raised from 4 to 5 ($p = 4$). Let u_c, u_d, u_e be the three parameter values defining the two segments shown. Assuming the original multiplicity of u_d is 1, then three knot insertions are required to form the two Bézier segments (note that $\mathbf{C}(u_d) = \mathbf{P}_k^0$), and three removals are now necessary. However, we can skip the first two and compute $\mathbf{P}_{k-1}^3$ and $\mathbf{P}_k^3$ directly. This requires computing only two points in the form of Eq. (5.29), and no checking for equality of points is necessary. This compares to the six point computations and the three point equality checks required in the general case. Locally the knot vector has the form

$$\ldots, u_c, u_c, \underbrace{u_d, \ldots, u_d}_{p+1}, \underbrace{u_e, \ldots, u_e}_{p+1}, \ldots$$

where u_c has multiplicity of at least 2.

Algorithm A5.9 raises the degree from p to $p + t$, $t \geq 1$, by computing $\hat{n}$, $\hat{U}$, and the new $\mathbf{Q}_i$ (nh, Uh, and Qw); it uses Eq. (5.36) to degree elevate the Bézier segments. Min() and Max() compute the minimum and the maximum of two integers, respectively, and Bin(i,j) computes $\binom{i}{j}$, the binomial coefficient, which may be precomputed and stored for further efficiency. Let p be the degree of the original curve. The required local arrays are:

bezalfs[p+t+1][p+1] : coefficients for degree elevating the Bézier segments;

bpts[p+1] : pth-degree Bézier control points of the current segment;

ebpts[p+t+1] : $(p+t)$th-degree Bézier control points of the current segment;

Nextbpts[p-1] : leftmost control points of the next Bézier segment;

alphas[p-1] : knot insertion αs.

```
ALGORITHM A5.9
DegreeElevateCurve(n,p,U,Pw,t,nh,Uh,Qw)
  { /*  Degree elevate a curve t times.  */
    /*  Input:  n,p,U,Pw,t  */
    /*  Output: nh,Uh,Qw  */
  m = n+p+1;
  ph = p+t;    ph2 = ph/2;
   /* Compute Bézier degree elevation coefficients */
  bezalfs[0][0] = bezalfs[ph][p] = 1.0;
  for (i=1; i<=ph2; i++)
    {
    inv = 1.0/Bin(ph,i);
    mpi = Min(p,i);
```

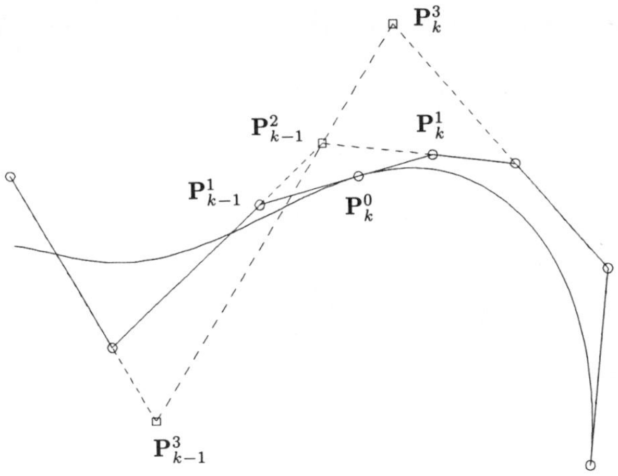

Figure 5.36. Removal of three knots from a quartic curve.

```
      for (j=Max(0,i-t); j<=mpi; j++)
        bezalfs[i][j] = inv*Bin(p,j)*Bin(t,i-j);
      }
    for (i=ph2+1; i<=ph-1; i++)
      {
      mpi = Min(p,i);
      for (j=Max(0,i-t); j<=mpi; j++)
        bezalfs[i][j] = bezalfs[ph-i][p-j];
      }
    mh = ph;   kind = ph+1;
    r = -1;   a = p;
    b = p+1;   cind = 1;
    ua = U[0];
    Qw[0] = Pw[0];
    for (i=0; i<=ph; i++)   Uh[i] = ua;
      /* Initialize first Bézier seg */
    for (i=0; i<=p; i++)   bpts[i] = Pw[i];
    while (b < m)   /* Big loop thru knot vector */
      {
      i = b;
      while (b < m && U[b] == U[b+1])   b = b+1;
      mul = b-i+1;
      mh = mh+mul+t;
      ub = U[b];
      oldr = r;    r = p-mul;
         /* Insert knot u(b) r times */
      if (oldr > 0)   lbz = (oldr+2)/2;   else   lbz = 1;
```

```
if (r > 0)   rbz = ph-(r+1)/2;   else   rbz = ph;
if (r > 0)
  { /* Insert knot to get Bézier segment */
  numer = ub-ua;
  for (k=p; k>mul; k--)
    alfs[k-mul-1] = numer/(U[a+k]-ua);
  for (j=1; j<=r; j++)
    {
    save = r-j;   s = mul+j;
    for (k=p; k>=s; k--)
      {
      bpts[k] = alfs[k-s]*bpts[k] +
                (1.0-alfs[k-s])*bpts[k-1];
      }
    Nextbpts[save] = bpts[p];
    }
  } /* End of "insert knot" */
for (i=lbz; i<=ph; i++)   /* Degree elevate Bezier */
  { /* Only points lbz,...,ph are used below */
  ebpts[i] = 0.0;
  mpi = Min(p,i);
  for (j=Max(0,i-t); j<=mpi; j++)
    ebpts[i] = ebpts[i] + bezalfs[i][j]*bpts[j];
  } /* End of degree elevating Bezier */
if (oldr > 1)
  { /* Must remove knot u=U[a] oldr times */
  first = kind-2;   last = kind;
  den = ub-ua;
  bet = (ub-Uh[kind-1])/den;
  for (tr=1; tr<oldr; tr++)
    { /* Knot removal loop */
    i = first;   j = last;   kj = j-kind+1;
    while (j-i > tr)  /* Loop and compute the new */
      {  /* control points for one removal step */
      if (i < cind)
        {
        alf = (ub-Uh[i])/(ua-Uh[i]);
        Qw[i] = alf*Qw[i] + (1.0-alf)*Qw[i-1];
        }
      if( j >= lbz)
        {
        if( j-tr <= kind-ph+oldr )
          {
          gam = (ub-Uh[j-tr])/den;
          ebpts[kj] = gam*ebpts[kj]+(1.0-gam)*ebpts[kj+1];
```

```
                {
                else
                {
                ebpts[kj] = bet*ebpts[kj]+(1.0-bet)*ebpts[kj+1];
                {
              }
            i = i+1;   j = j-1;   kj = kj-1;
            }
          first = first-1;    last = last+1;
          }
        }  /* End of removing knot, u=U[a] */
      if (a != p)  /* Load the knot ua */
        for (i=0; i<ph-oldr; i++)
          {  Uh[kind] = ua;    kind = kind+1;  }
      for (j=lbz; j<=rbz; j++)  /* Load ctrl pts into Qw */
        {  Qw[cind] = ebpts[j];   cind = cind+1;  }
      if (b < m)
        {  /* Set up for next pass thru loop */
        for (j=0; j<r; j++)     bpts[j] = Nextbpts[j];
        for (j=r; j<=p; j++)    bpts[j] = Pw[b-p+j];
        a = b;    b = b+1;    ua = ub;
        }
        else
           /* End knot */
          for (i=0; i<=ph; i++)  Uh[kind+i] = ub;
      }  /* End of while-loop (b < m) */
    nh = mh-ph-1;
    }
```

Several curve degree elevation examples are shown in Figures 5.37a–5.37d. The original third-degree curve (Figure 5.37a) is raised to fourth-, fifth-, and seventh-degrees in Figures 5.37b, 5.37c, and 5.37d, respectively. Note that the control polygon converges to the curve as the degree is raised.

Let $\mathbf{S}^w(u,v) = \sum_{i=0}^{n}\sum_{j=0}^{m} N_{i,p}(u)N_{j,q}(v)\mathbf{P}_{i,j}^w$ be a NURBS surface. Degree elevation is accomplished for surfaces by applying it to the rows/columns of control points. In particular, we elevate the degree p (u direction) by applying Algorithm `A5.9` to each of the $m+1$ columns of control points. The v direction degree q is elevated by applying Algorithm `A5.9` to each of the $n+1$ rows of control points. An efficient organization of a surface degree elevation algorithm which requires storage of Bézier strips is Algorithm `A5.10`.

```
ALGORITHM A5.10
DegreeElevateSurface(n,p,U,m,q,V,Pw,dir,t,nh,Uh,mh,Vh,Qw)
  {  /*  Degree elevate a surface t times.  */
     /*  Input:  n,p,U,m,q,V,Pw,dir,t  */
     /*  Output: nh,Uh,mh,Vh,Qw  */
```

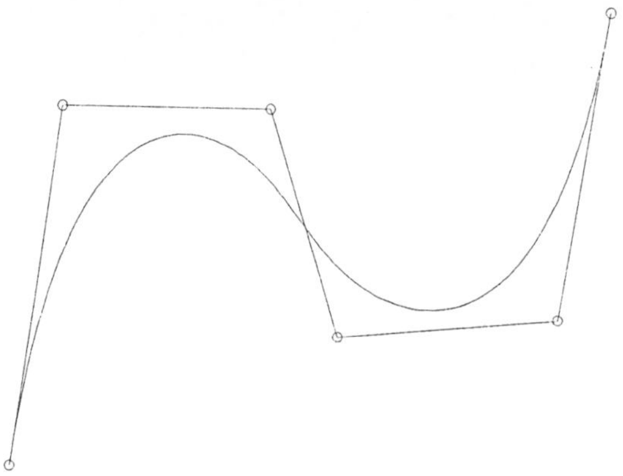

(a)

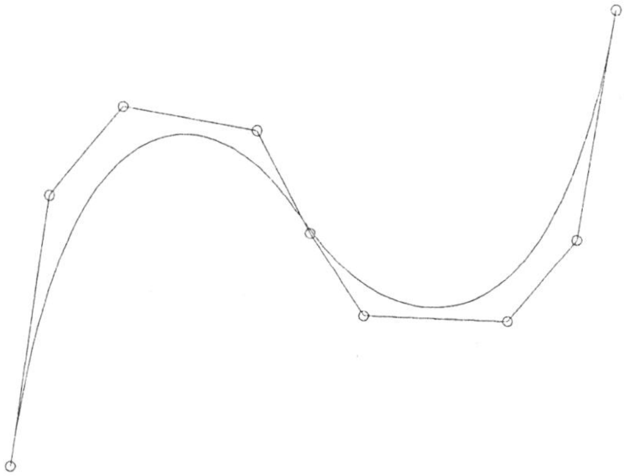

(b)

Figure 5.37. Curve degree elevation example. (a) The original cubic curve defined over $\{0,0,0,0,{}^4/_{10},{}^7/_{10},1,1,1,1\}$; (b) the degree is elevated by one; (c) the degree is elevated by two; (d) the degree is elevated by four.

```
if (dir == U_DIRECTION)
  {
  allocate memory for Bezier and NextBezier strips;
  initialize knot vectors and first row of control points;
  initialize Bezier strip;
  set variables;
  while(b<m)
    {
    get multiplicity;
    get ub, r, oldr, etc;
    save alfas
```

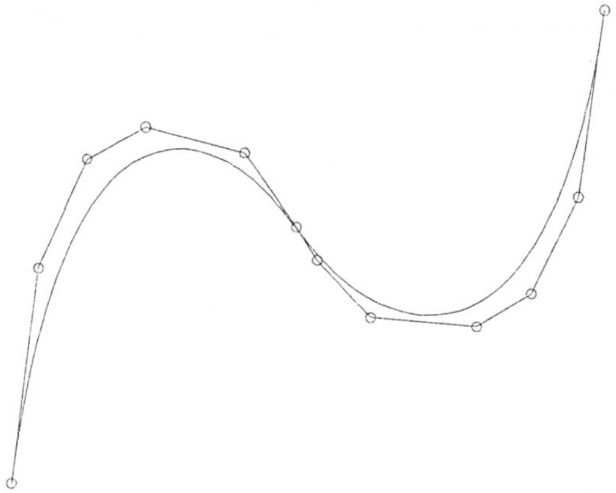

(c)

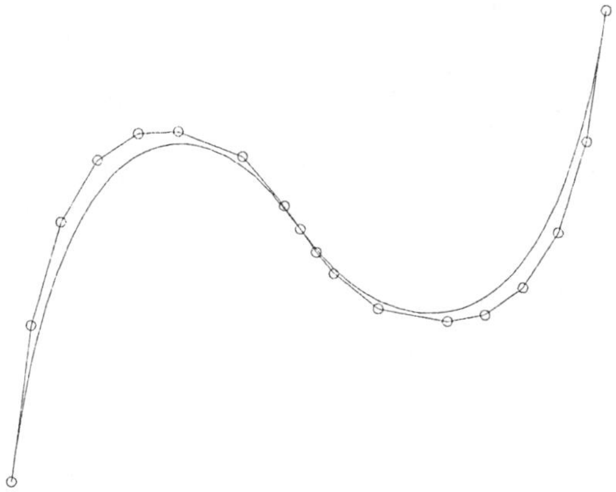

(d)

Figure 5.37. (*Continued.*)

```
        for (j=0; j<=m; j++)
          {
          insert knot;
          degree elevate Bezier row[j];
          remove knot;
          save new control points;
          initialize for next pass through;
          }
        update knot vector;
        update variables;
        get end knots;
        }
      }
```

```
    if (dir == V_DIRECTION)
      {
      /* Similar code as above with u- and v-directional
        parameters switched */
      }
    }
```

Surface degree elevation examples are shown in Figures 5.38a–5.38e. The original $(3,2)$th-degree surface (Figure 5.38a) is raised to $(4,3)$, $(5,4)$, $(6,6)$, and $(9,9)$th-degrees in Figures 5.38b–5.38e, respectively; the original net is shown dashed, and the degree elevated net is drawn solid.

5.6 Degree Reduction

Let $\mathbf{C}(u) = \sum_{i=0}^{n} N_{i,p}(u)\mathbf{Q}_i$ be a pth-degree B-spline curve on the knot vector

$$U = \{\underbrace{a,\ldots,a}_{p+1},\underbrace{u_1,\ldots,u_1}_{m_1},\ldots,\underbrace{u_s,\ldots,u_s}_{m_s},\underbrace{b,\ldots,b}_{p+1}\}$$

As usual, $\mathbf{C}(u)$ can be rational or nonrational; we drop the w superscript for the remainder of this section. $\mathbf{C}(u)$ is *degree reducible* if it has a precise representation of the form

$$\mathbf{C}(u) = \hat{\mathbf{C}}(u) = \sum_{i=0}^{\hat{n}} N_{i,p-1}(u)\,\mathbf{P}_i \tag{5.37}$$

on the knot vector

$$\hat{U} = \{\underbrace{a,\ldots,a}_{p},\underbrace{u_1,\ldots,u_1}_{m_1-1},\ldots,\underbrace{u_s,\ldots,u_s}_{m_s-1},\underbrace{b,\ldots,b}_{p}\} \tag{5.38}$$

Clearly

$$\hat{n} = n - s - 1 \tag{5.39}$$

Note that m_i can be 1, which implies that the knot u_i is not present in $\hat{U}$. This means that u_i was precisely removable from $\mathbf{C}(u)$. Although it is always possible to degree elevate a curve, clearly a curve may not be degree reducible. The situation is similar to knot removal in that the problem is over-determined, that is, any algorithm for degree reduction must produce more equations than unknown $\mathbf{P}_i$. Due to floating point round-off error, one can never expect $\hat{\mathbf{C}}(u)$ to coincide precisely with $\mathbf{C}(u)$, and therefore our algorithm must measure the error $E(u) = \mid \mathbf{C}(u) - \hat{\mathbf{C}}(u) \mid$ and declare $\mathbf{C}(u)$ to be degree reducible only if

$$\max_u E(u) \le \texttt{TOL}$$

for some user-specified tolerance, TOL. We consider only *precise* degree reduction in most of this section, i.e., we assume that TOL is very small. The main application is to reverse the degree elevation process. For example, degree reduction should be applied to each constituent piece when decomposing a composite

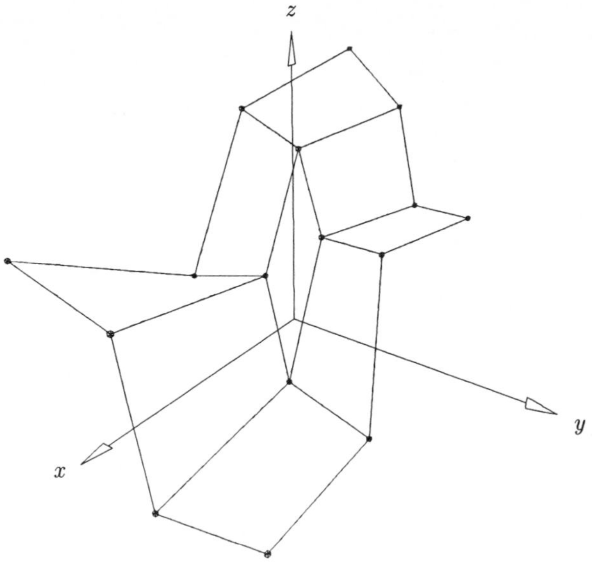

(a)

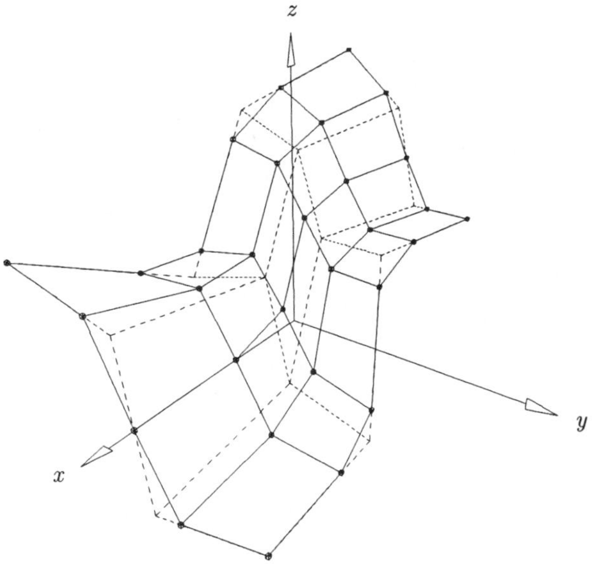

(b)

Figure 5.38. Surface degree elevation example. (a) The original (cubic $\times$ quadratic) surface net, the surface defined over $U = \{0,0,0,0,1,1,1,1\}$, and $V = \{0,0,0,{}^1/_2,1,1,1\}$; (b) the degree elevated by one in both directions; (c) the degree elevated by two in both directions; (d) the degree elevated by three in the u direction, by four in the v direction; (e) the degree elevated by six in the u direction, by seven in the v direction.

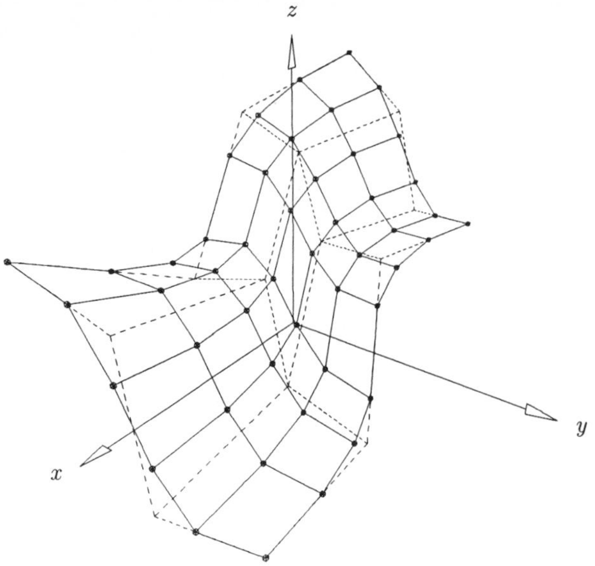

(c)

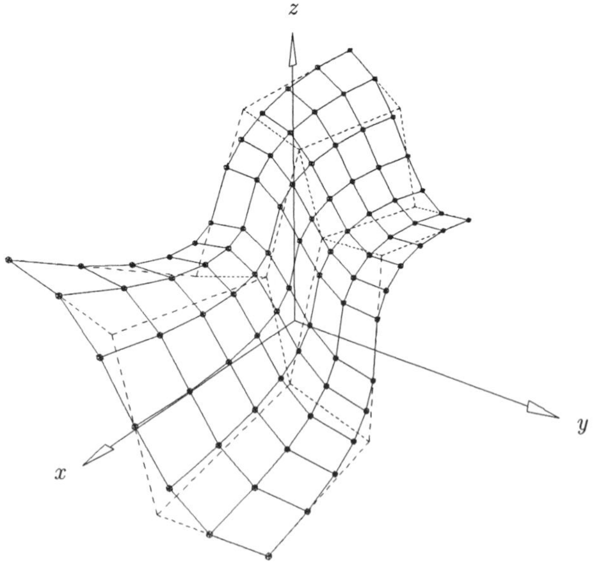

(d)

Figure 5.38. (*Continued.*)

curve, because degree elevation may have been required in the composition process. The material in this section is taken from [Pieg95].

Degree reduction of Bézier curves is relatively well understood, and there exist a number of algorithms (e.g., see references [Forr72; Dann85; Lach88; Watk88;

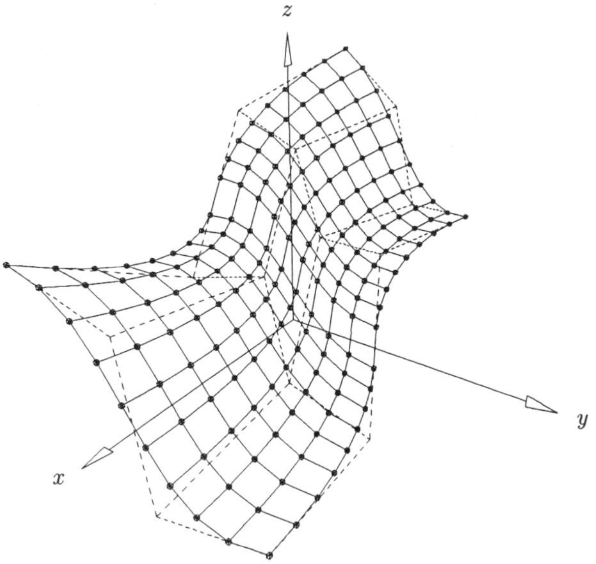

(e)

Figure 5.38. (*Continued.*)

Wein92; Eck93]). Following the strategy developed in the previous section for degree elevation, we present a three-step algorithm for degree reduction of B-spline curves:

```
repeat
  extract the ith Bézier segment from the B-spline curve,
  degree reduce the ith Bézier piece,
  remove unnecessary knots between the (i − 1)th and the
    ith segments,
until done
```

Error is produced in both the Bézier degree reduction and the knot removal steps, and our algorithm accumulates both types of error and exits immediately if TOL is exceeded on any knot span. Figures 5.39a–5.39h show walk-through examples explaining how the algorithm works. The details of each step are:

a. original fourth-degree B-spline curve defined over the knot vector

$$U = \{0,0,0,0,0,u_1,u_1,u_2,u_2,1,1,1,1,1\}$$

The coordinate system (u, E) is used to graph the error over each knot span as a function of u as the algorithm sweeps out the entire knot vector;

b. the knot u_1 is inserted twice, bringing the total multiplicity to four; the first Bézier piece is obtained;

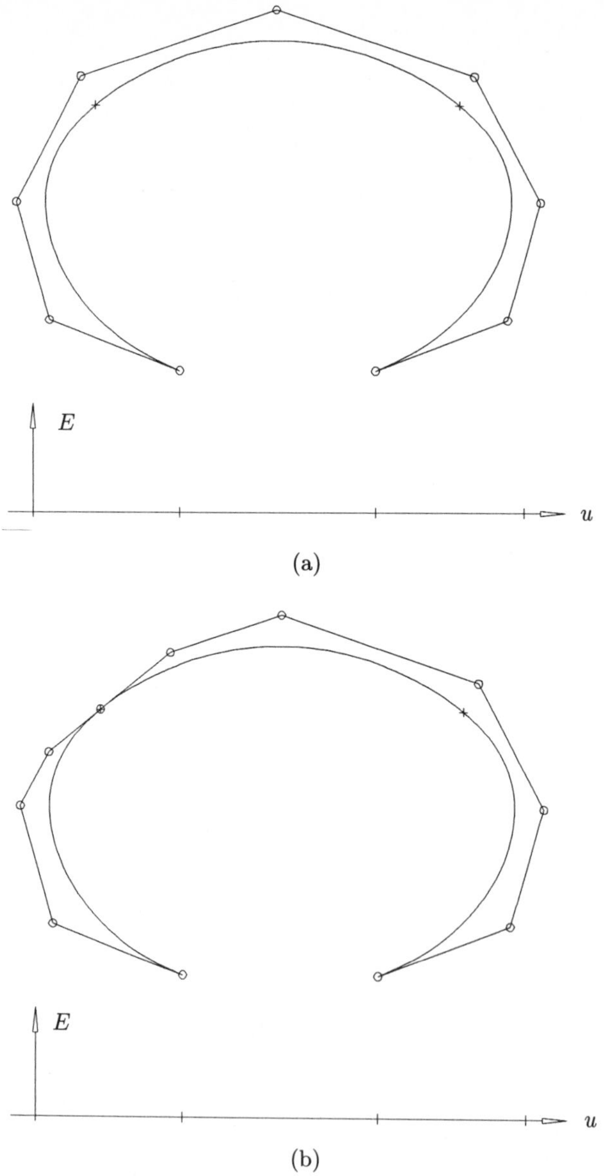

Figure 5.39. Degree reduction of a B-spline curve from fourth-degree to third-degree. (a) Fourth-degree B-spline curve to be degree reduced; (b) first Bézier segment is extracted.

c. the first Bézier segment is degree reduced, which replaces the first five control points by four new ones; this is the first time error is introduced as graphed in the (u, E) system. The solid curve is the original curve, whereas the dashed one is the approximation;

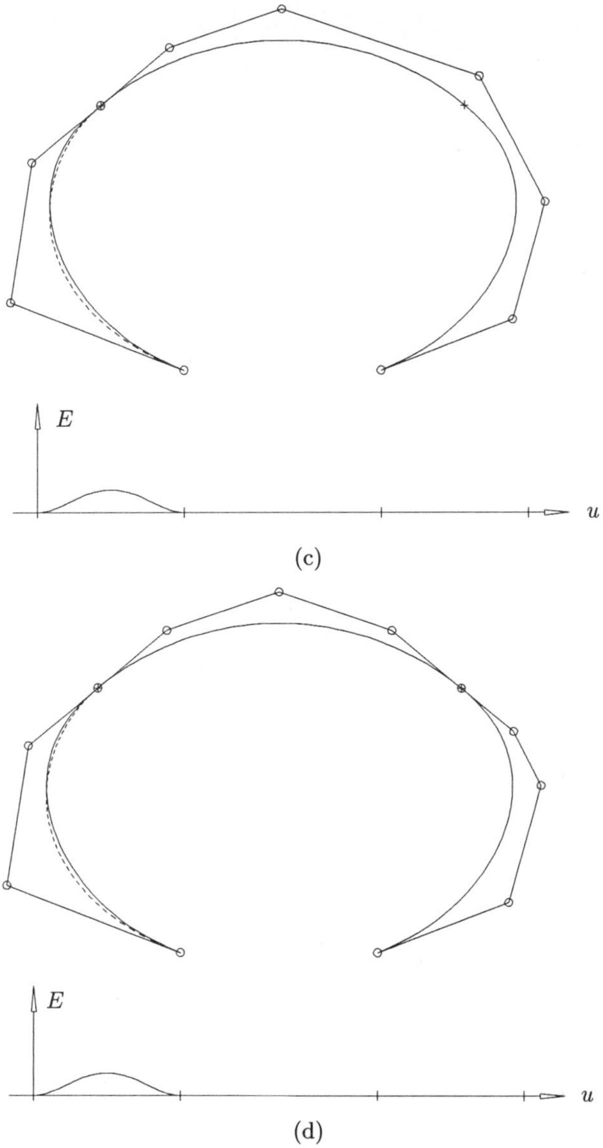

Figure 5.39. *Continued.* (c) first Bézier segment is degree reduced; (d) second Bézier segment is extracted.

d. the knot u_2 is inserted twice to obtain the second Bézier segment;

e. the second Bézier segment is degree reduced. Now there is error over two segments; both are Bézier degree reduction errors;

f. two occurrences of the knot u_1 are removed; notice how knot removal introduces additional error that affects more than one knot span;

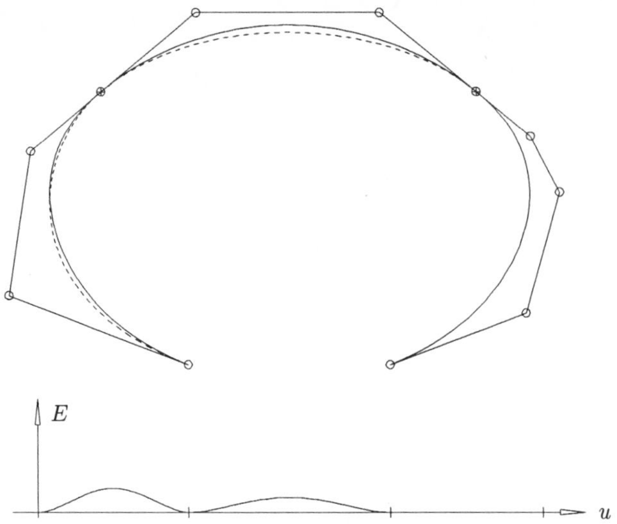

(e)

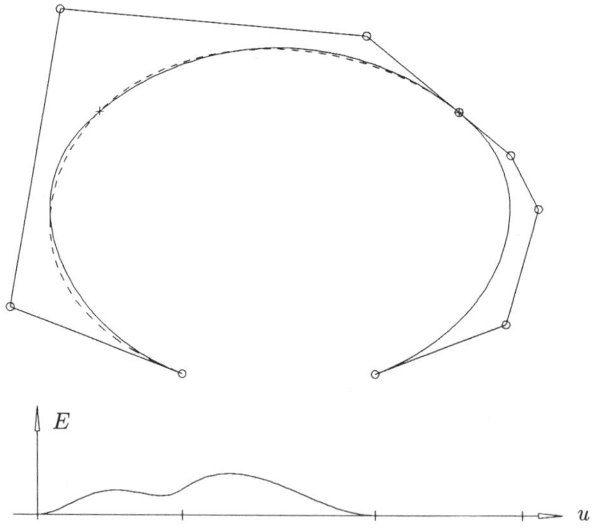

(f)

Figure 5.39. *Continued.* (e) second Bézier segment is degree reduced; (f) first interior multiple knot is removed twice.

g. the last Bézier segment is degree reduced;

h. two occurrences of u_2 are removed, yielding the final curve.

Curve decomposition, knot removal, and bounding the knot removal error were covered in Sections 5.3 and 5.4.

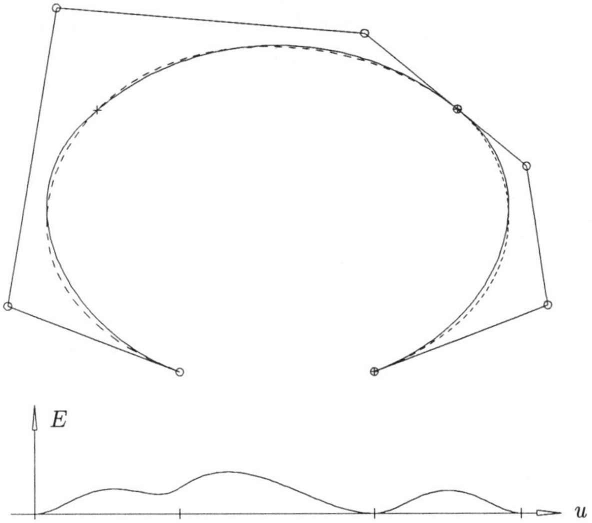

(g)

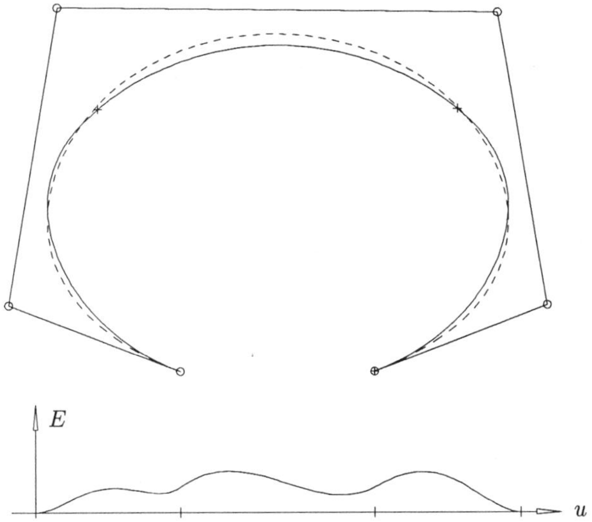

(h)

Figure 5.39. *Continued.* (g) third Bézier segment is degree reduced; (h) second interior multiple knot is removed twice.

We focus now on Bézier degree reduction. Let

$$\mathbf{C}(u) = \sum_{i=0}^{p} B_{i,p}(u)\,\mathbf{Q}_i$$

be a pth degree Bézier curve, and denote its degree reduced counterpart by

$$\hat{\mathbf{C}}(u) = \sum_{i=0}^{p-1} B_{i,p-1}(u)\,\mathbf{P}_i$$

We compute the unknown $\mathbf{P}_i$ by turning around the Bézier degree elevation formula, Eqs. (5.34) and (5.35); let

$$r = \frac{p-1}{2} \tag{5.40}$$

(integer division) and denote the degree elevation coefficients by α_i, that is

$$\alpha_i = \frac{i}{p}$$

(we need coefficients for degree elevation from $p-1$ to p). There are two cases to consider, p is even, and p is odd. Assume first that p is even. Solving Eq. (5.35) for the $\mathbf{P}_i$, we obtain

$$\begin{aligned} \mathbf{P}_0 &= \mathbf{Q}_0 \\ \mathbf{P}_i &= \frac{\mathbf{Q}_i - \alpha_i \mathbf{P}_{i-1}}{1-\alpha_i} \qquad i = 1,\ldots,r \\ \mathbf{P}_i &= \frac{\mathbf{Q}_{i+1} - (1-\alpha_{i+1})\mathbf{P}_{i+1}}{\alpha_{i+1}} \qquad i = p-2,\ldots,r+1 \\ \mathbf{P}_{p-1} &= \mathbf{Q}_p \end{aligned} \tag{5.41}$$

Now assume p is odd; then the $\mathbf{P}_i$ are computed as

$$\begin{aligned} \mathbf{P}_0 &= \mathbf{Q}_0 \\ \mathbf{P}_i &= \frac{\mathbf{Q}_i - \alpha_i \mathbf{P}_{i-1}}{1-\alpha_i} \qquad i = 1,\ldots,r-1 \\ \mathbf{P}_i &= \frac{\mathbf{Q}_{i+1} - (1-\alpha_{i+1})\mathbf{P}_{i+1}}{\alpha_{i+1}} \qquad i = p-2,\ldots,r+1 \\ \mathbf{P}_r &= \frac{1}{2}\left(\mathbf{P}_r^L + \mathbf{P}_r^R\right) \\ \mathbf{P}_{p-1} &= \mathbf{Q}_p \end{aligned} \tag{5.42}$$

where

$$\begin{aligned} \mathbf{P}_r^L &= \frac{\mathbf{Q}_r - \alpha_r \mathbf{P}_{r-1}}{1-\alpha_r} \\ \mathbf{P}_r^R &= \frac{\mathbf{Q}_{r+1} - (1-\alpha_{r+1})\mathbf{P}_{r+1}}{\alpha_{r+1}} \end{aligned}$$

Note that the odd case differs from the even case only in that, for symmetry reasons, the middle control point, $\mathbf{P}_r$, is computed as the average of two components computed from the left and right, respectively. In general, the resulting $(p-1)$th degree curve, $\hat{\mathbf{C}}(u)$, is an approximation to $\mathbf{C}(u)$; they coincide only when $\mathbf{C}(u)$ is precisely degree reducible. Piegl and Tiller [Pieg95] derive the error bounds for the approximation

p even:

$$\left|\mathbf{C}(u) - \hat{\mathbf{C}}(u)\right| = \left|B_{r+1,p}(u)\left[\mathbf{Q}_{r+1} - \frac{1}{2}(\mathbf{P}_r + \mathbf{P}_{r+1})\right]\right| \tag{5.43}$$

p odd:

$$\left|\mathbf{C}(u) - \hat{\mathbf{C}}(u)\right| = \frac{1}{2}\left(1-\alpha_r\right)\left|\left(B_{r,p}(u) - B_{r+1,p}(u)\right)\left(\mathbf{P}_r^L - \mathbf{P}_r^R\right)\right| \tag{5.44}$$

Figures 5.40a and 5.40b show examples of reducing the degree of a Bézier curve from seven to six, and six to five, respectively. The error curves are graphed on the bottom of the figures. We remark that:

- Equations (5.43) and (5.44) express the *parametric* error (distance between points at corresponding parameter values); the maximums of geometric and parametric errors are not necessarily at the same u value;
- even if $\mathbf{C}(u)$ is not degree reducible, Eqs. (5.41) and (5.42) produce $p/2$ precise control points from the left and $p/2$ precise ones from the right, in the sense that if $\hat{\mathbf{C}}(u)$ is degree elevated to yield $\bar{\mathbf{C}}(u)$, then $\mathbf{C}(u)$ and $\bar{\mathbf{C}}(u)$ have the same first and last $p/2$ control points. Hence, $\mathbf{C}(u)$ and $\hat{\mathbf{C}}(u)$ have the same derivatives up to order $p/2-1$ at both ends. This is an important property from the standpoint of B-spline degree reduction, since it implies that up to $C^{p/2-1}$ continuity is maintained in the Bézier degree reduction steps, which in turn implies that the first $p/2-1$ knot removal steps produce no error;
- for p even the maximum error occurs at $u = 1/2$ (see Figure 5.40b); for p odd the error is zero at $u = 1/2$, and it has two peaks a bit to the left and right of $u = 1/2$ (Figure 5.40a). The odd case is analyzed in more detail elsewhere by Piegl and Tiller [Pieg95].

We now present an algorithm to degree reduce a B-spline curve, subject to a maximum error tolerance, `TOL`. If the curve is rational, then `TOL` should be adjusted as in Eq. (5.30). We maintain an error vector, e_i, $i = 0, \ldots, m-1$, which we use to accumulate error for each knot span. The e_i are initialized to zero. When the ith span is Bézier degree reduced, the incurred error is added to e_i. For simplicity we drop the scalar functions (which are bounded by 1) from Eqs. (5.43) and (5.44) and use maximum error bounds

$$\left|\mathbf{C}(u) - \hat{\mathbf{C}}(u)\right| \le \left|\mathbf{Q}_{r+1} - \frac{1}{2}\left(\mathbf{P}_r + \mathbf{P}_{r+1}\right)\right| \tag{5.45}$$

and

$$\left|\mathbf{C}(u) - \hat{\mathbf{C}}(u)\right| \le \left|\mathbf{P}_r^L - \mathbf{P}_r^R\right| \tag{5.46}$$

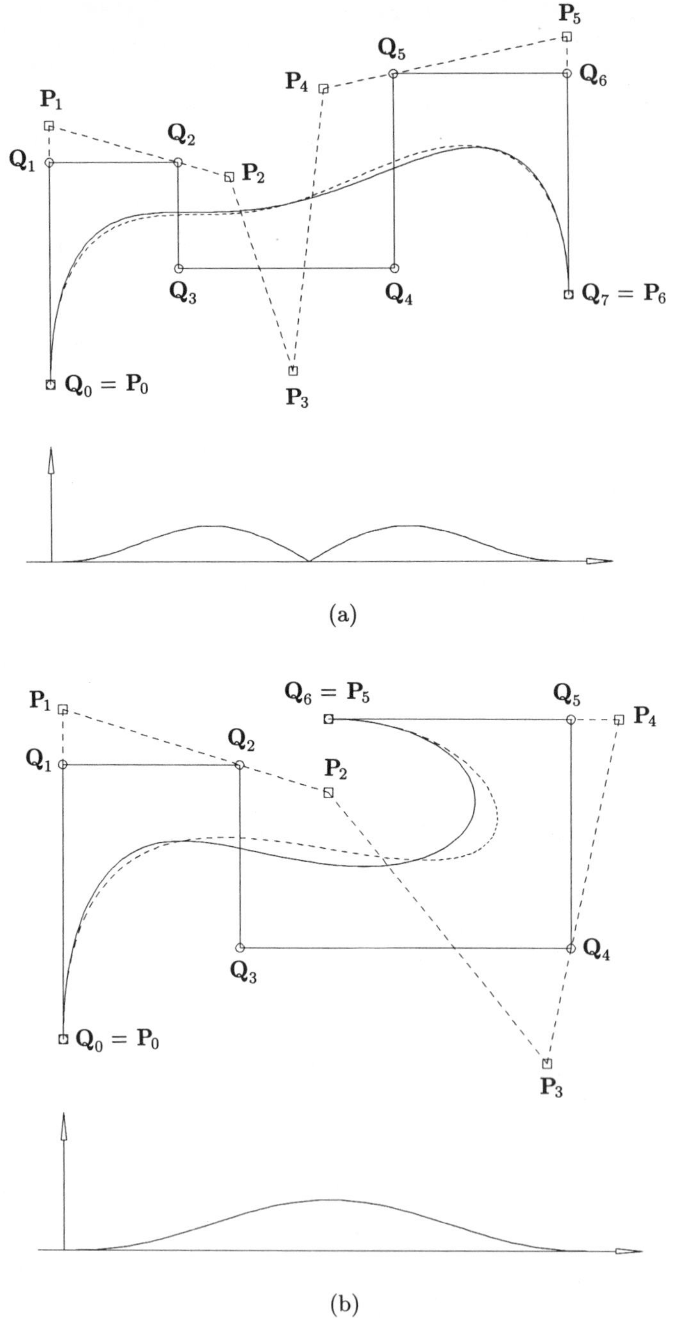

Figure 5.40. Bézier degree reduction. (a) From degree seven to degree six; (b) from degree six to degree five.

The algorithm in [Pieg95] computes tighter error bounds for both the Bézier degree reduction and knot removal steps. When removing a knot, the maximum knot removal error is added to each e_i whose span is affected by the removal. The local arrays used are:

`bpts[p+1]`	:	Bézier control points of the current segment;
`Nextbpts[p-1]`	:	leftmost control points of the next Bézier segment;
`rbpts[p]`	:	degree reduced Bézier control points;
`alphas[p-1]`	:	knot insertion alphas;
`e[m]`	:	error vector.

A supporting routine, `BezDegreeReduce(bpts,rbpts,MaxErr)`, which implements Bézier degree reduction and computation of the maximum error, is used. This routine uses Eqs. (5.41), (5.42), (5.45), and (5.46). A return code of 1 indicates the curve was not degree reducible; if the curve is reducible, $\hat{n}$, $\hat{U}$, and the $\mathbf{P}_i$ are computed (`nh, Uh, Pw`) and a 0 code is returned.

```
ALGORITHM A5.11
DegreeReduceCurve(n,p,U,Qw,nh,Uh,Pw)
  { /*  Degree reduce a curve from p to p-1.  */
    /*  Input:  n,p,U,Qw  */
    /*  Output: nh,Uh,Pw  */
  ph = p-1;   mh = ph;   /* Initialize some variables */
  kind = ph+1;   r = -1;   a = p;
  b = p+1;   cind = 1;   mult = p;
  m = n+p+1;   Pw[0] = Qw[0];
  for (i=0; i<=ph; i++)  /* Compute left end of knot vector */
    Uh[i] = U[0];
  for (i=0; i<=p; i++)   /* Initialize first Bézier segment */
    bpts[i] = Qw[i];
  for (i=0; i<m; i++)    /* Initialize error vector */
    e[i] = 0.0;
      /* Loop through the knot vector */
  while (b < m)
    { /* First compute knot multiplicity */
    i = b;
    while (b < m && U[b] == U[b+1])   b = b+1;
    mult = b-i+1;   mh = mh+mult-1;
    oldr = r;   r = p-mult;
    if (oldr > 0)  lbz = (oldr+2)/2;  else  lbz = 1;
        /* Insert knot U[b] r times */
    if (r > 0)
      {
      numer = U[b]-U[a];
      for (k=p; k>=mult; k--)
```

```
        alphas[k-mult-1] = numer/(U[a+k]-U[a]);
      for (j=1; j<=r; j++)
        {
        save = r-j;   s = mult+j;
        for (k=p; k>=s; k--)
          bpts[k] = alphas[k-s]*bpts[k]
                              + (1.0-alphas[k-s])*bpts[k-1];
        Nextbpts[save] = bpts[p];
        }
      }
        /* Degree reduce Bézier segment */
    BezDegreeReduce(bpts,rbpts,MaxErr);
    e[a] = e[a]+MaxErr;
    if (e[a] > TOL)
      return(1);    /* Curve not degree reducible */
        /* Remove knot U[a] oldr times */
    if (oldr > 0)
      {
      first = kind;   last = kind;
      for (k=0; k<oldr; k++)
        {
        i = first;   j = last;   kj = j-kind;
        while (j-i > k)
          {
          alfa = (U[a]-Uh[i-1])/(U[b]-Uh[i-1]);
          beta = (U[a]-Uh[j-k-1])/(U[b]-Uh[j-k-1]);
          Pw[i-1] = (Pw[i-1]-(1.0-alfa)*Pw[i-2])/alfa;
          rbpts[kj] = (rbpts[kj]-beta*rbpts[kj+1])/(1.0-beta);
          i = i+1;   j = j-1;   kj = kj-1;
          }
           /* Compute knot removal error bounds (Br) */
        if (j-i < k)  Br = Distance4D(Pw[i-2],rbpts[kj+1]);
          else
          {
          delta = (U[a]-Uh[i-1])/(U[b]-Uh[i-1]);
          A = delta*rbpts[kj+1]+(1.0-delta)*Pw[i-2];
          Br = Distance4D(Pw[i-1],A);
          }
           /* Update the error vector */
        K = a+oldr-k;   q = (2*p-k+1)/2;
        L = K-q;
        for (ii=L; ii<=a; ii++)
          {  /* These knot spans were affected */
          e[ii] = e[ii] + Br;
          if (e[ii] > TOL)
```

```
          return(1);    /* Curve not degree reducible */
        }
      first = first-1;    last = last+1;
      }  /* End for (k=0; k<oldr; k++) loop */
    cind = i-1;
    }  /* End if (oldr > 0) */
      /* Load knot vector and control points */
  if (a != p)
    for (i=0; i<ph-oldr; i++)
      {  Uh[kind] = U[a];    kind = kind+1;  }
  for (i=lbz; i<=ph; i++)
    {  Pw[cind] = rbpts[i];    cind = cind+1;  }
      /* Set up for next pass through */
  if (b < m)
    {
    for (i=0; i<r; i++)     bpts[i] = Nextbpts[i];
    for (i=r; i<=p; i++)    bpts[i] = Qw[b-p+i];
    a = b;     b = b+1;
    }
  else
    for (i=0; i<=ph; i++)   Uh[kind+i] = U[b];
  }  /* End of while (b < m) loop */
nh = mh-ph-1;
return(0);
}
```

Figure 5.41 shows an example of reducing the degree from five to four. The original knot vector is

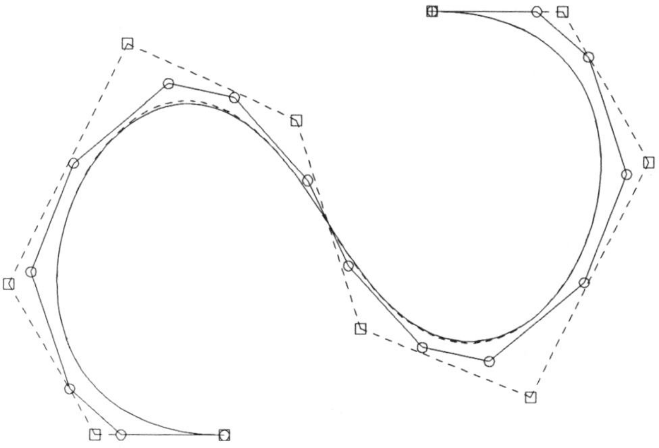

Figure 5.41. Degree reduction of a B-spline curve from degree five to four.

$$U = \{0,0,0,0,0,0,0.15,0.15,0.3,0.3,0.5,0.5,\\ 0.7,0.7,0.85,0.85,1,1,1,1,1,1\}$$

The solid curve is the original curve, whereas the dashed one is the degree reduced curve. Figure 5.42a shows a cubic curve defined on the knot vector

$$U = \left\{0,0,0,0,\frac{3}{10},\frac{3}{10},\frac{1}{2},\frac{1}{2},\frac{7}{10},\frac{7}{10},1,1,1,1\right\}$$

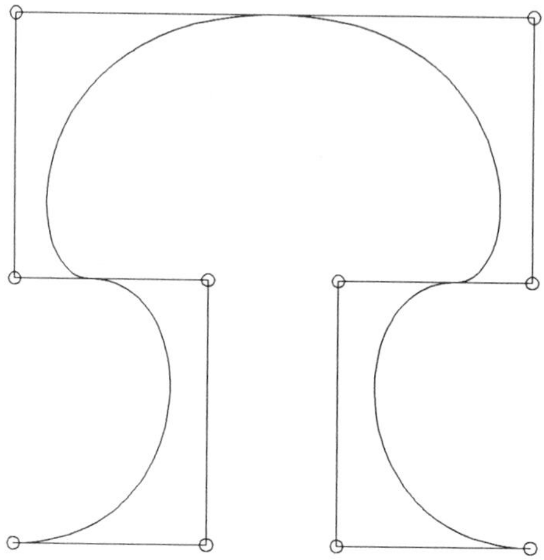

(a)

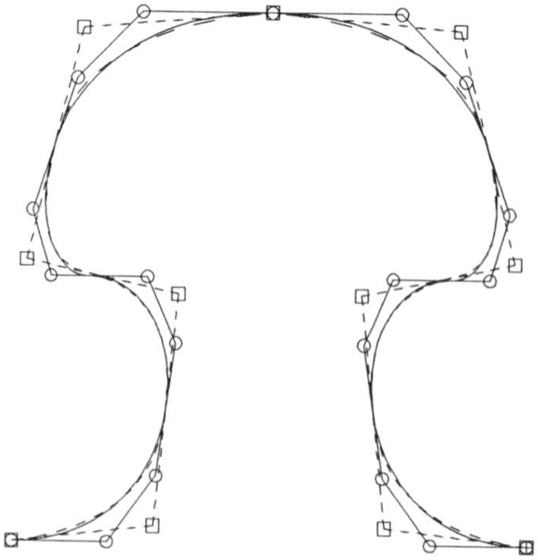

(b)

Figure 5.42. A cubic curve. (a) The cubic curve is not degree reducible; (b) the curve is degree reducible after knot refinement.

It is not possible to approximate this curve with a second-degree B-spline curve to within a reasonable tolerance. After refining the knot vector to

$$U^{(r)} = \{0,0,0,0,0.15,0.15,0.3,0.3,0.4,0.4,0.5,0.5,0.5,\\ 0.6,0.6,0.7,0.7,0.85,0.85,1,1,1,1\}$$

a reasonable approximation is possible, as shown in Figure 5.42b. Notice the discontinuity at $u = 1/2$. This is due to the triple knot in the original curve. The refinement brings out an interesting point: the quality of the approximation can be improved by introducing extra knots with at least multiplicity two. Hence, together with knot refinement, the tools of this section can be used to develop algorithms to approximate high-degree curves with lower-degree curves.

Finally, we remark that the u- or v-degree of a surface can be reduced by applying these curve techniques to the rows or columns of control points.

EXERCISES

5.1. Let $p = 2$ and $U = \{0,0,0,1,2,3,4,4,5,5,5\}$. $\mathbf{C}(u) = \sum_{i=0}^{7} N_{i,2}(u)\mathbf{P}_i$, a B-spline curve, is defined on U by the control points $\{(-6,-1),(-5,2),(-3,3),(-1,2),(0,0),(3,1),(3,3),(1,5)\}$. Using repeated knot insertion, compute $\mathbf{C}(5/4)$ and $\mathbf{C}'(5/4)$. Check that Eqs. (5.12) – (5.14) and (5.16) – (5.18) hold true for this example. Sketch the curve and its control polygon.

5.2. Use the same curve as in Exercise 5.1. What value of u must be inserted as a knot in order to cause the point $(-3/4, 3/2)$ to become a control point?

5.3. Consider the B-spline surface

$$\mathbf{S}(u,v) = \sum_{i=0}^{7}\sum_{j=0}^{8} N_{i,2}(u)N_{j,3}(v)\,\mathbf{P}_{i,j}$$

where
$$U = \left\{0,0,0,\frac{1}{5},\frac{3}{10},\frac{3}{5},\frac{4}{5},\frac{9}{10},1,1,1\right\}$$

and
$$V = \left\{0,0,0,0,\frac{1}{10},\frac{2}{5},\frac{1}{2},\frac{7}{10},\frac{4}{5},1,1,1,1\right\}$$

Suppose you want to modify the surface shape slightly in the region corresponding to the rectangular area of parameter space given by $3/10 < u < 6/10$ and $1/2 < v < 7/10$. You want to do this by adding knots (control points) until you have at least one control point which you can freely move, without changing the continuity of the surface with respect to u and v, and without changing the surface shape outside of this rectangular area. What knots must you add to U and V? State clearly how many and what values.

5.4. Consider the B-spline surface

$$\mathbf{S}(u,v) = \sum_{i=0}^{3}\sum_{j=0}^{2} N_{i,2}(u)N_{j,2}(v)\,\mathbf{P}_{i,j}$$

where
$$U = \left\{0,0,0,\frac{1}{2},1,1,1\right\}$$

and
$$V = \{0,0,0,1,1,1\}$$

and

$$\mathbf{P}_{0,0} = (0,0,0) \quad \mathbf{P}_{1,0} = (3,0,3) \quad \mathbf{P}_{2,0} = (6,0,3) \quad \mathbf{P}_{3,0} = (9,0,0)$$
$$\mathbf{P}_{0,1} = (0,2,2) \quad \mathbf{P}_{1,1} = (3,2,5) \quad \mathbf{P}_{2,1} = (6,2,5) \quad \mathbf{P}_{3,1} = (9,2,2)$$
$$\mathbf{P}_{0,2} = (0,4,0) \quad \mathbf{P}_{1,2} = (3,4,3) \quad \mathbf{P}_{2,2} = (6,4,3) \quad \mathbf{P}_{3,2} = (9,4,0)$$

Compute $\mathbf{S}(3/10, 6/10)$ using knot insertion. Compare this with Exercise 3.8.

5.5. Let $p = 3$ and $U = \{0,0,0,0,1,1,1,2,2,2,2\}$ as in the example of Figure 5.26. Assume the control points $\mathbf{P}_i^0 = \{(-1,0),\ (-1,1),\ (-1/2, 3/2),\ (1/4, 3/2),\ (1, 3/2),\ (2,1),\ (2,0)\}$. Determine how many times $u = 1$ is removable, and compute the new control points. You can do this by using Eq. (5.29), or by tracing through Algorithm A5.8.

CHAPTER

SIX

Advanced Geometric Algorithms

6.1 Point Inversion and Projection for Curves and Surfaces

In this chapter we cover various topics which are rather fundamental in implementing NURBS geometry.

Given a point $\mathbf{P} = (x, y, z)$, assumed to lie on the NURBS curve $\mathbf{C}(u)$ of degree p, *point inversion* is the problem of finding the corresponding parameter, $\bar{u}$, such that $\mathbf{C}(\bar{u}) = \mathbf{P}$. Theoretically, point inversion can be solved in closed form if $p \leq 4$. The steps are:

1. using the strong convex hull property (P4.10), determine which spans of $\mathbf{C}(u)$ can possibly contain $\mathbf{P}$;
2. using knot insertion or refinement, extract the candidate spans and convert them to power basis form;
3. each span results in three polynomial equations in one unknown; if the three equations have a common solution, then $\mathbf{P}$ lies on that segment of the curve.

As an example of Step 3, assume $p = 2$. Then a span $\mathbf{r}(u)$ is given by the vector function (in four-dimensional space):

$$\mathbf{r}(u) = \mathbf{a}_0^w + \mathbf{a}_1^w u + \mathbf{a}_2^w u^2 \tag{6.1}$$

Let $\mathbf{a}_i^w = (w_i x_i, w_i y_i, w_i z_i, w_i)$. Projecting Eq. (6.1) to three-dimensional space and setting it equal to $\mathbf{P} = (x, y, z)$, we obtain

$$\frac{w_2 x_2 u^2 + w_1 x_1 u + w_0 x_0}{w_2 u^2 + w_1 u + w_0} = x$$

$$\frac{w_2 y_2 u^2 + w_1 y_1 u + w_0 y_0}{w_2 u^2 + w_1 u + w_0} = y$$

$$\frac{w_2 z_2 u^2 + w_1 z_1 u + w_0 z_0}{w_2 u^2 + w_1 u + w_0} = z$$

which yields

$$w_2(x_2 - x)u^2 + w_1(x_1 - x)u + w_0(x_0 - x) = 0$$
$$w_2(y_2 - y)u^2 + w_1(y_1 - y)u + w_0(y_0 - y) = 0$$
$$w_2(z_2 - z)u^2 + w_1(z_1 - z)u + w_0(z_0 - z) = 0 \qquad (6.2)$$

This method has its disadvantages, for example:

- Equation (6.2) cannot be solved in closed form for $p > 4$, and the solution for $p = 3$ and $p = 4$ is not without problems on a computer;
- there are numerical tolerance problems, e.g., one cannot expect the three solutions of Eq. (6.2) to be exactly equal; but when should they be considered equal? The problem is exacerbated when the point **P** is not precisely on the curve (a common occurrence);
- the software implementation of the previous solution is rather involved.

A simpler and completely adequate method is to use Newton iteration to minimize the distance between **P** and $\mathbf{C}(u)$ (see Figures 6.1a and 6.1b). **P** is considered to be on the curve if the minimum distance is less than a specified tolerance, ϵ_1. This effectively solves the more general problem of *point projection* to a curve. To obtain a start value, u_0, for the Newton iteration:

- if the point is known to lie on the curve (within tolerance), use the strong convex hull property to determine candidate spans; if it is a more general point projection problem, choose all spans as candidates;
- evaluate curve points at n equally spaced parameter values on each candidate span, and compute the distance of each point from **P**. Choose u_0 to be the value yielding the point closest to **P**; the number n is generally chosen by some heuristic method. We emphasize that a good start value is important in achieving reliable convergence.

Now assume we have the start value, u_0, and form the dot product function

$$f(u) = \mathbf{C}'(u) \cdot (\mathbf{C}(u) - \mathbf{P})$$

The distance from **P** to $\mathbf{C}(u)$ is minimum when $f(u) = 0$, whether **P** is on the curve or not (Figures 6.1a and 6.1b). Denote by u_i the parameter obtained at the ith Newton iteration. Then

$$u_{i+1} = u_i - \frac{f(u_i)}{f'(u_i)} = u_i - \frac{\mathbf{C}'(u_i) \cdot (\mathbf{C}(u_i) - \mathbf{P})}{\mathbf{C}''(u_i) \cdot (\mathbf{C}(u_i) - \mathbf{P}) + |\,\mathbf{C}'(u_i)\,|^2} \qquad (6.3)$$

Two zero tolerances can be used to indicate convergence:

ϵ_1 : a measure of Euclidean distance;

ϵ_2 : a zero cosine measure.

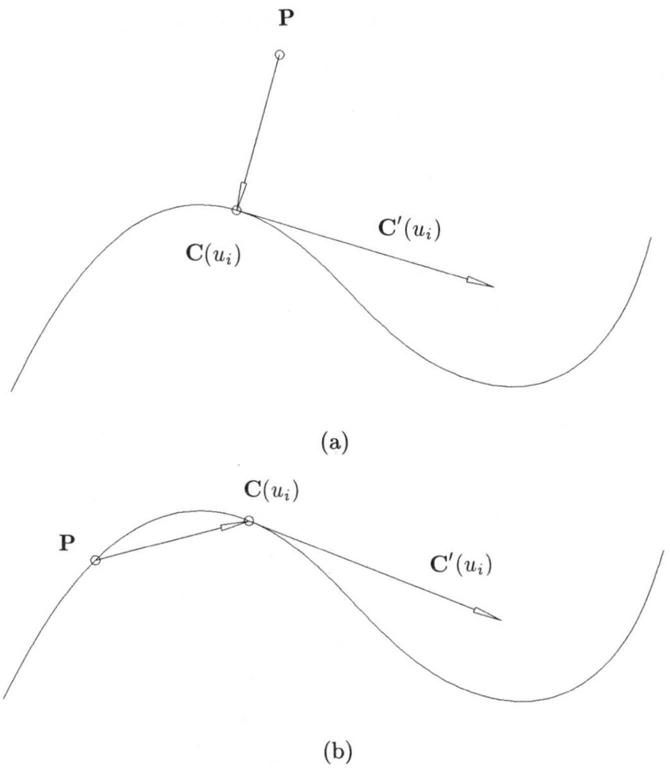

Figure 6.1. (a) Point projection; (b) point inversion.

Convergence criteria are then given by

$$
\begin{aligned}
&|\,(u_{i+1}-u_i)\,\mathbf{C}'(u_i)\,| \le \epsilon_1\\
&|\,\mathbf{C}(u_i)-\mathbf{P}\,| \le \epsilon_1\\
&\frac{|\,\mathbf{C}'(u_i)\cdot(\mathbf{C}(u_i)-\mathbf{P})\,|}{|\,\mathbf{C}'(u_i)\,|\,|\,\mathbf{C}(u_i)-\mathbf{P}\,|} \le \epsilon_2
\end{aligned}
\tag{6.4}
$$

The criteria are checked in the following order:

1. point coincidence:

$$|\,\mathbf{C}(u_i)-\mathbf{P}\,| \le \epsilon_1$$

2. zero cosine:

$$\frac{|\,\mathbf{C}'(u_i)\cdot(\mathbf{C}(u_i)-\mathbf{P})\,|}{|\,\mathbf{C}'(u_i)\,|\,|\,\mathbf{C}(u_i)-\mathbf{P}\,|} \le \epsilon_2$$

If at least one of these conditions is not satisfied, a new value, u_{i+1}, is computed using Eq. (6.3). Then two more conditions are checked:

3. ensure that the parameter stays within the range ($u_{i+1} \in [a,b]$)

   if the curve is not closed:

$$\text{if } (u_{i+1} < a) \qquad u_{i+1} = a$$
$$\text{if } (u_{i+1} > b) \qquad u_{i+1} = b$$

   if the curve is closed:

$$\text{if } (u_{i+1} < a) \qquad u_{i+1} = b - (a - u_{i+1})$$
$$\text{if } (u_{i+1} > b) \qquad u_{i+1} = a + (u_{i+1} - b)$$

4. the parameter does not change significantly, e.g., the point is off the end of the curve

$$|\,(u_{i+1} - u_i)\,\mathbf{C}'(u_i)\,| \leq \epsilon_1$$

If any of conditions (1), (2), or (4) is satisfied, the iteration is halted. Figure 6.2 shows the projection of a set of points onto a NURBS curve.

Point inversion and projection for surfaces are analogous. Form the vector function

$$\mathbf{r}(u,v) = \mathbf{S}(u,v) - \mathbf{P}$$

and the two scalar equations

$$f(u,v) = \mathbf{r}(u,v)\cdot\mathbf{S}_u(u,v) = 0$$
$$g(u,v) = \mathbf{r}(u,v)\cdot\mathbf{S}_v(u,v) = 0 \qquad (6.5)$$

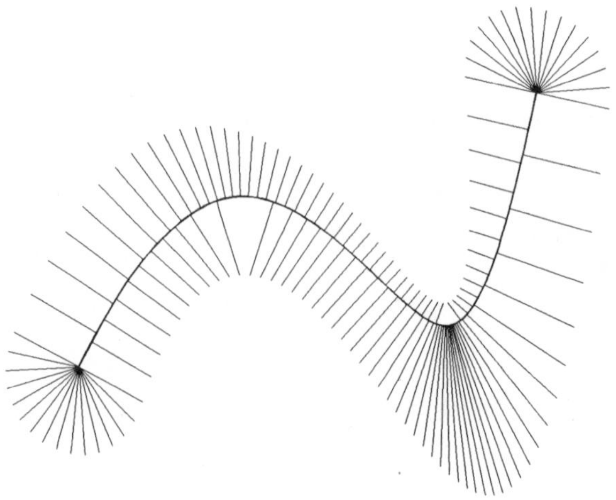

Figure 6.2. Projecting a set of points onto a NURBS curve.

We must solve Eq. (6.5). Let

$$\delta_i = \begin{bmatrix} \Delta u \\ \Delta v \end{bmatrix} = \begin{bmatrix} u_{i+1} - u_i \\ v_{i+1} - v_i \end{bmatrix}$$

$$J_i = \begin{bmatrix} f_u & f_v \\ g_u & g_v \end{bmatrix} = \begin{bmatrix} |\,\mathbf{S}_u\,|^2 + \mathbf{r}\cdot\mathbf{S}_{uu} & \mathbf{S}_u\cdot\mathbf{S}_v + \mathbf{r}\cdot\mathbf{S}_{uv} \\ \mathbf{S}_u\cdot\mathbf{S}_v + \mathbf{r}\cdot\mathbf{S}_{vu} & |\,\mathbf{S}_v\,|^2 + \mathbf{r}\cdot\mathbf{S}_{vv} \end{bmatrix}$$

$$\kappa_i = -\begin{bmatrix} f(u_i, v_i) \\ g(u_i, v_i) \end{bmatrix}$$

where all the functions in the matrix J_i are evaluated at (u_i, v_i). At the ith iteration we must solve the 2×2 system of linear equations in the unknown δ_i, given by

$$J_i \delta_i = \kappa_i \tag{6.6}$$

From δ_i we obtain

$$\begin{aligned} u_{i+1} &= \Delta u + u_i \\ v_{i+1} &= \Delta v + v_i \end{aligned} \tag{6.7}$$

Convergence criteria are given by

$$|\,(u_{i+1} - u_i)\,\mathbf{S}_u(u_i, v_i) + (v_{i+1} - v_i)\,\mathbf{S}_v(u_i, v_i)\,| \le \epsilon_1$$

$$|\,\mathbf{S}(u_i, v_i) - \mathbf{P}\,| \le \epsilon_1$$

$$\frac{|\,\mathbf{S}_u(u_i, v_i)\cdot(\mathbf{S}(u_i, v_i) - \mathbf{P})\,|}{|\,\mathbf{S}_u(u_i, v_i)\,|\,|\,\mathbf{S}(u_i, v_i) - \mathbf{P}\,|} \le \epsilon_2 \qquad \frac{|\,\mathbf{S}_v(u_i, v_i)\cdot(\mathbf{S}(u_i, v_i) - \mathbf{P})\,|}{|\,\mathbf{S}_v(u_i, v_i)\,|\,|\,\mathbf{S}(u_i, v_i) - \mathbf{P}\,|} \le \epsilon_2 \tag{6.8}$$

Again, the conditions are checked by

1. point coincidence:

$$|\,\mathbf{S}(u_i, v_i) - \mathbf{P}\,| \le \epsilon_1$$

2. zero cosine:

$$\frac{|\,\mathbf{S}_u(u_i, v_i)\cdot(\mathbf{S}(u_i, v_i) - \mathbf{P})\,|}{|\,\mathbf{S}_u(u_i, v_i)\,|\,|\,\mathbf{S}(u_i, v_i) - \mathbf{P}\,|} \le \epsilon_2 \qquad \frac{|\,\mathbf{S}_v(u_i, v_i)\cdot(\mathbf{S}(u_i, v_i) - \mathbf{P})\,|}{|\,\mathbf{S}_v(u_i, v_i)\,|\,|\,\mathbf{S}(u_i, v_i) - \mathbf{P}\,|} \le \epsilon_2$$

If these conditions are not satisfied, a new value (u_{i+1}, v_{i+1}) is computed using Eq. (6.7). Then two more conditions are checked:

3. ensure that the parameters stay in range ($u_{i+1} \in [a, b]$ and $v_{i+1} \in [c, d]$):

   if the surface is not closed in the u direction:

$$\begin{aligned} &\text{if } (u_{i+1} < a) \qquad u_{i+1} = a \\ &\text{if } (u_{i+1} > b) \qquad u_{i+1} = b \end{aligned}$$

if the surface is not closed in the v direction:

$$\text{if } (v_{i+1} < c) \qquad v_{i+1} = c$$
$$\text{if } (v_{i+1} > d) \qquad v_{i+1} = d$$

if the surface is closed in the u direction:

$$\text{if } (u_{i+1} < a) \qquad u_{i+1} = b - (a - u_{i+1})$$
$$\text{if } (u_{i+1} > b) \qquad u_{i+1} = a + (u_{i+1} - b)$$

if the surface is closed in the v direction:

$$\text{if } (v_{i+1} < c) \qquad v_{i+1} = d - (c - v_{i+1})$$
$$\text{if } (v_{i+1} > d) \qquad v_{i+1} = c + (v_{i+1} - d)$$

4. parameters do not change significantly, that is

$$|\,(u_{i+1} - u_i)\,\mathbf{S}_u(u_i, v_i) + (v_{i+1} - v_i)\,\mathbf{S}_v(u_i, v_i)\,| \le \epsilon_1$$

Iteration is halted if any of conditions (1), (2), or (4) is satisfied. Figure 6.3 shows the projection of a set of points from the control net onto a NURBS surface.

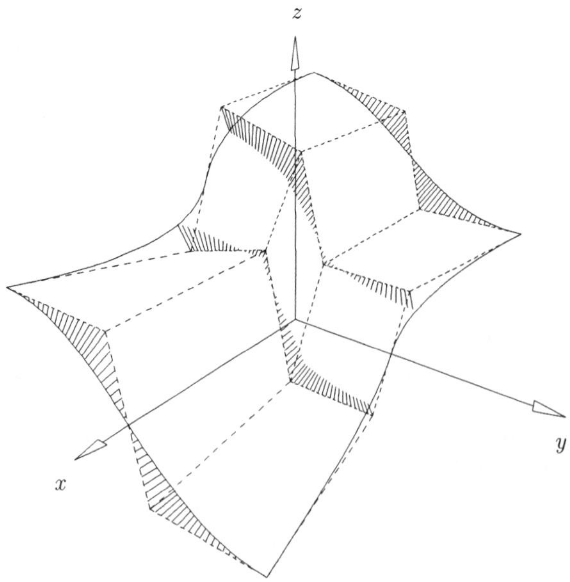

Figure 6.3. Projecting points of the control net onto a NURBS surface.

6.2 Surface Tangent Vector Inversion

Let $(\bar{u}, \bar{v})$ be a fixed parameter point and $\mathbf{P} = \mathbf{S}(\bar{u}, \bar{v})$ its image on the surface $\mathbf{S}(u, v)$ (see Figure 6.4). Let $\mathbf{T} = (dx, dy, dz)$ be a vector starting at $\mathbf{P}$ and lying in the tangent plane of $\mathbf{S}(u, v)$ at $\mathbf{P}$. Denote by $\mathbf{S}_u$ and $\mathbf{S}_v$ the first partial derivatives of $\mathbf{S}(u, v)$ at $(\bar{u}, \bar{v})$. If $\mathbf{S}_u \times \mathbf{S}_v \neq 0$, it follows from elementary differential geometry [DoCa76] that there exists a vector $\mathbf{W} = (du, dv)$ in the uv plane such that

$$\mathbf{T} = \mathbf{S}_u du + \mathbf{S}_v dv \tag{6.9}$$

Tangent vector inversion is the process of determining the vector $\mathbf{W}$. Equation (6.9) expands into three equations in two unknowns, that is

$$\begin{bmatrix} x_u & x_v \\ y_u & y_v \\ z_u & z_v \end{bmatrix} \begin{bmatrix} du \\ dv \end{bmatrix} = \begin{bmatrix} dx \\ dy \\ dz \end{bmatrix} \tag{6.10}$$

which we write as

$$M\mathbf{W} = \mathbf{T}$$

Equation (6.10) has a unique and exact solution (generally such a system does not) which we obtain by multiplying through by M^T (the transpose of M)

$$(M^T M)\,\mathbf{W} = M^T\mathbf{T}$$

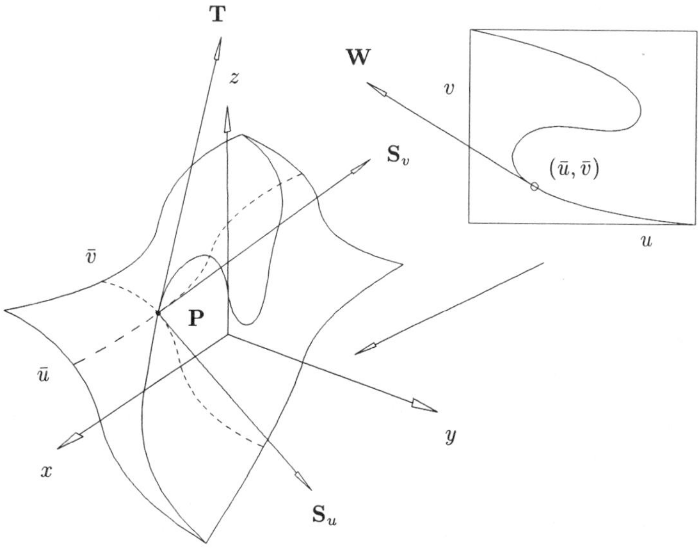

Figure 6.4. Surface tangent vector inversion.

or

$$\begin{bmatrix} |\mathbf{S}_u|^2 & \mathbf{S}_u\cdot\mathbf{S}_v \\ \mathbf{S}_u\cdot\mathbf{S}_v & |\mathbf{S}_v|^2 \end{bmatrix} \begin{bmatrix} du \\ dv \end{bmatrix} = \begin{bmatrix} \mathbf{S}_u\cdot\mathbf{T} \\ \mathbf{S}_v\cdot\mathbf{T} \end{bmatrix} \tag{6.11}$$

Solving this 2×2 system of equations yields the unknowns du and dv.

6.3 Transformations and Projections of Curves and Surfaces

Transformations and projections of curves and surfaces are common in geometric modeling and computer graphics. Transformations include translations, rotations, scalings, shears, and reflections. Parallel and perspective projections are essential in viewing three-dimensional geometry on a video screen or other two-dimensional output devices. There are many excellent discussions of transformations and projections in the literature, e.g., [Faux81; Fole90; Roge90]. In this section we assume the reader is familiar with the general concepts, and we elaborate only on the application of these concepts to NURBS curves and surfaces.

All transformations and projections are performed on NURBS curves and surfaces by applying operations to the control points and weights; hence, it suffices to restrict the discussion to curves. Equations (4.1) and (4.5) represent two different ways to think of a NURBS curve, namely, as a piecewise rational curve in Euclidean space, or as a nonrational B-spline curve in homogeneous space. The first method uses the B-spline basis functions to blend weighted three-dimensional control points; the second method uses the functions to blend four-dimensional control points. Correspondingly, there exist two methods for performing transformations and projections:

- apply the operations to the three-dimensional control points of $\mathbf{C}(u)$; for a perspective projection, new weights must also be computed;
- apply a 4×4 matrix to the four-dimensional control points of $\mathbf{C}^w(u)$.

Let

$$\mathbf{C}(u) = \frac{\sum_{i=0}^{n} N_{i,p}(u) w_i \mathbf{P}_i}{\sum_{i=0}^{n} N_{i,p}(u) w_i} = \sum_{i=0}^{n} R_{i,p}(u)\mathbf{P}_i \tag{6.12}$$

With the exception of perspective, all transformations and projections of $\mathbf{C}(u)$ are performed by applying the operation to the three-dimensional control points, $\mathbf{P}_i$; the weights, w_i, do not change. This follows from the Affine Invariance Property, P4.9 (which follows from the form of Eq. [6.12]). Let us consider projections. Figure 6.5 shows a general parallel projection of the control point, $\mathbf{P}_i$, to a projection plane given by the reference point, $\mathbf{Q}$, and the unit length normal vector, $\mathbf{N}$. $\bar{\mathbf{P}}_i$ denotes the projection of $\mathbf{P}_i$. If the direction of the projection is given by the vector $\mathbf{W}$, then

$$\bar{\mathbf{P}}_i = \mathbf{P}_i + \alpha\mathbf{W} \tag{6.13}$$

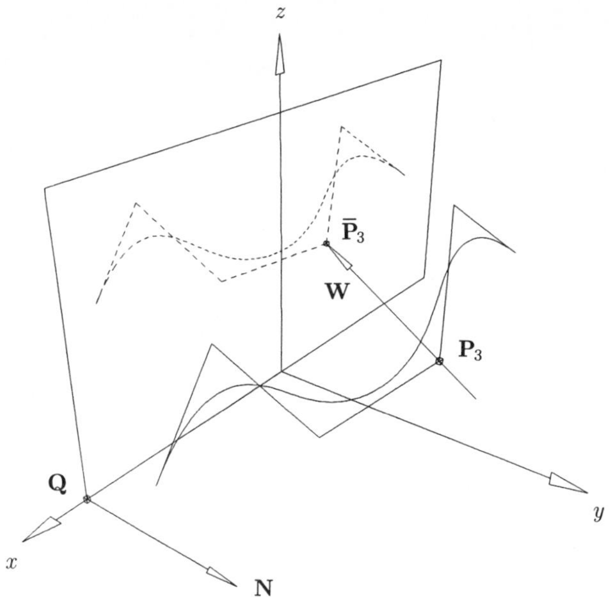

Figure 6.5. Parallel projection of NURBS curves.

From Eq. (6.13) we have

$$\alpha \mathbf{W} = \bar{\mathbf{P}}_i - \mathbf{P}_i - \mathbf{Q} + \mathbf{Q}$$

and

$$\alpha(\mathbf{N} \cdot \mathbf{W}) = \mathbf{N} \cdot (\bar{\mathbf{P}}_i - \mathbf{Q}) + \mathbf{N} \cdot (\mathbf{Q} - \mathbf{P}_i)$$

Since $\bar{\mathbf{P}}_i$ lies on the projection plane, $\mathbf{N} \cdot (\bar{\mathbf{P}}_i - \mathbf{Q}) = 0$, from which follows

$$\alpha = \frac{\mathbf{N} \cdot (\mathbf{Q} - \mathbf{P}_i)}{\mathbf{N} \cdot \mathbf{W}}$$

and finally

$$\bar{\mathbf{P}}_i = \mathbf{P}_i + \left(\frac{\mathbf{N} \cdot (\mathbf{Q} - \mathbf{P}_i)}{\mathbf{N} \cdot \mathbf{W}} \right) \mathbf{W} \tag{6.14}$$

The corresponding formula for surfaces is

$$\bar{\mathbf{P}}_{i,j} = \mathbf{P}_{i,j} + \left(\frac{\mathbf{N} \cdot (\mathbf{Q} - \mathbf{P}_{i,j})}{\mathbf{N} \cdot \mathbf{W}} \right) \mathbf{W} \tag{6.15}$$

Figure 6.6 shows a perspective projection. As before, let the projection plane be defined by $\mathbf{Q}$ and $\mathbf{N}$. Denote the eye position by $\mathbf{E}$. Then

$$\bar{\mathbf{P}}_i = (1 - \alpha)\mathbf{P}_i + \alpha \mathbf{E} \tag{6.16}$$

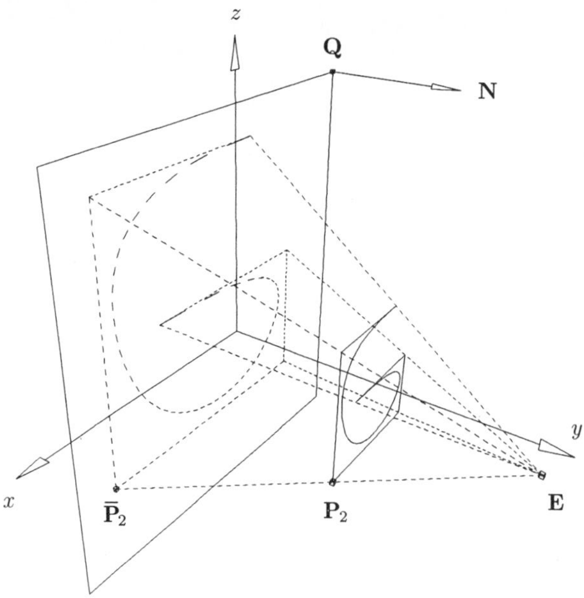

Figure 6.6. Perspective projection of NURBS curves.

It follows that

$$\alpha(\mathbf{E}-\mathbf{P}_i)=\bar{\mathbf{P}}_i-\mathbf{P}_i-\mathbf{Q}+\mathbf{Q}$$

and $\mathbf{N}\cdot(\bar{\mathbf{P}}_i-\mathbf{Q})=0$ implies that

$$\alpha=\frac{\mathbf{N}\cdot(\mathbf{Q}-\mathbf{P}_i)}{\mathbf{N}\cdot(\mathbf{E}-\mathbf{P}_i)}$$

From

$$1-\alpha=1-\frac{\mathbf{N}\cdot(\mathbf{Q}-\mathbf{P}_i)}{\mathbf{N}\cdot(\mathbf{E}-\mathbf{P}_i)}=\frac{\mathbf{N}\cdot(\mathbf{E}-\mathbf{P}_i-\mathbf{Q}+\mathbf{P}_i)}{\mathbf{N}\cdot(\mathbf{E}-\mathbf{P}_i)}=\frac{\mathbf{N}\cdot(\mathbf{E}-\mathbf{Q})}{\mathbf{N}\cdot(\mathbf{E}-\mathbf{P}_i)}$$

we obtain

$$\bar{\mathbf{P}}_i=\frac{\mathbf{N}\cdot(\mathbf{E}-\mathbf{Q})}{\mathbf{N}\cdot(\mathbf{E}-\mathbf{P}_i)}\mathbf{P}_i+\frac{\mathbf{N}\cdot(\mathbf{Q}-\mathbf{P}_i)}{\mathbf{N}\cdot(\mathbf{E}-\mathbf{P}_i)}\mathbf{E} \tag{6.17}$$

Equation (6.17) is the formula for computing the new control points of the projected curve.

We now derive the formula for the new weights. Let

$$\mathbf{P}=\mathbf{C}(u)=\sum_{i=0}^{n}R_{i,p}(u)\mathbf{P}_i$$

be an arbitrary point on $\mathbf{C}(u)$, and denote by $\bar{\mathbf{P}}$ the perspective projection of $\mathbf{P}$

onto the plane given by $\mathbf{Q}$ and $\mathbf{N}$. Recalling that

$$\sum_{i=0}^{n} R_{i,p}(u) = 1$$

for all u, we obtain

$$\bar{\mathbf{P}} = \frac{\mathbf{N}\cdot(\mathbf{E}-\mathbf{Q})}{\mathbf{N}\cdot(\mathbf{E}-\mathbf{P})}\mathbf{P} + \frac{\mathbf{N}\cdot(\mathbf{Q}-\mathbf{P})}{\mathbf{N}\cdot(\mathbf{E}-\mathbf{P})}\mathbf{E}$$

$$= \frac{\sum R_{i,p}(\mathbf{N}\cdot(\mathbf{E}-\mathbf{Q})\mathbf{P}_i) + \sum R_{i,p}(\mathbf{N}\cdot(\mathbf{Q}-\mathbf{P}_i))\,\mathbf{E}}{\sum R_{i,p}(\mathbf{N}\cdot(\mathbf{E}-\mathbf{P}_i))}$$

$$= \frac{\sum R_{i,p}(\mathbf{N}\cdot(\mathbf{E}-\mathbf{P}_i))\left(\dfrac{\mathbf{N}\cdot(\mathbf{E}-\mathbf{Q})}{\mathbf{N}\cdot(\mathbf{E}-\mathbf{P}_i)}\right)\mathbf{P}_i}{\sum R_{i,p}(\mathbf{N}\cdot(\mathbf{E}-\mathbf{P}_i))}$$

$$+ \frac{\sum R_{i,p}(\mathbf{N}\cdot(\mathbf{E}-\mathbf{P}_i))\left(\dfrac{\mathbf{N}\cdot(\mathbf{Q}-\mathbf{P}_i)}{\mathbf{N}\cdot(\mathbf{E}-\mathbf{P}_i)}\right)\mathbf{E}}{\sum R_{i,p}(\mathbf{N}\cdot(\mathbf{E}-\mathbf{P}_i))}$$

Setting

$$\bar{w}_i = w_i\left(\mathbf{N}\cdot(\mathbf{E}-\mathbf{P}_i)\right) \tag{6.18}$$

and recalling that

$$R_{i,p} = \frac{N_{i,p}w_i}{\sum N_{i,p}w_i}$$

we obtain

$$\bar{\mathbf{P}} = \frac{\sum N_{i,p}\bar{w}_i\left(\dfrac{\mathbf{N}\cdot(\mathbf{E}-\mathbf{Q})}{\mathbf{N}\cdot(\mathbf{E}-\mathbf{P}_i)}\mathbf{P}_i + \dfrac{\mathbf{N}\cdot(\mathbf{Q}-\mathbf{P}_i)}{\mathbf{N}\cdot(\mathbf{E}-\mathbf{P}_i)}\mathbf{E}\right)}{\sum N_{i,p}\bar{w}_i}$$

$$= \frac{\sum N_{i,p}(u)\bar{w}_i\bar{\mathbf{P}}_i}{\sum N_{i,p}(u)\bar{w}_i} \tag{6.19}$$

Equation (6.19) shows that the control points and weights given by Eqs. (6.17) and (6.18) are those of the projected curve. The formulas for surfaces are

$$\bar{\mathbf{P}}_{i,j} = \frac{\mathbf{N}\cdot(\mathbf{E}-\mathbf{Q})}{\mathbf{N}\cdot(\mathbf{E}-\mathbf{P}_{i,j})}\mathbf{P}_{i,j} + \frac{\mathbf{N}\cdot(\mathbf{Q}-\mathbf{P}_{i,j})}{\mathbf{N}\cdot(\mathbf{E}-\mathbf{P}_{i,j})}\mathbf{E} \tag{6.20}$$

and

$$\bar{w}_{i,j} = w_{i,j}[\mathbf{N}\cdot(\mathbf{E}-\mathbf{P}_{i,j})] \tag{6.21}$$

Figure 6.7 shows parallel projection of NURBS surfaces.

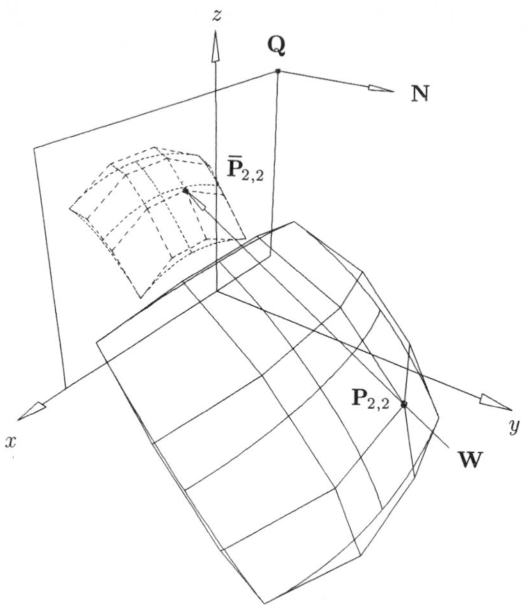

Figure 6.7. Parallel projection of NURBS surfaces.

Now let $\mathbf{C}^w(u) = \sum_{i=0}^{n} N_{i,p}(u)\mathbf{P}_i^w$. All transformations and projections can be packed into one 4×4 matrix of the form

$$A = \begin{bmatrix} B & T \\ P & a_{3,3} \end{bmatrix} = \begin{bmatrix} b_{0,0} & b_{0,1} & b_{0,2} & t_0 \\ b_{1,0} & b_{1,1} & b_{1,2} & t_1 \\ b_{2,0} & b_{2,1} & b_{2,2} & t_2 \\ p_0 & p_1 & p_2 & a_{3,3} \end{bmatrix} \tag{6.22}$$

where the vectors T and P represent translation and perspective, respectively, and the 3×3 matrix, B, contains rotation, scaling, shear, reflection through a coordinate plane, and projection to a coordinate plane. The matrix A is to be applied to all control points $\mathbf{P}_i^w$ of $\mathbf{C}^w(u)$.

Examples

Let $\mathbf{P}_i^w = (w_i x_i, w_i y_i, w_i z_i, w_i)$, and denote a transformed homogeneous control point by $\bar{\mathbf{P}}_i^w = A\mathbf{P}_i^w$.

Ex6.1 Translate $\mathbf{C}^w(u)$ by the vector $\mathbf{V} = (x, y, z)$. Then

$$\bar{\mathbf{P}}_i^w = \begin{bmatrix} 1 & 0 & 0 & x \\ 0 & 1 & 0 & y \\ 0 & 0 & 1 & z \\ 0 & 0 & 0 & 1 \end{bmatrix} \begin{bmatrix} w_i x_i \\ w_i y_i \\ w_i z_i \\ w_i \end{bmatrix} = \begin{bmatrix} w_i(x_i + x) \\ w_i(y_i + y) \\ w_i(z_i + z) \\ w_i \end{bmatrix}$$

Ex6.2 Apply a rotation matrix R to $\mathbf{C}^w(u)$

$$\bar{\mathbf{P}}_i^w = \begin{bmatrix} r_{0,0} & r_{0,1} & r_{0,2} & 0 \\ r_{1,0} & r_{1,1} & r_{1,2} & 0 \\ r_{2,0} & r_{2,1} & r_{2,2} & 0 \\ 0 & 0 & 0 & 1 \end{bmatrix} \begin{bmatrix} w_i x_i \\ w_i y_i \\ w_i z_i \\ w_i \end{bmatrix} = \begin{bmatrix} w_i(r_{0,0}x_i + r_{0,1}y_i + r_{0,2}z_i) \\ w_i(r_{1,0}x_i + r_{1,1}y_i + r_{1,2}z_i) \\ w_i(r_{2,0}x_i + r_{2,1}y_i + r_{2,2}z_i) \\ w_i \end{bmatrix}$$

Ex6.3 Perspective projection: Let $\mathbf{E} = (0, 0, d)$ be the eye position lying on the z-axis, a distance d from the origin. Let the xy plane be the projection plane. Then

$$\bar{\mathbf{P}}_i^w = \begin{bmatrix} d & 0 & 0 & 0 \\ 0 & d & 0 & 0 \\ 0 & 0 & 0 & 0 \\ 0 & 0 & -1 & d \end{bmatrix} \begin{bmatrix} w_i x_i \\ w_i y_i \\ w_i z_i \\ w_i \end{bmatrix} = \begin{bmatrix} w_i d x_i \\ w_i d y_i \\ 0 \\ w_i(d - z_i) \end{bmatrix} \tag{6.23}$$

6.4 Reparameterization of NURBS Curves and Surfaces

Let $\mathbf{C}(u) = \big(x(u), y(u), z(u)\big)$ be an arbitrary parametric curve on $u \in [a, b]$, and assume that $u = f(s)$ is a scalar-valued function on $s \in [c, d]$ satisfying:

- $f'(s) > 0$ for all $s \in [c, d]$ ($f(s)$ is strictly increasing);
- $a = f(c)$ and $b = f(d)$ ($f(s)$ maps $[c, d]$ onto $[a, b]$).

The composition of $\mathbf{C}(u)$ and $f(s)$, given by

$$\mathbf{C}(s) = \mathbf{C}\big(f(s)\big) = \Big(x\big(f(s)\big), y\big(f(s)\big), z\big(f(s)\big)\Big)$$

is called a *reparameterization* of $\mathbf{C}(u)$ (see Figure 6.8).

$\mathbf{C}(s)$ is geometrically the same curve as $\mathbf{C}(u)$, but parametrically they are different. Applications of reparameterization include:

- Internal point mapping: Given parameter values $u_0, \ldots, u_n$ and $s_0, \ldots, s_n$, where $a < u_0 < \cdots < u_n < b$ and $c < s_0 < \cdots < s_n < d$, determine a function $u = f(s)$ such that $u_i = f(s_i)$, $i = 0, \ldots, n$. Then form $\mathbf{C}\big(f(s)\big)$. This forces the curve points $\mathbf{C}(u_i)$ to be assumed at the new parameter values, s_i;
- Modification of end derivatives: Reparameterization changes the curve derivatives; this follows from the Chain Rule, e.g.

$$\mathbf{C}'(s) = \mathbf{C}'(u) f'(s) \qquad \mathbf{C}''(s) = \mathbf{C}'(u) f''(s) + \mathbf{C}''(u)\big(f'(s)\big)^2$$

  Note that only the magnitudes of the end first derivatives change, but magnitudes and directions of the end second and higher derivatives change;
- Modification of end weights: If $\mathbf{C}^w(u) = \sum_{i=0}^{n} N_{i,p}(u)\mathbf{P}_i^w$ is a NURBS

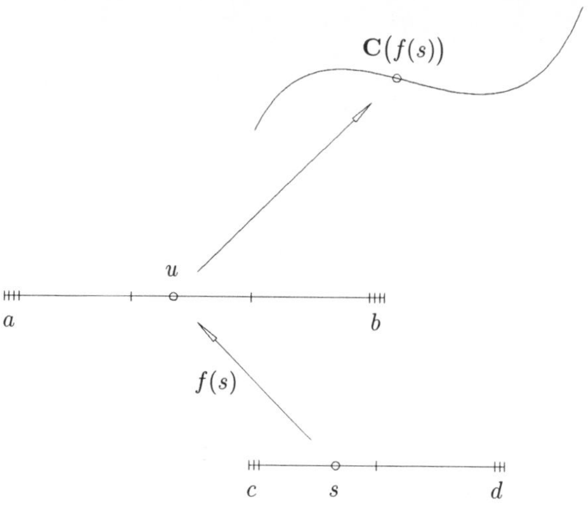

Figure 6.8. Curve reparameterization.

curve, it is sometimes useful to modify the end weights, w_0 and w_n, to have specific values without changing the curve geometry. We shall see that this is possible and in fact is simply equivalent to a reparameterization of $\mathbf{C}(u)$.

Examples

Ex6.4 Let

$$\mathbf{C}(u) = \big(x(u), y(u)\big) = (u, -2u^2 + 2u) \tag{6.24}$$

on $u \in [0,1]$, and assume we want a parameter $s \in [0,1]$ such that $u = 1/2$ corresponds to $s = 6/10$, that is

$$\mathbf{C}\Big(u = \frac{1}{2}\Big) = \mathbf{C}\Big(s = \frac{6}{10}\Big) = \Big(\frac{1}{2}, \frac{1}{2}\Big)$$

Then $u = f(s)$ must satisfy three constraints

$$0 = f(0) \qquad \frac{1}{2} = f\left(\frac{6}{10}\right) \qquad 1 = f(1)$$

We choose $f(s)$ to be a quadratic polynomial

$$u = f(s) = as^2 + bs + c$$

The first constraint implies $c = 0$, and the last two yield the linear equations

$$\frac{1}{2} = \frac{9}{25}a + \frac{6}{10}b$$

$$1 = a + b \tag{6.25}$$

Solving Eq. (6.25) yields

$$a = \frac{5}{12} \qquad b = \frac{7}{12}$$

thus

$$u = f(s) = \frac{5}{12}s^2 + \frac{7}{12}s \tag{6.26}$$

Substituting Eq. (6.26) into Eq. (6.24), we obtain the reparameterized curve

$$\mathbf{C}(s) = \left(\frac{5}{12}s^2 + \frac{7}{12}s, -\frac{25}{72}s^4 - \frac{35}{36}s^3 + \frac{11}{72}s^2 + \frac{7}{6}s\right) \tag{6.27}$$

The reader should verify that

$$\mathbf{C}(s = 0) = \mathbf{C}(u = 0) = (0, 0)$$
$$\mathbf{C}\left(s = \frac{6}{10}\right) = \mathbf{C}\left(u = \frac{1}{2}\right) = \left(\frac{1}{2}, \frac{1}{2}\right)$$
$$\mathbf{C}(s = 1) = \mathbf{C}(u = 1) = (0, 0)$$

Note also that the derivatives have changed. For example, differentiating Eqs. (6.24) and (6.27) directly yields

$$\mathbf{C}'(u = 0) = (1, 2) \qquad \mathbf{C}'(s = 0) = \left(\frac{7}{12}, \frac{7}{6}\right)$$

Figure 6.9 shows the curve and its first derivatives with respect to u and s at $u = s = 0$.

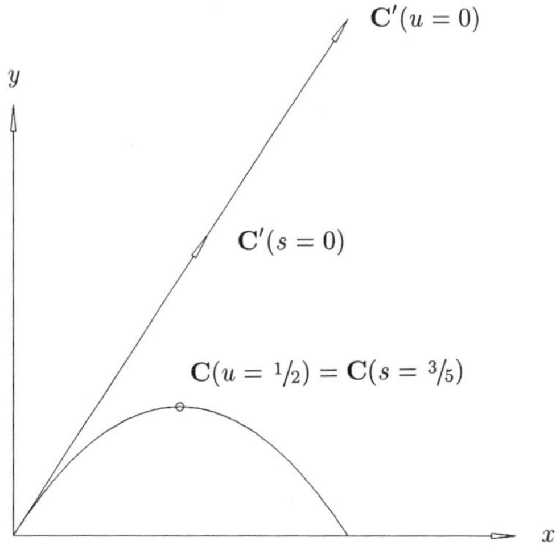

Figure 6.9. The reparameterized curve of Example **Ex6.4**.

Ex6.5 Consider the circular arc given by

$$\mathbf{C}(u) = \left(\frac{1-u^2}{1+u^2}, \frac{2u}{1+u^2} \right) \tag{6.28}$$

on $u \in [0,1]$. This arc is centered at the origin, has radius 1, and sweeps an angle of 90° (see Chapter 1, Eq. [1.2], Figure 1.2, Example 1.8, and Figure 1.19a). It is easy to check that

$$\mathbf{C}\left(u = \frac{1}{2}\right) = \left(\frac{6}{10}, \frac{8}{10}\right)$$

and

$$\mathbf{C}'(u=0) = (0,2)$$
$$\mathbf{C}'(u=1) = (-1,0) \tag{6.29}$$

We want a reparameterization, $\mathbf{C}(s)$, of $\mathbf{C}(u)$ which is more symmetric, namely, $\mathbf{C}(s)$ should satisfy

$$\mid \mathbf{C}'(s=0) \mid = \mid \mathbf{C}'(s=1) \mid \tag{6.30}$$

We choose a linear rational function of the form

$$u = f(s) = \frac{as+b}{cs+d} \qquad s \in [0,1] \tag{6.31}$$

Clearly, we can assume that $d = 1$, and the conditions $f(0) = 0$ and $f(1) = 1$ imply $b = 0$ and $c = a - 1$. Hence, $f(s)$ has the form

$$u = \frac{as}{(a-1)s+1} \tag{6.32}$$

The condition given by Eq. (6.30) determines a. From Eq. (6.29) and $\mathbf{C}'(s) = \mathbf{C}'(u)\, f'(s)$, we require

$$2f'(s=0) = f'(s=1) \tag{6.33}$$

Differentiating Eq. (6.32) yields

$$f'(s) = \frac{a}{\left((a-1)s+1\right)^2}$$

and from Eq. (6.33) we obtain $2a = {}^1\!/_a$. It follows that $2a^2 - 1 = 0$, thus $a = \pm\sqrt{2}/2$. Choosing $a = -\sqrt{2}/2$ causes a zero in the denominator of Eq. (6.32) in the interval $s \in [0,1]$, hence we select $a = \sqrt{2}/2$. Thus, we obtain

$$u = f(s) = \frac{\sqrt{2}s}{(\sqrt{2}-2)s+2} \tag{6.34}$$

Substituting Eq. (6.34) into Eq. (6.28) yields

$$\mathbf{C}(s) = \left(\frac{(1-\sqrt{2})s^2 + (\sqrt{2}-2)s + 1}{(2-\sqrt{2})s^2 + (\sqrt{2}-2)s + 1}, \frac{(1-\sqrt{2})s^2 + \sqrt{2}s}{(2-\sqrt{2})s^2 + (\sqrt{2}-2)s + 1} \right) \tag{6.35}$$

The reader can verify that $\mathbf{C}(s)$ satisfies Eq. (6.30) and also the condition

$$\mathbf{C}\left(s = \frac{1}{2}\right) = \left(\frac{\sqrt{2}}{2}, \frac{\sqrt{2}}{2}\right) \tag{6.36}$$

that is, $s = 1/2$ maps to the midpoint of the circular arc.

Note that:

- if $\mathbf{C}(u)$ is a pth-degree polynomial (rational) curve and $f(s)$ is a qth-degree polynomial (rational) function, then $\mathbf{C}(s)$ is a pqth-degree polynomial (rational) curve. In particular, a linear reparameterization function of the form $u = as + b$ or $u = (as+b)/(cs+d)$ does not raise the degree of the curve;
- a linear rational function of the form $u = (as+b)/(cs+d)$ converts a polynomial curve to a rational curve of the same degree.

We now discuss the problem of reparameterizing a NURBS curve with a polynomial function. Let $\mathbf{C}^w(u) = \sum_{i=0}^{n} N_{i,p}(u)\mathbf{P}_i^w$ be a pth-degree NURBS curve on $u \in [a,b]$, and $u = f(s)$ a qth-degree polynomial on $s \in [c,d]$. For now let us assume $\mathbf{C}^w(u)$ has no internal knots, therefore U has the form

$$U = \{\underbrace{a,\ldots,a}_{p+1},\underbrace{b,\ldots,b}_{p+1}\}$$

The reparameterized curve $\mathbf{C}^w(s)$ has degree pq and is defined on the knot vector

$$S = \{\underbrace{c,\ldots,c}_{pq+1},\underbrace{d,\ldots,d}_{pq+1}\} \tag{6.37}$$

The $pq+1$ new control points can be computed by repeated application of the Chain Rule and the formulas for the end derivatives of a B-spline curve. We illustrate this by example.

Example

`Ex6.6` Let $\mathbf{C}(u) = \sum_{i=0}^{2} N_{i,2}(u)\mathbf{P}_i$, $U = \{0,0,0,1,1,1\}$, be the B-spline representation of the parabolic arc of Example `Ex6.4` (see Figures 6.9 and

6.10). The control points are $\{(0,0),(1/2,1),(1,0)\}$, and the reparameterization function is

$$u = f(s) = \frac{5}{12}s^2 + \frac{7}{12}s \quad \text{on} \quad s \in [0,1]$$

The reparameterized curve, of degree four, is given by

$$\mathbf{C}(s) = \sum_{i=0}^{4} N_{i,4}(s)\,\mathbf{Q}_i \qquad S = \{0,0,0,0,0,1,1,1,1,1\} \tag{6.38}$$

Clearly (see Figure 6.10)

$$\mathbf{Q}_0 = \mathbf{P}_0 \qquad \mathbf{Q}_4 = \mathbf{P}_2$$

From $\mathbf{C}'(s) = \mathbf{C}'(u)f'(s)$ and Eq. (3.7) we obtain

$$\begin{aligned}\mathbf{C}'(s=0) &= \frac{4}{1-0}(\mathbf{Q}_1 - \mathbf{Q}_0) = \mathbf{C}'(u=0)f'(s=0)\\ &= \frac{2}{1-0}(\mathbf{P}_1 - \mathbf{P}_0)\left(\frac{7}{12}\right)\end{aligned}$$

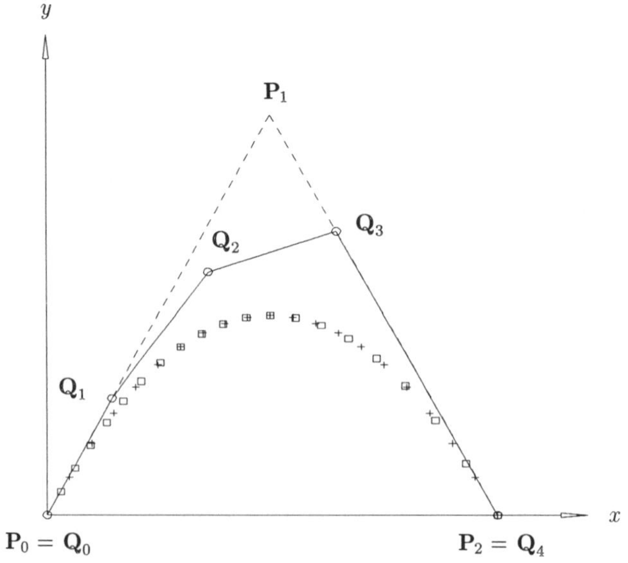

Figure 6.10. The reparameterized B-spline curve of Example Ex6.6; + shows the original parameterization and □ illustrates the new parameterization.

from which follows

$$\mathbf{Q}_1 = \frac{7}{24}(\mathbf{P}_1 - \mathbf{P}_0) + \mathbf{Q}_0 = \left(\frac{7}{48}, \frac{7}{24}\right)$$

Similarly, $4(\mathbf{Q}_4 - \mathbf{Q}_3) = 2(\mathbf{P}_2 - \mathbf{P}_1)(17/12)$, and

$$\mathbf{Q}_3 = \mathbf{Q}_4 - \frac{17}{24}(\mathbf{P}_2 - \mathbf{P}_1) = \left(\frac{31}{48}, \frac{17}{24}\right)$$

From $\mathbf{C}''(s) = \mathbf{C}'(u)f''(s) + \mathbf{C}''(u)\big(f'(s)\big)^2$ and Eq. (3.9), and after noting that

$$\mathbf{C}'(u=0) = (1,2) \qquad \mathbf{C}''(u=0) = (0,-4)$$

$$f'(s=0) = \frac{7}{12} \qquad f''(s=0) = \frac{5}{6}$$

we obtain

$$\mathbf{C}''(s=0) = 12(\mathbf{Q}_0 - 2\mathbf{Q}_1 + \mathbf{Q}_2) = \frac{5}{6}(1,2) + \left(\frac{7}{12}\right)^2 (0,-4)$$

from which follows

$$\mathbf{Q}_2 = \frac{5}{72}(1,2) + \frac{49}{1728}(0,-4) + 2\left(\frac{7}{48}, \frac{7}{24}\right) = \left(\frac{156}{432}, \frac{263}{432}\right)$$

Hence, the general procedure for reparameterizing a pth-degree curve $\mathbf{C}^w(u)$ having no internal knots, with a qth-degree polynomial, $f(s)$, is to:

1. set $\mathbf{Q}_0 = \mathbf{P}_0$ and $\mathbf{Q}_{pq} = \mathbf{P}_p$;
2. let $\mathbf{C}^{w(i)}$ denote the ith derivative of $\mathbf{C}^w(u)$, and let $m_\ell = (pq+1)/2$ (integer arithmetic), and $m_r = pq - pq/2 - 1$. Compute the derivatives $\mathbf{C}^{w(i)}(u=a)$ for $i = 1,\ldots,m_\ell$, and $\mathbf{C}^{w(i)}(u=b)$ for $i = 1,\ldots,m_r$; note that the differentiation is carried out in homogeneous space;
3. let $f^{(i)}$ denote the ith derivative of $f(s)$; compute the derivatives $f^{(i)}(s = c)$ for $i = 1,\ldots,m_\ell$, and $f^{(i)}(s=d)$ for $i = 1,\ldots,m_r$;
4. using repeated application of the Chain Rule (which expresses $\mathbf{C}^{w(i)}(s)$ in terms of $\mathbf{C}^{w(i)}(u)$ and $f^{(i)}(s)$) and Eqs. (6.41) and (6.42), compute the new control points $\mathbf{Q}_1,\ldots,\mathbf{Q}_{m_\ell}$ and $\mathbf{Q}_{pq-1},\ldots,\mathbf{Q}_{pq-m_r}$.

Applying the Chain Rule four times yields

$$\mathbf{C}^{w(1)}(s) = \mathbf{C}^{w(1)}(u)f^{(1)}(s)$$

$$\mathbf{C}^{w(2)}(s) = \mathbf{C}^{w(1)}(u)f^{(2)}(s) + \mathbf{C}^{w(2)}(u)\big(f^{(1)}(s)\big)^2$$

$$\mathbf{C}^{w(3)}(s) = \mathbf{C}^{w(1)}(u)f^{(3)}(s) + 3\mathbf{C}^{w(2)}(u)f^{(1)}(s)f^{(2)}(s) + \mathbf{C}^{w(3)}(u)\big(f^{(1)}(s)\big)^3$$

$$\mathbf{C}^{w(4)}(s) = \mathbf{C}^{w(1)}(u)f^{(4)}(s) + \mathbf{C}^{w(2)}(u)\Big[4f^{(1)}(s)f^{(3)}(s) + 3\big(f^{(2)}(s)\big)^2\Big]$$
$$+ 6\mathbf{C}^{w(3)}(u)\big(f^{(1)}(s)\big)^2 f^{(2)}(s) + \mathbf{C}^{w(4)}(u)\big(f^{(1)}(s)\big)^4 \qquad (6.39)$$

The general formula

$$\mathbf{C}^{w(n)}(s) = \sum_{j=0}^{n} \sum_{\substack{k_1+k_2+\cdots+k_n=j \\ k_1+2k_2+\cdots+nk_n=n \\ k_1,k_2,\ldots,k_n\geq 0}} \mathbf{C}^{w(j)}(u) \frac{n!}{k_1!(1!)^{k_1}\cdots k_n!(n!)^{k_n}} \Big(f^{(1)}(s)\Big)^{k_1} \cdots \Big(f^{(n)}(s)\Big)^{k_n} \qquad (6.40)$$

is due to Faa di Bruno (see [Knut73], page 50). Although this formula is elegant, its implementation is not straightforward. The difficulty is in obtaining the n-tuples that satisfy the conditions

$$k_1 + k_2 + \cdots + k_n = j$$
$$k_1 + 2k_2 + \cdots + nk_n = n \qquad k_1, k_2, \ldots, k_n \geq 0$$

To illustrate this we use Eq. (6.40) to derive the first four derivatives given in Eq. (6.39):

`n=1`: $k_1 = 1$ must hold:

$$j = 0 : k_1 = 0 \rightarrow \text{ no solution}$$
$$j = 1 : k_1 = 1 \rightarrow (1)$$

which yields

$$\mathbf{C}^{w(1)}(s) = \mathbf{C}^{w(1)}(u)f^{(1)}(s)$$

`n=2`: $k_1 + 2k_2 = 2$ must hold:

$$j = 0 : k_1 + k_2 = 0 \rightarrow \text{ no solution}$$
$$j = 1 : k_1 + k_2 = 1 \rightarrow (0,1)$$
$$j = 2 : k_1 + k_2 = 2 \rightarrow (2,0)$$

yielding $\mathbf{C}^{w(2)}(s) = \mathbf{C}^{w(1)}(u)f^{(2)}(s) + \mathbf{C}^{w(2)}(u)\Big(f^{(1)}(s)\Big)^2$

`n=3`: $k_1 + 2k_2 + 3k_3 = 3$ must hold:

$$j = 0 : k_1 + k_2 + k_3 = 0 \rightarrow \text{ no solution}$$
$$j = 1 : k_1 + k_2 + k_3 = 1 \rightarrow (0,0,1)$$
$$j = 2 : k_1 + k_2 + k_3 = 2 \rightarrow (1,1,0)$$
$$j = 3 : k_1 + k_2 + k_3 = 3 \rightarrow (3,0,0)$$

from which we obtain

$$\mathbf{C}^{w(3)}(s) = \mathbf{C}^{w(1)}(u)f^{(3)}(s) + 3\mathbf{C}^{w(2)}(u)f^{(1)}(s)f^{(2)}(s) + \mathbf{C}^{w(3)}(u)\Big(f^{(1)}(s)\Big)^3$$

n=4: $k_1 + 2k_2 + 3k_3 + 4k_4 = 4$ must hold:

$$j = 0 : k_1 + k_2 + k_3 + k_4 = 0 \rightarrow \text{ no solution}$$

$$j = 1 : k_1 + k_2 + k_3 + k_4 = 1 \rightarrow (0,0,0,1)$$

$$j = 2 : k_1 + k_2 + k_3 + k_4 = 2 \rightarrow (1,0,1,0) \quad \text{and} \quad (0,2,0,0)$$

$$j = 3 : k_1 + k_2 + k_3 + k_4 = 3 \rightarrow (2,1,0,0)$$

$$j = 4 : k_1 + k_2 + k_3 + k_4 = 4 \rightarrow (4,0,0,0)$$

from which we obtain

$$\mathbf{C}^{w(4)}(s) = \mathbf{C}^{w(1)}(u)f^{(4)}(s) + \mathbf{C}^{w(2)}(u)\left[4f^{(1)}(s)f^{(3)}(s) + 3\big(f^{(2)}(s)\big)^2\right]$$
$$+ 6\mathbf{C}^{w(3)}(u)\Big(f^{(1)}(s)\Big)^2 f^{(2)}(s) + \mathbf{C}^{w(4)}(u)\Big(f^{(1)}(s)\Big)^4$$

Given the derivatives of $\mathbf{C}^w(s)$ in terms of those of $\mathbf{C}^w(u)$ and $f(s)$, the general formulas for $\mathbf{Q}_i^w$ are

$$\mathbf{Q}_i^w = \frac{(pq-i)!\Delta s^i}{(pq)!}\mathbf{C}^{w(i)}(s=c) + \sum_{j=0}^{i-1}(-1)^{i+j-1}\binom{i}{j}\mathbf{Q}_j^w \tag{6.41}$$

where $\Delta s^i = (d-c)^i$, $i = 1,\ldots,m_\ell$, and

$$\mathbf{Q}_{pq-i}^w = (-1)^i\frac{(pq-i)!\Delta s^i}{(pq)!}\mathbf{C}^{w(i)}(s=d) + \sum_{j=0}^{i-1}(-1)^{i+j-1}\binom{i}{j}\mathbf{Q}_{pq-j}^w \tag{6.42}$$

for $i = 1,\ldots,m_r$. For example, the first five control points from the left are

$$\begin{aligned}
\mathbf{Q}_0^w &= \mathbf{P}_0^w \\
\mathbf{Q}_1^w &= \frac{\Delta s}{pq}\mathbf{C}^{w(1)}(s=c) + \mathbf{Q}_0^w \\
\mathbf{Q}_2^w &= \frac{\Delta s^2}{pq(pq-1)}\mathbf{C}^{w(2)}(s=c) - \mathbf{Q}_0^w + 2\mathbf{Q}_1^w \\
\mathbf{Q}_3^w &= \frac{\Delta s^3}{pq(pq-1)(pq-2)}\mathbf{C}^{w(3)}(s=c) + \mathbf{Q}_0^w - 3\mathbf{Q}_1^w + 3\mathbf{Q}_2^w \\
\mathbf{Q}_4^w &= \frac{\Delta s^4}{pq(pq-1)(pq-2)(pq-3)}\mathbf{C}^{w(4)}(s=c) - \mathbf{Q}_0^w + 4\mathbf{Q}_1^w - 6\mathbf{Q}_2^w + 4\mathbf{Q}_3^w
\end{aligned} \tag{6.43}$$

and from the right are

$$\mathbf{Q}^w_{pq} = \mathbf{P}^w_n$$

$$\mathbf{Q}^w_{pq-1} = -\frac{\Delta s}{pq}\mathbf{C}^{w(1)}(s=d) + \mathbf{Q}^w_{pq}$$

$$\mathbf{Q}^w_{pq-2} = \frac{\Delta s^2}{pq(pq-1)}\mathbf{C}^{w(2)}(s=d) - \mathbf{Q}^w_{pq} + 2\mathbf{Q}^w_{pq-1}$$

$$\mathbf{Q}^w_{pq-3} = -\frac{\Delta s^3}{pq(pq-1)(pq-2)}\mathbf{C}^{w(3)}(s=d) + \mathbf{Q}^w_{pq} - 3\mathbf{Q}^w_{pq-1} + 3\mathbf{Q}^w_{pq-2}$$

$$\mathbf{Q}^w_{pq-4} = \frac{\Delta s^4}{pq(pq-1)(pq-2)(pq-3)}\mathbf{C}^{w(4)}(s=d) - \mathbf{Q}^w_{pq} + 4\mathbf{Q}^w_{pq-1} - 6\mathbf{Q}^w_{pq-2} + 4\mathbf{Q}^w_{pq-3} \tag{6.44}$$

A linear reparameterization function

$$u = \alpha s + \beta \qquad s \in [c,d] \tag{6.45}$$

is an interesting special case. Examining Eq. (6.39), note that

$$\mathbf{C}^{w(i)}(s) = \mathbf{C}^{w(i)}(u)\left(f^{(1)}(s)\right)^i = \alpha^i \mathbf{C}^{w(i)}(u) \tag{6.46}$$

Then $$\mathbf{Q}^w_1 = \frac{\Delta s}{pq}\mathbf{C}^{w(1)}(s) + \mathbf{Q}^w_0 = \frac{\alpha \Delta s}{\Delta u}(\mathbf{P}^w_1 - \mathbf{P}^w_0) + \mathbf{P}^w_0 \tag{6.47}$$

From $a = \alpha c + \beta$ and $b = \alpha d + \beta$ we obtain

$$\alpha = \frac{b-a}{d-c} = \frac{\Delta u}{\Delta s} \tag{6.48}$$

Substituting Eq. (6.48) into Eq. (6.47) yields

$$\mathbf{Q}^w_1 = \mathbf{P}^w_1$$

Using Eqs. (6.41), (6.46), and (6.48), one can show by induction that

$$\mathbf{Q}^w_i = \mathbf{P}^w_i \qquad \text{for all } i \tag{6.49}$$

Hence, neither the degree nor the (homogeneous) control points change; the linear function of Eq. (6.45) simply changes the parameter bounds from $[a,b]$ to $[c,d]$.

Now let $\mathbf{C}^w(u)$ be an arbitrary pth-degree NURBS curve on $u \in [a,b]$ with knot vector U, and let $u = f(s)$ be a qth-degree piecewise polynomial reparameterization function on $s \in [c,d]$. Now $f(s)$ can be in any form, but for convenience of terminology let us assume that it is in B-spline form, i.e.

$$u = f(s) = \sum_{i=0}^{n} N_{i,q}(s) f_i \tag{6.50}$$

where the $\{f_i\}$ are scalars. Denote the knot vector by S; then $\mathbf{C}^w(f(s))$ is a pqth-degree NURBS curve on $s \in [c,d]$, and its knots and control points can be computed as follows:

1. let $\{s_i\}$ denote the set of distinct internal knots of $f(s)$, and let $\{u_i\} = \{f(s_i)\}$ denote their images; use knot refinement to insert all u_i and all original internal knots of U until they all have multiplicity p. $\mathbf{C}^w(u)$ is then in piecewise Bézier form; denote the refined knot vector by U';
2. let
$$s = g(u) = f^{-1}(s) \tag{6.51}$$
be the inverse function of $f(s)$; then form the new knot vector, S', whose distinct knots are the images $s_i = g(u_i)$ of the distinct knots of U'. All internal knots in S' appear with multiplicity pq;
3. use Eqs. (6.39)–(6.44) and the Δs_i obtained from the new s knots in Step 2 to compute the new control points of $\mathbf{C}^w(s)$, which is also in piecewise Bézier form;
4. apply knot removal to $\mathbf{C}^w(s)$ and S' to obtain the minimal representation of $\mathbf{C}^w(s)$. The continuity of $\mathbf{C}^w(s)$ and the multiplicities of its knots are known, hence general knot removal (as in Algorithm `A5.5`) is not required. Let s_i be a knot in S', and let $u_i = f(s_i)$; denote by m_i^u and m_i^s the multiplicities of u_i and s_i in the original knot vectors U and S, respectively ($m_i^u, m_i^s \geq 0$). Then the multiplicity m_i of s_i in S' is

$$\begin{aligned} m_i &= pq - p + m_i^u \qquad \text{if } m_i^s = 0 \\ m_i &= pq - q + m_i^s \qquad \text{if } m_i^u = 0 \\ m_i &= \max(pq - p + m_i^u, pq - q + m_i^s) \qquad \text{if } m_i^u \neq 0,\ m_i^s \neq 0 \end{aligned} \tag{6.52}$$

If $u = f(s) = \alpha s + \beta$, then $s = g(u) = (u-\beta)/\alpha$. The (homogeneous) control points do not change, and the new knots are obtained from the original ones by

$$s_i = g(u_i) \tag{6.53}$$

For example, the knot vectors $U = \{0,0,0,1/3,1,1,1\}$ and $S' = \{1,1,1,3,7,7,7\}$ are equivalent (define the same curve), since $s = 6u + 1$ maps U to S'.

Figures 6.11a–6.11d show reparameterization examples. The curve is a cubic B-spline curve defined on $U = \{0,0,0,0,\ 1/2,1,1,1,1\}$. In Figure 6.11a the reparameterization function (shown in the upper right corner) is defined by the scalars $F = \{0,\ 2/5, 1\}$, on the knot vector $S = \{0,0,0,\ 1,1,1\}$. Figure 6.11b shows reparameterization defined by $F = \{0,\ 2/5,\ 9/10, 1\}$ and $S = \{0,0,0,\ 1/2,1,1,1\}$. In Figure 6.11c the function is given by $F = \{0,\ 1/2,\ 7/10,\ 9/10, 1\}$ and $S = \{0,0,0,\ 1/2,\ 1/2,\ 1,1,1\}$. Reparameterization with a linear B-spline function, given by $F = \{0,1\}$ and $S = \{0,0,1,1\}$, is depicted in Figure 6.11d.

We turn now to reparameterization with rational (or piecewise rational) functions of the form

$$u = f(s) = \frac{g(s)}{h(s)} \tag{6.54}$$

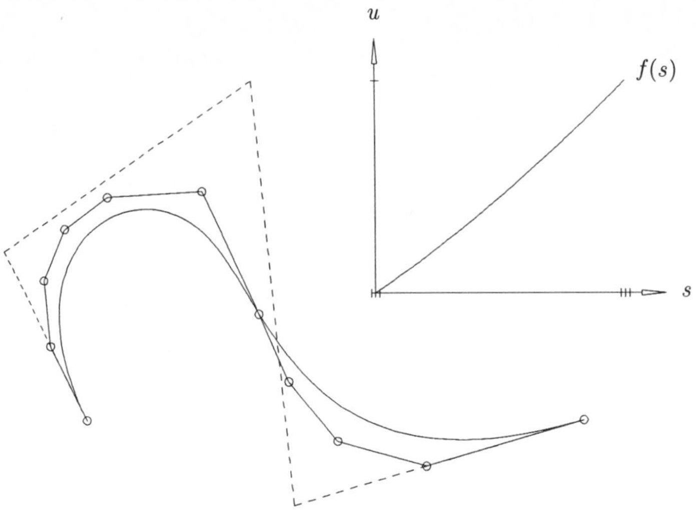

(a)

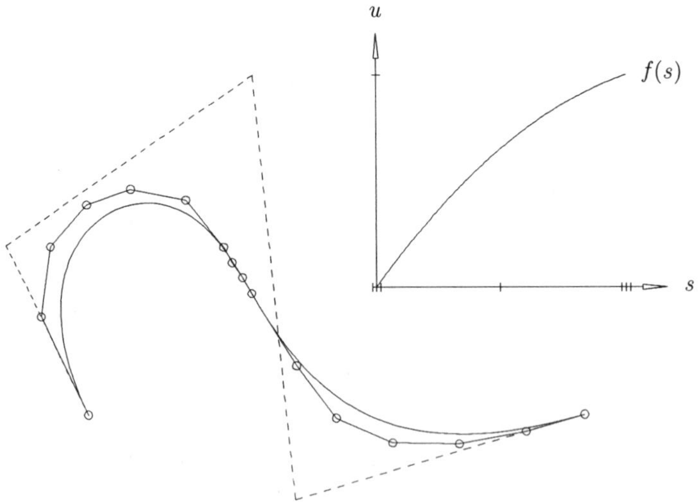

(b)

Figure 6.11. B-spline curve reparameterized with quadratic B-spline functions. (a) $F = \{0, {}^2\!/_5, 1\}$, $S = \{0,0,0,1,1,1\}$; (b) $F = \{0, {}^2\!/_5, {}^9\!/_{10}, 1\}$, $S = \{0,0,0, {}^1\!/_2, 1,1,1\}$.

As previously, if either $\mathbf{C}^w(u)$ or $f(s)$ has internal knots we can reparameterize in three steps:

1. insert knots to obtain $\mathbf{C}^w(u)$ as a piecewise Bézier curve;
2. reparameterize the Bézier segments;
3. remove unnecessary knots.

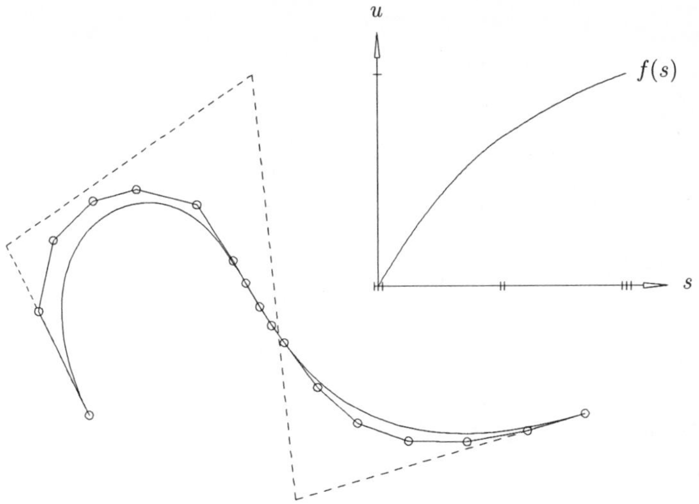

(c)

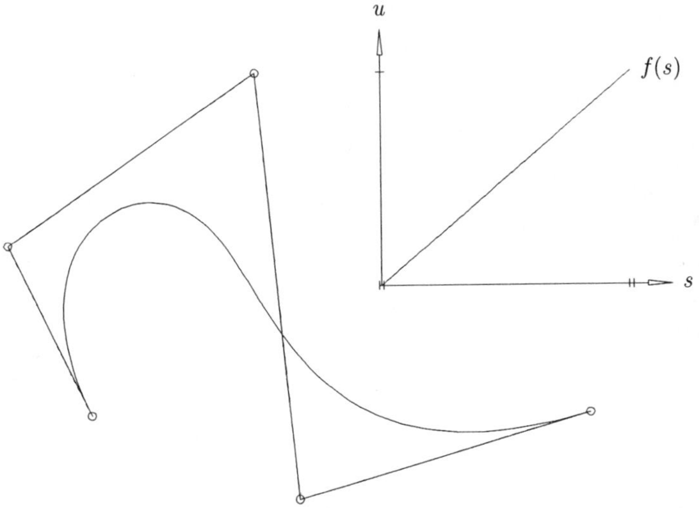

(d)

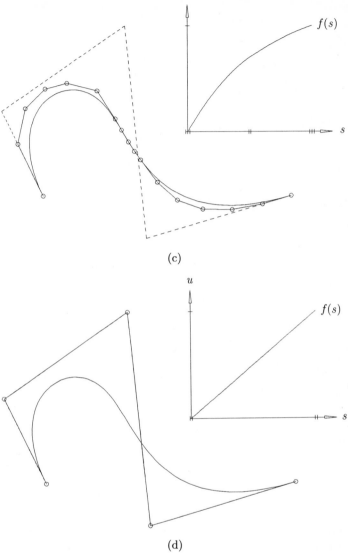

Figure 6.11. (*Continued.*) (c) $F = \{0, 1/2, 7/10, 9/10, 1\}$, $S = \{0, 0, 0, 1/2, 1/2, 1, 1, 1\}$; (d) $F = \{0, 1\}$, $S = \{0, 0, 1, 1\}$.

Hence, we can assume that $\mathbf{C}^w(u)$ and $f(s)$ have no internal knots. Theoretically, one can reparameterize with a rational function using a technique similar to that used for polynomial functions. Let $r(u) = \sum_{i=0}^{p} a_i u^i$ be a pth-degree polynomial function. Then

$$r(s) = r\left(\frac{g(s)}{h(s)}\right) = \sum_{i=0}^{p} a_i \left(\frac{g(s)}{h(s)}\right)^i$$

and $$\bar{r}(s) = \big(h(s)\big)^p r(s) = \sum_{i=0}^{p} a_i \big(g(s)\big)^i \big(h(s)\big)^{p-i}$$

If $g(s)$ and $h(s)$ are qth-degree polynomials, then $\bar{r}(s)$ is a pqth-degree polynomial. Now let

$$\mathbf{C}^w(u) = \big(wx(u), wy(u), wz(u), w(u)\big)$$

be a pth-degree polynomial curve in homogeneous space. Then

$$\mathbf{C}^w(s) = \mathbf{C}^w\left(\frac{g(s)}{h(s)}\right) = \left[wx\left(\frac{g(s)}{h(s)}\right), \ldots, w\left(\frac{g(s)}{h(s)}\right)\right]$$

and

$$\bar{\mathbf{C}}^w(s) = \big(h(s)\big)^p \mathbf{C}^w(s) = \left[\big(h(s)\big)^p wx\left(\frac{g(s)}{h(s)}\right), \ldots, \big(h(s)\big)^p w\left(\frac{g(s)}{h(s)}\right)\right]$$

Concerning $\bar{\mathbf{C}}^w(s)$, note that

- $\bar{\mathbf{C}}^w(s)$ is a pqth-degree polynomial curve in homogeneous space;
- $\bar{\mathbf{C}}^w(s)$ and $\mathbf{C}^w(s)$ are different curves in homogeneous space, but they project to the same curve in Euclidean space, i.e., $\bar{\mathbf{C}}(s) = \mathbf{C}(s)$;
- using $\bar{\mathbf{C}}^w(s) = \big(h(s)\big)^p \mathbf{C}^w({}^{g(s)}/_{h(s)})$, the Chain Rule, and end derivative formulas, one can compute the new homogeneous control points of $\bar{\mathbf{C}}^w(s)$.

The fundamental difference between reparameterization with a rational versus a polynomial function is:

- if $f(s)$ is polynomial then $\mathbf{C}^w(u)$ (and hence $\mathbf{C}(u)$) is reparameterized, but $\mathbf{C}^w(u)$ is not changed geometrically; furthermore, the end weights of $\mathbf{C}(u)$ do not change;
- if $f(s)$ is rational then a different curve, $\bar{\mathbf{C}}^w(s)$, is generated, which projects to the same (but reparameterized) curve, $\mathbf{C}(u)$. In general, the end weights of $\mathbf{C}(u)$ will change.

Example

Ex6.7 The circular arc given by Eq. (6.35) has a Bézier representation. Clearly, the Euclidean control points, $\{\mathbf{P}_i\} = \{(1,0),(1,1),(0,1)\}$, remain the same. The weights are determined by equating the power basis and Bézier forms of the denominator function of Eq. (6.35)

$$\left(2-\sqrt{2}\right)s^2 + \left(\sqrt{2}-2\right)s + 1 = (1-s)^2 w_0 + 2s(1-s)w_1 + s^2 w_2$$

Substituting $s = 0, 1, {}^1/_2$, and solving for the w_i yields

$$\{w_i\} = \left\{1, \frac{\sqrt{2}}{2}, 1\right\} \tag{6.55}$$

Figure 6.12 shows the new curve, $\bar{\mathbf{C}}^w(s)$, and its projection, $\mathbf{C}(s)$. Compare this figure with Figure 1.22.

In practice, it is generally not necessary to use rational reparameterization functions of degree greater than one. Lee and Lucian [Lee91] give an excellent description of reparameterization using a linear rational function. We summarize their results here. Let

$$\mathbf{C}(u) = \frac{\sum_{i=0}^{n} N_{i,p}(u) w_i \mathbf{P}_i}{\sum_{i=0}^{n} N_{i,p}(u) w_i} \qquad u \in [a,b]$$

$$s = g(u) = \frac{\alpha u + \beta}{\gamma u + \delta}$$

$$u = f(s) = \frac{-\delta s + \beta}{\gamma s - \alpha} \qquad s \in [c,d]$$

$\big(f(s)$ is the inverse of $g(u)\big)$. Let

$$\mu(u) = \gamma u + \delta \qquad \lambda(s) = \gamma s - \alpha$$

To ensure that $g(u)$ and $f(s)$ are well-behaved, we assume

$$\alpha\delta - \gamma\beta > 0$$

$$\mu(u) \neq 0 \quad \text{for all} \;\; u \in [a,b]$$

$$\lambda(s) \neq 0 \quad \text{for all} \;\; s \in [c,d]$$

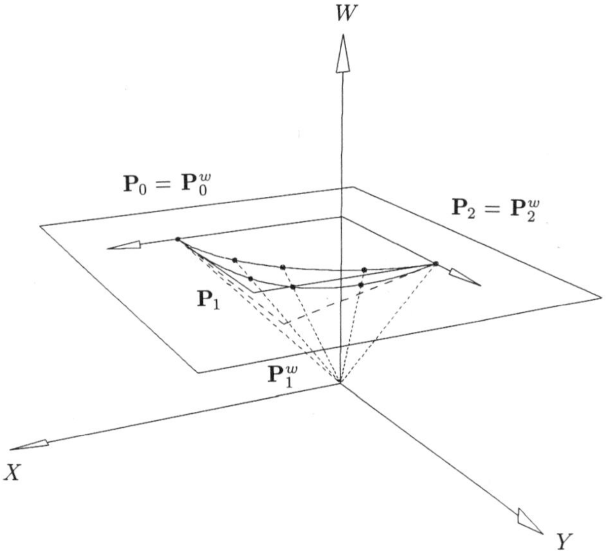

Figure 6.12. Homogeneous representation of the circular arc using weights $\{1, \sqrt{2}/2, 1\}$.

The reparameterized curve $\mathbf{C}(s)$ is obtained as follows:

1. the control points $\{\mathbf{P}_i\}$ do not change;
2. the new knots are the images under $g(u)$ of the original knots, $s_i = g(u_i)$;
3. the new weights $\{\bar{w}_i\}$ (modulo a common nonzero factor) are obtained by either

$$\bar{w}_i = w_i \prod_{j=1}^{p} \lambda(s_{i+j}) \tag{6.56}$$

or

$$\bar{w}_i = \frac{w_i}{\prod_{j=1}^{p} \mu(u_{i+j})} \tag{6.57}$$

s_{i+j} and u_{i+j} are the new and old knots, respectively.

Figures 6.13a through 6.13c show reparameterization examples. The third-degree NURBS curve is defined originally on the knot vector $U = \{0,0,0,0,{}^3/_{10}, {}^7/_{10}, 1,1,1,1\}$. In Figures 6.13a and 6.13b all the weights are initially equal to one. In Figure 6.13c the original weights are $W = \{1, {}^1/_2, 2, 3, {}^1/_2, 1\}$. In Figure 6.13a the rational function is

$$g(u) = \frac{2u+1}{3u+2}$$

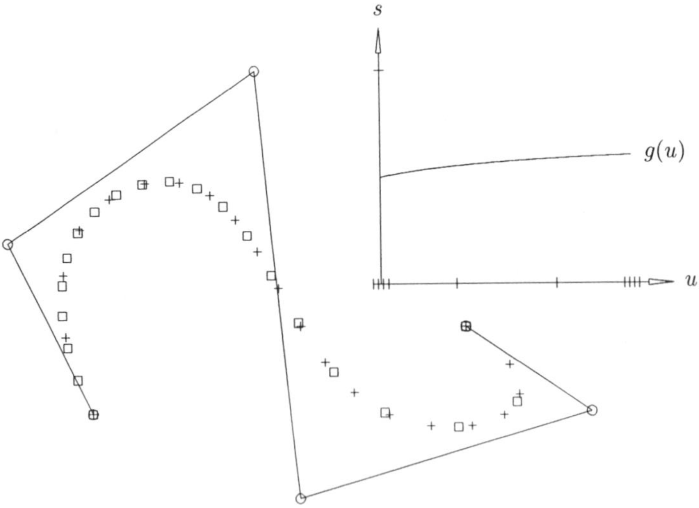

(a)

Figure 6.13. Rational reparameterization of NURBS curves; + shows the original parameterization, and □ illustrates the new parameterization. (a) $g(u) = {}^{(2u+1)}/_{(3u+2)}$; (b) $g(u) = {}^{2u}/_{(3u+1)}$; (c) $g(u) = {}^{(2u-1)}/_{(3u+2)}$.

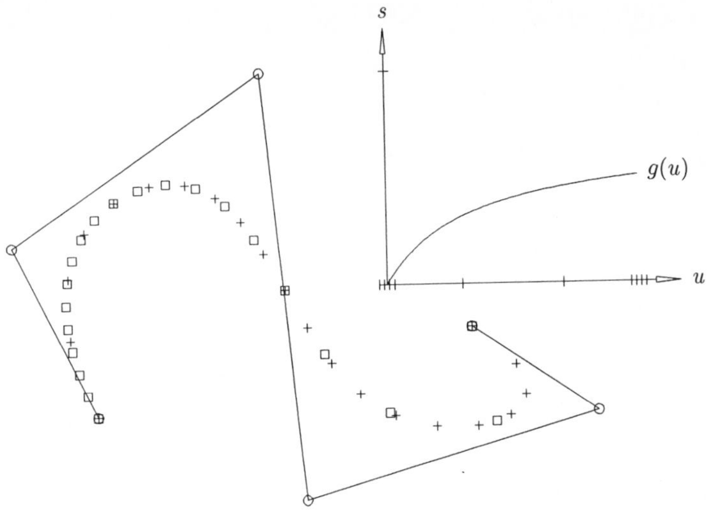

(b)

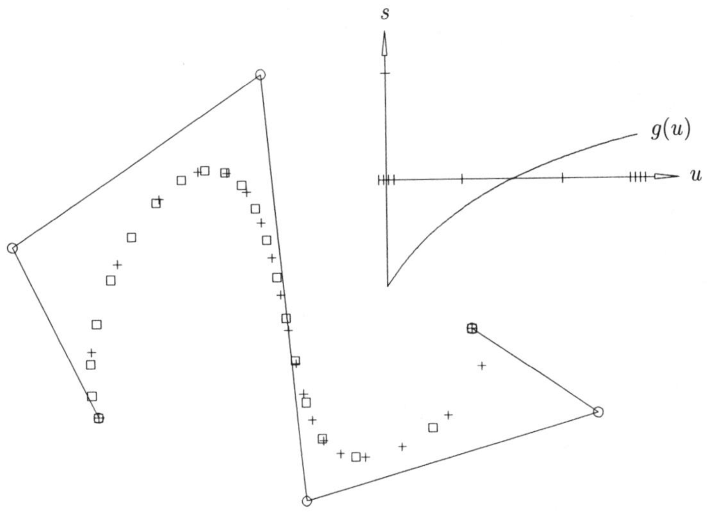

(c)

Figure 6.13. (*Continued.*)

resulting in a new knot vector

$$U = \{0.5, 0.5, 0.5, 0.5, 0.55, 0.58, 0.6, 0.6, 0.6, 0.6\}$$

and weights

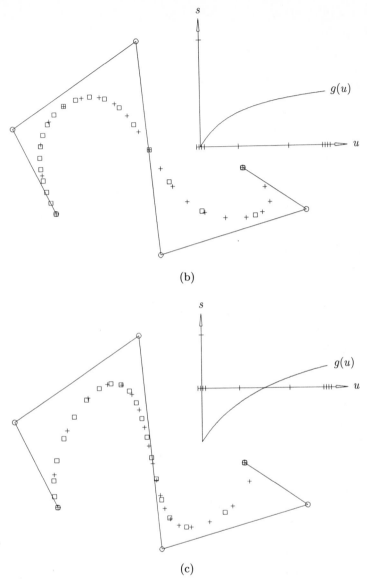

$$W = \{0.125, 0.08, 0.04, 0.01, 0.009, 0.008\}$$

+ shows the original parameterization, and □ marks the new one. Figure 6.13b applies

$$g(u) = \frac{2u}{3u+1}$$

yielding $$U = \{0,0,0,0,0.31,0.45,0.5,0.5,0.5,0.5\}$$

and $$W = \{1.0,0.52,0.16,0.04,0.02,0.01\}$$

Again, + shows the original and □ shows the new parameterization. Finally, in Figure 6.13c the function

$$g(u) = \frac{2u-1}{3u+2}$$

yields $$U = \{-0.5,-0.5,-0.5,-0.5,-0.13,0.09,0.2,0.2,0.2,0.2\}$$

and $$W = \{0.125,0.04,0.08,0.05,0.004,0.008\}$$

The formulas for surfaces are similar. For example, Eq. (6.56) generalizes to

$$\bar{w}_{i,j} = w_{i,j} \prod_{k=1}^{p} \lambda(s_{i+k}) \qquad j = 0,\ldots,m$$

in the u direction, and

$$\bar{w}_{i,j} = w_{i,j} \prod_{\ell=1}^{q} \lambda(t_{j+\ell}) \qquad i = 0,\ldots,n$$

in the v direction, where

$$s = g(u) = \frac{\alpha_u u + \beta_u}{\gamma_u u + \delta_u} \qquad t = h(v) = \frac{\alpha_v v + \beta_v}{\gamma_v v + \delta_v}$$

and $$\lambda(s) = \gamma_u s - \alpha_u \qquad \lambda(t) = \gamma_v t - \alpha_v$$

Equation (6.57) is generalized in a similar fashion.

Figures 6.14a–6.14d show surface reparameterization examples. The test surface is a (3×2)-degree surface defined over

$$U = \{0,0,0,0,1,1,1,1\} \qquad V = \{0,0,0,\tfrac{1}{2},1,1,1\}$$

with weights all equal to one. The reparameterization functions are

$$g(u) = \frac{2u+1}{3u+2} \qquad h(v) = \frac{2v+1}{3v+2}$$

Figure 6.14a shows the original surface; note the even distribution of the parameter lines. In Figure 6.14b the surface was reparameterized in the u direction, in

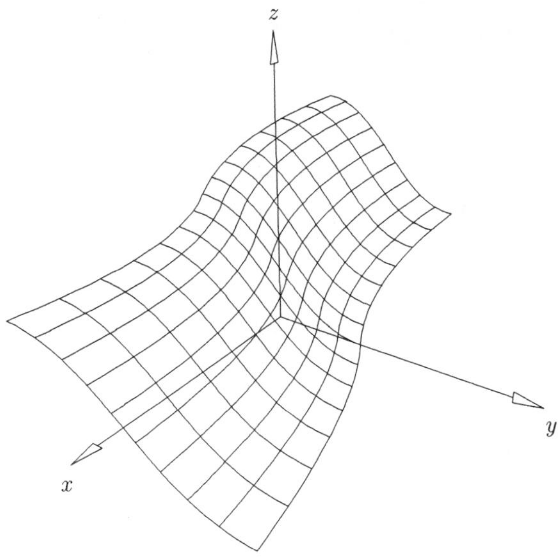

(a)

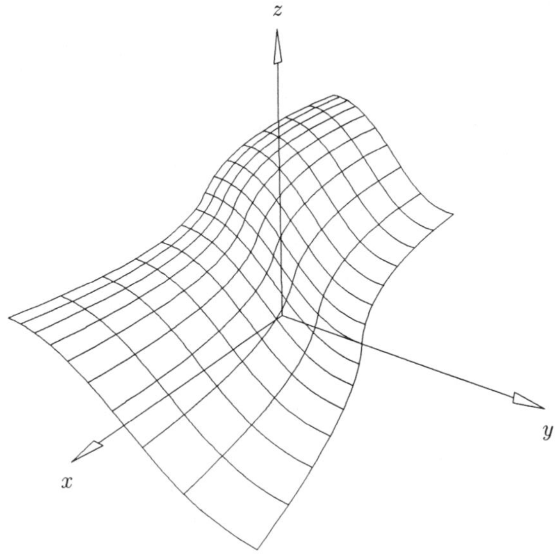

(b)

Figure 6.14. Rational reparameterization of NURBS surfaces using $g(u) = {}^{(2u+1)}/_{(3u+2)}$. (a) Original surface; (b) reparameterization in the u direction; (c) reparameterization in the v direction; (d) reparameterization in both directions.

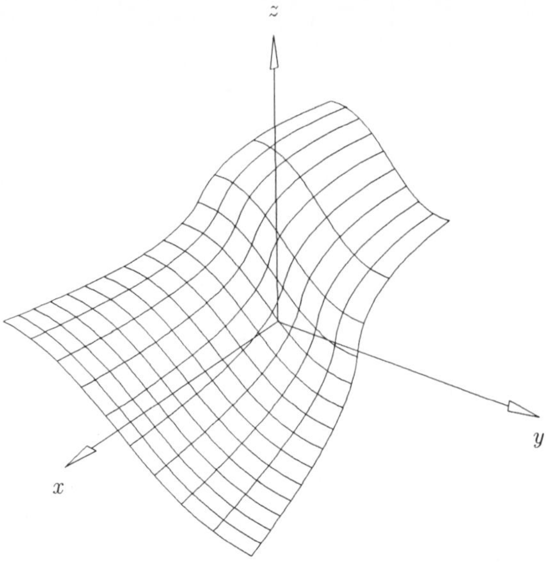

(c)

Figure 6.14. (*Continued.*)

Figure 6.14c in the v direction, and in Figure 6.14d in both directions. Note the uneven distribution of parameter lines in Figures 6.14b–6.14d.

Now assume that the end weights of $\mathbf{C}(u)$ are not equal, i.e., $w_0 \neq w_n$. Since the linear rational function $s = g(u)$ has three degrees of freedom, it should be possible to determine $g(u)$ satisfying the three conditions

$$c = g(a) \qquad d = g(b) \qquad \bar{w}_0 = \bar{w}_n$$

Lee and Lucian [Lee91] derive a function satisfying these conditions

$$s = g(u) = \frac{\sqrt[p]{w_0}(b-u)c + \sqrt[p]{w_n}(u-a)d}{\sqrt[p]{w_0}(b-u) + \sqrt[p]{w_n}(u-a)} \tag{6.58}$$

Figure 6.15 shows a reparameterization example to make end weights equal. The original third-degree NURBS curve is defined by

$$U = \left\{0,0,0,0,\frac{3}{10},\frac{7}{10},1,1,1,1\right\} \qquad W = \{2,8,3,4,2,5\}$$

The new interval chosen is $[c,d] = [{}^1\!/_{10}, {}^4\!/_5]$. The reparameterization function computed by Eq. (6.58) is

$$g(u) = \frac{1.242u + 0.126}{0.45u + 1.26}$$

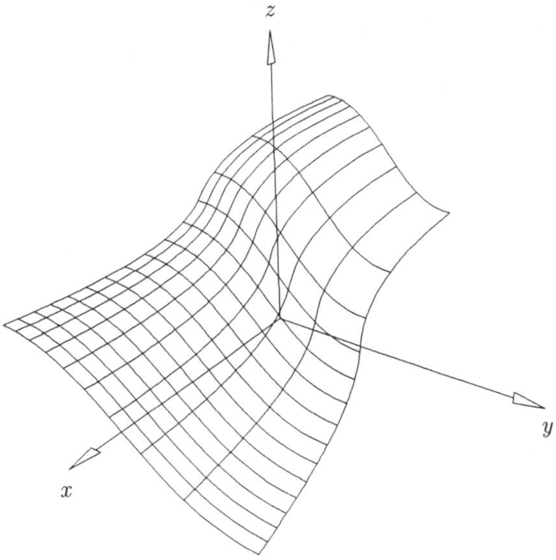

(d)

Figure 6.14. (*Continued.*)

resulting in new knots and weights

$$U' = \{0.1, 0.1, 0.1, 0.1, 0.36, 0.63, 0.8, 0.8, 0.8, 0.8\}$$

$$W' = \{1, 3.61, 1.08, 1.06, 0.43, 1\}$$

where the end weights were chosen to be one. Again, + marks the original parameterization and □ the new parameterization.

We gave examples in Chapter 4 which showed that arbitrary changes in weights generally changed the shape of a rational NURBS curve (e.g., see Figures 4.2 and 4.4). In this section we changed weights without modifying the curve shape, the only change being in the parameterization of the curve. This suggests that for a given curve there must exist a relationship among the weights which determines the curve shape, that is, weight changes which maintain this relationship result in a reparameterization of the curve but not a change in shape. These relationships are called *shape invariants* or *shape factors*. For rational Bézier curves they depend only on the degree; for NURBS curves they depend on the degree and the knots. In general, the derivation of these shape invariants is quite complicated (see [Forr68; Vers75; Patt85; Lee87; Pieg91a]). We give a few here for reference; the c_i denote constants.

- Quadratic Bézier curve (conic):

$$\frac{w_0 w_2}{w_1^2} = c_1 \tag{6.59}$$

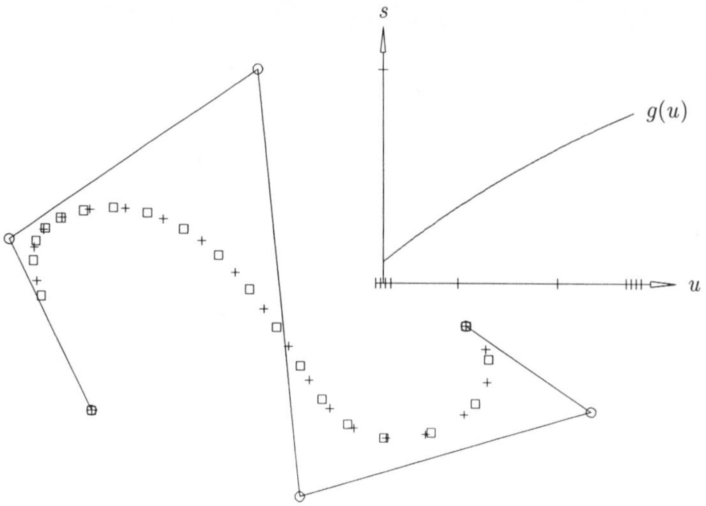

Figure 6.15. Curve reparameterization to make end weights equal.

Consider the circular arc, defined by either $\{w_i\} = \{1, 1, 2\}$ (Figure 1.19b) or $\{w_i\} = \{1, \sqrt{2}/2, 1\}$ (Eq. [6.55])

$$2 = \frac{(1)(2)}{1^2} = \frac{(1)(1)}{\left(\frac{\sqrt{2}}{2}\right)^2} = 2$$

Assuming fixed control points, any three weights which when substituted into Eq. (6.59) yield the value 2 produce the circular arc;

- Cubic Bézier curve:

$$\frac{w_0 w_2}{w_1^2} = c_1 \qquad \frac{w_1 w_3}{w_2^2} = c_2 \tag{6.60}$$

- A pth-degree Bézier curve:

$$\frac{w_0 w_2}{w_1^2} = c_1, \ldots, \frac{w_{p-2} w_p}{w_{p-1}^2} = c_{p-1} \tag{6.61}$$

- Quadratic NURBS curve $\mathbf{C}^w(u) = \sum_{i=0}^{n} N_{i,2}(u)\mathbf{P}_i^w$ on $U = \{u_0, \ldots, u_m\}$:

$$\frac{(u_{i+2} - u_{i+1})w_{i-1} + (u_{i+1} - u_i)w_i}{(u_{i+3} - u_{i+1})(u_{i+2} - u_i)w_i^2} \times \frac{(u_{i+3} - u_{i+2})w_i + (u_{i+2} - u_{i+1})w_{i+1}}{(u_{i+3} - u_{i+1})(u_{i+2} - u_i)w_i^2} = c_i \tag{6.62}$$

for $i = 1, \ldots, n-1$.

We conclude the reparameterization of curves with mention of another interesting technique. Fuhr and Kallay [Fuhr92] develop a technique to interpolate a set of function values using a C^1 continuous piecewise linear rational function. Their method can be used to obtain C^1 continuous reparameterizations which do not raise the degree, but which map arbitrarily many internal points, $u_i = f(s_i)$.

A NURBS surface $\mathbf{S}^w(u,v) = \sum_{i=0}^{n}\sum_{j=0}^{m} N_{i,p}(u)N_{j,q}(v)\mathbf{P}_{i,j}^w$ can be reparameterized in either the u, the v, or both directions. For example, it would be reparameterized with a polynomial function in the u direction by mapping the u knots to s knots (Eqs. [6.51] and [6.52]), and applying Eqs. (6.39) through (6.44) to the $m+1$ columns of control points.

6.5 Curve and Surface Reversal

In this section we use reparameterization to reverse the direction of a NURBS curve and the direction of the normal vectors of a surface.

Let $\mathbf{C}^w(u) = \sum_{i=0}^{n} N_{i,p}(u)\mathbf{P}_i^w$ be a NURBS curve on $u \in [a,b]$, and $u = f(s)$ a reparameterization function on $s \in [c,d]$. In Section 6.4 we assumed that $f'(s) > 0$ on $s \in [c,d]$. This was implicitly used in Example `Ex6.6` and in the derivation of Eqs. (6.41) through (6.44) and Eq. (6.49).

The concepts of Section 6.4 still apply if we assume $f'(s) < 0$ on $s \in [c,d]$. In particular, let

$$u = f(s) = -s + a + b \qquad s \in [a,b] \tag{6.63}$$

Observe that

$$b = f(a) \qquad a = f(b) \tag{6.64}$$

and that $f'(s) = -1$ on $s \in [a,b]$. The inverse of $f(s)$ is

$$s = g(u) = -u + a + b \tag{6.65}$$

From Eq. (6.53), the knots of $\mathbf{C}^w(s)$ are computed by

$$s_{m-p-i} = -u_{p+i} + a + b \qquad i = 1,\ldots,m-2p-1 \tag{6.66}$$

where u_i are the knots of $\mathbf{C}^w(u)$, $0 \le i \le m$. For example, if $U = \{0,0,0,1,3,6,6,8,8,8\}$, then $S = \{0,0,0,2,2,5,7,8,8,8\}$.

The control points $\mathbf{Q}_i^w$ of $\mathbf{C}^w(s)$ are computed as

$$\mathbf{Q}_0^w = \mathbf{C}^w\big(f(s=a)\big) = \mathbf{C}^w(u=b) = \mathbf{P}_n^w$$

$$\begin{aligned}
\mathbf{Q}_1^w &= \frac{s_{p+1}-a}{p}\mathbf{C}^{w(1)}(s=a) + \mathbf{Q}_0^w \\
&= \frac{b-u_{m-p-1}}{p}\mathbf{C}^{w(1)}(u=b)f'(s=a) + \mathbf{P}_n^w \\
&= \frac{b-u_{m-p-1}}{p}\,\frac{p}{b-u_{m-p-1}}(\mathbf{P}_n^w - \mathbf{P}_{n-1}^w)(-1) + \mathbf{P}_n^w \\
&= \mathbf{P}_{n-1}^w
\end{aligned}$$

In general

$$\mathbf{Q}_i^w = \mathbf{P}_{n-i}^w \tag{6.67}$$

The effect of Eqs. (6.63)–(6.67) is to reverse the direction of the curve. This is shown in Figure 6.16; note that the parameterization does not change.

Let $\mathbf{S}^w(u,v) = \sum_{i=0}^{n}\sum_{j=0}^{m} N_{i,p}(u)N_{j,q}(v)\,\mathbf{P}_{i,j}^w$ be a NURBS surface with knot vectors $U = \{u_0,\ldots,u_r\}$ and $V = \{v_0,\ldots,v_s\}$. A surface's parameterization can also be reversed. More specifically, u reversal produces

$$\mathbf{S}^w(s,v) = \sum_{i=0}^{n}\sum_{j=0}^{m} N_{i,p}(s)N_{j,q}(v)\,\mathbf{Q}_{i,j}^w \tag{6.68}$$

on S and V, where

$$s_{r-p-i} = -u_{p+i} + u_0 + u_r \qquad i = 1,\ldots,r-2p-1 \tag{6.69}$$

and

$$\mathbf{Q}_{i,j}^w = \mathbf{P}_{n-i,j}^w \qquad i = 0,\ldots,n \quad j = 0,\ldots,m \tag{6.70}$$

Analogously, v reversal produces

$$\mathbf{S}^w(u,t) = \sum_{i=0}^{n}\sum_{j=0}^{m} N_{i,p}(u)N_{j,q}(t)\,\mathbf{Q}_{i,j}^w \tag{6.71}$$

on U and T, where

$$t_{s-q-j} = -v_{q+j} + v_0 + v_s \qquad j = 1,\ldots,s-2q-1 \tag{6.72}$$

and

$$\mathbf{Q}_{i,j}^w = \mathbf{P}_{i,m-j}^w \qquad i = 0,\ldots,n \quad j = 0,\ldots,m \tag{6.73}$$

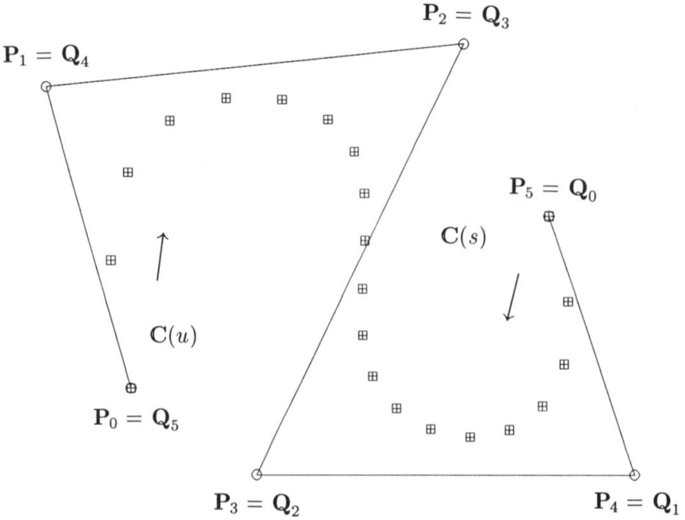

Figure 6.16. Curve reversal; no parameterization change occurs.

At an arbitrary parameter point (u,v), the surface normal vector is given by

$$\mathbf{N}(u,v) = \mathbf{S}_u(u,v) \times \mathbf{S}_v(u,v) \tag{6.74}$$

Clearly, the direction of $\mathbf{N}(u,v)$ can be reversed by reversing either $\mathbf{S}_u(u,v)$ or $\mathbf{S}_v(u,v)$ (but not both). This is accomplished by applying either Eqs. (6.68)–(6.70) or Eqs. (6.71)–(6.73), respectively.

Figures 6.17a–6.17c show surface reversal examples. In Figure 6.17a the original degree (3×2) surface is shown, as well as $\mathbf{S}_u$, $\mathbf{S}_v$, and $\mathbf{N}$. In Figures 6.17b and 6.17c the parameterizations are reversed in the u and v directions, respectively. Note that the normal vector is reversed in each case.

6.6 Conversion Between B-spline and Piecewise Power Basis Forms

The steps to convert a B-spline curve or surface to piecewise power basis form are:

1. use knot refinement, e.g., Algorithms `A5.4`–`A5.7`, to decompose the curve or surface into piecewise Bézier form;
2. applying matrix multiplications (change of basis) convert each Bézier curve segment (or surface patch) to power basis form;
3. apply matrix multiplications to reparameterize the power basis forms obtained in Step 2.

As usual, all equations are applied to four-dimensional control points and power basis coefficients; for convenience, we drop all w superscripts. Step 1 requires no further elaboration.

Suppose the jth curve segment, $\mathbf{C}_j(u)$, is defined on $u \in [u_j, u_{j+1}]$. Now the Bézier control points, $\mathbf{P}_i$, $i = 0,\ldots,p$, obtained in Step 1 for $\mathbf{C}_j(u)$ are valid, but our definition of a Bézier curve requires a $[0,1]$ parameterization (Eqs. [1.7] and [1.8]). Let

$$u = (u_{j+1} - u_j)s + u_j \tag{6.75}$$

Then $0 \le s \le 1$, and the jth segment has the Bézier form

$$\mathbf{C}_j(s) = \sum_{i=0}^{p} B_{i,p}(s)\mathbf{P}_i = [B_{i,p}(s)]^T[\mathbf{P}_i] = \left[\, s^i \,\right]^T M_p[\mathbf{P}_i] \tag{6.76}$$

where $[B_{i,p}(s)]^T$ and $\left[\, s^i \,\right]^T$ are $1 \times (p+1)$ row vectors of scalar values, M_p is a $(p+1)\times(p+1)$ matrix of scalars, and $[\mathbf{P}_i]$ is a $(p+1)\times 1$ column vector of four-dimensional points. Setting

$$[\mathbf{a}_i] = M_p[\mathbf{P}_i] \tag{6.77}$$

we obtain

$$\mathbf{C}_j(s) = \left[\, s^i \,\right]^T [\mathbf{a}_i] \tag{6.78}$$

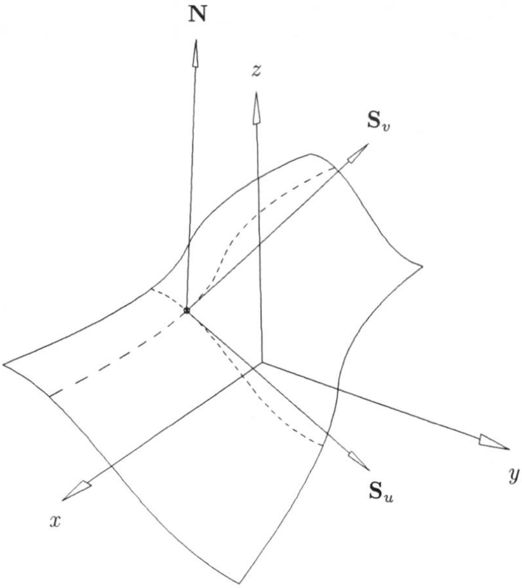

(a)

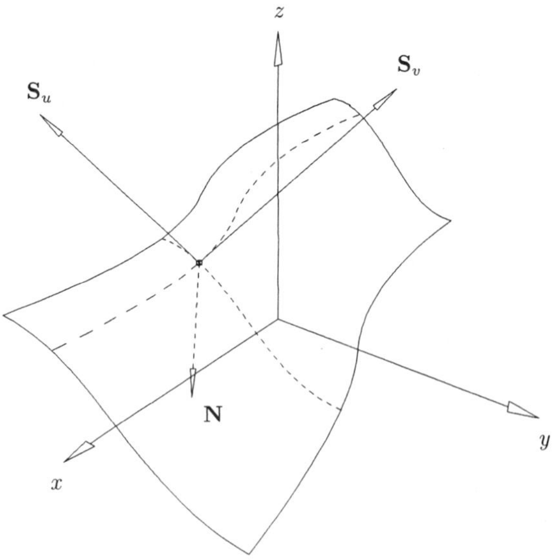

(b)

Figure 6.17. Surface reversal. (a) Original surface showing partial derivatives and the normal vector; (b) parameterization is reversed in the u direction; (c) parameterization is reversed in the v direction.

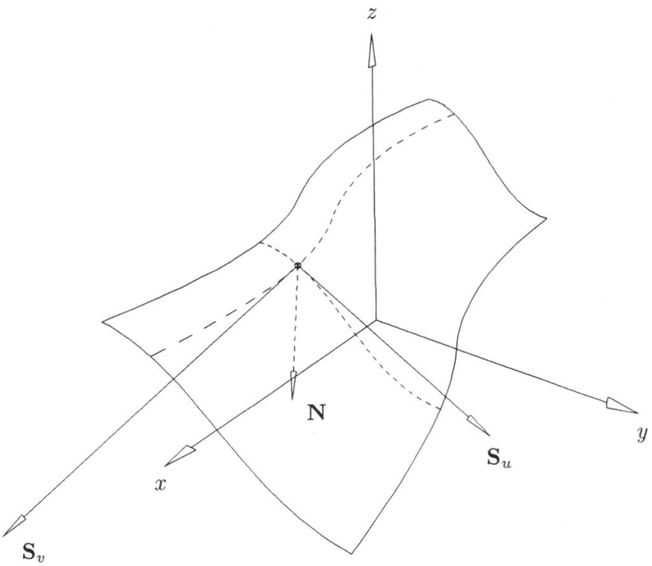

(c)

Figure 6.17. (*Continued.*)

which is the power basis form of the jth segment in the parameter s.

We now derive the matrices M_p for arbitrary p. As a warm-up and for reference, we compute the first three matrices. From Eq. (6.76) it follows that

$$[B_{i,p}(s)]^T = \left[\, s^i \,\right]^T M_p \tag{6.79}$$

For $p = 1, 2, 3$, and from Eq. (1.8), we obtain

$$[\,1-s \quad s\,] = [\,1 \quad s\,] \begin{bmatrix} 1 & 0 \\ -1 & 1 \end{bmatrix}$$

$$[\,(1-s)^2 \quad 2s(1-s) \quad s^2\,] = [\,1 \quad s \quad s^2\,] \begin{bmatrix} 1 & 0 & 0 \\ -2 & 2 & 0 \\ 1 & -2 & 1 \end{bmatrix}$$

$$[\,(1-s)^3 \quad 3s(1-s)^2 \quad 3s^2(1-s) \quad s^3\,] = [\,1 \quad s \quad s^2 \quad s^3\,] \begin{bmatrix} 1 & 0 & 0 & 0 \\ -3 & 3 & 0 & 0 \\ 3 & -6 & 3 & 0 \\ -1 & 3 & -3 & 1 \end{bmatrix} \tag{6.80}$$

Now we derive the general formula. Let $M_p(i, j)$ denote the element of M_p in the ith row and the jth column. From Eq. (1.8) we have

$$(1-s)^p = \binom{p}{0} s^0 (1-s)^p = B_{0,p}(s) = \left[\, s^i \,\right]^T [M_p(i,0)]$$

$$= [\,1 \quad s \quad \cdots \quad s^p\,] \begin{bmatrix} M_p(0,0) \\ \vdots \\ M_p(p,0) \end{bmatrix}$$

From elementary algebra, expanding $(1-s)^p$ yields the binomial coefficients with alternating signs; hence

$$M_p(i,0) = (-1)^i \binom{p}{i} \qquad i = 0, \ldots, p \tag{6.81}$$

In general, the kth column of M_p is defined by

$$\binom{p}{k} s^k (1-s)^{p-k} = B_{k,p}(s) = \left[\, s^i \,\right]^T [M_p(i,k)]$$

Examining $\binom{p}{k} s^k (1-s)^{p-k}$ reveals that

- expanding the term $(1-s)^{p-k}$ yields the binomial coefficients

$$(-1)^j \binom{p-k}{j} \qquad j = 0, \ldots, p-k$$

- multiplying by s^k causes $M_p(j,k) = 0$ for $j = 0, \ldots, k-1$, and the values above are shifted down the column by k rows;
- all elements of the kth column are multiplied by $\binom{p}{k}$.

In summary, for $k = 0, \ldots, p$, the kth column of M_p is given by

$$M_p(j,k) = \begin{cases} 0 & j = 0, \ldots, k-1 \\ (-1)^{j-k} \binom{p}{k} \binom{p-k}{j-k} & j = k, \ldots, p \end{cases} \tag{6.82}$$

We leave it as an exercise to prove that

$$M_p(j,k) = M_p(p-k, p-j) \tag{6.83}$$

Note additional properties of the matrix M_p:

- the diagonal elements are the binomial coefficients for degree p;
- the elements in the last row and in the first column are also the degree p binomial coefficients, but with alternating signs;
- the elements in each row and each column sum to zero except in the first row and last column.

Equation (6.83) says that M_p is symmetric about the diagonal which runs from the bottom left element to the top right element.

Algorithm A6.1 computes M_p efficiently. An array bin[i][j], which contains the precomputed binomial coefficients, is used.

```
ALGORITHM A6.1
  BezierToPowerMatrix(p,M)
    { /*  Compute pth degree Bézier matrix  */
       /*  Input:  p  */
       /*  Output: M  */
    for (i=0; i<p; i++)  /* Set upper triangle to zero */
      for (j=i+1; j<=p; j++)    M[i][j] = 0.0;
    M[0][0] = M[p][p] = 1.0;  /* Set corner elements */
    if (p mod 2)  M[p][0] = -1.0;
      else        M[p][0] = 1.0;
    sign = -1.0;
    for (i=1; i<p; i++)  /* Compute first column, last row, */
      {           /* and the diagonal */
      M[i][i] = bin[p][i];
      M[i][0] = M[p][p-i] = sign*M[i][i];
      sign = -sign;
      }
    /* Compute remaining elements */
    k1 = (p+1)/2;     pk = p-1;
    for (k=1; k<k1; k++)
      {
      sign = -1.0;
      for (j=k+1; j<=pk; j++)
        {
        M[j][k] = M[pk][p-j] = sign*bin[p][k]*bin[p-k][j-k];
        sign = -sign;
        }
      pk = pk-1;
      }
    }
```

We now come to Step 3 of converting a B-spline curve to piecewise power basis, namely, reparameterizing Eq. (6.78) to obtain

$$\mathbf{C}_j(u) = \left[u^i\right]^T \left[\mathbf{b}_i\right] \tag{6.84}$$

the power basis segment in the original parameter, u. We work through the details for $p = 2$, then give the general formula without proof. Solving Eq. (6.75) for s yields

$$s = \frac{1}{u_{j+1} - u_j} u - \frac{u_j}{u_{j+1} - u_j} = cu + d \tag{6.85}$$

For $p = 2$, substituting $s = cu + d$ into Eq. (6.78) and equating the result with Eq. (6.84) yields

$$\left[s^i\right]^T [\mathbf{a}_i] = \left[(cu+d)^i\right]^T [\mathbf{a}_i] = \left[1 \quad cu+d \quad c^2u^2+2cdu+d^2\right]^T [\mathbf{a}_i]$$
$$= \left[1 \quad u \quad u^2\right] R [\mathbf{a}_i] = \left[1 \quad u \quad u^2\right][\mathbf{b}_i] \qquad (6.86)$$

where
$$R = \begin{bmatrix} 1 & d & d^2 \\ 0 & c & 2cd \\ 0 & 0 & c^2 \end{bmatrix}$$

From Eq. (6.86) it follows that

$$R [\mathbf{a}_i] = [\mathbf{b}_i] \qquad (6.87)$$

The $[\mathbf{b}_i]$ are the desired power basis coefficients.

In general, for $s = cu + d$ the pth-degree reparameterization matrix is given by

$$R_p = [r_{i,j}]$$

where
$$r_{i,j} = \begin{cases} 0 & j < i \\ \binom{j}{i} c^i d^{j-i} & i \le j \quad i,j = 0,\ldots,p \end{cases} \qquad (6.88)$$

Combining Eqs. (6.77) and (6.87), we obtain

$$[\mathbf{b}_i] = R_p M_p [\mathbf{P}_i] \qquad (6.89)$$

for the power basis coefficients in terms of the Bézier control points. Figure 6.18 shows an example of B-spline to power basis conversion. A cubic NURBS curve with three segments was converted to piecewise power basis form. Figure 6.18 illustrates the curve and marks its second segment. Note that the segment is defined by the middle four control points. The middle curve segment is also shown, as are the vector coefficients, $\mathbf{b}_0$, $\mathbf{b}_1$, $\mathbf{b}_2$, and $\mathbf{b}_3$, which are scaled by $^1/_{10}$ to make them fit into the figure. Note that the vector coefficients have no geometric relationship with the curve. The polynomial piece is defined on $[\,^3/_{10}, {}^7/_{10}]$.

We complete the discussion of B-spline to power basis conversion with two final remarks:

- the IGES parametric splines (Entities 112 and 114) [IGE93] assume a parameterization for each segment starting at zero; this implies $d = 0$ in Eq. (6.85), and hence R_p reduces to a diagonal matrix with elements

$$r_{i,j} = \begin{cases} 0 & i \ne j \\ c^i & i = j \end{cases} \qquad i = 0,\ldots,p \qquad (6.90)$$

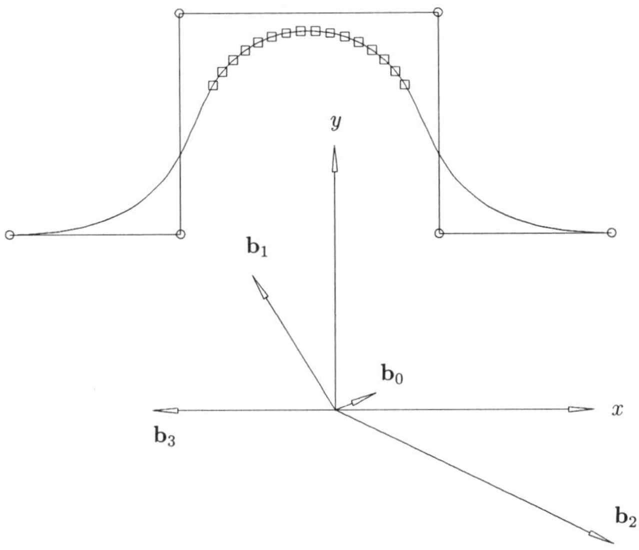

Figure 6.18. Converting a NURBS curve into a piecewise polynomial curve represented in power basis form.

- for surfaces, Eq. (6.89) becomes

$$[\,\mathbf{b}_{i,j}\,] = R_p M_p\,[\,\mathbf{P}_{i,j}\,]\,M_q^T R_q^T \tag{6.91}$$

  where R_p and R_q^T are the reparameterization matrices taking u to s, and v to t, respectively $(0 \le s,t \le 1)$.

Figures 6.19a and 6.19b show B-spline surface to power basis conversion. The test surface is a degree (3×2) surface defined on

$$U = \left\{0,0,0,0,\frac{3}{10},\frac{7}{10},1,1,1,1\right\} \qquad V = \left\{0,0,0,\frac{3}{10},\frac{3}{5},1,1,1\right\}$$

Three polynomial patches are shown in Figure 6.19a: patch $(0,2)$ defined on $[0, {}^3\!/_{10}] \times [{}^3\!/_5, 1]$; patch $(1,1)$ defined on $[{}^3\!/_{10}, {}^7\!/_{10}] \times [{}^3\!/_{10}, {}^3\!/_5]$; and patch $(2,0)$ defined on $[{}^7\!/_{10}, 1] \times [0, {}^3\!/_{10}]$. Figure 6.19b illustrates some of the vector coefficients defining the patch $(1,1)$ in power basis form. The vectors are scaled by ${}^1\!/_2$ for better visualization. Note the lack of any geometric relationship between the patch geometry and the vector coefficients. Compare this figure with Figure 5.25 in Chapter 5.

We now discuss the conversion of a piecewise power basis curve or surface to B-spline form. The steps are:

1. apply matrix multiplications to reparameterize the power basis segments (patches) to the interval $[0,1]$;

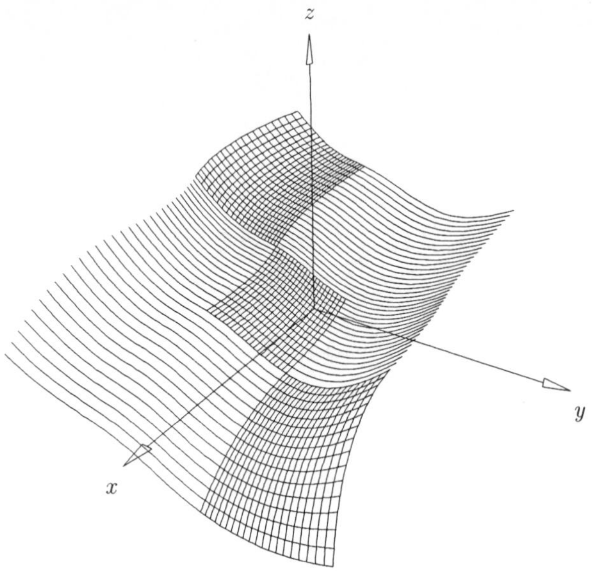

(a)

Figure 6.19. Converting a NURBS surface into a collection of polynomial patches represented in power basis form. (a) Patches with indexes (0,2), (1,1), and (2,0) are shown; (b) some of the vector coefficients defining patch (1,1).

2. apply matrix multiplications to convert each power basis segment (patch) to Bézier form;
3. piece the segments (patches) together to form a B-spline curve or surface, with all internal knots having multiplicity equal to the degree (or degree plus one if C^0 continuity cannot be assumed); the values of the knots are those given by the parameter bounds of the original power basis segments (patches);
4. use knot removal to obtain the minimal representation of the B-spline curve or surface (Algorithm `A5.8` for curves, or see [Till92] for a surface algorithm).

Steps 3 and 4 require no further elaboration. Consider curves first. Let

$$\mathbf{C}_j(u) = \left[\, u^i \,\right]^T [\, \mathbf{a}_i \,] \tag{6.92}$$

be the power basis form of the jth curve segment, with $u \in [u_j, u_{j+1}]$. We need the corresponding Bézier form of the segment

$$\mathbf{C}_j(s) = [\, B_{i,p}(s) \,]^T [\, \mathbf{P}_i \,] = \left[\, s^i \,\right]^T M_p [\, \mathbf{P}_i \,]$$

$$= \left[\, u^i \,\right]^T R_p M_p [\, \mathbf{P}_i \,] = \left[\, u^i \,\right]^T [\, \mathbf{a}_i \,] = \mathbf{C}_j(u)$$

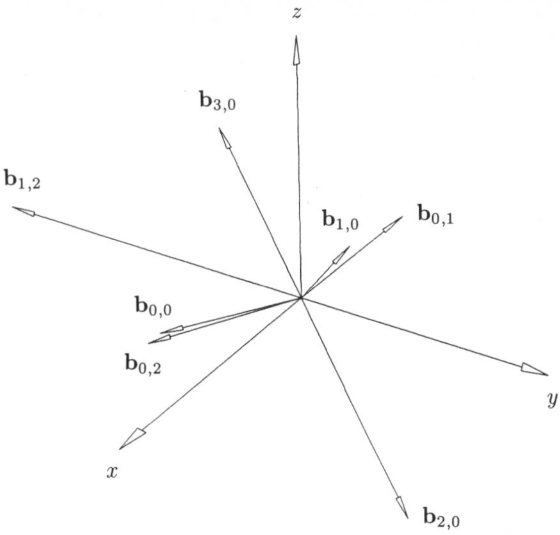

(b)

Figure 6.19. (*Continued.*)

where $s \in [0,1]$. Hence

$$[\,\mathbf{a}_i\,] = R_p M_p\,[\,\mathbf{P}_i\,]$$

and

$$[\,\mathbf{P}_i\,] = M_p^{-1} R_p^{-1}\,[\,\mathbf{a}_i\,] \tag{6.93}$$

Figures 6.20a through 6.20c show examples of power basis to NURBS conversion. Figure 6.20a illustrates a piecewise cubic power basis curve defined on $s_0 < s_1 < s_2 < s_3$. In Figure 6.20b each piece is converted to Bézier form, that is, it is a B-spline curve with triple internal knots. Figure 6.20c shows the B-spline curve after knot removal. Note that the original curve was C^2 continuous at s_1, but only C^1 continuous at s_2; thus, s_2 is a double knot in the final knot vector. It is easy to invert the matrices M_1, M_2, and M_3, shown in Eq. (6.80), to obtain

$$M_1^{-1} = \begin{bmatrix} 1 & 0 \\ 1 & 1 \end{bmatrix}$$

$$M_2^{-1} = \begin{bmatrix} 1 & 0 & 0 \\ 1 & \frac{1}{2} & 0 \\ 1 & 1 & 1 \end{bmatrix}$$

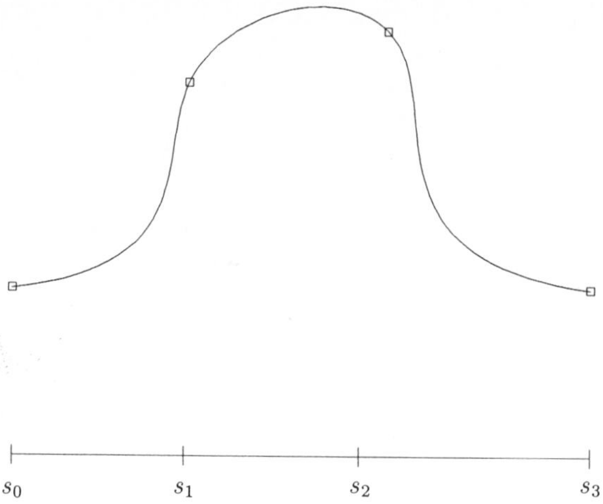

(a)

Figure 6.20. Converting a piecewise polynomial curve into NURBS form. (a) Piecewise polynomial defined over $s_0 < s_1 < s_2 < s_3$; (b) converting each piece into Bézier form; (c) the NURBS representation after knot removal.

$$M_3^{-1} = \begin{bmatrix} 1 & 0 & 0 & 0 \\ 1 & \frac{1}{3} & 0 & 0 \\ 1 & \frac{2}{3} & \frac{1}{3} & 0 \\ 1 & 1 & 1 & 1 \end{bmatrix} \tag{6.94}$$

Given M_p, the formula for the kth column of M_p^{-1} is

$$M_p^{-1}(j,k) = \begin{cases} 0 & j = 0,\ldots,k-1 \\ \dfrac{1}{M_p(k,k)} & j = k \\ \dfrac{-\sum\limits_{i=k}^{j-1} M_p(j,i)M_p^{-1}(i,k)}{M_p(j,j)} & j = k+1,\ldots,p \end{cases} \tag{6.95}$$

As was M_p, M_p^{-1} is symmetric about the diagonal running from the bottom left element to the top right element, hence

$$M_p^{-1}(j,k) = M_p^{-1}(p-k, p-j) \tag{6.96}$$

Algorithm `A6.2` computes M_p^{-1} (denoted by `MI`).

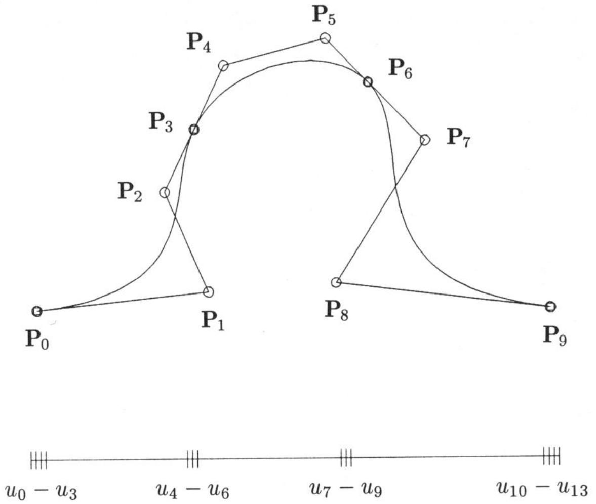

(b)

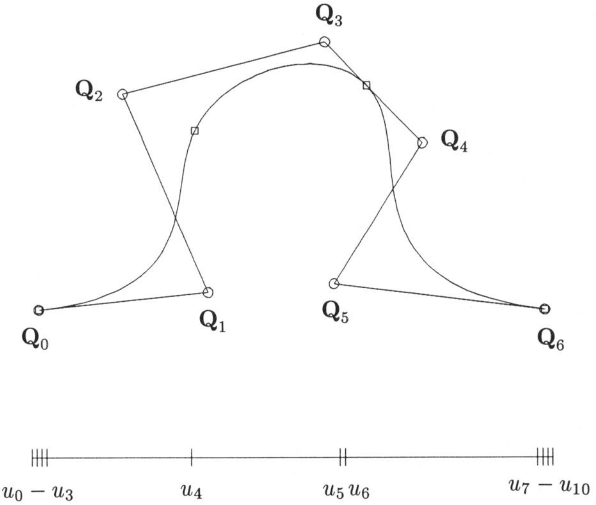

(c)

Figure 6.20. (*Continued.*)

```
ALGORITHM A6.2
  PowerToBezierMatrix(p,M,MI)
    { /* Compute inverse of pth-degree Bézier matrix  */
      /* Input:  p,M  */
      /* Output: MI  */
```

```
for (i=0; i<p; i++)  /* Set upper triangle to zero */
  for (j=i+1; j<=p; j++)   MI[i][j] = 0.0;
/* Set first col, last row, and diagonal */
for (i=0; i<=p; i++)
  {
  MI[i][0] = MI[p][i] = 1.0;
  MI[i][i] = 1.0/M[i][i];
  }
/* Compute remaining elements */
k1 = (p+1)/2;    pk = p-1;
for (k=1; k<k1; k++)
  {
  for (j=k+1; j<=pk; j++)
    {
    d = 0.0;
    for (i=k; i<j; i++)  d = d-M[j][i]*MI[i][k];
    MI[j][k] = d/M[j][j];
    MI[pk][p-j] = MI[j][k];
    }
  pk = pk-1;
  }
}
```

Recalling Eqs. (6.85) and (6.86), we have $s = cu + d$ and

$$\left[\, s^i \,\right]^T = \left[\, (cu+d)^i \,\right]^T = \left[\, u^i \,\right]^T R_p \tag{6.97}$$

Inverting Eq. (6.85) yields

$$u = \frac{1}{c}s - \frac{d}{c} = (u_{j+1} - u_j)s + u_j = \gamma s + \delta$$

From Eq. (6.97) we have

$$\left[\, u^i \,\right]^T = \left[\, (\gamma s + \delta)^i \,\right]^T = \left[\, s^i \,\right]^T R_p^{-1}$$

which implies that R_p^{-1} is simply R_p with c replaced by γ and d by δ. To summarize

$$R_p^{-1} = [\, r_{i,j} \,]$$

with

$$r_{i,j} = \begin{cases} 0 & j < i \\ \binom{j}{i}\gamma^i \delta^{j-i} & i \le j \quad i,j = 0,\ldots,p \end{cases} \tag{6.98}$$

where

$$\gamma = u_{j+1} - u_j \qquad \delta = u_j$$

We conclude with two remarks:

- for the IGES parametric splines, $\delta = 0$ and R_p^{-1} reduces to the diagonal matrix [IGE93] with elements

$$r_{i,j} = \begin{cases} 0 & i \neq j \\ \gamma^i & i = j \end{cases} \qquad i = 0, \ldots, p \tag{6.99}$$

- for surfaces Eq. (6.93) becomes

$$[\,\mathbf{P}_{i,j}\,] = M_p^{-1} R_p^{-1} \,[\,\mathbf{a}_{i,j}\,]\,(R_q^{-1})^T (M_q^{-1})^T$$

  where R_p^{-1} and $(R_q^{-1})^T$ are the reparameterization matrices taking s to u and t to v, respectively $(0 \leq s, t \leq 1)$.

Figures 6.21a–6.21c illustrate power basis to NURBS surface conversion. The test surface is a collection of nine degree (3×2) polynomial patches shown in Figure 6.21a. Figure 6.21b illustrates the piecewise Bézier representation. Knot removal produces the surface shown in Figure 6.21c.

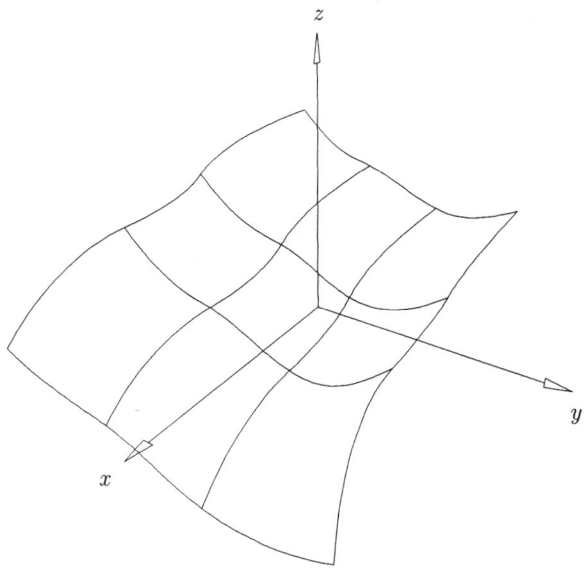

(a)

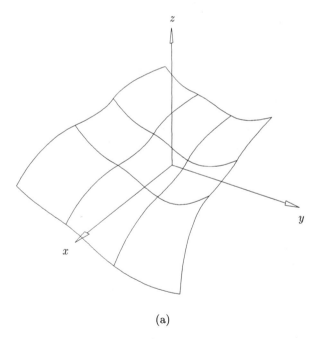

Figure 6.21. Converting a piecewise polynomial surface into NURBS form. (a) Piecewise polynomial surface; (b) converting each patch into Bézier form; (c) the NURBS representation after knot removal.

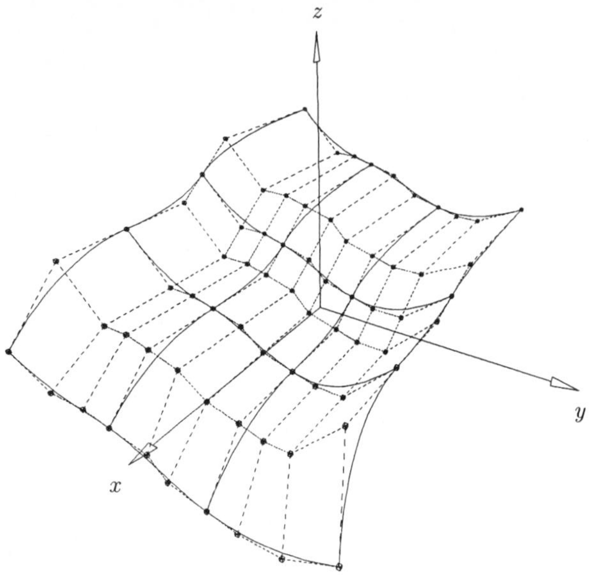

(b)

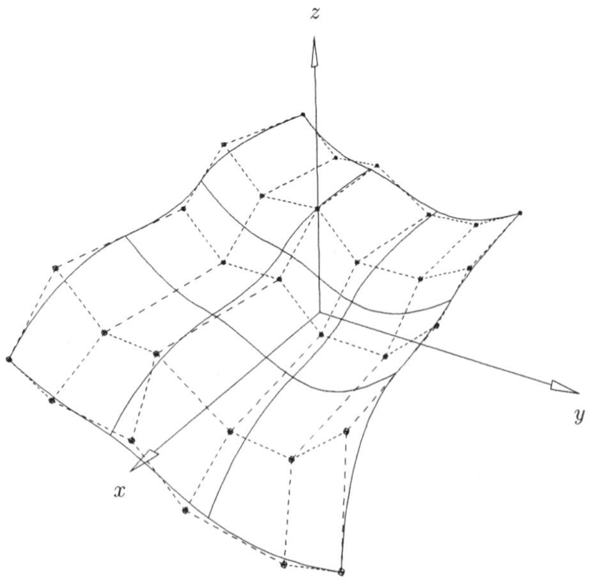

(c)

Figure 6.21. (*Continued.*)

Exercises

6.1. Consider the perspective projection of Example Ex6.3. The Euclidean coordinates of $\bar{\mathbf{P}}_i^w$ are

$$\bar{\mathbf{P}}_i = \left(\frac{dx_i}{d - z_i}, \frac{dy_i}{d - z_i}, 0\right)$$

Carry out the projection using Eqs. (6.17) and (6.18); compare the results.

6.2. Use a quadratic function $u = f(s) = as^2 + bs + c$ to reparameterize the Bézier circular arc $\mathbf{C}(u)$ given by $\{\mathbf{P}_i\} = \{(1,0),(1,1),(0,1)\}$ and $\{w_i\} = \{1,1,2\}$, so that

$$\mathbf{P} = \mathbf{C}\left(s = \frac{1}{2}\right) = \left(\frac{\sqrt{2}}{2}, \frac{\sqrt{2}}{2}\right)$$

Three steps are required:

- determine the u value at which $\mathbf{P}$ is attained. Hint: use Eq. (6.28);
- compute the coefficients a, b, c of $f(s)$;
- use Eq. (6.38) to determine the new homogeneous control points.

Have the end weights changed?

6.3. A cubic curve $\mathbf{C}^w(u)$ on $U = \{0,0,0,0,1,1,3,5,7,7,7,7\}$ is reparameterized with a nonrational quadratic NURBS function, $f(s)$, on $S = \{0,0,0,2,3,6,6,7,7,7\}$. What will the knot vector of the reparameterized curve $\mathbf{C}^w(s)$ look like? What is the continuity of $\mathbf{C}^w(s)$ at the various knots?

6.4. Check Eq. (6.34) and Eqs. (6.55)–(6.58) against one another, that is:

- using Eq. (6.34), do Eq. (6.56) and Eq. (6.57) yield Eq. (6.55);
- does Eq. (6.58) produce Eq. (6.34)?

Remember, all weights can be multiplied by a common factor.

6.5. Derive Eq. (6.83).

6.6. Let the cubic curve $\mathbf{C}(u)$ be defined by $U = \{0,0,0,0,1,2,2,2,2\}$ and the control points $\{\mathbf{P}_i\} = \{(0,0),(1,1),(3,2),(5,1),(4,-1)\}$. Use knot insertion (by hand) to decompose the curve into two Bézier segments, then convert the two segments to power basis form. Check your result by computing some endpoint and end derivative values from the power basis segments, and from the original B-spline curve.

6.7. Let $s = cu + d$. Form R_3 and R_3^{-1}, and verify that $R_3 R_3^{-1} = I$ (I is the identity matrix).

CHAPTER

SEVEN

Conics and Circles

7.1 Introduction

The conic sections and circles play a fundamental role in CADCAM applications. Undoubtedly one of the greatest advantages of NURBS is their capability of precisely representing conic sections and circles, as well as free-form curves and surfaces. We assume a knowledge of conics and circles; the purpose of this chapter is to study them in the framework of their representation as NURBS curves. In Section 7.2 we review various forms and properties of conics which are required in subsequent sections. Section 7.3 covers the quadratic rational Bézier representation of conic and circular arcs; Section 7.4 introduces infinite control points. In Sections 7.5 and 7.6 we present algorithms for constructing the NURBS representation of arbitrary circles and conics, respectively, including full circles and ellipses. Section 7.7 covers conversions between the various representation forms, and Section 7.8 gives examples of higher order circle representations.

7.2 Various Forms for Representing Conics

There are many ways to define and represent the conics. We start by giving a geometric definition, and then use it to derive the general implicit (algebraic) equations of the conics in the xy plane (see [Lawr72]). A conic is the locus of a point moving so that its distance from a fixed point (the *focus*) is proportional to its distance to a fixed line (the *directrix*), that is (see Figure 7.1)

$$\text{Conic } = \left\{ \mathbf{P} \,\middle|\, \frac{\mathbf{PF}}{\mathbf{PD}} = e \right\}$$

where e is a constant of proportionality called the *eccentricity*. The eccentricity

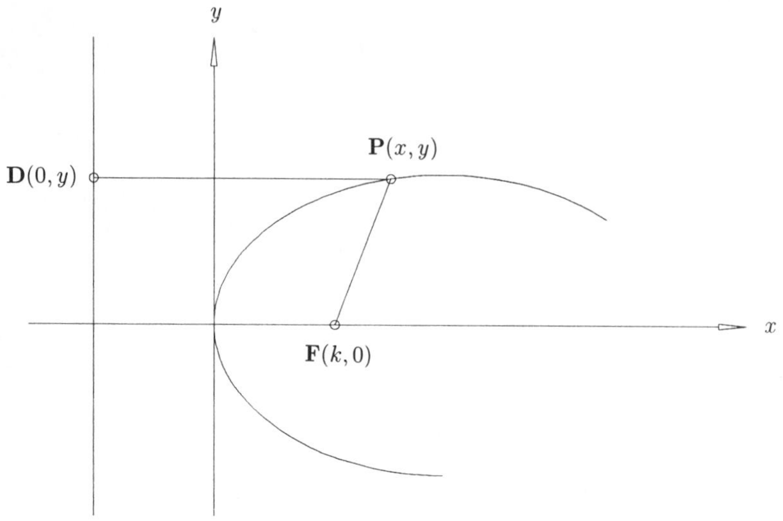

Figure 7.1. Conic definition via the focus and the directrix.

determines the type of conic, i.e.

$$e = \begin{cases} = 1 & \text{parabola} \\ < 1 & \text{ellipse} \\ > 1 & \text{hyperbola} \end{cases}$$

If the directrix is chosen to be the line $x = 0$ and the focus to be $\mathbf{F} = (k, 0)$, then

$$e = \frac{\sqrt{(x-k)^2 + y^2}}{|\, x \,|} \tag{7.1}$$

where $|\, x \,| = \mathbf{PD}$ and $\mathbf{D} = (0, y)$. Squaring and rearranging Eq. (7.1) yields

$$\left(1 - e^2\right)x^2 - 2kx + y^2 + k^2 = 0 \tag{7.2}$$

that is, a conic lying in the xy plane is represented by a second-degree algebraic equation. Conversely, it can be shown that any second-degree algebraic equation represents a conic. Let this equation be written as

$$ax^2 + by^2 + 2hxy + 2fx + 2gy + c = 0 \tag{7.3}$$

Let $\alpha = ab - h^2$, and let

$$D = \begin{vmatrix} a & h & f \\ h & b & g \\ f & g & c \end{vmatrix}$$

be the determinant of the 3×3 matrix formed from the coefficients of Eq. (7.3). Using α and D, a complete classification of the conics is

$\alpha = 0$	$D \neq 0$			parabola
	$D = 0$	$b \neq 0$	$g^2 - bc > 0$	2 parallel real lines
			$g^2 - bc = 0$	2 parallel coincident lines
			$g^2 - bc < 0$	2 parallel imaginary lines
		$b = h = 0$	$f^2 - ac > 0$	2 parallel real lines
			$f^2 - ac = 0$	2 parallel coincident lines
			$f^2 - ac < 0$	2 parallel imaginary lines
$\alpha > 0$	$D = 0$			point ellipse
	$D \neq 0$		$-bD > 0$	real ellipse
			$-bD < 0$	imaginary ellipse
$\alpha < 0$	$D \neq 0$			hyperbola
	$D = 0$			2 intersecting lines

By means of simple transformations, Eq. (7.2) can be restated in one of the standard forms. For $e \neq 1$ we use the transformation

$$x' = x - \frac{k}{1 - e^2} \qquad y' = y$$

Substituting into Eq. (7.2) and dropping the primes yields

$$\frac{x^2}{a^2} + \frac{y^2}{b^2} = 1 \tag{7.4}$$

where

$$a = \frac{ke}{1 - e^2} \qquad b^2 = a^2(1 - e^2)$$

There are two cases:

- Ellipse (see Figure 7.2): $e < 1$ implies $a, b > 0$, and Eq. (7.4) becomes

$$\frac{x^2}{a^2} + \frac{y^2}{b^2} = 1 \qquad a > b > 0 \tag{7.5}$$

  In this position the origin is the *center* of the ellipse. The x-axis is the *major axis*, and the y-axis is the *minor axis*. The points $(-a, 0)$, $(a, 0)$, $(0, -b)$, $(0, b)$ are the *vertices*. The distances a and b are the *major* and *minor radii*, respectively. If $a = b$ Eq. (7.5) represents a circle (this is the limiting case, $e \to 0$, $k \to \infty$).

- Hyperbola (Figure 7.3): $e > 1$ implies $a < 0$ and $b^2 < 0$ (b is imaginary). Setting $b = \mid b \mid$, Eq. (7.4) yields

$$\frac{x^2}{a^2} - \frac{y^2}{b^2} = 1 \qquad a, b > 0 \tag{7.6}$$

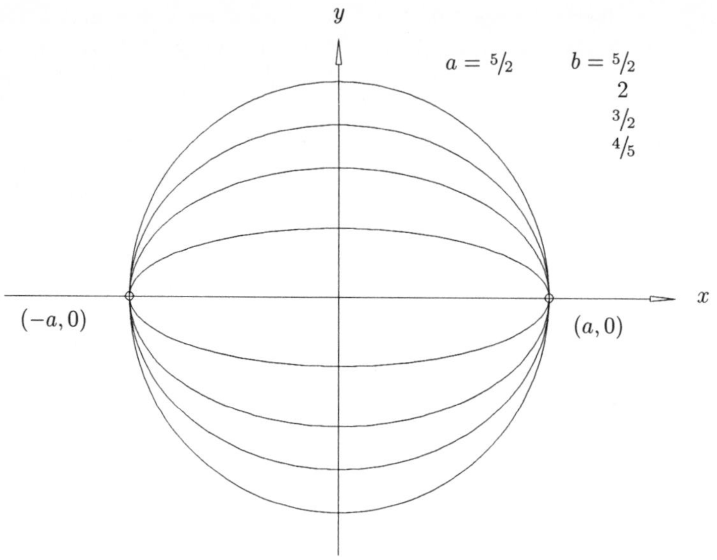

Figure 7.2. Ellipses defined by different parameters ($a = 5/2, b = \{5/2, 2, 3/2, 4/5\}$).

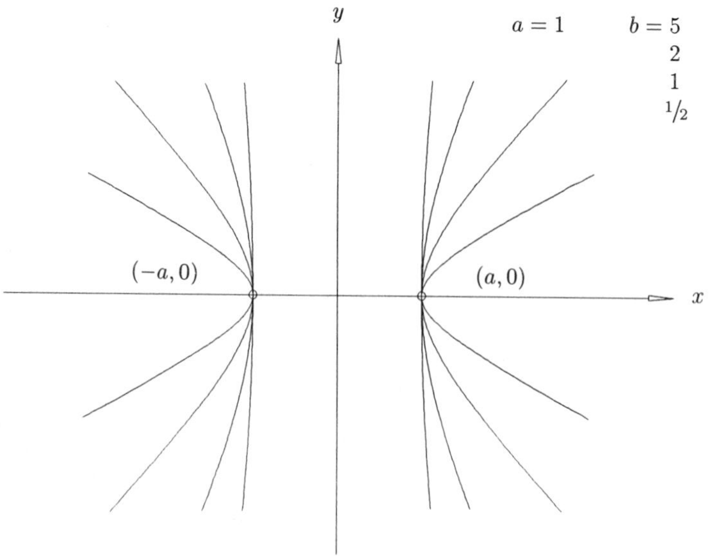

Figure 7.3. Hyperbolas defined by different parameters ($a = 1, b = \{5, 2, 1, 1/2\}$).

In this position the origin is the *center* of the hyperbola. The x-axis is the *transverse axis*, and the y-axis is called the *semiconjugate* or *imaginary axis*. The points $(-a, 0)$ and $(a, 0)$ are the *vertices*. The distances a and b are called the *major* and *minor* (or *imaginary*) *radii*, respectively. Note that the hyperbola has two branches separated by the imaginary axis.

Similarly, $e = 1$ and the transformations

$$x' = x - \frac{1}{2}k \qquad y' = y$$

yield the parabola

$$y^2 = 4ax \qquad a = \frac{1}{2}k > 0 \tag{7.7}$$

with focus $\mathbf{F} = (a, 0)$ and directrix $x + a = 0$ (see Figure 7.4). The parabola has no center. In standard position its *axis* is the x-axis, the origin is its *vertex*, and a is its *focal distance*.

Two parametric representations of the conics are important in CADCAM applications: rational and maximum inscribed area forms. We discuss the rational form first. The equations

$$x(u) = a\frac{1 - u^2}{1 + u^2}$$

$$y(u) = b\frac{2u}{1 + u^2} \qquad -\infty < u < \infty \tag{7.8}$$

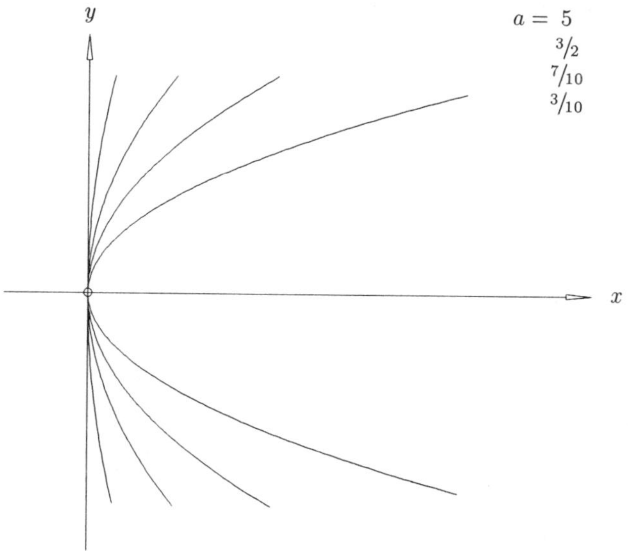

Figure 7.4. Parabolas defined by different parameters ($a = \{5, {}^3/_2, {}^7/_{10}, {}^3/_{10}\}$).

represent an ellipse in standard position (Figure 7.5 shows points on the segment $0 \le u \le 1$). This can be seen by substituting Eq. (7.8) into Eq. (7.5)

$$\frac{a^2\left(\frac{1-u^2}{1+u^2}\right)^2}{a^2} + \frac{b^2\left(\frac{2u}{1+u^2}\right)^2}{b^2} = \frac{1-2u^2+u^4+4u^2}{1+2u^2+u^4} = 1$$

Note that $\big(x(0), y(0)\big) = (a, 0)$, $\big(x(1), y(1)\big) = (0, b)$, and the vertex $(-a, 0)$ is approached in the limit as $u \to -\infty$ or $u \to \infty$. The equations

$$\begin{aligned} x(u) &= a\frac{1+u^2}{1-u^2} \\ y(u) &= b\frac{2u}{1-u^2} \qquad -\infty < u < \infty \end{aligned} \tag{7.9}$$

represent a hyperbola in standard position (Figure 7.6). The interval $u \in (-1, 1)$ corresponds to the right branch; the left branch is traced out by $u \in (-\infty, -1)$ and $u \in (1, \infty)$. $\mathbf{C}(-1)$ and $\mathbf{C}(1)$ represent points at infinity. Finally

$$\begin{aligned} x(u) &= au^2 \\ y(u) &= 2au \qquad -\infty < u < \infty \end{aligned} \tag{7.10}$$

parameterizes the parabola in standard position (see Figure 7.7). Let $\mathbf{C}(u) = \big(x(u), y(u), 0\big)$ be a conic in standard position, embedded in three-dimensional Euclidean space. By applying an arbitrary 3×3 rotation matrix and an arbitrary

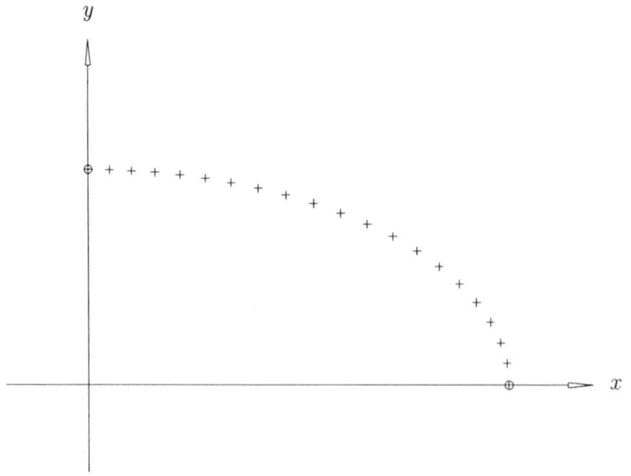

Figure 7.5. Rational parameterization of an elliptic arc (Eq. [7.8]).

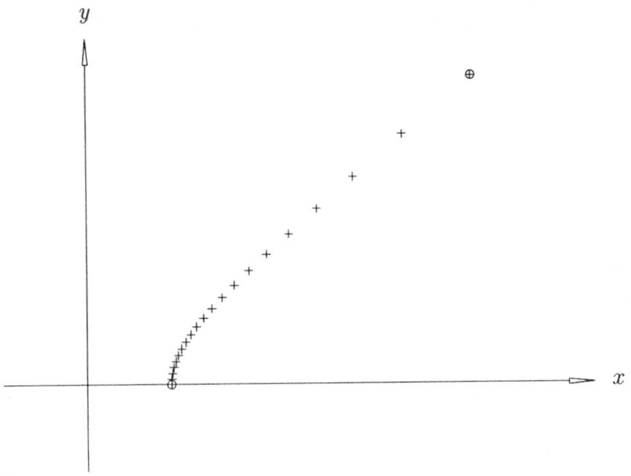

Figure 7.6. Rational parameterization of a hyperbolic arc (Eq. [7.9]).

translation vector, it is easy to see that a general conic in three-dimensional space has the form

$$x(u) = \frac{a_0 + a_1 u + a_2 u^2}{w_0 + w_1 u + w_2 u^2} = \frac{\sum_{i=0}^{2} a_i u^i}{\sum_{i=0}^{2} w_i u^i}$$

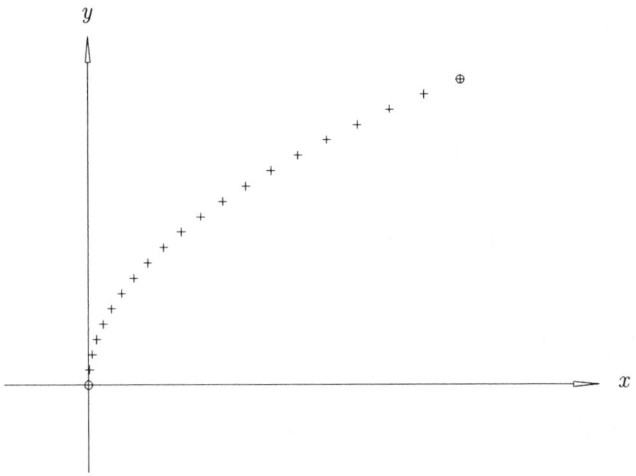

Figure 7.7. Parameterization of a parabolic arc (Eq. [7.10]).

$$y(u) = \frac{b_0 + b_1 u + b_2 u^2}{w_0 + w_1 u + w_2 u^2} = \frac{\sum_{i=0}^{2} b_i u^i}{\sum_{i=0}^{2} w_i u^i}$$

$$z(u) = \frac{c_0 + c_1 u + c_2 u^2}{w_0 + w_1 u + w_2 u^2} = \frac{\sum_{i=0}^{2} c_i u^i}{\sum_{i=0}^{2} w_i u^i} \qquad -\infty < u < \infty \tag{7.11}$$

Setting

$$x_i = \frac{a_i}{w_i}$$

$$y_i = \frac{b_i}{w_i}$$

$$z_i = \frac{c_i}{w_i}$$

and

$$\mathbf{a}_i = (x_i, y_i, z_i)$$

we obtain

$$\mathbf{C}(u) = \frac{w_0 \mathbf{a}_0 + w_1 \mathbf{a}_1 u + w_2 \mathbf{a}_2 u^2}{w_0 + w_1 u + w_2 u^2} = \frac{\sum_{i=0}^{2} w_i \mathbf{a}_i u^i}{\sum_{i=0}^{2} w_i u^i} \tag{7.12}$$

the rational power basis form of the conic. Setting

$$\mathbf{a}_i^w = (w_i x_i, w_i y_i, w_i z_i, w_i) \tag{7.13}$$

yields

$$\mathbf{C}^w(u) = \sum_{i=0}^{2} \mathbf{a}_i^w u^i \tag{7.14}$$

the homogeneous form of the rational power basis conic. Furthermore, any equation in the form of Eq. (7.11) is a conic. This fact will follow from Sections 7.3 and 7.7.

The rational forms can represent rather poor parameterizations of a conic, in the sense that evenly spaced parameter values can map into very unevenly spaced points on the curve. Figures 7.5 to 7.7 show points on sections of the conics given by Eqs. (7.8)–(7.10). The points are images of evenly spaced values of u. From Chapter 6 we know that the parameterization of a rational curve can be changed (and possibly improved) by a reparameterization with a linear rational function.

Now suppose $\mathbf{C}(u) = \big(x(u), y(u)\big)$ is a parametric representation of a conic in standard position. For each type of conic we now give functions $x(u), y(u)$, which yield a good parameterization in the sense that if for arbitrary integer n and parameter bounds a and b we compute n equally spaced parameter values

$$a = u_1, \ldots, u_n = b \qquad u_{i+1} - u_i = \text{constant}, \quad i = 1, \ldots, n-1$$

then the point sequence $\mathbf{C}(u_1), \ldots, \mathbf{C}(u_n)$ forms the $(n-1)$-sided polygon on $\mathbf{C}(u)$, whose closure has the maximum inscribed area. The ellipse is given by

$$\begin{aligned} x(u) &= a\cos u \\ y(u) &= b\sin u \qquad 0 \le u \le 2\pi \end{aligned} \tag{7.15}$$

(see Figure 7.8). If $a = b$ Eq. (7.15) represents a circle, and the parameterization is uniform. The hyperbola uses the hyperbolic functions

$$\sinh u = \frac{e^u - e^{-u}}{2}$$

$$\cosh u = \frac{e^u + e^{-u}}{2}$$

Its equations are (Figure 7.9)

$$\begin{aligned} x(u) &= a\cosh u \\ y(u) &= b\sinh u \qquad -\infty < u < \infty \end{aligned} \tag{7.16}$$

Equation (7.16) traces out the right branch; the left branch is traced out by

$$\begin{aligned} x(u) &= -a\cosh u \\ y(u) &= -b\sinh u \qquad -\infty < u < \infty \end{aligned}$$

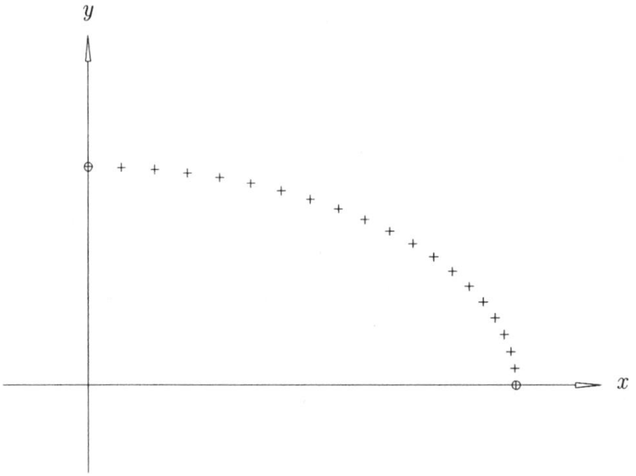

Figure 7.8. Maximum area parameterization of an ellipse (Eq. [7.15]).

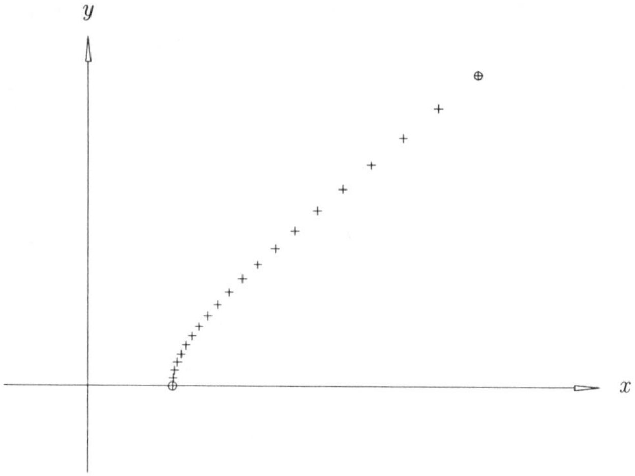

Figure 7.9. Maximum area parameterization of a hyperbola (Eq. [7.16]).

A parametric parabola is given by the equation (Figure 7.7)

$$\begin{aligned} x(u) &= au^2 \\ y(u) &= 2au \qquad -\infty < u < \infty \end{aligned} \tag{7.17}$$

which is the same as Eq. (7.10).

Equations (7.15)–(7.17) can be extended to represent conics in three-dimensional space. Let $\{\mathbf{O}, \mathbf{X}, \mathbf{Y}\}$ be the local coordinate system of the conic in three-dimensional space ($\mathbf{O}$ is a point, and $\mathbf{X}$ and $\mathbf{Y}$ are orthogonal unit length vectors). The conics are defined as (Figure 7.10)

- Ellipse: with $\mathbf{O}$ as the center, $\mathbf{X}$ as the major and $\mathbf{Y}$ as the minor axis, the equation of the ellipse is

$$\mathbf{C}(u) = \mathbf{O} + a\cos u\mathbf{X} + b\sin u\mathbf{Y} \tag{7.18}$$

- Hyperbola: with $\mathbf{O}$ as the center, $\mathbf{X}$ as the transverse axis, and $\mathbf{Y}$ as the imaginary axis, the equation of the left branch of the hyperbola is

$$\mathbf{C}(u) = \mathbf{O} - a\cosh u\mathbf{X} - b\sinh u\mathbf{Y} \tag{7.19}$$

- Parabola: with $\mathbf{O}$ as the vertex and $\mathbf{X}$ as the axis, $\mathbf{Y}$ gives the tangent direction of the parabola at its vertex. The equation of the parabola is

$$\mathbf{C}(u) = \mathbf{O} + au^2\mathbf{X} + 2au\mathbf{Y} \tag{7.20}$$

Equations (7.18)–(7.20) are the conic forms specified in the new Standard for the Exchange of Product Model Data (STEP) [STEP94].

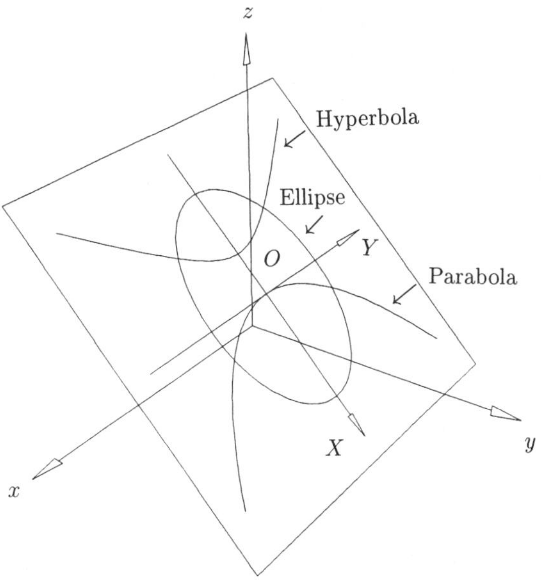

Figure 7.10. Ellipse, parabola, and hyperbola in three-dimensional space.

Almost any book on analytic geometry covers the implicit equation form of the conics in detail, including the classification of conic types, degenerate cases, and the transformations into standard position (Eqs. [7.5]–[7.7]), for example see [Salm79; Coxe80; Ilyi84]. A few modern CADCAM geometry books cover the conics in some detail, particularly the rational and maximum inscribed area parametric forms, e.g., see Rogers [Roge90] and Beach [Beac91]. The maximum inscribed area property of Eqs. (7.15)–(7.17) was first given by [Smit71]. Liming's two books ([Limi44, 79]) contain a wealth of information on conic constructions and the use of conics in engineering design.

7.3 The Quadratic Rational Bézier Arc

The quadratic rational Bézier arc has the form

$$\mathbf{C}(u) = \frac{(1-u)^2 w_0\,\mathbf{P}_0 + 2u(1-u)\,w_1\,\mathbf{P}_1 + u^2 w_2\,\mathbf{P}_2}{(1-u)^2 w_0 + 2u(1-u)w_1 + u^2 w_2}$$

$$= R_{0,2}(u)\,\mathbf{P}_0 + R_{1,2}(u)\,\mathbf{P}_1 + R_{2,2}(u)\,\mathbf{P}_2 \tag{7.21}$$

where
$$R_{i,2}(u) = \frac{B_{i,2}(u)w_i}{\displaystyle\sum_{j=0}^{2} B_{j,2}(u)w_j} \qquad u \in [0,1]$$

To show that Eq. (7.21) is a conic, introduce a local, oblique coordinate system

$$\{\mathbf{P}_1, \mathbf{S}, \mathbf{T}\} \tag{7.22}$$

with

$$\mathbf{S} = \mathbf{P}_0 - \mathbf{P}_1 \qquad \mathbf{T} = \mathbf{P}_2 - \mathbf{P}_1$$

(see Figure 7.11). For arbitrary $u \in [0,1]$ the point $\mathbf{C}(u)$ lies in the triangle $\mathbf{P}_0\mathbf{P}_1\mathbf{P}_2$, hence can be written as

$$\mathbf{C}(u) = \mathbf{P}_1 + \alpha(u)\mathbf{S} + \beta(u)\mathbf{T} = \alpha(u)\mathbf{P}_0 + \big(1 - \alpha(u) - \beta(u)\big)\mathbf{P}_1 + \beta(u)\mathbf{P}_2 \tag{7.23}$$

Comparing this with Eq. (7.21) we find that

$$\alpha(u) = R_{0,2}(u) \qquad \beta(u) = R_{2,2}(u) \tag{7.24}$$

Using the identity

$$B_{0,2}(u)\, B_{2,2}(u) = \left(\frac{B_{1,2}(u)}{2}\right)^2$$

and Eq. (7.23), and denoting the denominator function in Eq. (7.21) by $w(u)$, we obtain

$$\begin{aligned}\alpha(u)\beta(u) = R_{0,2}(u)R_{2,2}(u) &= \frac{w_0 w_2\, B_{0,2}(u)B_{2,2}(u)}{\big(w(u)\big)^2} \\ &= w_0 w_2 \frac{\big(B_{1,2}(u)\big)^2}{4\big(w(u)\big)^2} = \frac{w_0 w_2}{w_1^2} \frac{\big(w_1 B_{1,2}(u)\big)^2}{4\big(w(u)\big)^2} \\ &= \frac{w_0 w_2}{w_1^2} \frac{1}{4} \big(R_{1,2}(u)\big)^2\end{aligned}$$

Setting

$$k = \frac{w_0 w_2}{w_1^2} \tag{7.25}$$

and using Eq. (7.23) produces

$$\alpha(u)\beta(u) = \frac{1}{4} k \big(1 - \alpha(u) - \beta(u)\big)^2 \tag{7.26}$$

Equation (7.26) is the implicit (second-degree) equation of a conic in the oblique coordinate system $\{\mathbf{P}_1, \mathbf{S}, \mathbf{T}\}$. Note that the constant, k, of Eq. (7.25) is the *conic shape factor* given in Chapter 6, Eq. (6.59). Equation (7.26) says that k determines the conic; if the three weights are changed in such a way that k is not changed, then only the parameterization changes, not the curve.

The type of conic can be determined by looking at the denominator $w(u)$ of Eq. (7.21), which can be written as

$$\begin{aligned} w(u) &= (1-u)^2 w_0 + 2u(1-u)w_1 + u^2 w_2 \\ &= (w_0 - 2w_1 + w_2)u^2 + 2(w_1 - w_0)u + w_0 \end{aligned} \tag{7.27}$$

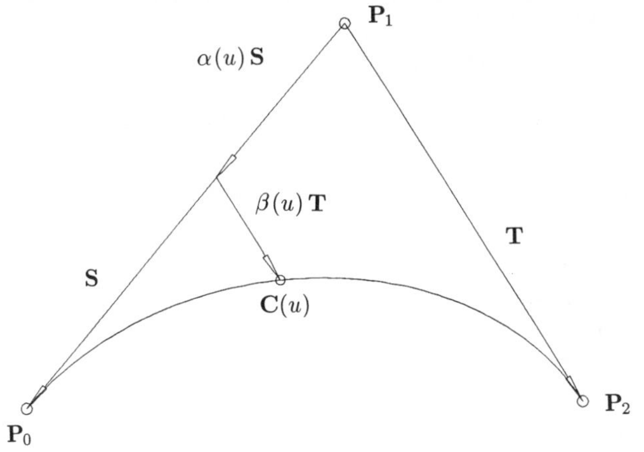

Figure 7.11. Local coordinate system for rational quadratic Bézier curve.

The roots of Eq. (7.27) are

$$u_{1,2} = \frac{w_0 - w_1 \pm w_1\sqrt{1-k}}{w_0 - 2w_1 + w_2} \tag{7.28}$$

where k is the conic shape factor. Equation (7.25) says that any two weights can be chosen arbitrarily; the conic is then determined by the third weight. It is customary to choose $w_0 = w_2 = 1$; this is called the *normal parameterization.* Then if $w_1 = 1$, Eq. (7.21) is a parabola. Assuming $w_1 \neq 1$, Eq. (7.28) implies that

- if $k > 1$, then Eq. (7.27) has no real solutions; there are no points at infinity on the curve, hence it is an ellipse;
- if $k = 1$, Eq. (7.27) has one real solution; there is one point on the curve at infinity, and the curve is a parabola;
- if $k < 1$, Eq. (7.27) has two roots; the curve has two points at infinity, and it is a hyperbola.

Expressing these conditions in terms of w_1, we have:

- ${w_1}^2 < 1$ $(-1 < w_1 < 1) \Longrightarrow$ ellipse;
- ${w_1}^2 = 1$ $(w_1 = 1$ or $-1) \Longrightarrow$ parabola;
- ${w_1}^2 > 1$ $(w_1 > 1$ or $w_1 < -1) \Longrightarrow$ hyperbola.

(see Figure 7.12).

Notice that w_1 can be zero or negative. $w_1 = 0$ yields a straight line segment from $\mathbf{P}_0$ to $\mathbf{P}_2$, and $w_1 < 0$ yields the complementary arc, traversed in the reverse order (see [Lee87] for a simple proof). Notice also that the convex hull property does not hold if $w_1 < 0$.

Varying w_1 yields a family of conic arcs having $\mathbf{P}_0$ and $\mathbf{P}_2$ as endpoints and end tangents parallel to $\mathbf{P}_0\mathbf{P}_1$ and $\mathbf{P}_1\mathbf{P}_2$. However, specifying a weight is not a convenient design tool. A more convenient way to select a conic from the family is to specify a third point on the conic, which is attained at some parameter value, say $u = 1/2$. This point is called the *shoulder point* of the conic, $\mathbf{S} = \mathbf{C}(1/2)$ (see Figure 7.12). Substitution of $u = 1/2$ into Eq. (7.21) yields

$$\mathbf{S} = \frac{1}{1+w_1}\mathbf{M} + \frac{w_1}{1+w_1}\mathbf{P}_1 \tag{7.29}$$

where $\mathbf{M}$ is the midpoint of the chord $\mathbf{P}_0\mathbf{P}_2$. Due to our choice of $w_0 = w_2 = 1$, it follows that the tangent to the conic at $\mathbf{S}$ is parallel to $\mathbf{P}_0\mathbf{P}_2$, i.e., the conic attains its maximum distance from $\mathbf{P}_0\mathbf{P}_2$ at $\mathbf{S} = \mathbf{C}(1/2)$. Let s be a new parameter that gives a linear interpolation between $\mathbf{M}$ and $\mathbf{P}_1$. Then for some value of s we have

$$\mathbf{S} = (1-s)\mathbf{M} + s\mathbf{P}_1 \tag{7.30}$$

From Eqs. (7.29) and (7.30) it follows that

$$s = \frac{w_1}{1+w_1} \qquad w_1 = \frac{s}{1-s} \tag{7.31}$$

The parameter s is a good shape design tool. The designer can move his shoulder point (which determines the fullness of the curve) linearly from $\mathbf{M}$ to $\mathbf{P}_1$. $s = 0$ yields a line segment, $0 < s < 1/2$ yields an ellipse, $s = 1/2$ yields a parabola, and $1/2 < s < 1$ yields a hyperbola.

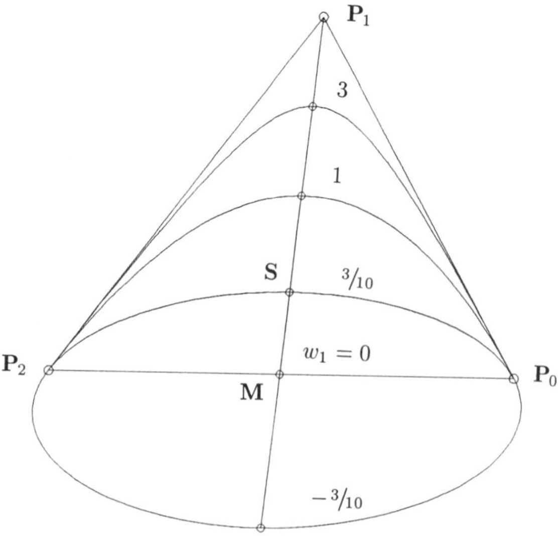

Figure 7.12. Various conic arcs defined by $w_1 = \{3, 1, 3/10, 0, -3/10\}$.

A circular arc of sweep angle less than 180° is also represented by Eq. (7.21). For symmetry $\mathbf{P}_0\mathbf{P}_1\mathbf{P}_2$ must be an isosceles triangle, with $\mathbf{P}_0\mathbf{P}_1 = \mathbf{P}_1\mathbf{P}_2$. Because the circle is a special case of an ellipse, we expect that $0 < w_1 < 1$. Consider Figure 7.13. From Eq. (7.31) it follows that

$$w_1 = \frac{s}{1-s} = \frac{\mathbf{MS}}{\mathbf{SP}_1} \tag{7.32}$$

Let $\theta = \angle\mathbf{P}_1\mathbf{P}_2\mathbf{M}$. From symmetry the arc $\mathbf{P}_2\mathbf{S}$ is the same as $\mathbf{SP}_0$, hence the angle $\angle\mathbf{SP}_2\mathbf{M}$ bisects θ. From the properties of bisectors it follows that

$$w_1 = \frac{\mathbf{MS}}{\mathbf{SP}_1} = \frac{\mathbf{MP}_2}{\mathbf{P}_1\mathbf{P}_2} = \frac{e}{f} = \cos\theta \tag{7.33}$$

Much of the material in this section goes back to the work of Coons and Forrest [Coon67; Ahuj68; Forr68]. It can also be found in [Lee87; Pieg87a].

7.4 Infinite Control Points

In this section we introduce infinite control points, a concept which we use to construct circular and elliptical arcs sweeping 180°. Versprille [Vers75] mentions infinite control points briefly, and Piegl uses them to construct a number of different curves and surfaces [Pieg87c, 88a, 88b].

The notion of a point at infinity is common in projective geometry [Ahuj68; Coxe74; Ries81]. The point $\mathbf{P}^w = (x, y, z, 0)$ in four-dimensional space (x, y, and

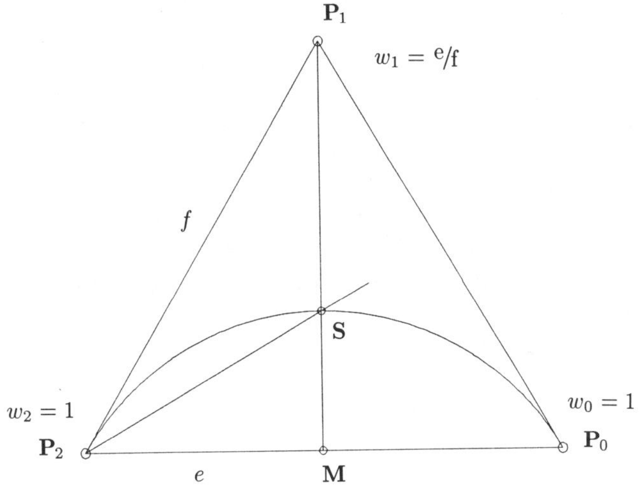

Figure 7.13. Quadratic rational Bézier representation of a circular arc sweeping less than 180°.

z not all zero) is called a *point at infinity.* It is illustrated in three-dimensional space by a direction vector from the origin through the three-dimensional point (x, y, z). Thus, $\mathbf{P} = H\{\mathbf{P}^w\}$ is a direction vector (see Eq. [1.16]). To emphasize this we use the notation $\vec{\mathbf{P}}$.

Assume $\mathbf{P}_j^w = (x_j, y_j, z_j, 0)$ is an infinite control point of a curve $\mathbf{C}(u)$. Then

$$\mathbf{C}^w(u) = \sum_{i=0}^{n} N_{i,p}(u)\mathbf{P}_i^w$$

can be written as

$$\mathbf{C}(u) = \frac{\left(\sum\limits_{j\neq i=0}^{n} N_{i,p}(u)w_i\mathbf{P}_i\right) + N_{j,p}(u)\vec{\mathbf{P}}_j}{\sum\limits_{j\neq i=0}^{n} N_{i,p}(u)w_i}$$

$$= \frac{\sum\limits_{j\neq i} N_{i,p}(u)w_i\mathbf{P}_i}{w(u)} + \frac{N_{j,p}(u)\vec{\mathbf{P}}_j}{w(u)}$$

$$= \bar{\mathbf{C}}(u) + f(u)\vec{\mathbf{P}}_j \tag{7.34}$$

Hence, for fixed u_0, $\mathbf{C}(u_0)$ is $\bar{\mathbf{C}}(u_0)$, which lies in the convex hull of the control points $\mathbf{P}_0, \ldots, \mathbf{P}_{j-1}, \mathbf{P}_{j+1}, \ldots, \mathbf{P}_n$, plus a nonnegative scale factor of the vector $\vec{\mathbf{P}}_j$ (see Figure 7.14). Increasing the magnitude of $\vec{\mathbf{P}}_j$ pulls the curve toward its direction. Note in Figure 7.14 that the curve $\bar{\mathbf{C}}(u)$ touches the control polygon on the segments $\mathbf{P}_1\mathbf{P}_3$ and $\mathbf{P}_3\mathbf{P}_4$. $\mathbf{C}(u)$ is a cubic curve with two distinct internal knots (multiplicity 1). The points at which $\bar{\mathbf{C}}(u)$ touches the control polygon correspond to $\bar{\mathbf{C}}(u)$ evaluated at these internal knot values.

We warn the reader at this point that in the projective geometry sense we are not rigorously correct in stating that $\mathbf{P}^w = (x, y, z, 0)$ is a point at infinity. In projective geometry terminology, the points (x, y, z, w) and $(\alpha x, \alpha y, \alpha z, \alpha w)$, $\alpha \neq 0$, are the same, that is, a point in projective space is what mathematicians call an *equivalence class.* This means that $\vec{\mathbf{P}}_j = (x_j, y_j, z_j, 0)$ and $\vec{\mathbf{P}}_j^* = (\alpha x_j, \alpha y_j, \alpha z_j, 0)$ are two *representations* of the same point in projective space. However, substituting $\vec{\mathbf{P}}_j$ and $\vec{\mathbf{P}}_j^*$ into Eq. (7.34) clearly results in two different curves. In this book we do not delve into projective geometry, thus we choose to sacrifice mathematical rigor for clarity. Strictly speaking, our infinite control point is just a representative of a projective point, whose last coordinate happens to be zero.

Example

Ex7.1 We represent the semicircle of radius r, centered at the origin, with an infinite control point (see Figure 7.15). Let $\mathbf{P}_0^w = (r, 0, 1)$, $\mathbf{P}_1^w = (0, r, 0)$, and $\mathbf{P}_2^w = (-r, 0, 1)$. Then

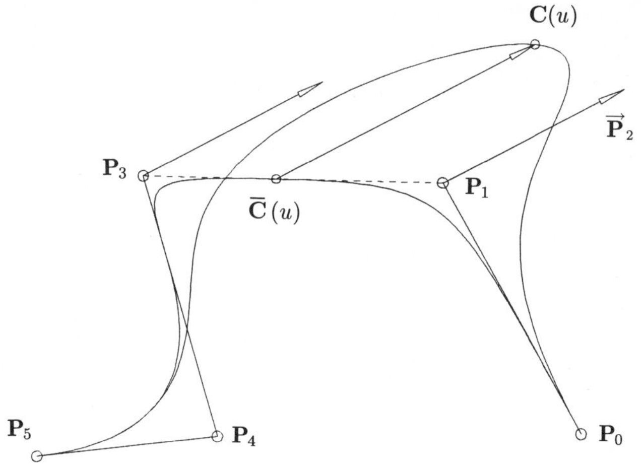

Figure 7.14. NURBS curve with an infinite control point $\vec{P_2}$; notice the stronger convex hull property.

$$\mathbf{C}(u) = \frac{(1-u)^2 w_0 \mathbf{P}_0 + u^2 w_2 \mathbf{P}_2}{(1-u)^2 w_0 + u^2 w_2} + \frac{2u(1-u)}{(1-u)^2 w_0 + u^2 w_2} \vec{\mathbf{P}}_1$$

$$= \frac{(1-u)^2 \mathbf{P}_0 + u^2 \mathbf{P}_2}{1-2u+2u^2} + \frac{2u(1-u)}{1-2u+2u^2} \vec{\mathbf{P}}_1$$

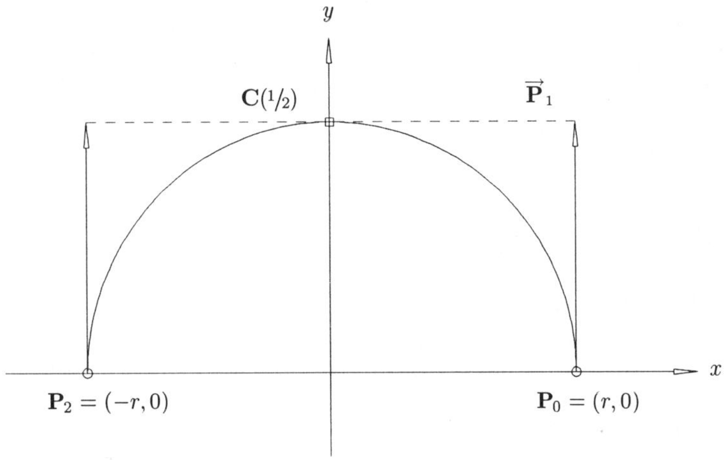

Figure 7.15. A semicircle defined by using an infinite control point.

and it follows that

$$x(u) = \frac{r(1-2u)}{1-2u+2u^2} \qquad y(u) = \frac{2ru(1-u)}{1-2u+2u^2}$$

The reader can verify that $\big(x(u)\big)^2 + \big(y(u)\big)^2 = r^2$ for all u. Notice that

$$\mathbf{C}\left(\frac{1}{2}\right) = (0, r)$$

is the point on the arc farthest from the chord $\mathbf{P}_0\mathbf{P}_2$, and the derivative at this point, $\mathbf{C}'(1/2)$, is parallel to $\mathbf{P}_0\mathbf{P}_2$, i.e., the shoulder point concept of Section 7.3 also holds when $\mathbf{P}_1^w$ is an infinite control point.

Note that there is a difference between infinite control points and zero weights. Figure 7.12 shows that $w_1 = 0$ yields a straight line from $\mathbf{P}_0$ to $\mathbf{P}_2$. Substituting $w_1 = 0$ into Eq. (7.21) and assuming the normal parameterization yields

$$\mathbf{C}(u) = R_{0,2}(u)\mathbf{P}_0 + R_{2,2}(u)\mathbf{P}_2 = \frac{(1-u)^2\mathbf{P}_0 + u^2\mathbf{P}_2}{(1-u)^2 + u^2}$$

that is, $R_{1,2}(u) \equiv 0$, and $\mathbf{C}(u)$ is a straight line from $\mathbf{P}_0$ to $\mathbf{P}_2$; see also Figures 4.2, 4.3c, 4.4, 4.5d, and 4.6. If we think of our NURBS curves in terms of homogeneous control points

$$\mathbf{C}^w(u) = \sum_{i=0}^{n} N_{i,p}(u)\mathbf{P}_i^w \tag{7.35}$$

then we represent an infinite control point by $\mathbf{P}_j^w = (x_j, y_j, z_j, 0)$, and we set w_j to zero by setting $\mathbf{P}_j^w = (0,0,0,0)$. Although one must be careful in dealing with such points individually, they generally cause no problems in B-spline algorithms derived from Eq. (7.35). For example, the point evaluation and knot insertion algorithms of previous chapters (Algorithms `A4.1` and `A5.1`) have no problem with zero weights or infinite control points (assuming, of course, not all weights are zero).

7.5 Construction of Circles

In this section we develop algorithms for constructing circular arcs of arbitrary sweep angle, including full circles. The construction of a general NURBS circular arc is more complicated than first expected, and there are many ways to do it. Much of the material in this section is taken from [Pieg89b], which is a detailed study of the NURBS circle.

We discuss only quadratic representations in this section. Higher degree representations are useful, for example, when an arc of greater than or equal to 180° is desired, without internal knots and without the use of negative weights or infinite control points. Such representations can be obtained using degree elevation (see Section 7.8).

From Section 7.3 we know how to construct an arc of less than 180°, and clearly we can construct arcs of arbitrary sweep angle by simply piecing together smaller arcs using multiple knots. When deciding how to do this, there are four trade-offs to consider: continuity, parameterization, convex hull, and number of control points required. The last three are related, in the sense that parameterization and characteristics of the convex hull can be improved by increasing the number of control points. We clarify these trade-offs with some examples. For simplicity, all examples are in the xy plane, centered at the origin, and have radius 1.

Examples

`Ex7.2` A full circle using a nine-point square control polygon: Example `Ex6.7` and Figure 6.12 (and Section 7.3) show the 90° arc in the first quadrant is obtained using $\{\mathbf{P}_i\} = \{(1,0),(1,1),(0,1)\}$ and $\{w_i\} = \{1, \sqrt{2}/2, 1\}$. By piecing four of these arcs together using double knots, we obtain the full circle of Figures 7.16a and 7.16b. The knots, weights, and control points are

$$U = \left\{0,0,0,\frac{1}{4},\frac{1}{4},\frac{1}{2},\frac{1}{2},\frac{3}{4},\frac{3}{4},1,1,1\right\}$$

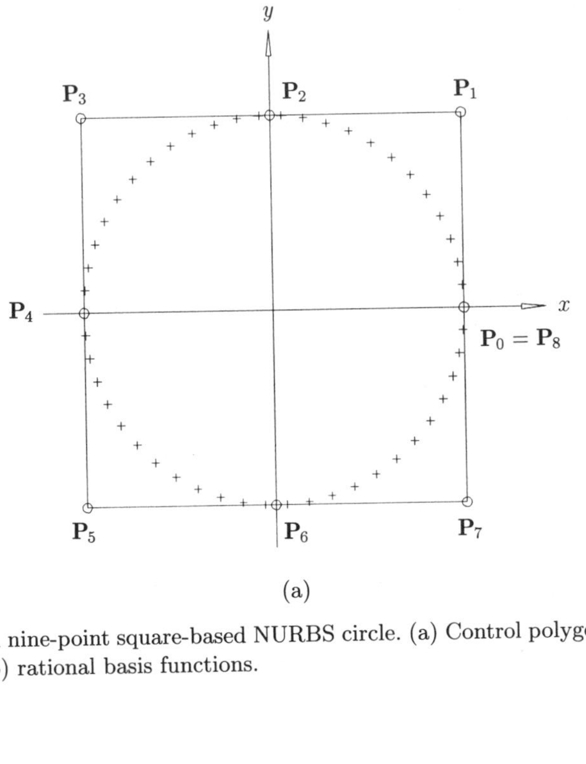

(a)

Figure 7.16. A nine-point square-based NURBS circle. (a) Control polygon and parameterization; (b) rational basis functions.

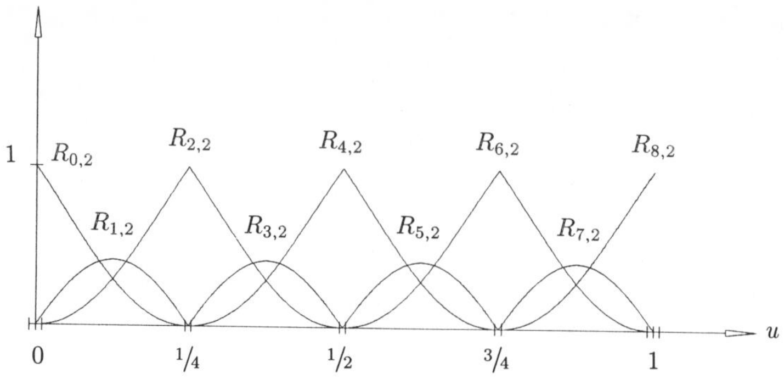

(b)

Figure 7.16. (*Continued.*)

$$\{w_i\} = \left\{1, \frac{\sqrt{2}}{2}, 1, \frac{\sqrt{2}}{2}, 1, \frac{\sqrt{2}}{2}, 1, \frac{\sqrt{2}}{2}, 1\right\}$$

$$\{\mathbf{P}_i\} =$$

$$\{(1,0),(1,1),(0,1),(-1,1),(-1,0),(-1,-1),(0,-1),(1,-1),(1,0)\}$$

To indicate parameterization, points are marked on the circle; they were computed at equally spaced parameter values. The circumscribing square forms a fairly tight convex hull. Now consider continuity at $u = 1/4$ ($u = 1/2$ and $u = 3/4$ are analogous). We can write either

$$\mathbf{C}^w(u) = \sum_{i=0}^{n} N_{i,2}(u)\mathbf{P}_i^w \quad \text{or} \quad \mathbf{C}(u) = \sum_{i=0}^{n} R_{i,2}(u)\mathbf{P}_i$$

Clearly, the basis functions $N_{2,2}(u)$ and $R_{2,2}(u)$ are only C^0 continuous at $u = 1/4$ (see Figure 7.16b). $\mathbf{C}^w(u)$ is also only C^0 continuous, that is, the four parabolic arcs in homogeneous space are linked together around the cone, and where each pair meet there is a cusp. Analytically, this can be seen by computing the first derivative of $\mathbf{C}^w(u)$ at $u = 1/4$ from the left and right. Applying Eq. (3.7) to just the w coordinate yields

$$w'\left(\frac{1}{4}\right)_{\text{left}} = \frac{2}{\frac{1}{4} - 0}(w_2 - w_1) = 8\left(1 - \frac{\sqrt{2}}{2}\right)$$

and

$$w'\left(\frac{1}{4}\right)_{\text{right}} = \frac{2}{\frac{1}{2} - \frac{1}{4}}(w_3 - w_2) = 8\left(\frac{\sqrt{2}}{2} - 1\right)$$

Clearly, the two derivatives are not equal. Surprisingly, $\mathbf{C}(u)$ is C^1 continuous. Using Eqs. (4.9) and (4.10) we obtain

$$\mathbf{C}'\left(\frac{1}{4}\right)_{\text{left}} = \frac{2}{\frac{1}{4}-0}\,\frac{\sqrt{2}/2}{1}\,(\mathbf{P}_2-\mathbf{P}_1) = \left(-4\sqrt{2},0\right)$$

and
$$\mathbf{C}'\left(\frac{1}{4}\right)_{\text{right}} = \frac{2}{\frac{1}{2}-\frac{1}{4}}\,\frac{\sqrt{2}/2}{1}\,(\mathbf{P}_3-\mathbf{P}_2) = \left(-4\sqrt{2},0\right)$$

With regard to the first three criteria, this is quite a good representation of the full circle.

Ex7.3 A full circle using a seven-point triangular control polygon: From elementary geometry it is easy to see that an arc of 120° requires a control triangle whose base angle, $\angle \mathbf{P}_1\mathbf{P}_0\mathbf{P}_2$, is equal to 60°. From Eq. (7.33), $w_1 = \cos 60° = 1/2$. By piecing together three such arcs we obtain the full circle of Figures 7.17a and 7.17b, with

$$U = \left\{0,0,0,\frac{1}{3},\frac{1}{3},\frac{2}{3},\frac{2}{3},1,1,1\right\}$$

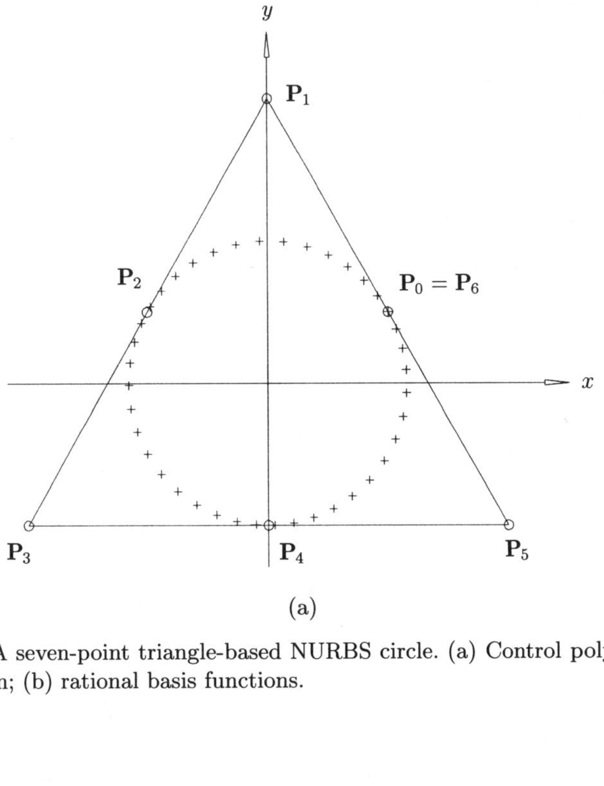

(a)

Figure 7.17. A seven-point triangle-based NURBS circle. (a) Control polygon and parameterization; (b) rational basis functions.

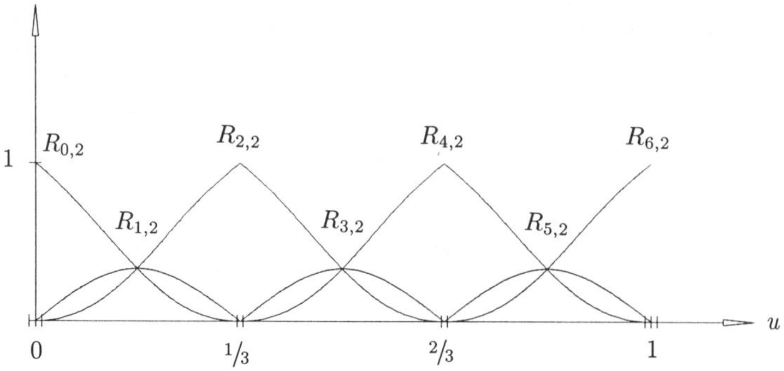

(b)

Figure 7.17. (*Continued.*)

$$\{w_i\} = \left\{1, \frac{1}{2}, 1, \frac{1}{2}, 1, \frac{1}{2}, 1\right\}$$

$$\{\mathbf{P}_i\} =$$

$$\left\{\left(a, \frac{1}{2}\right), (0,2), \left(-a, \frac{1}{2}\right), (-2a,-1), (0,-1), (2a,-1), \left(a, \frac{1}{2}\right)\right\}$$

where $a = \cos 30°$. Points on the circle are marked to show parameterization, which is not quite as good as in Figure 7.16a. The convex hull is also looser. The reader can verify that $\mathbf{C}(u)$ is C^1 continuous at $u = 1/3$ and $u = 2/3$, in spite of the fact that the basis functions are C^0 continuous there (see Figure 7.17b).

Ex7.4 An arc of 240°: Setting w_1 negative yields the complementary arc. Thus, we obtain the 240° arc of Figures 7.18a and 7.18b using

$$U = \{0,0,0,1,1,1\}$$

$$\{w_i\} = \left\{1, -\frac{1}{2}, 1\right\}$$

$$\{\mathbf{P}_i\} = \left\{\left(a, \frac{1}{2}\right), (0,2), \left(-a, \frac{1}{2}\right)\right\}$$

Negative weights are generally undesirable, because we lose the convex hull property, and dividing by zero can occur when computing points on the curve. However, it is important to note that for the circle and ellipse, $w(u) > 0$ for all $u \in [0,1]$. This follows from $w_0 = w_2 = 1$, $|\, w_1 \,| < 1$, and $w(u) = (1-u)^2 + 2u(1-u)w_1 + u^2$ (geometrically, the parabolic arc $\mathbf{C}^w(u)$ lies on the cone above the $W = 0$ plane). Thus, no problems arise when using Algorithm `A4.1` to evaluate points on this arc. Let us insert a knot at $u = 1/2$. Using Eq. (5.11)

$$\alpha_1 = \frac{\frac{1}{2} - 0}{1 - 0} = \frac{1}{2} \qquad \alpha_2 = \frac{\frac{1}{2} - 0}{1 - 0} = \frac{1}{2}$$

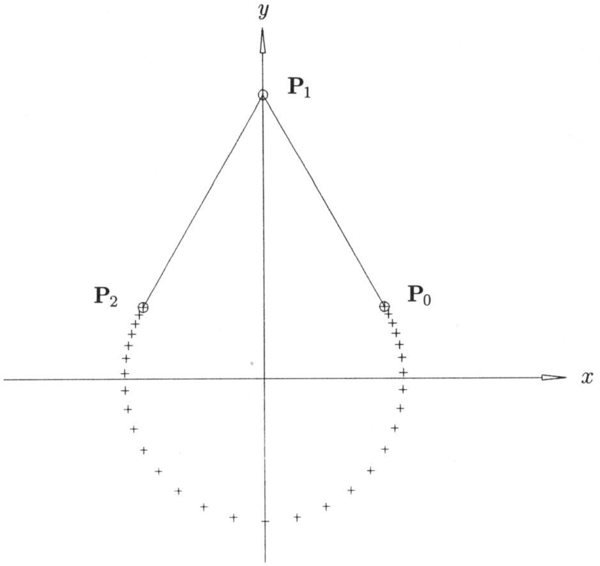

(a)

Figure 7.18. Arc of 240° using a negative weight. (a) Control polygon and parameterization; (b) rational basis functions.

The new control points, $\mathbf{Q}_i^w$, are

$$\mathbf{Q}_0^w = \mathbf{P}_0^w \qquad \mathbf{Q}_3^w = \mathbf{P}_2^w$$

$$\mathbf{Q}_1^w = \frac{1}{2}\mathbf{P}_1^w + \frac{1}{2}\mathbf{P}_0^w = \left(\frac{a}{2}, -\frac{1}{4}, \frac{1}{4}\right)$$

$$\mathbf{Q}_2^w = \frac{1}{2}\mathbf{P}_2^w + \frac{1}{2}\mathbf{P}_1^w = \left(-\frac{a}{2}, -\frac{1}{4}, \frac{1}{4}\right)$$

Thus (see Figures 7.19a and 7.19b)

$$U = \left\{0, 0, 0, \frac{1}{2}, 1, 1, 1\right\}$$

$$\{w_i\} = \left\{1, \frac{1}{4}, \frac{1}{4}, 1\right\}$$

$$\{\mathbf{Q}_i\} = \left\{\left(a, \frac{1}{2}\right), (2a, -1), (-2a, -1), \left(-a, \frac{1}{2}\right)\right\}$$

is a representation of the 240° arc without negative weights. The parameterization is not particularly good. $\mathbf{C}^w(u)$ and $\mathbf{C}(u)$ are C^2 continuous on $u \in [0, 1]$; inserting the knot did not change this.

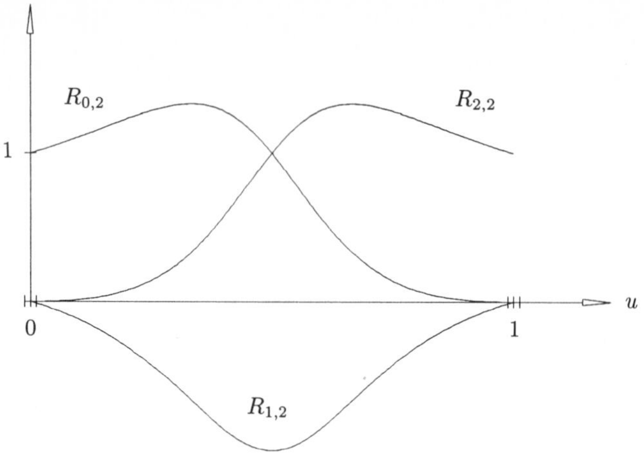

(b)

Figure 7.18. (*Continued.*)

`Ex7.5` A semicircle using four control points: Consider the semicircle of Example `Ex7.1` and Figure 7.15, with $r = 1$. Inserting the knot $u = 1/2$ one time, we obtain (as in Example `Ex7.4`)

$$\alpha_1 = \alpha_2 = \frac{1}{2}$$

$$\mathbf{Q}_0^w = \mathbf{P}_0^w \qquad \mathbf{Q}_3^w = \mathbf{P}_2^w$$

$$\mathbf{Q}_1^w = \frac{1}{2}\mathbf{P}_1^w + \frac{1}{2}\mathbf{P}_0^w = \left(-\frac{1}{2}, \frac{1}{2}, \frac{1}{2}\right)$$

$$\mathbf{Q}_2^w = \frac{1}{2}\mathbf{P}_2^w + \frac{1}{2}\mathbf{P}_1^w = \left(\frac{1}{2}, \frac{1}{2}, \frac{1}{2}\right)$$

Thus (see Figures 7.20a and 7.20b)

$$U = \left\{0, 0, 0, \frac{1}{2}, 1, 1, 1\right\}$$

$$\{w_i\} = \left\{1, \frac{1}{2}, \frac{1}{2}, 1\right\}$$

$$\{\mathbf{Q}_i\} = \{(1,0), (1,1), (-1,1), (-1,0)\}$$

`Ex7.6` A full circle using a seven-point square control polygon: Two semicircles such as in Example `Ex7.5` can be pieced together to form a seven-point square circle (see Figures 7.21a and 7.21b)

$$U = \left\{0, 0, 0, \frac{1}{4}, \frac{1}{2}, \frac{1}{2}, \frac{3}{4}, 1, 1, 1\right\}$$

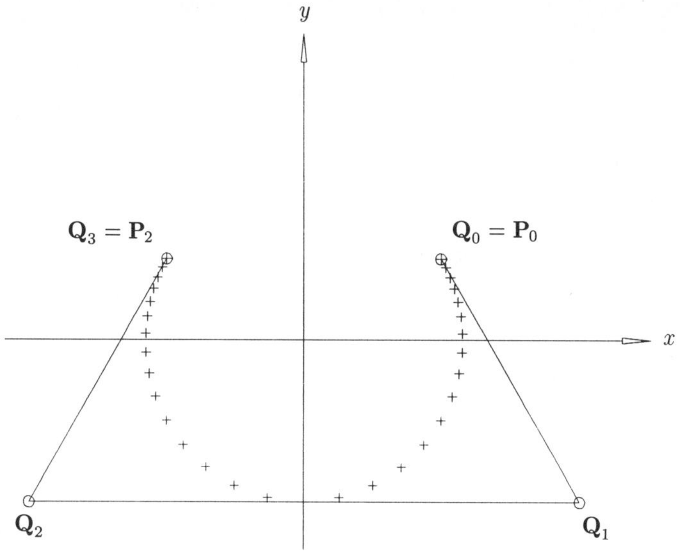

(a)

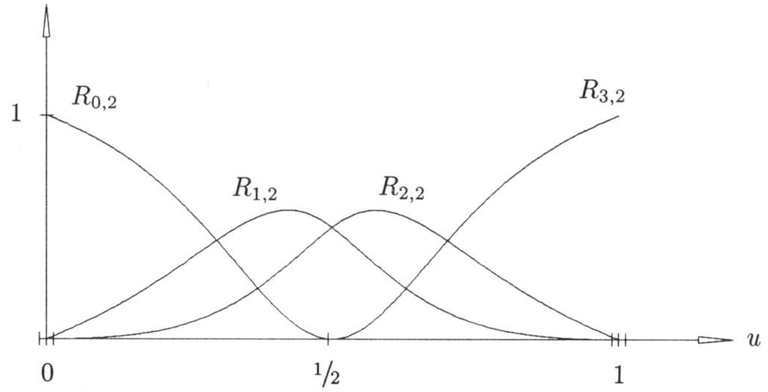

(b)

Figure 7.19. Arc of Figure 7.18 after inserting $u = 1/2$ one time. (a) Control polygon and parameterization; (b) rational basis functions.

$$\{w_i\} = \left\{1, \frac{1}{2}, \frac{1}{2}, 1, \frac{1}{2}, \frac{1}{2}, 1\right\}$$

$\mathbf{C}(u)$ is C^1 continuous at $u = 1/2$ and C^2 continuous everywhere else. The parameterization is not as good as that of Example `Ex7.2` and Figure 7.16a.

Algorithm `A7.1` constructs a NURBS circular arc in three-dimensional space of arbitrary sweep angle θ ($0° < \theta \leq 360°$). It pieces together equal arcs of sweep

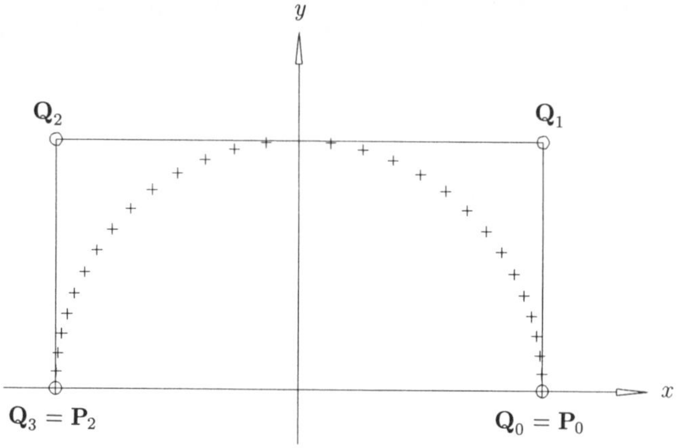

(a)

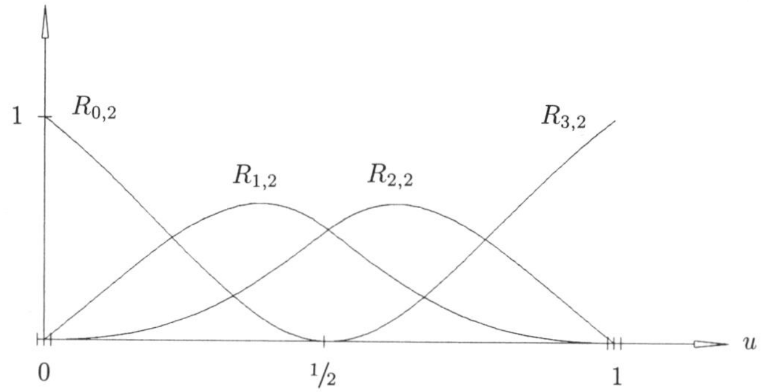

(b)

Figure 7.20. Semicircle of Figure 7.15 after inserting $u = 1/2$ one time. (a) Control polygon and parameterization; (b) rational basis functions.

angle $d\theta$, $\min(\theta, 45°) < d\theta \leq 90°$, using double knots, and weights computed by Eq. (7.33). The resulting arc of angle θ is C^1 continuous, has a tight convex hull, and has a good parameterization.

Designers are offered many different interfaces to specify circular arcs, but no matter what the interface is, the following data can be easily generated:

- $\mathbf{O}$: center of circle (origin of local coordinate system);
- $\mathbf{X}$: unit length vector lying in the plane of definition of the circle;
- $\mathbf{Y}$: unit length vector in the plane of definition of the circle, and orthogonal to $\mathbf{X}$;
- r : radius.
- θ_s, θ_e : start and end angles, measured with respect to $\mathbf{X}$.

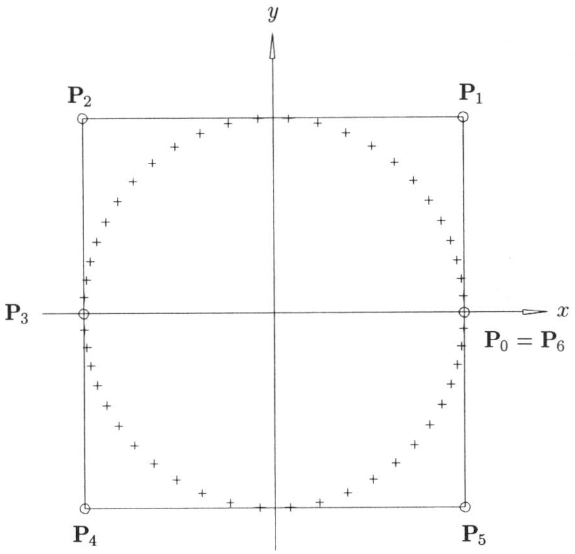

(a)

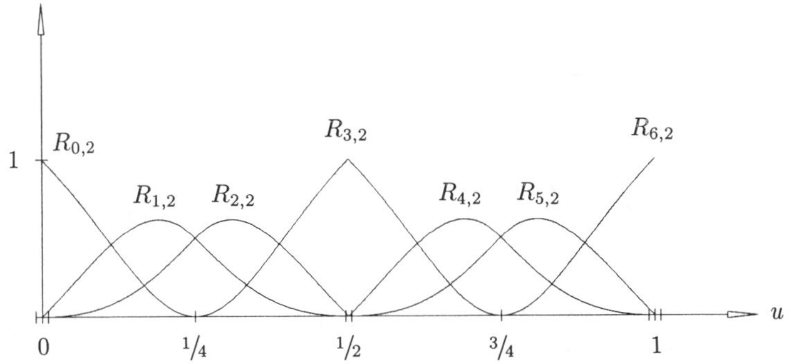

(b)

Figure 7.21. A seven-point square-based NURBS circle. (a) Control polygon and parameterization; (b) rational basis functions.

The arc is then represented by

$$\mathbf{C}(u) = \mathbf{O} + r\cos u\,\mathbf{X} + r\sin u\,\mathbf{Y} \qquad \theta_s \le u \le \theta_e \tag{7.36}$$

The resulting arc is oriented counter-clockwise in the local coordinate system defined by **O**, **X**, and **Y**. We assume a utility routine `Intersect3DLines(P0,T0, P2,T2,alf0,alf2,P1)`, which computes the intersection ($\mathbf{P}_1$) of two lines in three-dimensional space given by the point/tangent pairs $[\mathbf{P}_0, \mathbf{T}_0]$ and $[\mathbf{P}_2, \mathbf{T}_2]$. It returns the integer value 1 if the lines are parallel, 0 otherwise. α_0 and α_2 are the parametric locations of $\mathbf{P}_1$ along the lines $[\mathbf{P}_0, \mathbf{T}_0]$ and $[\mathbf{P}_2, \mathbf{T}_2]$, respectively. α_0, α_2, and the integer return value are not used in Algorithm A7.1, but they are used in Section 7.6. Pw=w*P denotes multiplication of a Euclidean point by a weight (Pw=P if $w = 1$). The algorithm computes the knots and weighted control points for the NURBS circular arc.

```
ALGORITHM A7.1
  MakeNurbsCircle(O,X,Y,r,ths,the,n,U,Pw)
    { /*  Create arbitrary NURBS circular arc  */
      /*  Input:  O,X,Y,r,ths,the  */
      /*  Output: n,U,Pw  */
    if (the < ths)   the = 360.0 + the;
    theta = the-ths;
    if (theta <= 90.0)   narcs = 1;   /* get number of arcs */
      else
        if (theta <= 180.0)   narcs = 2;
          else
            if (theta <= 270.0)   narcs = 3;
              else
                narcs = 4;
    dtheta = theta/narcs;
    n = 2*narcs;      /* n+1 control points */
    w1 = cos(dtheta/2.0);    /* dtheta/2 is base angle */
    P0 = O + r*cos(ths)*X + r*sin(ths)*Y;
    T0 = -sin(ths)*X + cos(ths)*Y; /* Initialize start values */
    Pw[0] = P0;
    index = 0;   angle = ths;
    for (i=1; i<=narcs; i++)    /* create narcs segments */
      {
      angle = angle + dtheta;
      P2 = O + r*cos(angle)*X + r*sin(angle)*Y;
      Pw[index+2] = P2;
      T2 = -sin(angle)*X + cos(angle)*Y;
      Intersect3DLines(P0,T0,P2,T2,dummy,dummy,P1);
      Pw[index+1] = w1*P1;
      index = index + 2;
      if (i < narcs)   {  P0 = P2;    T0 = T2;  }
      }
    j = 2*narcs+1;    /* load the knot vector */
    for (i=0; i<3; i++)
      {  U[i] = 0.0;   U[i+j] = 1.0;  }
    switch (narcs)
      {
      case 1:  break;
      case 2:  U[3] = U[4] = 0.5;
               break;
```

```
        case 3:  U[3] = U[4] = 1.0/3.0;
                 U[5] = U[6] = 2.0/3.0;
                 break;
        case 4:  U[3] = U[4] = 0.25;
                 U[5] = U[6] = 0.5;
                 U[7] = U[8] = 0.75;
                 break;
      }
   }
```

Figures 7.22a–7.22d show circular arc representations using one, two, three, and four segments, respectively.

We close this section with some miscellaneous remarks on NURBS circles. A different algorithm is given by Piegl and Tiller [Pieg89b] for constructing a circular arc of arbitrary sweep angle. It is based on using infinite control points and negative weights, and then using knot insertion to remove them (as in Examples Ex7.4–Ex7.6). The resulting arcs may require fewer control points and double knots than with Algorithm A7.1, but the parameterization is generally not as good. It is also proven that it is impossible to represent a full circle using a quadratic NURBS with positive weights without a double internal knot [Pieg89b].

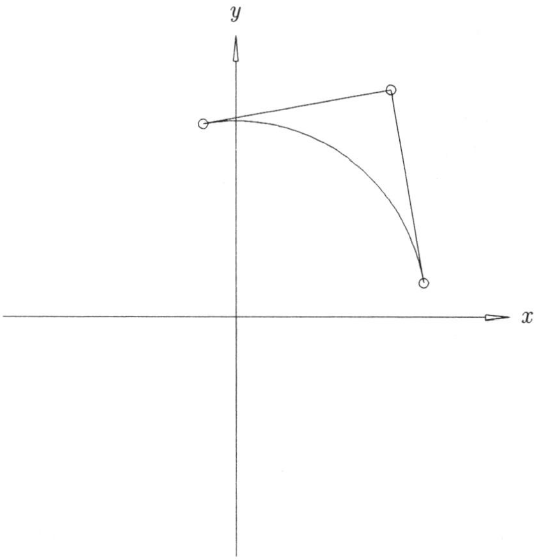

(a)

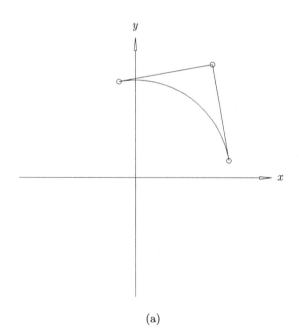

Figure 7.22. Circular arcs of different sweep angles. (a) $\theta_s = 10°$, $\theta_e = 100°$; (b) $\theta_s = 30°$, $\theta_e = 170°$; (c) $\theta_s = 20°$, $\theta_e = 250°$; (d) $\theta_s = 40°$, $\theta_e = 330°$.

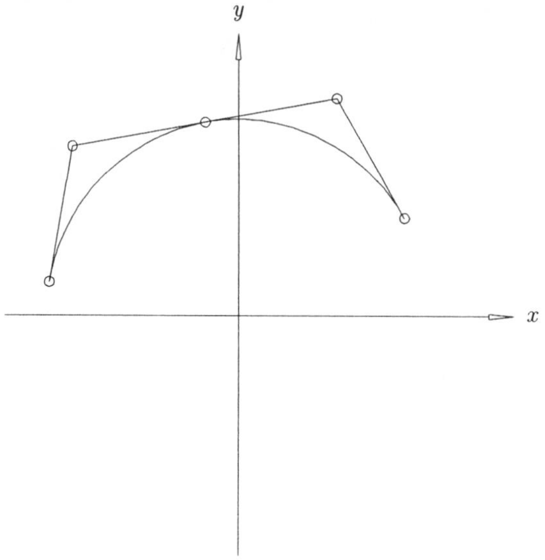

(b)

Figure 7.22. (*Continued.*)

7.6 Construction of Conics

In this section we develop algorithms for constructing conics, discussing only quadratic representations. Parabolic and hyperbolic arcs can always be represented with one rational Bézier curve (no internal knots) and positive weights. As was the case for circles, we may have to piece segments together with internal knots to obtain arbitrary elliptical arcs using only positive weights. In doing this, the issues again are continuity, parameterization, convex hull, and number of control points.

We consider first an arbitrary open conic arc in three-dimensional space. There are many ways to specify a conic arc. In CADCAM applications, two of the most common are:

- the defining geometric parameters such as radii, axes, focal distance, etc., together with specification of start and end points; this leads effectively to representation by Eqs. (7.15)–(7.17);
- specification of start and end points, $\mathbf{P}_0$ and $\mathbf{P}_2$, together with the tangent directions at those two points, $\mathbf{T}_0$ and $\mathbf{T}_2$, plus one additional point on the arc $\mathbf{P}$ (see Figure 7.23).

If the data is available in the form given in item 1, it is easy to derive $\mathbf{P}_0$, $\mathbf{T}_0$, $\mathbf{P}_2$, $\mathbf{T}_2$, and $\mathbf{P}$; thus we assume throughout this section that the data is given as specified in item 2.

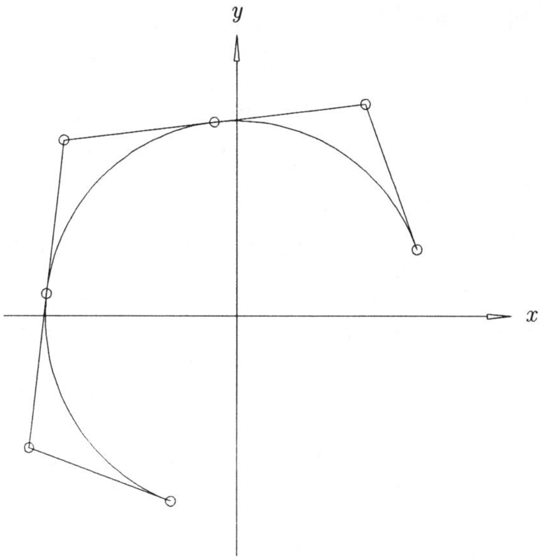

(c)

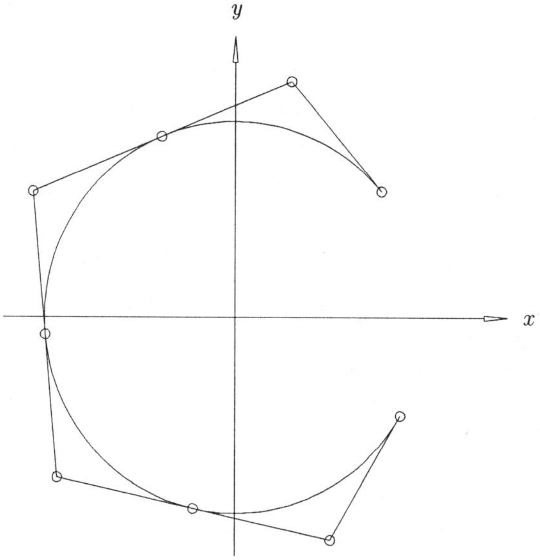

(d)

Figure 7.22. (*Continued.*)

$\mathbf{P}_1$ (Figure 7.23) is easily obtained by intersecting lines $[\mathbf{P}_0, \mathbf{T}_0]$ and $[\mathbf{P}_2, \mathbf{T}_2]$. Setting $w_0 = w_2 = 1$, the only missing item is w_1. Allowing w_1 to be negative, or $\mathbf{P}_1$ to be infinite (temporarily), we can obtain any conic arc with one rational Bézier curve. If necessary, we then split this Bézier arc at suitable locations to obtain positive weights and multiple segments with good parameterization and convex hull characteristics.

The additional point $\mathbf{P}$ determines the conic and hence w_1. Substituting $\mathbf{P} = \mathbf{C}(u)$ into the left side of Eq. (7.21) yields three equations in the two unknowns, u and w_1 (which can be solved). But geometric arguments yield a more efficient algorithm (see Piegl [Pieg87b]). First assume that $\mathbf{P}_1$ is finite. The conic we seek can be considered as a perspective view of the parabola determined by $\mathbf{P}_0$, $\mathbf{P}_1$, and $\mathbf{P}_2$, with $\mathbf{P}_1$ being the center of the perspective. Any pair of conic segments lying in this triangle can be mapped onto one another, including the line $[\mathbf{P}_0, \mathbf{P}_2]$ (degenerate conic) onto the conic we seek. Hence, $\mathbf{P}$ and $\mathbf{Q}$ (Figure 7.23) are corresponding points under this transformation. Now the line $\mathbf{L}(u) = [\mathbf{P}_0, \mathbf{P}_2]$ is obtained by setting $w_1 = 0$ (not using an infinite control point), yielding

$$\mathbf{L}(u) = \frac{(1-u)^2\mathbf{P}_0 + u^2\mathbf{P}_2}{(1-u)^2 + u^2} \tag{7.37}$$

$\mathbf{L}(u)$ is a convex combination of $\mathbf{P}_0$ and $\mathbf{P}_2$, thus the ratio of distances $|\,\mathbf{P}_0\mathbf{Q}\,|$ to $|\,\mathbf{Q}\mathbf{P}_2\,|$ is $u^2 : (1-u)^2$, from which it follows that

$$u = \frac{a}{1+a} \qquad a = \sqrt{\frac{|\,\mathbf{P}_0\mathbf{Q}\,|}{|\,\mathbf{Q}\mathbf{P}_2\,|}} \tag{7.38}$$

(Compare Figure 7.23 and this argument with Figure 4.6 and Eq. [4.4]). Substituting u and $\mathbf{P}$ into Eq. (7.21), we easily obtain w_1, i.e.

$$w_1 = \frac{(1-u)^2(\mathbf{P}-\mathbf{P}_0)\cdot(\mathbf{P}_1-\mathbf{P}) + u^2(\mathbf{P}-\mathbf{P}_2)\cdot(\mathbf{P}_1-\mathbf{P})}{2u(1-u)\,|\,\mathbf{P}_1-\mathbf{P}\,|^2} \tag{7.39}$$

Piegl [Pieg87b] derives w_1 using techniques from projective geometry.

Now suppose $\mathbf{P}_1$ ($\vec{\mathbf{P}}_1$) is infinite ($\mathbf{T}_0$ and $\mathbf{T}_2$ are parallel). In this case, $w_1 = 0$ and $\vec{\mathbf{P}}_1$ is parallel to $\mathbf{T}_0$. Only the magnitude of $\vec{\mathbf{P}}_1$ is unknown. Consider Figure 7.24. The perspective center is now at infinity, and u is obtained exactly as before: $[\mathbf{P}, \mathbf{T}_0]$ (which is $[\mathbf{P}, \vec{\mathbf{P}}_1]$) is intersected with $[\mathbf{P}_0, \mathbf{P}_2]$ to yield $\mathbf{Q}$, and u is then computed from Eq. (7.38). For a rational quadratic Bézier curve with $w_0 = w_2 = 1$, Eq. (7.34) reduces to

$$\mathbf{C}(u) = \frac{(1-u)^2\mathbf{P}_0 + u^2\mathbf{P}_2}{(1-u)^2 + u^2} + \frac{2u(1-u)}{(1-u)^2 + u^2}\vec{\mathbf{P}}_1 = \bar{\mathbf{C}}(u) + f(u)\vec{\mathbf{P}}_1 \tag{7.40}$$

Let u_0 be the parameter yielding $\mathbf{Q}$. Then

$$\mathbf{P} = \mathbf{Q} + f(u_0)\vec{\mathbf{P}}_1$$

and

$$\vec{\mathbf{P}}_1 = \frac{1}{f(u_0)}(\mathbf{P}-\mathbf{Q}) \qquad f(u_0) = \frac{2u_0(1-u_0)}{(1-u_0)^2 + u_0^2} \tag{7.41}$$

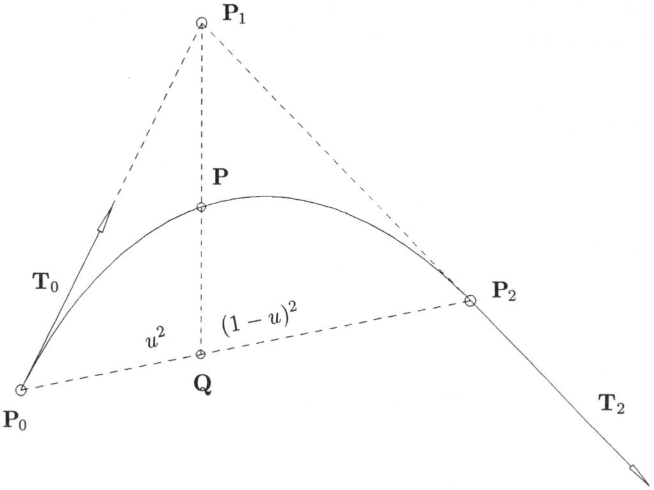

Figure 7.23. A general conic segment defined by endpoints, end tangents, and one additional point lying on the curve.

Based on Eqs. (7.38), (7.39), and (7.41), we now give an algorithm to construct one rational Bézier conic arc. Since w_1 can be negative or $\mathbf{P}_1$ infinite, this algorithm handles any conic arc except a full ellipse. We make use of the

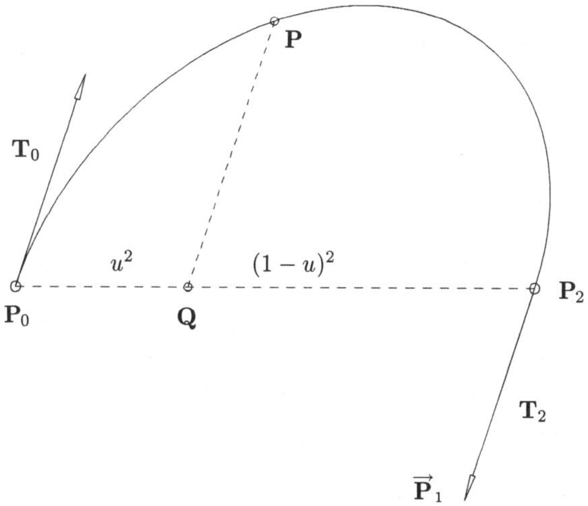

Figure 7.24. A 180° elliptical arc defined by endpoints, end tangents, and one additional point.

α_0,α_2 values computed in Intersect3DLines. We further assume a function Dot(V1,V2) which returns the dot product of the vectors $\mathbf{V}_1$ and $\mathbf{V}_2$.

```
ALGORITHM A7.2
  MakeOneArc(P0,T0,P2,T2,P,P1,w1)
    { /*  Create one Bézier conic arc  */
      /*  Input:  P0,T0,P2,T2,P  */
      /*  Output: P1,w1  */
    V02 = P2-P0;
    i = Intersect3DLines(P0,T0,P2,T2,dummy,dummy,P1);
    if (i == 0)
      { /* finite control point */
      V1P = P-P1;
      Intersect3DLines(P1,V1P,P0,V02,alf0,alf2,dummy);
      a = sqrt(alf2/(1.0-alf2));
      u = a/(1.0+a);
      num = (1.0-u)*(1.0-u)*Dot(P-P0,P1-P) + u*u*Dot(P-P2,P1-P);
      den = 2.0*u*(1.0-u)*Dot(P1-P,P1-P);
      w1 = num/den;
      return;
      }
      else
      { /* infinite control point, 180 degree arc */
      w1 = 0.0;
      Intersect3DLines(P,T0,P0,V02,alf0,alf2,dummy);
      a = sqrt(alf2/(1.0-alf2));
      u = a/(1.0+a);
      b = 2.0*u*(1.0-u);
      b = -alf0*(1.0-b)/b;
      P1 = b*T0;
      return;
      }
    }
```

Algorithm A7.2 is adequate for parabolic and hyperbolic arcs, and for elliptical arcs for which $w_1 > 0$ and whose sweep angle is not too large. Splitting an ellipse into segments is not as easy as was the case for circles. We do not know the major and minor axes and radii, and an equation of the form of Eq. (7.36) is not available with our input. A convenient point at which to split is the shoulder point, $\mathbf{S}$. To split the arc $\mathbf{P}_0\mathbf{P}_1\mathbf{P}_2$ we make use of the rational deCasteljau algorithm, Eq. (1.19). There are two steps in splitting the ellipse (see Figures 7.25a–7.25c):

1. Split at $u = 1/2$. Using the deCasteljau Algorithm to obtain

$$\mathbf{Q}_1^w = \frac{1}{2}\mathbf{P}_0^w + \frac{1}{2}\mathbf{P}_1^w \qquad \mathbf{R}_1^w = \frac{1}{2}\mathbf{P}_1^w + \frac{1}{2}\mathbf{P}_2^w$$

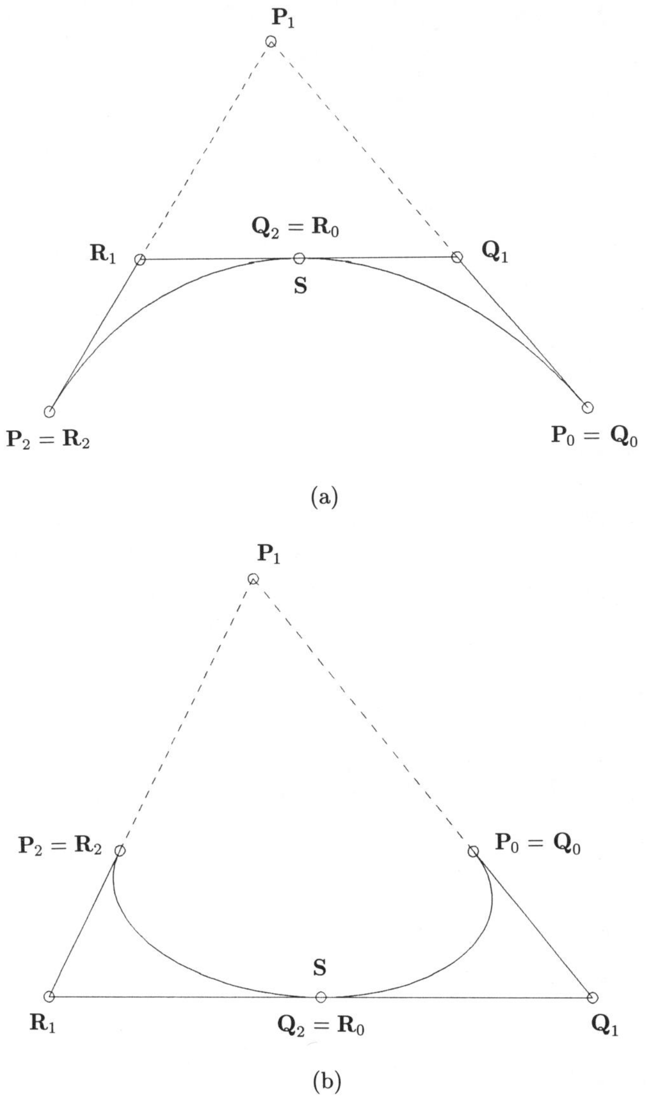

Figure 7.25. Splitting a conic curve. (a) Arc sweeping less than 180°; (b) arc sweeping more than 180°; (c) arc sweeping 180°.

and recalling that $w_0 = w_2 = 1$, it follows that

$$\mathbf{Q}_1 = \frac{\mathbf{P}_0 + w_1 \mathbf{P}_1}{1 + w_1} \qquad \mathbf{R}_1 = \frac{w_1 \mathbf{P}_1 + \mathbf{P}_2}{1 + w_1} \tag{7.42}$$

and

$$w_q = w_r = \frac{1}{2}(1 + w_1) \tag{7.43}$$

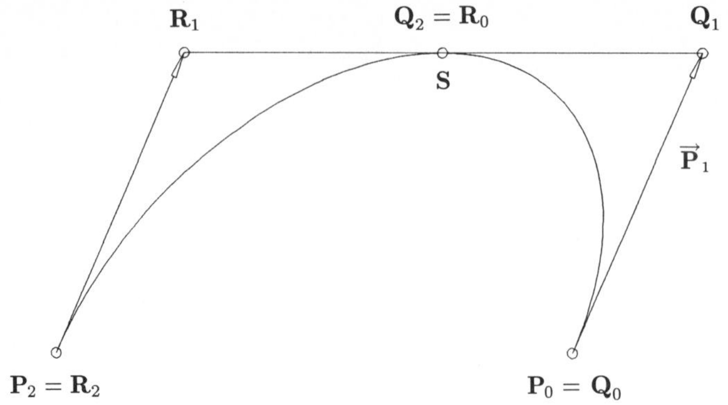

(c)

Figure 7.25. (*Continued.*)

where w_q and w_r are the weights at $\mathbf{Q}_1$ and $\mathbf{R}_1$, respectively. A second application of the deCasteljau Algorithm yields

$$\mathbf{R}_0 = \mathbf{Q}_2 = \mathbf{S} = \frac{1}{2}(\mathbf{Q}_1 + \mathbf{R}_1) \tag{7.44}$$

and

$$w_s = \frac{1}{2}(1 + w_1) \tag{7.45}$$

2. Reparameterize so that the end weights are 1 for both of the two new segments. After splitting, the weights for the first segment are

$$w_0 = 1 \quad w_q = \frac{1}{2}(1 + w_1) \quad w_s = \frac{1}{2}(1 + w_1)$$

We want the weights to be

$$w_0 = 1 \quad w_{q_1} \quad w_{q_2} = 1$$

where w_{q_1} is to be determined. Using the conic shape factor (Eq. [6.59])

$$\frac{w_0 w_s}{w_q^2} = \frac{w_0 w_{q2}}{w_{q1}^2}$$

which implies that

$$w_{q1} = \sqrt{\frac{1 + w_1}{2}} \tag{7.46}$$

Due to symmetry, we also have

$$w_{r_1} = \sqrt{\frac{1 + w_1}{2}} \tag{7.47}$$

Figures 7.25a and 7.25b illustrate ellipse splitting with positive and negative weights. The preceding process also works for infinite control points (see Figure 7.25c); however, the resulting formulas

$$\mathbf{Q}_1 = \mathbf{P}_0 + \vec{\mathbf{P}}_1 \quad \mathbf{R}_1 = \mathbf{P}_2 + \vec{\mathbf{P}}_1 \tag{7.48}$$

$$\mathbf{R}_0 = \mathbf{Q}_2 = \mathbf{S} = \frac{1}{2}(\mathbf{Q}_1 + \mathbf{R}_1) \tag{7.49}$$

$$w_{q_1} = w_{r_1} = \frac{\sqrt{2}}{2} \tag{7.50}$$

are even simpler. Equation (7.50) should not be surprising, as the semiellipse of Figure 7.25c is obtained by applying an affine transformation (specifically, a nonuniform scaling) to a semicircle. Such transformations do not change the weights. We leave it as an exercise for the reader to write a routine `SplitArc(P0,P1,w1,P2,Q1,S,R1,wqr)` which implements Eqs. (7.42)–(7.50).

Making use of Algorithm `A7.2` and `SplitArc()`, we now present an algorithm which constructs an arbitrary open conic arc in three-dimensional space. The resulting NURBS curve consists of either one, two, or four segments connected with C^1 continuity. The output is the knots (`U`), the number of control points less 1 (`n`), and the control points in homogeneous form (`Pw`). We assume a utility, `Angle(P,Q,R)`, which returns the angle $\angle \mathbf{PQR}$.

```
ALGORITHM A7.3
  MakeOpenConic(P0,T0,P2,T2,P,n,U,Pw)
    { /*  Construct open conic arc in 3D  */
      /*  Input:  P0,T0,P2,T2,P  */
      /*  Output: n,U,Pw  */
    MakeOneArc(P0,T0,P2,T2,P,P1,w1);
    if (w1 <= -1.0)       /* parabola or hyperbola */
      return(error);      /* outside convex hull */
    if (w1 >= 1.0)    /* classify type & number of segments */
      nsegs = 1;      /* hyperbola or parabola, one segment */
      else
      {   /* ellipse, determine number of segments */
      if (w1 > 0.0 && Angle(P0,P1,P2) > 60.0)   nsegs = 1;
      else
      if (w1 < 0.0 && angle(P0,P1,P2) > 90.0)   nsegs = 4;
        else        nsegs = 2;
      }
    n = 2*nsegs;
    j = 2*nsegs+1;
    for (i=0; i<3; i++)    /* load end knots */
      { U[i] = 0.0;    U[i+j] = 1.0;  }
    Pw[0] = P0;    Pw[n] = P2;    /* load end ctrl pts */
    if (nsegs == 1)
```

```
    {
    Pw[1] = w1*P1;
    return;
    }
  SplitArc(P0,P1,w1,P2,Q1,S,R1,wqr);
  if (nsegs == 2)
    {
    Pw[2] = S;
    Pw[1] = wqr*Q1;    Pw[3] = wqr*R1;
    U[3] = U[4] = 0.5;
    return;
    }
    /* nsegs == 4 */
  Pw[4] = S;
  w1 = wqr;
  SplitArc(P0,Q1,w1,S,HQ1,HS,HR1,wqr);
  Pw[2] = HS;
  Pw[1] = wqr*HQ1;    Pw[3] = wqr*HR1;
  SplitArc(S,R1,w1,P2,HQ1,HS,HR1,wqr);
  Pw[6] = HS;
  Pw[5] = wqr*HQ1;    Pw[7] = wqr*HR1;
  for (i=0; i<2; i++)    /* load the remaining knots */
    {
    U[i+3] = 0.25;   U[i+5] = 0.5;   U[i+7] = 0.75;
    }
  return;
  }
```

Figures 7.26a and 7.26b show examples using two and four segments, respectively.

Algorithm A7.3 produces ellipses which have good parameterization. For applications where parameterization is not considered important, a simpler algorithm which produces C^2 continuous curves with equally good convex hulls (see [Pieg90]) is:

1. call MakeOneArc (Algorithm A7.2);
2. insert knots at appropriate locations to cut the corners and to eliminate negative weights or an infinite control point (e.g., at $u = 1/2$, or $u = 1/3$ and $u = 2/3$).

For comparison, Figure 7.26c shows an elliptic arc which was constructed using

- Algorithm A7.3 (points marked by □);
- MakeOneArc, with subsequent insertion of $u = 1/2$ one time (points marked by $+$).

There remains the problem of full ellipses. If the major and minor axes and radii are known, a rectangular control polygon is appropriate. The weights and

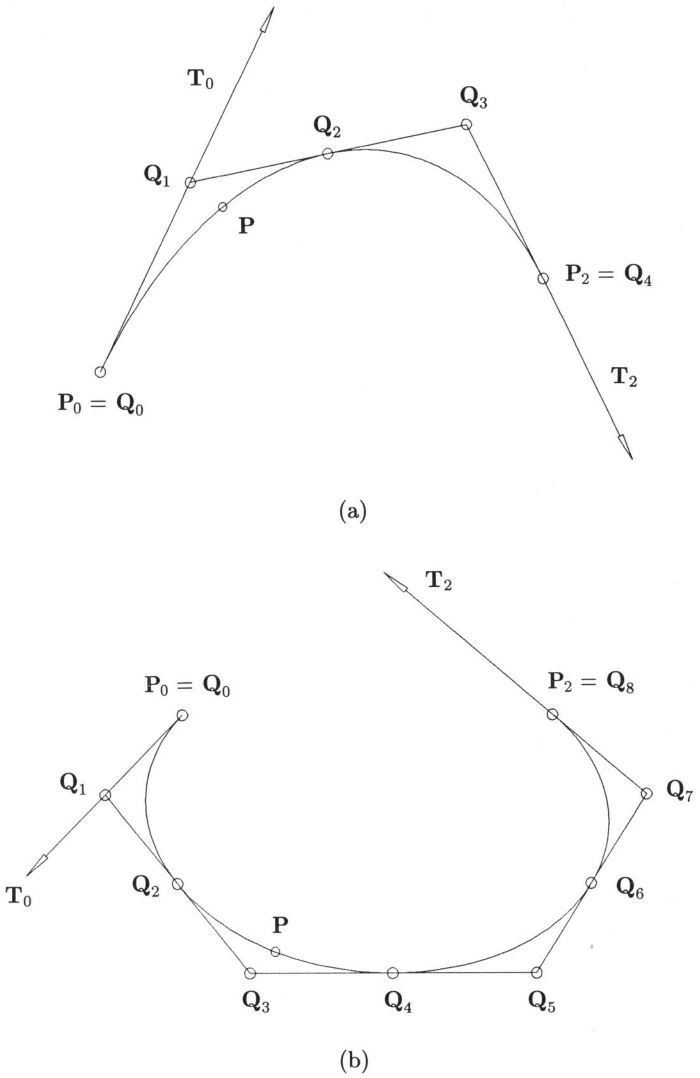

Figure 7.26. NURBS representation of conic segments. (a) Arc sweeping less than 180°; (b) arc sweeping more than 180°; (c) comparison between representations obtained by curve splitting (□) and knot insertion (+).

knots are the same as those of the circle in Example `Ex7.2` (Figure 7.16a), or a configuration analogous to Example `Ex7.6` (Figure 7.21a) can be used.

If input data is $\mathbf{P}_0, \mathbf{T}_0, \mathbf{P}_2, \mathbf{T}_2, \mathbf{P}$, together with the knowledge that the conic is a full ellipse (starting and ending at $\mathbf{P}_0$), then an appropriate construction is:

1. call `MakeOneArc` to get the rational Bézier representation of one segment of the ellipse (with positive weight w_1);

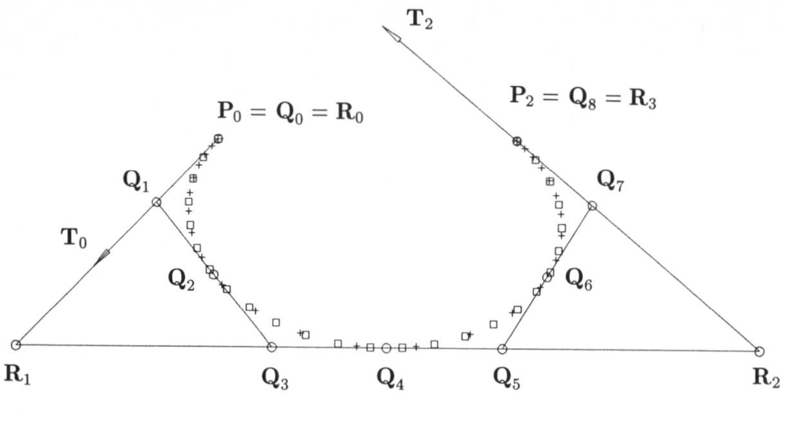

Figure 7.26. (*Continued.*)

2. compute the center of the ellipse $\mathbf{C}$;
3. compute the major and minor axes, (unit) vectors $(\mathbf{U}, \mathbf{V})$, along with the major and minor radii (r_1, r_2);
4. compute the control points

$$\begin{aligned}
\mathbf{Q}_0 &= \mathbf{C} + r_1\mathbf{U} \quad (= \mathbf{Q}_8) \\
\mathbf{Q}_1 &= \mathbf{Q}_0 + r_2\mathbf{V} \\
\mathbf{Q}_2 &= \mathbf{C} + r_2\mathbf{V} \\
\mathbf{Q}_3 &= \mathbf{Q}_2 - r_1\mathbf{U} \\
\mathbf{Q}_4 &= \mathbf{C} - r_1\mathbf{U} \\
\mathbf{Q}_5 &= \mathbf{Q}_4 - r_2\mathbf{V} \\
\mathbf{Q}_6 &= \mathbf{C} - r_2\mathbf{V} \\
\mathbf{Q}_7 &= \mathbf{Q}_6 + r_1\mathbf{U}
\end{aligned}$$

The details of Steps 2 and 3 are given in the next section, and the results are illustrated in Figure 7.28.

7.7 Conic Type Classification and Form Conversion

In previous sections we presented five forms for representing conics:

- implicit equation (Eqs. [7.3] and [7.5]–[7.7]);
- maximum inscribed area forms (Eqs. [7.15]–[7.17]);

- quadratic rational power basis (Eqs. [7.8]–[7.14]);
- quadratic rational Bézier (Eq. [7.21]);
- quadratic NURBS form.

In this section we discuss conic-type classification and form conversion, that is, given a curve in one of these forms, determine what type of conic it is – ellipse, parabola, or hyperbola – and convert it to another form. When we refer to the implicit form we assume that the conic is in the xy plane; otherwise the conic can be in three-dimensional space.

Consider the first two forms. If a conic is in standard position and can be described by one of Eqs. (7.5)–(7.7), its type is obvious. If it is not in standard position (Eq. [7.3]), then its type is determined by the values of α and D (determinant) as described in Section 7.2, and it can easily be transformed into standard position. For the maximum inscribed area forms, the conic type is inherent in the definition. Note that the maximum area form is quite similar to the standard position implicit form, in that their defining equations are given in terms of the conics' so-called *geometric characteristics*, i.e., axes, vertices, center, radii, etc. Hence, the conversion between these two forms is trivial.

Conversion between the quadratic rational power basis (Eq. [7.14]) and Bézier forms is given by the methods of Chapter 6, in particular Eqs. (6.89) and (6.93). Their rational counterparts are

$$[\,\mathbf{a}_i^w\,] = R_2 M_2\,[\,\mathbf{P}_i^w\,] \tag{7.51}$$

and

$$[\,\mathbf{P}_i^w\,] = M_2^{-1} R_2^{-1}\,[\,\mathbf{a}_i^w\,] \tag{7.52}$$

where M_2 and R_2 are the quadratic (3×3) Bézier and reparameterization matrices, respectively. The type of a Bézier conic is easily gleaned from the conic shape factor, Eq. (7.25). The type of a power basis conic is computed from Eqs. (7.52) and (7.25). For simplicity, assume our power basis segment is defined on $0 \le u \le 1$, with R_2 the identity matrix. Denote by w_i^a the power basis weights (Eq. [7.14]), and by w_i^P the Bézier weights. Then from Eqs. (6.94) and (7.52) we find that

$$[\,w_i^P\,] = M_2^{-1}\,[\,w_i^a\,] = \begin{bmatrix} 1 & 0 & 0 \\ 1 & \dfrac{1}{2} & 0 \\ 1 & 1 & 1 \end{bmatrix} [\,w_i^a\,]$$

from which it follows that

$$\begin{aligned} w_0^P &= w_0^a \\ w_1^P &= w_0^a + \frac{1}{2} w_1^a \\ w_2^P &= w_0^a + w_1^a + w_2^a \end{aligned} \tag{7.53}$$

When substituted into Eq. (7.25), these w_i^P yield the conic type.

A quadratic NURBS curve with internal knots may or may not represent a unique conic (it is a conic, line, or point on each span). The classification of a quadratic NURBS curve is a three-step process:

1. using Eq. (6.62), compute the conic shape factor of each nondegenerate segment;
2. if all shape factors indicate a common type (all $c_i < 1, = 1$, or > 1), decompose the curve into Bézier segments;
3. compute the geometric characteristics of each segment and compare them.

Notice that all shape factors can indicate a common type, and in fact may even be equal, but the curve may still not be a unique conic. As an example, recall that the weights of a circular arc depend only on the sweep angle (Eq. [7.33]); hence one could piece together circular arcs of different radii, but with equal sweep angles and shape factors.

Based on this discussion, for classification and conversion purposes the five forms can be put into two groups:

1. implicit and maximum inscribed area forms;
2. quadratic rational power basis, Bézier, and NURBS forms.

Conic representations are easily obtained within a group if certain data is available, that is

- geometric characteristics (Group 1);
- start points and end points, together with their tangent directions and an additional point, $\mathbf{P}_0, \mathbf{T}_0, \mathbf{P}_2, \mathbf{T}_2, \mathbf{P}$ (Group 2).

Using Algorithms `A7.1`–`A7.3`, conversion from a form in Group 1 to one in Group 2 is easy because it involves only point and tangent computation from Eqs. (7.3) and (7.5)–(7.7) or (7.15)–(7.17). Conversion from Group 2 to Group 1 requires more work. Beach [Beac91] derives the formulas for converting from the rational power basis to implicit form (Eq. [7.3]). We show here how to convert from rational Bézier form to Eq. (7.3), and how to compute the geometric characteristics of a conic from its rational Bézier form.

Let $\mathbf{C}(u)$ be the rational Bézier conic given by Eq. (7.21). Recalling Eqs. (7.22) through (7.26) and Figure 7.11

$$\alpha(u)\beta(u) = \frac{1}{4}k\big(1 - \alpha(u) - \beta(u)\big)^2 \tag{7.54}$$

is the implicit equation of the conic in the oblique coordinate system given by $\{\mathbf{P}_1, \mathbf{S}, \mathbf{T}\}$, where

$$k = \frac{w_0 w_2}{{w_1}^2} \qquad \alpha(u) = R_{0,2}(u) \qquad \beta(u) = R_{2,2}(u)$$

In order to obtain Eq. (7.3) from Eq. (7.54) we need to express α and β in terms of Cartesian coordinates x and y. Equation (7.20) says that $\alpha(u)$ and $\beta(u)$

are the barycentric coordinates of the point $\mathbf{C}(u)$ in the triangle $\{\mathbf{P}_0, \mathbf{P}_1, \mathbf{P}_2\}$. Fixing an arbitrary u_0, let $\alpha = \alpha(u_0)$, $\beta = \beta(u_0)$, and $\mathbf{P} = \mathbf{C}(u_0) = (x, y)$. Then

$$\alpha = \frac{\text{area}\,(\mathbf{P}, \mathbf{P}_1, \mathbf{P}_2)}{\text{area}\,(\mathbf{P}_0, \mathbf{P}_1, \mathbf{P}_2)} \qquad \beta = \frac{\text{area}\,(\mathbf{P}, \mathbf{P}_0, \mathbf{P}_1)}{\text{area}\,(\mathbf{P}_0, \mathbf{P}_1, \mathbf{P}_2)}$$

from which it follows that

$$\alpha = \frac{(y - y_1)(x_2 - x_1) - (x - x_1)(y_2 - y_1)}{(y_0 - y_1)(x_2 - x_1) - (x_0 - x_1)(y_2 - y_1)}$$

$$\beta = \frac{(y - y_1)(x_0 - x_1) - (x - x_1)(y_0 - y_1)}{(y_2 - y_1)(x_0 - x_1) - (x_2 - x_1)(y_0 - y_1)} \tag{7.55}$$

Now let

$$h_0 = x_0 - x_1 \qquad h_1 = x_2 - x_1$$

$$h_2 = y_0 - y_1 \qquad h_3 = y_2 - y_1$$

and

$$g_1 = h_2 h_1 - h_0 h_3$$

Then

$$\alpha = \frac{h_1(y - y_1) - h_3(x - x_1)}{g_1} \qquad \beta = \frac{h_0(y - y_1) - h_2(x - x_1)}{-g_1} \tag{7.56}$$

Finally, setting $s_1 = h_0 - h_1$ and $s_2 = h_3 - h_2$, and substituting Eq. (7.56) into Eq. (7.54), yields the six coefficients of Eq. (7.3), i.e.

$$\begin{aligned}
a &= s_2^2 + \frac{4}{k} h_2 h_3 \\
b &= s_1^2 + \frac{4}{k} h_0 h_1 \\
h &= s_1 s_2 - \frac{2}{k}(h_0 h_3 + h_1 h_2) \\
f &= -h y_1 - a x_1 + g_1 s_2 \\
g &= -h x_1 - b y_1 + g_1 s_1 \\
c &= b y_1^2 + 2h x_1 y_1 + a x_1^2 - 2 g_1 (y_1 s_1 + x_1 s_2) + g_1^2
\end{aligned} \tag{7.57}$$

We turn now to the computation of the geometric characteristics from the rational Bézier form. We present the formulas here without proof: although not difficult, the derivations are involved. For the proofs we refer the reader to Lee's elegant article [Lee87], which is the source of this material.

We are given a quadratic rational Bézier conic, defined by Eq. (7.21), with all $w_i > 0$. We assume the conic is not degenerate. We define the symbols

$$\mathbf{S} = \mathbf{P}_0 - \mathbf{P}_1 \qquad \mathbf{T} = \mathbf{P}_2 - \mathbf{P}_1$$

$$k = \frac{w_0 w_2}{w_1^2} \qquad \epsilon = \frac{k}{2(k-1)}$$

$$\alpha = |\,\mathbf{S}\,|^2 \qquad \beta = \mathbf{S}\cdot\mathbf{T} \qquad \gamma = |\,\mathbf{T}\,|^2$$

$$\delta = \alpha\gamma - \beta^2 = |\,\mathbf{S}\times\mathbf{T}\,|^2$$

$$\zeta = \alpha + \gamma + 2\beta = |\,\mathbf{S}+\mathbf{T}\,|^2$$

$$\eta = \alpha + \gamma - 2\beta = |\,\mathbf{S}-\mathbf{T}\,|^2$$

For the parabola we have the formulas

$$\text{Axis} \ : \ \frac{1}{\sqrt{\zeta}}(\mathbf{S}+\mathbf{T}) \tag{7.58}$$

$$\text{Focus} \ : \ \mathbf{P}_1 + \frac{\gamma\mathbf{S}+\alpha\mathbf{T}}{\zeta} \tag{7.59}$$

$$\text{Vertex} \ : \ \mathbf{P}_1 + \left(\frac{\gamma+\beta}{\zeta}\right)^2\mathbf{S} + \left(\frac{\alpha+\beta}{\zeta}\right)^2\mathbf{T} \tag{7.60}$$

The center of an ellipse or hyperbola is given by

$$\text{Center} \ : \ \mathbf{P}_1 + \epsilon(\mathbf{S}+\mathbf{T}) \tag{7.61}$$

Let $\lambda_1 \le \lambda_2$ be the solutions to the quadratic equation

$$2\delta\lambda^2 - (k\eta + 4\beta)\lambda + 2(k-1) = 0$$

The roots of this equation are real. For an ellipse, $\lambda_2 \ge \lambda_1 > 0$ and $\epsilon > 0$. For a hyperbola, $\lambda_1 < 0 < \lambda_2$ and $\epsilon < 0$. The major and minor radii are

$$\text{Ellipse} \ : \ r_1 = \sqrt{\frac{\epsilon}{\lambda_1}} \qquad r_2 = \sqrt{\frac{\epsilon}{\lambda_2}} \tag{7.62}$$

$$\text{Hyperbola} \ : \ r_1 = \sqrt{\frac{\epsilon}{\lambda_1}} \qquad r_2 = \sqrt{\frac{-\epsilon}{\lambda_2}} \tag{7.63}$$

Define the following

$$\text{if} \quad \left|\frac{k}{2} - \gamma\lambda_1\right| > \left|\frac{k}{2} - \alpha\lambda_1\right|$$

$$\bar{x} = \frac{k}{2} - \gamma\lambda_1 \qquad \bar{y} = \beta\lambda_1 - \frac{k}{2} + 1$$

$$\text{else} \quad \bar{x} = \beta\lambda_1 - \frac{k}{2} + 1 \qquad \bar{y} = \frac{k}{2} - \alpha\lambda_1$$

and

$$\rho = \alpha\bar{x}^2 + 2\beta\bar{x}\bar{y} + \gamma\bar{y}^2$$

$$x_0 = \frac{\bar{x}}{\rho} \qquad y_0 = \frac{\bar{y}}{\rho}$$

Then the points $\mathbf{Q}_1$ and $\mathbf{Q}_2$

$$\mathbf{Q}_1 = \mathbf{P}_1 + (\epsilon + r_1 x_0)\mathbf{S} + (\epsilon + r_1 y_0)\mathbf{T}$$

$$\mathbf{Q}_2 = \mathbf{P}_1 + (\epsilon - r_1 x_0)\mathbf{S} + (\epsilon - r_1 y_0)\mathbf{T} \qquad (7.64)$$

lie on the major axis of the ellipse or on the transverse axis of the hyperbola. The other orthogonal axis is easily obtained, and the vertices of the ellipse or the hyperbola are computed from the center, the radii, and the axis directions.

Note that for the circle, which is a special case of the ellipse, Eq. (7.62) yields $r_1 = r_2$. An algorithm should check for this case, because it makes no sense to apply Eq. (7.64) to a circle.

Figures 7.27a–7.27c illustrate these formulas. Figure 7.27a shows a parabolic arc along with the vertex (**V**), focus (**F**), and axis vector (**A**). In Figure 7.27b an elliptical arc is depicted, with center (**C**), negative major axis (−**U**), and minor axis (**V**). Figure 7.27c shows the hyperbolic case. Again, center (**C**), major (**U**) and minor (**V**) axes are computed. This figure also shows how to compute the asymptotes of the arc, $\mathcal{A}_1$ and $\mathcal{A}_2$, i.e., the lines that are tangential to the curve at two points at infinity.

Finally, Figure 7.28 shows how to compute the NURBS representation of a full ellipse, given an arc in Bézier form (see the four steps given at the end of the previous section).

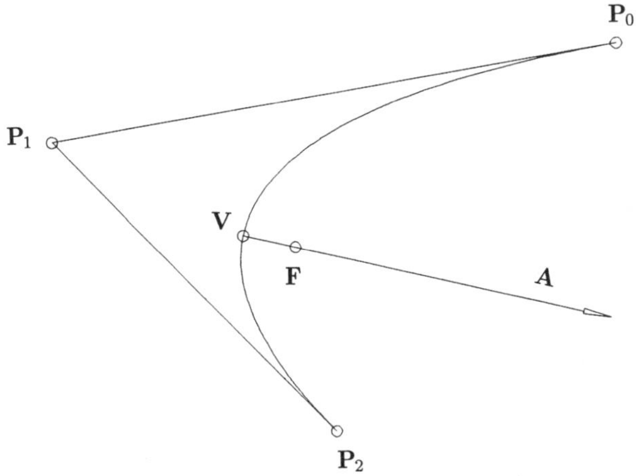

(a)

Figure 7.27. Geometric data computed from the Bézier representation. (a) A parabola with vertex (**V**), focus (**F**), and axis (**A**); (b) an ellipse with center (**C**), negative major axis (−**U**), and minor axis (**V**); (c) a hyperbola with center (**C**), major axis (**U**), minor axis (**V**), and the two asymptotes ($\mathcal{A}_1$ and $\mathcal{A}_2$).

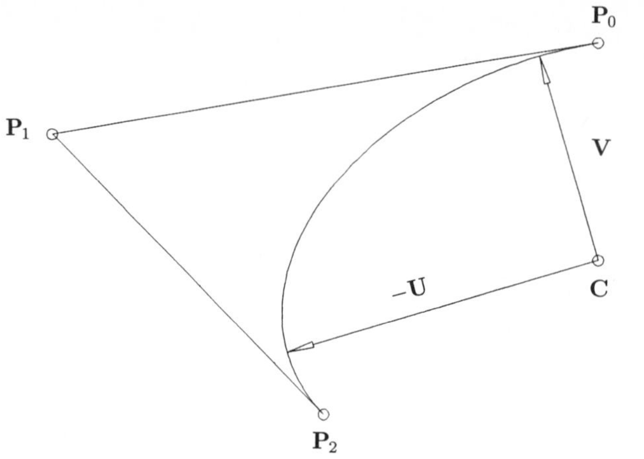

(b)

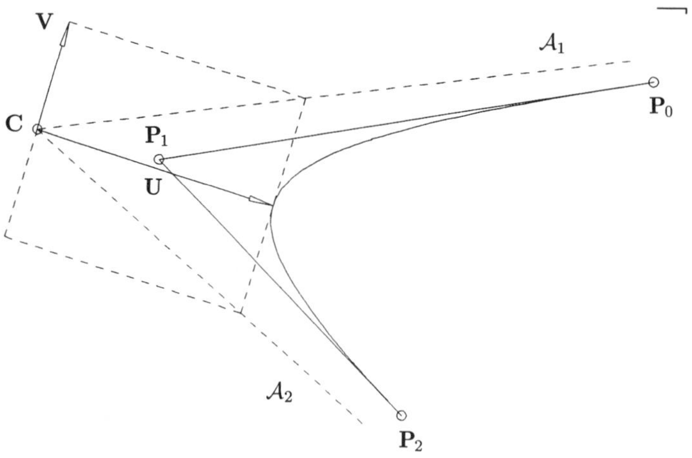

(c)

Figure 7.27. (*Continued.*)

7.8 Higher Order Circles

In some applications it is useful to represent full circles or circular arcs of sweep angle greater than 180° with one rational Bézier segment (no internal knots), no infinite control points, and no negative weights. In previous sections we eliminated infinite control points and negative weights by using knot insertion. Degree elevation also does the trick. A few examples are:

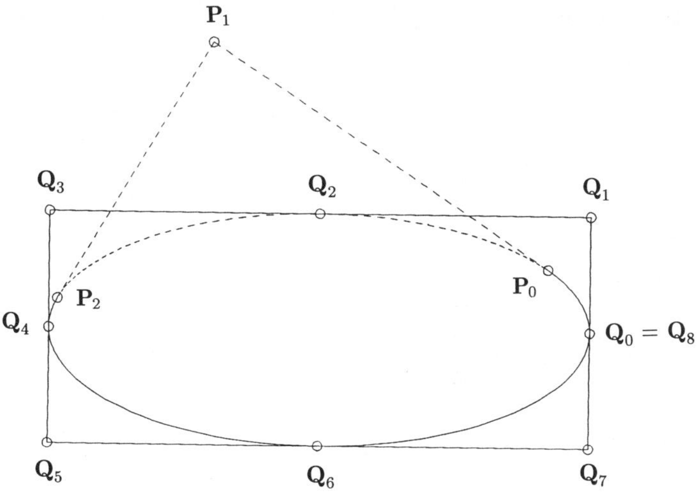

Figure 7.28. NURBS representation of a full ellipse given in Bézier form (dashed line).

Examples

Ex7.7 The semicircle of Example Ex7.1 can be degree elevated to yield

$$\mathbf{Q}_0^w = \mathbf{P}_0^w \qquad \mathbf{Q}_3^w = \mathbf{P}_2^w$$

$$\mathbf{Q}_1^w = \frac{1}{3}\mathbf{P}_0^w + \frac{2}{3}\mathbf{P}_1^w = \left(\frac{1}{3}, \frac{2}{3}, \frac{1}{3}\right)$$

$$\mathbf{Q}_2^w = \frac{2}{3}\mathbf{P}_1^w + \frac{1}{3}\mathbf{P}_2^w = \left(-\frac{1}{3}, \frac{2}{3}, \frac{1}{3}\right)$$

Thus (see Figure 7.29)

$$U = \{0,0,0,0,1,1,1,1\}$$

$$\{w_i\} = \left\{1, \frac{1}{3}, \frac{1}{3}, 1\right\}$$

$$\{\mathbf{Q}_i\} = \{(1,0),(1,2),(-1,2),(-1,0)\}$$

Ex7.8 The arc of 240° given in Example Ex7.4 is degree elevated to yield (see Figure 7.30):

$$U = \{0,0,0,0,1,1,1,1\}$$

$$\{w_i\} = \left\{1, \frac{1}{6}, \frac{1}{6}, 1\right\}$$

$$\{\mathbf{Q}_i\} = \left\{\left(a, \frac{1}{2}\right), (2a,-3), (-2a,-3), \left(-a, \frac{1}{2}\right)\right\}$$

with $a = \sqrt{3}/2$.

The following fourth- and fifth-degree full circle constructions are due to Chou [Chou95] and Strotman [Stro91].

Ex7.9 We write the semicircle (with radius 1) in the complex plane as

$$z = e^{i\pi u} = f(u) = g(u) + h(u)i \qquad 0 \le u \le 1 \tag{7.65}$$

Squaring Eq. (7.65), we obtain the full circle

$$e^{i2\pi u} = (g^2 - h^2) + (2gh)i \qquad 0 \le u \le 1 \tag{7.66}$$

From Example Ex7.1 we know that

$$g(u) = \frac{1-2u}{1-2u+2u^2} \qquad h(u) = \frac{2u(1-u)}{1-2u+2u^2} \tag{7.67}$$

Substituting Eq. (7.67) into Eq. (7.66) and returning to the real xy plane, we obtain

$$x(u) = \frac{1-4u+8u^3-4u^4}{1-4u+8u^2-8u^3+4u^4}$$

$$y(u) = \frac{4u(1-3u+2u^2)}{1-4u+8u^2-8u^3+4u^4} \tag{7.68}$$

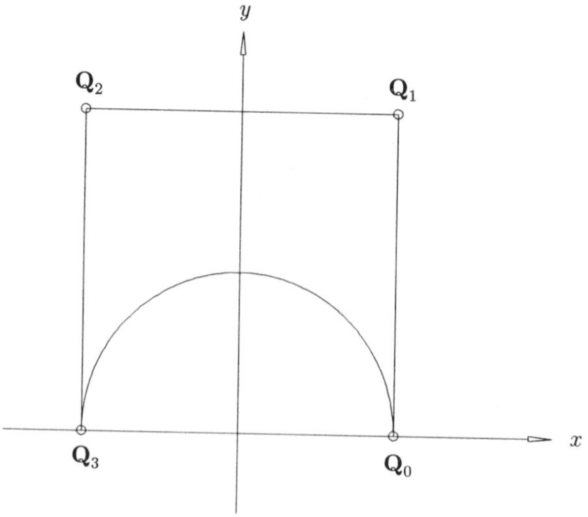

Figure 7.29. Rational cubic Bézier representation of the semicircle.

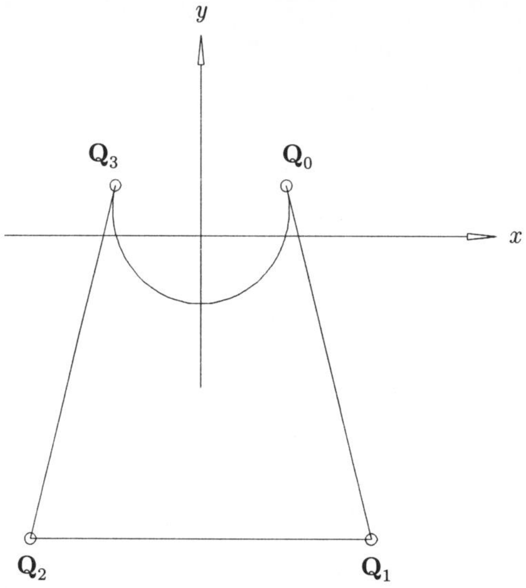

Figure 7.30. Rational cubic Bézier representation of an arc sweeping 240°.

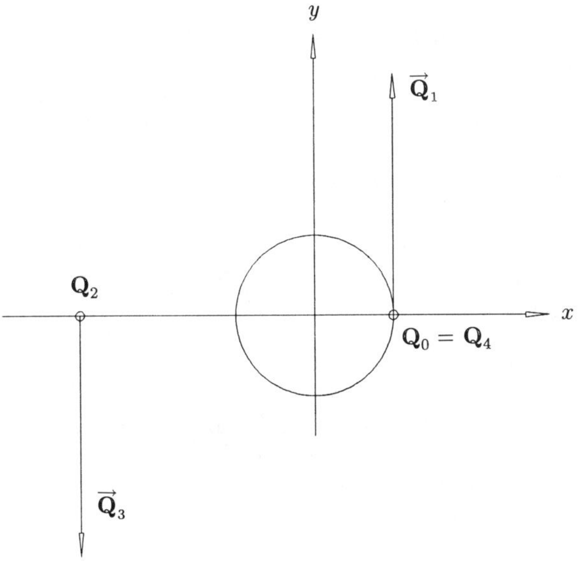

Figure 7.31. Rational quartic representation of the full circle using two infinite control points.

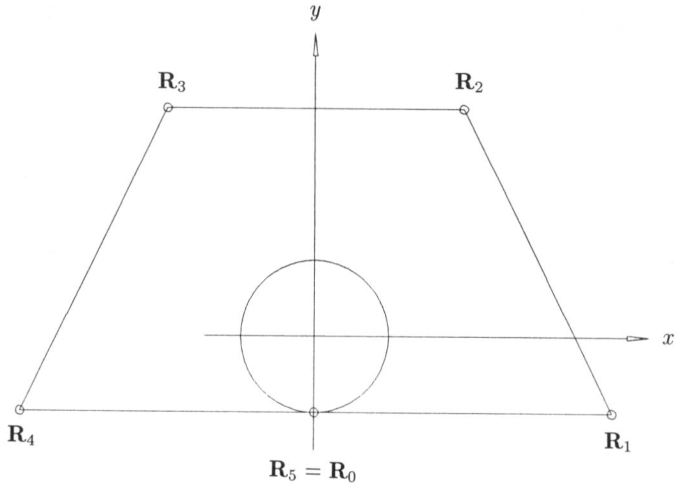

Figure 7.32. Rational quintic representation of the full circle using only finite control points.

Converting to Bézier form yields

$$\{\mathbf{Q}_i^w\} = \{(3,0,3),(0,3,0),(-3,0,1),(0,-3,0),(3,0,3)\}$$

This is a fourth-degree full circle with two infinite control points (see Figure 7.31).

`Ex7.10` Simple degree elevation of the fourth-degree circle of Example `Ex7.9` yields

$$\mathbf{R}_0^w = (0,-5,5) \quad \mathbf{R}_1^w = (4,-1,1) \quad \mathbf{R}_2^w = (2,3,1)$$
$$\mathbf{R}_3^w = (-2,3,1) \quad \mathbf{R}_4^w = (-4,-1,1) \quad \mathbf{R}_5^w = (0,-5,5)$$

This is a fifth-degree Bézier full circle using only finite control points and positive weights (see Figure 7.32).

Chou [Chou95] proves that it is impossible to obtain a fourth-degree Bézier full circle using only positive weights and finite control points.

Finally, we remind the reader that circles are simply perspective projections of curves which lie on a right circular cone. Thus any such curves, including nonplanar ones, will do. The possibilities are endless.

Exercises

7.1. Prove the statement made in Section 7.3, "Due to our choice of $w_0 = w_2 = 1$, it follows that the tangent to the conic at $\mathbf{S} = \mathbf{C}(1/2)$ is parallel to $\mathbf{P}_0\mathbf{P}_2$." Hint: Use Eqs. (7.25) and (7.26) and the properties of similar triangles.

7.2. Consider Figure 7.13 and Eq. (7.33). They imply that w_1 depends only on the sweep angle (not radius). Consider what happens to w_1 in the two limiting cases:

- hold $\mathbf{P}_0$ and $\mathbf{P}_2$ fixed and let $\mathbf{P}_1$ go to infinity;
- fix a circle, and let $\mathbf{P}_0$ and $\mathbf{P}_2$ come together.

7.3. The two concepts of "setting a weight to zero" and "infinite coefficients" also exist for the rational power basis representation. Is one of these concepts being used to obtain Eqs. (7.8) and (7.9)? If so, which one?

7.4. Another representation of the full circle is obtained by using the nine-point square control polygon and the knots of Example `Ex7.2` but with weights $\{w_i\} = \{1, 1, 2, 1, 1, 1, 2, 1, 1\}$. Investigate the continuity at $u = 1/2$. Use formulas from Chapter 5 to remove the knot $u = 1/2$ as many times as possible. Compare this with Example `Ex7.2` and explain the results. Visualize the two circles lying on the cone in homogeneous space.

7.5. Use Eqs. (7.53) and (7.25) to verify that Eqs. (7.8) and (7.9) represent an ellipse and a hyperbola, respectively.

7.6. A NURBS curve is defined by

$$U = \left\{0, 0, 0, \frac{1}{2}, 1, 1, 1\right\}$$

$$\mathbf{P}_i = \{(1,0), (1,1), (-2,1), (-2,-1)\}$$

$$w_i = \left\{1, \frac{1}{2}, \frac{1}{2}, 1\right\}$$

Is this curve a unique conic?

CHAPTER

EIGHT

Construction of Common Surfaces

8.1 Introduction

Sections 2 through 5 of this chapter cover the NURBS representation of the four surface types: bilinear surfaces, general cylinders (extruded surfaces), ruled surfaces, and surfaces of revolution. As the reader surely realizes by now, these representations are not unique. Considerations such as parameterization, convex hull, continuity, software design, application area, data exchange, and even personal taste can influence the choice of representation method. Our presentation closely follows the constructions given by Piegl and Tiller [Pieg87a]. Section 6 uses nonuniform scaling to obtain additional surfaces such as the ellipsoid and elliptic paraboloid. Section 7 presents a method for constructing a three-sided patch on a sphere, whose boundary curves are circles whose radii are equal to the radius of the sphere. This patch is useful as a corner fillet surface.

In order to clearly indicate the degree in this chapter, we use the notation $R_{i,p;j,q}(u,v)$ for the i,jth rational basis function of degree $p \times q$ (compare this with Eq. [4.12]).

8.2 Bilinear Surfaces

Let $\mathbf{P}_{0,0}, \mathbf{P}_{1,0}, \mathbf{P}_{0,1}, \mathbf{P}_{1,1}$ be four points in three-dimensional space. We want to construct a NURBS representation of the surface obtained by bilinearly interpolating between the four line segments, $\mathbf{P}_{0,0}\mathbf{P}_{1,0}$, $\mathbf{P}_{0,1}\mathbf{P}_{1,1}$, $\mathbf{P}_{0,0}\mathbf{P}_{0,1}$, and $\mathbf{P}_{1,0}\mathbf{P}_{1,1}$. Clearly, the desired (nonrational) surface is given by

$$\mathbf{S}(u,v) = \sum_{i=0}^{1}\sum_{j=0}^{1} N_{i,1}(u)N_{j,1}(v)\,\mathbf{P}_{i,j} \tag{8.1}$$

with

$$U = V = \{0,0,1,1\}$$

Equation (8.1) represents a simple linear interpolation between the opposite boundary lines in each of the two directions. In Figure 8.1a the four points lie in a common plane, hence the surface is that portion of the plane bounded by the four line segments. Figure 8.1b shows a hyperbolic paraboloid obtained by linear interpolations between the nonparallel diagonals of a cube.

8.3 The General Cylinder

Let $\mathbf{W}$ be a vector of unit length and $\mathbf{C}(u) = \sum_{i=0}^{n} R_{i,p}(u)\mathbf{P}_i$ be a pth-degree NURBS curve on the knot vector, U, with weights w_i. We want the representation of the general cylinder, $\mathbf{S}(u,v)$, obtained by sweeping $\mathbf{C}(u)$ a distance d along $\mathbf{W}$. Denoting the parameter for the sweep direction by v, $0 \le v \le 1$, clearly $\mathbf{S}(u,v)$ must satisfy two conditions

- for fixed $\bar{u}$, $\mathbf{S}(\bar{u},v)$ is a straight line segment from $\mathbf{C}(\bar{u})$ to $\mathbf{C}(\bar{u}) + d\mathbf{W}$;
- for fixed $\bar{v}$

$$\mathbf{S}(u,\bar{v}) = \mathbf{C}(u) + \bar{v}d\mathbf{W} = \sum_{i=0}^{n} R_{i,p}(\mathbf{P}_i + \bar{v}d\mathbf{W})$$

(the translational invariance property).

The desired representation is

$$\mathbf{S}(u,v) = \sum_{i=0}^{n}\sum_{j=0}^{1} R_{i,p;j,1}(u,v)\,\mathbf{P}_{i,j} \tag{8.2}$$

on knot vectors U and V, where $V = \{0,0,1,1\}$ and U is the knot vector of $\mathbf{C}(u)$. The control points are given by $\mathbf{P}_{i,0} = \mathbf{P}_i$ and $\mathbf{P}_{i,1} = \mathbf{P}_i + d\mathbf{W}$, and the weights are $w_{i,0} = w_{i,1} = w_i$. A general cylinder is shown in Figure 8.2.

A right circular cylinder is obtained by translating the NURBS circle a distance d along a vector normal to the plane of the circle. Any of the circle representations given in Chapter 7 will do. Figure 8.3 shows a right circular cylinder whose underlying circle is the quadratic, nine-point, square control polygon representation of Example Ex7.2 and Figure 7.16a. The cylinder is defined by

$$\mathbf{S}(u,v) = \sum_{i=0}^{8}\sum_{j=0}^{1} R_{i,2;j,1}(u,v)\,\mathbf{P}_{i,j} \tag{8.3}$$

where $V = \{0,0,1,1\}$ and U and the weights ($w_{i,0}$ and $w_{i,1}$) are those given for the circle in Example Ex7.2. Note that the control net forms the circumscribing box of the cylinder.

Cylinders with circular and conic cross sections of sweep angle less than 360° are obtained by translating the control points computed by Algorithms A7.1 and A7.3. Figure 8.4 shows an elliptic cylinder.

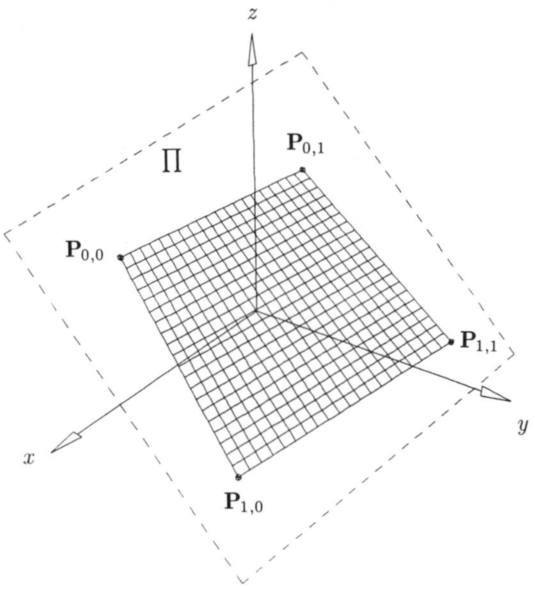

(a)

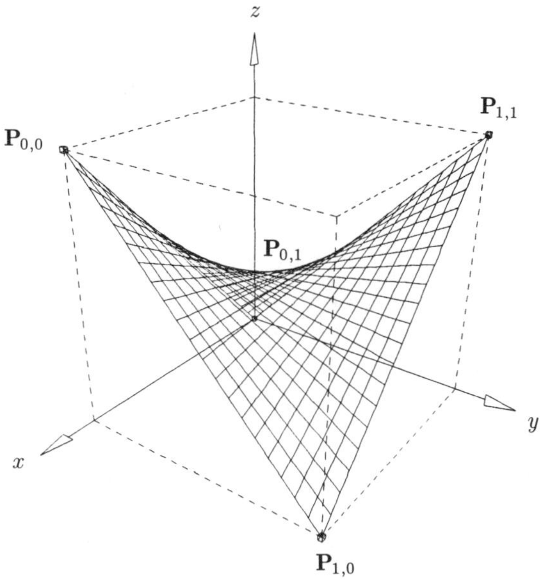

(b)

Figure 8.1. Bilinear surfaces. (a) Straight line boundaries lying in the plane Π; (b) nonplanar straight line boundaries (defined by diagonals of a cube) yielding a hyperbolic paraboloid.

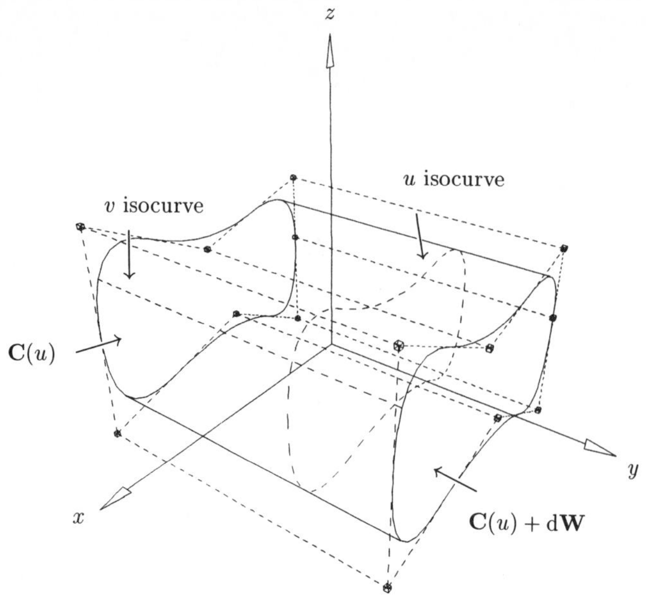

Figure 8.2. A general cylinder obtained by translating $\mathbf{C}(u)$ a distance d along $\mathbf{W}$.

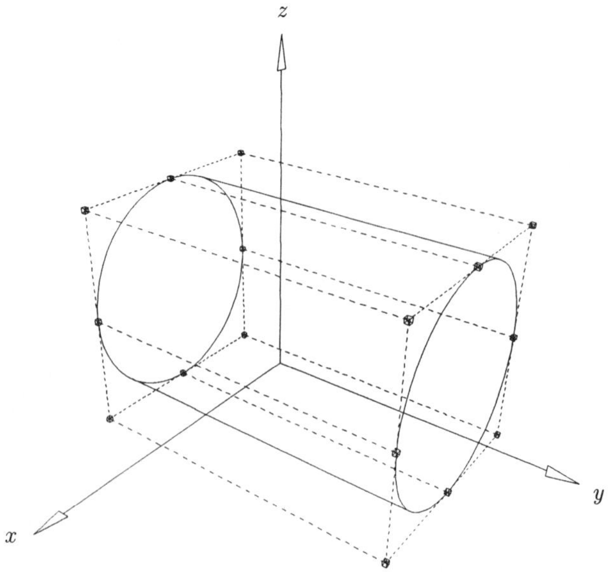

Figure 8.3. A right circular cylinder.

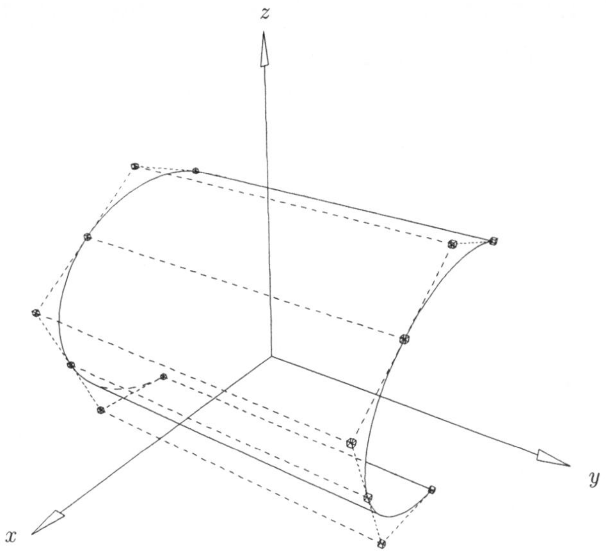

Figure 8.4. An elliptic cylindrical patch.

8.4 The Ruled Surface

Assume we have two NURBS curves

$$\mathbf{C}_k(u) = \sum_{i=0}^{n_k} R_{i,p_k}(u)\mathbf{P}_i^k \qquad k = 1,2$$

defined on knot vectors $U^k = \{u_0^k, \ldots, u_{m_k}^k\}$. We want a surface which is ruled in the v direction, i.e., it is a linear interpolation between $\mathbf{C}_1(u)$ and $\mathbf{C}_2(u)$. Furthermore, we require that the interpolation be between points of equal parameter value, i.e., for fixed $\bar{u}$, $\mathbf{S}(\bar{u}, v)$ is a straight line segment connecting the points $\mathbf{C}_1(\bar{u})$ and $\mathbf{C}_2(\bar{u})$. The desired surface form is

$$\mathbf{S}(u,v) = \sum_{i=0}^{n}\sum_{j=0}^{1} R_{i,p;j,1}(u,v)\,\mathbf{P}_{i,j} \tag{8.4}$$

where $V = \{0,0,1,1\}$. n, U, p, $w_{i,j}$, and $\mathbf{P}_{i,j}$ must all be determined.

Because of the tensor product nature of the surface, the two boundary curves, $\mathbf{C}_k(u)$, must have the same degree and be defined on the same knot vector. Hence, the algorithm for determining n, U, p, $w_{i,j}$ and $\mathbf{P}_{i,j}$ is

1. ensure that the two curves are defined on the same parameter range, i.e., $u_0^1 = u_0^2$ and $u_{m_1}^1 = u_{m_2}^2$;

2. if $p_1 = p_2$, then set $p = p_1$; otherwise, set p to the larger of p_1, p_2, and raise the degree of the lower degree curve to p (Algorithm A5.9);
3. if the knot vectors U^1 and U^2 are not identical, merge them to obtain the knot vector U; more precisely, u_j is in U if it is in either U^1 or U^2. The maximum multiplicity of u_j in U^1 or U^2 is also carried over to U. For example, if $U^1 = \{0,0,0,1,2,2,4,4,4\}$ and $U^2 = \{0,0,0,1,2,3,4,4,4\}$, then $U = \{0,0,0,1,2,2,3,4,4,4\}$;
4. using U, apply knot refinement (Algorithm A5.4) to both curves, $\mathbf{C}_k(u)$; this step yields the final values of n, $w_{i,j}$, and $\mathbf{P}_{i,j}$.

Figures 8.5a–8.5e show the process of constructing a ruled surface between a degree two and a degree three curve.

The general cone is also a ruled surface. Let $\mathbf{P}$ be the vertex point of the cone, and let

$$\mathbf{C}_1(u) = \sum_{i=0}^{n} R_{i,p}(u)\mathbf{P}_i^1$$

be its base curve. Define the curve

$$\mathbf{C}_2(u) = \sum_{i=0}^{n} R_{i,p}(u)\mathbf{P}_i^2$$

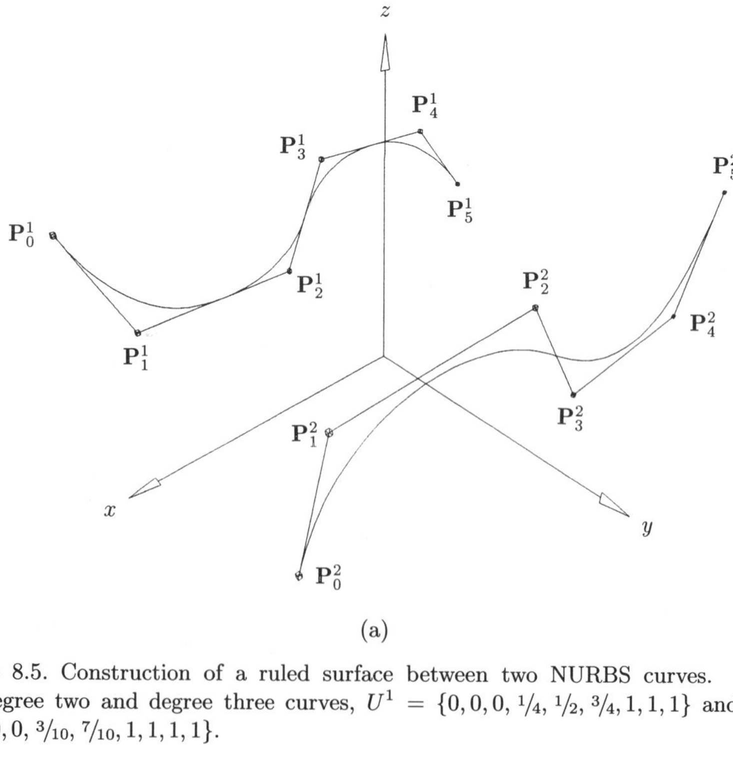

Figure 8.5. Construction of a ruled surface between two NURBS curves. (a) Input degree two and degree three curves, $U^1 = \{0,0,0,1/4,1/2,3/4,1,1,1\}$ and $U^2 = \{0,0,0,0,3/10,7/10,1,1,1,1\}$.

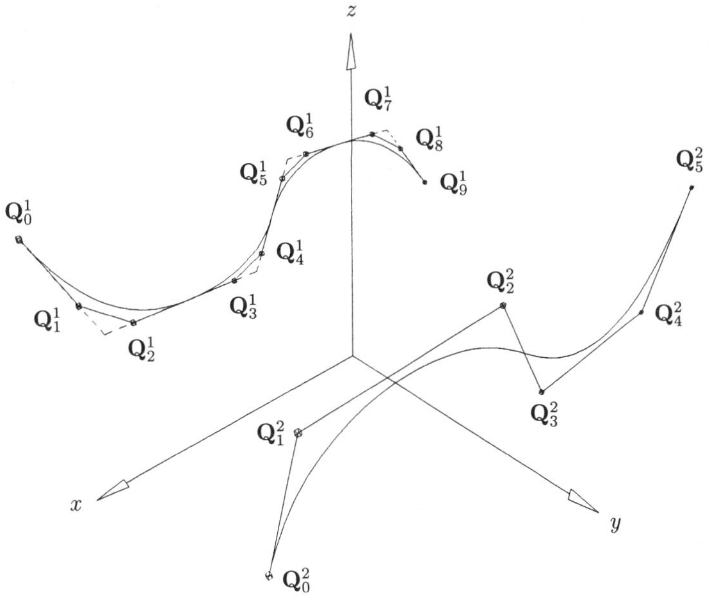

(b)

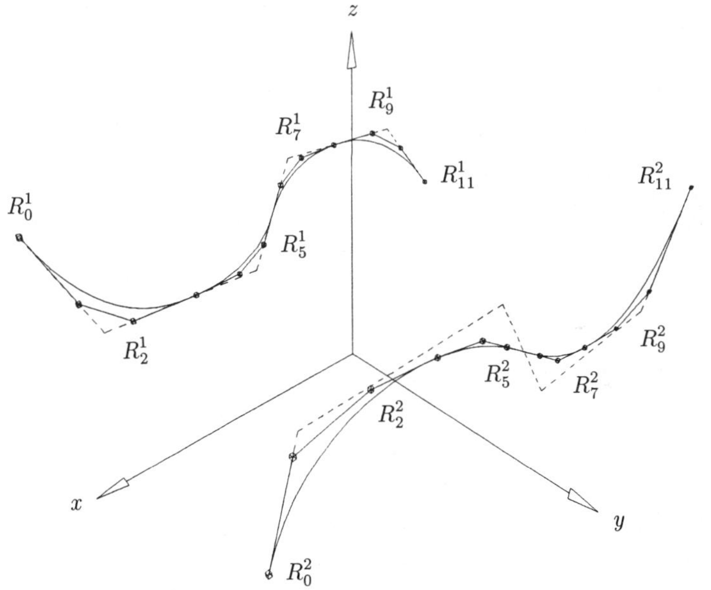

(c)

Figure 8.5. (*Continued.*) (b) degree elevation of degree two curve; (c) knot refined curves after merging the knot vectors; surface knot vector is $U = \{0, 0, 0, 0, {}^1\!/_4, {}^1\!/_4, {}^3\!/_{10}, {}^1\!/_2, {}^1\!/_2, {}^7\!/_{10}, {}^3\!/_4, {}^3\!/_4, 1, 1, 1, 1\}$.

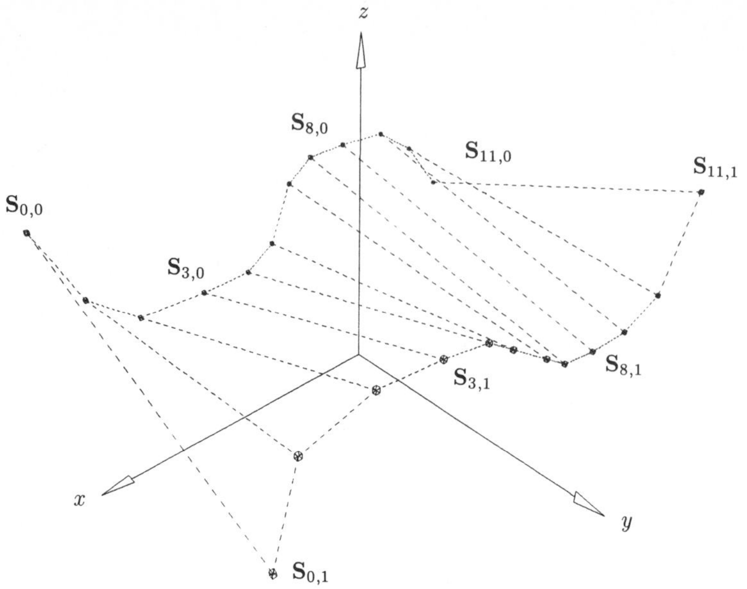

(d)

Figure 8.5. (*Continued.*) (d) control net of ruled surface.

with $\mathbf{P}_i^2 = \mathbf{P}$ and $w_i^2 = w_i^1$ for all i (a degenerate curve). The ruled surface between $\mathbf{C}_1(u)$ and $\mathbf{C}_2(u)$ is the desired cone. Figure 8.6 shows a right circular cone, and Figures 8.7a–8.7c show some exotic ruled surfaces defined by lines and circles.

We emphasize again that the rulings (straight line segments) on the NURBS surface are between points of equal parameter value, not points of equal relative arc length. In general, ruling according to relative arc length yields a geometrically different surface, and this cannot be achieved using NURBS. As a consequence, mathematically precise conversion between NURBS and an IGES ruled surface (Type 118), Form 0 [IGE93] is not possible.

8.5 The Surface of Revolution

Let $\mathbf{C}(v) = \sum_{j=0}^{m} R_{j,q}(v)\mathbf{P}_j$ be a qth-degree NURBS curve on the knot vector V. $\mathbf{C}(v)$ is called the *generatrix*, and it is to be revolved about an axis. At the end of this section we present an algorithm which can revolve $\mathbf{C}(v)$ through an arbitrary angle about an arbitrary axis. However, for the sake of simplicity let us now assume that $\mathbf{C}(v)$ lies in the xz plane, and that we revolve $\mathbf{C}(v)$ a full 360° about the z-axis. The required surface, $\mathbf{S}(u,v)$, has characteristics such that (see Figure 8.8):

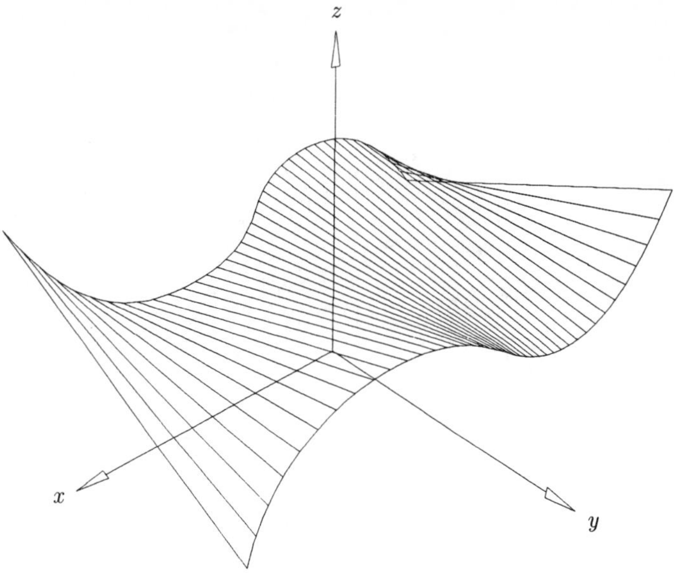

(e)

Figure 8.5. (*Continued.*) (e) ruled surface.

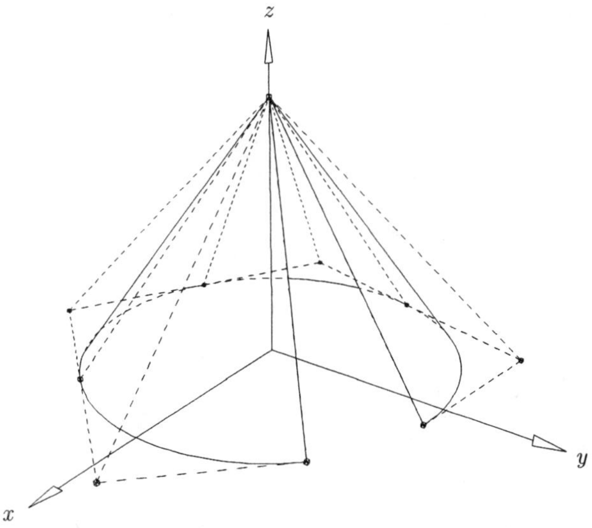

Figure 8.6. A right circular conical patch.

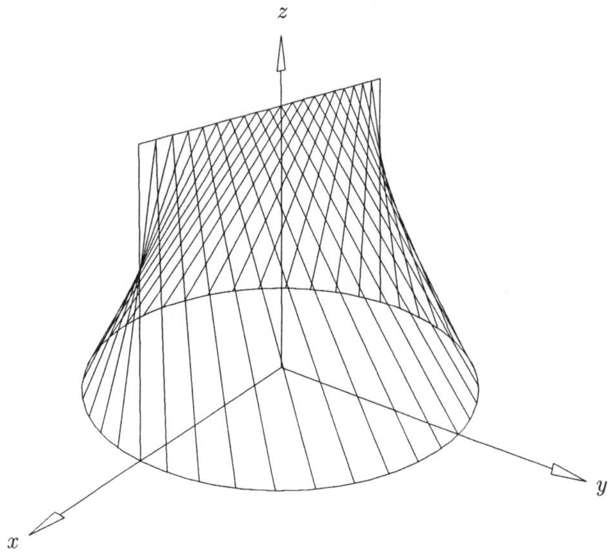

(a)

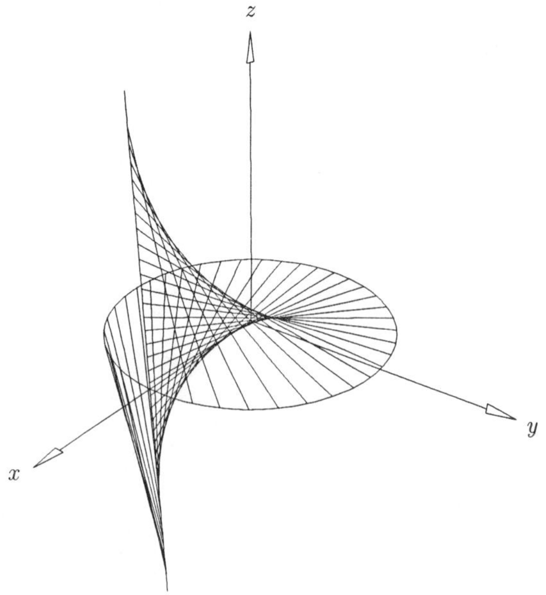

(b)

Figure 8.7. Ruled surfaces defined by circles and lines. (a) Degree two ruled surface (conoid); (b) degree three ruled surface.

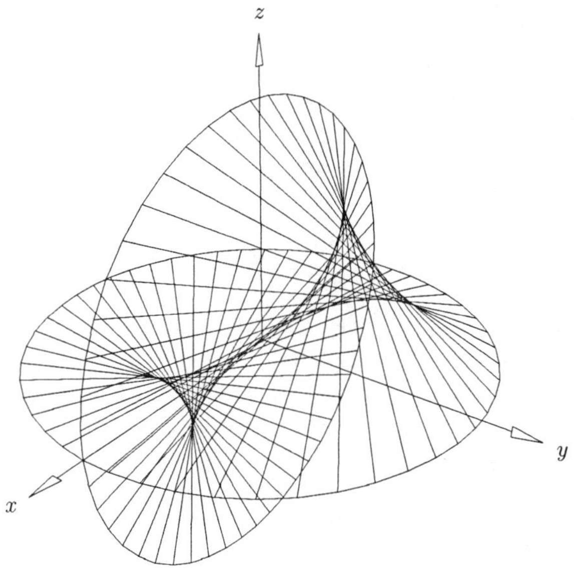

(c)

Figure 8.7. (*Continued.*) (c) degree four ruled surface.

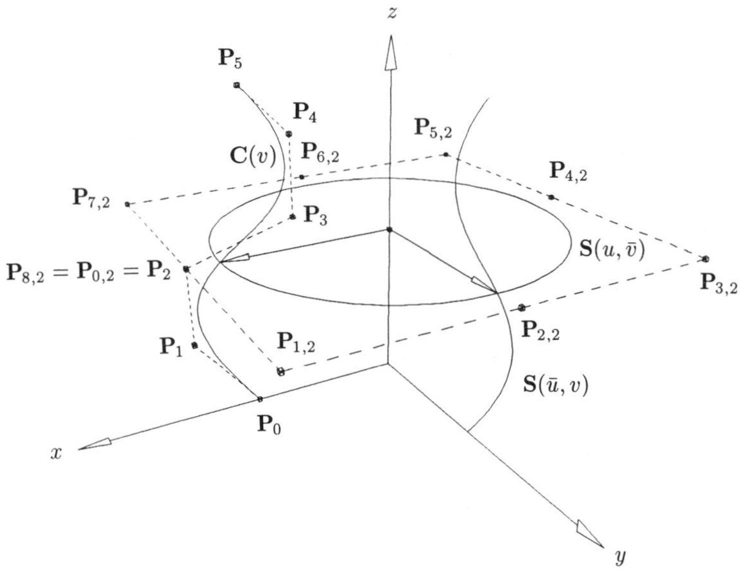

Figure 8.8. Definition of a surface of revolution.

- for fixed $\bar{u}$, $\mathbf{S}(\bar{u}, v)$ is the curve $\mathbf{C}(v)$ rotated some angle about the z-axis;
- for fixed $\bar{v}$, $\mathbf{S}(u, \bar{v})$ is a full circle which lies in a plane perpendicular to the z-axis, with its center on the z-axis.

Let us use the nine-point circle representation, with $U = \{0, 0, 0, 1/4, 1/4, 1/2, 1/2, 3/4, 3/4, 1, 1, 1\}$ and weights $w_i = \{1, \sqrt{2}/2, 1, \sqrt{2}/2, 1, \sqrt{2}/2, 1, \sqrt{2}/2, 1\}$. Then the required surface has the form

$$\mathbf{S}(u, v) = \sum_{i=0}^{8} \sum_{j=0}^{m} R_{i,2;j,q}(u, v)\, \mathbf{P}_{i,j} \tag{8.5}$$

The knot vectors are U and V. The control points and weights are determined as follows (see Figure 8.8): For $i = 0$, $\mathbf{P}_{i,j} = \mathbf{P}_{0,j} = \mathbf{P}_j$. Because of the circular nature of $\mathbf{S}(u, \bar{v})$, the $\mathbf{P}_{i,j}$ for fixed j, $0 \le i \le 8$, all lie in the plane $z = z_j$. They lie on the square of width $2x_j$, with center on the z-axis. The weights are defined by taking the products of the w_j and the circle weights, w_i, i.e., for fixed j, $w_{0,j} = w_j$, $w_{1,j} = (\sqrt{2}/2) w_j$, $w_{2,j} = w_j$, $w_{3,j} = (\sqrt{2}/2) w_j, \ldots, w_{8,j} = w_j$. Figures 8.9a and 8.9b show the control net and the corresponding surface of revolution generated by Eq. (8.5) and the curve of Figure 8.8.

It is not entirely obvious that Eq. (8.5) represents the desired surface of revolution, hence we sketch a proof here. Fixing $u = \bar{u}$ and using the unprojected form of Eq. (8.5), we write

$$\mathbf{S}^w(\bar{u}, v) = \sum_{j=0}^{m} N_{j,q}(v) \left(\sum_{i=0}^{8} N_{i,2}(\bar{u})\, \mathbf{P}_{i,j}^w \right) = \sum_{j=0}^{m} N_{j,q}(v)\, \mathbf{Q}_j^w$$

with

$$\mathbf{Q}_j^w = \sum_{i=0}^{8} N_{i,2}(\bar{u})\, \mathbf{P}_{i,j}^w \qquad 0 \le j \le m$$

But this says that $\mathbf{Q}_j$ is just $\mathbf{P}_{0,j}$ ($= \mathbf{P}_j$) rotated about the z-axis through some fixed angle, θ, corresponding to $\bar{u}$. Hence, from the rotational invariance of NURBS curves, it follows that $\mathbf{S}(\bar{u}, v)$ is just $\mathbf{C}(v)$ rotated about the z-axis through θ. This completes the proof.

Several common surfaces are surfaces of revolution. A torus is obtained by revolving a full circle about the z-axis (Figure 8.10). A sphere is obtained by revolving about the z-axis a half circle whose endpoints lie on the z-axis (see Figure 8.11). Notice that the control points at the north and south poles of the sphere are repeated nine times: $\mathbf{P}_{0,0} = \cdots = \mathbf{P}_{8,0}$ and $\mathbf{P}_{0,4} = \cdots = \mathbf{P}_{8,4}$. Hence, the partial derivatives at these poles with respect to u are identically zero. However, the normal vectors clearly exist there.

We now present an algorithm which constructs a NURBS surface of revolution through an arbitrary angle, `theta`, about an arbitrary axis (see Figure 8.12). The axis is specified by a point, `S`, and a unit length vector, `T`. For convenience, we separate weights and three-dimensional control points in this algorithm; `m,Pj[],wj[]` define the generatrix curve, and `n,U,Pij[][],wij[][]` are computed (see Eq. [8.5]). We assume four utility functions:

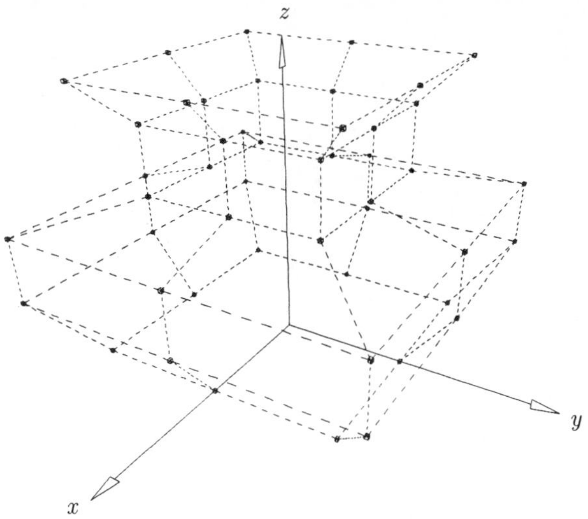

(a)

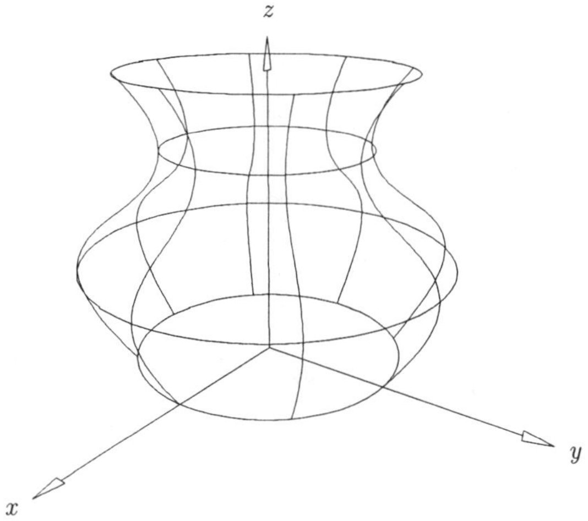

(b)

Figure 8.9. (a.) A control net for a surface of revolution; (b) a surface of revolution.

`PointToLine()` : projects a point to a line;

`VecNormalize()` : normalizes a vector and returns its magnitude;

`VecCrossProd()` : computes the vector cross product;

`Intersect3DLines()` : intersects two three-dimensional lines.

Note the similarity between this algorithm and Algorithm `A7.1`.

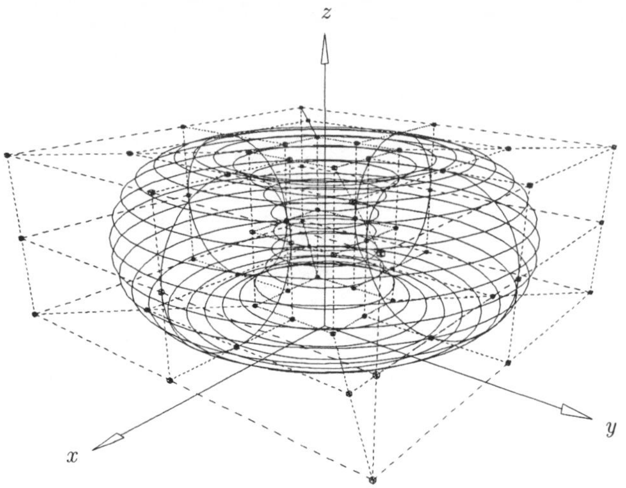

Figure 8.10. A torus as a surface of revolution.

```
ALGORITHM A8.1
  MakeRevolvedSurf(S,T,theta,m,Pj,wj,n,U,Pij,wij)
    { /*  Create NURBS surface of revolution  */
      /*  Input:  S,T,theta,m,Pj,wj  */
      /*  Output: n,U,Pij,wij  */
    if (theta <= 90.0)   narcs = 1;
      else
        if (theta <= 180.0)
          { narcs = 2;   U[3] = U[4] = 0.5;  }
          else
            if (theta <= 270.0)
              {
              narcs = 3;
              U[3] = U[4] = 1.0/3.0;
              U[5] = U[6] = 2.0/3.0;
              }
              else
              {
              narcs = 4;
              U[3] = U[4] = 0.25;
              U[5] = U[6] = 0.5;
              U[7] = U[8] = 0.75;
              }
    dtheta = theta/narcs;
    j = 3 + 2*(narcs-1);   /* load end knots */
    for (i=0; i<3; j++,i++)
```

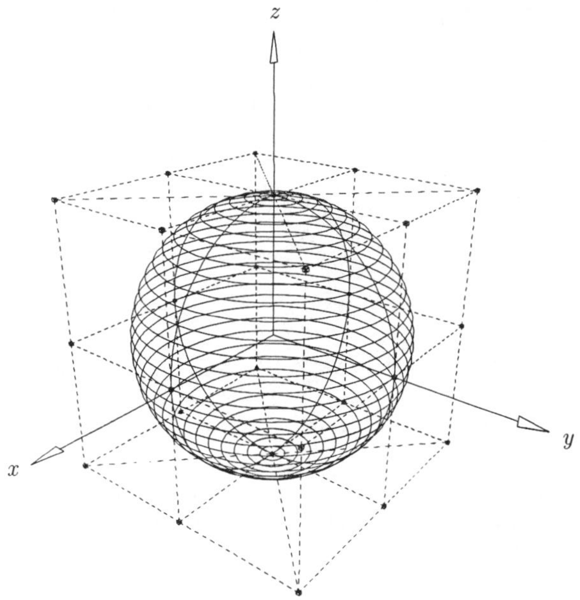

Figure 8.11. A sphere as a surface of revolution.

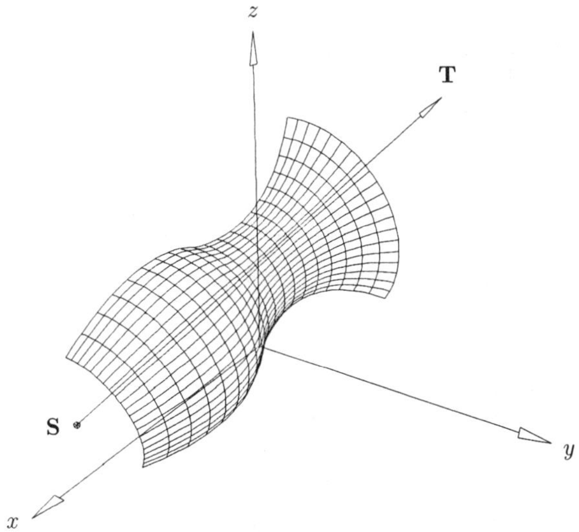

Figure 8.12. A general surface of revolution through an arbitrary angle about an arbitrary axis.

```
    { U[i] = 0.0;   U[j] = 1.0;  }
  n = 2*narcs;
  wm = cos(dtheta/2.0);    /* dtheta/2 is base angle */
  angle = 0.0;   /* Compute sines and cosines only once */
  for (i=1; i<=narcs; i++)
    {
    angle = angle + dtheta;
    cosines[i] = cos(angle);
    sines[i] = sin(angle);
    }
  for (j=0; j<=m; j++)
    /* Loop and compute each u row of ctrl pts and weights */
    {
    PointToLine(S,T,Pj[j],O);
    X = Pj[j]-O;
    r = VecNormalize(X);    VecCrossProd(T,X,Y);
    Pij[0][j] = P0 = Pj[j];   /* Initialize first */
    wij[0][j] = wj[j];        /* ctrl pt and weight */
    T0 = Y;   index = 0;   angle = 0.0;
    for (i=1; i<=narcs; i++)   /* compute u row */
      {
      P2 = O + r*cosines[i]*X + r*sines[i]*Y;
      Pij[index+2][j] = P2;
      wij[index+2][j] = wj[j];
      T2 = -sines[i]*X + cosines[i]*Y;
      Intersect3DLines(P0,T0,P2,T2,Pij[index+1][j]);
      wij[index+1][j] = wm*wj[j];
      index = index + 2;
      if (i < narcs)   { P0 = P2;   T0 = T2;  }
      }
    }
}
```

Figure 8.13 shows a general toroidal patch as a surface of revolution used to round off a sharp corner.

8.6 Nonuniform Scaling of Surfaces

Let $\mathbf{P} = (p_i)$, $i = 1, 2, 3$, be a point in three-dimensional space, and let $F = (f_i)$, $i = 1, 2, 3$, be three real numbers (*scale factors*), one for each coordinate. Scaling $\mathbf{P}$ about the origin by the factors F yields the point

$$\bar{\mathbf{P}} = (\bar{p}_i) \qquad \bar{p}_i = f_i p_i, \;\; i = 1, 2, 3 \tag{8.6}$$

If $\mathbf{C} = (c_i)$ is an arbitrary point, then $\mathbf{P}$ is scaled about $\mathbf{C}$ by the equation

$$\bar{\mathbf{P}} = (\bar{p}_i) \qquad \bar{p}_i = f_i p_i + (1 - f_i)c_i, \;\; i = 1, 2, 3 \tag{8.7}$$

The scaling is called *uniform* if the three f_i are equal; otherwise, it is *nonuniform*.

Several interesting surfaces can be obtained by applying a nonuniform scaling to a surface of revolution. Figure 8.14 shows an ellipsoid, centered at the origin, which has an implicit equation of the form

$$\frac{x^2}{a^2} + \frac{y^2}{b^2} + \frac{z^2}{c^2} = 1 \tag{8.8}$$

The three coordinate planes cut the surface in three ellipses. The ellipsoid is constructed by first producing the unit radius sphere, centered at the origin, and then scaling it about the origin with the factors $F = (a, b, c)$.

Figure 8.15b shows an elliptic paraboloid. The xz and yz planes cut the surface in parabolas; the xy plane cuts it in an ellipse. It has the implicit equation

$$\frac{x^2}{a^2} + \frac{y^2}{b^2} = cz \tag{8.9}$$

The elliptic paraboloid of Figure 8.15b is obtained from the paraboloid of revolution shown in Figure 8.15a by scaling about the origin with the factors $F = (a, b, 1)$.

A nonuniform scaling is performed on a NURBS surface by applying the scale factors to the three-dimensional control points. If the control points are stored in

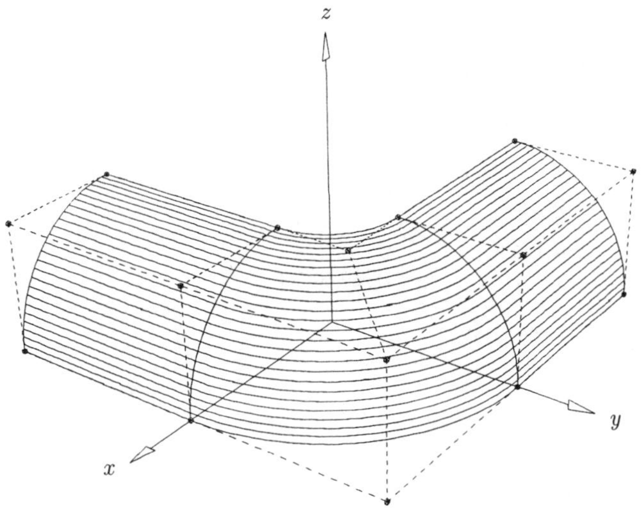

Figure 8.13. A toroidal patch as a surface of revolution used to round a sharp corner.

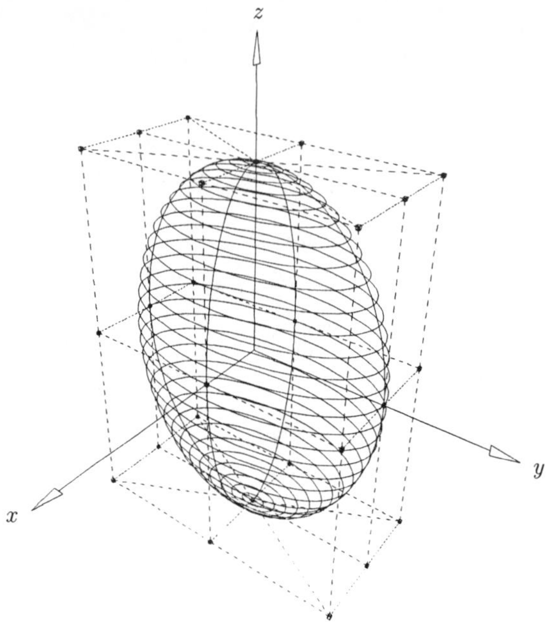

Figure 8.14. An ellipsoid obtained by scaling a sphere.

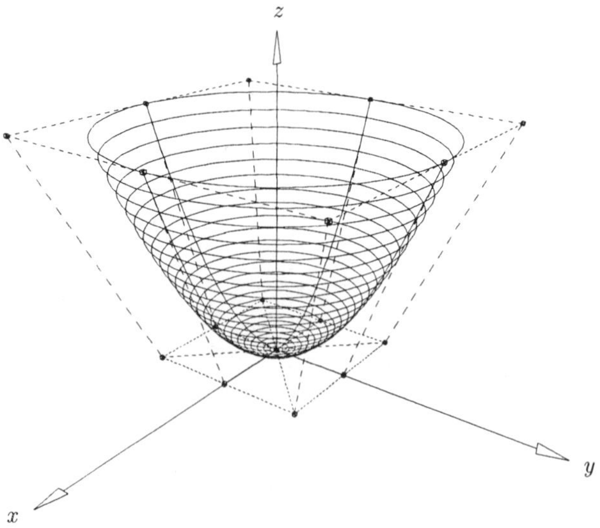

(a)

Figure 8.15. Paraboloids. (a) A paraboloid of revolution; (b) an elliptic paraboloid.

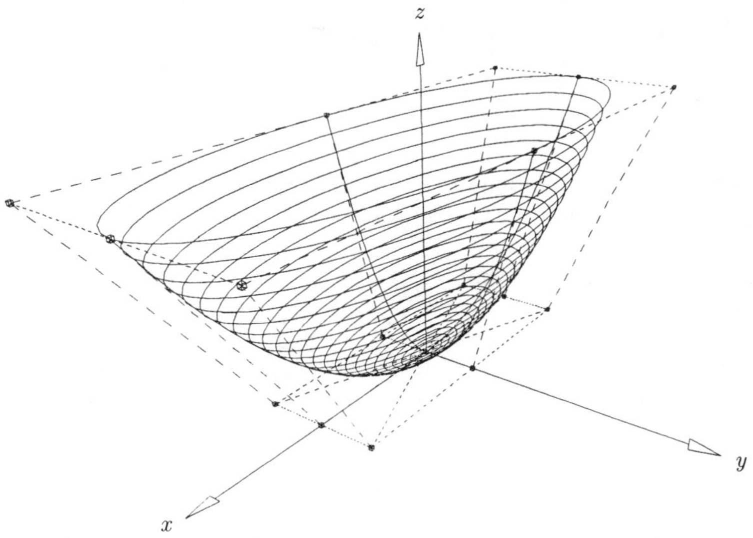

(b)

Figure 8.15. (*Continued.*)

three-dimensional (unweighted) form, then Eq. (8.6) or Eq. (8.7) can be applied directly. The weights do not change. If the control points are stored in four-dimensional form

$$\mathbf{P}^w = (p_1^w, p_2^w, p_3^w, w) = (p_i^w, w) \qquad i = 1,2,3$$

then only the first three coordinates change. Equation (8.6) becomes

$$\bar{\mathbf{P}}^w = (\bar{p}_i^w, w) \qquad \bar{p}_i^w = f_i p_i^w, \;\; i = 1,2,3 \tag{8.10}$$

and Eq. (8.7) becomes

$$\bar{\mathbf{P}}^w = (\bar{p}_i^w, w) \qquad \bar{p}_i^w = f_i p_i^w + (1 - f_i) w c_i, \;\; i = 1,2,3 \tag{8.11}$$

8.7 A Three-sided Spherical Surface

When three surfaces intersect, the result is three edge curves meeting at a corner point (see Figure 8.16a). Since sharp edges and corners are often undesirable in manufactured parts, surfaces are required which "smooth" or "round off" the sharp edges and corners. These are called *fillet* surfaces. A common conceptual method of obtaining fillet surfaces is the rolling marble model. If a marble with radius R is rolled along all the edge curves and into the corner, the surfaces $\mathbf{S}_4$–$\mathbf{S}_7$ of Figure 8.16b are obtained. $\mathbf{S}_4$–$\mathbf{S}_6$ are *edge fillets*, and $\mathbf{S}_7$ is a *corner fillet.* Cross sections of $\mathbf{S}_4$–$\mathbf{S}_6$ perpendicular to the directions of the respective edge curves are circular arcs of radius R, whose arc length varies as the angle between the surfaces varies along an edge. In general, these surfaces are quite complex and cannot be represented precisely in NURBS form. Using NURBS, they are usually approximated to within some user-specified tolerance. The corner fillet, $\mathbf{S}_7$, is a three-sided *patch*, lying on a sphere of radius R. We use the term patch to mean a subsurface of some larger surface. The three boundary curves are circular arcs of radius R, whose centers coincide with the center of the sphere. Furthermore, assuming the surfaces do not meet tangentially, the arcs have sweep angles less than 180° and therefore can each be represented with one Bézier segment with all positive weights. The corner fillet is precisely representable as a (4×2)-degree NURBS surface, with one degenerate boundary.

In addition to obtaining a corner fillet surface, the method presented here is a simple and specific case of a more general technique to construct tensor product patches on quadric surfaces. A *quadric surface* is any surface having a second-order implicit equation of the form

$$S(x,y,z) = ax^2 + by^2 + cz^2 + dxy + exz + fyz + gx + hy + iz + j = 0 \qquad (8.12)$$

Spheres, ellipsoids, hyperboloids, paraboloids, and circular cylinders and cones are examples of quadric surfaces. All of these, and many other important surfaces such as tori and a surface of revolution whose generating curve is quadratic, are generated by two families of curves of maximum degree 2. For example, a sphere is generated by two families of circles (circles of latitude and longitude), and the right circular cylinder by a family of straight lines and a family of circles. The techniques of Sections 8.2–8.6 can be used to construct patches on these surfaces if the patch boundary curves are portions of curves comprising the two generating families. The resulting surface patch is biquadratic. If the patch boundaries do not follow the generating families (as in the case of the general corner fillet), then the situation is more complex, and the patch may not even be representable as a NURBS surface. Some results and algorithms have been obtained for the case that the underlying surface is quadric and the patch boundaries are conic sections, e.g., see [Geis90; Boeh91; Hosc92a].

We now show how to construct a corner fillet. Although the details are rather messy, the method is conceptually quite simple; we simply compose two mappings. Without loss of generality we assume that the underlying sphere has radius R and is centered at $(0,0,R)$ (see Figure 8.17). The well-known *stereographic projection* (see [Coxe67; DoCa76]) yields a rational parametric representation of the sphere $\mathbf{S}_1(u,v) = \big(x(u,v), y(u,v), z(u,v)\big)$, where

$$x(u,v) = \frac{4R^2u}{u^2+v^2+4R^2}$$

$$y(u,v) = \frac{4R^2v}{u^2+v^2+4R^2}$$

$$z(u,v) = \frac{2R(u^2+v^2)}{u^2+v^2+4R^2} \qquad (8.13)$$

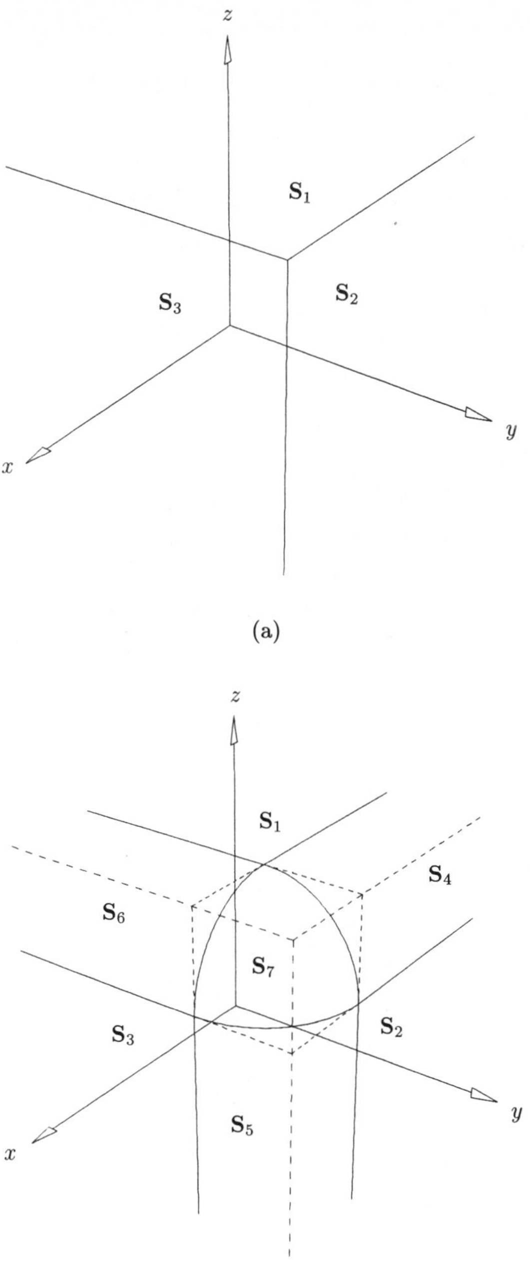

(b)

Figure 8.16. Rounding edges and a corner. (a) Three edges and a corner formed by three intersecting planes; (b) three edge fillet surfaces and one corner fillet surface formed by rolling a marble; the rounded corner and the three edges are shown dashed.

that is, a (u, v) point maps into the (x, y, z) point which is at the intersection of the sphere and the line segment from $(u, v, 0)$ to $(0, 0, 2R)$ (see Figure 8.17). Under this projection we have the following correspondences:

- straight lines passing through the origin of the xy plane map to longitudinal circles on the sphere;
- all other circles on the sphere correspond to circles in the xy plane.

The three boundaries of the fillet surface are circular arcs of radius R, with centers at $(0, 0, R)$. Denote these arcs by $\mathbf{C}_1(t), \mathbf{C}_2(s), \mathbf{C}_3(t)$, with $0 \leq s,\ t \leq 1$. Without loss of generality we assume that the patch boundaries are positioned and oriented as (see Figure 8.18):

- $\mathbf{C}_1(t)$ and $\mathbf{C}_3(t)$ start at the origin: $\mathbf{C}_1(0) = \mathbf{C}_3(0) = (0, 0, 0)$;
- $\mathbf{C}_1(t)$ lies in the xz plane;
- $\mathbf{C}_1(1) = \mathbf{C}_2(0)$ and $\mathbf{C}_2(1) = \mathbf{C}_3(1)$.

Then the projection of the fillet patch yields a flat surface, $\mathbf{S}_2(s, t) = \big(u(s, t), v(s, t), 0\big)$ in the xy plane. The $s = 0$ and $s = 1$ boundaries of $\mathbf{S}_2(s, t)$ are straight lines, the $t = 0$ boundary is degenerate, and the $t = 1$ boundary is a circular arc. Hence, $\mathbf{S}_2(s, t)$ has degree $(2, 1)$ and the composition mapping $\mathbf{S}(s, t) = \mathbf{S}_1 \circ \mathbf{S}_2$ yields a (4×2)-degree rational Bézier representation of the fillet surface.

Clearly, general formulas can be derived for computing the control points and weights of $\mathbf{S}(s, t)$. However, as most terms are zero anyway, we specifically derive the formulas for each coordinate and weight separately. The computation is:

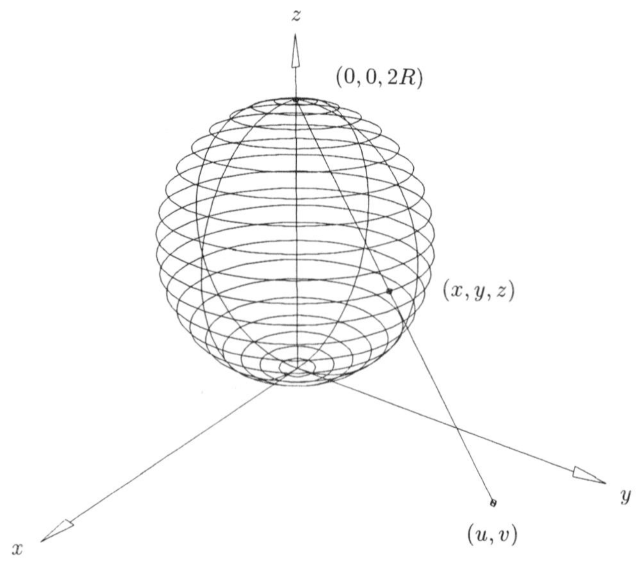

Figure 8.17. Stereographic projection.

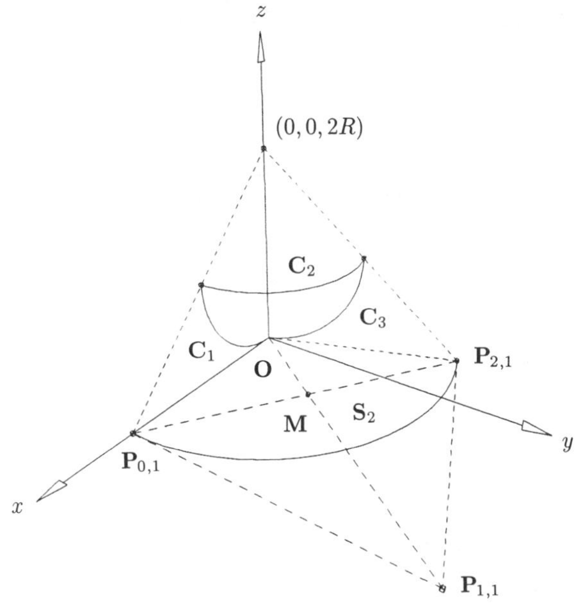

Figure 8.18. The flat surface $\mathbf{S}_2$ obtained by projecting the fillet surface onto the xy plane.

1. obtain the Bézier representation of $\mathbf{S}_2(s,t)$;
2. convert $\mathbf{S}_2(s,t)$ to power basis form;
3. substitute the power basis coefficients of $\mathbf{S}_2(s,t)$ into $\mathbf{S}_1(u,v)$ (Eq. [8.13]) to obtain the power basis form of the fillet patch, $\mathbf{S}(s,t)$;
4. convert $\mathbf{S}(s,t)$ to Bézier form.

The Bézier representation of $\mathbf{S}_2(s,t)$ requires six four-dimensional control points, $\mathbf{P}^w_{i,j}$, $0 \le i \le 2$, $0 \le j \le 1$. Clearly, $\mathbf{P}_{0,0} = \mathbf{P}_{1,0} = \mathbf{P}_{2,0} = (0,0,0)$, with $w_{0,0} = w_{2,0} = 1$. $w_{1,0}$ is set equal to $w_{1,1}$, which must still be computed later. $\mathbf{P}^w_{i,1}$, $0 \le i \le 2$, are the control points of the circular arc which is the projection of $\mathbf{C}_2(s)$. They are obtained as follows:

1. project the three points $\mathbf{C}_2(0)$, $\mathbf{C}_2(1/2)$, and $\mathbf{C}_2(1)$ to the circular arc in the xy plane. Let (x,y,z) be the coordinates of one of these points; then the uv coordinates of the projection are computed by the formula

$$\alpha = \frac{-2R}{z-2R} \qquad u = \alpha x, \;\; v = \alpha y \tag{8.14}$$

   This yields $\mathbf{P}^w_{0,1}$ and $\mathbf{P}^w_{2,1}$ ($w_{0,1} = w_{2,1} = 1$).

2. compute the center ($\mathbf{O}$ in Figure 8.18) and the radius, r, of the projected arc; for example, $\mathbf{O}$ is found by intersecting the perpendicular bisectors

of two of the chords formed by the projections of the three points, $\mathbf{C}_2(0)$, $\mathbf{C}_2(1/2)$, and $\mathbf{C}_2(1)$;

3. then compute $\mathbf{P}^w_{1,1}$ by (see Figure 8.18):
   - compute $\mathbf{M} = 1/2(\mathbf{P}_{0,1} + \mathbf{P}_{2,1})$;
   - $\mathbf{P}_{1,1}$ is the inverse of $\mathbf{M}$ with respect to the projected circular arc (see [Coxe67]), hence $\mathbf{OM} \cdot \mathbf{OP}_{1,1} = r^2$; from this we get

$$\mathbf{P}_{1,1} = (1-\alpha)\mathbf{O} + \alpha\mathbf{M}$$

where

$$\alpha = \frac{r^2}{|\,\mathbf{OM}\,|^2};$$

   - from Eq. (7.33), $w_{1,1} = \cos \angle \mathbf{P}_{1,1}\mathbf{P}_{2,1}\mathbf{P}_{0,1}$.

Let $[\mathbf{a}^w_{i,j}]$ denote the power basis coefficients of $\mathbf{S}^w_2(s,t)$. From Eq. (6.91) it follows that

$$[\,\mathbf{a}^w_{i,j}\,] = M_2\,[\,\mathbf{P}^w_{i,j}\,]\,M_1^T$$

where M_2 and M_1 are the second- and first-order Bézier matrices, respectively (Eq. [6.80]). Applying the matrix multiplications yields

$$\begin{aligned}
\mathbf{a}^w_{0,0} &= \mathbf{P}^w_{0,0}\\
\mathbf{a}^w_{0,1} &= \mathbf{P}^w_{0,1} - \mathbf{P}^w_{0,0}\\
\mathbf{a}^w_{1,0} &= 2(\mathbf{P}^w_{1,0} - \mathbf{P}^w_{0,0})\\
\mathbf{a}^w_{1,1} &= 2(\mathbf{P}^w_{1,1} + \mathbf{P}^w_{0,0} - \mathbf{P}^w_{0,1} - \mathbf{P}^w_{1,0})\\
\mathbf{a}^w_{2,0} &= \mathbf{P}^w_{0,0} - 2\mathbf{P}^w_{1,0} + \mathbf{P}^w_{2,0}\\
\mathbf{a}^w_{2,1} &= \mathbf{P}^w_{0,1} + \mathbf{P}^w_{2,1} - \mathbf{P}^w_{0,0} - \mathbf{P}^w_{2,0} + 2(\mathbf{P}^w_{1,0} - \mathbf{P}^w_{1,1})
\end{aligned} \tag{8.15}$$

Now let

$$\mathbf{a}^w_{i,j} = (u_{i,j}, v_{i,j}, h_{i,j}) \tag{8.16}$$

(note that the $u_{i,j}$ and $v_{i,j}$ are weighted). The z coordinate is zero, and to avoid a conflict later we use h instead of w for a weight. Denote the control points of the circular arc by $\mathbf{P}^w_{i,1} = (\alpha_i, \beta_i, \gamma_i)$, $0 \le i \le 2$ (α_i and β_i weighted). Assuming corner weights to be 1, and considering the fact that $\mathbf{C}_1(t)$ lies in the xz plane and $\mathbf{C}_1(0) = (0,0,0)$, it follows that the only nonzero $u_{i,j}$, $v_{i,j}$, and $h_{i,j}$ are

$$\begin{aligned}
u_{0,1} &= \alpha_0\\
u_{1,1} &= 2(\alpha_1 - \alpha_0)\\
u_{2,1} &= \alpha_2 + \alpha_0 - 2\alpha_1\\
v_{1,1} &= 2\beta_1\\
v_{2,1} &= \beta_2 - 2\beta_1\\
h_{0,0} &= 1\\
h_{1,0} &= 2(\gamma_1 - 1)\\
h_{2,0} &= 2(1 - \gamma_1)
\end{aligned} \tag{8.17}$$

Using Eqs. (8.16) and (8.17) and the power basis form

$$\mathbf{S}_2^w(s,t) = \begin{bmatrix} 1 & s & s^2 \end{bmatrix} \begin{bmatrix} \mathbf{a}_{i,j}^w \end{bmatrix} \begin{bmatrix} 1 \\ t \end{bmatrix} \tag{8.18}$$

we obtain

$$\mathbf{S}_2(s,t) = \big(u(s,t), v(s,t)\big)$$

with

$$u(s,t) = \frac{U(s,t)}{H(s,t)} \qquad v(s,t) = \frac{V(s,t)}{H(s,t)} \tag{8.19}$$

and

$$U(s,t) = u_{0,1}t + u_{1,1}st + u_{2,1}s^2t$$

$$V(s,t) = v_{1,1}st + v_{2,1}s^2t$$

$$H(s,t) = h_{0,0} + h_{1,0}s + h_{2,0}s^2 \tag{8.20}$$

Substituting Eqs. (8.19) and (8.20) into Eq. (8.13), we have

$$\mathbf{S}(s,t) = \big(x(s,t), y(s,t), z(s,t)\big) \tag{8.21}$$

with

$$x(s,t) = \frac{X(s,t)}{W(s,t)} \quad y(s,t) = \frac{Y(s,t)}{W(s,t)} \quad z(s,t) = \frac{Z(s,t)}{W(s,t)} \tag{8.22}$$

and

$$\begin{aligned} X(s,t) &= 4R^2U(s,t)H(s,t) \\ &= 4R^2(u_{0,1}t + u_{1,1}st + u_{2,1}s^2t)(h_{0,0} + h_{1,0}s + h_{2,0}s^2) \\ &= 4R^2[u_{0,1}h_{0,0}t + (u_{1,1}h_{0,0} + u_{0,1}h_{1,0})st \\ &\quad + (u_{2,1}h_{0,0} + u_{1,1}h_{1,0} + u_{0,1}h_{2,0})s^2t \\ &\quad + (u_{2,1}h_{1,0} + u_{1,1}h_{2,0})s^3t + u_{2,1}h_{2,0}s^4t] \end{aligned} \tag{8.23}$$

$$\begin{aligned} Y(s,t) &= 4R^2V(s,t)H(s,t) \\ &= 4R^2(v_{1,1}st + v_{2,1}s^2t)(h_{0,0} + h_{1,0}s + h_{2,0}s^2) \\ &= 4R^2[v_{1,1}h_{0,0}st + (v_{2,1}h_{0,0} + v_{1,1}h_{1,0})s^2t \\ &\quad + (v_{1,1}h_{2,0} + v_{2,1}h_{1,0})s^3t + v_{2,1}h_{2,0}s^4t] \end{aligned} \tag{8.24}$$

$$\begin{aligned} Z(s,t) &= 2R\left[U(s,t)^2 + V(s,t)^2\right] \\ &= 2R\left[u_{0,1}^2t^2 + 2u_{0,1}u_{1,1}st^2 + (u_{1,1}^2 + 2u_{0,1}u_{2,1} + v_{1,1}^2)s^2t^2\right. \\ &\quad \left. + 2(u_{1,1}u_{2,1} + v_{1,1}v_{2,1})s^3t^2 + (u_{2,1}^2 + v_{2,1}^2)s^4t^2\right] \end{aligned} \tag{8.25}$$

$$\begin{aligned} W(s,t) &= U(s,t)^2 + V(s,t)^2 + 4R^2H(s,t)^2 \\ &= 4R^2h_{0,0}^2 + 8R^2h_{0,0}h_{1,0}s + 4R^2(h_{1,0}^2 + 2h_{0,0}h_{2,0})s^2 + u_{0,1}^2t^2 \\ &\quad + 8R^2h_{1,0}h_{2,0}s^3 + 2u_{0,1}u_{1,1}st^2 + 4R^2h_{2,0}^2s^4 \\ &\quad + (u_{1,1}^2 + 2u_{0,1}u_{2,1} + v_{1,1}^2)s^2t^2 \\ &\quad + 2(u_{1,1}u_{2,1} + v_{1,1}v_{2,1})s^3t^2 + (u_{2,1}^2 + v_{2,1}^2)s^4t^2 \end{aligned} \tag{8.26}$$

Denote by

$$\mathbf{S}^w(s,t) = [\,s^i\,][\,\mathbf{b}^w_{i,j}\,][\,t^j\,]^T \qquad 0 \le i \le 4 \quad 0 \le j \le 2 \tag{8.27}$$

the power basis representation of $\mathbf{S}^w(s,t)$, and let $\mathbf{b}^w_{i,j} = (x_{i,j}, y_{i,j}, z_{i,j}, w_{i,j})$. Most of the coordinates of the $\mathbf{b}^w_{i,j}$ are zero. The only nonzero elements are

$$\begin{aligned}
x_{0,1} &= 4R^2 u_{0,1} h_{0,0} \\
x_{1,1} &= 4R^2 (u_{1,1} h_{0,0} + u_{0,1} h_{1,0}) \\
x_{2,1} &= 4R^2 (u_{2,1} h_{0,0} + u_{1,1} h_{1,0} + u_{0,1} h_{2,0}) \\
x_{3,1} &= 4R^2 (u_{2,1} h_{1,0} + u_{1,1} h_{2,0}) \\
x_{4,1} &= 4R^2 u_{2,1} h_{2,0}
\end{aligned} \tag{8.28}$$

$$\begin{aligned}
y_{1,1} &= 4R^2 v_{1,1} h_{0,0} \\
y_{2,1} &= 4R^2 (v_{2,1} h_{0,0} + v_{1,1} h_{1,0}) \\
y_{3,1} &= 4R^2 (v_{1,1} h_{2,0} + v_{2,1} h_{1,0}) \\
y_{4,1} &= 4R^2 v_{2,1} h_{2,0}
\end{aligned} \tag{8.29}$$

$$\begin{aligned}
z_{0,2} &= 2R u_{0,1}^2 \\
z_{1,2} &= 4R u_{0,1} u_{1,1} \\
z_{2,2} &= 2R (u_{1,1}^2 + 2u_{0,1} u_{2,1} + v_{1,1}^2) \\
z_{3,2} &= 4R (u_{1,1} u_{2,1} + v_{1,1} v_{2,1}) \\
z_{4,2} &= 2R (u_{2,1}^2 + v_{2,1}^2)
\end{aligned} \tag{8.30}$$

$$\begin{aligned}
w_{0,0} &= 4R^2 h_{0,0}^2 \\
w_{1,0} &= 8R^2 h_{0,0} h_{1,0} \\
w_{2,0} &= 4R^2 (h_{1,0}^2 + 2h_{0,0} h_{2,0}) \\
w_{3,0} &= 8R^2 h_{1,0} h_{2,0} \\
w_{4,0} &= 4R^2 h_{2,0}^2 \\
w_{0,2} &= u_{0,1}^2 \\
w_{1,2} &= 2u_{0,1} u_{1,1} \\
w_{2,2} &= u_{1,1}^2 + 2u_{0,1} u_{2,1} + v_{1,1}^2 \\
w_{3,2} &= 2(u_{1,1} u_{2,1} + v_{1,1} v_{2,1}) \\
w_{4,2} &= u_{2,1}^2 + v_{2,1}^2
\end{aligned} \tag{8.31}$$

Equations (8.27)–(8.31) give the power basis form of the fillet surface $\mathbf{S}^w(s,t)$. The Bézier (NURBS) representation is obtained by applying Eq. (6.100), that is

$$[\,\mathbf{P}^w_{i,j}\,] = M_4^{-1}\,[\,\mathbf{b}^w_{i,j}\,]\,(M_2^{-1})^T$$

Algorithm `A6.2` is used to compute M_4^{-1} and M_2^{-1}.

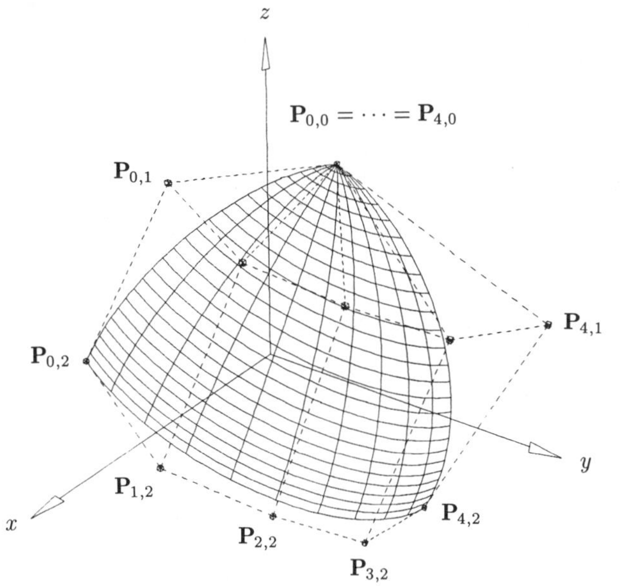

Figure 8.19. A corner fillet surface – an arbitrary spherical patch whose boundaries are great circles of the sphere.

We now summarize the complete algorithm. Input to the algorithm are three boundary arcs, $\mathbf{C}_1$, $\mathbf{C}_2$, and $\mathbf{C}_3$, arbitrarily positioned and oriented in space but joined at their endpoints. Output is a (4×2)-degree rational Bézier fillet patch.

```
ALGORITHM A8.2
  MakeCornerFilletSurf(C1,C2,C3,Pwij)
    { /* Create NURBS corner fillet surface */
      /* Input: C1,C2,C3 */
      /* Output: Pwij */
    1. Compute the common radius and center point of the three
       boundary arcs.
    2. Using translation, rotation and possibly curve reversal
       (see Chapter 6), position and orient the boundary arcs
       as in Figure 8.18. Note that, in fact, only C2 must
       actually be positioned and oriented, as only it is
       required in order to compute the three control points
       P^w_{i,1} = (α_i,β_i,γ_i).
    3. Compute the (α_i,β_i,γ_i) as described above.
    4. Convert S^w_2(s,t) from Bézier to power basis form
       (Eq. [8.17]).
    5. Compute the power basis form of the fillet patch
       S^w = S^w_1 ∘ S^w_2 (Eqs. [8.27]-[8.31]).
```

6. `Convert` $\mathbf{S}^w(s,t)$ `to rational Bézier form (Eq. [8.32] and Algorithm A6.2).`
7. `Rotate/translate` $\mathbf{S}(s,t)$ `back to the correct location in three-dimensional space (the inverse transformation of Step 2).`

}

Figure 8.19 shows a corner fillet patch constructed by Algorithm `A8.2`.

CHAPTER

NINE

Curve and Surface Fitting

9.1 Introduction

In Chapters 7 and 8 we showed how to construct NURBS representations of common and relatively simple curves and surfaces such as circles, conics, cylinders, surfaces of revolution, etc. These entities can be specified with only a few data items, e.g., center point, height, radius, axis of revolution, etc. Moreover, the few data items uniquely specify the geometric entity. In this chapter we enter the realm of free-form (or sculptured) curves and surfaces. We study *fitting*, i.e., the construction of NURBS curves and surfaces which fit a rather arbitrary set of geometric data, such as points and derivative vectors. We distinguish two types of fitting, *interpolation* and *approximation*. In interpolation we construct a curve or surface which satisfies the given data precisely, e.g., the curve passes through the given points and assumes the given derivatives at the prescribed points. Figure 9.1 shows a curve interpolating five points and the first derivative vectors at the endpoints. In approximation, we construct curves and surfaces which do not necessarily satisfy the given data precisely, but only approximately. In some applications – such as generation of point data by use of coordinate measuring devices or digitizing tablets, or the computation of surface/surface intersection points by marching methods – a large number of points can be generated, and they can contain measurement or computational noise. In this case it is important for the curve or surface to capture the "shape" of the data, but not to "wiggle" its way through every point. In approximation it is often desirable to specify a maximum bound on the deviation of the curve or surface from the given data, and to specify certain *constraints*, i.e., data which is to be satisfied precisely. Figure 9.2 shows a curve approximating a set of $m+1$ points. A maximum deviation bound, E, was specified, and the perpendicular distance, e_i, is the approximation error obtained by projecting $\mathbf{Q}_i$ on to the curve. The e_i of each point, $\mathbf{Q}_i$, is less than E. The endpoints $\mathbf{Q}_0$ and $\mathbf{Q}_m$ were specified as constraints, with the result that $e_0 = e_m = 0$.

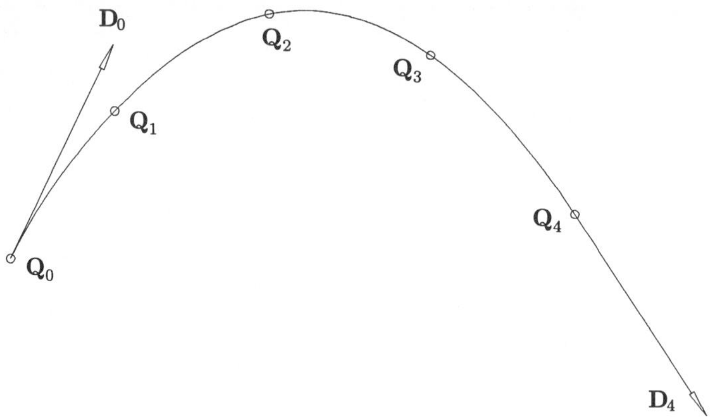

Figure 9.1. A curve interpolating five points and two end derivatives.

There are many subtleties in fitting, and literally hundreds of papers have been written on this topic. Many of the techniques are heuristic, and there are usually no unique or clear-cut "right" answers. A fundamental problem is that the given data never specifies a unique solution. There are infinitely many NURBS curves which can interpolate the seven data items in Figure 9.1, or approximate the $m+1$ items in Figure 9.2. How often has the implementor of a fitting algorithm been told by a designer using the software: "but that's not the curve I wanted!". And the reply is often: "well, it's mathematically correct; it satisfies the data you gave me!".

Input to a fitting problem generally consists of geometric data, such as points and derivatives. Output is a NURBS curve or surface, i.e., control points, knots, and weights. Furthermore, either the degree p $\big($or (p,q) for surfaces$\big)$ must be input or the algorithm must select an appropriate degree. If C^r continuity is

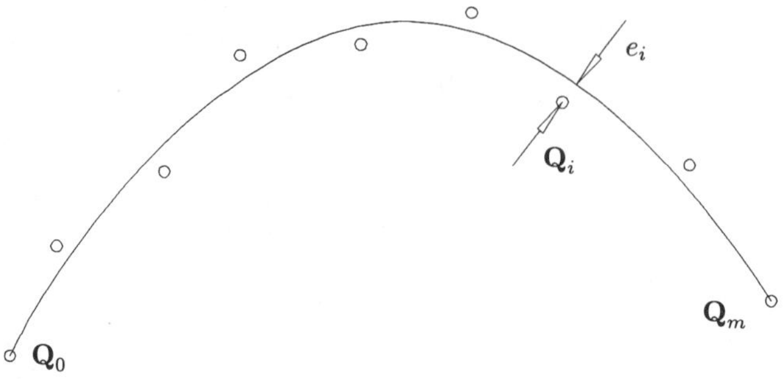

Figure 9.2. A curve approximating $m+1$ points; the curve is constrained to pass through the endpoints, $\mathbf{Q}_0$ and $\mathbf{Q}_m$.

desired for a curve, then the chosen degree p must satisfy

$$p \geq r + 1 \tag{9.1}$$

(assuming no interior knots of multiplicity > 1). Assuming no other requirements, choosing $p = r + 1$ is generally adequate for interpolation. For approximation, choosing $p > r + 1$ may produce better results. For example, suppose we want a C^1 continuous curve approximation to point data representing a twisted curve in three-dimensional space. Using a cubic will likely yield a curve with much fewer control points than a quadratic, although a quadratic gives us the desired continuity. Very little has been published on setting the weights in the fitting process. Most often, all weights are simply set to 1. Indeed, for interpolation there is probably little reason to do otherwise (an exception being when fitting with piecewise circular arcs [Hosc92b]). For approximation, allowing weights to be arbitrary should produce curves and surfaces with fewer control points; we present one such algorithm. Finally, there are many methods for choosing the knots, most of them heuristic.

Most fitting algorithms fall into one of two categories: *global* or *local*. With a global algorithm, a system of equations or an optimization problem is set up and solved. If the given data consists of only points and derivatives, and if the control points are the only unknowns (degree, knots, and weights have been preselected), then the system is linear and hence easy to solve. If more esoteric data, such as curvature, is given, or knots and/or weights are also system unknowns, then the resulting system is nonlinear. Theoretically, a perturbation of any one input data item can change the shape of the entire curve or surface; however, the magnitude of the change decreases with increasing distance from the affected data item. Local algorithms are more geometric in nature, constructing the curve or surface segment-wise, using only local data for each step. A perturbation in a data item only changes the curve or surface locally. These algorithms are usually computationally less expensive than global methods. They can also deal with cusps, straight line segments, and other local data anomalies better. However, achieving desired levels of continuity at segment boundaries is more of a headache, and local methods often result in multiple interior knots.

In subsequent sections we present a number of global and local methods of curve and surface interpolation and approximation. The methods were chosen for their proven utility, and because they represent a broad cross section of techniques. We emphasize that this chapter does not treat interactive curve and surface design, although many of the techniques covered here are applicable to that topic. Interactive design in a NURBS framework generally takes one (or both) of the following approaches:

- given a NURBS curve or surface, interactively change its shape by modifying weights and/or control points; these techniques are treated in Chapter 11;
- interactively construct a NURBS curve or surface. Local fitting techniques are particularly well-suited to this task. Polynomial or rational segments

of any type (e.g., Hermite, Bézier) can be individually constructed and shaped. In addition to local controls, some methods provide global controls, such as a global tension parameter. Whatever the method, if the result is a piecewise polynomial or rational curve or surface, it generally can be converted to NURBS form as the final step.

9.2 Global Interpolation

In this section we present methods to interpolate a curve to point and derivative data, and to interpolate a surface to point data.

9.2.1 GLOBAL CURVE INTERPOLATION TO POINT DATA

Suppose we are given a set of points $\{\mathbf{Q}_k\}$, $k = 0, \ldots, n$, and we want to interpolate these points with a pth-degree nonrational B-spline curve. If we assign a parameter value, $\bar{u}_k$, to each $\mathbf{Q}_k$, and select an appropriate knot vector $U = \{u_0, \ldots, u_m\}$, we can set up the $(n+1) \times (n+1)$ system of linear equations

$$\mathbf{Q}_k = \mathbf{C}(\bar{u}_k) = \sum_{i=0}^{n} N_{i,p}(\bar{u}_k)\,\mathbf{P}_i \tag{9.2}$$

The control points, $\mathbf{P}_i$, are the $n+1$ unknowns. Let r be the number of coordinates in the $\mathbf{Q}_k$ (typically 2, 3, or 4). Note that this method is independent of r; Eq. (9.2) has one coefficient matrix, with r right hand sides and, correspondingly, r solution sets for the r coordinates of the $\mathbf{P}_i$.

The problem of choosing the $\bar{u}_k$ and U remains, and their choice affects the shape and parameterization of the curve. Throughout this section we assume that the parameter lies in the range $u \in [0, 1]$. Three common methods of choosing the $\bar{u}_k$ are:

- equally spaced:

$$\bar{u}_0 = 0 \qquad \bar{u}_n = 1$$

$$\bar{u}_k = \frac{k}{n} \qquad k = 1, \ldots, n-1 \tag{9.3}$$

  This method is not recommended, as it can produce erratic shapes (such as loops) when the data is unevenly spaced;

- chord length: Let d be the total chord length

$$d = \sum_{k=1}^{n} |\,\mathbf{Q}_k - \mathbf{Q}_{k-1}\,| \tag{9.4}$$

  Then $\qquad \bar{u}_0 = 0 \qquad \bar{u}_n = 1$

$$\bar{u}_k = \bar{u}_{k-1} + \frac{|\,\mathbf{Q}_k - \mathbf{Q}_{k-1}\,|}{d} \qquad k = 1, \ldots, n-1 \tag{9.5}$$

This is the most widely used method, and it is generally adequate. It also gives a "good" parameterization to the curve, in the sense that it approximates a uniform parameterization.

- centripetal method: Let

$$d = \sum_{k=1}^{n} \sqrt{|\,\mathbf{Q}_k - \mathbf{Q}_{k-1}\,|}$$

Then $\bar{u}_0 = 0 \qquad \bar{u}_n = 1$

$$\bar{u}_k = \bar{u}_{k-1} + \frac{\sqrt{|\,\mathbf{Q}_k - \mathbf{Q}_{k-1}\,|}}{d} \qquad k = 1, \ldots, n-1 \tag{9.6}$$

This is a newer method (see [Lee89]) which gives better results than the chord length method when the data takes very sharp turns.

Knots can be equally spaced, that is,

$$u_0 = \cdots = u_p = 0 \qquad u_{m-p} = \cdots = u_m = 1$$

$$u_{j+p} = \frac{j}{n-p+1} \qquad j = 1, \ldots, n-p \tag{9.7}$$

However, this method is not recommended; if used in conjunction with Eqs. (9.5) or (9.6) it can result in a singular system of equations (Eq. [9.2]). We recommend the following technique of *averaging*

$$u_0 = \cdots = u_p = 0 \qquad u_{m-p} = \cdots = u_m = 1$$

$$u_{j+p} = \frac{1}{p} \sum_{i=j}^{j+p-1} \bar{u}_i \qquad j = 1, \ldots, n-p \tag{9.8}$$

With this method the knots reflect the distribution of the $\bar{u}_k$. Furthermore, using Eq. (9.8) combined with Eq. (9.5) or (9.6) to compute the $\bar{u}_k$ leads to a system (Eq. [9.2]) which is totally positive and banded with a semibandwidth less than p (see [DeBo78]), that is, $N_{i,p}(\bar{u}_k) = 0$ if $|\,i - k\,| \geq p$. Hence, it can be solved by Gaussian elimination without pivoting.

Figure 9.3 shows control points, parameters, and the knot vector of a cubic curve interpolating seven points. Parameters were chosen by the chord length method, and the knots were obtained by averaging the parameters (Eq. [9.8]). In Figure 9.4 a comparison of different parameterizations is illustrated. Figure 9.5 shows the same comparison using more "wildly" scattered data points. In both cases a cubic curve is passed through seven points, using uniform parameters and uniform knots (solid curve and top knot vector – see Eqs. [9.3] and [9.7]); chord length parameters and knots obtained by averaging (dashed curve and middle

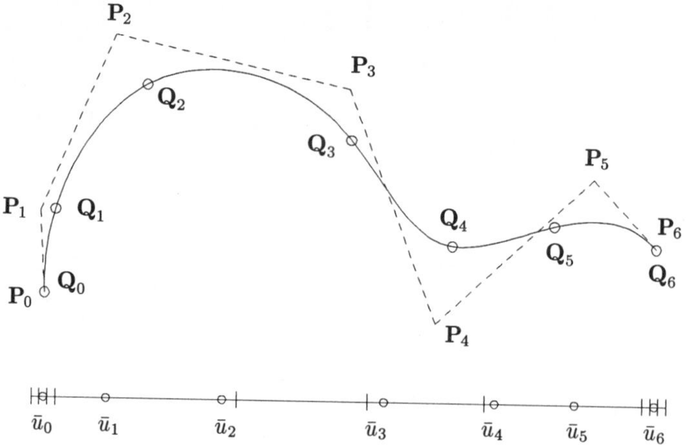

Figure 9.3. A curve interpolation example using chord length parameterization and a knot vector obtained by averaging parameters.

knot vector – see Eqs. [9.5] and [9.8]); and centripetal parameters and knots obtained by averaging (dotted curve and bottom knot vector – see Eqs. [9.6] and [9.8]). In Figure 9.5 notice how the chord length and centripetal parameterized curves adapt to the changes in point spacing.

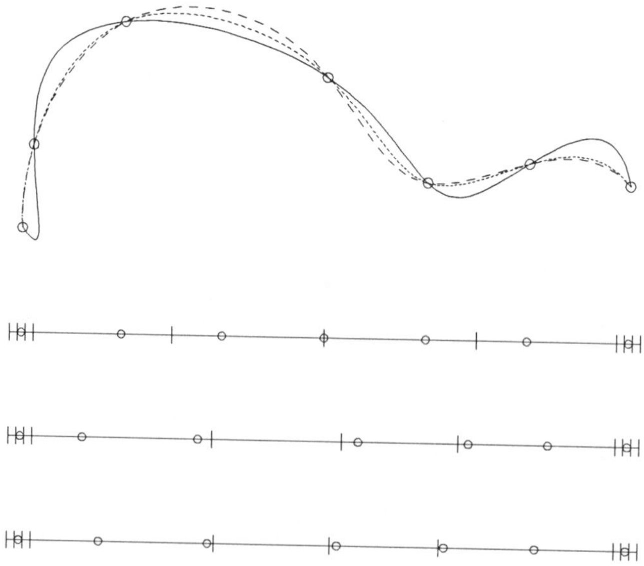

Figure 9.4. A curve interpolation example with different parameterizations and knot vectors.

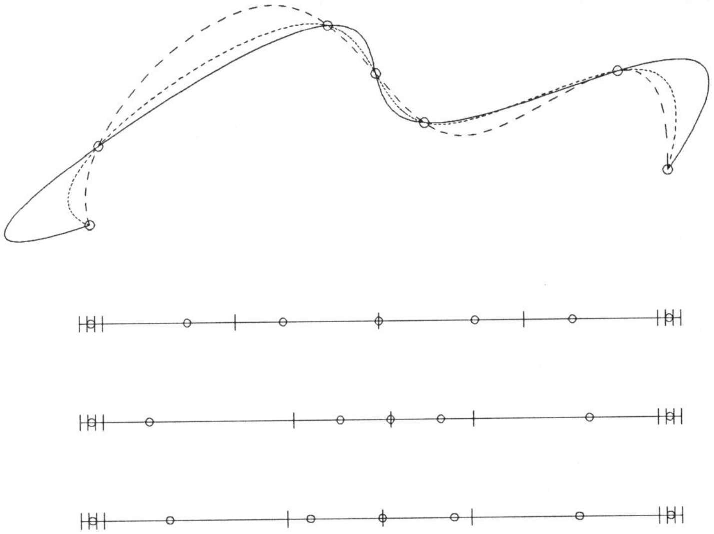

Figure 9.5. A curve interpolation example with different parameterizations and knot vectors.

Figure 9.6 illustrates interpolation with different degrees; solid, dashed, and dotted curves have degrees 2, 3, and 4, respectively. Figure 9.7 shows the inability of the global interpolant to handle collinear point sets.

Once the $\bar{u}_k$ and the knots are computed, the $(n+1)\times(n+1)$ coefficient matrix of the system (Eq. [9.2]) is set up by evaluating the nonzero basis functions at each $\bar{u}_k$, $k=0,\ldots,n$; use Algorithms A2.1 and A2.2.

Example

Ex9.1 Let $\{\mathbf{Q}_k\} = \{(0,0),(3,4),(-1,4),(-4,0),(-4,-3)\}$, and assume that we want to interpolate the $\mathbf{Q}_k$ with a cubic curve. We use Eqs. (9.5) and (9.8) to compute the $\bar{u}_k$ and u_j, and then set up the system of linear equations, Eq. (9.2). The separate chord lengths are

$$|\mathbf{Q}_1-\mathbf{Q}_0|=5 \quad |\mathbf{Q}_2-\mathbf{Q}_1|=4 \quad |\mathbf{Q}_3-\mathbf{Q}_2|=5 \quad |\mathbf{Q}_4-\mathbf{Q}_3|=3$$

and the total chord length is $d=17$. Thus

$$\bar{u}_0=0 \quad \bar{u}_1=\frac{5}{17} \quad \bar{u}_2=\frac{9}{17} \quad \bar{u}_3=\frac{14}{17} \quad \bar{u}_4=1$$

Using Eq. (9.8)

$$u_4=\frac{1}{3}\left(\frac{5}{17}+\frac{9}{17}+\frac{14}{17}\right)=\frac{28}{51}$$

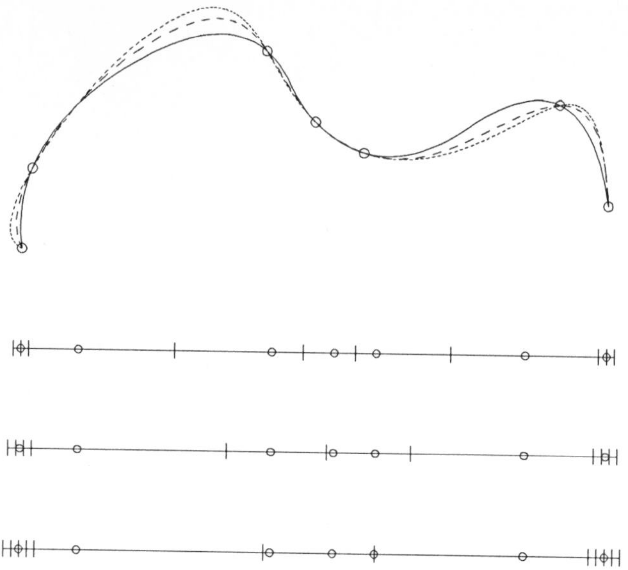

Figure 9.6. A curve interpolation with different degrees using chord length parameterization and knots obtained by averaging.

hence
$$U = \left\{0,0,0,0,\frac{28}{51},1,1,1,1\right\}$$

The system of linear equations is

$$\begin{bmatrix} 1 & 0 & 0 & 0 & 0 \\ N_{0,3}\left(\frac{5}{17}\right) & N_{1,3}\left(\frac{5}{17}\right) & N_{2,3}\left(\frac{5}{17}\right) & N_{3,3}\left(\frac{5}{17}\right) & 0 \\ N_{0,3}\left(\frac{9}{17}\right) & N_{1,3}\left(\frac{9}{17}\right) & N_{2,3}\left(\frac{9}{17}\right) & N_{3,3}\left(\frac{9}{17}\right) & 0 \\ 0 & N_{1,3}\left(\frac{14}{17}\right) & N_{2,3}\left(\frac{14}{17}\right) & N_{3,3}\left(\frac{14}{17}\right) & N_{4,3}\left(\frac{14}{17}\right) \\ 0 & 0 & 0 & 0 & 1 \end{bmatrix} \begin{bmatrix} \mathbf{P}_0 \\ \mathbf{P}_1 \\ \mathbf{P}_2 \\ \mathbf{P}_3 \\ \mathbf{P}_4 \end{bmatrix}$$
$$= \begin{bmatrix} \mathbf{Q}_0 \\ \mathbf{Q}_1 \\ \mathbf{Q}_2 \\ \mathbf{Q}_3 \\ \mathbf{Q}_4 \end{bmatrix}$$

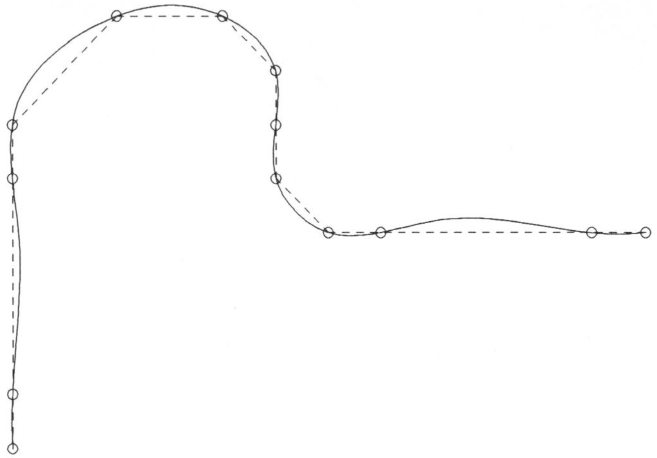

Figure 9.7. A global cubic curve interpolant to data containing collinear points (see the dashed line).

We now summarize the global interpolation algorithm. We assume two utility routines to solve the system of linear equations:

- `LUDecomposition(A,q,sbw)` to decompose the $q \times q$ coefficient matrix with semibandwidth `sbw` into lower and upper triangular components; for simplicity we assume `A` is an $q \times q$ square array, but a utility should be used which only stores the nonzero band;
- `ForwardBackward(A,q,sbw,rhs,sol)` to perform the forward/backward substitution (see [Pres88]); `rhs[]` is the right hand side of the system (the coordinates of the $\mathbf{Q}_k$), and `sol[]` is the solution vector (coordinates of the $\mathbf{P}_i$).

The algorithm also makes use of `FindSpan()` and `BasisFuns()` from Chapter 2.

```
ALGORITHM A9.1
  GlobalCurveInterp(n,Q,r,p,m,U,P)
    { /* Global interpolation through n+1 points */
      /* Input: n,Q,r,p */
      /* Output: m,U,P */
    m = n+p+1;
    Compute the uk;    /* Eq.(9.5) or (9.6) */
    Compute the knot vector U;   /* Eq.(9.8) */
    Initialize array A to zero;
    for (i=0; i<=n; i++)
      { /* Set up coefficient matrix */
      span = FindSpan(n,p,uk[i],U);
      BasisFuns(span,uk[i],p,U,A[i][span-p]); /* Get ith row */
      }
```

```
LUDecomposition(A,n+1,p-1);
for (i=0; i<r; i++)   /* r is the number of coordinates */
  {
  for (j=0; j<=n; j++)   rhs[j] = ith coordinate of Q[j];
  ForwardBackward(A,n+1,p-1,rhs,sol);
  for (j=0; j<=n; j++)   ith coordinate of P[j] = sol[j];
  }
}
```

9.2.2 GLOBAL CURVE INTERPOLATION WITH END DERIVATIVES SPECIFIED

It is not uncommon for derivative vectors to be specified as input data. In this case, the solution process is similar to Algorithm A9.1:

1. compute parameters $\bar{u}_k$ corresponding to the points $\mathbf{Q}_k$;
2. compute a knot vector U;
3. evaluate the basis functions to set up a system of linear equations, with the control points as unknowns;
4. solve the system.

Only Steps 2 and 3 are slightly different from the previous case. Each derivative gives rise to one additional knot and control point, and hence to one additional linear equation. The derivative formulas of Chapters 2 and 3 are used to set up the additional equations, e.g., Eqs. (2.7),(2.10), and (3.3)–(3.10). We now illustrate this with examples using first derivatives.

Again let $\{\mathbf{Q}_k\}$, $k = 0, \ldots, n$, be points, and assume that $\mathbf{D}_0$ and $\mathbf{D}_n$ are the first derivative vectors at the start point and end point of the curve, respectively. We want to interpolate this data with a pth-degree curve

$$\mathbf{C}(u) = \sum_{i=0}^{n+2} N_{i,p}(u)\,\mathbf{P}_i$$

As before, compute the $\bar{u}_k$, $k = 0, \ldots, n$, using Eq. (9.5) or Eq. (9.6). Then set $m = n + p + 3$ and obtain the $m + 1$ knots by

$$u_0 = \cdots = u_p = 0 \qquad u_{m-p} = \cdots = u_m = 1$$

$$u_{j+p+1} = \frac{1}{p} \sum_{i=j}^{j+p-1} \bar{u}_i \qquad j = 0, \ldots, n - p + 1 \tag{9.9}$$

Notice that Eq. (9.9) is analogous to Eq. (9.8) except that we pick up two additional knots by running j from 0 to $n - p + 1$. As before, Eq. (9.2) yields $n + 1$ equations

$$\mathbf{Q}_k = \mathbf{C}(\bar{u}_k) = \sum_{i=0}^{n+2} N_{i,p}(\bar{u}_k)\,\mathbf{P}_i \tag{9.10}$$

Equations (3.7) produce two additional equations, i.e.

$$-\mathbf{P}_0 + \mathbf{P}_1 = \frac{u_{p+1}}{p}\mathbf{D}_0 \tag{9.11}$$

$$-\mathbf{P}_{n+1} + \mathbf{P}_{n+2} = \frac{1 - u_{m-p-1}}{p}\mathbf{D}_n \tag{9.12}$$

Inserting Eqs. (9.11) and (9.12) into Eq. (9.10) as the second and next to last equations, respectively, yields an $(n+3) \times (n+3)$ banded linear system. Figure 9.8 shows cubic curve interpolants with end tangents specified. The small, medium, and large magnitudes of the derivatives produce the solid, the dashed, and the dotted curves, respectively. Figure 9.9 illustrates interpolants to the same data points, but with different end tangent directions and magnitudes for the derivatives.

9.2.3 CUBIC SPLINE CURVE INTERPOLATION

The previous method (Eqs. [9.9]–[9.12]) is valid for any degree $p > 1$. If $p = 3$, there is an algorithm which is more efficient and yields the traditional C^2 cubic spline. The $\bar{u}_k$ are computed as previously. The knots are

$$\begin{aligned} &u_0 = \cdots = u_3 = 0 && u_{n+3} = \cdots = u_{n+6} = 1 \\ &u_{j+3} = \bar{u}_j && j = 1, \ldots, n-1 \end{aligned} \tag{9.13}$$

In other words, the interpolation of the $\mathbf{Q}_k$ occurs at the knots. The first two and last two equations are, respectively

$$\mathbf{P}_0 = \mathbf{Q}_0$$

$$-\mathbf{P}_0 + \mathbf{P}_1 = \frac{u_4}{3}\mathbf{D}_0 \tag{9.14}$$

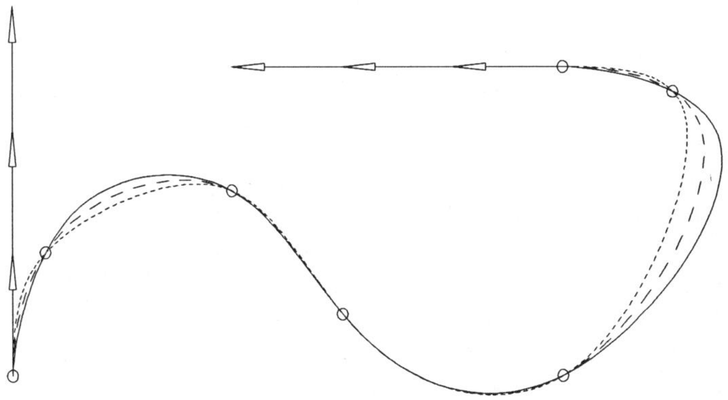

Figure 9.8. Global cubic curve interpolants with varying end derivative magnitudes.

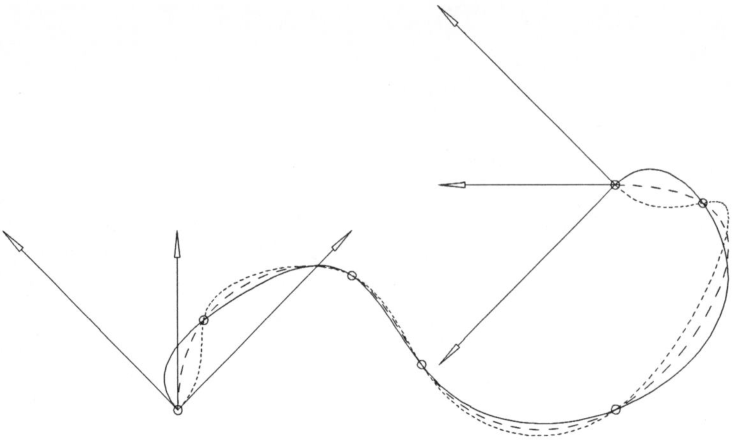

Figure 9.9. A global cubic curve interpolation with different end derivative directions.

and

$$-\mathbf{P}_{n+1} + \mathbf{P}_{n+2} = \frac{1 - u_{n+2}}{3}\,\mathbf{D}_n$$
$$\mathbf{P}_{n+2} = \mathbf{Q}_n \tag{9.15}$$

These can be solved directly. Recalling that there are only three nonzero cubic basis functions at an interior knot, the remaining $n-1$ equations have the form

$$\mathbf{Q}_k = \mathbf{C}(\bar{u}_k) = N_{k,3}(\bar{u}_k)\mathbf{P}_k + N_{k+1,3}(\bar{u}_k)\mathbf{P}_{k+1} + N_{k+2,3}(\bar{u}_k)\mathbf{P}_{k+2} \tag{9.16}$$

for $k = 1, \ldots, n-1$. Setting

$$a_k = N_{k,3}(\bar{u}_k) \quad b_k = N_{k+1,3}(\bar{u}_k) \quad c_k = N_{k+2,3}(\bar{u}_k)$$

yields the tridiagonal system

$$\begin{bmatrix} \mathbf{R}_2 \\ \mathbf{R}_3 \\ \vdots \\ \mathbf{R}_{n-1} \\ \mathbf{R}_n \end{bmatrix} = \begin{bmatrix} \mathbf{Q}_1 - a_1\mathbf{P}_1 \\ \mathbf{Q}_2 \\ \vdots \\ \mathbf{Q}_{n-2} \\ \mathbf{Q}_{n-1} - c_{n-1}\mathbf{P}_{n+1} \end{bmatrix}$$

$$= \begin{bmatrix} b_1 & c_1 & 0 & \cdots & 0 & 0 & 0 \\ a_2 & b_2 & c_2 & \cdots & 0 & 0 & 0 \\ \vdots & \vdots & \vdots & \ddots & \vdots & \vdots & \vdots \\ 0 & 0 & 0 & \cdots & a_{n-2} & b_{n-2} & c_{n-2} \\ 0 & 0 & 0 & \cdots & 0 & a_{n-1} & b_{n-1} \end{bmatrix} \begin{bmatrix} \mathbf{P}_2 \\ \mathbf{P}_3 \\ \vdots \\ \mathbf{P}_{n-1} \\ \mathbf{P}_n \end{bmatrix} \tag{9.17}$$

This system can be solved by a simple algorithm which computes the rows of the matrix in Eq. (9.17) on-the-fly. It requires two local arrays, `R[]` and `dd[]`, of length $n+1$, and an array `abc[]` of length 4, which stores $a_k, b_k, c_k, 0$. It assumes that $\mathbf{P}_0$, $\mathbf{P}_1$, $\mathbf{P}_{n+1}$, $\mathbf{P}_{n+2}$ are already computed and loaded into array `P`. The algorithm can be adapted to handle points with any number of coordinates.

```
ALGORITHM A9.2
  SolveTridiagonal(n,Q,U,P)
    { /*  Solve tridiagonal system for C2 cubic spline  */
      /*  Input:  n,Q,U,P[0],P[1],P[n+1],P[n+2]   */
      /*  Output: P  */
    for (i=3; i<n; i++)   R[i] = Q[i-1];
    BasisFuns(4,U[4],3,U,abc);
    den = abc[1];
    P[2] = (Q[1]-abc[0]*P[1])/den;
    for (i=3; i<n; i++)
      {
      dd[i] = abc[2]/den;
      BasisFuns(i+2,U[i+2],3,U,abc);
      den = abc[1]-abc[0]*dd[i];
      P[i] = (R[i]-abc[0]*P[i-1])/den;
      }
    dd[n] = abc[2]/den;
    BasisFuns(n+2,U[n+2],3,U,abc);
    den = abc[1]-abc[0]*dd[n];
    P[n] = (Q[n-1]-abc[2]*P[n+1]-abc[0]*P[n-1])/den;
    for (i=n-1; i>=2; i--)   P[i] = P[i]-dd[i+1]*P[i+1];
    }
```

Figure 9.10 shows data interpolated with this cubic spline algorithm.

Often, only tangent directions but not magnitudes for derivative vectors are specified. We denote unit length tangent vectors by $\mathbf{T}_0$ and $\mathbf{T}_n$. In this case, magnitudes α_0 and α_n must be estimated. Set

$$\mathbf{D}_0 = \alpha_0 \mathbf{T}_0 \qquad \mathbf{D}_n = \alpha_n \mathbf{T}_n \tag{9.18}$$

and proceed as before. A reasonable choice is to set α_0 and α_n equal to the total chord length, d, as computed in Eq. (9.4). In an interactive environment, α_0 and α_n can be used as additional shape controls.

9.2.4 GLOBAL CURVE INTERPOLATION WITH FIRST DERIVATIVES SPECIFIED

Suppose now that the first derivative, $\mathbf{D}_k$, is given at every point, $\mathbf{Q}_k$, $k = 0, \ldots, n$. There are $2(n+1)$ data items and that many unknown control points.

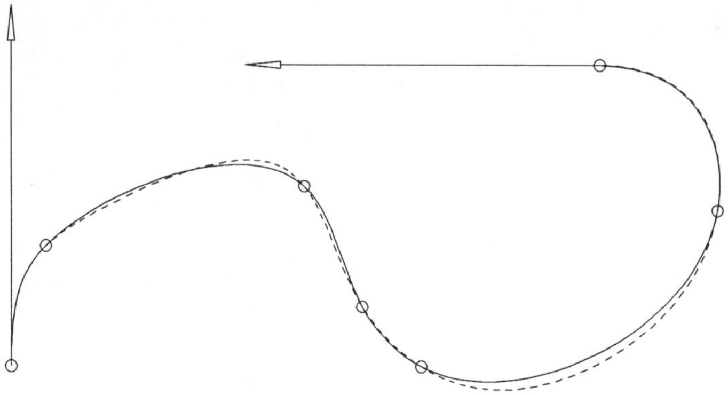

Figure 9.10. A cubic spline interpolant (solid line) compared to a regular cubic interpolant (dashed line) obtained by using chord length parameterization and knots computed by averaging.

The $n+1$ equations expressing the $\mathbf{Q}_k$ are

$$\mathbf{Q}_k = \mathbf{C}(\bar{u}_k) = \sum_{i=0}^{2n+1} N_{i,p}(\bar{u}_k)\mathbf{P}_i \tag{9.19}$$

and from Eqs. (2.10) and (3.3), the $n+1$ equations expressing the $\mathbf{D}_k$ are

$$\mathbf{D}_k = \mathbf{C}'(\bar{u}_k) = \sum_{i=0}^{2n+1} N'_{i,p}(\bar{u}_k)\mathbf{P}_i \tag{9.20}$$

The parameters $\bar{u}_k$ are computed using Eq. (9.5) or Eq. (9.6). The number of knots is

$$2(n+1)+p+1 \tag{9.21}$$

and they should be chosen to reflect the distribution of the $\bar{u}_k$. For $p=2$ and $p=3$, satisfactory choices are

$$U = \left\{0,0,0,\frac{\bar{u}_1}{2},\bar{u}_1,\frac{\bar{u}_1+\bar{u}_2}{2},\bar{u}_2,\ldots,\bar{u}_{n-1},\frac{\bar{u}_{n-1}+1}{2},1,1,1\right\} \tag{9.22}$$

and $$U = \left\{0,0,0,0,\frac{\bar{u}_1}{2},\frac{2\bar{u}_1+\bar{u}_2}{3},\frac{\bar{u}_1+2\bar{u}_2}{3},\ldots,\frac{\bar{u}_{n-2}+2\bar{u}_{n-1}}{3},\frac{\bar{u}_{n-1}+1}{2},1,1,1,1\right\} \tag{9.23}$$

respectively. Equations (9.19) and (9.20) are merged in an alternating fashion to yield a $2(n+1)\times 2(n+1)$ banded linear system. For example, let $p=3$. Denote the first and last interior knots of Eq. (9.23) by

$$u_4 = \frac{\bar{u}_1}{2} \qquad u_{m-p-1} = \frac{\bar{u}_{n-1}+1}{2}$$

The system of equations is

$$
\begin{aligned}
&\mathbf{P}_0 &&= \mathbf{Q}_0 \\
&-\mathbf{P}_0 + \mathbf{P}_1 &&= \frac{u_4}{3}\mathbf{D}_0 \\
&N_{1,3}(\bar{u}_1)\mathbf{P}_1 + \cdots + N_{4,3}(\bar{u}_1)\mathbf{P}_4 &&= \mathbf{Q}_1 \\
&N'_{1,3}(\bar{u}_1)\mathbf{P}_1 + \cdots + N'_{4,3}(\bar{u}_1)\mathbf{P}_4 &&= \mathbf{D}_1 \\
&\qquad\vdots \\
&N_{2n-3,3}(\bar{u}_{n-1})\mathbf{P}_{2n-3} + \cdots + N_{2n,3}(\bar{u}_{n-1})\mathbf{P}_{2n} &&= \mathbf{Q}_{n-1} \\
&N'_{2n-3,3}(\bar{u}_{n-1})\mathbf{P}_{2n-3} + \cdots + N'_{2n,3}(\bar{u}_{n-1})\mathbf{P}_{2n} &&= \mathbf{D}_{n-1} \\
&-\mathbf{P}_{2n} + \mathbf{P}_{2n+1} &&= \frac{1 - u_{m-p-1}}{3}\mathbf{D}_n \\
&\mathbf{P}_{2n+1} &&= \mathbf{Q}_n
\end{aligned}
\tag{9.24}
$$

Use Algorithm A2.3 (`DersBasisFuns()`) to compute the $N_{i,3}(\bar{u}_k)$ and $N'_{i,3}(\bar{u}_k)$.

If unit length tangent vectors $\mathbf{T}_k$ are given instead of the $\mathbf{D}_k$, then magnitudes α_k must be estimated. Setting all $\alpha_k = d$, where d is the total chord length, is a reasonable choice. Figure 9.11 shows quadratic (solid line) and cubic (dashed line) curve interpolants to points and derivatives. Figure 9.12 illustrates a comparison among different curve interpolants obtained by using various derivative magnitudes at the data points. The solid curve applies $\alpha_k = d$ (middle tangent);

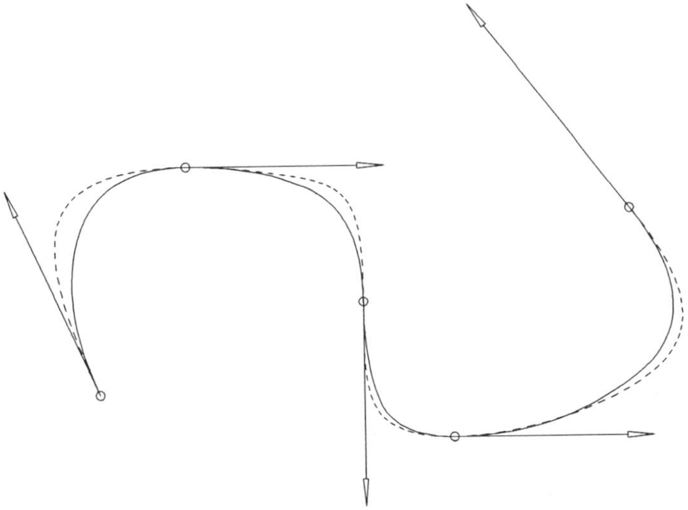

Figure 9.11. Quadratic (solid line) and cubic (dashed line) curve interpolants with derivatives specified at each data point.

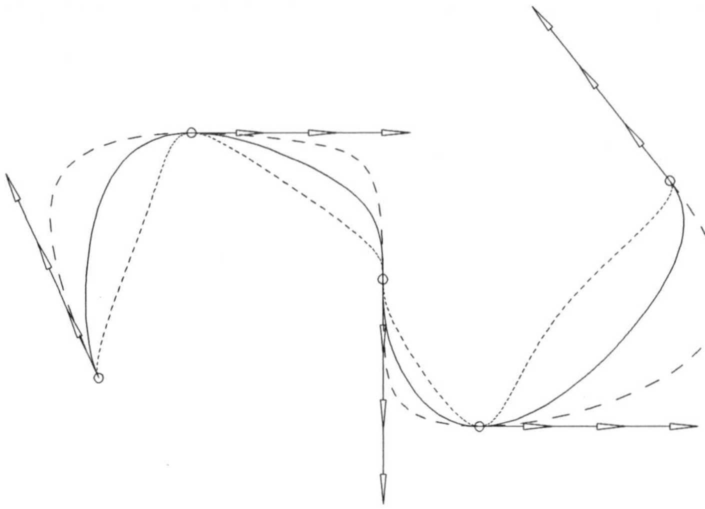

Figure 9.12. Cubic curve interpolants with varying tangent derivatives at each point.

the dashed curve has $\alpha_k = {}^3\!/_2\, d$ (large tangent); and the dotted curve was obtained by $\alpha_k = {}^1\!/_2\, d$ (small tangent). Figure 9.13 shows the control points of a quadratic curve interpolant to specified points and first derivatives.

9.2.5 GLOBAL SURFACE INTERPOLATION

We now turn to global interpolation of surfaces. We are given a set of $(n+1) \times (m+1)$ data points $\{\mathbf{Q}_{k,\ell}\}$, $k = 0, \ldots, n$ and $\ell = 0, \ldots, m$, and we want to construct a nonrational (p,q)th-degree B-spline surface interpolating these points, i.e.

$$\mathbf{Q}_{k,\ell} = \mathbf{S}(\bar{u}_k, \bar{v}_\ell) = \sum_{i=0}^{n} \sum_{j=0}^{m} N_{i,p}(\bar{u}_k) N_{j,q}(\bar{v}_\ell)\, \mathbf{P}_{i,j} \qquad (9.25)$$

Again, the first order of business is to compute reasonable values for the $(\bar{u}_k, \bar{v}_\ell)$ and the knot vectors U and V. We show how to compute the $\bar{u}_k$; the $\bar{v}_\ell$ are analogous. A common method is to use Eq. (9.5) or Eq. (9.6) to compute parameters $\bar{u}_0^\ell, \ldots, \bar{u}_n^\ell$ for each ℓ, and then to obtain each $\bar{u}_k$ by averaging across all $\bar{u}_k^\ell$, $\ell = 0, \ldots, m$, that is

$$\bar{u}_k = \frac{1}{m+1} \sum_{\ell=0}^{m} \bar{u}_k^\ell \qquad k = 0, \ldots, n$$

where for each fixed ℓ, $\bar{u}_k^\ell$, $k = 0, \ldots, n$, was computed by Eq. (9.5) or Eq. (9.6). An efficient algorithm using Eq. (9.5) follows. It computes both the $\bar{u}_k$ and $\bar{v}_\ell$. It requires one local array,`cds[]`, of length $\max(n+1, m+1)$, to store chordal

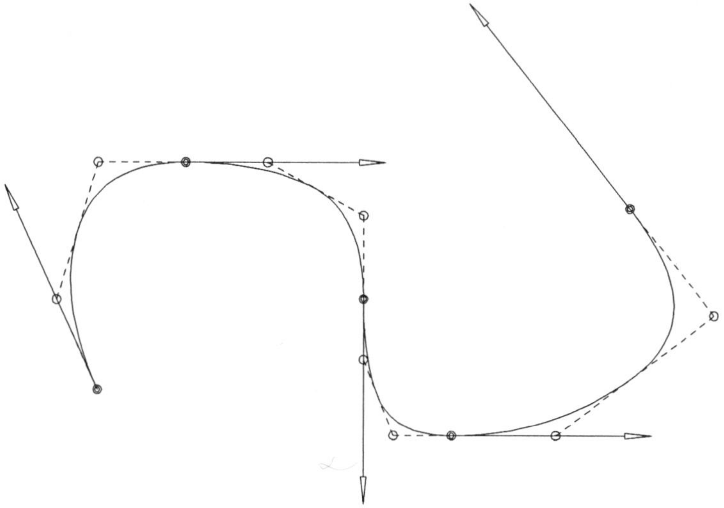

Figure 9.13. Control points of a quadratic B-spline curve interpolant to data with specified derivatives.

distances $|\mathbf{Q}_{k,\ell} - \mathbf{Q}_{k-1,\ell}|$, $k = 1, \ldots, n$ (and similarly for the v direction). The function `Distance3D()` computes the distance between two three-dimensional points. This algorithm handles the case when the total chord length of a row is equal to zero, a necessary condition if a three-sided surface is being constructed.

```
ALGORITHM A9.3
  SurfMeshParams(n,m,Q,uk,vl)
    { /*  Compute parameters for  */
      /*        global surface interpolation  */
      /*  Input:  n,m,Q  */
      /*  Output: uk,vl  */
     /* First get the uk */
    num = m+1;    /* number of nondegenerate rows */
    uk[0] = 0.0;     uk[n] = 1.0;
    for (k=1; k<n; k++)   uk[k] = 0.0;
    for (l=0; l<=m; l++)
      {
      total = 0.0;   /* total chord length of row */
      for (k=1; k<=n; k++)
        {
        cds[k] = Distance3D(Q[k][l],Q[k-1][l]);
        total = total + cds[k];
        }
      if (total == 0.0)   num = num-1;
```

```
        else
          {
          d = 0.0;
          for (k=1; k<n; k++)
            {
            d = d + cds[k];
            uk[k] = uk[k] + d/total;
            }
          }
      }
    if (num == 0)    return(error);
    for (k=1; k<n; k++)    uk[k] = uk[k]/num;
       /* Now do the same for vl */
    }
```

Once the $(\bar{u}_k, \bar{v}_\ell)$ are computed, the knot vectors U and V can be obtained by Eq. (9.8).

Now to the computation of the control points. Clearly, Eq. (9.25) represents $(n+1)\times(m+1)$ linear equations in the unknown $\mathbf{P}_{i,j}$. However, since $\mathbf{S}(u,v)$ is a tensor product surface, the $\mathbf{P}_{i,j}$ can be obtained more simply and efficiently as a sequence of curve interpolations. For fixed ℓ write Eq. (9.25) as

$$\mathbf{Q}_{k,\ell} = \sum_{i=0}^{n} N_{i,p}(\bar{u}_k)\left(\sum_{j=0}^{m} N_{j,q}(\bar{v}_\ell)\,\mathbf{P}_{i,j}\right) = \sum_{i=0}^{n} N_{i,p}(\bar{u}_k)\,\mathbf{R}_{i,\ell} \tag{9.26}$$

where

$$\mathbf{R}_{i,\ell} = \sum_{j=0}^{m} N_{j,q}(\bar{v}_\ell)\,\mathbf{P}_{i,j} \tag{9.27}$$

Notice that Eq. (9.26) is just curve interpolation through the points $\mathbf{Q}_{k,\ell}$, $k = 0,\ldots,n$. The $\mathbf{R}_{i,\ell}$ are the control points of the isoparametric curve on $\mathbf{S}(u,v)$ at fixed $v=\bar{v}_\ell$. Now fixing i and letting ℓ vary, Eq. (9.27) is curve interpolation through the points $\mathbf{R}_{i,0},\ldots,\mathbf{R}_{i,m}$, with $\mathbf{P}_{i,0},\ldots,\mathbf{P}_{i,m}$ as the computed control points. Thus, the algorithm to obtain all the $\mathbf{P}_{i,j}$ is (see Figure 9.14a–9.14d):

1. using U and the $\bar{u}_k$, do $m+1$ curve interpolations through $\mathbf{Q}_{0,\ell},\ldots,\mathbf{Q}_{n,\ell}$ (for $\ell=0,\ldots,m$); this yields the $\mathbf{R}_{i,\ell}$ (Figure 9.14b);
2. using V and the $\bar{v}_\ell$, do $n+1$ curve interpolations through $\mathbf{R}_{i,0},\ldots,\mathbf{R}_{i,m}$ (for $i=0,\ldots,n$); this yields the $\mathbf{P}_{i,j}$ (Figure 9.14c).

Figure 9.14d portrays the resulting surface. Clearly, the algorithm is symmetric; the same surface is obtained by:

1. doing $n+1$ curve interpolations through the $\mathbf{Q}_{k,0},\ldots,\mathbf{Q}_{k,m}$ to obtain the $\mathbf{R}_{k,j}$ (control points of isoparametric curves $\mathbf{S}(\bar{u}_k,v)$);
2. then doing $m+1$ curve interpolations through the $\mathbf{R}_{0,j},\ldots,\mathbf{R}_{n,j}$ to obtain the $\mathbf{P}_{i,j}$.

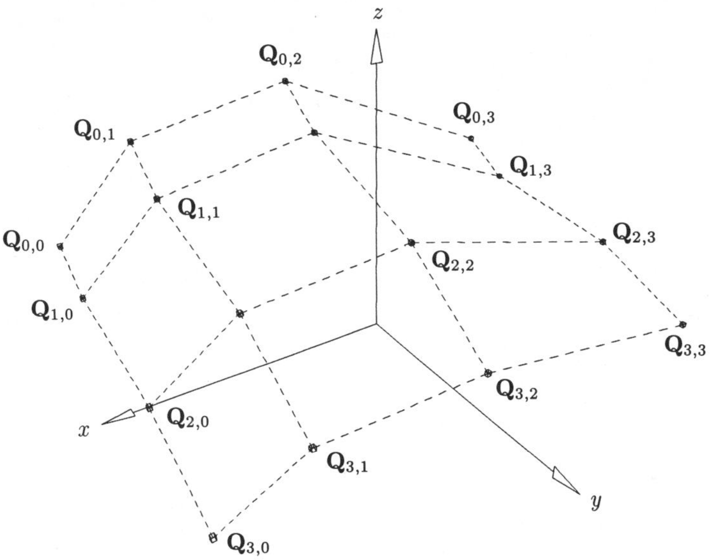

(a)

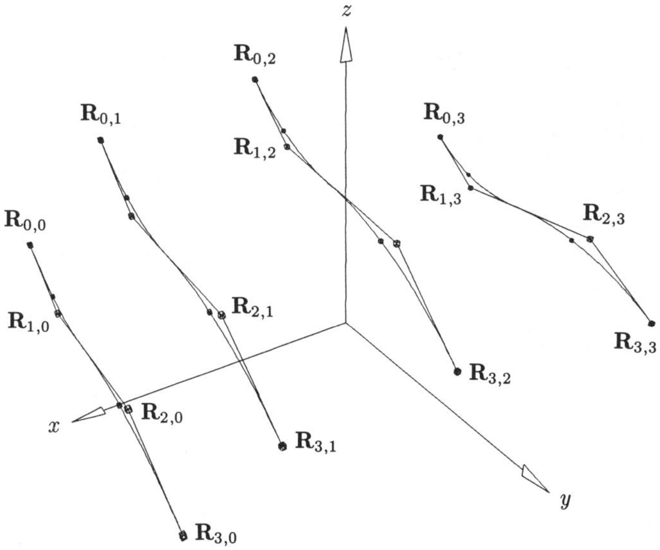

(b)

Figure 9.14. Global surface interpolation. (a) The data points; (b) interpolating the u-directional data points; (c) interpolating in the v direction through control points of u-directional interpolants; (d) the surface interpolant showing control points.

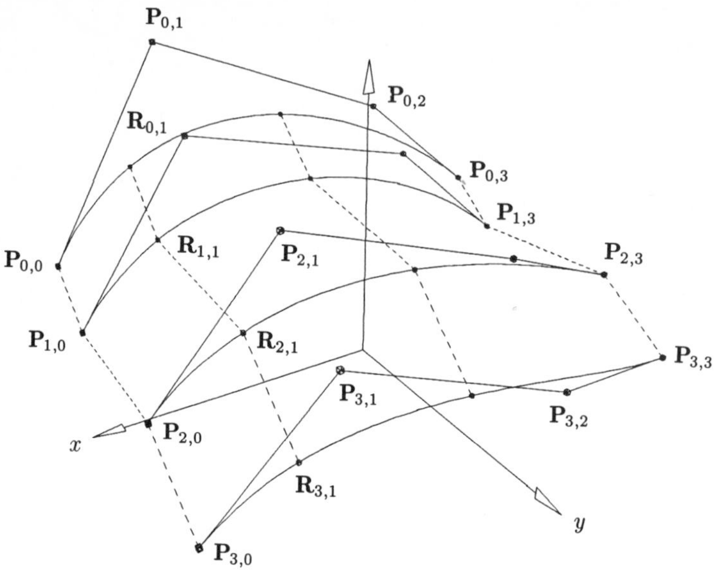

(c)

Figure 9.14. (*Continued.*)

Summarizing, surface interpolation proceeds as follows:

```
ALGORITHM A9.4
  GlobalSurfInterp(n,m,Q,p,q,U,V,P)
    { /*  Global surface interpolation  */
      /*  Input:  n,m,Q,p,q  */
      /*  Output: U,V,P  */
    SurfMeshParams(n,m,Q,uk,vl);  /* get parameters */
    Compute U using Eq.(9.8);
    Compute V using Eq.(9.8);
    for (l=0; l<=m; l++)
      {
      Do curve interpolation through Q[0][l],...,Q[n][l];
      This yields R[0][l],...,R[n][l];
      }
    for (i=0; i<=n; i++)
      {
      Do curve interpolation through R[i][0],...,R[i][m];
      This yields P[i][0],...,P[i][m];
      }
    }
```

Several surface interpolation examples are shown in Figures 9.15–9.18. The data set is shown in Figure 9.15. Surfaces with different parameterizations and

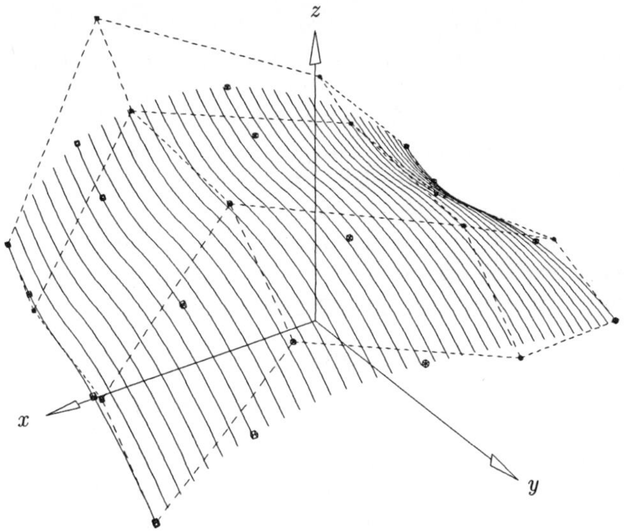

(d)

Figure 9.14. (*Continued.*)

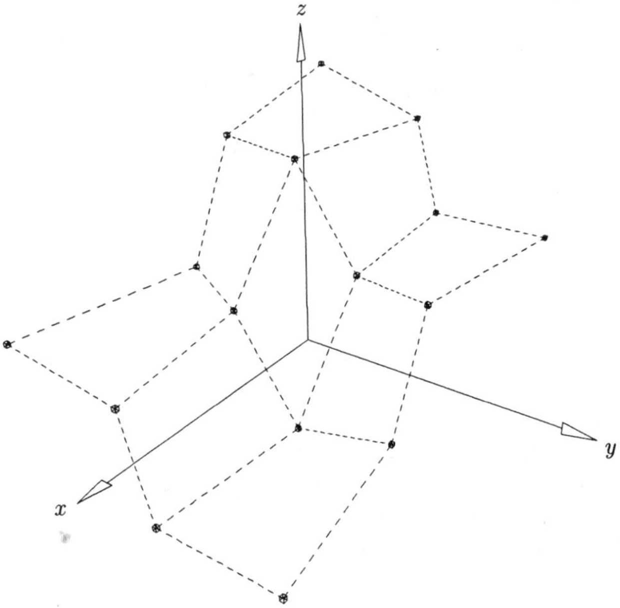

Figure 9.15. Data points to test surface interpolation.

knot vectors are illustrated in Figures 9.16a–9.16c. The degree is $(2,3)$, and the parameterizations and knot vectors are uniform (Figure 9.16a); chord length, knots obtained by averaging (Figure 9.16b); and centripetal, knots obtained by averaging (Figure 9.16c). In Figure 9.17 surface interpolants with different degrees are depicted. The degrees in each are: Figure 9.17a, degree $(2,3)$; Figure 9.17b, degree (3,2); and Figure 9.17c, degree $(3,3)$. In Figure 9.18 the inability to handle coplanar data is demonstrated.

Derivative constraints can also be incorporated into global surface interpolation. Conceptually, the derivative formulas of Chapters 2 and 3 can be used to define one additional linear equation for each derivative constraint specified. Unfortunately, if the number of data constraints is not the same in every row or column it becomes more difficult to solve for the unknown surface control points using curve interpolations in two directions, as described previously. However, with clever use of curve knot insertion and surface knot removal, one can adapt Algorithm `A9.4` to handle partial derivative constraints at individual data points. Finally, local surface interpolation methods (see Section 9.3) are well-suited to handling derivative constraints, as they require derivatives at every point anyway.

9.3 Local Interpolation

In this section we present local interpolation of curves and surfaces to point and tangent data. We start with some preliminary concepts.

9.3.1 LOCAL CURVE INTERPOLATION PRELIMINARIES

Let $\{\mathbf{Q}_k\}$, $k = 0,\ldots,n$, be given. By local curve interpolation we mean a method which constructs n polynomial or rational curve segments, $\mathbf{C}_i(u)$, $i = 0,\ldots,n-1$, such that $\mathbf{Q}_i$ and $\mathbf{Q}_{i+1}$ are the endpoints of $\mathbf{C}_i(u)$. Neighboring segments are joined with some prescribed level of continuity, and the construction proceeds segment-wise, generally from left to right. Any equations which arise are local to only a few neighboring segments. In the framework of NURBS, we construct the segments using polynomial or rational Bézier curves, then obtain a NURBS curve by selecting a suitable knot vector.

Now let $\bar{u}_i$ denote the start parameter of $\mathbf{C}_i(u)$ and the end parameter of $\mathbf{C}_{i-1}(u)$. $\mathbf{C}_i(u)$ and $\mathbf{C}_{i-1}(u)$ meet at $\bar{u}_i$ with G^1 *continuity* (G for *geometric*) if their tangent directions coincide there, that is, if $\mathbf{C}'_i(\bar{u}_i)$ and $\mathbf{C}'_{i-1}(\bar{u}_i)$ are pointing in the same direction. However, their magnitudes may be different. G^1 continuity implies that the curve is visually continuous (smooth) but may have a discontinuity in the parameterization. For a deeper study of G^n continuity, $n \geq 1$, we refer the reader to Barsky and DeRose [Bars89, 90]. Local fitting algorithms are designed to provide some level of either G or C continuity; in this chapter we present only algorithms providing G^1 or C^1 continuity. Local methods yielding higher continuity are not widely used. Although G^2 and C^2

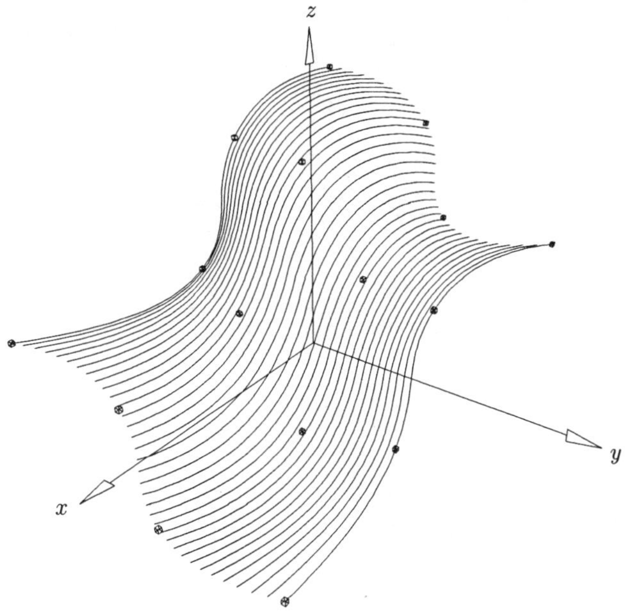

(a)

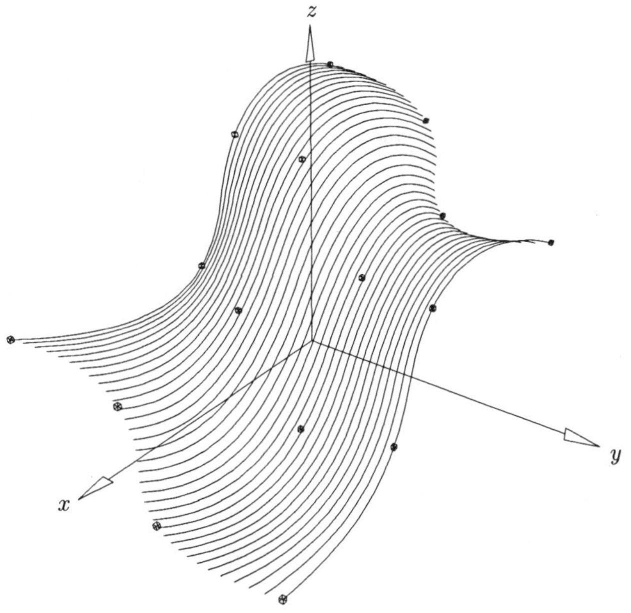

(b)

Figure 9.16. A surface interpolation with degree (2, 3) surfaces obtained by using different parameterizations and knot vectors.

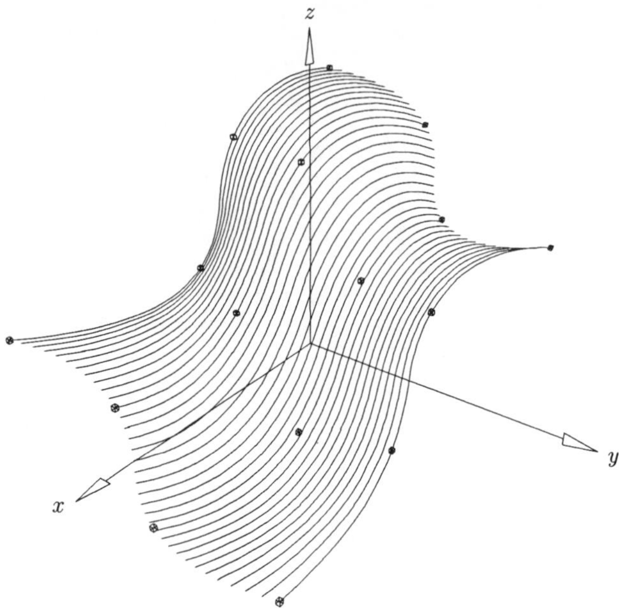

(c)

Figure 9.16. (*Continued.*)

are possible with cubics, higher degree must be used if a reasonable amount of flexibility is to be maintained.

Obtaining the Bézier segments, $\mathbf{C}_i(u)$, requires computation of the inner Bézier control points, one point for quadratics, two for cubics. These control points lie on the lines which are tangent to the curve at the $\mathbf{Q}_k$; thus, we require tangent vectors $\mathbf{T}_k$ at each $\mathbf{Q}_k$. In some cases they can be input along with the $\mathbf{Q}_k$; e.g., they are easily obtained when computing points of intersection between two surfaces. However, if not input then they must be computed as part of the fitting algorithm. A number of methods exist; Boehm et al [Boeh84] gives a survey of various methods. Let

$$\Delta\bar{u}_k = \bar{u}_k - \bar{u}_{k-1} \quad \mathbf{q}_k = \mathbf{Q}_k - \mathbf{Q}_{k-1} \quad \mathbf{d}_k = \frac{\mathbf{q}_k}{\Delta\bar{u}_k}$$

All methods have one of two forms

$$\mathbf{D}_k = (1-\alpha_k)\mathbf{d}_k + \alpha_k\mathbf{d}_{k+1} \tag{9.28}$$

or

$$\mathbf{T}_k = \frac{\mathbf{V}_k}{|\,\mathbf{V}_k\,|} \qquad \mathbf{V}_k = (1-\alpha_k)\mathbf{q}_k + \alpha_k\mathbf{q}_{k+1} \tag{9.29}$$

(see Figure 9.19). Notice that Eq. (9.28) assumes that values for the $\bar{u}_k$ have been assigned. The vectors $\mathbf{D}_k$ can be viewed as estimates for the derivatives.

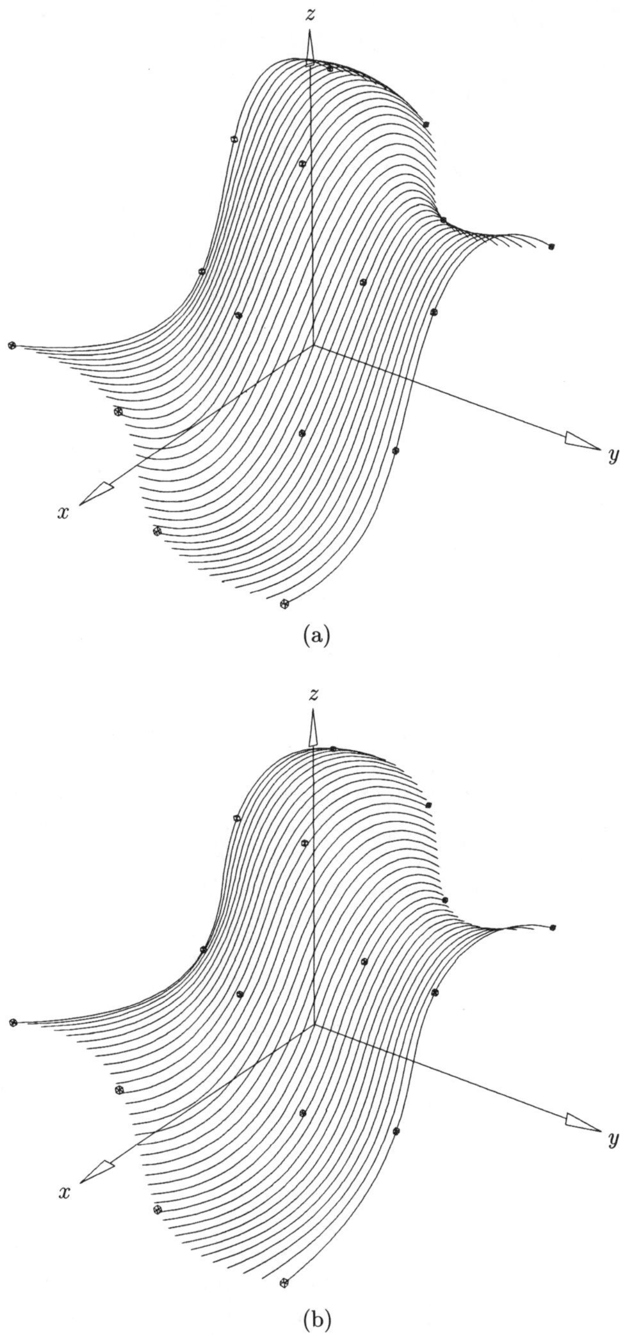

Figure 9.17. Surface interpolants using different degrees; the parameterization is chord length and knot vector obtained by averaging.

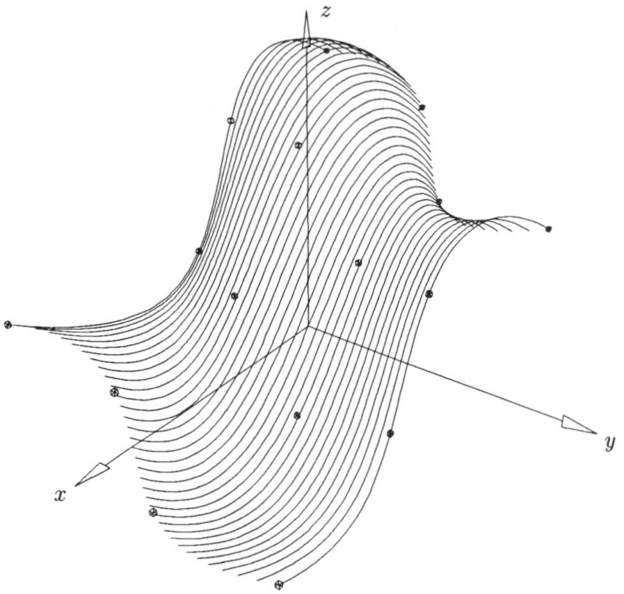

(c)

Figure 9.17. (*Continued.*)

Equation (9.29) does not use parameters $\bar{u}_k$, and the resulting vectors should be viewed as tangent directions only. Assignment of magnitudes and parameters must be done in conjunction with one another; they are not independent. Notice also that we use the notation $\mathbf{T}$ strictly for *unit length* tangent vectors. Equations (9.28) and (9.29) are linear interpolations. The various schemes differ in the way they compute the interpolation parameter α_k; it typically depends on either three or five neighboring points. For example, the Bessel method [DeBo78] is a three-point method using

$$\alpha_k = \frac{\Delta \bar{u}_k}{\Delta \bar{u}_k + \Delta \bar{u}_{k+1}} \qquad k = 1, \ldots, n-1 \tag{9.30}$$

together with Eq. (9.28). Setting

$$\alpha_k = \frac{|\mathbf{q}_{k-1} \times \mathbf{q}_k|}{|\mathbf{q}_{k-1} \times \mathbf{q}_k| + |\mathbf{q}_{k+1} \times \mathbf{q}_{k+2}|} \qquad k = 2, \ldots, n-2 \tag{9.31}$$

together with Eq. (9.29) yields a five-point method to obtain $\mathbf{T}_k$ [Akim70; Renn82; Pieg87d]. It has the advantage that three collinear points, $\mathbf{Q}_{k-1}$, $\mathbf{Q}_k$, $\mathbf{Q}_{k+1}$, yield a $\mathbf{T}_k$ which is parallel to the line segment. The denominator of Eq. (9.31) vanishes if $\mathbf{Q}_{k-2}, \mathbf{Q}_{k-1}, \mathbf{Q}_k$ are collinear and $\mathbf{Q}_k, \mathbf{Q}_{k+1}, \mathbf{Q}_{k+2}$ are collinear. This implies either a corner at $\mathbf{Q}_k$ or a straight line segment from $\mathbf{Q}_{k-2}$ to $\mathbf{Q}_{k+2}$. In these cases α_k can be defined in a number of ways; we choose

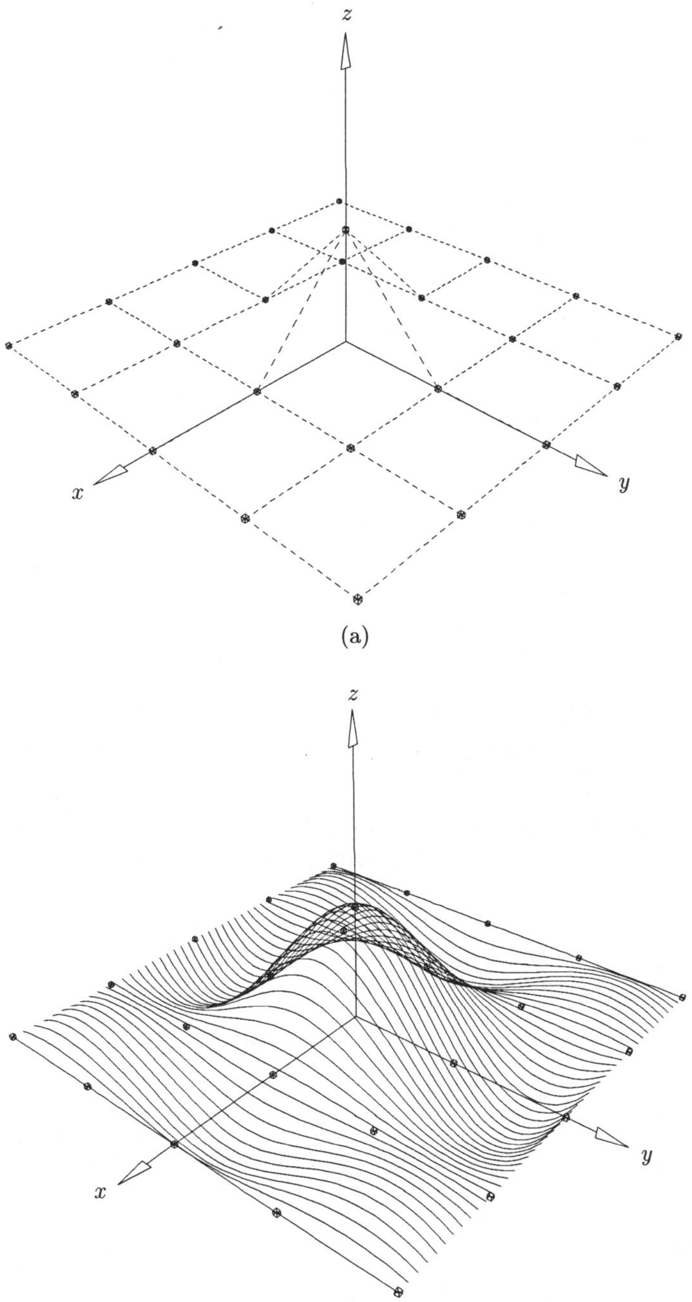

(a)

(b)

Figure 9.18. Global surface interpolation example. (a) Data containing coplanar points; (b) interpolating surface.

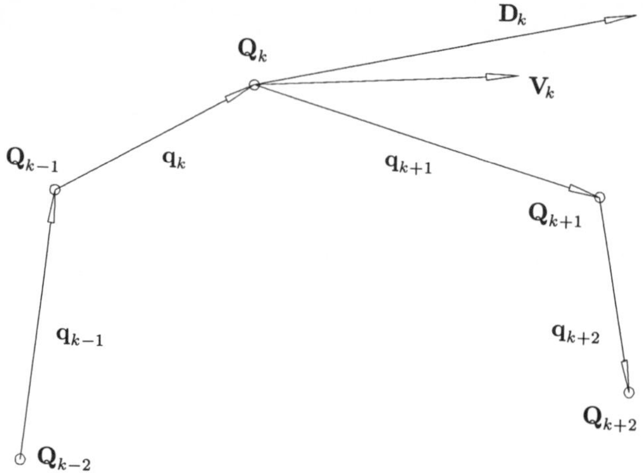

Figure 9.19. Computation of tangent ($\mathbf{V}_k$) and derivative ($\mathbf{D}_k$) vectors for local curve interpolation.

- $\alpha_k = 1$, which implies $\mathbf{V}_k = \mathbf{q}_{k+1}$; this produces a corner at $\mathbf{Q}_k$ if one is implied by the data;
- $\alpha_k = 1/2$, which implies $\mathbf{V}_k = 1/2(\mathbf{q}_k + \mathbf{q}_{k+1})$; this choice smoothes out a corner if one is implied.

Based on these choices, a local curve interpolation routine can accept an input flag, indicating whether or not to preserve corners. All methods require special treatment at the ends. For the three-point scheme we can set

$$\mathbf{D}_0 = 2\mathbf{d}_1 - \mathbf{D}_1 \qquad \mathbf{D}_n = 2\mathbf{d}_n - \mathbf{D}_{n-1} \tag{9.32}$$

and for the five-point scheme we can use

$$\begin{aligned} \mathbf{q}_0 &= 2\mathbf{q}_1 - \mathbf{q}_2 & \mathbf{q}_{-1} &= 2\mathbf{q}_0 - \mathbf{q}_1 \\ \mathbf{q}_{n+1} &= 2\mathbf{q}_n - \mathbf{q}_{n-1} & \mathbf{q}_{n+2} &= 2\mathbf{q}_{n+1} - \mathbf{q}_n \end{aligned} \tag{9.33}$$

to substitute into Eqs. (9.31) and (9.29) in order to obtain $\mathbf{T}_0, \mathbf{T}_1$ and $\mathbf{T}_{n-1}, \mathbf{T}_n$. We are now ready to present several local interpolation methods.

9.3.2 LOCAL PARABOLIC CURVE INTERPOLATION

We start with a simple two-dimensional, nonrational, quadratic scheme. Let $\{\mathbf{Q}_k\}$, $k = 0, \ldots, n$, be points in the xy plane. Use some tangent estimation scheme to compute the corresponding $\{\mathbf{T}_k\}$, e.g., Eqs. (9.29), (9.31), and (9.33). Let L_k denote the directed line defined by $(\mathbf{Q}_k, \mathbf{T}_k)$, and $\mathbf{R}_k$ the intersection point of L_{k-1} and L_k. Assume for the moment that the intersection exists, and that

$$\gamma_{k-1} > 0 \qquad \gamma_k < 0 \tag{9.34}$$

where
$$\mathbf{R}_k = \mathbf{Q}_{k-1} + \gamma_{k-1}\mathbf{T}_{k-1} \qquad \mathbf{R}_k = \mathbf{Q}_k + \gamma_k\mathbf{T}_k$$

(we drop this restriction later). Then we choose as our control points

$$\mathbf{Q}_0, \mathbf{R}_1, \mathbf{Q}_1, \mathbf{R}_2, \ldots, \mathbf{R}_n, \mathbf{Q}_n \tag{9.35}$$

Let $\bar{u}_0 = 0$ and $\bar{u}_n = 1$. If $\{\bar{u}_i\}$, $i = 1, \ldots, n-1$, is any sequence of numbers satisfying $\bar{u}_{i-1} < \bar{u}_i < \bar{u}_{i+1}$, then the control points of Eq. (9.35), together with the knot vector

$$U = \{0, 0, 0, \bar{u}_1, \bar{u}_1, \bar{u}_2, \bar{u}_2, \ldots, \bar{u}_{n-1}, \bar{u}_{n-1}, 1, 1, 1\} \tag{9.36}$$

define a nonrational, G^1 continuous, quadratic B-spline curve interpolating the $\{\mathbf{Q}_k\}$ (see Figure 9.20). The choice of the internal knots does not affect the shape of the curve, only the parameterization. It is possible to choose the knots so that the resulting curve is C^1 continuous; in doing so, we can remove the control points $\mathbf{Q}_1, \ldots, \mathbf{Q}_{n-1}$ and one occurrence of each of the interior knots. We simply equate start and end derivatives at $\mathbf{Q}_{k-1}$ (using Eq. [3.7] transformed to the intervals $[\bar{u}_{k-2}, \bar{u}_{k-1}]$ and $[\bar{u}_{k-1}, \bar{u}_k]$) and obtain the formula

$$\bar{u}_0 = 0 \qquad \bar{u}_1 = 1$$

$$\bar{u}_k = \bar{u}_{k-1} + (\bar{u}_{k-1} - \bar{u}_{k-2})\frac{|\,\mathbf{R}_k - \mathbf{Q}_{k-1}\,|}{|\,\mathbf{Q}_{k-1} - \mathbf{R}_{k-1}\,|} \qquad k = 2, \ldots, n \tag{9.37}$$

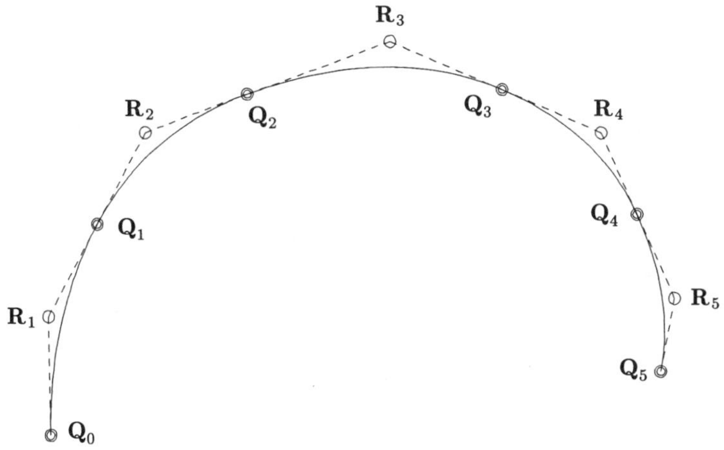

Figure 9.20. G^1 continuous quadratic curve interpolant.

The C^1 continuous curve interpolating the $\{\mathbf{Q}_k\}$ is then defined by the control points

$$\mathbf{Q}_0, \mathbf{R}_1, \mathbf{R}_2, \ldots, \mathbf{R}_{n-1}, \mathbf{R}_n, \mathbf{Q}_n \tag{9.38}$$

and the knots

$$U = \left\{0, 0, 0, \frac{\bar{u}_1}{\bar{u}_n}, \frac{\bar{u}_2}{\bar{u}_n}, \ldots, \frac{\bar{u}_{n-2}}{\bar{u}_n}, \frac{\bar{u}_{n-1}}{\bar{u}_n}, 1, 1, 1\right\} \tag{9.39}$$

One must pay a price for the C^1 continuity and the reduction in the number of control points, namely in the parameterization; Figures 9.21a and 9.21b show this. The curve in these figures is marked at equally spaced parameter values. In Figure 9.21a the knots were computed using Eq. (9.37) and in Figure 9.21b using the chord length parameterization (Eq. [9.5]). Note the spacing of the $\mathbf{Q}_k$.

We now drop the restriction given in Eq. (9.34) and detail two special cases which arise when computing the $\mathbf{R}_k$:

- $\mathbf{T}_{k-1}$ and $\mathbf{T}_k$ are parallel, hence $\mathbf{R}_k$ cannot be computed by intersection; this can indicate collinear segments, an inflection point, or a 180° turn in the curve;
- $\mathbf{R}_k$ can be computed, but γ_{k-1} and γ_k do not satisfy Eq. (9.34); this indicates either an inflection point or a turn of more than 180°.

The collinear segments case applies if $\mathbf{T}_{k-1}$ and $\mathbf{T}_k$ are both parallel to the chord $\mathbf{Q}_{k-1}\mathbf{Q}_k$. We handle this case simply by setting

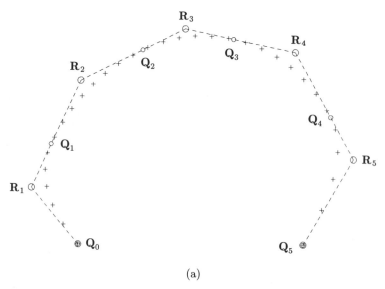

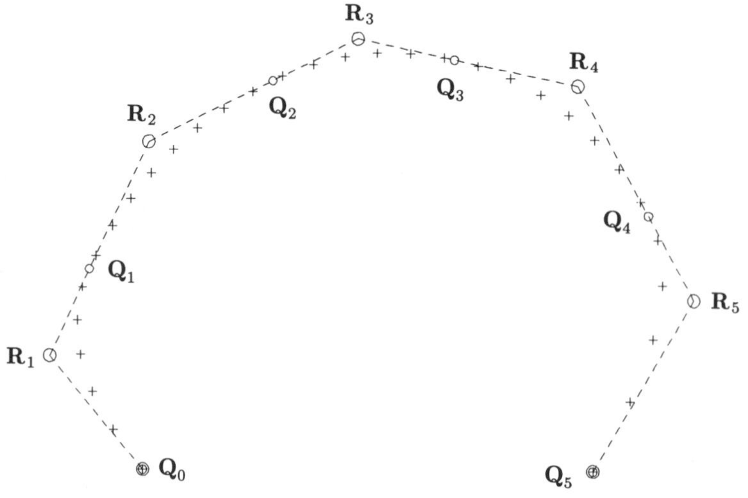

(a)

Figure 9.21. Parameterizations of the curve interpolant in Figure 9.20. (a) C^1 parameterization (Eqs. [9.39]–[9.41]); (b) G^1 parameterization using chord length parameters.

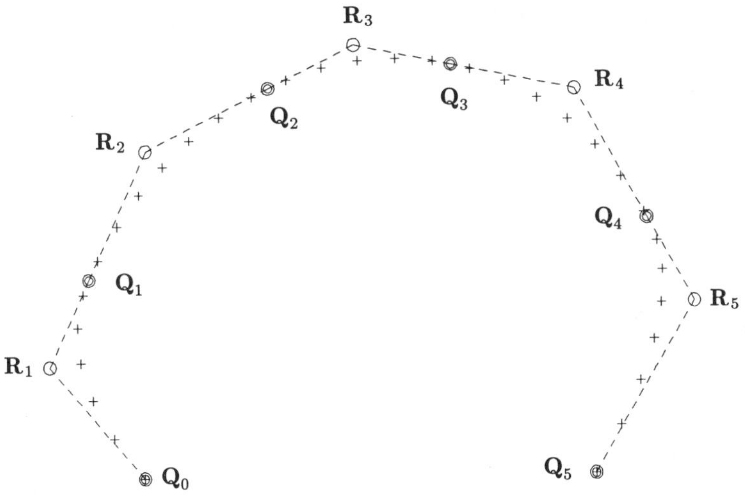

(b)

Figure 9.21. (*Continued.*)

$$\mathbf{R}_k = \frac{1}{2}(\mathbf{Q}_{k-1} + \mathbf{Q}_k) \tag{9.40}$$

All other special cases are handled by creating two parabolic segments between $\mathbf{Q}_{k-1}$ and $\mathbf{Q}_k$, instead of one. Thus, we must compute three additional points, $\mathbf{R}'_k$, $\mathbf{Q}'_k$ and $\mathbf{R}'_{k+1}$ (see Figures 9.22a and 9.22b). Setting

$$\mathbf{R}'_k = \mathbf{Q}_{k-1} + \gamma_k \mathbf{T}_{k-1} \qquad \mathbf{R}'_{k+1} = \mathbf{Q}_k - \gamma_{k+1}\mathbf{T}_k \tag{9.41}$$

and

$$\mathbf{Q}'_k = \frac{\gamma_k \mathbf{R}'_{k+1} + \gamma_{k+1}\mathbf{R}'_k}{\gamma_k + \gamma_{k+1}} \tag{9.42}$$

it remains to determine reasonable choices for γ_k and γ_{k+1}. If $\mathbf{T}_{k-1}$ and $\mathbf{T}_k$ are parallel (but not to $\mathbf{Q}_{k-1}\mathbf{Q}_k$), then set

$$\gamma_k = \gamma_{k+1} = \frac{1}{2} \mid \mathbf{Q}_{k-1}\mathbf{Q}_k \mid \tag{9.43}$$

This is illustrated in Figure 9.22a for the case of a 180° turn. Now consider the case when $\mathbf{T}_{k-1}$ and $\mathbf{T}_k$ are not parallel, but Eq. (9.34) does not hold (see Figure 9.22b). Intuitively, γ_k and γ_{k+1} should depend on the angles θ_{k-1} and θ_k subtended by the chord $\mathbf{Q}_{k-1}\mathbf{Q}_k$ and the tangents $\mathbf{T}_{k-1}$ and $\mathbf{T}_k$, respectively ($0 \le \theta_{k-1},\ \theta_k \le 90°$). Figure 9.22c shows a parabola defined by an isosceles triangle. For this figure one can easily derive

$$\gamma_k = \gamma_{k+1} = \frac{1}{4}\frac{\mid \mathbf{Q}_{k-1}\mathbf{Q}_k \mid}{\cos\theta}$$

This suggests setting

$$\gamma_k = \frac{1}{4}\frac{\mid \mathbf{Q}_{k-1}\mathbf{Q}_k \mid}{\alpha\cos\theta_k + (1-\alpha)\cos\theta_{k-1}}$$

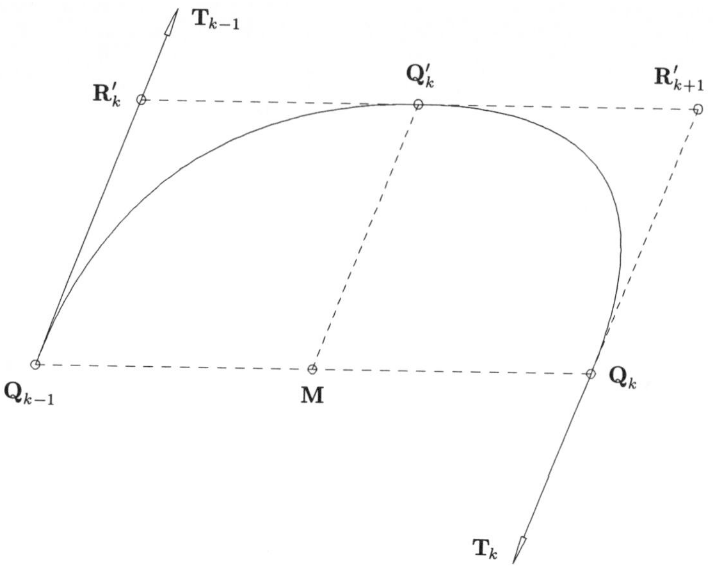

(a)

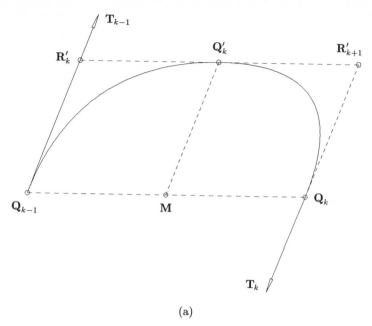

Figure 9.22. Computing piecewise parabolic arcs to tangents at neighboring data points. (a) Parallel end tangents; (b) a turning point implied by tangents $\mathbf{T}_{k-1}$ and $\mathbf{T}_k$; (c) parabola defined by an isosceles control triangle.

$$\gamma_{k+1} = \frac{1}{4} \frac{|\,\mathbf{Q}_{k-1}\mathbf{Q}_k\,|}{\alpha \cos\theta_{k-1} + (1-\alpha)\cos\theta_k} \tag{9.44}$$

where α is some constant between 0 and 1. Based on experimental observation, we choose $\alpha = 2/3$. The two curve segments of Figure 9.22b are obtained using Eqs. (9.41), (9.42), and (9.44).

Figures 9.23–9.25 show several examples. In Figure 9.23a the tangents are computed by Bessel's method [DeBo78], while in Figure 9.23b Akima's method [Akim70] is used. Note how collinearity is maintained in Figure 9.23b. In Figure 9.24a the "no corner" option was selected, resulting in a (perhaps unwanted) smooth connection of each segment. Figure 9.24b shows the corner preserving case, using the same algorithm with only a different flag setting. Figure 9.25 shows the profile of a shoe sole, obtained using this interpolation method.

9.3.3 LOCAL RATIONAL QUADRATIC CURVE INTERPOLATION

The preceding method can be modified to produce rational quadratic curves. All weights at the $\mathbf{Q}_k$ are set to 1; weights at the $\mathbf{R}_k$ can be freely chosen. For example, some applications may desire that the segments be more "circular" rather than parabolic. More specifically, for $k = 1, \ldots, n$, a conic arc is defined

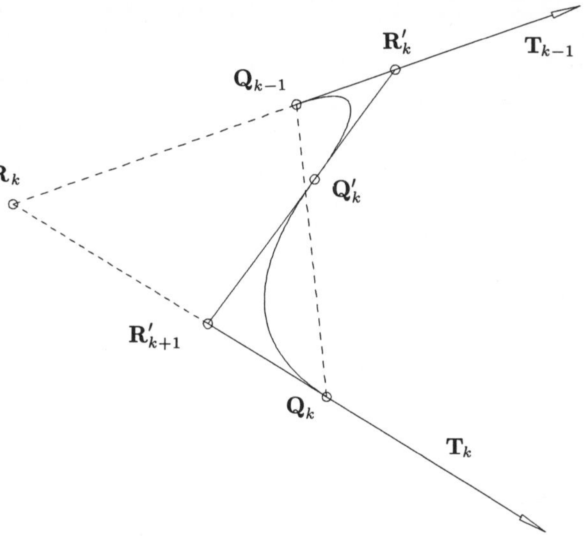

(b)

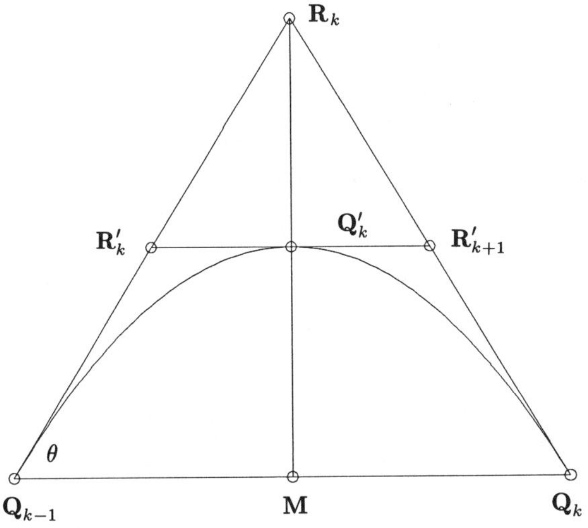

(c)

Figure 9.22. (*Continued.*)

by $\mathbf{Q}_{k-1}$, $\mathbf{R}_k, \mathbf{Q}_k$, and the weight w_k at $\mathbf{R}_k$. The w_k can be set as follows:

1. if $\mathbf{Q}_{k-1}$, $\mathbf{R}_k$, and $\mathbf{Q}_k$ are collinear, set $w_k = 1$;
2. if the triangle is isosceles $\big(\mid \mathbf{Q}_{k-1}\mathbf{R}_k \mid = \mid \mathbf{Q}_k\mathbf{R}_k \mid\big)$, set w_k according to Eq. (7.33) (a precise circular arc);

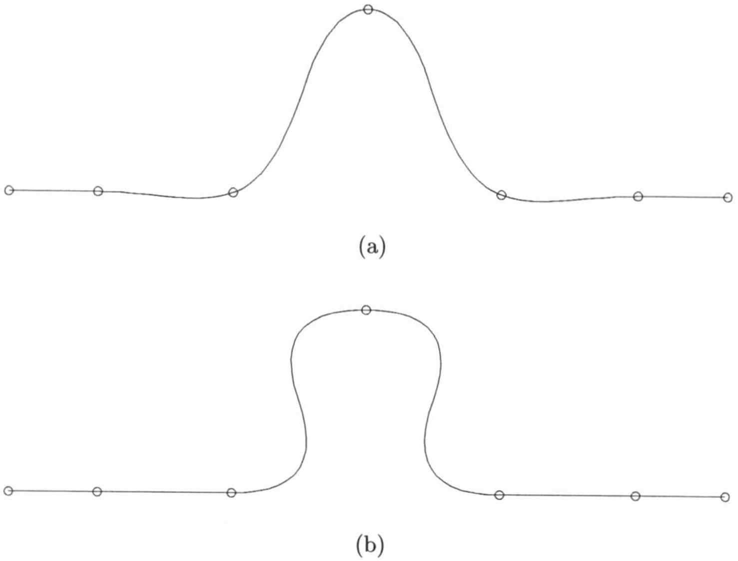

Figure 9.23. Local quadratic curve interpolants. (a) Tangents computed by Bessel's method; (b) tangents computed by Akima's method.

3. if the triangle is not isosceles, set w_k as follows (see Figure 9.26):
   a. let $\mathbf{M} = \frac{1}{2}(\mathbf{Q}_{k-1} + \mathbf{Q}_k)$;
   b. set $\mathbf{S}_1$ to be the intersection of $\mathbf{MR}_k$, with the bisector of the angle $\angle \mathbf{R}_k \mathbf{Q}_{k-1} \mathbf{Q}_k$;
   c. set $\mathbf{S}_2$ to be the intersection of $\mathbf{MR}_k$, with the bisector of the angle $\angle \mathbf{Q}_{k-1} \mathbf{Q}_k \mathbf{R}_k$;
   d. set $\mathbf{S} = \frac{1}{2}(\mathbf{S}_1 + \mathbf{S}_2)$;
   e. with $\mathbf{S}$ as the shoulder point, use Eqs. (7.30) and (7.31) to compute the w_k.

Recognition of the special cases in computing $\mathbf{R}_k$ is exactly as detailed; however, the computation of $\mathbf{R}'_k$ and $\mathbf{R}'_{k+1}$ is slightly different. Referring again to Figure 9.22c but assuming the isosceles triangle defines a circular arc, it follows from Eqs. (7.31)–(7.33) that

$$\gamma_k = \frac{1}{2} \frac{|\,\mathbf{Q}_{k-1}\mathbf{Q}_k\,|}{1+\cos\theta}$$

Thus, we set

$$\gamma_k = \frac{1}{2} \frac{|\,\mathbf{Q}_{k-1}\mathbf{Q}_k\,|}{1+\alpha\cos\theta_k + (1-\alpha)\cos\theta_{k-1}}$$

$$\gamma_{k+1} = \frac{1}{2} \frac{|\,\mathbf{Q}_{k-1}\mathbf{Q}_k\,|}{1+\alpha\cos\theta_{k-1} + (1-\alpha)\cos\theta_k} \tag{9.45}$$

where α is the same constant as in Eq. (9.44).

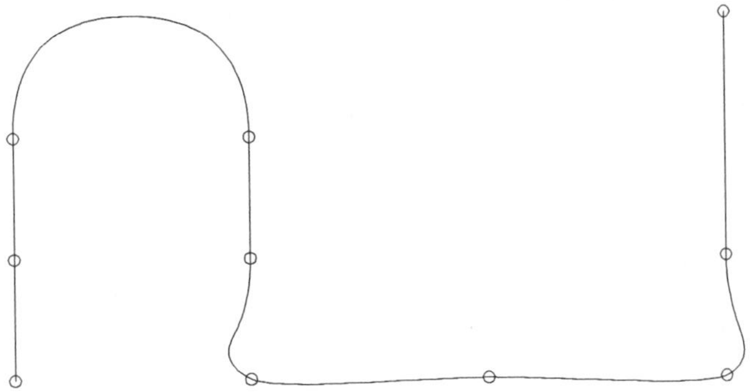

(a)

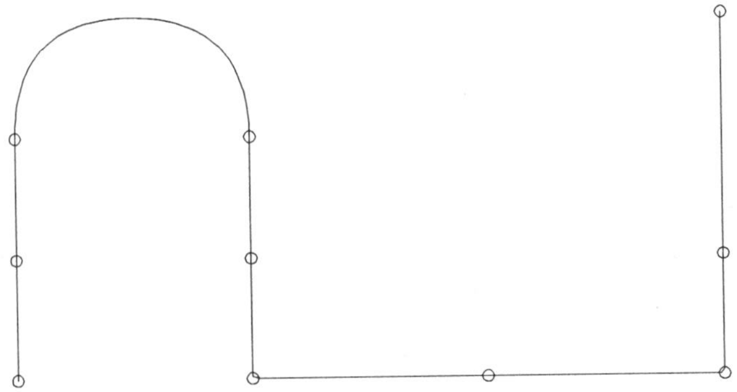

(b)

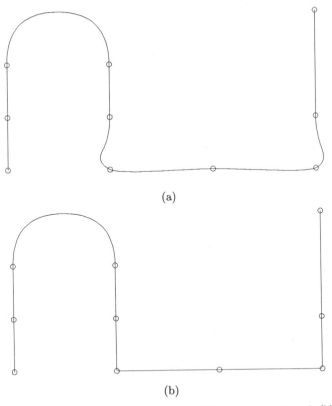

Figure 9.24. Local quadratic curve interpolants. (a) No corner is allowed; (b) the corner is maintained.

Figure 9.27 shows an example of rational quadratic curve interpolation. Notice that circles are precisely reproduced from four points, and the two corners are preserved by setting the corner flag.

9.3.4 LOCAL CUBIC CURVE INTERPOLATION

Cubics easily handle three-dimensional data and inflection points without special treatment. We begin by deriving a general fact about cubic Bézier curves, which is of interest in its own right. Let $\mathbf{P}_0$ and $\mathbf{P}_3$ be two endpoints, and $\mathbf{T}_0$ and $\mathbf{T}_3$ be the corresponding tangent directions with unit length. It is possible to construct a cubic Bézier curve, $\mathbf{C}(u)$, $u \in [0,1]$, with these endpoints and tangent directions, and satisfying

$$\alpha = |\,\mathbf{C}'(0)\,| = \left|\,\mathbf{C}'\left(\frac{1}{2}\right)\right| = |\,\mathbf{C}'(1)\,| \tag{9.46}$$

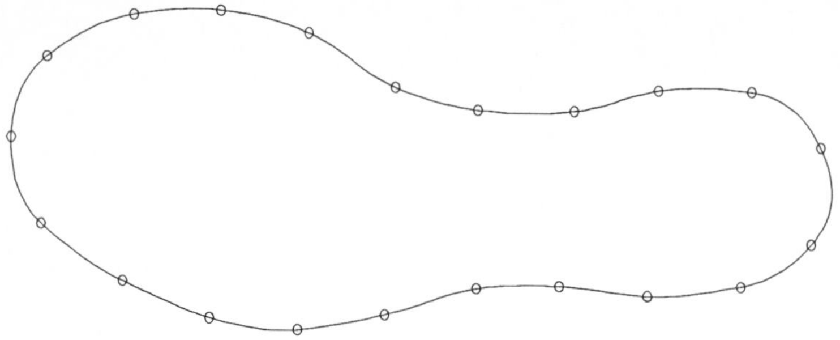

Figure 9.25. A piecewise G^1 parabolic curve interpolant.

(see Figure 9.28), that is, the speed is equal at the start point, midpoint, and endpoint of the curve. Equations (9.46) and (1.10) imply that

$$\mathbf{P}_1 = \mathbf{P}_0 + \frac{1}{3}\alpha\mathbf{T}_0 \qquad \mathbf{P}_2 = \mathbf{P}_3 - \frac{1}{3}\alpha\mathbf{T}_3 \tag{9.47}$$

We apply the deCasteljau Algorithm of Chapter 1 at $u = 1/2$, and, recalling the notation used in that algorithm (see Figure 1.17), we write $\mathbf{P}_0^3 = \mathbf{C}(1/2)$. By backing out of the deCasteljau algorithm one can derive

$$\mathbf{P}_1^2 - \mathbf{P}_0^3 = \frac{1}{8}(\mathbf{P}_3 + \mathbf{P}_2 - \mathbf{P}_1 - \mathbf{P}_0) \tag{9.48}$$

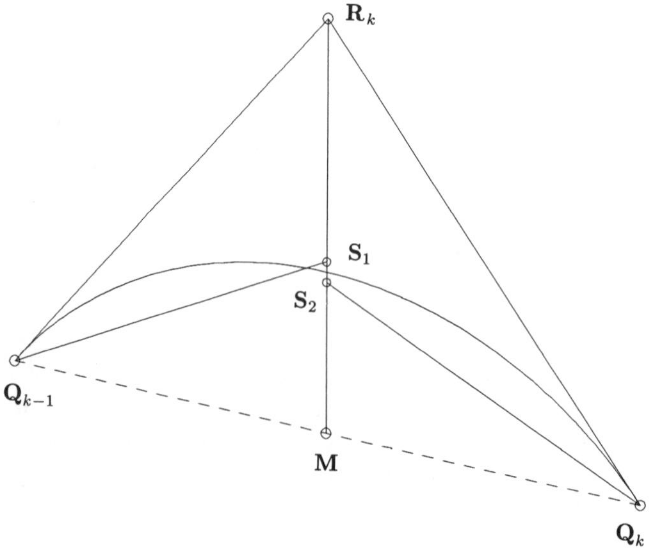

Figure 9.26. Choosing the weight (shoulder point) for rational quadratic interpolation.

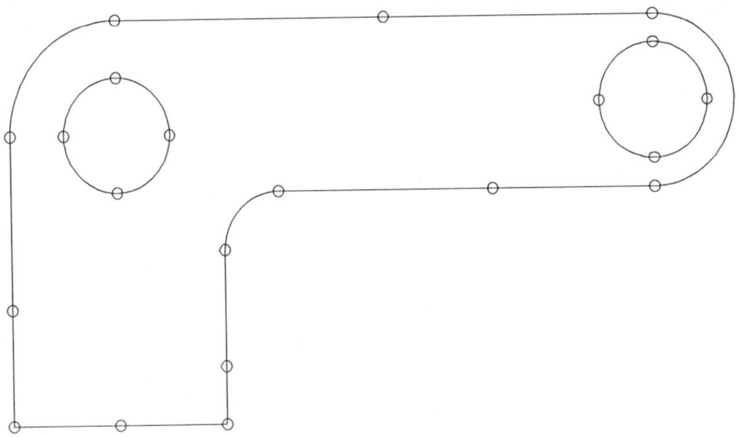

Figure 9.27. Rational quadratic curve interpolants; circles are precisely reproduced, and corners are maintained.

Applying Eq. (1.10) and considering the bisection of the parameter range, it follows that

$$\mathbf{C}'\left(\frac{1}{2}\right) = 6\left(\mathbf{P}_1^2 - \mathbf{P}_0^3\right) \tag{9.49}$$

Setting the speed equal to α, substituting Eq. (9.48) into Eq. (9.49), and using Eq. (9.47), we obtain

$$\begin{aligned}\frac{8}{6}\alpha &= |\,\mathbf{P}_3 + \mathbf{P}_2 - \mathbf{P}_1 - \mathbf{P}_0\,| \\ &= |\,\mathbf{P}_3 + \left(\mathbf{P}_3 - \frac{1}{3}\alpha\mathbf{T}_3\right) - \left(\mathbf{P}_0 + \frac{1}{3}\alpha\mathbf{T}_0\right) - \mathbf{P}_0\,|\end{aligned}$$

which leads to

$$16\alpha^2 = \alpha^2|\,\mathbf{T}_0 + \mathbf{T}_3\,|^2 - 12\alpha(\mathbf{P}_3 - \mathbf{P}_0)\cdot(\mathbf{T}_0 + \mathbf{T}_3) + 36|\,\mathbf{P}_3 - \mathbf{P}_0\,|^2$$

and finally

$$a\alpha^2 + b\alpha + c = 0 \tag{9.50}$$

where

$$a = 16 - |\,\mathbf{T}_0 + \mathbf{T}_3\,|^2 \quad b = 12(\mathbf{P}_3 - \mathbf{P}_0)\cdot(\mathbf{T}_0 + \mathbf{T}_3) \quad c = -36|\,\mathbf{P}_3 - \mathbf{P}_0\,|^2$$

Equation (9.50) has two real solutions for α, one positive and one negative. Substituting the positive solution into Eq. (9.47) yields the desired $\mathbf{P}_1$ and $\mathbf{P}_2$.

We now return to the cubic interpolation problem. Let $\{\mathbf{Q}_k\}$, $k = 0, \ldots, n$, be a set of three-dimensional data points. If tangent vectors are not given, compute them (Eqs. [9.29], [9.31], and [9.33]). We must construct a cubic Bézier

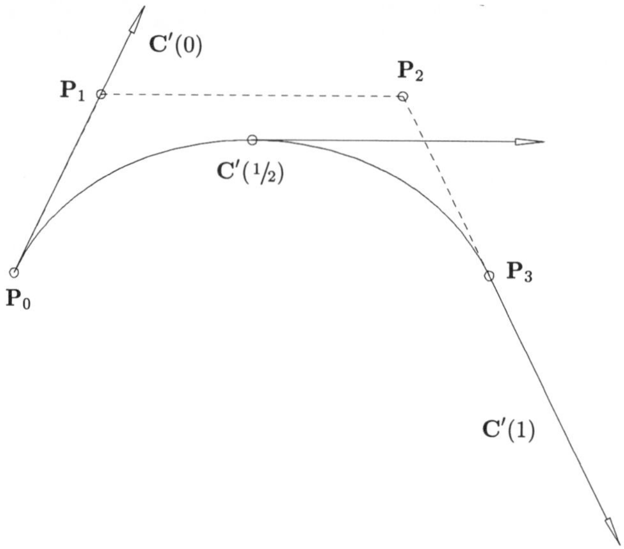

Figure 9.28. A cubic Bézier curve with equal tangent magnitudes at parameters 0, ½, and 1.

curve segment, $\mathbf{C}_k(u)$, between each pair, $\mathbf{Q}_k$, $\mathbf{Q}_{k+1}$. Denote the Bézier control points by

$$\mathbf{P}_{k,0} = \mathbf{Q}_k \quad \mathbf{P}_{k,1} \quad \mathbf{P}_{k,2} \quad \mathbf{P}_{k,3} = \mathbf{Q}_{k+1} \tag{9.51}$$

We must determine suitable locations for $\mathbf{P}_{k,1}$ and $\mathbf{P}_{k,2}$ along $\mathbf{T}_k$ and $\mathbf{T}_{k+1}$, respectively. It is possible to obtain a C^1 continuous cubic and to achieve a good approximation to a uniform parameterization. The method is due to Renner [Renn82]. True uniform parameterization means constant speed over the entire parameter range. We construct a curve with equal speed at each $\mathbf{Q}_k$ and at the midpoint of each Bézier segment. Set $\bar{u}_0 = 0$. Now, for $k = 0, \ldots, n-1$, the $\bar{u}_{k+1}$ and the two inner control points of $\mathbf{C}_k(u)$ are computed as follows:

1. use Eq. (9.50) to compute α and Eq. (9.47) to compute $\mathbf{P}_{k,1}$ and $\mathbf{P}_{k,2}$;
2. set

$$\bar{u}_{k+1} = \bar{u}_k + 3\,|\,\mathbf{P}_{k,1} - \mathbf{P}_{k,0}\,| \tag{9.52}$$

This algorithm yields n Bézier segments, each having speed equal to 1 at their end- and midpoints with respect to their parameter ranges, $[\bar{u}_k, \bar{u}_{k+1}]$. Thus, a C^1 continuous cubic B-spline curve interpolating the $\mathbf{Q}_k$ is defined by the control points (see Figure 9.29)

$$\mathbf{Q}_0, \mathbf{P}_{0,1}, \mathbf{P}_{0,2}, \mathbf{P}_{1,1}, \mathbf{P}_{1,2}, \ldots, \mathbf{P}_{n-2,2,}, \mathbf{P}_{n-1,1}, \mathbf{P}_{n-1,2,}, \mathbf{Q}_n \tag{9.53}$$

and the knots

$$U = \left\{0,0,0,0,\frac{\bar{u}_1}{\bar{u}_n},\frac{\bar{u}_1}{\bar{u}_n},\frac{\bar{u}_2}{\bar{u}_n},\frac{\bar{u}_2}{\bar{u}_n},\ldots,\frac{\bar{u}_{n-1}}{\bar{u}_n},\frac{\bar{u}_{n-1}}{\bar{u}_n},1,1,1,1\right\} \tag{9.54}$$

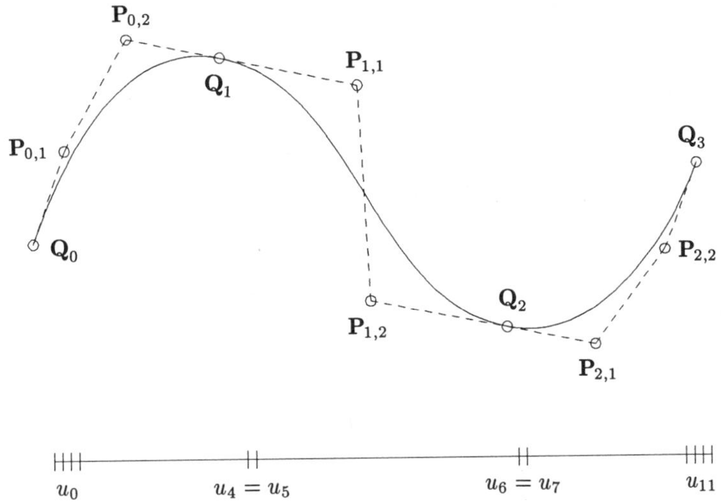

Figure 9.29. C^1 local cubic curve interpolant.

Figure 9.30 shows an example of cubic curve interpolation using this method. The curve is marked at points corresponding to equally spaced parameter values. Figure 9.31 is another example of this interpolation, using the same data set as in Figure 9.7. Notice how collinear points are fitted by straight cubic segments.

9.3.5 LOCAL BICUBIC SURFACE INTERPOLATION

A $C^{(1,1)}$ continuous, bicubic, local surface interpolation scheme is also possible (C^1 continuous in both the u and the v directions). Let $\{\mathbf{Q}_{k,\ell}\}$, $k = 0, \ldots, n$

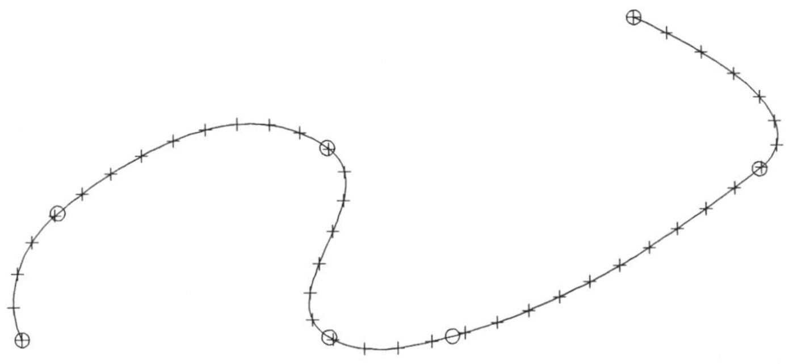

Figure 9.30. Parameterization of a local cubic curve interpolant; the points are computed at equally spaced parameter values.

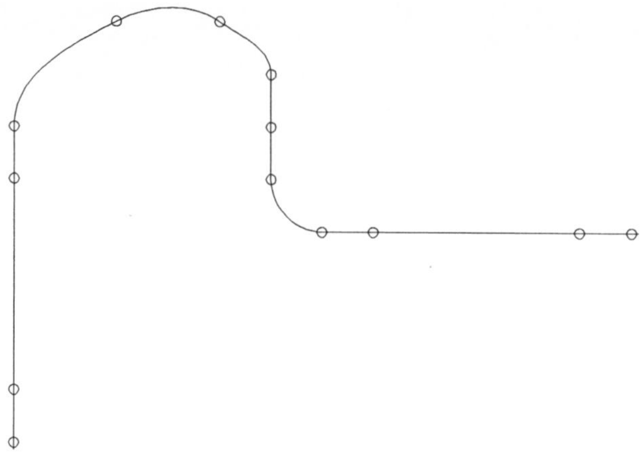

Figure 9.31. The cubic curve interpolant to data shown in Figure 9.7; note how collinearity is preserved.

and $\ell = 0, \ldots, m$, be a set of data points, and let $\{(\bar{u}_k, \bar{v}_\ell)\}$ be the corresponding parameter pairs, computed by chord length averaging (as in Algorithm A9.3). The following method produces a bicubic surface, $\mathbf{S}(u,v)$, satisfying

$$\mathbf{S}(\bar{u}_k, \bar{v}_\ell) = \sum_{i=0}^{2n+1} \sum_{j=0}^{2m+1} N_{i,3}(\bar{u}_k) N_{j,3}(\bar{v}_\ell) \mathbf{P}_{i,j} \qquad (9.55)$$

We obtain the surface by constructing nm bicubic Bézier patches, $\{\mathbf{B}_{k,\ell}(u,v)\}$, $k = 0, \ldots, n-1$, $\ell = 0, \ldots, m-1$, where $\mathbf{Q}_{k,\ell}$, $\mathbf{Q}_{k+1,\ell}$, $\mathbf{Q}_{k,\ell+1}$, $\mathbf{Q}_{k+1,\ell+1}$ are the corner points of the patch, and the patches join with $C^{(1,1)}$ continuity across their boundaries. Except for the surface boundaries, all rows and columns of control points containing the original $\{\mathbf{Q}_{k,\ell}\}$ are removed (see Figures 9.32b and 9.32c), leaving $(2n+2)(2m+2)$ control points in the final B-spline surface. The knot vectors are

$$U = \{0,0,0,0,\bar{u}_1,\bar{u}_1,\bar{u}_2,\bar{u}_2,\ldots,\bar{u}_{n-1},\bar{u}_{n-1},1,1,1,1\}$$
$$V = \{0,0,0,0,\bar{v}_1,\bar{v}_1,\bar{v}_2,\bar{v}_2,\ldots,\bar{v}_{m-1},\bar{v}_{m-1},1,1,1,1\} \qquad (9.56)$$

A bicubic Bézier patch has 16 control points. The 12 boundary control points are obtained by initially looping through the $m+1$ rows and $n+1$ columns of data and using a cubic curve interpolation scheme. The scheme is slightly different from the one detailed previously, because we already have the parameters $\{(\bar{u}_k, \bar{v}_\ell)\}$. Notice that these had to be computed up front, since all rows (columns) must have the same parameterization in a tensor product surface. Thus, we can still force C^1 continuity at the segment endpoints, but we cannot force equal speed at the midpoint of the Bézier curve segments. More specifically, let $\ell = \ell_0$ be fixed, and consider the cubic curve interpolating the points

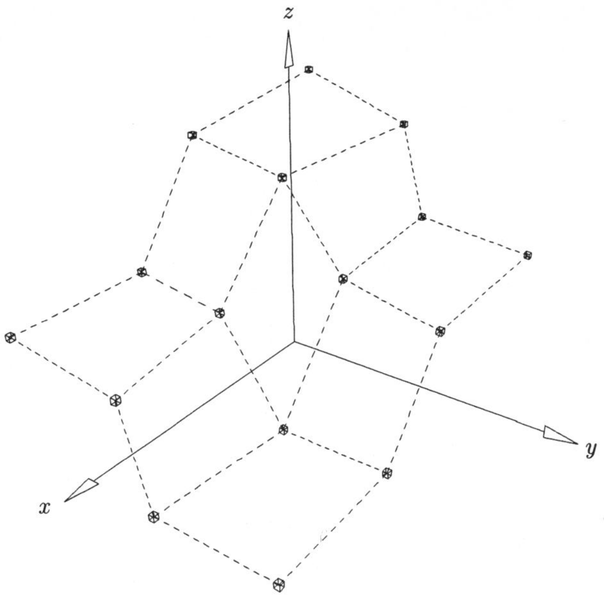

(a)

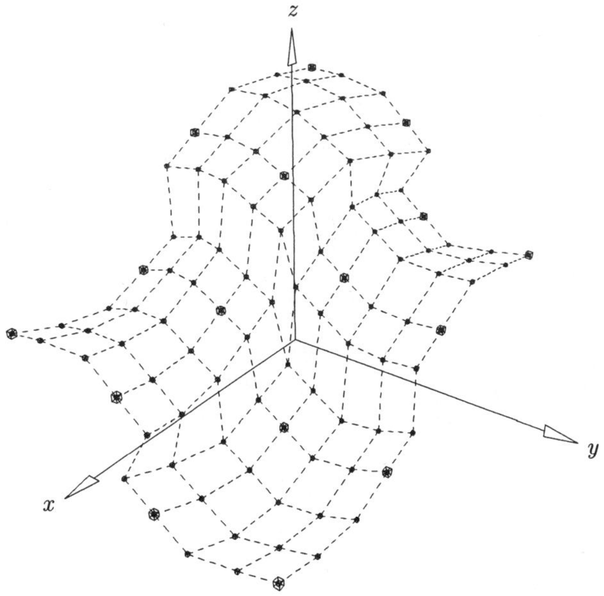

(b)

Figure 9.32. $C^{(1,1)}$ local bicubic surface interpolation. (a) The data set; (b) the Bézier net of the interpolant.

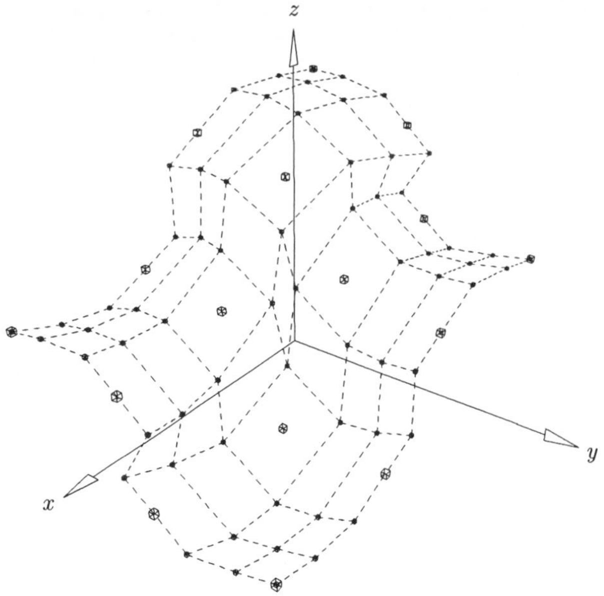

(c)

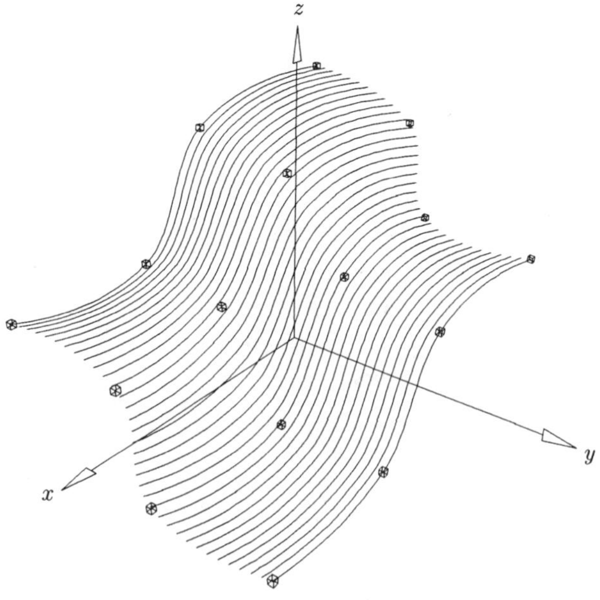

(d)

Figure 9.32. (*Continued.*) (c) a B-spline net (large cubes mark data points, and the small ones are the B-spline control points); (d) the surface interpolant.

$\mathbf{Q}_{0,\ell_0}, \ldots, \mathbf{Q}_{n,\ell_0}$. Let r_{ℓ_0} denote the total chord length of the ℓ_0th row. At each point, $\mathbf{Q}_{k,\ell_0}$, compute the $\mathbf{T}^u_{k,\ell_0}$ (the unit tangent in the u direction) as previously (Eqs. [9.29],[9.31], and [9.33]). Then the interior Bézier points on this row are computed by

$$\mathbf{P}^{k,\ell_0}_{1,0} = \mathbf{Q}_{k,\ell_0} + a\mathbf{T}^u_{k,\ell_0} \qquad \mathbf{P}^{k,\ell_0}_{2,0} = \mathbf{Q}_{k+1,\ell_0} - a\mathbf{T}^u_{k+1,\ell_0} \tag{9.57}$$

where
$$a = \frac{r_{\ell_0}(\bar{u}_{k+1} - \bar{u}_k)}{3} = \frac{r_{\ell_0}\Delta\bar{u}_{k+1}}{3}$$

The resulting curve is C^1 continuous, with derivative magnitude equal to r_{ℓ_0} at all $\mathbf{Q}_{k,\ell_0}$. The same technique is applied to the $n+1$ columns of data.

It remains to compute the four interior control points of each Bézier patch. This requires estimates for the mixed partial derivative, $\mathbf{D}^{uv}_{k,\ell}$, at each $\mathbf{Q}_{k,\ell}$, as well as Eq. (3.24) (and analogous formulas for the other three corners). We derive a formula for $\mathbf{D}^{uv}_{k,\ell}$ based on the three-point Bessel method (Eqs. [9.28], [9.30], and [9.32]). Let r_ℓ and s_k denote the total chord length of the ℓth row (kth column). Then

$$\mathbf{D}^u_{k,\ell} = r_\ell\mathbf{T}^u_{k,\ell} \qquad \mathbf{D}^v_{k,\ell} = s_k\mathbf{T}^v_{k,\ell} \tag{9.58}$$

Then set
$$\mathbf{d}^{vu}_{k,\ell} = (1-\alpha_k)\frac{\mathbf{D}^v_{k,\ell} - \mathbf{D}^v_{k-1,\ell}}{\Delta\bar{u}_k} + \alpha_k\frac{\mathbf{D}^v_{k+1,\ell} - \mathbf{D}^v_{k,\ell}}{\Delta\bar{u}_{k+1}}$$

and
$$\mathbf{d}^{uv}_{k,\ell} = (1-\beta_\ell)\frac{\mathbf{D}^u_{k,\ell} - \mathbf{D}^u_{k,\ell-1}}{\Delta\bar{v}_\ell} + \beta_\ell\frac{\mathbf{D}^u_{k,\ell+1} - \mathbf{D}^u_{k,\ell}}{\Delta\bar{v}_{\ell+1}}$$

with
$$\alpha_k = \frac{\Delta\bar{u}_k}{\Delta\bar{u}_k + \Delta\bar{u}_{k+1}} \qquad \beta_\ell = \frac{\Delta\bar{v}_\ell}{\Delta\bar{v}_\ell + \Delta\bar{v}_{\ell+1}}$$

Finally
$$\mathbf{D}^{uv}_{k,\ell} = \frac{\alpha_k\mathbf{d}^{uv}_{k,\ell} + \beta_\ell\mathbf{d}^{vu}_{k,\ell}}{\alpha_k + \beta_\ell} \tag{9.59}$$

The appropriate end formulas (Eq. [9.32]) must be used on the boundaries. The four interior control points of the (k,ℓ)th patch are now computed using Eqs. (9.59) and (3.24)

$$\mathbf{P}^{k,\ell}_{1,1} = \gamma\mathbf{D}^{uv}_{k,\ell} + \mathbf{P}^{k,\ell}_{0,1} + \mathbf{P}^{k,\ell}_{1,0} - \mathbf{P}^{k,\ell}_{0,0}$$

$$\mathbf{P}^{k,\ell}_{2,1} = -\gamma\mathbf{D}^{uv}_{k+1,\ell} + \mathbf{P}^{k,\ell}_{3,1} - \mathbf{P}^{k,\ell}_{3,0} + \mathbf{P}^{k,\ell}_{2,0}$$

$$\mathbf{P}^{k,\ell}_{1,2} = -\gamma\mathbf{D}^{uv}_{k,\ell+1} + \mathbf{P}^{k,\ell}_{1,3} - \mathbf{P}^{k,\ell}_{0,3} + \mathbf{P}^{k,\ell}_{0,2}$$

$$\mathbf{P}^{k,\ell}_{2,2} = \gamma\mathbf{D}^{uv}_{k+1,\ell+1} + \mathbf{P}^{k,\ell}_{2,3} + \mathbf{P}^{k,\ell}_{3,2} - \mathbf{P}^{k,\ell}_{3,3}$$

where
$$\gamma = \frac{\Delta\bar{u}_{k+1}\Delta\bar{v}_{\ell+1}}{9}$$

We now summarize with an algorithm. For the sake of efficiency, the sequence of events is slightly different than detailed here. The algorithm requires local arrays: td[n+1][m+1][3], which contains the $\mathbf{T}^u_{k,\ell}$, $\mathbf{T}^v_{k,\ell}$, and $\mathbf{D}^{uv}_{k,\ell}$; ub[n+1] and vb[m+1], which contain the parameter values; and r[m+1] and s[n+1], which store the total chord lengths of the rows and columns, respectively.

```
ALGORITHM A9.5
  LocalSurfInterp(n,m,Q,U,V,P)
    { /* Local surface interpolation */
    { /* through (n+1)(m+1) points  */
      /* Input:  n,m,Q  */
      /* Output: U,V,P  */
    total = 0.0;   /* get ub[], r[] and u direction tangents */
    for (k=0; k<=n; k++)   ub[k] = 0.0;
    for (l=0; l<=m; l++)
      {
      Compute and load T^u_{0,l} into td[0][l][0];
      r[l] = 0.0;
      for (k=1; k<=n; k++)
        {
        Compute and load T^u_{k,l} into td[k][l][0]
            /* Eqs.(9.31) and (9.33) */
        d = | Q_{k,l} - Q_{k-1,l} |;
        ub[k] = ub[k]+d;
        r[l] = r[l]+d;
        }
      total = total + r[l];
      }
    for (k=1; k<n; k++)   ub[k] = ub[k-1]+ub[k]/total;
    ub[n] = 1.0;
    total = 0.0;   /* get vb[], s[] and v direction tangents */
    for (l=0; l<=m; l++)   vb[l] = 0.0;
    for (k=0; k<=n; k++)
      {
      Compute and load T^v_{k,0} into td[k][0][1];
      s[k] = 0.0;
      for (l=1; l<=m; l++)
        {
        Compute and load T^v_{k,l} into td[k][l][1]
            /* Eqs.(9.31) and (9.33) */
        d = | Q_{k,l} - Q_{k,l-1} |;
        vb[l] = vb[l]+d;
        s[k] = s[k]+d;
        }
      total = total + s[k];
      }
```

```
for (l=1; l<m; l++)   vb[l] = vb[l-1]+vb[l]/total;
vb[m] = 1.0;
Load the U knot vector;
Load the V knot vector;
Compute all Bézier control points along each row and
    column of data points.
for (k=0; k<=n; k++)
  for (l=0; l<=m; l++)
    {
    Compute the D^{uv}_{k,ℓ} by Eq.(9.59) and load into td[k][l][2].
    }
for (k=0; k<n; k++)
  for (l=0; l<m; l++)
    {
    Compute the four inner control points of the (k,l)th
        Bezier patch and load them into P.
    }
Load the NURBS control points by discarding Bézier points
    along inner rows and columns.   /* Figure 9.32c */
}
```

Figure 9.32 shows the surface construction process. In Figure 9.32a data points are shown marked by small cubes. Figure 9.32b illustrates the control points of the Bézier patches. Eliminating Bézier points along inner rows and columns yields the NURBS surface control net depicted in Figure 9.32c. The surface is shown in Figure 9.32d.

This interpolation scheme easily generates closed $C^{(1,1)}$ continuous surfaces. Figures 9.33a and 9.33b show an example of a surface interpolation where the data indicates a closed surface in one direction. In Figures 9.34a and 9.34b the surface is closed in both directions (a toroidal-like interpolant). A nice property of this method is that flat (planar) patches are generated where the data points indicate planarity. An example of this is shown in Figures 9.35a and 9.35b.

Obtaining pleasing surfaces when the data is unevenly spaced is more difficult for surfaces than for curves. Figures 9.36a and 9.36b show an interpolation to very unevenly spaced data. Although the surface is not particularly pleasing, the results using the global methods of the previous section are not much different.

9.4 Global Approximation

Approximation is more difficult than interpolation. In interpolation, the number of control points is automatically determined by the chosen degree and the number of data items, knot placement is straightforward, and there is no curve or surface error to be checked. In approximation, a curve/surface error bound, E, is input along with the data to be fit. It is usually not known in advance how many control points are required to obtain the desired accuracy, E, and

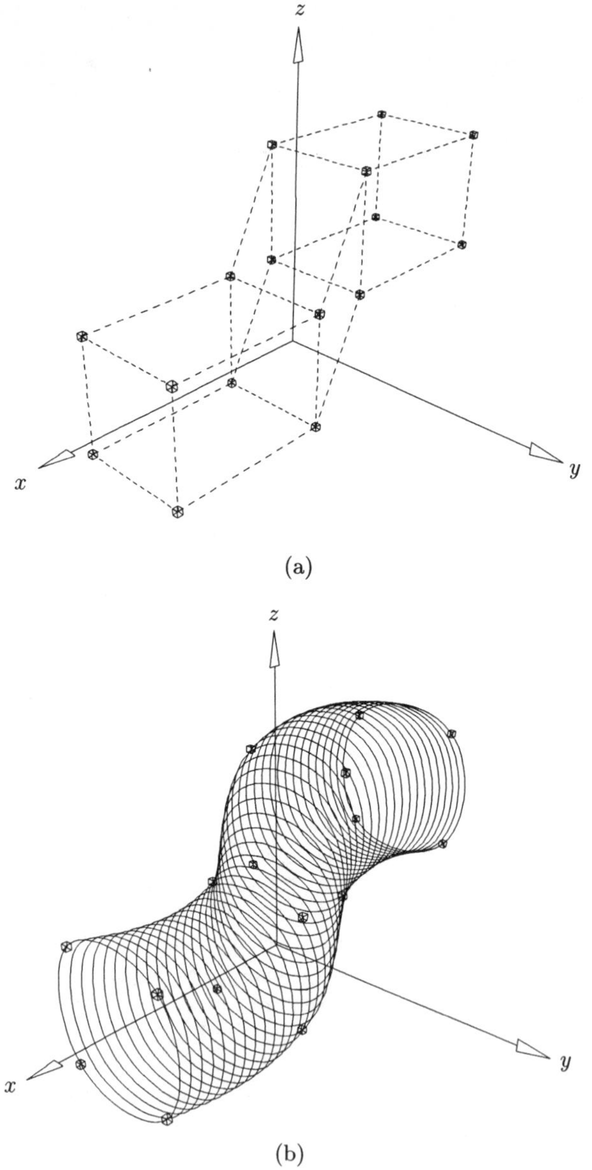

Figure 9.33. A surface interpolation example using a local bicubic surface interpolant. (a) Data points; (b) an interpolating surface.

hence approximation methods are generally iterative. Roughly speaking, global methods proceed in one of two ways:

1a. start with the minimum or a small number of control points;

b. fit an approximating curve or surface to the data, using a global fit method;

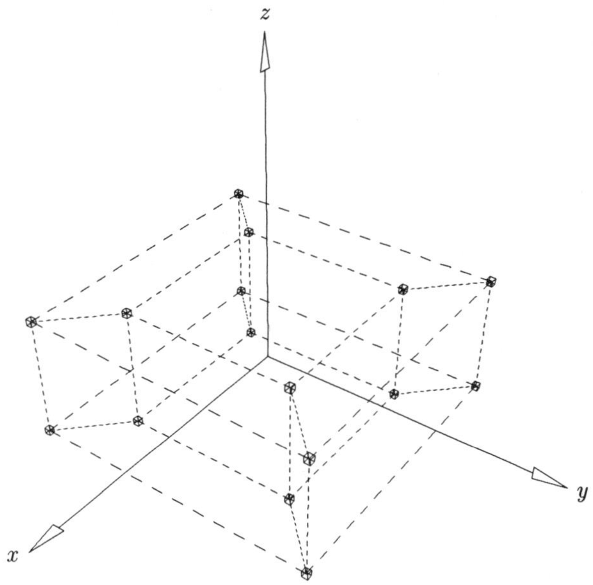

(a)

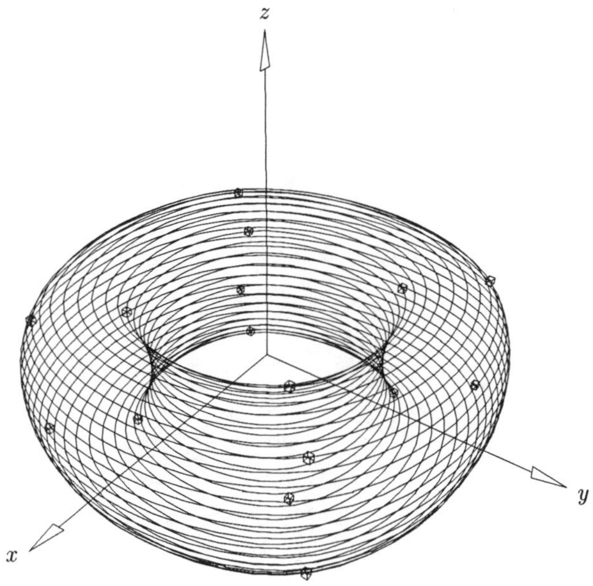

(b)

Figure 9.34. A surface interpolation example using a local bicubic surface interpolant. (a) Data points; (b) interpolating surface.

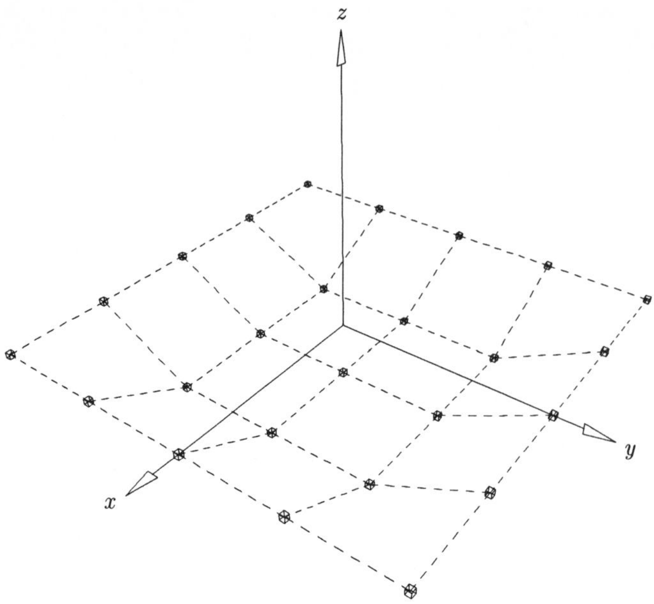

(a)

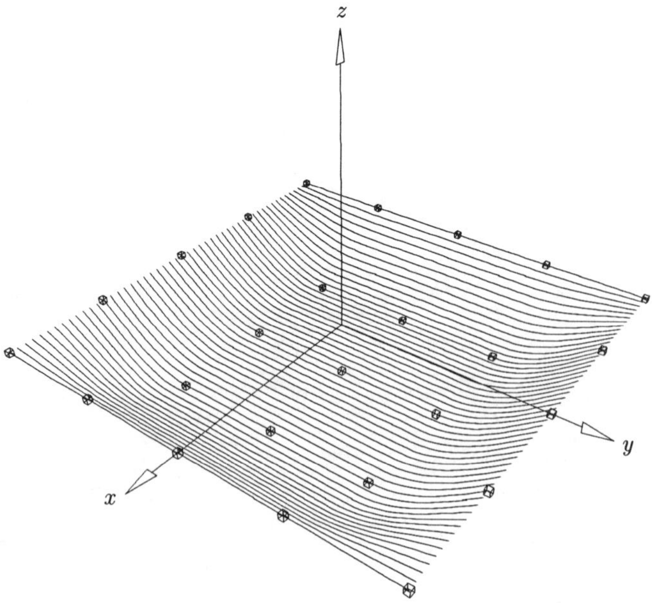

(b)

Figure 9.35. A surface interpolation example using a local bicubic surface interpolant. (a) Data points; (b) an interpolating surface.

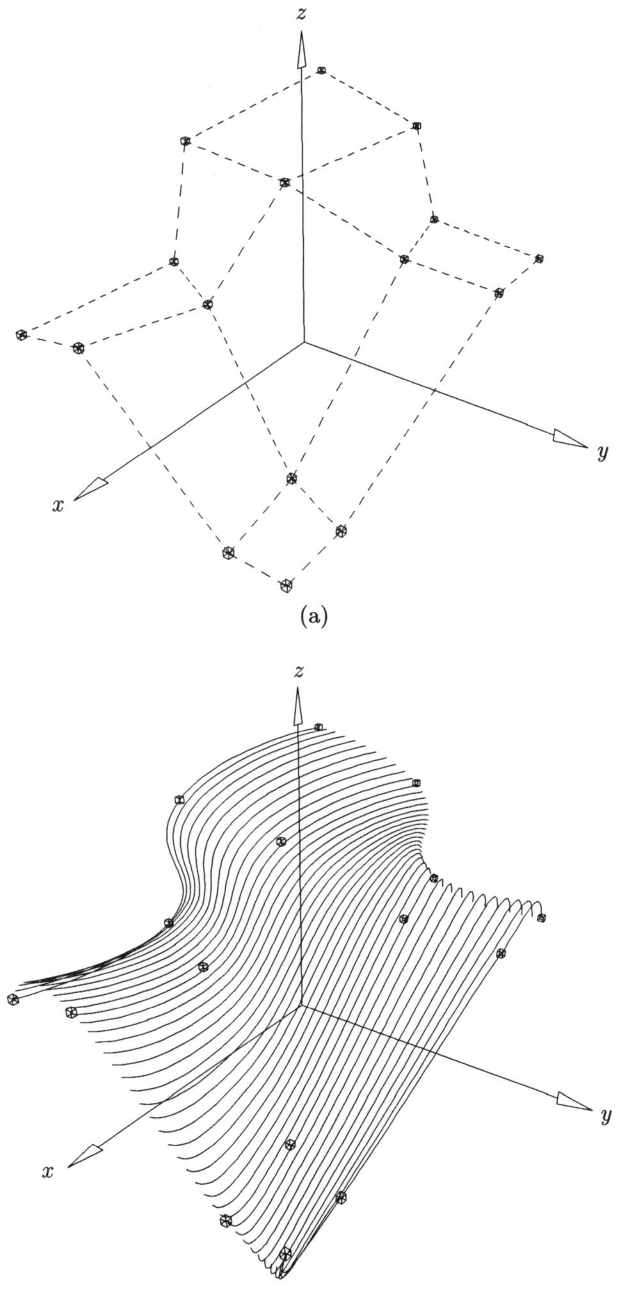

(b)

Figure 9.36. A surface interpolation example using a local bicubic surface interpolant. (a) Data points; (b) an interpolating surface.

c. check the deviation of the curve/surface from the data;

d. if the deviation everywhere is less than E, return; else increase the number of control points and go back to Step 1(b).

2a. start with the maximum or "many" control points, enough that the first approximation satisfies E;

b. fit a curve/surface to the data using a global method;

c. check if the deviation E is satisfied everywhere;

d. if E is no longer satisfied return the previous curve or surface, else reduce the number of control points and go back to Step 2(b).

We return to these two methods in Section 9.4.4, and in particular we give an example of the second type. Clearly, approximation is also more expensive than interpolation. Multiple fits are required, and deviation checking can be expensive.

A central ingredient in both of these methods is that given a *fixed number* of control points, say n, we fit an approximating curve (surface) to the data. There are many ways to do this. For example, a nonlinear optimization problem can be set up, with the control points, parameters ($\bar{u}_k$), knots, and even the weights as unknowns. The objective function to be minimized must measure the error in some way, e.g., least squares or maximum deviation (e.g., see [Laur93]). In Sections 9.4.1–9.4.3, we present curve and surface fitting methods in which a fixed number of control points are the only unknowns, and they are solved using linear least squares techniques.

9.4.1 LEAST SQUARES CURVE APPROXIMATION

To avoid the nonlinear problem, we set the weights to 1, and precompute values for the parameters and knots. We then set up and solve the (unique) linear least squares problem for the unknown control points. We start with a simple curve fit to point data. Assume that $p \geq 1$, $n \geq p$, and $\mathbf{Q}_0, \ldots, \mathbf{Q}_m$ $(m > n)$ are given. We seek a pth degree nonrational curve

$$\mathbf{C}(u) = \sum_{i=0}^{n} N_{i,p}(u)\mathbf{P}_i \qquad u \in [0,1] \tag{9.61}$$

satisfying that:

- $\mathbf{Q}_0 = \mathbf{C}(0)$ and $\mathbf{Q}_m = \mathbf{C}(1)$;
- the remaining $\mathbf{Q}_k$ are approximated in the least squares sense, i.e.

$$\sum_{k=1}^{m-1} |\,\mathbf{Q}_k - \mathbf{C}(\bar{u}_k)\,|^2 \tag{9.62}$$

is a minimum with respect to the $n+1$ variables, $\mathbf{P}_i$; the $\{\bar{u}_k\}$ are the precomputed parameter values.

We emphasize that the resulting curve generally does not pass precisely through $\mathbf{Q}_k$, and $\mathbf{C}(\bar{u}_k)$ is not the closest point on $\mathbf{C}(u)$ to $\mathbf{Q}_k$. Let

$$\mathbf{R}_k = \mathbf{Q}_k - N_{0,p}(\bar{u}_k)\,\mathbf{Q}_0 - N_{n,p}(\bar{u}_k)\,\mathbf{Q}_m \qquad k = 1, \ldots, m-1 \tag{9.63}$$

Then set

$$\begin{aligned} f &= \sum_{k=1}^{m-1} |\,\mathbf{Q}_k - \mathbf{C}(\bar{u}_k)\,|^2 = \sum_{k=1}^{m-1} |\mathbf{R}_k - \sum_{i=1}^{n-1} N_{i,p}(\bar{u}_k)\,\mathbf{P}_i|^2 \\ &= \sum_{k=1}^{m-1} \left(\mathbf{R}_k - \sum_{i=1}^{n-1} N_{i,p}(\bar{u}_k)\,\mathbf{P}_i\right) \cdot \left(\mathbf{R}_k - \sum_{i=1}^{n-1} N_{i,p}(\bar{u}_k)\,\mathbf{P}_i\right) \\ &= \sum_{k=1}^{m-1} \Bigg[\mathbf{R}_k \cdot \mathbf{R}_k - 2\sum_{i=1}^{n-1} N_{i,p}(\bar{u}_k)(\mathbf{R}_k \cdot \mathbf{P}_i) \\ &\qquad + \left(\sum_{i=1}^{n-1} N_{i,p}(\bar{u}_k)\,\mathbf{P}_i\right) \cdot \left(\sum_{i=1}^{n-1} N_{i,p}(\bar{u}_k)\,\mathbf{P}_i\right)\Bigg] \end{aligned}$$

f is a scalar-valued function of the $n-1$ variables, $\mathbf{P}_1, \ldots, \mathbf{P}_{n-1}$. Now we apply the standard technique of linear least squares fitting [DeBo78; Vand83; Lanc86]; to minimize f we set the derivatives of f with respect to the $n-1$ points, $\mathbf{P}_\ell$, equal to zero. The ℓth derivative is

$$\frac{\partial f}{\partial \mathbf{P}_\ell} = \sum_{k=1}^{m-1} \left(-2N_{\ell,p}(\bar{u}_k)\mathbf{R}_k + 2N_{\ell,p}(\bar{u}_k)\sum_{i=1}^{n-1} N_{i,p}(\bar{u}_k)\,\mathbf{P}_i\right)$$

which implies that

$$-\sum_{k=1}^{m-1} N_{\ell,p}(\bar{u}_k)\mathbf{R}_k + \sum_{k=1}^{m-1}\sum_{i=1}^{n-1} N_{\ell,p}(\bar{u}_k)N_{i,p}(\bar{u}_k)\,\mathbf{P}_i = 0$$

It follows that

$$\sum_{i=1}^{n-1} \left(\sum_{k=1}^{m-1} N_{\ell,p}(\bar{u}_k)N_{i,p}(\bar{u}_k)\right) \mathbf{P}_i = \sum_{k=1}^{m-1} N_{\ell,p}(\bar{u}_k)\mathbf{R}_k \tag{9.64}$$

Equation (9.64) is one linear equation in the unknowns $\mathbf{P}_1, \ldots, \mathbf{P}_{n-1}$. Letting $\ell = 1, \ldots, n-1$ yields the system of $n-1$ equations in $n-1$ unknowns

$$(N^T N)\mathbf{P} = \mathbf{R} \tag{9.65}$$

where N is the $(m-1) \times (n-1)$ matrix of scalars

$$N = \begin{bmatrix} N_{1,p}(\bar{u}_1) & \cdots & N_{n-1,p}(\bar{u}_1) \\ \vdots & \ddots & \vdots \\ N_{1,p}(\bar{u}_{m-1}) & \cdots & N_{n-1,p}(\bar{u}_{m-1}) \end{bmatrix} \tag{9.66}$$

$\mathbf{R}$ is the vector of $n-1$ points

$$\mathbf{R} = \begin{bmatrix} N_{1,p}(\bar{u}_1)\mathbf{R}_1 + \cdots + N_{1,p}(\bar{u}_{m-1})\mathbf{R}_{m-1} \\ \vdots \\ N_{n-1,p}(\bar{u}_1)\mathbf{R}_1 + \cdots + N_{n-1,p}(\bar{u}_{m-1})\mathbf{R}_{m-1} \end{bmatrix} \tag{9.67}$$

and

$$\mathbf{P} = \begin{bmatrix} \mathbf{P}_1 \\ \vdots \\ \mathbf{P}_{n-1} \end{bmatrix}$$

Note that Eq. (9.65) is one coefficient matrix, with three right hand sides and three sets of unknowns (x, y, z coordinates). In order to set up Eqs. (9.66) and (9.67), a knot vector $U = \{u_0, \ldots, u_r\}$ and parameters $\{\bar{u}_k\}$ are required. The $\{\bar{u}_k\}$ can be computed using Eq. (9.5). The placement of the knots should reflect the distribution of the $\{\bar{u}_k\}$. If d is a positive real number, denote by $i = \text{int}(d)$ the largest integer such that $i \le d$. We need a total of $n+p+2$ knots; there are $n-p$ internal knots, and $n-p+1$ internal knot spans. Let

$$d = \frac{m+1}{n-p+1} \tag{9.68}$$

Then define the internal knots by

$$\begin{aligned} i &= \text{int}(jd) \qquad \alpha = jd - i \\ u_{p+j} &= (1-\alpha)\bar{u}_{i-1} + \alpha\bar{u}_i \qquad j = 1, \ldots, n-p \end{aligned} \tag{9.69}$$

Equation (9.69) guarantees that every knot span contains at least one $\bar{u}_k$, and under this condition deBoor [DeBo78] shows that the matrix $(N^T N)$ in Eq. (9.65) is positive definite and well-conditioned. It can be solved by Gaussian elimination without pivoting. Furthermore, $(N^T N)$ has a semibandwidth less than $p+1$ (if $N_{i,j}$ is the element in the ith row, jth column, then $N_{i,j} = 0$ if $|\, i-j \,| > p$). Finally, concerning implementation, note that the matrix N (Eq. [9.66]) can be very large, and most of its elements are zero; in some applications it is not uncommon for $m = 1000$ and $n = 100$. Hence, the implementor may want to develop a storage scheme that stores only the nonzero elements of N. Once $(N^T N)$ and $\mathbf{R}$ (Eq. [9.67]) are computed, N can be deallocated. Similarly, only the nonzero band of $(N^T N)$ should be stored.

Figures 9.37a–9.37c show examples of simple least squares curve fits. In Figure 9.37a seven control points were specified. Figure 9.37b shows a nine control point fit, whereas Figure 9.37c depicts an eleven control point fit. Notice that, in a distance sense, the approximation improves as the number of control points increases. However, as the number of control points approaches the number of data points, undesirable shapes can occur if the data exhibits noise or unwanted wiggles.

Mile End Library
Queen Mary University of London
Reading Week 3rd-9th Nov

Extended Reading Week Loans
One Week Loans borrowed or renewed
from Thursday 30th Oct
will be due back on Monday 10th Nov

Borrowed Items 10/11/2014 11:05
XXXXXX5577

Item Title	Due Date
* The NURBS book	09/03/2015

* Indicates items borrowed today
PLEASE NOTE
If you still have overdue books on loan
you may have more fines to pay

Don't forget to renew your loans
if you are going away for Reading Week

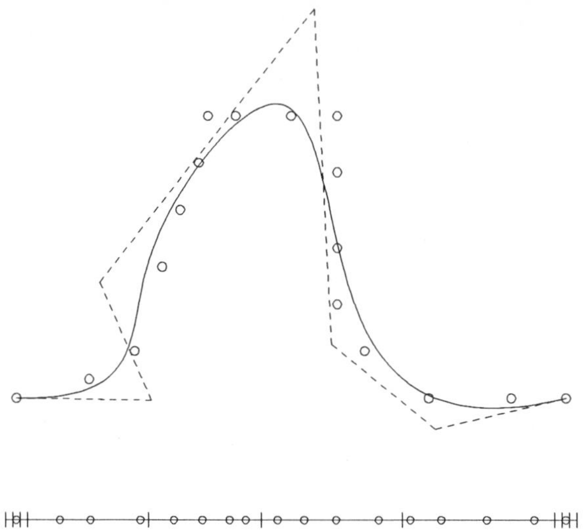

(a)

Figure 9.37. Global curve fitting. (a) Seven control points; (b) nine control points; (c) eleven control points.

9.4.2 WEIGHTED AND CONSTRAINED LEAST SQUARES CURVE FITTING

We now present a very general, weighted and constrained least squares curve fitting method. It is a NURBS adaptation of an algorithm by Smith et al [Smit74]. Let $\{\mathbf{Q}_i\}$, $i = 0, \ldots, r$, be the points to be approximated. Optionally, the first derivative $\mathbf{D}_i$ at any $\mathbf{Q}_i$ can be specified. Let $\{\mathbf{D}_{i(j)}\}$, $j = 0, \ldots, s$, be the set of derivatives; $-1 \le s \le r$, where $s = -1$, means no derivatives are specified. Furthermore, any $\mathbf{Q}_i$ or $\mathbf{D}_{i(j)}$ can be constrained (precisely interpolated). We divide the $\{\mathbf{Q}_i\}$ and $\{\mathbf{D}_{i(j)}\}$ into unconstrained and constrained sets. Denote by $\mathbf{Q}^u_{i(0)}, \ldots, \mathbf{Q}^u_{i(r_u)}$ and $\mathbf{D}^u_{i(0)}, \ldots, \mathbf{D}^u_{i(s_u)}$ the unconstrained items, and by $\mathbf{Q}^c_{i(0)}, \ldots, \mathbf{Q}^c_{i(r_c)}$ and $\mathbf{D}^c_{i(0)}, \ldots, \mathbf{D}^c_{i(s_c)}$ the constrained items (s_u, s_c, or r_c equal to -1 means no data corresponding to this index). Note that $r = r_u + r_c + 1$ and $s = s_u + s_c + 1$. We also allow a positive weight to be assigned to each unconstrained item, hence we have $w^q_{i(0)}, \ldots, w^q_{i(r_u)}$ and $w^d_{i(0)}, \ldots, w^d_{i(s_u)}$ ($w^q_i, w^d_i > 0$). These weights allow additional influence over the "tightness" of the approximation to each data item relative to its neighbors. $w^q_i, w^d_i = 1$ is the default. Increasing a weight increases the tightness of the approximation to that item, whereas decreasing the weight loosens the approximation to that item. Notice that these weights have nothing to do with weights in the NURBS sense.

Now let $m_u = r_u + s_u + 1$ and $m_c = r_c + s_c + 1$. We want to approximate the unconstrained data in the least squares sense and interpolate the constrained

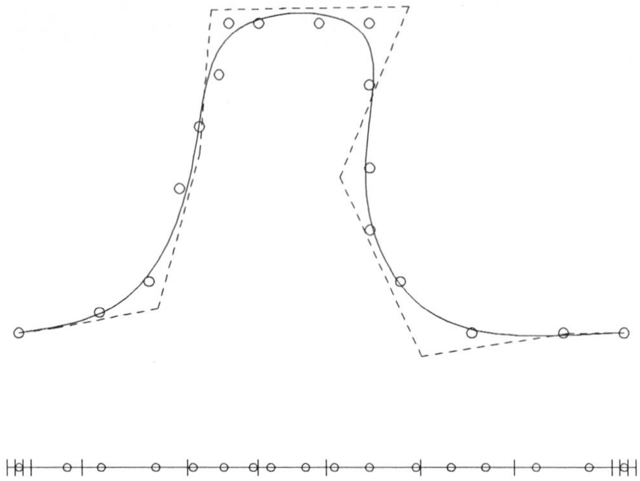

(b)

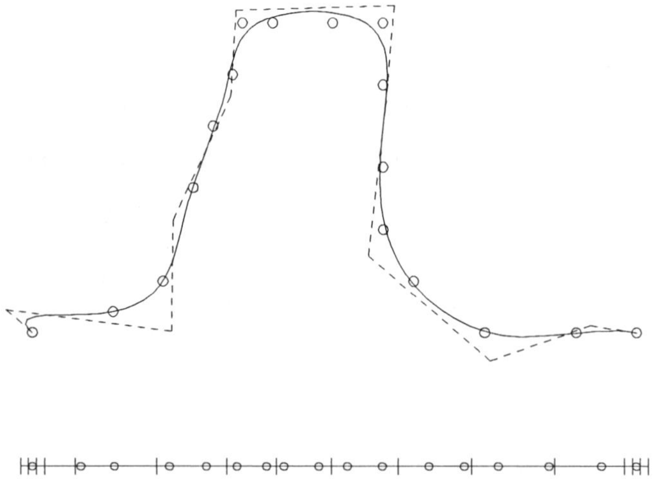

(c)

Figure 9.37. (*Continued.*)

data with a pth degree nonrational curve, $\mathbf{C}(u)$, with $n+1$ control points. The next algorithm requires that

$$m_c < n \qquad m_c + n < m_u + 1 \tag{9.70}$$

Now let:

$\mathbf{S}_k, k = 0, \ldots, m_u$, be the kth unconstrained data item (a $\mathbf{Q}^u$ or a $\mathbf{D}^u$);

$\mathbf{T}_k, k = 0, \ldots, m_c$, be the kth constrained data item (a $\mathbf{Q}^c$ or a $\mathbf{D}^c$);

$w_k, k = 0, \ldots, m_u$, be the kth weight (a w^q or a w^d).

Define the vectors/matrices:

$\mathbf{S} = [\mathbf{S}_k]$ (a vector with $m_u + 1$ elements);

$\mathbf{T} = [\mathbf{T}_k]$ (a vector with $m_c + 1$ elements);

$W = [w_k]$ (an $(m_u + 1) \times (m_u + 1)$ diagonal matrix, with the w_k on the diagonal);

$\mathbf{P} = [\mathbf{P}_k]$ (the vector of $n + 1$ unknown control points);

$N = [ND_{i,p}(\bar{u}_k)]$, where $ND_{i,p}(\bar{u}_k)$ is the ith basis function or its first derivative, evaluated at $\bar{u}_k$, which is a parameter value corresponding to an unconstrained data item; this is an $(m_u + 1) \times (n + 1)$ matrix of scalars;

$M = [MD_{i,p}(\bar{u}_k)]$, where $MD_{i,p}(\bar{u}_k)$ is the ith basis function or its first derivative, evaluated at $\bar{u}_k$, which is a parameter value corresponding to a constrained data item; this is an $(m_c+1) \times (n+1)$ matrix of scalars.

The $\bar{u}_k$ can be computed using Eq. (9.5), and the knots u_j according to Eq. (9.68) and Eq. (9.69) (replace m by r in Eq. [9.68]).

Determining the curve is basically a constrained minimization problem, involving $n + 1$ unknowns (the $\mathbf{P}_i$) and $m_c + 1$ constraints. The standard method of solution is to use Lagrange multipliers (see [Kapl52]). The idea is to introduce $m_c + 1$ additional unknowns, λ_k (the Lagrange multipliers), thereby obtaining a partitioned $(n + m_c + 2) \times (n + m_c + 2)$ system of equations. From this system a solution is first obtained for the $m_c + 1$ λ_k and subsequently for the $n+1$ $\mathbf{P}_i$. Let

$$\mathbf{A} = [\lambda_k]$$

be the vector of Lagrange multipliers; note that each λ_k is a vector with the same dimensionality as the $\{\mathbf{Q}_i\}$ and $\{\mathbf{D}_{i(j)}\}$.

The unconstrained equations are

$$N\mathbf{P} = \mathbf{S}$$

and the constrained equations are

$$M\mathbf{P} = \mathbf{T}$$

The error in the unconstrained equations is $\mathbf{S} - N\mathbf{P}$, and we want to minimize the sum of the weighted squares of this error, subject to $M\mathbf{P} = \mathbf{T}$. Hence, using Lagrange multipliers we want to minimize the expression

$$(\mathbf{S}^T - \mathbf{P}^T N^T) W (\mathbf{S} - N\mathbf{P}) + \mathbf{A}^T (M\mathbf{P} - \mathbf{T})$$

with respect to the unknowns, $\mathbf{A}$ and $\mathbf{P}$. Differentiating and setting equal to zero yields

$$-2(\mathbf{S}^T W N - \mathbf{P}^T N^T W N) + \mathbf{A}^T M = 0$$

$$M\mathbf{P} - \mathbf{T} = 0$$

Transposing and factoring 2 out of $\mathbf{A}$ yields

$$N^T W N \mathbf{P} + M^T \mathbf{A} = N^T W \mathbf{S} \qquad (9.71)$$

$$M\mathbf{P} = \mathbf{T} \qquad (9.72)$$

or in partitioned matrix form

$$\begin{bmatrix} N^T W N & M^T \\ M & 0 \end{bmatrix} \begin{bmatrix} \mathbf{P} \\ \mathbf{A} \end{bmatrix} = \begin{bmatrix} N^T W \mathbf{S} \\ \mathbf{T} \end{bmatrix} \qquad (9.73)$$

We must solve Eq. (9.73) for $\mathbf{A}$ and $\mathbf{P}$. There is a unique solution if $N^T W N$ and $M(N^T W N)^{-1} M^T$ are both invertible. This is seen by solving Eq. (9.71) for $\mathbf{P}$, that is

$$\mathbf{P} = \left(N^T W N\right)^{-1} N^T W \mathbf{S} - \left(N^T W N\right)^{-1} M^T \mathbf{A} \qquad (9.74)$$

Multiplying by M yields

$$M\mathbf{P} = M\left(N^T W N\right)^{-1} N^T W \mathbf{S} - M\left(N^T W N\right)^{-1} M^T \mathbf{A}$$

Finally, from Eq. (9.72) we find that

$$M\left(N^T W N\right)^{-1} M^T \mathbf{A} = M\left(N^T W N\right)^{-1} N^T W \mathbf{S} - \mathbf{T} \qquad (9.75)$$

or

$$\mathbf{A} = \left(M\left(N^T W N\right)^{-1} M^T\right)^{-1} \left(M\left(N^T W N\right)^{-1} N^T W \mathbf{S} - \mathbf{T}\right) \qquad (9.76)$$

Hence, we solve first for $\mathbf{A}$ and then for $\mathbf{P}$ by substituting $\mathbf{A}$ into Eq. (9.74).

Algorithm `A9.6` implements weighted and constrained least squares curve fitting. The input is:

`Q[r+1]`: an array containing the points to be fit (constrained and unconstrained);

`r`: the upper index of `Q[]`;

`Wq[r+1]`: `Wq[i] > 0` means $\mathbf{Q}_i$ is unconstrained, and `Wq[i]` is the weight w_i^q; `Wq[i] < 0` means $\mathbf{Q}_i$ is to be constrained;

`D[s+1]`: an array containing the derivatives; `s = -1` means no derivatives are specified;

`s`: there are $s+1$ derivatives in `D[]`;

`I[s+1]`: an integer array; `I[j]` gives the index into `Q[]` of the point corresponding to the derivative in `D[j]` (i.e., `D[j]`$= \mathbf{D}_{i(j)}$);

`Wd[s+1]`: `Wd[j] > 0` means `D[j]` is unconstrained, and `Wd[j]` is the weight $w_{i(j)}^d$; `Wd[j] < 0` means `D[j]` is to be constrained;

`n`: a fit with $n+1$ control points;

`p`: a fit with degree p curve.

The knots U and control points P are output. The algorithm uses `LUDecomposition()` and `ForwardBackward()` to invert the matrix $(N^T WN)$ and to solve for the Lagrange multipliers, **A**. $(N^T WN)$ has a semibandwidth less than $p+1$, due to the way in which the algorithm constructs N. In general **A** can have full bandwidth, but it is usually a small matrix. The appropriate algorithms from Chapter 2 are used to determine knot spans and to compute basis functions and their derivatives. The following local arrays are required:

ub[r+1]: the parameters;

N[mu+1][n+1],M[mc+1][n+1],S[mu+1],T[mc+1],A[mc+1]: the arrays corresponding to the matrices defined previously (except S[], which is $W\mathbf{S}$);

W[mu+1]: the weights; since the matrix W is diagonal, only a vector of length $m_u + 1$ is required;

funs[2][p+1]: contains the basis functions, and their derivatives where specified (see Algorithms A2.2 and A2.3).

Furthermore, several local arrays are required for temporary storage of matrices computed in Eqs. (9.71)–(9.76).

```
ALGORITHM A9.6
  WCLeastSquaresCurve(Q,r,Wq,D,s,I,Wd,n,p,U,P)
    { /* Weighted & constrained least squares curve fit  */
      /* Input:  Q,r,Wq,D,s,I,Wd,n,p  */
      /* Output: U,P  */
    ru = -1;    rc = -1;
    for (i=0; i<=r; i++)
      if (Wq[i] > 0.0)    ru = ru+1;
        else              rc = rc+1;
    su = -1;    sc = -1;
    for (j=0; j<=s; j++)
      if (Wd[j] > 0.0)    su = su+1;
        else              sc = sc+1;
    mu = ru+su+1;    mc = rc+sc+1;
    if (mc >= n || mc+n >= mu+1)   return(error);
    Compute and load parameters ū_k into ub[] (Eq.[9.5]);
    Compute and load the knots into U[] (Eqs.[9.68],[9.69]);
         /* Now set up arrays N,W,S,T,M */
    j = 0;   /* current index into I[] */
    mu2 = 0;   mc2 = 0;   /* counters up to mu and mc */
    for (i=0; i<=r; i++)
      {
      span = FindSpan(n,p,ub[i],U);
      dflag = 0;
      if (j <= s)
        if (i == I[j])   dflag = 1;
```

```
    if (dflag == 0)     BasisFuns(span,ub[i],p,U,funs);
      else              DersBasisFuns(span,ub[i],p,1,U,funs);
    if (Wq[i] > 0.0)
      {  /* Unconstrained point */
      W[mu2] = Wq[i];
      Load the mu2th row of N[][] from funs[0][];
      S[mu2] = W[mu2]*Q[i];
      mu2 = mu2+1;
      }
      else
      {  /* Constrained point */
      Load the mc2th row of M[][] from funs[0][];
      T[mc2] = Q[i];
      mc2 = mc2+1;
      }
    if (dflag == 1)
      {  /* Derivative at this point */
      if (Wd[j] > 0.0)
        {  /* Unconstrained derivative */
        W[mu2] = Wd[j];
        Load the mu2th row of N[][] from funs[1][];
        S[mu2] = W[mu2]*D[j];
        mu2 = mu2+1;
        }
        else
        {  /* Constrained derivative */
        Load the mc2th row of M[][] from funs[1][];
        T[mc2] = D[j];
        mc2 = mc2+1;
        }
      j = j+1;
      }
    }  /* End of for-loop i=0,...,r */
  Compute the matrices N^T W N and N^T W S;
  LUDecomposition(N^T W N,n+1,p);
  if (mc < 0)
    {  /* No constraints */
    Use ForwardBackward() to solve for the control points P[].
        Eq.(9.71) reduces to (N^T W N) P = N^T W S.
    return;
    }
  Compute the inverse (N^T W N)^{-1}, using ForwardBackward().
  Do matrix operations to get: M (N^T W N)^{-1} M^T and
      M (N^T W N)^{-1} (N^T W S) - T;
  Solve Eq.(9.75) for the Lagrange multipliers, load into A[];
```

Then $\mathbf{P} = \left(N^T W N\right)^{-1}\left(\left(N^T W \mathbf{S}\right) - M^T \mathbf{A}\right)$, Eq.(9.74);
}

Figures 9.38–9.43 show several examples of weighted and constrained curve fitting. Figure 9.38 shows an unconstrained fit with all weights set to 1. In Figure 9.39 the weights w_4^q, w_5^q, w_6^q, and w_7^q were increased to 100 each, resulting in a curve pull towards the data points $\mathbf{Q}_4, \ldots, \mathbf{Q}_7$. Note that, despite the misleading graphics, the curve does not pass through the endpoints. Figure 9.40 shows a constrained fit with point (marked with squares) as well as derivative (arrowed vectors) constraints. The curve passes through the square-marked points and is tangential to the specified vectors at these points. In Figure 9.41 two additional weights were introduced, $w_5^q = 100$ and $w_{15}^q = 100$. Figure 9.42 shows the same curve as in Figure 9.40, except that two new inner derivatives were used. Similarly, Figure 9.43 is the same as Figure 9.42 except that the weights $w_4^q = 50$ and $w_{16}^q = 20$ were added.

9.4.3 LEAST SQUARES SURFACE APPROXIMATION

We turn now to surface approximation with a fixed number of control points. Let $\{\mathbf{Q}_{k,\ell}\}$, $k = 0, \ldots, r$ and $\ell = 0, \ldots, s$, be the $(r+1) \times (s+1)$ set of points to be approximated by a (p,q)th degree nonrational surface, with $(n+1) \times (m+1)$ control points. Although it is possible to set up and solve a general least squares surface fitting problem, linear or nonlinear, and with or without weights and constraints, the task is much more complex than for curves. We present a surface approximation scheme here which builds upon our least squares curve scheme, is

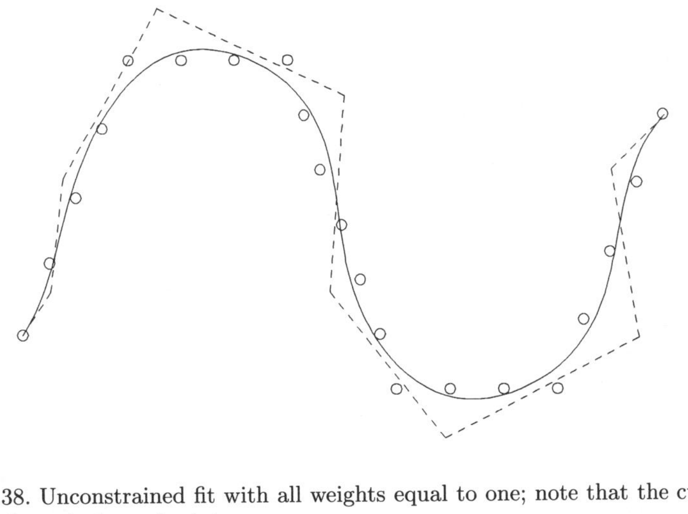

Figure 9.38. Unconstrained fit with all weights equal to one; note that the curve does not pass through the endpoints.

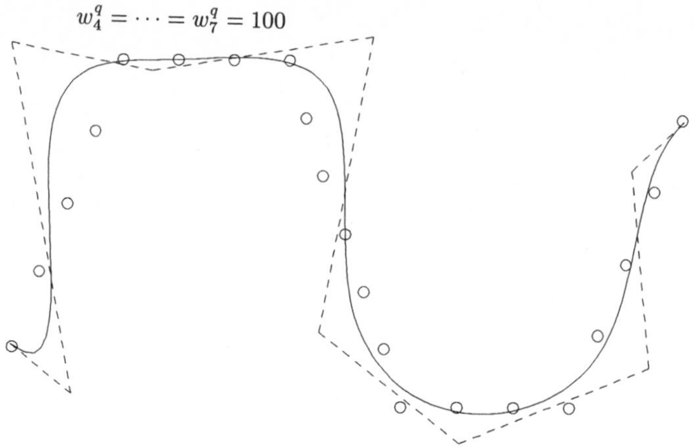

Figure 9.39. Unconstrained fit with weights $w_4^q = w_5^q = w_6^q = w_7^q = 100$; the curve does not pass through the endpoints.

very simple, and is quite adequate for most applications. As was done for global surface interpolation, we simply fit curves across the data in one direction, then fit curves through the resulting control points across the other direction.

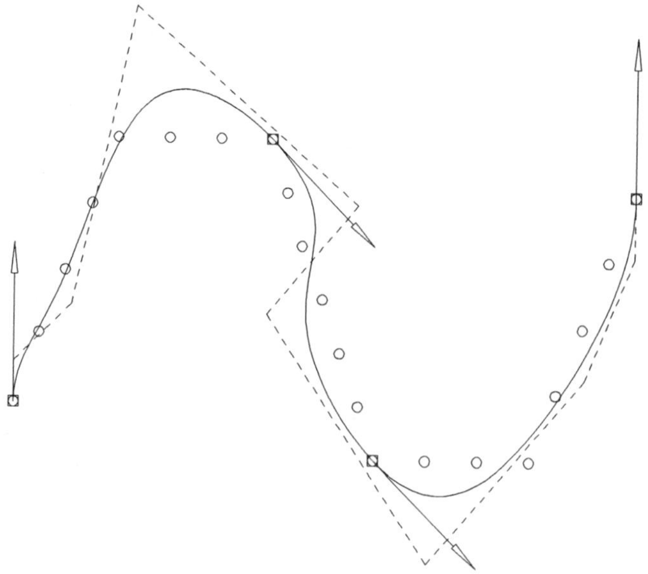

Figure 9.40. A constrained curve fit; point constraints are marked by squares, tangent constraints are shown by arrows, and all weights are one.

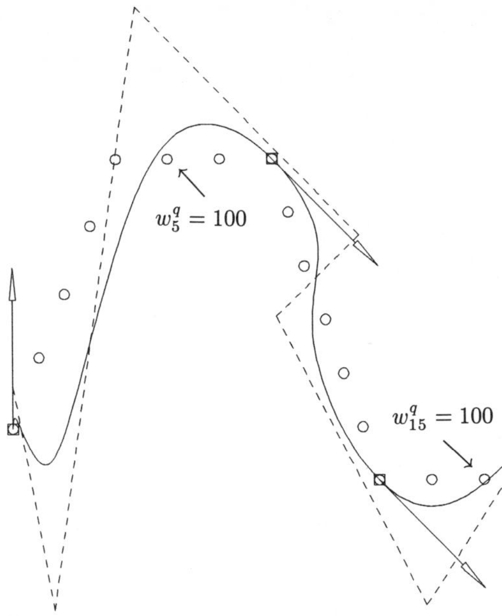

Figure 9.41. The curve from Figure 9.40, with weights $w_5^q = w_{15}^q = 100$.

Algorithm `A9.7` interpolates the corner points $\mathbf{Q}_{0,0}$, $\mathbf{Q}_{r,0}$, $\mathbf{Q}_{0,s}$, and $\mathbf{Q}_{r,s}$ precisely, and approximates the remaining $\{\mathbf{Q}_{k,l}\}$. It uses repeated least squares curve fits given by Eqs. (9.63) and (9.65)–(9.67). It fits the $s+1$ rows of data

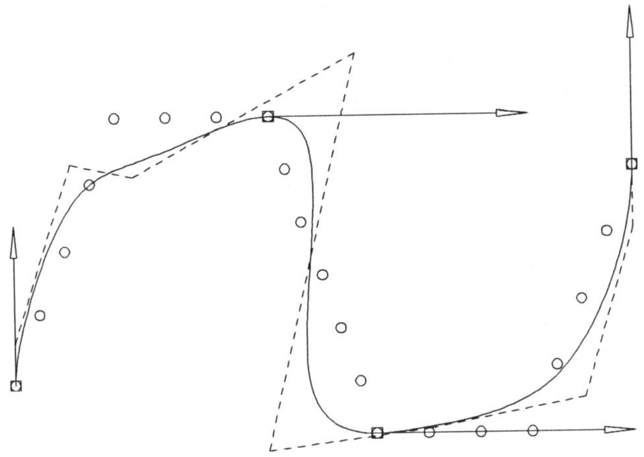

Figure 9.42. The curve from Figure 9.40, but using two new tangent constraints.

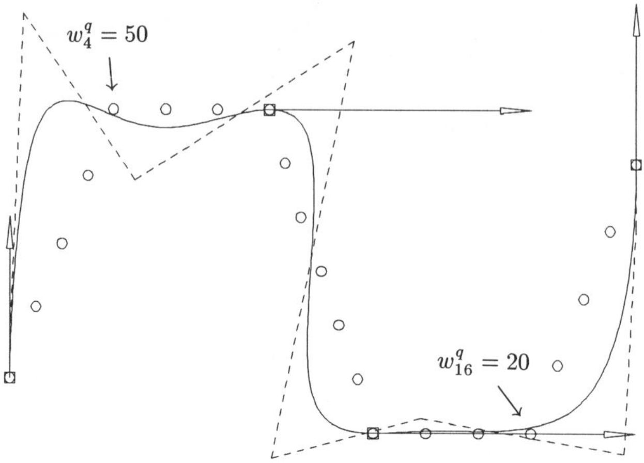

Figure 9.43. The curve from Figure 9.42, but with weights $w_4^q = 50$ and $w_{16}^q = 20$.

first, storing the resulting control points in the local array, `Temp[n+1][s+1]`. Then it fits across these control points to produce the $(n+1) \times (m+1)$ surface control points. Notice that the matrices N and N^TN only have to be computed once for each direction, and the LU decomposition of N^TN is only done once for each direction. We require local arrays `Nu[r-1][n-1]` and `NTNu[n-1][n-1]` for the u direction fits, and `Nv[s-1][m-1]` and `NTNv[m-1][m-1]` for the v direction fits. The vector $\mathbf{R}$ of Eq. (9.68) is stored in `Ru[n-1]` and `Rv[m-1]`.

```
ALGORITHM A9.7
  GlobalSurfApproxFixednm(r,s,Q,p,q,n,m,U,V,P)
    { /* Global surface approx with fixed num of ctrl pts */
      /* Input: r,s,Q,p,q,n,m */
      /* Output: U,V,P */
    SurfMeshParams(r,s,Q,ub,vb);
    Compute knots U by Eqs.(9.68),(9.69);
    Compute knots V by Eqs.(9.68),(9.69);
    Compute Nu[][] and NTNu[][] using Eq.(9.66);
    LUDecomposition(NTNu,n-1,p);
    for (j=0; j<=s; j++)
      { /* u direction fits */
      Temp[0][j] = Q_{0,j};     Temp[n][j] = Q_{r,j};
      Compute and load Ru[] (Eqs.[9.63],[9.67]);
      Call ForwardBackward() to get the control points
          Temp[1][j],...,Temp[n-1][j];
      }
    Compute Nv[][] and NTNv[][] using Eq.(9.66);
    LUDecomposition(NTNv,m-1,q);
```

```
for (i=0; i<=n; i++)
  { /* v direction fits */
  P[i][0] = Temp[i][0];     P[i][m] = Temp[i][s];
  Compute and load Rv[] (Eqs.[9.63],[9.67]);
  Call ForwardBackward() to get the control points
      P[i][1],...,P[i][m-1];
  }
}
```

Figures 9.44–9.47 illustrate surface fitting. Figure 9.44 shows the original data joined by straight lines. Figure 9.45a depicts a degree $(2,3)$ least squares surface fit using a (5×6) control net. The error of approximation is shown in Figure 9.45b. Figure 9.46a shows an approximation with an (8×8) net. Its quality of approximation is much better, as seen in Figure 9.46b. For comparison, Figure 9.47 shows a degree $(2,3)$ global interpolation (using chord length parameters) to the data in Figure 9.44.

Of course, one can fit the $r+1$ columns first, and then fit across the resulting $m+1$ rows of control points. In general the results are not the same. We know of no criteria to decide in advance which approach will yield the "best" fit for a particular set of data. Clearly, this technique can easily be extended to accomodate point and derivative constraints and weighting on the boundaries. Interior constraints are more difficult. Suppose $\mathbf{Q}_{k_0,\ell_0}$, $0 < k_0 < r$ and $0 < \ell_0 < s$, is to be constrained. The point is constrained during the u direction

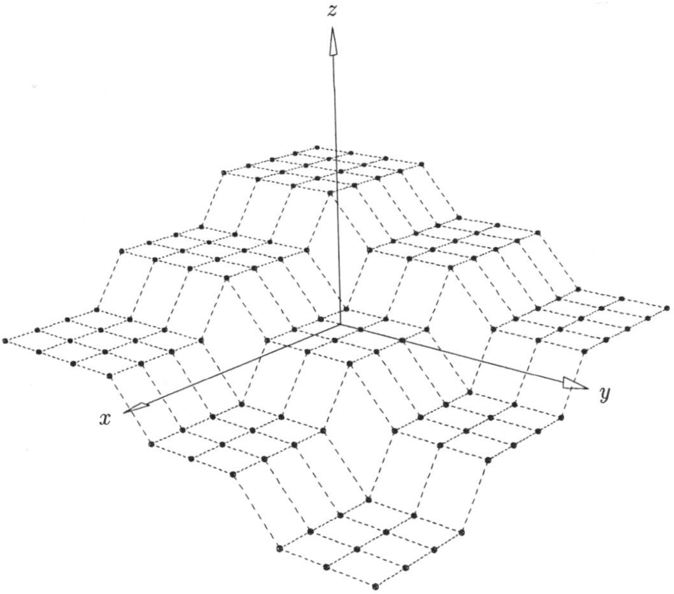

Figure 9.44. Data set for surface approximation.

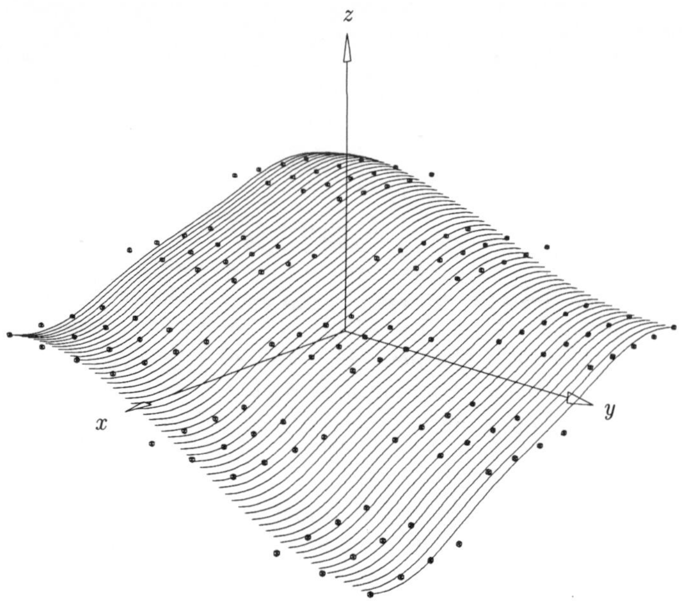

(a)

Figure 9.45. A least squares surface fit with a degree $(2,3)$ surface using a (5×6) control net. (a) Surface approximant; (b) error surface (error measured at data points).

curve fit, as in Algorithm `A9.6`. Then, if $\bar{u}_{k_0} \in [u_i, u_{i+1})$, the points $\texttt{Temp}[i-p][\ell_0], \ldots, \texttt{Temp}[i][\ell_0]$ must be constrained in the v direction fitting.

9.4.4 APPROXIMATION TO WITHIN A SPECIFIED ACCURACY

We now return to the problem of approximating data to within some user-specified error bound, E. As indicated at the beginning of this section, iterative methods either start with few control points, fit, check deviation, and add control points if necessary (Type 1); or they start with many control points, fit, check deviation, and discard control points if possible (Type 2). The least squares based methods given earlier are appropriate for the fitting step. The deviation checking step usually measures maximum distance, either as

$$\max_{0\le k\le m} |\,\mathbf{Q}_k - \mathbf{C}(\bar{u}_k)\,| \quad \text{or} \quad \max_{\substack{0\le k\le r\\ 0\le \ell\le s}} |\,\mathbf{Q}_{k,\ell} - \mathbf{S}(\bar{u}_k,\bar{v}_\ell)\,| \tag{9.77}$$

or as

$$\max_{0\le k\le m}\left(\min_{0\le u\le 1} |\,\mathbf{Q}_k - \mathbf{C}(u)\,|\right) \quad \text{or} \quad \max_{\substack{0\le k\le r\\ 0\le \ell\le s}}\left(\min_{\substack{0\le u\le 1\\ 0\le v\le 1}} |\,\mathbf{Q}_{k,\ell} - \mathbf{S}(u,v)\,|\right) \tag{9.78}$$

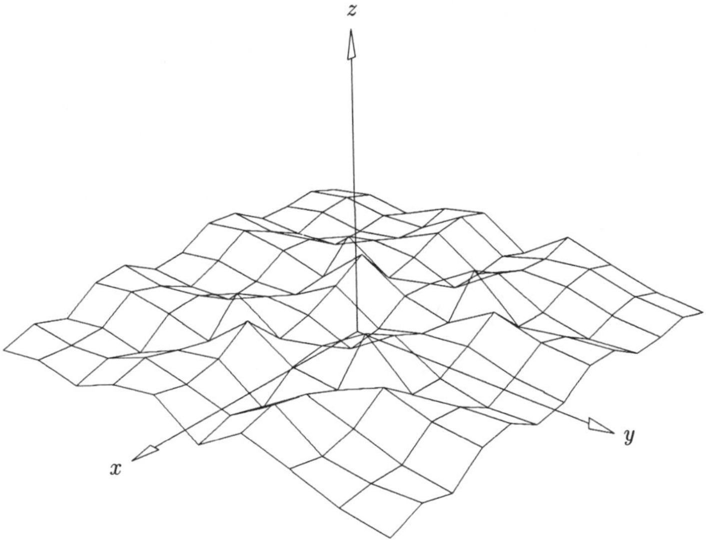

(b)

Figure 9.45. (*Continued.*)

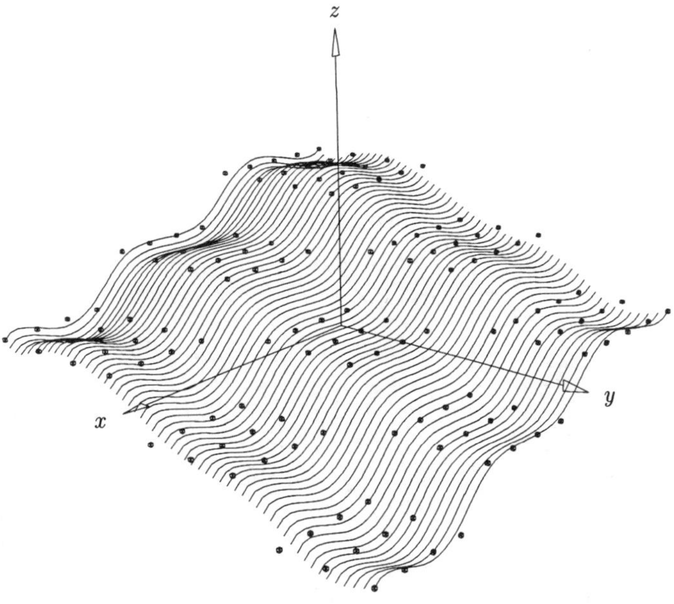

(a)

Figure 9.46. A least squares surface fit with a degree (2, 3) surface using an (8×8) control net. (a) Surface approximant; (b) error surface (error measured at data points).

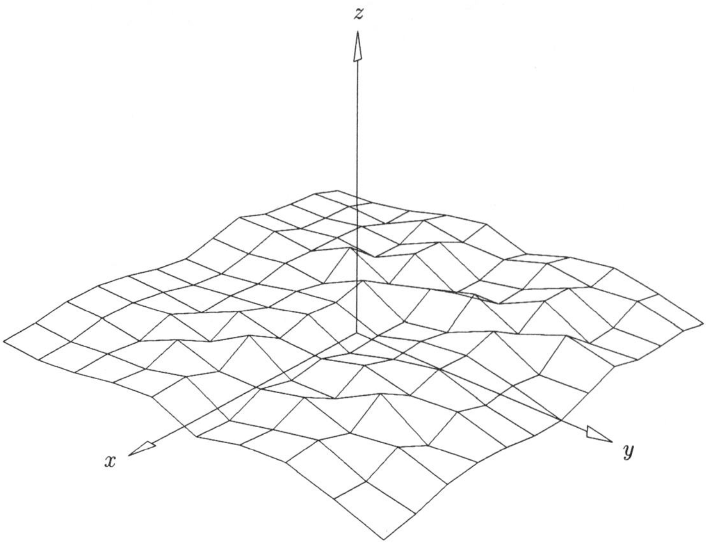

(b)

Figure 9.46. (*Continued.*)

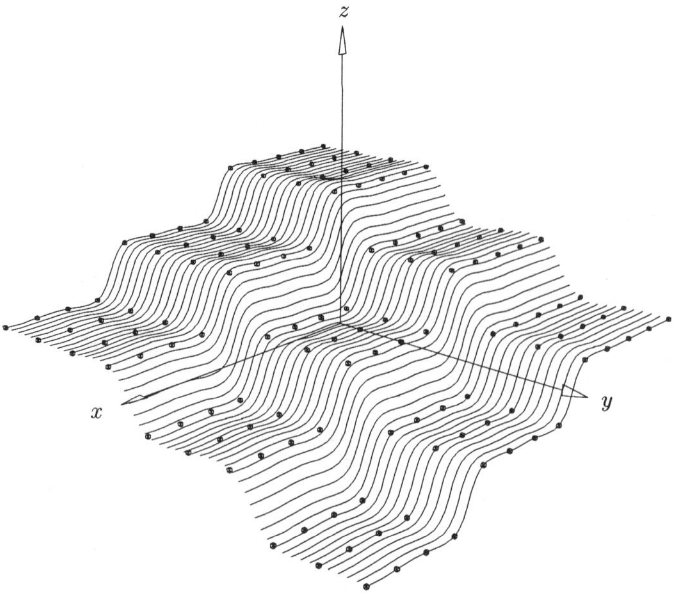

Figure 9.47. The surface interpolating points shown in Figure 9.44.

We call Eq. (9.78) the *max norm deviation*. It uses Eqs. (6.4)–(6.9) to compute the minimum distance from each $\mathbf{Q}_k$ ($\mathbf{Q}_{k,\ell}$) to $\mathbf{C}(u)$ ($\mathbf{S}(u,v)$). The $\bar{u}_k$ ($\bar{u}_k, \bar{v}_\ell$) serve as good start points for the Newton iterations. Obviously, Eq. (9.78) is more expensive to apply than Eq. (9.77). However, it is usually what a user wants measured, and it generally leads to curves and surfaces with fewer control points, since

$$\min_{0 \le u \le 1} |\mathbf{Q}_k - \mathbf{C}(u)| \le |\mathbf{Q}_k - \mathbf{C}(\bar{u}_k)| \tag{9.79}$$

We emphasize that both Type 1 and Type 2 methods can fail to converge, and this eventuality must be dealt with in a software implementation.

A Type 1 curve approximation method can proceed as follows. Start with $p+1$ control points (the minimum). Fit a curve using Eqs. (9.63) and (9.65)–(9.67), or Algorithm A9.6 if interior constraints are desired. After each fit, use Eq. (9.78) to check if the curve deviation is less than E. A record is maintained for each knot span, indicating whether or not it has converged; a span $[u_j, u_{j+1})$ has converged if Eq. (9.78) is satisfied for all k such that $\bar{u}_k \in [u_j, u_{j+1})$. After each fit and subsequent deviation check, a knot is added at the midpoint of each nonconvergent span, thus adding control points. This algorithm must deal with the case in which a span can become empty as knots are added (i.e., the span contains no $\bar{u}_k$), thus producing a singular system of equations in the fitting step.

A Type 1 surface approximation method can be implemented in a similar fashion, with an efficiency improvement. During the deviation check, determine the row ℓ_0 and column k_0 which have the greatest numbers of points with deviations greater than E. Then extract isoparametric curves $\mathbf{C}_{\bar{u}_{k_0}}(v)$ and $\mathbf{C}_{\bar{v}_{\ell_0}}(u)$, and independently approximate them to within E. This yields new (increased) knot vectors, U and V, to use for the next surface fit. Using this method, usually only a few surface fits and subsequent deviation checks are required.

We now develop a Type 2 curve approximation method, which combines least squares fitting with the knot removal techniques of Chapter 5. First we need a few more knot removal tools. Let u_r be an interior knot of a pth degree nonrational curve, $\mathbf{C}(u)$, $u_r \ne u_{r+1}$, and denote the multiplicity of u_r by s, i.e., $u_{r-s+j} = u_r$ for $j = 1, \ldots, s$. Let $\hat{\mathbf{C}}(u)$ denote the curve obtained by removing one occurrence of u_r. Recall that the new control points, $\mathbf{P}_i^1$ and $\mathbf{P}_j^1$, are computed from the left and the right, respectively, by Eq. (5.28). After removal, $\hat{\mathbf{C}}(u)$ differs from $\mathbf{C}(u)$; Tiller [Till92] derives error bounds for two cases:

- assume $(p+s) \bmod 2 = 0$; set $k = (p+s)/2$ and

$$B_r = |\mathbf{P}_{r-k} - \alpha_{r-k}\mathbf{P}^1_{r-k+1} - (1-\alpha_{r-k})\mathbf{P}^1_{r-k-1}| \tag{9.80}$$

where $$\alpha_{r-k} = \frac{u_r - u_{r-k}}{u_{r-k+p+1} - u_{r-k}}$$

Then $$|\mathbf{C}(u) - \hat{\mathbf{C}}(u)| \le N_{r-k,p}(u) B_r \qquad \text{for } u \in [0,1] \tag{9.81}$$

- assume $(p+s) \bmod 2 = 1$; set $k = (p+s+1)/2$ and

$$B_r = |\mathbf{P}^1_{r-k} - \mathbf{P}^1_{r-k+1}| \tag{9.82}$$

Then $$|\mathbf{C}(u) - \hat{\mathbf{C}}(u)| \leq (1-\alpha_{r-k+1})N_{r-k+1,p}(u)B_r \qquad \text{for } u \in [0,1] \tag{9.83}$$

with $$\alpha_{r-k+1} = \frac{u_r - u_{r-k+1}}{u_{r-k+p+2} - u_{r-k+1}}$$

The B_r are just the distances computed in knot removal Algorithm A5.8. Algorithm A9.8 is a modification of Algorithm A5.8 to compute just the B_r.

```
ALGORITHM A9.8
GetRemovalBndCurve(n,p,U,P,u,r,s,Br)
  { /*  Get knot removal error bound (nonrational)  */
    /*  Input:  n,p,U,P,u,r,s  */
    /*  Output: Br  */
  ord = p+1;
  last = r-s;
  first = r-p;
  off = first-1; /* difference in index between temp and P */
  temp[0] = P[off];   temp[last+1-off] = P[last+1];
  i = first;      j=last;
  ii = 1;     jj = last-off;
  while (j-i > 0)
    { /* Compute new control points for one removal step */
    alfi = (u-U[i])/(U[i+ord]-U[i]);
    alfj = (u-U[j])/(U[j+ord]-U[j]);
    temp[ii] = (P[i]-(1.0-alfi)*temp[ii-1])/alfi;
    temp[jj] = (P[j]-alfj*temp[jj+1])/(1.0-alfj);
    i = i+1;     ii = ii+1;
    j = j-1;     jj = jj-1;
    } /* End of while-loop */
  if (j-i < 0)  /* now get bound */
    {   /* Eq.(9.82) */
    Br = Distance3D(temp[ii-1],temp[jj+1]);
    }
    else
    {   /* Eq.(9.80) */
    alfi = (u-U[i])/(U[i+ord]-U[i]);
    Br = Distance3D(P[i],alfi*temp[ii+1]+(1.0-alfi)
                                              *temp[ii-1]);
    }
  }
```

Now let $\{\mathbf{Q}_k\}$ be a set of points and $\{\bar{u}_k\}$ the associated set of parameters. Denote by $\{e_k\}$ a set of errors associated with the points, and let E be a maximum error bound. Given a curve $\mathbf{C}(u)$ with the property that the max norm deviation of each $\mathbf{Q}_k$ from $\mathbf{C}(u)$ is less than or equal to e_k, Algorithm A9.9 removes (roughly) as many knots as possible from $\mathbf{C}(u)$ while maintaining $e_k \leq E$ for all k. It also updates the $\{e_k\}$, i.e., it accumulates the error. Output is the new curve, represented by $\hat{n}$, $\hat{U}$, and $\hat{\mathbf{P}}_i$. The algorithm maintains two lists, the knot removal error, B_r, for each *distinct* interior knot; and for each basis function, $N_{i,p}(u)$, the range of indices representing the parameters $\bar{u}_k$ which fall within the domain of that function. Clearly, when a knot is removed these lists must be updated; however, the effect is local. The bound, B_r, of only a few neighboring knots changes, and only a few neighboring basis functions (and their domains) change. Suppose we remove u_r, which has multiplicity s before removal. After removal there is one less basis function, and in the *new* numbering scheme the range of $\bar{u}_k$ indices for only the basis functions

$$N_{i,p}(u) \qquad i = r-p-1, \ldots, r-s \tag{9.84}$$

must be recomputed. B_r values change for all knots whose old span index lies in the range

$$\max\{r-p, p+1\}, \ldots, \min\{r+p-s+1, n\} \tag{9.85}$$

Example

Ex9.3 See Figure 9.48: Let the cubic curve be defined by $\mathbf{P}_0, \ldots, \mathbf{P}_{11}$ and $U = \{0,0,0,0,1,2,3,4,4,5,6,7,8,8,8,8\}$. Suppose we remove one occurrence of the knot $u_8 = 4$ ($r = 8$, $s = 2$). By Eq. (9.85) new B_r values must be computed for knots $2,3,4,5,6$. By Eq. (9.84) new $\bar{u}_k$ ranges of indices must be computed for $N_{4,3}$, $N_{5,3}$, and $N_{6,3}$.

Ex9.4 See Figure 9.49: Let the cubic curve be defined by $\mathbf{P}_0, \ldots, \mathbf{P}_{10}$ and $U = \{0,0,0,0,1,2,3,4,5,6,7,8,8,8,8\}$. Suppose we remove the knot $u_7 = 4$ ($r = 7$, $s = 1$). By Eq. (9.85) new B_r values must be computed for knots 1,2,3,5,6,7 (all remaining interior knots). By Eq. (9.84) new $\bar{u}_k$ ranges of indices must be computed for $N_{3,3}$, $N_{4,3}$, $N_{5,3}$, and $N_{6,3}$.

```
ALGORITHM A9.9
RemoveKnotsBoundCurve(n,p,U,P,ub,ek,E,nh,Uh,Ph)
  { /* Remove knots from curve, bounded */
    /* Input: n,p,U,P,ub,ek,E */
    /* Output: ek,nh,Uh,Ph */
  Inf = ∞;   /* Big number */
  Get the values Br for all distinct interior knots (A9.8).
  For each basis function, get range of parameter indices.
  while (1)
    {
    Find knot with the smallest Br bound.  Set r and s.
```

```
        if (Br == Inf)  break;    /* Finished */
        Using Eqs.(9.81),(9.83), and Algorithm A2.4 to compute
            NewError[k], form temp[k] = ek[k]+NewError[k] at
            all ub[k] values falling within the relevant domain.
        If knot is removable   /* All temp[k] <= E */
          {
          Update ek[] :  ek[k] = temp[k] for relevant range.
          Call routine similar to A5.8 to remove knot
              (remove without tolerance check).
          If no more internal knots, break.   /* Finished */
          Using Eq.(9.84), compute new index ranges for
              affected basis functions.
          Using Eq.(9.85), compute new error bounds for the
              relevant knots.
          }
          else
          {
          Set this Br to Inf.
          }
        }
    }
```

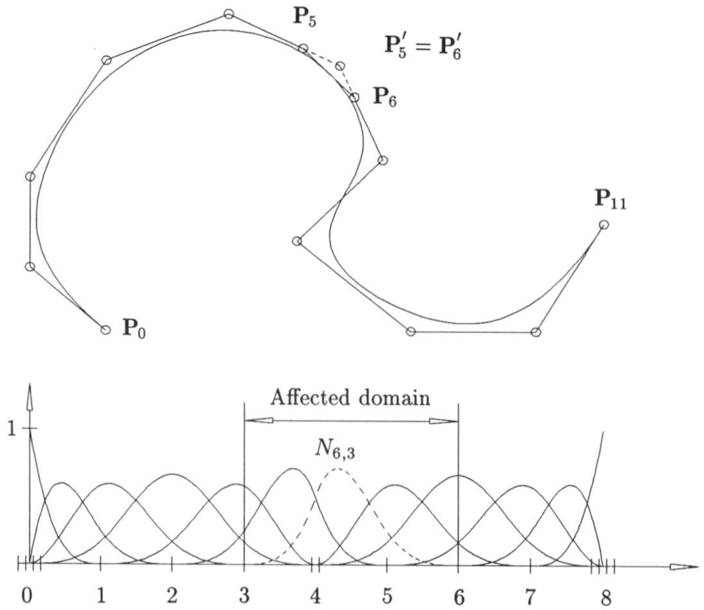

Figure 9.48. Removal of the knot $u_8 = 4$ one time.

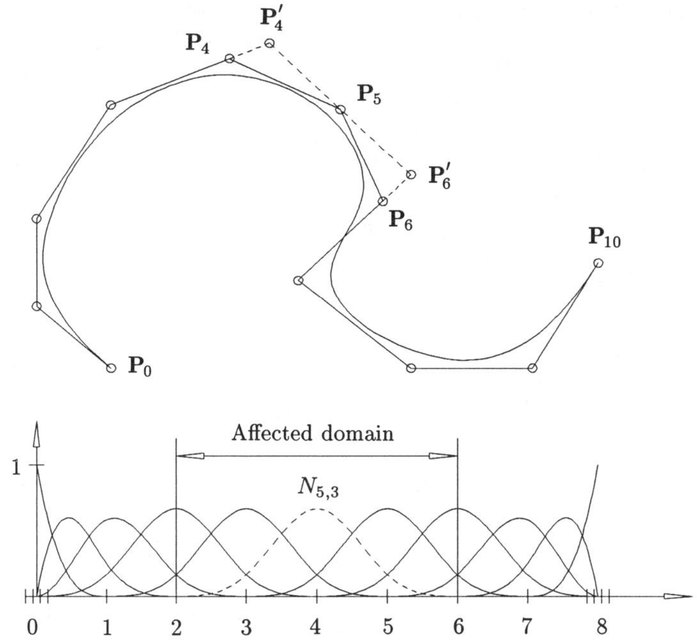

Figure 9.49. Removal of the knot $u_7 = 4$ one time.

We can now put together a Type 2 curve approximation method.

```
ALGORITHM A9.10
GlobalCurveApproxErrBnd(m,Q,p,E,n,U,P)
  { /* Global curve approximation to within bound E */
    /* Input: m,Q,p,E */
    /* Output: n,U,P */
  Compute ū_k and load into ub[] (Eq.[9.5]).
  Set U and P to be the degree 1 curve interpolating the Q_k:
      U = {0,0,ū_1,...,ū_{m-1},1,1} and P_k = Q_k.
  Initialize the e_k: ek[0],...,ek[m] = 0.
  n = m;
  for (deg=1; deg<=p; deg++)
    {
    RemoveKnotsBoundCurve(n,p,U,P,ub,ek,E,nh,Uh,Ph);
    if (deg == p)   break;
    Let U be the knot vector obtained by degree elevating Uh
        from deg to deg+1 (increase all multiplicities by 1).
        Reset n (Eq.[5.32]).
    Fit a least squares curve to the Q_k, using n, ub, degree
        deg+1, and knot vector U; this yields new ctrl pts P.
```

```
    Using Eqs.(6.4),(6.5), project all Q_k to current curve
        to get R_k = C(u_k). Then update ek[] and ub[]:
        e_k = | Q_k, R_k | and ū_k = u_k.
    } /* End of for-loop */
  if (n == nh)   return(n,U,P);
  Set U = Uh and n = nh, and fit one final time with degree p
      and knots U.
  Project the Q_k and update ek[] and ub[].
  RemoveKnotsBoundCurve(n,p,U,P,ub,ek,E,nh,Uh,Ph);
  return(nh,Uh,Ph);
  }
```

The advantages of starting with a linear curve and working up to degree p are three-fold:

- geometric characteristics (e.g., cusps and discontinuities in curvature) inherent in the data tend to be captured at the appropriate stage; if the data is known to be smooth, then Algorithm A9.10 can be started at degree 2 (quadratic interpolation before entering the for-loop);
- the evolving curve tends to "settle" into a natural parameterization;
- a general rule when globally fitting large numbers of points is that the higher the degree, and the more knots (interpolation is the limit), the worse the wiggle; Algorithm 9.10 reduces the number of knot spans as it increases the degree, thereby tending to decrease wiggle in the final curve.

Figure 9.50a shows a cubic curve fitting example using Algorithm A9.10. The tolerance is $E = {}^7\!/_{100}$. Figure 9.50b shows the parameterization of this curve, along with the control polygon. Note the mix of double and single knots, as apparent by the alternating touching and nontouching polygon legs. Figure 9.51 shows another example of cubic curve approximation, with $E = {}^8\!/_{100}$.

The max norm error bound E is guaranteed in the knot removal steps of Algorithm A9.10. The error resulting from the least squares fit is guaranteed to be less than or equal to the error in the previous (knot removed curve) *in the least squares sense.* In practice it also seems to always be better in the max norm sense. In any case, the max norm error can be easily monitored during the point projection step when the e_k and $\bar{u}_k$ are updated.

Constraints can be easily incorporated into the algorithm by using Algorithm A9.6 for the fitting, and by initializing the relevant e_k to ∞ and not updating it (or its $\bar{u}_k$). Lyche [Lych87, 88] used similar knot removal techniques for curve and surface approximation and data reduction.

An analogous Type 2 surface approximation method can be developed. Let

$$\mathbf{S}(u,v) = \sum_{i=0}^{n} \sum_{j=0}^{m} N_{i,p}(u) N_{j,q}(v) \mathbf{P}_{i,j} \qquad (u,v) \in [0,1] \times [0,1]$$

be a (p,q)th degree B-spline surface. Assume u_r is a u knot of multiplicity s,

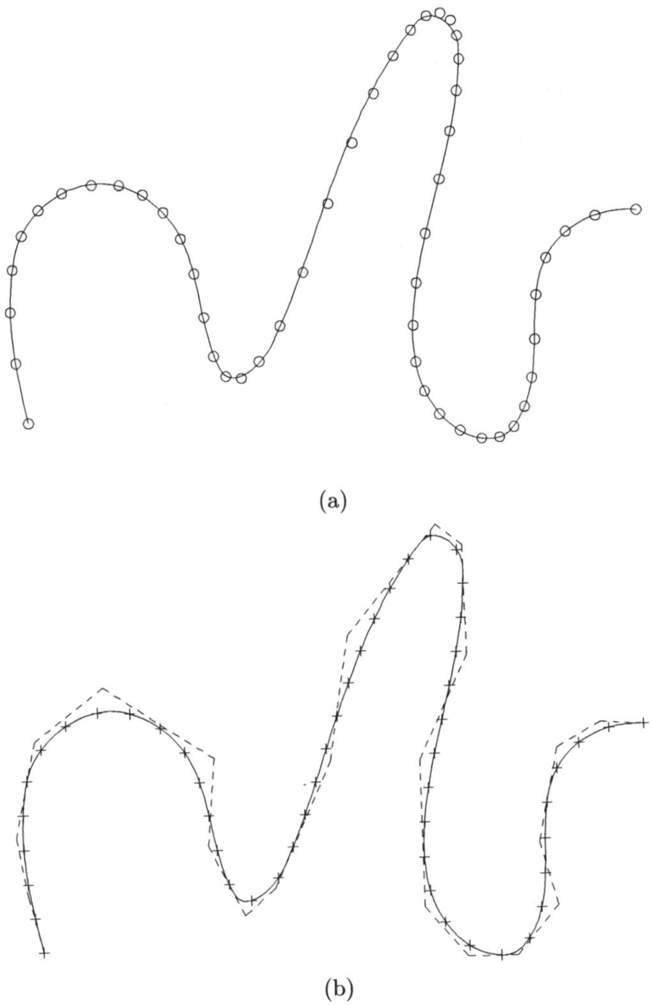

Figure 9.50. A cubic curve fit using algorithm **A9.10**.

and let $\hat{\mathbf{S}}(u,v)$ denote the surface obtained by removing one occurrence of u_r. Considering the tensor product structure of $\mathbf{S}(u,v)$, and using the techniques of Tiller [Till92], it can be shown that:

- if $(p+s) \mod 2 = 0$, set $k = (p+s)/2$ and

$$B_r^j = | \mathbf{P}_{r-k,j} - \alpha_{r-k}\mathbf{P}^1_{r-k+1,j} - (1-\alpha_{r-k})\mathbf{P}^1_{r-k-1,j} | \qquad j = 0,\ldots,m \tag{9.86}$$

where

$$\alpha_{r-k} = \frac{u_r - u_{r-k}}{u_{r-k+p+1} - u_{r-k}}$$

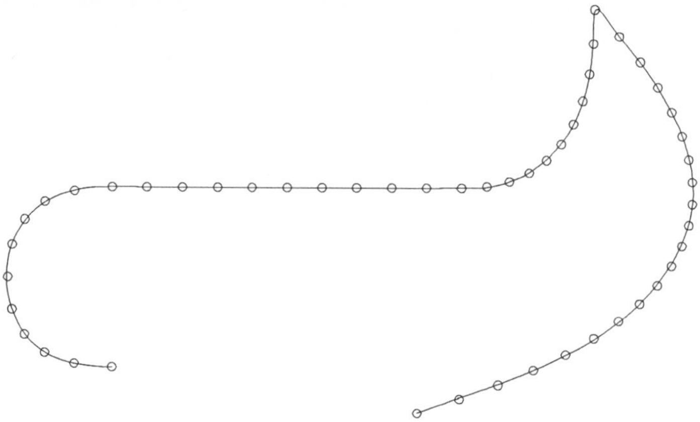

Figure 9.51. A cubic curve fit using algorithm `A9.10` and $E = {}^{8}/_{100}$.

Then $$|\,\mathbf{S}(u,v) - \hat{\mathbf{S}}(u,v)\,| \le N_{r-k,p}(u) \sum_{j=0}^{m} N_{j,q}(v) B_r^j$$
$$\text{for } (u,v) \in [0,1] \times [0,1] \qquad (9.87)$$

- if $(p+s) \bmod 2 = 1$, set $k = {}^{(p+s+1)}/_{2}$ and

$$B_r^j = |\,\mathbf{P}^1_{r-k,j} - \mathbf{P}^1_{r-k+1,j}\,| \qquad j = 0,\ldots,m \qquad (9.88)$$

Then $$|\,\mathbf{S}(u,v) - \hat{\mathbf{S}}(u,v)\,| \le (1 - \alpha_{r-k+1}) N_{r-k+1,p}(u) \sum_{j=0}^{m} N_{j,q}(v) B_r^j$$
$$\text{for } (u,v) \in [0,1] \times [0,1] \qquad (9.89)$$

with $$\alpha_{r-k+1} = \frac{u_r - u_{r-k+1}}{u_{r-k+p+2} - u_{r-k+1}}$$

Analogous equations hold for v direction knot removal. Using these equations, one can develop a knot removal stategy for surfaces similar to Algorithms `A9.8` and `A9.9`. This, combined with the least squares based surface fitting algorithm `A9.7`, provides a method for approximating a set of points $\{\mathbf{Q}_{k,\ell}\}$ to within an E tolerance.

Figures 9.52a–9.52e show several examples of surface approximation. The data set to be approximated is shown in Figure 9.52a. Figure 9.52b shows a degree $(2,2)$ surface that is an interpolant obtained by using $E = 0$. Increasing E to ${}^{1}/_{2}$ yields the surface in Figure 9.52c. Further increasing E to 1 produces the surface of Figure 9.52d. Finally, a degree $(3,3)$ approximation using $E = 1$ is shown in Figure 9.52e.

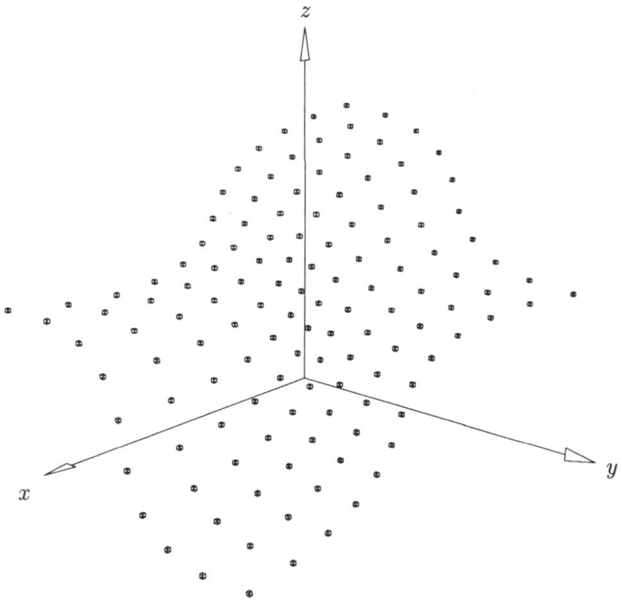

(a)

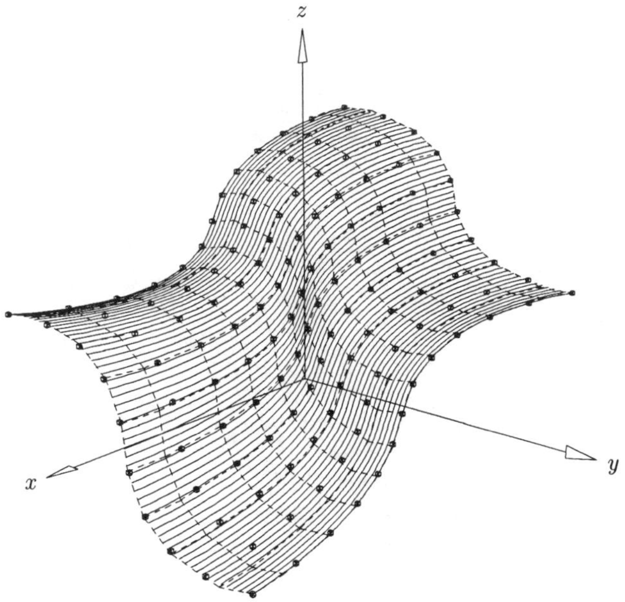

(b)

Figure 9.52. Various surface fitting examples using the extension of algorithm A9.10 to surfaces.

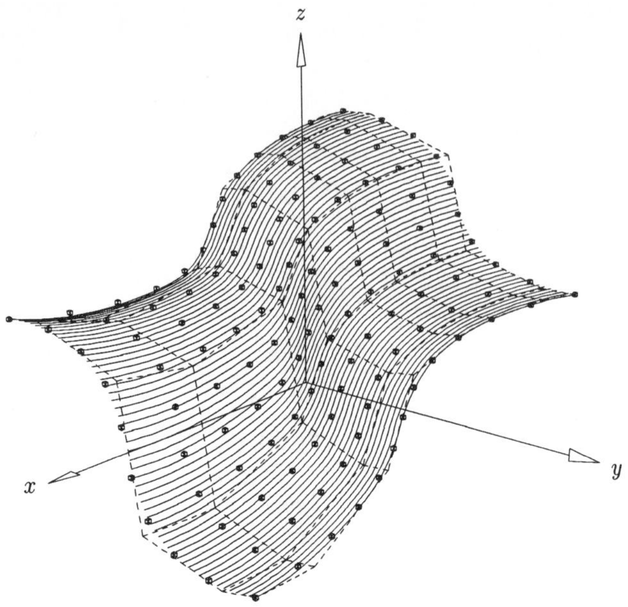

(c)

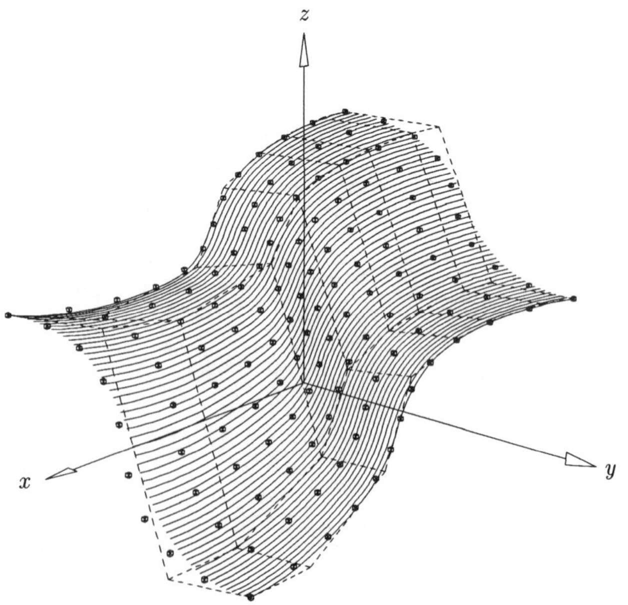

(d)

Figure 9.52. (*Continued.*)

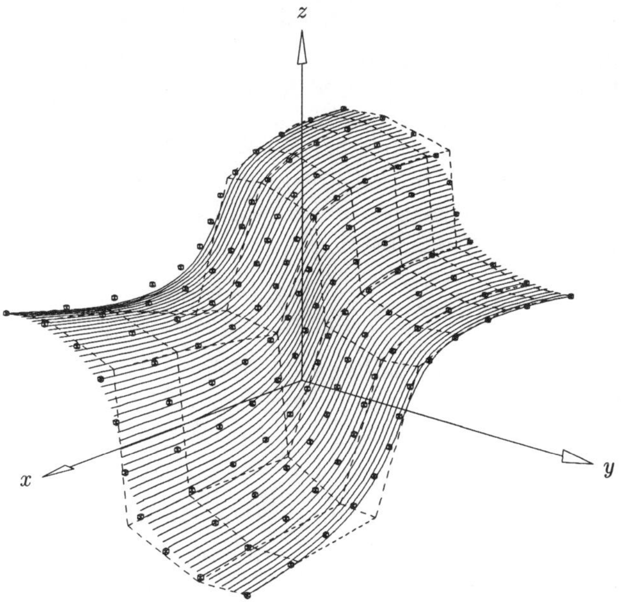

(e)

Figure 9.52. (*Continued.*)

Algorithm A9.10 and the corresponding surface algorithm are, in fact, data reduction algorithms, i.e., they work best on large data sets. They assume that during the knot removal phase (Algorithm A9.9) a significant number of knots can be removed. If this is not the case the least squares approximation step can fail, either because degree elevation requires more control points than there are data points, or because the many multiple knots make the system of equations singular. A simple fix is to restart the process with a higher degree curve.

9.5 Local Approximation

Let $\mathbf{Q}_0, \ldots, \mathbf{Q}_m$ and E be given. Here we give two examples of local curve approximation; the first produces a rational quadratic B-spline curve, and the second produces a nonrational cubic B-spline curve. In both cases the curves are G^1 continuous by construction; they can be made C^1 continuous, but this is not recommended for the quadratic case because it can produce very poor parameterizations. The quadratic curve fits planar data, while the cubic curve fits arbitrary three-dimensional data. The algorithms are variations on the methods presented in [Pieg87b; Chou92].

A good approximation algorithm attempts to generate as few segments as possible. One way to do this is to let $k_s = 0$, then find the largest $k_e \leq m$

such that $\mathbf{Q}_{k_s}, \ldots, \mathbf{Q}_{k_e}$ can be fit to within the E tolerance by one pth degree segment. Once found, set $k_s = k_e$ and repeat the process to find the largest $k_e \leq m$ such that $\mathbf{Q}_{k_s}, \ldots, \mathbf{Q}_{k_e}$ can be fit with one pth degree segment. This continues until $k_s = m$. Since m is usually rather large in approximation, a binary search is much faster than a linear search. As a practical matter, it may be desirable to bound the number of data points which can be approximated by one segment. We denote this bound by $K_{\max}$, that is, the binary search algorithm is modified to guarantee that

$$k_e - k_s \leq K_{\max}$$

always holds. This is accomplished by initializing k_e to $k_s + K_{\max}$ at the start of each search for the next segment. There are two advantages to setting $K_{\max} < m$:

- for a fixed tolerance E, a smaller $K_{\max}$ produces a more accurate fit;
- if m is large and E is quite small (which is often the case), then the average number of points approximated with each segment is small relative to m; in this case the algorithm is much more efficient if $K_{\max}$ is set substantially smaller than m.

We develop routines `FitWithConic()` and `FitWithCubic()` in Sections 9.5.1 and 9.5.2, respectively. These routines attempt to fit the points $\mathbf{Q}_{k_s}, \ldots, \mathbf{Q}_{k_e}$ to within the tolerance E with a conic or cubic segment, respectively. If the fit is successful, the calling (search) routine either accepts the segment or it increases k_e and calls the fit routine again to try to find an even larger segment (depending on the search strategy). If the fit is unsuccessful, the calling routine decreases k_e and calls the fit routine again.

For both the quadratic and cubic cases, the knot vector is constructed as the segments are accepted. Double internal knots are used in both cases, producing G^1 quadratic and C^1 cubic curves. Accumulated chord lengths corresponding to segment boundaries are used for the knot values of quadratic curves; Eq. (9.37) is used to compute knots for cubic curves.

9.5.1 LOCAL RATIONAL QUADRATIC CURVE APPROXIMATION

We now develop the routine `FitWithConic()`. We assume points $\mathbf{Q}_{k_s}, \ldots, \mathbf{Q}_{k_e}$ lie in a unique plane, and that the end tangents $\mathbf{T}_s$ and $\mathbf{T}_e$ are given.

Consider Figure 9.53. Assume for the moment that

$$\mathbf{R} = \mathbf{Q}_{k_s} + \gamma_s \mathbf{T}_s \qquad \mathbf{R} = \mathbf{Q}_{k_e} + \gamma_e \mathbf{T}_e \tag{9.90}$$

with

$$\gamma_s > 0 \qquad \gamma_e < 0 \tag{9.91}$$

Then to determine an approximating conic, proceed in three steps:

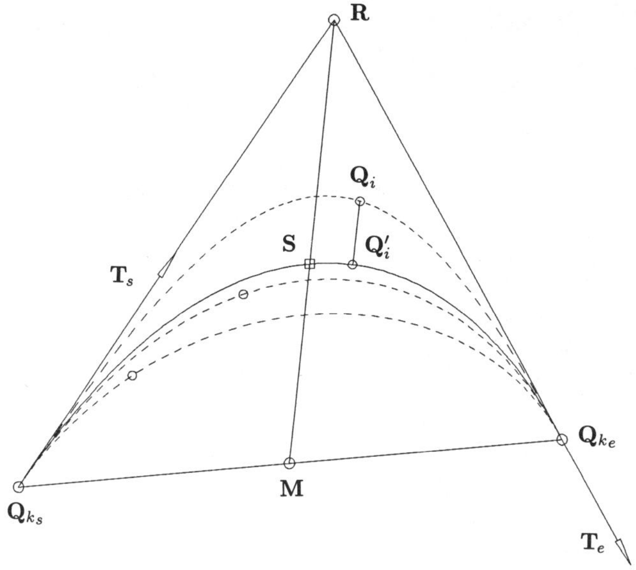

Figure 9.53. A curve fit and scatter check for conic curve fitting.

1. interpolate each point $\mathbf{Q}_i$, $i = k_s + 1, \ldots, k_e - 1$, with a conic, using $\mathbf{Q}_{k_s}$, $\mathbf{R}$, and $\mathbf{Q}_{k_e}$ as the control polygon, as in Algorithm A7.2. This yields the middle weight, w_i, and the corresponding shoulder point coordinate, $s_i = w_i/(1 + w_i)$;

2. compute an approximating conic by averaging the s_i, i.e.

$$s = \frac{1}{k_e - k_s - 1} \sum_{i=k_s+1}^{k_e-1} s_i \tag{9.92}$$

   By Eq. (7.30) the shoulder point of the approximating conic is $\mathbf{S} = (1 - s)\mathbf{M} + s\mathbf{R}$, and by Eq. (7.31) the middle weight is $w = s/(1 - s)$;

3. project each $\mathbf{Q}_i$ onto the approximating conic to check if all of them are within tolerance.

There are three special cases which are handled differently:

- $k_e - k_s = 1$, i.e., there are no interior points; the algorithm computes an interpolating segment between $\mathbf{Q}_{k_s}$ and $\mathbf{Q}_{k_e}$ exactly as described in Section 9.3.3;
- $\mathbf{T}_s$ and $\mathbf{T}_e$ are parallel; if they are parallel to the chord $\mathbf{Q}_{k_s}\mathbf{Q}_{k_e}$ and the points $\mathbf{Q}_{k_s}, \ldots, \mathbf{Q}_{k_e}$ are collinear, then a conic segment is returned which is actually a line segment; otherwise no fit is attempted;
- $\mathbf{R}$ is computed but Eq. (9.91) does not hold; no fit is attempted.

FitWithConic() returns the value 1 for a successful fit, or the value 0 for no fit. In the case of a successful fit, the weighted middle control point, $\mathbf{R}^w$, is also returned.

```
ALGORITHM A9.11
  FitWithConic(ks,ke,Q,Ts,Te,E,Rw)
    { /*  Fit to tolerance E with conic segment  */
      /*  Input:  ks,ke,Q,Ts,Te,E  */
      /*  Output: Rw  */
    if (ke-ks == 1)
      { /* No interior points to interpolate */
      Fit an interpolating segment as in Section 9.3.3.
      return(1);
      }
    i = Intersect3DLines(Q[ks],Ts,Q[ke],Te,alf1,alf2,R);
    if (i != 0)
      { /* No intersection */
      if (Q_ks,..., Q_ke not collinear)  return(0);
        else
          {
          Rw = (Q[ks]+Q[ke])/2.0;
          return(1);
          }
      }
    if (alf1 <= 0.0 || alf2 >= 0.0)   return(0);
    s = 0.0;     V = Q[ke]-Q[ks];
    for (i=ks+1; i<=ke-1; i++)
      { /* Get conic interpolating each interior point */
      V1 = Q[i] - R;
      j = Intersect3DLines(Q[ks],V,R,V1,alf1,alf2,dummy);
      if (j != 0 || alf1 <= 0.0 || alf1 >= 1.0 || alf2 <= 0.0)
        return(0);
      Compute the weight wi.   /* Algorithm A7.2 */
      s = s + wi/(1.0+wi);
      }
    s = s/(ke-ks-1);     w = s/(1.0-s);
    if (w < WMIN || w > WMAX)   /* system bounds on weights */
      return(0);
    Create Bezier segment with Q[ks],R,Q[ke] and w.
    for (i=ks+1; i<=ke-1; i++)
      {
      Project Q[i] onto the Bezier segment.
      if (distance > E)   return(0);
      }
    Rw = w*R;
    return(1);
    }
```

Figures 9.54a–9.54e show local quadratic curve fitting examples. The logarithmic spiral

$$r = \frac{1}{2}\, e^{\theta/5}$$

was sampled and approximated. Input parameters for Figures 9.54a–9.54d were:

Figure 9.54a	$E = 1/100,$	$K_{\max} = 50$
Figure 9.54b	$E = 1/1000,$	$K_{\max} = 50$
Figure 9.54c	$E = 1/10,$	$K_{\max} = 6$
Figure 9.54d	$E = 1/10,$	$K_{\max} = 10$

Figure 9.54e shows the parameterization of the curve in Figure 9.54b.

9.5.2 LOCAL NONRATIONAL CUBIC CURVE APPROXIMATION

We now develop `FitWithCubic()`. Let $\mathbf{P}_0 = \mathbf{Q}_{k_s}$ and $\mathbf{P}_3 = \mathbf{Q}_{k_e}$ denote the start and endpoints of the cubic Bézier segment, and $\mathbf{T}_s$ and $\mathbf{T}_e$ the start and end unit tangents (see Figure 9.55). We must determine the two inner control points, $\mathbf{P}_1$ and $\mathbf{P}_2$. Setting

$$\mathbf{P}_1 = \mathbf{P}_0 + \alpha \mathbf{T}_s \qquad \mathbf{P}_2 = \mathbf{P}_3 + \beta \mathbf{T}_e$$

we must determine values for α and β such that the cubic Bézier curve defined by $\mathbf{P}_0, \mathbf{P}_1, \mathbf{P}_2, \mathbf{P}_3$ passes within the E tolerance of all $\mathbf{Q}_k$, $k_s < k < k_e$. If $k_e - k_s = 1$, then theoretically, any α and β will do; however, they should be chosen so that the derivative magnitudes blend naturally with neighboring magnitudes. Using Eq. (9.29) and Exercise 9.2, reasonable estimates for the derivatives $\mathbf{D}_{k_s}$ and $\mathbf{D}_{k_e}$ at $\mathbf{Q}_{k_s}$ and $\mathbf{Q}_{k_e}$ are

$$\begin{aligned}
\mathbf{D}_{k_s} &= \mathbf{V}_{k_s} && \text{if } k_s = 0 \\
\mathbf{D}_j &= \frac{c_{j+1} - c_j}{c_j - c_{j-1}} \mathbf{V}_j && j \neq \{0, m\} \quad j = k_s \text{ or } j = k_e \\
\mathbf{D}_{k_e} &= \mathbf{V}_{k_e} && \text{if } k_e = m
\end{aligned} \tag{9.93}$$

where $\{c_j\}$ are the accumulated chord lengths. Then set

$$\alpha = \frac{|\,\mathbf{D}_{k_s}\,|}{3} \qquad \beta = -\frac{|\,\mathbf{D}_{k_e}\,|}{3} \tag{9.94}$$

Now assume $k_e - k_s > 1$. Our algorithm consists of three steps:

1. for each k, $k_s < k < k_e$, interpolate a cubic Bézier segment to the data $\mathbf{P}_0, \mathbf{T}_s$, $\mathbf{Q}_k$, $\mathbf{P}_3$, $\mathbf{T}_e$, thus obtaining an α_k and a β_k; the Bézier segments, $\mathbf{C}_k(u)$, are defined on the normalized interval $u \in [0,1]$;

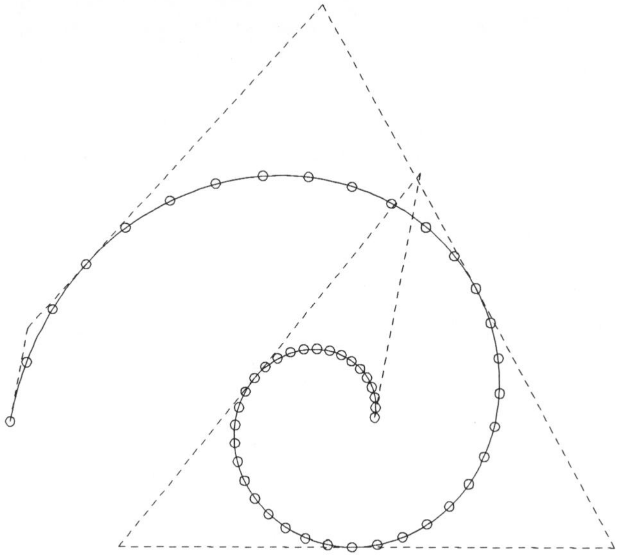

(a)

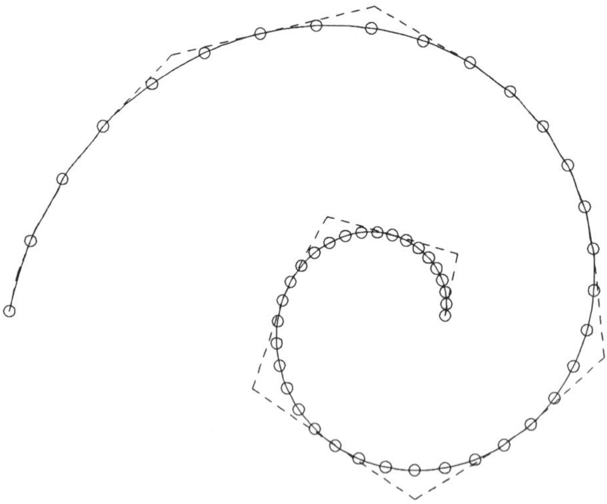

(b)

Figure 9.54. Local quadratic curve fitting examples.

2. average the α_ks and β_ks to obtain α and β; these define the candidate Bézier segment, $\mathbf{C}(u)$;
3. check if all $\mathbf{Q}_k$, $k_s < k < k_e$, are within E distance of $\mathbf{C}(u)$.

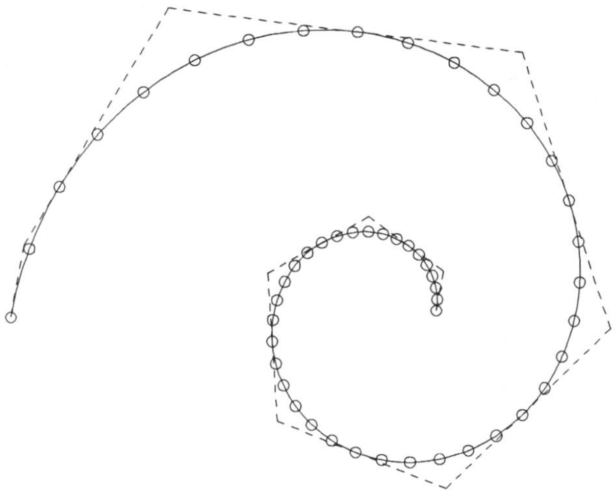

(c)

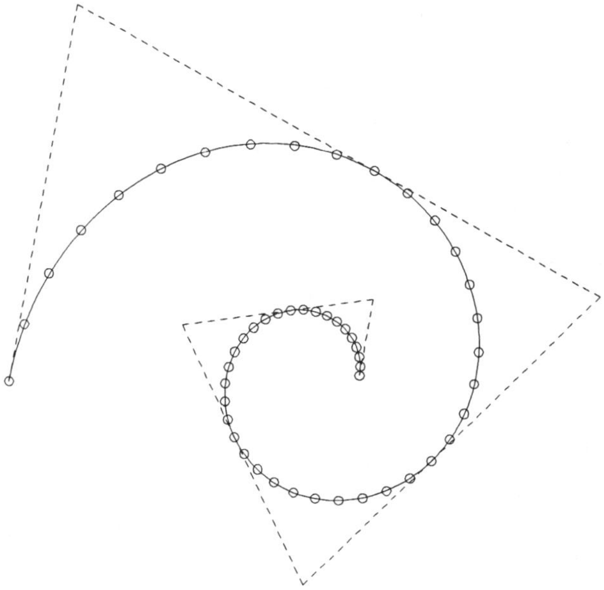

(d)

Figure 9.54. (*Continued.*)

Let $\mathbf{P} = \mathbf{Q}_k$ be the point to interpolate, and denote by $B_{i,3}$ the cubic Bernstein polynomials on $u \in [0,1]$. We write $\mathbf{P}$ as

$$\mathbf{P} = B_{0,3}\mathbf{P}_0 + B_{1,3}\mathbf{P}_1 + B_{2,3}\mathbf{P}_2 + B_{3,3}\mathbf{P}_3$$

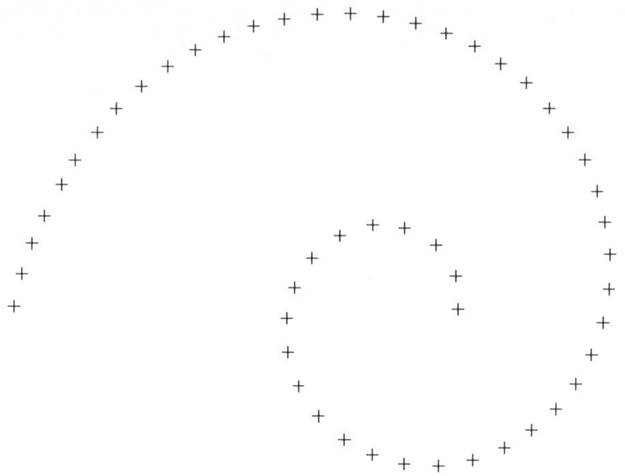

(e)

Figure 9.54. (*Continued.*)

$$= \mathbf{P}_0(B_{0,3} + B_{1,3}) + \alpha\mathbf{T}_s B_{1,3} + \beta\mathbf{T}_e B_{2,3} + \mathbf{P}_3(B_{2,3} + B_{3,3}) \quad (9.95)$$

and finally

$$\mathbf{P} = \mathbf{P}_c + a\mathbf{T}_s + b\mathbf{T}_e \quad (9.96)$$

where the point

$$\mathbf{P}_c = \mathbf{P}_0(B_{0,3} + B_{1,3}) + \mathbf{P}_3(B_{2,3} + B_{3,3}) \quad (9.97)$$

lies on the line $\mathbf{P}_0\mathbf{P}_3$, and

$$a = \alpha B_{1,3} \qquad b = \beta B_{2,3} \quad (9.98)$$

Thus

$$\alpha = \frac{a}{B_{1,3}} \qquad \beta = \frac{b}{B_{2,3}} \quad (9.99)$$

Consider Figure 9.55. Equation (9.96) says that we obtain $\mathbf{P}$ by starting at $\mathbf{P}_c$, going along a direction parallel to $\mathbf{T}_s$ for some distance (to $\mathbf{P}_d$), then continuing from there in the opposite direction of $\mathbf{T}_e$ for another distance. Since $\mathbf{T}_s$ and $\mathbf{T}_e$ have unit length, it follows that

$$a =| \mathbf{P}_c\mathbf{P}_d | \qquad b = - | \mathbf{P}_d\mathbf{P} | \quad (9.100)$$

Hence, we must compute $\mathbf{P}_c$ and $\mathbf{P}_d$, then a and b from Eq. (9.100), and finally α and β from Eq. (9.99).

There are two cases to consider, coplanar and not coplanar. First assume the vectors $\mathbf{T}_s$, $\mathbf{T}_e$, and $\mathbf{P}_0\mathbf{P}_3$ are not coplanar. It turns out that there is a unique cubic Bézier curve passing through $\mathbf{P}$, and $\mathbf{P}_c$ and $\mathbf{P}_d$ can be constructed as follows (see Figure 9.55):

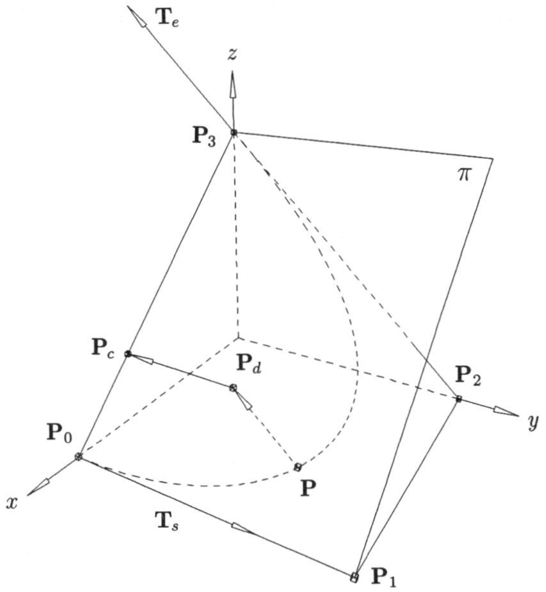

Figure 9.55. A unique cubic three-dimensional (twisted) Bézier curve specified by endpoints, end tangents, and one point on the curve.

1. let π be the plane defined by $\mathbf{P}_0$, $\mathbf{P}_3$, and $\mathbf{T}_s$;
2. intersect π with the line passing through $\mathbf{P}$ and parallel to $\mathbf{T}_e$ – this yields $\mathbf{P}_d$;
3. obtain $\mathbf{P}_c$ by intersecting the line $\mathbf{P}_0\mathbf{P}_3$ with the line passing through $\mathbf{P}_d$ and parallel to $\mathbf{T}_s$.

Equation (9.100) now yields a and b. In order to compute α and β by Eq. (9.99), we require the (unique) parameter value, $\hat{u}$, at which the curve passes through $\mathbf{P}$. From Eq. (9.97) and the fact that the $B_{i,3}$ sum to 1, we have

$$\mathbf{P}_c = \gamma \mathbf{P}_0 + (1-\gamma)\mathbf{P}_3 \tag{9.101}$$

where

$$\gamma = \frac{|\,\mathbf{P}_c\mathbf{P}_3\,|}{|\,\mathbf{P}_0\mathbf{P}_3\,|} = B_{0,3} + B_{1,3} \tag{9.102}$$

γ is computed as a quotient of directed distances, i.e., $\gamma \in [0,1]$ if and only if $\mathbf{P}_c$ lies between $\mathbf{P}_0$ and $\mathbf{P}_3$. The polynomial $B_{0,3} + B_{1,3}$ is cubic in u (the reader should sketch this function), and for any given $\gamma \in [0,1]$ there is a unique solution to Eq. (9.102) that lies within $[0,1]$. If $\gamma \notin [0,1]$, the fit is aborted (return "no fit" to the calling routine). The cubic equation, Eq. (9.102), can be solved by Newton iteration. One way to obtain good start values is to tabulate some number of $\hat{u}$ values corresponding to γ values between 0 and 1. Then, given any γ, a quick search in the table yields a start $\hat{u}$. Finally, substituting $\hat{u}$ into Eq. (9.99) yields α and β.

If $\mathbf{T}_s$, $\mathbf{T}_e$, and $\mathbf{P}_0\mathbf{P}_3$ are coplanar, then more than one cubic curve passing through $\mathbf{P}$ can exist, and the previous geometric construction of $\mathbf{P}_c$ and $\mathbf{P}_d$ fails. There are several special cases which complicate matters, hence we derive a set of equations which always yields α and β. We first assign a parameter, $\hat{u}$, to $\mathbf{P}$. A good estimate is obtained using chord length parameterization, i.e.

$$\begin{aligned} \hat{u}_{k_s} &= 0 \\ \hat{u}_k &= \hat{u}_{k-1} + \frac{c_k - c_{k-1}}{c_{k_e} - c_{k_s}} \end{aligned} \tag{9.103}$$

The $\hat{u}_k$ are, in fact, the normalized chord length parameters for the $\mathbf{Q}_k$ on $\mathbf{Q}_{k_s}, \ldots, \mathbf{Q}_{k_e}$. Now if $\mathbf{P} = \mathbf{Q}_k$, $k_s < k < k_e$, then $\hat{u} = \hat{u}_k$.

Next we compute the tangent $\mathbf{T}_p$ at $\mathbf{P}$ (Eqs. [9.29] and [9.31]). Let

$$s = 1 - \hat{u} \qquad t = \hat{u}$$

By definition

$$\mathbf{P} = s^3\mathbf{P}_0 + 3s^2t\mathbf{P}_1 + 3st^2\mathbf{P}_2 + t^3\mathbf{P}_3 \tag{9.104}$$

and recalling the deCasteljau algorithm (Eq. [1.12], Algorithm `A1.5`, and Figure 1.17) one can derive

$$\begin{aligned} \mathbf{P}_0^2 &= s^2\mathbf{P}_0 + 2st\mathbf{P}_1 + t^2\mathbf{P}_2 \\ \mathbf{P}_1^2 &= s^2\mathbf{P}_1 + 2st\mathbf{P}_2 + t^2\mathbf{P}_3 \end{aligned} \tag{9.105}$$

where $\mathbf{P}_0^2$ and $\mathbf{P}_1^2$ lie on the line defined by $\mathbf{P}$ and $\mathbf{T}_p$ (Figure 9.56). Thus

$$\begin{aligned} 0 &= \mathbf{T}_p \times \left(\mathbf{P}_1^2 - \mathbf{P}_0^2\right) \\ &= \mathbf{T}_p \times \left(t^2\mathbf{P}_3 + t(2s-t)\mathbf{P}_2 + s(s-2t)\mathbf{P}_1 - s^2\mathbf{P}_0\right) \end{aligned} \tag{9.106}$$

Substituting $\mathbf{P}_1 = \mathbf{P}_0 + \alpha\mathbf{T}_s$ and $\mathbf{P}_2 = \mathbf{P}_3 + \beta\mathbf{T}_e$ into Eqs. (9.104) and (9.106) yields

$$(3s^2t\mathbf{T}_s)\alpha + (3st^2\mathbf{T}_e)\beta = \mathbf{P} - (s^3 + 3s^2t)\mathbf{P}_0 - \left(t^3 + 3st^2\right)\mathbf{P}_3 \tag{9.107}$$

$$s(s-2t)(\mathbf{T}_p \times \mathbf{T}_s)\alpha + t(2s-t)(\mathbf{T}_p \times \mathbf{T}_e)\beta = 2st\big(\mathbf{T}_p \times (\mathbf{P}_0 - \mathbf{P}_3)\big) \tag{9.108}$$

Equation (9.107) involves the point constraint, $\mathbf{P}$, and Eq. (9.108) the tangent constraint, $\mathbf{T}_p$. They each contribute three equations in two unknowns, for a total of six equations (or four, when the data is xy planar). Some of the special cases are:

- if $\mathbf{T}_s \parallel \mathbf{T}_e$, then Eq. (9.107) yields only one equation; Eq. (9.108) supplies the necessary additional equation;

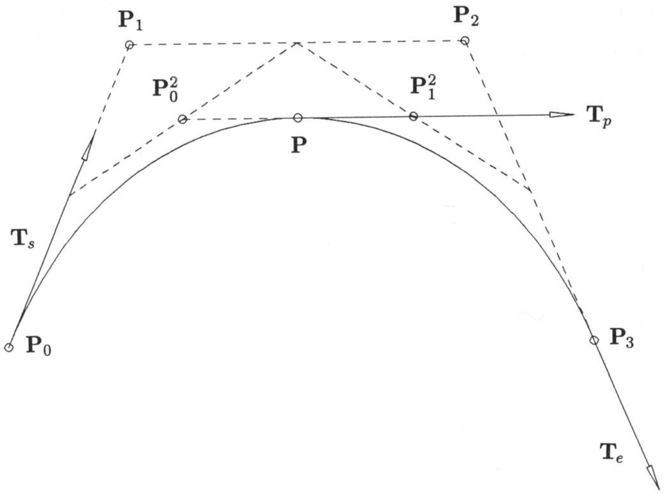

Figure 9.56. A planar cubic Bézier curve as specified by endpoints, end tangents, a point on the curve, and a tangent direction at this point.

- if $\mathbf{P} = (s^3 + 3s^2t)\mathbf{P}_0 + (t^3 + 3st^2)\mathbf{P}_3$, then Eq. (9.107) is a homogeneous system; in this case, $\alpha = \beta = 0$ may be the only solution, or there may exist infinitely many nontrivial solutions. Assuming we have ruled out the straight line case, we have $\mathbf{T}_p \times (\mathbf{P}_0 - \mathbf{P}_3) \neq 0$, hence Eq. (9.108) supplies the necessary nonhomogeneous equations.

A simple way to solve Eqs. (9.107) and (9.108), which avoids worrying about the special cases, is to put the six equations together and solve them by least squares. After solving, it must be checked that $\alpha > 0$ and $\beta < 0$; if this does not hold, the fit is aborted and control is returned to the calling program.

Once the equations are solved the α_ks and β_ks are simply averaged, that is

$$\alpha = \frac{1}{k_e - k_s - 1} \sum_{i=k_s+1}^{k_e-1} \alpha_i \qquad \beta = \frac{1}{k_e - k_s - 1} \sum_{i=k_s+1}^{k_e-1} \beta_i \tag{9.109}$$

The candidate cubic Bézier curve, $\mathbf{C}(u)$, is then defined by $\mathbf{P}_0$, $\mathbf{P}_1 = \mathbf{P}_0 + \alpha\mathbf{T}_s$, $\mathbf{P}_2 = \mathbf{P}_3 + \beta\mathbf{T}_e$, and $\mathbf{P}_3$.

We now must check if each $\mathbf{Q}_k$ is within E distance from the curve $\mathbf{C}(u)$ $(k_s < k < k_e)$. This requires Newton iterations, and the $\hat{u}$s computed previously are good start values. Recall that $\mathbf{Q}_k = \mathbf{C}_k(\hat{u}_k)$. Let $\Delta\alpha_k = \alpha_k - \alpha$ and $\Delta\beta_k = \beta_k - \beta$. Then from Eq. (9.95) we have

$$\begin{aligned} |\,\mathbf{Q}_k - \mathbf{C}(\hat{u}_k)\,| &= |\,\mathbf{C}_k(\hat{u}_k) - \mathbf{C}(\hat{u}_k)\,| \\ &= |\,\Delta\alpha_k B_{1,3}(\hat{u}_k)\mathbf{T}_s - \Delta\beta_k B_{2,3}(\hat{u}_k)\mathbf{T}_e\,| \end{aligned} \tag{9.110}$$

Equation (9.110) can be used as a fast acceptance test: if it is less than or equal to E, then Newton iterations are not required. If iterations are required, the technique given in Section 6.1 is appropriate.

The routine FitWithCubic() follows. It returns the value 1 for a successful fit, or the value 0 for no fit. We remark that the construction of $\mathbf{P}_c$ and $\mathbf{P}_d$ in the noncoplanar case is unstable when $\mathbf{T}_s$, $\mathbf{T}_e$, and $\mathbf{P}_0\mathbf{P}_3$ are close to being coplanar. Hence, this test should be made with a rather loose tolerance. The algorithm uses local arrays uh[], alfak[], betak[] to store the $\hat{u}_k$, α_k, and β_k.

```
ALGORITHM A9.12
  FitWithCubic(ks,ke,Q,Ts,Te,E,P1,P2)
    { /*  Fit to tolerance E with cubic segment  */
      /*  Input:  ks,ke,Q,Ts,Te,E  */
      /*  Output: P1,P2  */
    if (ke-ks == 1)
      { /* No interior points to interpolate */
      Compute α and β by Eqs.(9.93),(9.94).
      Set P_1 = Q_{k_s} + αT_s
      and P_2 = Q_{k_e} + βT_e
      return(1);
      }
    dk = ke-ks;
    line = Collinear(dk+1,Q[ks]);
    if (line == 1)
      { /* Collinear points case; create straight line */
      P1 = (2.0*Q[ks]+Q[ke])/3.0;
      P2 = (Q[ks]+2.0*Q[ke])/3.0;
      return(1);
      }
    for (k=1; k<dk; k++)
      {
      Get plane π defined by Q[ks],Q[ke],Ts.
      if (Line(Q[k+ks],Te) lies in π)
        { /* Coplanar case */
        Compute û_k by Eq.(9.103) and load into uh[k].
        Set up Eqs.(9.107) and (9.108) and solve for α_k and β_k
            (by least squares).
        if (α_k > 0 && β_k < 0)
          {
          alfak[k] = α_k;     betak[k] = β_k;
          }
          else
            return(0);
        }
        else
```

```
        { /* Noncoplanar case */
        Pd = Intersection of π with Line(Q[k+ks],Te);
        Pc = Intersection of Line(Q[ks],Q[ke]-Q[ks]) with
            Line(Pd,Ts);
        gamma = Distance3D(Pc,Q[ke])/Distance3D(Q[ks],Q[ke]);
        if (gamma < 0.0 || gamma > 1.0)   return(0);
        Use Newton iteration to solve Eq.(9.102) for uh[k].
        if (uh[k] < 0.0 || uh[k] > 1.0)   return(0);
          else
          {
          a = Distance3D(Pc,Pd);   b = -Distance3D(Pd,Q[k+ks]);
          Evaluate Bernstein polynomials and use Eq.(9.99)
            to get alfak[k] and betak[k].
          }
        }
      } /* End of for-loop: k=1,...,dk-1 */
        /* Step 2: average the α_ks and β_ks */
    alpha = beta = 0.0;
    for (k=1; k<dk; k++)
      { alpha = alpha+alfak[k];   beta = beta+betak[k]; }
    alpha = alpha/(dk-1);    beta = beta/(dk-1);
    P1 = Q[ks]+alpha*Ts;    P2 = Q[ke]+beta*Te;
        /* Step 3: check deviations */
    for (k=1; k<dk; k++)
      {
      u = uh[k];
      if (Eq.[9.110] less than E)   continue;
        else
        { /* Must do Newton iterations. u is start value */
        Project Q[k+ks] to curve to get error ek.
        if (ek > E)   break;
        }
      }
    if (k == dk)   return(1);   /* segment within tolerance */
      else         return(0);   /* not within tolerance */
    }
```

Figures 9.57 and 9.58 show examples of planar and nonplanar fits, respectively. The input data for Figure 9.57 was

Figure 9.57a	$E = {}^{1}\!/_{10}$,	$K_{\max} = 11$
Figure 9.57b	$E = {}^{1}\!/_{10}$,	$K_{\max} = 8$
Figure 9.57c	$E = {}^{1}\!/_{100}$,	$K_{\max} = 11$

Notice the change in the quality of the approximation from Figure 9.57a to Figure 9.57b. For the same tolerance, allowing a maximum of eight points per

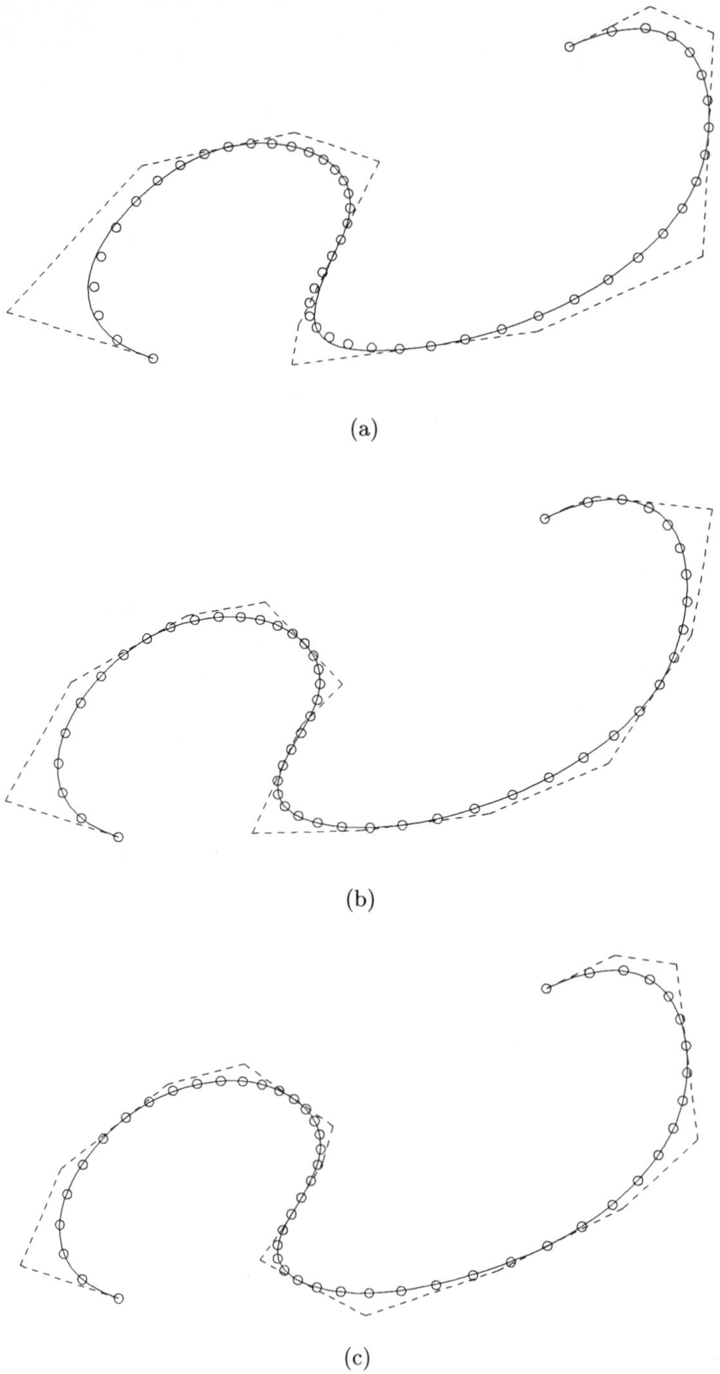

Figure 9.57. Local cubic approximation to planar data.

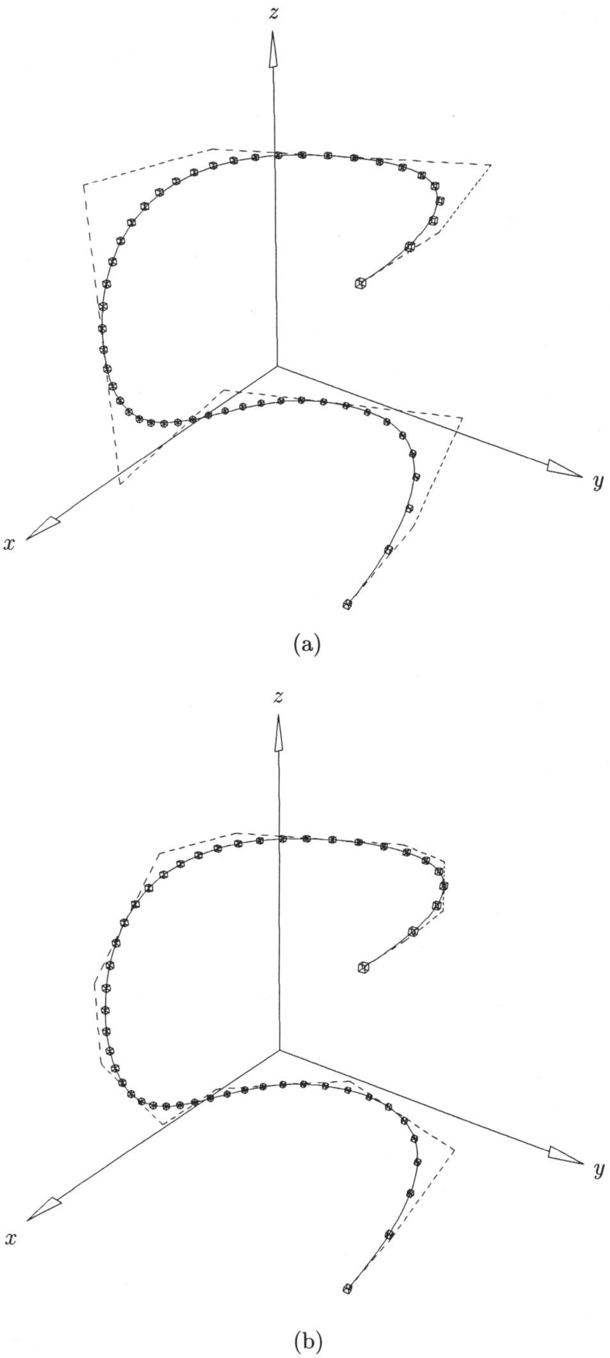

Figure 9.58. Local cubic approximation to three-dimensional data containing planar segments.

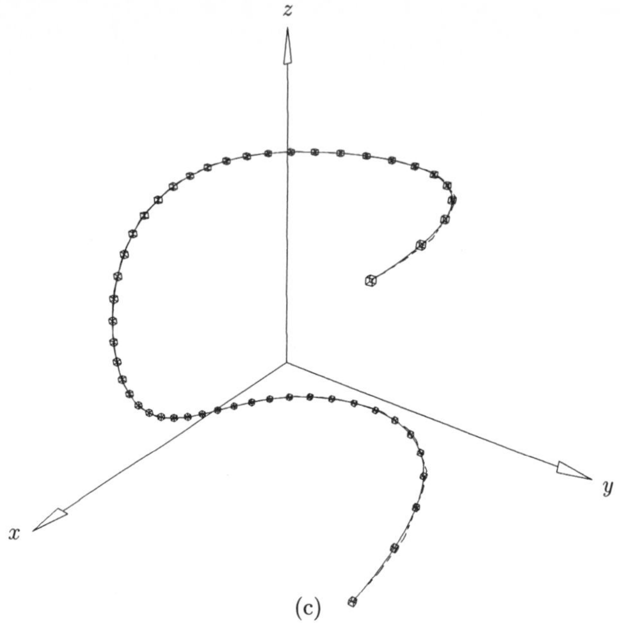

Figure 9.58. (*Continued.*)

segment instead of eleven improved the approximation noticeably. The input data for Figures 9.58a–9.58c was

Figure 9.58a	$E = 1/10,$	$K_{\max} = 20$
Figure 9.58b	$E = 1/100,$	$K_{\max} = 20$
Figure 9.58c	$E = 0,$	$K_{\max} = 20$

The zero tolerance resulted in an interpolatory curve. Given 51 points, one might expect 50 segments. However, only 25 segments were required, due to the fact that a cubic can always be constructed to pass through one interior point.

Exercises

9.1. You want to interpolate the points $\mathbf{Q}_{k,\ell}$, $k, \ell = 0, 1, 2, 3$ with a biquadratic surface ($p = q = 2$). Instead of using repeated curve interpolation, use Eq. (9.25) directly to set up a system of 16 linear equations in the 16 unknown $\mathbf{P}_{i,j}$s.

9.2. Assuming that the α_k were computed using Eq. (9.31), consider the unnormalized $\mathbf{V}_k$ of Eq. (9.29). Convince yourself that the quantities $\mathbf{V}_k/\Delta\bar{u}_k$ are good estimates for the derivatives, if the $\Delta\bar{u}_k$ are computed using Eq. (9.5) (the normalized relative chord length). Compute all the $\{\mathbf{V}_k\}$, $k = 0, \ldots, 4$, for $\{\mathbf{Q}_k\} = \{(0,0), (0,20), (20,40), (30,30), (30,20)\}$. What are their magnitudes? Compute the total chord length and the $\Delta\bar{u}_k$ according to Eq. (9.5). Do the quantities $\mathbf{V}_k/\Delta\bar{u}_k$ seem like reasonable estimates for derivatives?

9.3. Draw figures as in Figures 9.48 and 9.49 and determine which B_r values and parameter index ranges must be recomputed for two quadratic cases: $U = \{0, 0, 0, 1, 2, 3, 4, 5, 6, 6, 6\}$, with $r = 5$ and $s = 1$; and $U = \{0, 0, 0, 1, 2, 3, 3, 4, 5, 6, 6, 6\}$, with $r = 6$ and $s = 2$.

CHAPTER

TEN

Advanced Surface Construction Techniques

10.1 Introduction

In this chapter we cover several advanced surface construction techniques, namely swung, skinned, swept, Gordon, and Coons surfaces. Roughly speaking, the idea in this chapter is to take one or two curves, or sets of curves, and to create a NURBS surface which interpolates these curves; i.e., the given curves are isoparametric curves in the NURBS surface. Notice that this is fundamentally different from the interpolation to discrete point and derivative data presented in Chapter 9. In some of the constructions, it may not be obvious to the reader that the surfaces created do indeed satisfy the desired constraints. We leave it as an exercise for the reader to convince himself of this, either by mathematical proof or by software implementation.

10.2 Swung Surfaces

A swung surface is a generalization of a surface of revolution. Let

$$\mathbf{P}(u) = \sum_{i=0}^{n} R_{i,p}(u)\,\mathbf{P}_i \tag{10.1}$$

be a *profile curve* defined in the xz plane, and let

$$\mathbf{T}(v) = \sum_{j=0}^{m} R_{j,q}(v)\,\mathbf{T}_j \tag{10.2}$$

be a *trajectory curve* defined in the xy plane (see Figure 10.1). Denoting the nonzero coordinate functions of $\mathbf{P}(u)$ and $\mathbf{T}(v)$ by $P_x(u)$, $P_z(u)$, $T_x(v)$, and $T_y(v)$, we define the swung surface by [Wood87]

$$\mathbf{S}(u,v) = \big(\alpha P_x(u)T_x(v), \alpha P_x(u)T_y(v), P_z(u)\big) \tag{10.3}$$

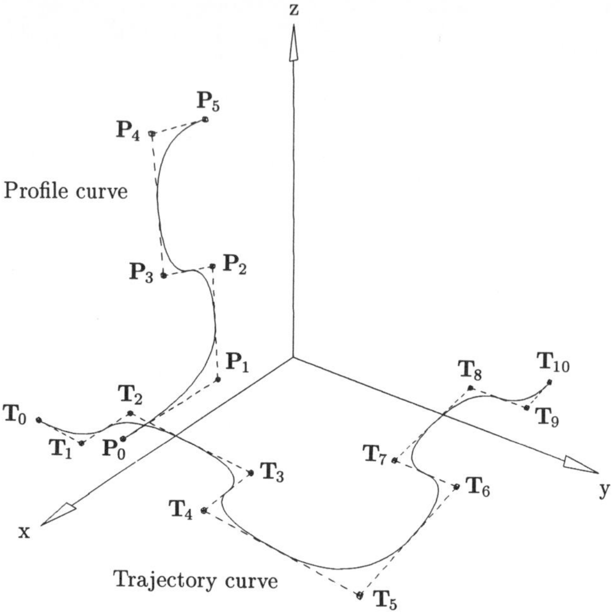

Figure 10.1. Profile and trajectory curves to define a swung surface.

Geometrically, $\mathbf{S}(u,v)$ is obtained by swinging $\mathbf{P}(u)$ about the z-axis and simultaneously scaling it according to $\mathbf{T}(v)$. α is an arbitrary scaling factor. Fixing u yields curves having the shape of $\mathbf{T}(v)$ but scaled in the x and y directions. Fixing $v = v_0$, the isoparametric curve, $\mathbf{C}_{v_0}(u)$, is obtained by rotating $\mathbf{P}(u)$ into the plane containing the vector $\big(T_x(v_0), T_y(v_0), 0\big)$, and scaling the x and y coordinates of the rotated curve with the factor $\alpha|\mathbf{T}(v_0)|$. The z coordinate remains unscaled. It follows from the transformation invariancy property of NURBS (P4.24) that $\mathbf{S}(u,v)$ has a NURBS representation given by

$$\mathbf{S}(u,v) = \sum_{i=0}^{n}\sum_{j=0}^{m} R_{i,p;j,q}(u,v)\,\mathbf{Q}_{i,j} \qquad (10.4)$$

where

$$\mathbf{Q}_{i,j} = (\alpha P_{i,x} T_{j,x}, \alpha P_{i,x} T_{j,y}, P_{i,z}) \qquad (10.5)$$

and

$$w_{i,j} = w_i w_j \qquad (10.6)$$

The U and V knot vectors for $\mathbf{S}(u,v)$ are those defining $\mathbf{P}(u)$ and $\mathbf{T}(v)$. Figures 10.2a–10.2c show examples of swinging. Figure 10.2a shows the control points of the swung surface defined by the curves in Figure 10.1 using $\alpha = 0.12$. The surface in Figure 10.2b is nonrational, whereas the surface of Figure 10.2c was obtained by applying the weights

$$w_1^P = w_4^P = 5 \qquad w_1^T = w_4^T = w_6^T = w_9^T = 5$$

where superscripts P and T refer to profile and trajectory curves, respectively.

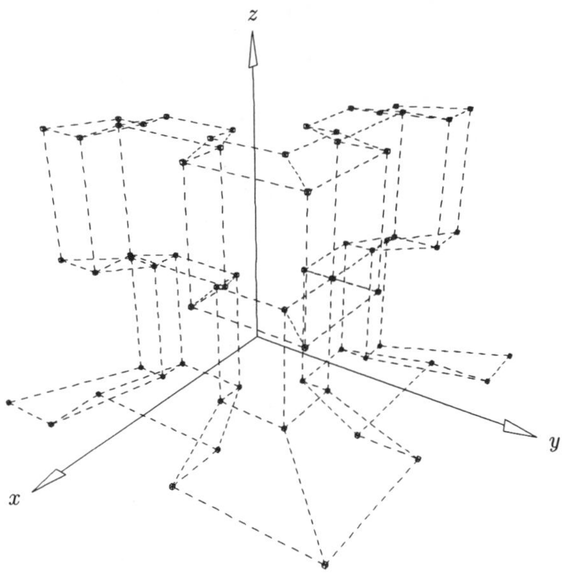

(a)

Figure 10.2. Swung surfaces. (a) Control net; (b) swung surface with no weights applied; (c) swung surface with some weights applied.

Note that both $\mathbf{P}(u)$ and $\mathbf{T}(v)$ can be either open or closed; correspondingly, $\mathbf{S}(u,v)$ can be open or closed in both u and v directions. Choosing $\alpha = 1$ and $\mathbf{T}(v)$ to be the circle with radius 1, centered at the origin, yields the surface of revolution given in Chapter 8.

10.3 Skinned Surfaces

Let $\{\mathbf{C}_k(u)\}$, $k = 0, \ldots, K$, be a set of curves. We call the $\mathbf{C}_k(u)$ *section curves.* In practice, they are usually planar cross sections, in the u direction, of the surface to be constructed. However, they can be three-dimensional. Furthermore, we do not assume planarity in this section. Skinning is a process of blending the section curves together to form a surface. The blend direction is the v direction, sometimes called the *longitudinal direction.* Although approximation across the section curves can be used, skinning methods usually interpolate through the $\mathbf{C}_k(u)$, with the result that the $\mathbf{C}_k(u)$ are isoparametric curves on the resulting skinned surface.

Skinning is simply a newer term for *lofting*, which dates back many decades, before computers. It was, and still is, widely used in the shipbuilding, automotive, and aircraft industries. One of the earliest computerized systems incorporating a lofting procedure was CONSURF, developed by A. Ball at the British Aircraft Corporation [Ball74, 75, 77]. That system was based on rational cubic

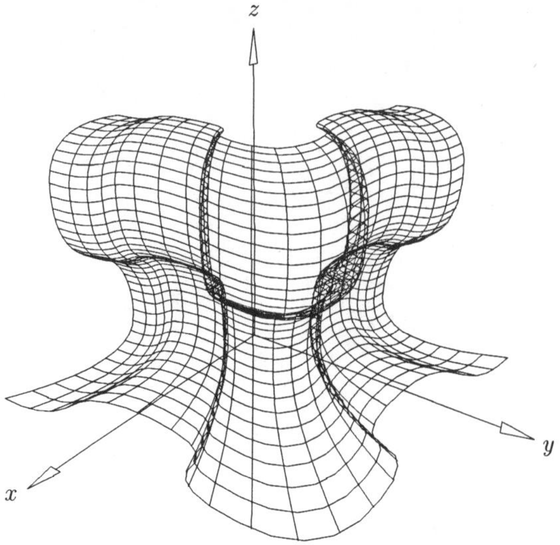

(b)

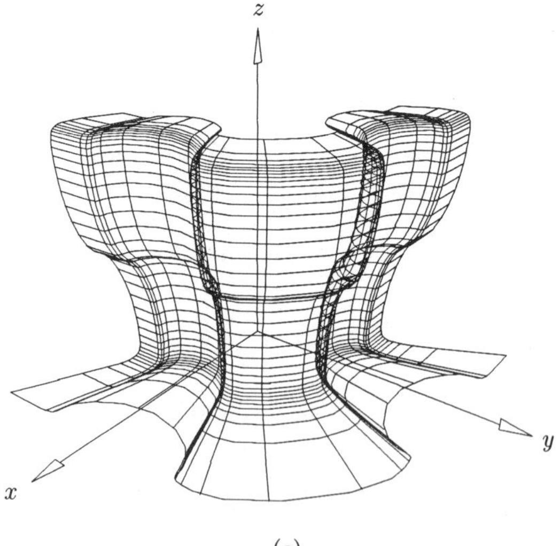

(c)

Figure 10.2. (*Continued.*)

curves. Filip and T. Ball [Fili89] describe a procedural method for lofting based on arbitrary parametric section curves. Detailed descriptions of skinning using B-splines are given in references [Till83; Wood87, 88; Hohm91].

Based on B-splines, we define skinning as follows. Let

$$\mathbf{C}_k^w(u) = \sum_{i=0}^{n} N_{i,p}(u)\,\mathbf{P}_{i,k}^w \qquad k = 0, \ldots, K \tag{10.7}$$

be the rational or nonrational section curves. We assume that all $\mathbf{C}_k^w(u)$ are defined on the same knot vector, U, and have common degree p. If necessary, the curves can be brought to a common p and U, as described in Section 8.4 (in fact, the ruled surface is a special case of a skinned surface). Then, for the v direction a degree q is chosen, and parameters $\{\bar{v}_k\}$, $k = 0, \ldots, K$, and a knot vector, V, are computed. These are then used to do $n+1$ curve interpolations across the control points of the section curves, yielding the control points $\mathbf{Q}_{i,j}^w$ of the skinned surface. Therefore, $\mathbf{Q}_{i,j}^w$ is the jth control point of the interpolating curve through $\mathbf{P}_{i,0}^w, \ldots, \mathbf{P}_{i,K}^w$. Note that if even one of the $\mathbf{C}_k^w(u)$ is rational, then the v direction interpolations through the $\mathbf{P}_{i,k}^w$ are carried out in four-dimensional space; otherwise, the three-dimensional points $\mathbf{P}_{i,k}$ are interpolated.

Figures 10.3a–10.3d show the skinning process. The original section curves are shown in Figure 10.3a and are defined on the knot vectors

$$\mathbf{C}_0(u): \quad \{0,0,1,1\} \qquad (p=1)$$

$$\mathbf{C}_1(u): \quad \left\{0,0,0,\frac{3}{10},\frac{1}{2},\frac{7}{10},1,1,1\right\} \qquad (p=2)$$

$$\mathbf{C}_2(u): \quad \left\{0,0,\frac{1}{5},\frac{2}{5},\frac{3}{5},\frac{4}{5},1,1\right\} \qquad (p=1)$$

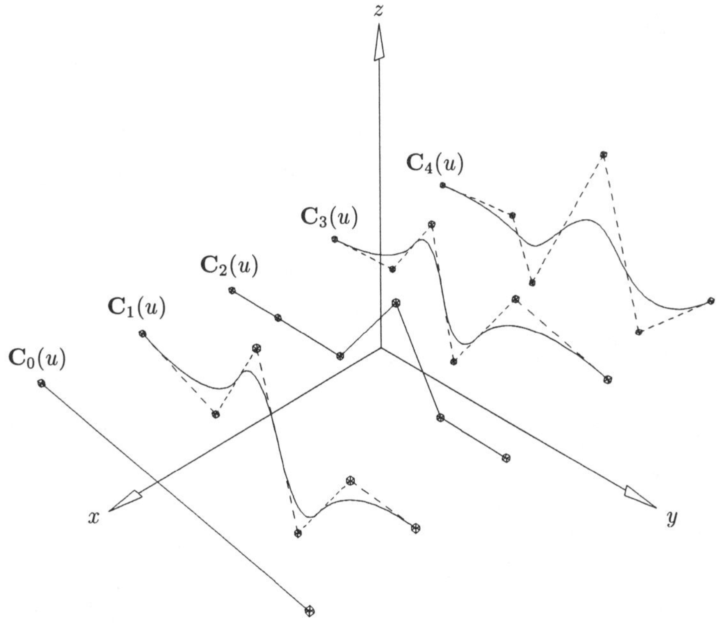

(a)

Figure 10.3. The process of surface skinning. (a) Cross-sectional curves; (b) cross-sectional curves made compatible; (c) control points; (d) skinned surface.

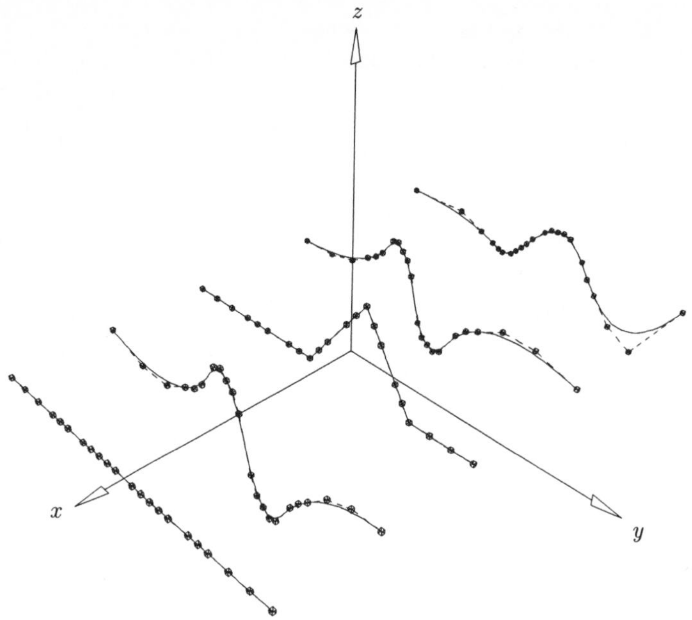

(b)

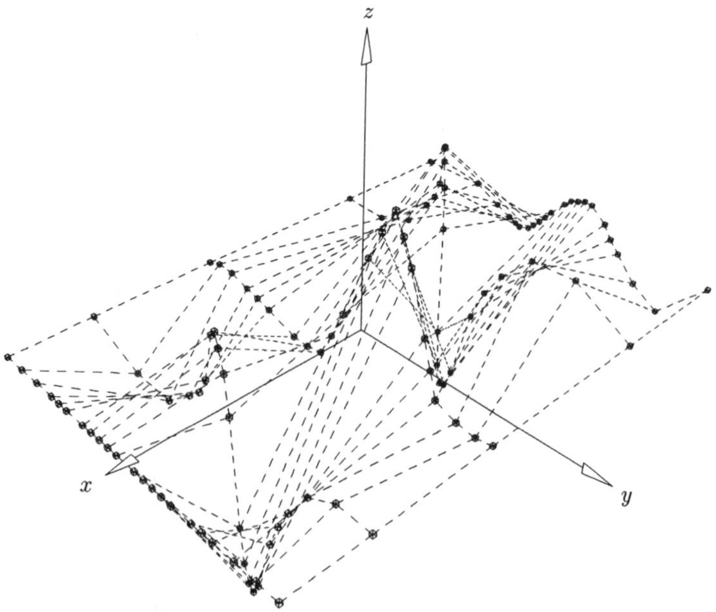

(c)

Figure 10.3. (*Continued.*)

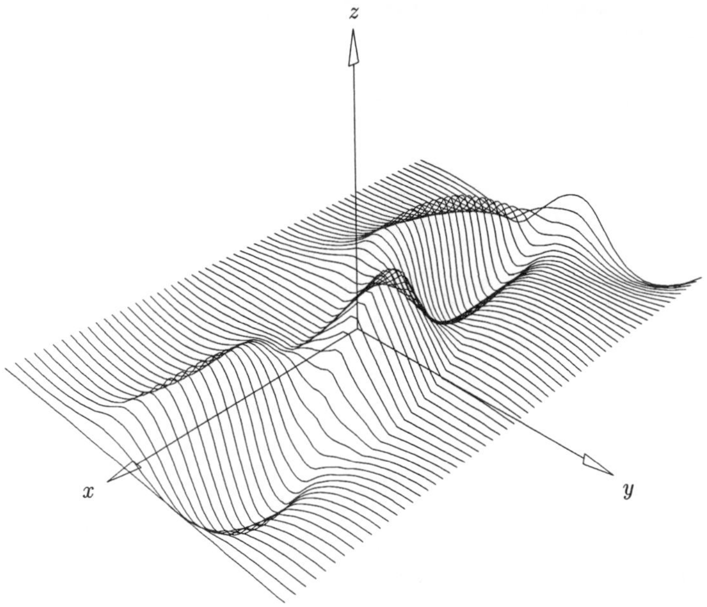

(d)

Figure 10.3. (*Continued.*)

$$\mathbf{C}_3(u): \quad \left\{0,0,0,\frac{3}{10},\frac{1}{2},\frac{7}{10},1,1,1\right\} \qquad (p=2)$$

$$\mathbf{C}_4(u): \quad \left\{0,0,0,0,\frac{3}{10},\frac{7}{10},1,1,1,1\right\} \quad (p=3)$$

After degree raising and knot refinement, the common knot vector is

$$\left\{0,0,0,0,\frac{1}{5},\frac{1}{5},\frac{1}{5},\frac{3}{10},\frac{3}{10},\frac{2}{5},\frac{2}{5},\frac{2}{5},\frac{1}{2},\frac{1}{2},\right.$$
$$\left.\frac{3}{5},\frac{3}{5},\frac{3}{5},\frac{7}{10},\frac{7}{10},\frac{4}{5},\frac{4}{5},\frac{4}{5},1,1,1,1\right\}$$

This raises the number of control points in the u direction to 22. The compatible curves are shown in Figure 10.3b. Note the significant number of new control points, the price one pays for flexibility. Figure 10.3c shows the control net of the skinned surface that is depicted in Figure 10.3d.

Although simple to formulate, it is quite difficult to implement a robust and usable skinning capability; and interactively designing skinned surfaces is often a tedious and iterative process. Surface shape is difficult to control; it depends on the number, shape, and positioning of the section curves (all of which the interactive designer usually controls), as well as on the method used for v-directional interpolations (which is usually embedded in the software and the designer cannot control). Often the design process consists of starting with a small number of section curves and then iteratively skinning, taking plane cuts to obtain additional section curves, modifying the new curves to obtain more desirable shapes, and reskinning. Finally, a skinned surface can exhibit unwanted self-intersections and twisting. However, in spite of these difficulties, skinning is a powerful and widely used surface design technique.

We turn our attention now to the v-directional interpolations. We assume for the moment that all section curves are nonrational; skinning across rational sections presents a host of problems, which we return to at the end of this section. Three items must be determined: the degree q, the parameters $\{\bar{v}_k\}$, and knots $V = \{v_i\}$. The degree q is arbitrary, the only restriction being $q \leq K$. The $\bar{v}_k$ are computed by averaging, for example

$$\bar{v}_0 = 0 \qquad \bar{v}_K = 1$$

$$\bar{v}_k = \bar{v}_{k-1} + \frac{1}{n+1} \sum_{i=0}^{n} \frac{|\mathbf{P}_{i,k} - \mathbf{P}_{i,k-1}|}{d_i} \qquad k = 1, \ldots, K-1 \tag{10.8}$$

where d_i denotes the total chord length of $\mathbf{P}_{i,0}, \ldots, \mathbf{P}_{i,K}$. The knots $\{v_i\}$ are then computed using Eq. (9.8). The skinned surface of Figure 10.3d was constructed using this method of interpolation.

Another common method is to use a so-called *spine curve* (also called a *path curve*), that is

$$\mathbf{C}_s(v) = \sum_{i=0}^{n_s} R_{i,p_s}(v)\, \mathbf{R}_i \tag{10.9}$$

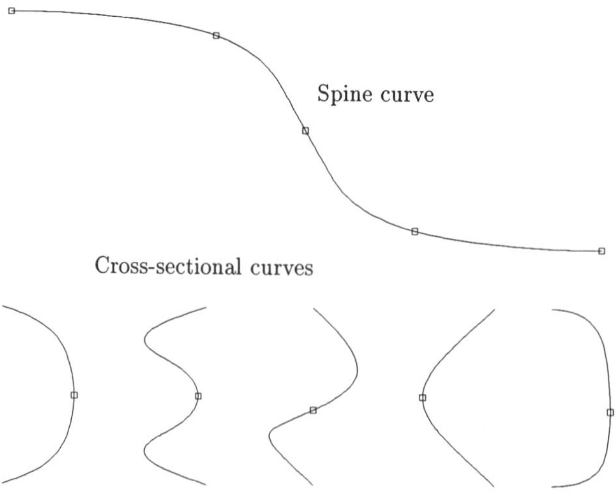

Figure 10.4. Spine curve and cross-sectional curves for spine-based skinning.

$\mathbf{C}_s(v)$ can be an arbitrary rational or nonrational, planar or nonplanar curve. The designer uses the spine curve to position and orient the section curves in space. Figure 10.4 shows the spine curve and five planar section curves to be positioned in three-dimensional space. One possible positioning is illustrated in Figure 10.5. The section curves are positioned at spine parameters

$$\hat{v}_k = \{0, 0.25, 0.5, 0.78, 1\}$$

and at section curve parameters

$$\hat{u}_k = \left\{\frac{1}{2}, \frac{1}{2}, \frac{1}{2}, \frac{1}{2}, \frac{1}{2}\right\}$$

Each section curve is oriented so that its plane is perpendicular to the tangent vector of the spine curve at the intersection of the spine curve and the section's plane. The spine curve can also aid in v-directional shape control by providing additional constraints for use in the v-directional interpolations. For example, spine tangent directions can be used: Let $\{\hat{v}_k\}$, $k = 0, \ldots, K$, be the v values of the points on $\mathbf{C}_s(v)$ where the section curves are positioned; for planar sections these are the v values corresponding to intersections of the spine with the section planes. These values are generally known, and they can be input to the skinning routine. Notice that, in general, $\hat{v}_k \neq \bar{v}_k$ if the $\bar{v}_k$ are computed using Eq. (10.8).

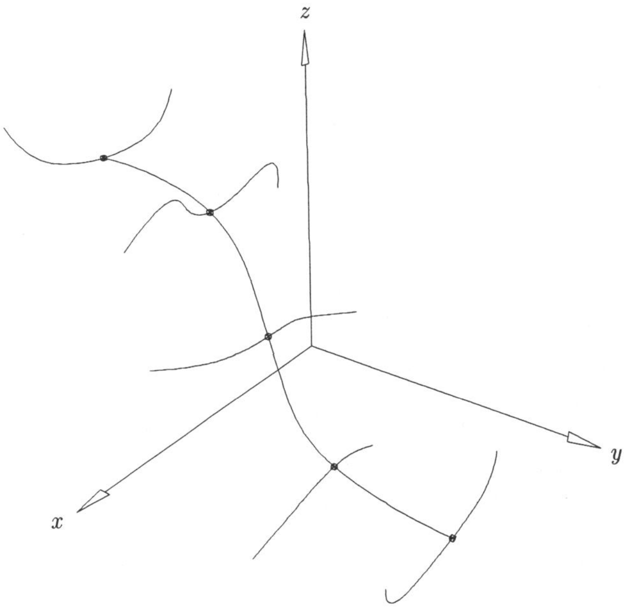

Figure 10.5. Section curves positioned along a spine curve.

Of course, one can set $\bar{v}_k = \hat{v}_k$, but this may not be a good idea if $\mathbf{C}_s(v)$ is poorly parameterized. Now let

$$\mathbf{P}_k = \mathbf{C}_s(\hat{v}_k) \qquad \mathbf{D}_k = \mathbf{C}'_s(\hat{v}_k) \qquad k = 0, \ldots, K$$

Then for each i and k we compute a derivative vector, $\mathbf{D}_{i,k}$. For each i this yields $2(K+1)$ interpolation constraints, $\mathbf{P}_{i,0}, \ldots, \mathbf{P}_{i,K}$ and $\mathbf{D}_{i,0}, \ldots, \mathbf{D}_{i,K}$. The $\mathbf{D}_{i,k}$ are computed by letting

$$d_k = |\mathbf{P}_k - \mathbf{P}_{k-1}| \qquad k = 1, \ldots, K$$

(see Figure 10.6). Then for $k = 1, \ldots, K-1$, set

$$\mathbf{D}_{i,k} = \frac{|\mathbf{P}_{i,k+1} - \mathbf{P}_{i,k}| + |\mathbf{P}_{i,k} - \mathbf{P}_{i,k-1}|}{d_{k+1} + d_k} \mathbf{D}_k \tag{10.10}$$

and at the ends

$$\mathbf{D}_{i,0} = \frac{|\mathbf{P}_{i,1} - \mathbf{P}_{i,0}|}{d_1} \mathbf{D}_0$$

$$\mathbf{D}_{i,K} = \frac{|\mathbf{P}_{i,K} - \mathbf{P}_{i,K-1}|}{d_K} \mathbf{D}_K \tag{10.11}$$

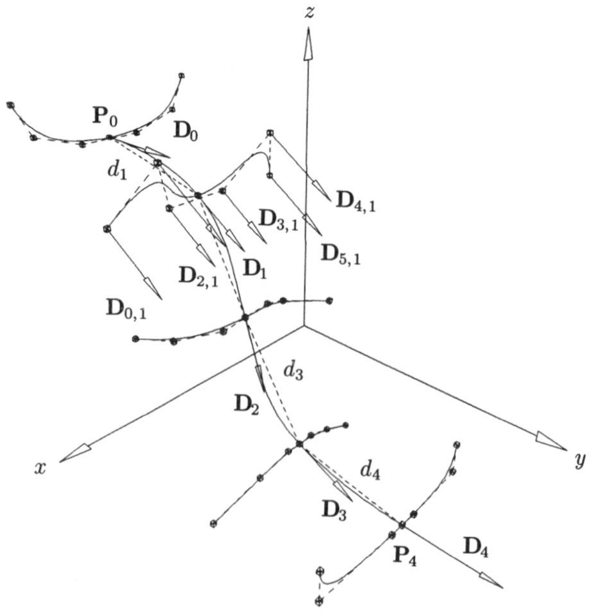

Figure 10.6. Computation of derivatives for spine skinning.

Hence, $\mathbf{D}_{i,k}$ is parallel to $\mathbf{D}_k$, but its magnitude is adjusted to reflect relative distances. Equations (10.10) and (10.11) ensure that

$$\mathbf{S}_v(u, \bar{v}_k) \parallel \mathbf{D}_k \qquad \text{for all } u \text{ and } k = 0, \ldots, K \tag{10.12}$$

that is, all partial derivatives with respect to v on the kth isoparametric curve are parallel to $\mathbf{D}_k$. This follows from the fact that these partial derivatives are linear combinations of the $\mathbf{D}_{i,k}$. Letting $m = 2K + 1$, we can now set up $m + 1$ linear equations for each fixed i (see Eqs. [9.19] and [9.20]), i.e.

$$\mathbf{P}_{i,k} = \sum_{j=0}^{m} N_{j,q}(\bar{v}_k)\,\mathbf{Q}_{i,j} \qquad \mathbf{D}_{i,k} = \sum_{j=0}^{m} N'_{j,q}(\bar{v}_k)\,\mathbf{Q}_{i,j} \tag{10.13}$$

The knot vector V must contain $m + q + 2$ knots; Eqs. (9.22) and (9.23) give suitable choices for the cases $q = 2$ and $q = 3$, respectively.

Figure 10.7a shows the control points of the skinned surface defined by the data in Figure 10.5, using cubic interpolation with specified tangents as shown in Figure 10.6; the surface is depicted in Figure 10.7b. The same data is interpolated in Figures 10.8a and 10.8b, without specified derivatives. Note the significant difference in surface shapes (Figures 10.7b and 10.8b). The positioning of section curves has a definite effect on surface shape, just as the positioning of data points in curve and surface interpolation; Figures 10.9a and 10.9b show two examples. In Figure 10.9a the spine and section curve parameters are

$$\hat{v}_k = \{0, 0.35, 0.5, 0.62, 1\} \qquad \hat{u}_k = \left\{\frac{1}{2}, \frac{1}{2}, \frac{1}{2}, \frac{1}{2}, \frac{1}{2}\right\}$$

and in Figure 10.9b they are

$$\hat{v}_k = \{0, 0.25, 0.5, 0.78, 1\} \qquad \hat{u}_k = \left\{\frac{1}{2}, \frac{3}{10}, \frac{1}{2}, \frac{9}{10}, \frac{1}{2}\right\}$$

We now consider the case in which some of the section curves are rational (Eq. [10.7]). The v interpolations must now be carried out in homogeneous space. Analogous to Eq. (10.8), the $\bar{v}_k$ are computed by averaging four-dimensional distances, that is

$$\bar{v}_0 = 0 \qquad \bar{v}_K = 1$$

$$\bar{v}_k = \bar{v}_{k-1} + \frac{1}{n+1}\sum_{i=0}^{n} \frac{|\mathbf{P}^w_{i,k} - \mathbf{P}^w_{i,k-1}|}{d^w_i} \qquad k = 1, \ldots, K-1 \tag{10.14}$$

where d^w_i denotes the total chord length of $\mathbf{P}^w_{i,0}, \ldots, \mathbf{P}^w_{i,K}$. The knots $\{v_i\}$ are again computed using Eq. (9.8). Interpolations through the $\mathbf{P}^w_{i,k}$ yield the control points $\mathbf{Q}^w_{i,j}$, $i = 0, \ldots, n$, $j = 0, \ldots, K$, of the skinned surface $\mathbf{S}^w(u, v)$. The isoparametric curves, $\mathbf{C}^w_{\bar{v}_k}(u) = \mathbf{S}^w(u, \bar{v}_k)$, are the original section curves, $\mathbf{C}^w_k(u)$. Although the designer may still use a spine curve to position and orient the

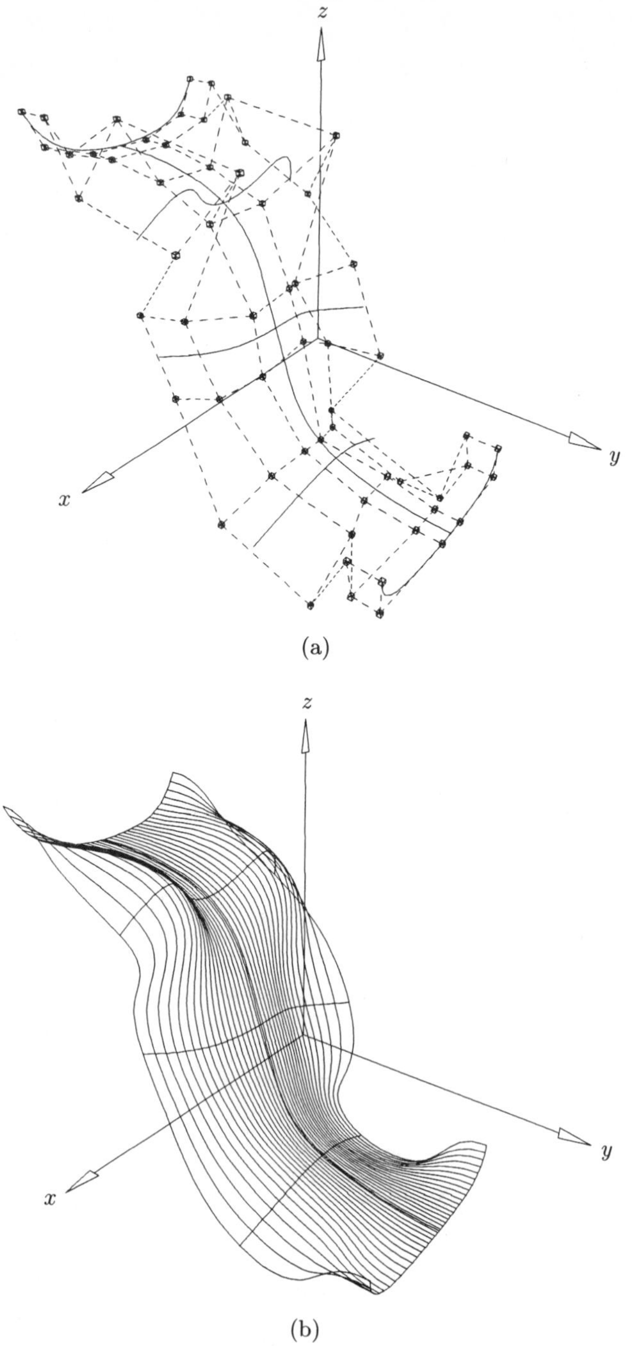

Figure 10.7. Spine skinning with spine controlled interpolation. (a) Control net; (b) skinned surface.

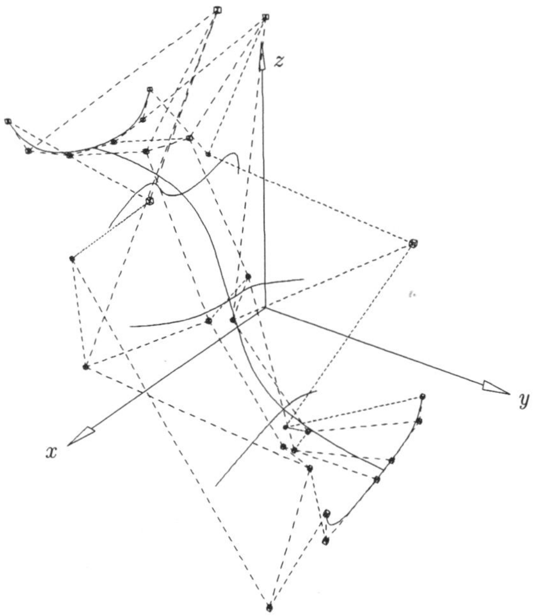

(a)

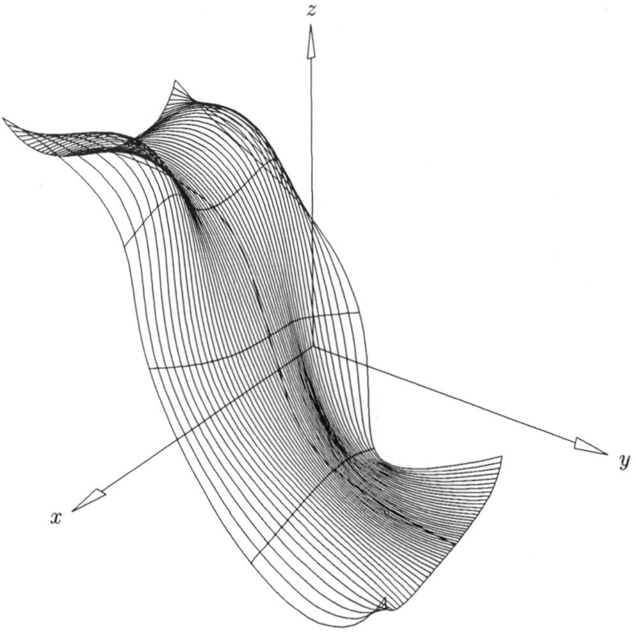

(b)

Figure 10.8. Spine skinning with no spine interpolation constraint. (a) Control net; (b) skinned surface.

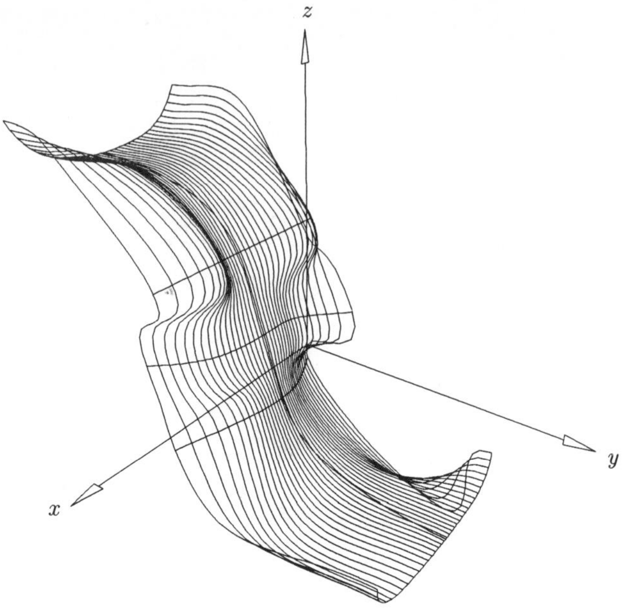

(a)

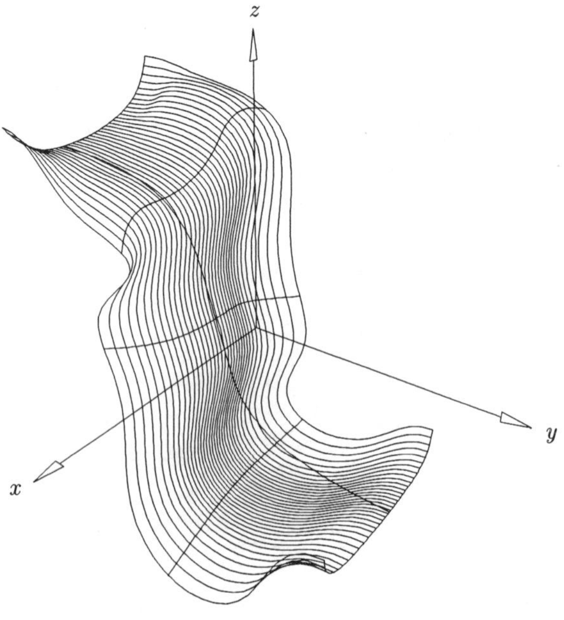

(b)

Figure 10.9. Spine skinning. (a) Section curves are positioned at different spine parameters; (b) section curves are positioned at different section curve parameters.

section curves, there is no obvious way to impose (linear) derivative constraints for the v direction interpolations to ensure that Eq. (10.12) is satisfied for all u and k.

Most often, skinning through rational section curves yields satisfactory results, but the reader should be aware that there exist several potential hazards, some of which do not seem to have very satisfying practical solutions. These problems all arise as a result of the fact that surface construction is taking place in homogeneous space, and corresponding three-dimensional and four-dimensional geometry can be radically different. For example, two three-dimensional curves can be smooth, similar in shape, and close to one another, while their four-dimensional counterparts may have cusps, have totally different shapes, and be far from one another. More specifically, some problems that can arise are:

- the v-directional surface parameterization may be rather poor. As a simple example, take two section curves, and multiply all the control points of one of them by a large weight. This does not change the three-dimensional curve geometry. The simple ruled (skinned) surface between the two sections is poorly parameterized in the v direction. The three-dimensional surface parameterization can be improved by using the projected control points, $\mathbf{P}_{i,k}$, to compute the $\bar{v}_k$ (as in Eq. [10.8]), but this can produce wild four-dimensional v-directional interpolations, resulting in undesirable geometry both in four-dimensional and three-dimensional space;
- for fixed i, the surface weights $w_{i,0}, \ldots, w_{i,K}$ result from interpolating the weights of the section control points, $\mathbf{P}^w_{i,0}, \ldots, \mathbf{P}^w_{i,K}$. Clearly, the interpolation can produce a negative or zero $w_{i,k}$, even though all the section weights are positive (e.g., see the explanation to Figure 10.10b below). This can cause problems, for example crash a system, downstream in a system not designed to handle such weights;
- the surface may not be as smooth as the section curves indicate. For example, let one section curve be the full circle given in Example `Ex7.2`. As shown in that example, the circle is C^1 continuous, although its homogeneous counterpart is only C^0 continuous at the double knots. Assuming that all other section curves are C^1, one expects the resulting skinned surface, $\mathbf{S}(u,v)$, to be C^1 continuous in the u direction. But $\mathbf{S}^w(u,v)$ is only C^0 continuous in the u direction, since it is formed by blending C^0 curves; in general, arbitrary u-directional isoparametric curves on $\mathbf{S}^w(u,v)$ are only C^0, and their projections to three-dimensional space may be only C^0 continuous. Figures 10.10a and 10.10b show an example of this. The four rational section curves are all C^1 continuous in three-dimensional space. They are quadratics, defined with a double knot at $u = 1/2$. The respective weights of the section curves are

$$\mathbf{C}_0 : \ \{1,2,1,1,1\}$$
$$\mathbf{C}_1 : \ \{1,1,1,3,1\}$$
$$\mathbf{C}_2 : \ \{1,1,1,1,1\}$$
$$\mathbf{C}_3 : \ \{1,4,1,2,1\}$$

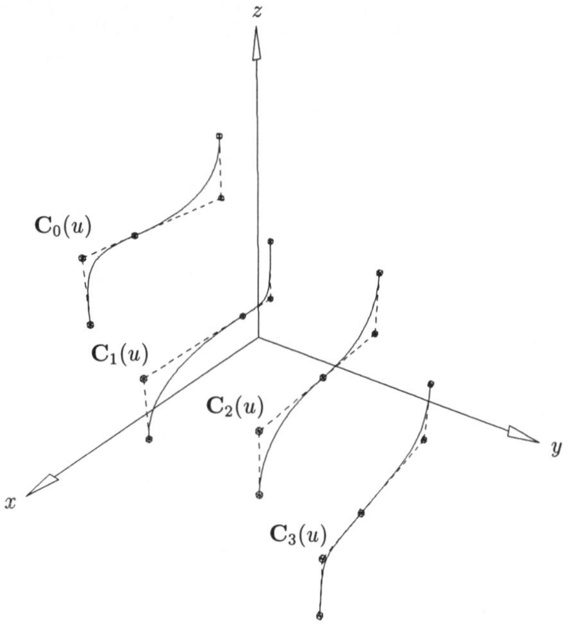

(a)

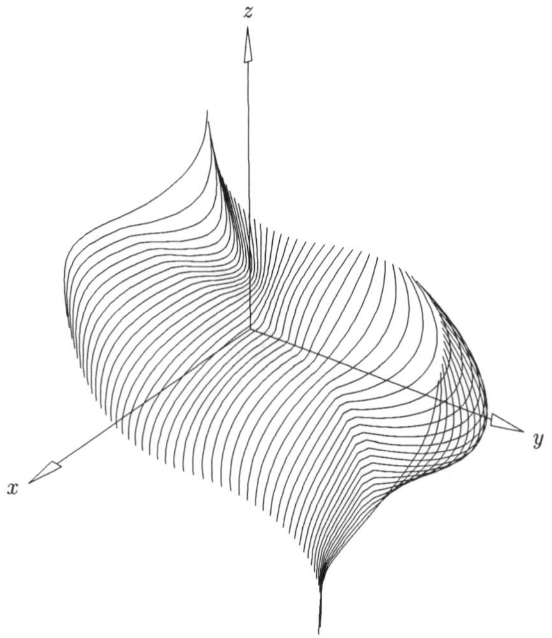

(b)

Figure 10.10. Rational skinning. (a) C^1 continuous section curves; (b) skinned surface.

$\mathbf{C}_0$, $\mathbf{C}_1$, and $\mathbf{C}_3$ are only C^0 continuous in four-dimensional space. After v-directional interpolations, the surface weights are:

$$w_{i,j} = \begin{bmatrix} 1 & 2 & 1 & 1 & 1 \\ 1 & 0.94 & 1 & 4.43 & 1 \\ 1 & 0.71 & 1 & -0.75 & 1 \\ 1 & 4 & 1 & 2 & 1 \end{bmatrix}$$

(note the negative weight at $\mathbf{P}_{3,2}$). The surface shown in Figure 10.10b exhibits only C^0 continuity in the u direction. To the authors' knowledge, the only solutions to this dilemma involve the use of higher degree section curves. For example, a full circle can be represented as a degree 5 NURBS curve with positive weights and no interior knots (Example `E7.10`), thereby eliminating the problem. Several solutions to this problem, all effectively raising the degree of the skinned surface, are discussed in [Hohm91]. A general solution is to use so-called *smoothing functions.* Suppose $\mathbf{C}_k^w(u)$ is a C^r continuous section curve on the knot vector U, whose projection $\mathbf{C}_k(u)$ is C^{r+s} continuous, $s > 0$. Let $f(u)$ be a B-spline scalar-valued function on U, such that

$$\hat{\mathbf{C}}_k^w(u) = f(u)\mathbf{C}_k^w(u) \tag{10.15}$$

is C^{r+s} continuous. $f(u)$ is called a smoothing function. For fixed u_0, $f(u_0)$ simply scales $\mathbf{C}_k^w(u_0)$ up or down the four-dimensional cone defined by $\mathbf{C}_k(u)$, that is, $\hat{\mathbf{C}}_k(u) = \mathbf{C}_k(u)$ for all u. Clearly, if all $\mathbf{C}_k^w(u)$ can be smoothed, then skinning through the corresponding $\hat{\mathbf{C}}_k^w(u)$ yields a C^{r+s} continuous surface which interpolates the three-dimensional section curves. However, we know of no general algorithm for determining $f(u)$. Differentiating Eq. (10.15) from the left and right yields a set of linear equations which express the desired continuity constraints at the knots. However, other considerations are:

- if $\mathbf{C}_k^w(u)$ is closed, then $\hat{\mathbf{C}}_k^w(u)$ should be closed;
- all weights of $\hat{\mathbf{C}}_k^w(u)$ should be positive;
- the weights of $\hat{\mathbf{C}}_k^w(u)$ should not vary wildly or become exceedingly large.

A degree $r + s$ function, $f(u)$, suffices to satisfy just the continuity constraints at the knots, but the other constraints generally force $f(u)$ to be of higher degree. Finally, once $f(u)$ is determined it must be multiplied with $\mathbf{C}_k^w(u)$. Multiplication of B-splines is not a trivial task. An algorithm similar to degree elevation (Algorithm `A5.9`) of Chapter 5 can be developed, i.e.,

1. decomposition of $f(u)$ and $\mathbf{C}_k^w(u)$ into Bézier segments;
2. multiplication of the segments;
3. recomposition of $\hat{\mathbf{C}}_k^w(u)$ into a NURBS curve (knot removal).

10.4 Swept Surfaces

Next we address the topic of sweeping a section curve along an arbitrary trajectory curve. Denote the trajectory by $\mathbf{T}(v)$ and the section curve by $\mathbf{C}(u)$. A general form of the swept surface is given by

$$\mathbf{S}(u,v) = \mathbf{T}(v) + M(v)\mathbf{C}(u) \tag{10.16}$$

where $M(v)$ is a 3×3 matrix incorporating rotation and nonuniform scaling of $\mathbf{C}(u)$ as a function of v. $\mathbf{T}(v)$ and $\mathbf{C}(u)$ may be arbitrary: nonrational or rational, planar or nonplanar, open or closed.

In general, Eq. (10.16) can produce nonsensical and unwanted surfaces with self-intersections, degeneracies, and discontinuities. Furthermore, in many cases $\mathbf{S}(u,v)$ is not precisely representable as a NURBS surface. In practice, most swept surfaces are one of two specific types:

1. $M(v)$ is the identity matrix for all v, that is, for each v, $\mathbf{C}(u)$ is just translated by $\mathbf{T}(v)$;
2. $M(v)$ is not the identity matrix.

Case 1 is described by the equation

$$\mathbf{S}(u,v) = \mathbf{T}(v) + \mathbf{C}(u) \tag{10.17}$$

which has a precise NURBS representation. We call this surface a *generalized translational sweep*. The general cylinder of Section 8.3 is a special case, with $\mathbf{T}(v)$ being a straight line. $\mathbf{S}(u,v)$ is constructed as follows. Let

$$\mathbf{T}(v) = \frac{\sum_{j=0}^{m} N_{j,q}(v) w_j^T \mathbf{T}_j}{\sum_{j=0}^{m} N_{j,q}(v) w_j^T} \qquad V = \{v_0, \ldots, v_s\}$$

and

$$\mathbf{C}(u) = \frac{\sum_{i=0}^{n} N_{i,p}(u) w_i^C \mathbf{Q}_i}{\sum_{i=0}^{n} N_{i,p}(u) w_i^C} \qquad U = \{u_0, \ldots, u_r\}$$

Then

$$\mathbf{S}(u,v) = \frac{\sum_{i=0}^{n}\sum_{j=0}^{m} N_{i,p}(u) N_{j,q}(v) w_{i,j} \mathbf{P}_{i,j}}{\sum_{i=0}^{n}\sum_{j=0}^{m} N_{i,p}(u) N_{j,q}(v) w_{i,j}}$$

is defined on knots U and V, and has control points

$$\mathbf{P}_{i,j} = \mathbf{T}_j + \mathbf{Q}_i \qquad i = 0, \ldots, n \quad j = 0, \ldots, m \tag{10.18}$$

and weights

$$w_{i,j} = w_i^C w_j^T \qquad i = 0, \ldots, n \quad j = 0, \ldots, m \tag{10.19}$$

Figures 10.11a and 10.11b show an example of translational sweep.

Now consider Case 2. Let $\{\mathbf{O}, \mathbf{X}, \mathbf{Y}, \mathbf{Z}\}$ denote our global coordinate system. To simplify matters, we introduce a local orthonormal coordinate system $\{\mathbf{o}(v), \mathbf{x}(v), \mathbf{y}(v), \mathbf{z}(v)\}$, which moves along $\mathbf{T}(v)$. For each v, $v_0 \le v \le v_s$, set

$$\mathbf{o}(v) = \mathbf{T}(v) \qquad \mathbf{x}(v) = \frac{\mathbf{T}'(v)}{|\mathbf{T}'(v)|} \tag{10.20}$$

Additionally, let $\mathbf{B}(v)$ be a vector-valued function satisfying $\mathbf{B}(v) \cdot \mathbf{x}(v) = 0$ for all v, and set

$$\mathbf{z}(v) = \frac{\mathbf{B}(v)}{|\mathbf{B}(v)|} \tag{10.21}$$

The determination of this function is a critical and nontrivial part of the sweeping

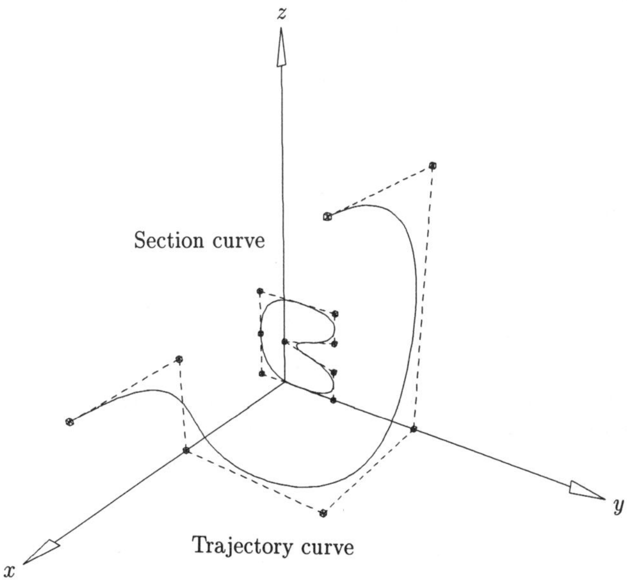

(a)

Figure 10.11. Translational sweeping. (a) Trajectory and section curves; (b) swept surface.

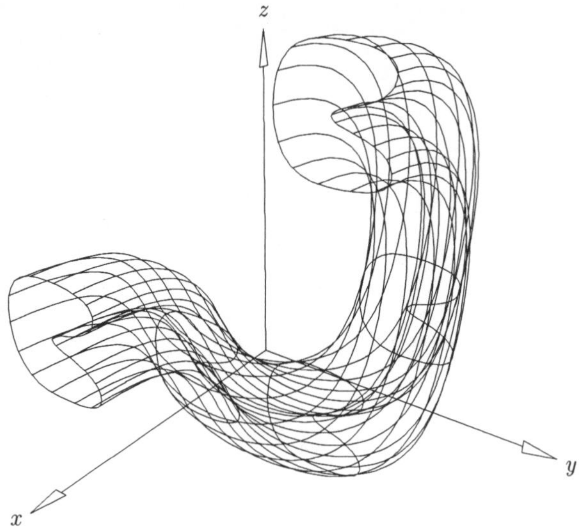

(b)

Figure 10.11. (*Continued.*)

process. We return to the question of how to determine $\mathbf{B}(v)$ at the end of this section; for now, we simply assume it is given. $\mathbf{y}(v)$ is then defined by

$$\mathbf{y}(v) = \mathbf{z}(v) \times \mathbf{x}(v) \tag{10.22}$$

In order to incorporate scaling we introduce a three-dimensional vector function

$$\mathbf{s}(v) = \big(s_x(v), s_y(v), s_z(v)\big) \tag{10.23}$$

The swept surface is now defined by

$$\mathbf{S}(u,v) = \mathbf{T}(v) + A(v)S(v)\mathbf{C}(u) \tag{10.24}$$

where $S(v)$ is a 3×3 diagonal matrix with diagonal elements $\big(s_x(v), s_y(v), s_z(v)\big)$, and $A(v)$ is the general transformation matrix taking $\{\mathbf{O},\mathbf{X},\mathbf{Y},\mathbf{Z}\}$ into $\{\mathbf{o}(v),$ $\mathbf{x}(v),\mathbf{y}(v),\mathbf{z}(v)\}$. The isoparametric curves on $\mathbf{S}(u,v)$ at fixed v values are instances of $\mathbf{C}(u)$, transformed by $A(v)S(v)$ and translated by $\mathbf{T}(v)$. If $\mathbf{C}(u)$ passes through the global origin at $u=\bar{u}$, then $\mathbf{T}(v)$ is the isoparametric curve $\mathbf{S}(u=\bar{u},v)$.

$\mathbf{S}(u,v)$ may not be representable in NURBS form. Clearly, if $A(v)$ and $S(v)$ can be precisely represented as rational B-spline functions, then so can $\mathbf{S}(u,v)$. $S(v)$ is generally no problem. If scaling is applied at all, then it is common to use a linear function or a higher degree B-spline approximation to a function which is linear with respect to the arc length parameter. However, $A(v)$ is generally not representable in NURBS form, even in the simple case that $\mathbf{z}(v) = \mathbf{Z}$ for all $v_0 \le v \le v_s$. Hence, we must construct a NURBS approximation to Eq. (10.24). Denote this approximation by $\hat{\mathbf{S}}(u,v)$. We present three methods:

- The first method is to use Eq. (10.24) to evaluate an $(n \times m)$ grid of points lying precisely on $\mathbf{S}(u,v)$, and then use either the interpolation or approximation techniques of Chapter 9 to construct a nonrational B-spline approximation, $\hat{\mathbf{S}}(u,v)$. A disadvantage with this method is that none of the u or v isoparametric curves on $\hat{\mathbf{S}}(u,v)$ are precise;
- Another method is given by Bloomenthal and Riesenfeld [Blom91] and by Coquillart [Coqu87a]; their method involves approximating the three-dimensional offset curves of the trajectory. Their algorithm interpolates $\mathbf{T}(v)$ as an isoparametric curve if $\mathbf{C}(u)$ passes through the origin; however, instances of $\mathbf{C}(u)$ are not interpolated, except at $v = v_0$ and $v = v_s$. Bloomenthal and Riesenfeld give error bounds for their method, based on error bounds for the offsetting process;
- A third method, which we present in more detail here, is to use skinning. We transform and place $K+1$ instances of $\mathbf{C}(u)$ along $\mathbf{T}(v)$, and then skin across these section curves. The accuracy of the resulting surface, $\hat{\mathbf{S}}(u,v)$, is increased by increasing K. Each instance of $\mathbf{C}(u)$ is interpolated as an isoparametric curve on $\hat{\mathbf{S}}(u,v)$. There are two strategies for the v-directional fitting. The first makes use of the B-spline structure of $\mathbf{T}(v)$. The trajectory's degree q and knot vector V are used for the fitting, hence they are inherited by $\hat{\mathbf{S}}(u,v)$. Furthermore, the parameters $\bar{v}_k$ for the fitting must be taken from $\mathbf{T}(v)$; if $\mathbf{T}(v)$ is rational, its weights must be factored in prior to the v-directional fitting. This method is required if $\mathbf{C}(u)$ passes through the global origin and it is desired that $\mathbf{T}(v)$ be an isoparametric curve in $\hat{\mathbf{S}}(u,v)$, but the method can be used in any case. The other method does not make use of $\mathbf{T}(v)$ other than to position the section curve; that is, the v-degree of $\hat{\mathbf{S}}(u,v)$ is input, parameters and knots are computed in some manner, and $\mathbf{T}(v)$'s weights need not be factored in.

Corresponding to the two methods of v-directional fitting, two sweeping algorithms follow. In both cases, the swept surface, $\hat{\mathbf{S}}(u,v)$, inherits its u-degree p and the knot vector U from $\mathbf{C}(u)$. `T` and `C` are the trajectory and section curves, and `Bv` and `sv` are input functions given by Eqs. (10.21) and (10.23), respectively. In Algorithm `A10.1` the v-degree `q` is not required; the number `K` is to be viewed as a minimum, because more instances of the section curve may be required depending on the number of knots defining $\mathbf{T}(v)$.

```
ALGORITHM A10.1
  SweepSurface1(T,C,Bv,sv,K,V,Pw)
    { /* Swept surface.  Trajectory interpolated.  */
      /* Input:  T,C,Bv,sv,K  */
      /* Output: V,Pw  */
    q = degree of T(v).
```

```
ktv = number of knots of $\mathbf{T}(v)$.
nsect = K+1;
if (ktv <= nsect+q)
  {  /* Must refine $\mathbf{T}(v)$'s knot vector */
  m = nsect+q-ktv+1;
  Insert m more knots into $\mathbf{T}(v)$'s knot vector.  Locations
    are not critical, recursively insert at the midpoint of
    the longest span will do.  New control points do not
    have to be computed, as we only require a refined
    set of knots.
  The resulting knot vector V is inherited by $\hat{\mathbf{S}}(u,v)$.
  }
  else
  {  /* $\mathbf{T}(v)$'s knot vector will do */
  V = $\mathbf{T}(v)$'s knot vector.
  if (ktv > nsect+q+1)    /* Must increase number of */
    nsect = ktv-q-1;      /* instances of $\mathbf{C}(u)$ */
  }
$\bar{v}_0$ = $\mathbf{T}(v)$'s minimum parameter value.
$\bar{v}_{nsect-1}$ = $\mathbf{T}(v)$'s maximum parameter value.
for (k=1; k<nsect-1; k++)    /* Compute parameters by */
  $\bar{v}_k = (v_{k+1} + \cdots + v_{k+q})/q$;    /* averaging knots */
for (k=0; k<nsect; k++)
  {  /* Transform and position section control points  */
  Let $\mathbf{Q}_i$ and $w_i$ be the control points and weights
    of $\mathbf{C}(u)$, $i = 0, \ldots, n$.
  Scale the control points $\mathbf{Q}_i$ by sv.
  Compute $\{\mathbf{o},\mathbf{x},\mathbf{y},\mathbf{z}\}(\bar{v}_k)$ from Eqs.(10.20)-(10.22).
  Compute the transformation matrix $A(\bar{v}_k)$ transforming the
    global system into $\{\mathbf{o},\mathbf{x},\mathbf{y},\mathbf{z}\}(\bar{v}_k)$.
  Apply $A(\bar{v}_k)$ to the scaled $\mathbf{Q}_i$.
  Reapply the weights $w_i$, and denote the resulting
    weighted control points by $\mathbf{Q}^w_{k,i}$.
  if ($\mathbf{T}(v)$ is rational)
    {  /* $w(v)$ is the weight function of $\mathbf{T}(v)$ */
        /* (4th coordinate) */
    $\mathbf{Q}^w_{k,i} = w(\bar{v}_k)\mathbf{Q}^w_{k,i}$;
    }
  }
for (i=0; i<=n; i++)
  {
  Interpolate across $\mathbf{Q}^w_{0,i}, \ldots, \mathbf{Q}^w_{\mathrm{nsect}-1,i}$ to obtain
    $\mathbf{P}^w_{0,i}, \ldots, \mathbf{P}^w_{\mathrm{nsect}-1,i}$.
  }
}
```

```
ALGORITHM A10.2
  SweepSurface2(T,C,Bv,sv,q,K,V,Pw)
    { /* Swept surface.  Trajectory not interpolated.  */
      /* Input:  T,C,Bv,sv,q,K  */
      /* Output: V,Pw  */
    Determine values v_0,...,v_K at which to place the
      instances of C(u).  A reasonable choice is to select the
      v_k so that the T(v_k) are approximately evenly
      spaced.
    for (k=0; k<=K; k++)
      { /* Transform and position section control points */
      Let Q_i and w_i be the control points and weights
        of C(u), i = 0,...,n.
      Scale the control points Q_i by sv.
      Compute {o,x,y,z}(v_k) from Eqs.(10.20)-(10.22).
      Compute the transformation matrix A(v_k) transforming the
        global system into {o,x,y,z}(v_k).
      Apply A(v_k) to the scaled Q_i.
      Reapply the weights w_i, and denote the resulting
        weighted control points by Q^w_{k,i}.
      }
    Determine v̄_0,...,v̄_K, the v-parameters for the
      v-directional interpolations (Eqs.[10.8] or [10.14]).
    Given q and the v̄_k, compute the knot vector V by averaging
      (Eq.[9.8]).
    for (i=0; i<=n; i++)
      {
      Interpolate across Q^w_{0,i},...,Q^w_{K,i} to obtain P^w_{0,i},...,P^w_{K,i}.
      }
    }
```

Figure 10.12a shows the trajectory and section curves, along with a start vector, $\mathbf{B}(v_0)$. The section curve does not pass through the global origin. Figures 10.12b and 10.12c show the results of sweeping by Algorithms A10.2 and A10.1, respectively. Since the section curve does not pass through the origin the trajectory is not contained in the surface, even in Figure 10.12c. Also note the larger number of section curve placements in Figure 10.12c. Figures 10.13a–10.13c show sweeping examples where the section curve passes through the origin (Figure 10.13a). No trajectory control was used (Algorithm A10.2). Figure 10.13b used no scaling, while Figure 10.13c used a piecewise linear B-spline scaling function defined by control points

$$\left\{\left(\frac{3}{10},\frac{3}{10},1\right),\left(\frac{3}{2},\frac{3}{2},\frac{1}{2}\right),\left(\frac{3}{10},\frac{3}{10},1\right),(1,1,2)\right\}$$

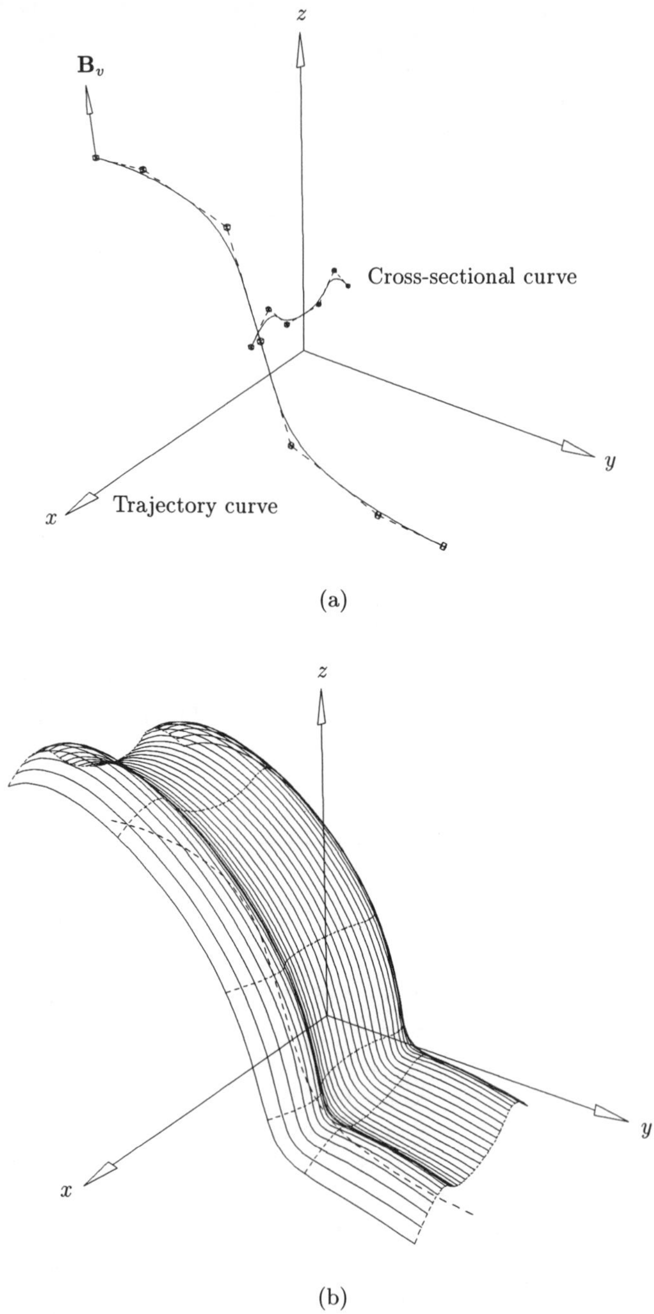

Figure 10.12. Sweeping examples. (a) Two-dimensional trajectory and the section curve not passing through the global origin; (b) swept surface with no trajectory controlled interpolation; (c) swept surface obtained by trajectory controlled interpolation.

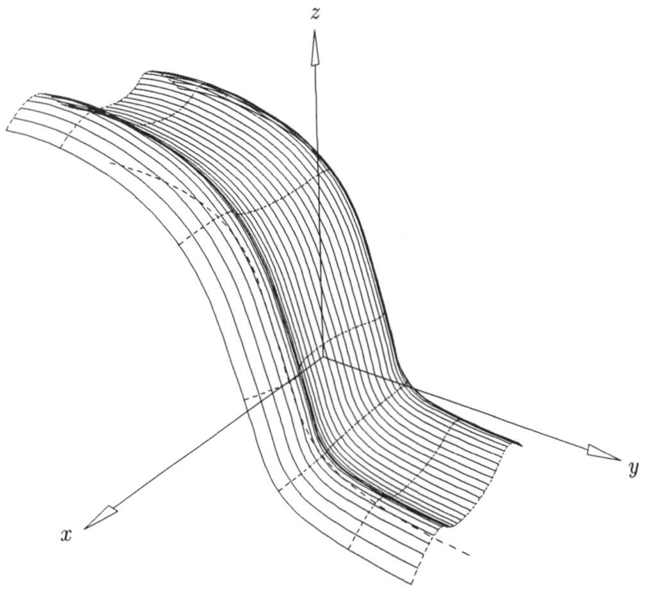

(c)

Figure 10.12. (*Continued.*)

and knots

$$V = \left\{0, 0, \frac{3}{10}, \frac{7}{10}, 1, 1\right\}$$

The previous two examples used a planar trajectory curve. Figure 10.14a shows a three-dimensional (twisted) trajectory. The trajectory was not maintained in Figure 10.14b (Algorithm A10.2), whereas the trajectory is an isocurve in the surface of Figure 10.14c (Algorithm A10.1). In both examples all section instances were scaled with the constant vector $(3/5, 3/5, 1)$.

The positioning and size of the section curve, as well as the shape (curvature) of the trajectory, have a dramatic effect on surface shape. Two examples are shown in Figures 10.15a and 10.15b. The trajectory is not interpolated in Figure 10.15a, but it is in Figure 10.15b. Both surfaces exhibit the so-called *offsetting phenomenon*, i.e., they have self-intersections and unwanted oscillations.

We return now to the problem of determining a suitable orientation function, $\mathbf{B}(v)$. If $\mathbf{T}(v)$ is a planar curve, the solution is simple: Let $\mathbf{B}(v)$ be a constant function whose value is a vector normal to the plane of $\mathbf{T}(v)$. For arbitrary trajectories the situation is more difficult. A common solution is to use the so-called *Frenet frame* [DoCa76; Klok86; Bron92; Silt92]. Assume $\mathbf{T}(v)$ is twice differentiable. Define $\mathbf{B}(v)$ by

$$\mathbf{B}(v) = \frac{\mathbf{T}'(v) \times \mathbf{T}''(v)}{|\mathbf{T}'(v) \times \mathbf{T}''(v)|} \tag{10.25}$$

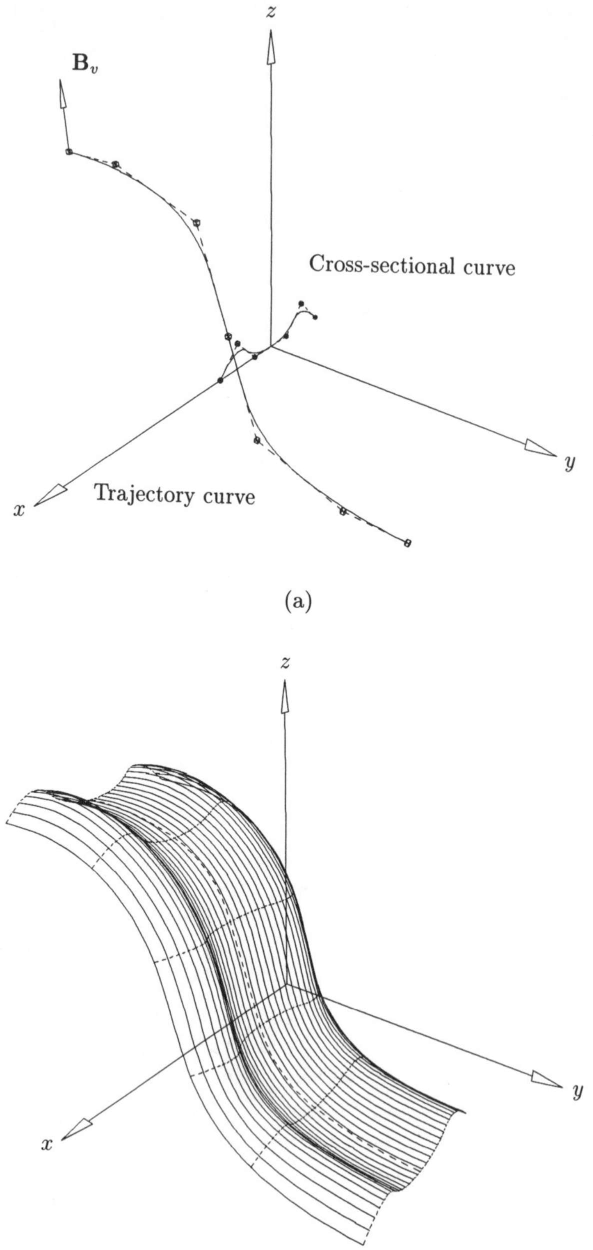

(b)

Figure 10.13. Sweeping examples. (a) Two-dimensional trajectory and section curve passing through the global origin; (b) swept surface with no scaling; (c) swept surface with scaled section curves.

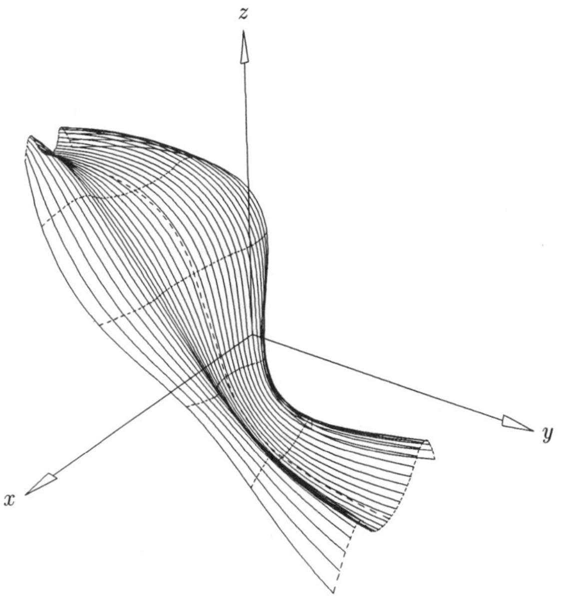

(c)

Figure 10.13. (*Continued.*)

and $\mathbf{N}(v)$ by

$$\mathbf{N}(v) = \mathbf{B}(v) \times \mathbf{T}'(v) \tag{10.26}$$

$\mathbf{T}'(v), \mathbf{N}(v)$, and $\mathbf{B}(v)$ are mutually orthogonal for all v, and when normalized they form a moving local coordinate system on $\mathbf{T}(v)$ called the Frenet frame. $\mathbf{B}(v)$ (or a NURBS approximation of it) can then be used in Eq. (10.21) and Algorithms `A10.1` and `A10.2`. There are several disadvantages to this method:

- $\mathbf{B}(v)$ is not defined by Eqs. (10.25) and (10.26) for linear segments or at inflection points (or more generally, where $\mathbf{T}''(v) \times \mathbf{T}'(v) = 0$);
- $\mathbf{B}(v)$ flips abruptly to the opposite direction at an inflection point;
- for three-dimensional trajectories, the vectors given by $\mathbf{B}(v)$ can rotate excessively around $\mathbf{T}(v)$, causing unwanted twisting of the resulting swept surface. Figure 10.16 shows this phenomenon; notice how the Frenet frame flips at the inflection point.

The first two problems can be dealt with rather easily [Klok86; Bron92; Silt92], but the rotation of $\mathbf{B}(v)$ depends solely on the shape of $\mathbf{T}(v)$, hence it cannot be avoided without changing the shape of $\mathbf{T}(v)$.

Siltanen and Woodward [Silt92] give an elegant method, called the *projection normal method*, that avoids these three problems. Let $v_0, \ldots, v_m$ be an increasing sequence of parameter values, with v_0 and v_m being the minimum and maximum values, respectively, in the domain of $\mathbf{T}(v)$. At each v_i we compute a vector, $\mathbf{B}_i$,

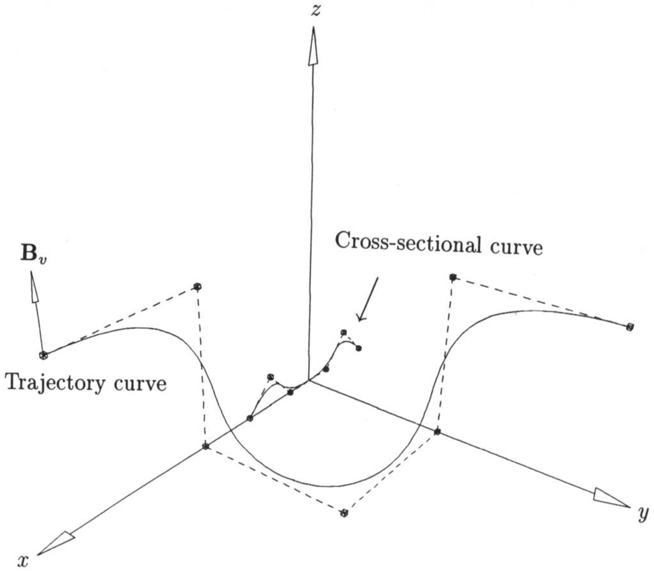

(a)

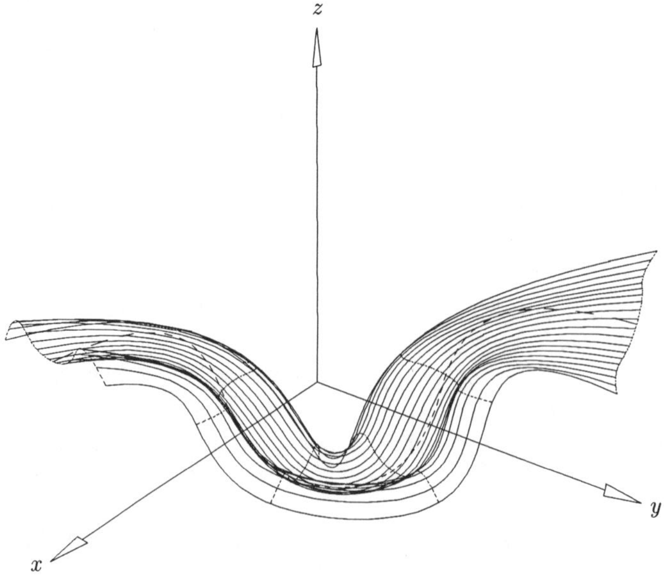

(b)

Figure 10.14. Sweeping examples with scaled section curves. (a) Three-dimensional trajectory and section curve; (b) trajectory is not interpolated; (c) trajectory is interpolated.

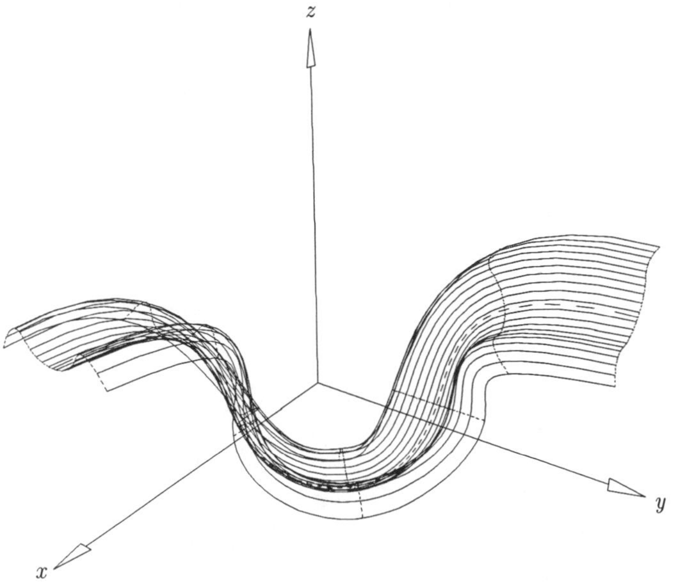

(c)

Figure 10.14. (*Continued.*)

and then use either interpolation or approximation to obtain the function $\mathbf{B}(v)$. We use Siltanen and Woodward's method to compute the $\mathbf{B}_i$. Set $\mathbf{B}_0$ to an arbitrary unit length vector orthogonal to $\mathbf{T}'(v_0)$. Then for $i = 1, \ldots, m$, compute

$$\mathbf{T}_i = \frac{\mathbf{T}'(v_i)}{|\mathbf{T}'(v_i)|}$$

and set

$$\mathbf{b}_i = \mathbf{B}_{i-1} - (\mathbf{B}_{i-1} \cdot \mathbf{T}_i)\mathbf{T}_i$$

$$\mathbf{B}_i = \frac{\mathbf{b}_i}{|\mathbf{b}_i|} \qquad (10.27)$$

In words, $\mathbf{B}_i$ is obtained by projecting $\mathbf{B}_{i-1}$ onto the plane defined by $\mathbf{T}_i$. Care must be taken to avoid points where $\mathbf{T}_i \parallel \mathbf{B}_{i-1}$. Notice that if $\mathbf{T}(v)$ is a closed curve, then in general the computed $\mathbf{B}_m$ is not equal to $\mathbf{B}_0$ (which is required). The solution is to set $\mathbf{B}_m = \bar{\mathbf{B}}_m = \mathbf{B}_0$, use the reverse of the previous technique to compute $\bar{\mathbf{B}}_{m-1}, \ldots, \bar{\mathbf{B}}_1$, and then set

$$\mathbf{B}_i = \frac{1}{2}(\mathbf{B}_i + \bar{\mathbf{B}}_i) \qquad i = 1, \ldots, m-1$$

The swept surfaces of Figures 10.12 to 10.15 used the projection normal method to compute the $\mathbf{B}_i$ vectors. Figures 10.17a and 10.17b show examples of how the

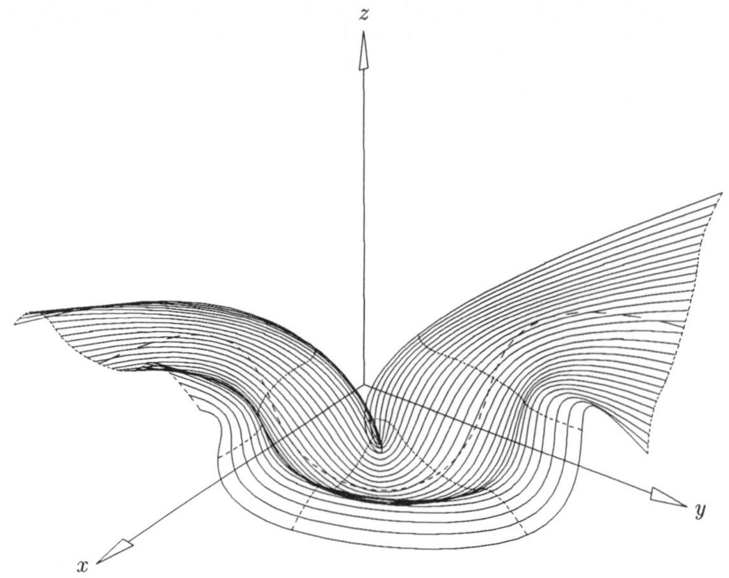

(a)

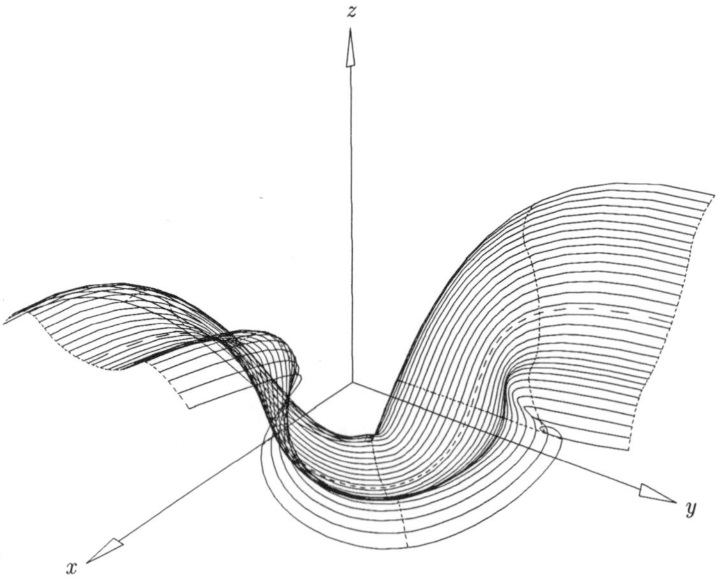

(b)

Figure 10.15. Sweeping examples. (a) Trajectory is not interpolated; (b) trajectory is interpolated.

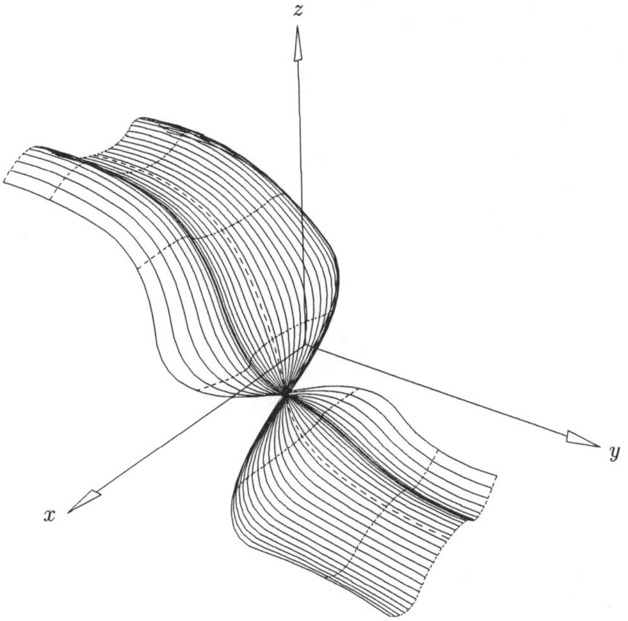

Figure 10.16. Sweeping example; section curve is placed by the Frenet frame.

$\mathbf{B}(v)$ vector (projection normal method) changes in comparison to the Frenet frame. In Figure 10.17a the trajectory is planar, whereas in Figure 10.17b it is twisted. In both cases the moving $\mathbf{B}(v)$ is drawn with a solid arrow, and the Frenet frame axes are plotted dashed.

Finally, Klok [Klok86] and Guggenheimer [Gugg89] present another method of obtaining a rotation minimizing $\mathbf{B}(v)$ as the solution to a differential equation with an initial condition. Additional reading on swept surfaces can be found in [Choi90; Akma92].

10.5 Interpolation of a Bidirectional Curve Network

Let

$$\mathbf{C}_k(u) = \sum_{i=0}^{n} N_{i,p}(u)\mathbf{P}_{k,i} \qquad k = 0,\ldots,r \quad u \in [0,1]$$

$$\mathbf{C}_\ell(v) = \sum_{j=0}^{m} N_{j,q}(v)\mathbf{P}_{\ell,j} \qquad \ell = 0,\ldots,s \quad v \in [0,1] \tag{10.28}$$

be two sets of nonrational B-spline curves satisfying the compatibility conditions (see Figure 10.18):

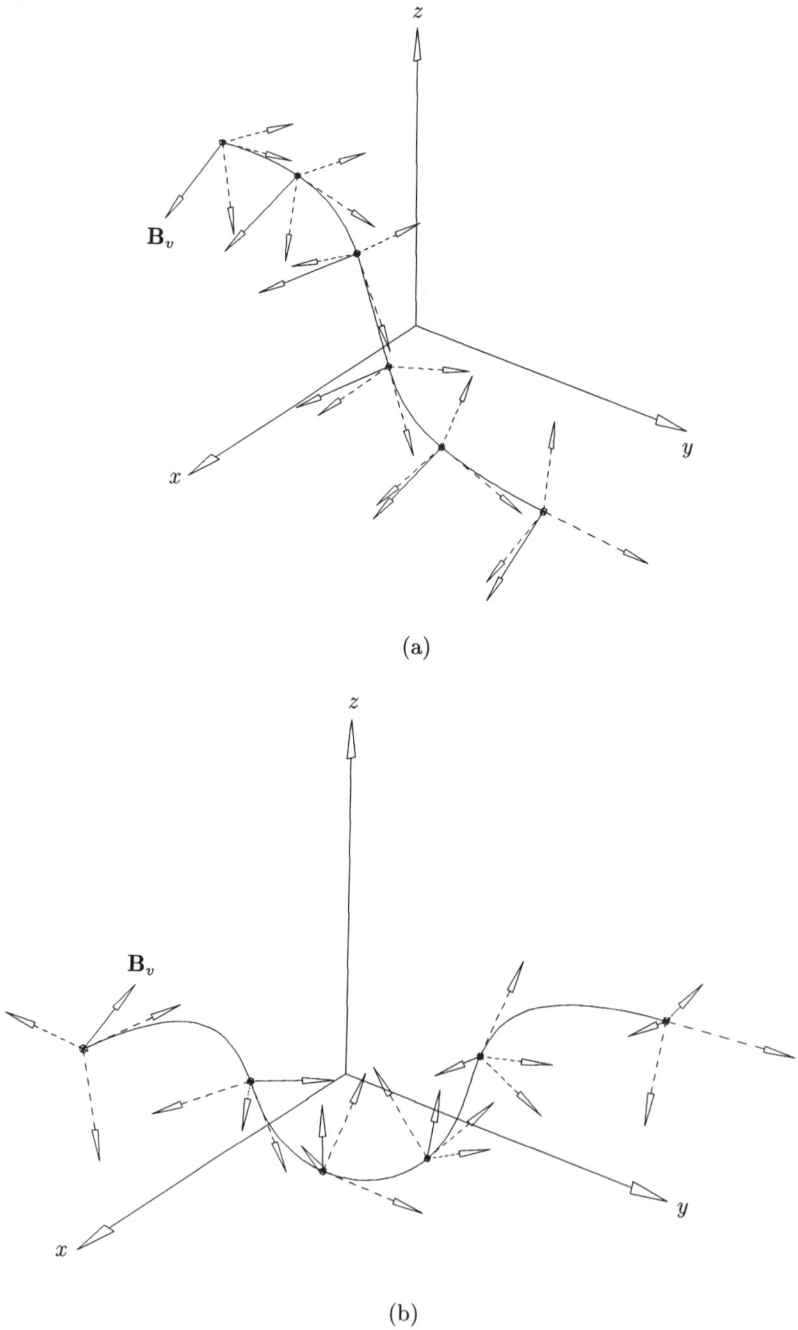

Figure 10.17. The change of $\mathbf{B}(v)$ and the Frenet frame along the trajectory. (a) Planar trajectory; (b) three-dimensional trajectory.

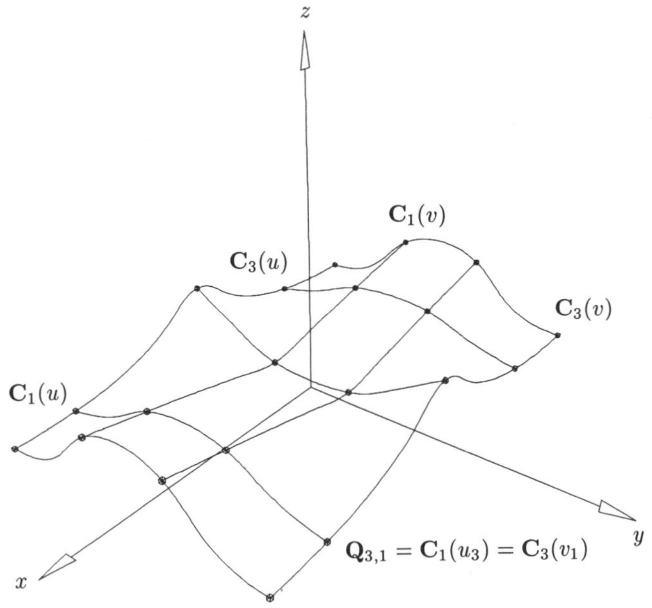

Figure 10.18. Compatible network of curves.

- as independent sets they are compatible in the B-spline sense, that is, all the $\mathbf{C}_k(u)$ are defined on a common knot vector, U^C, and all the $\mathbf{C}_\ell(v)$ are defined on a common knot vector, V^C;
- there exist parameters $0 = u_0 < u_1 < \cdots < u_{s-1} < u_s = 1$ and $0 = v_0 < v_1 < \cdots < v_{r-1} < v_r = 1$ such that

$$\mathbf{Q}_{\ell,k} = \mathbf{C}_k(u_\ell) = \mathbf{C}_\ell(v_k) \qquad k = 0,\ldots,r \quad \ell = 0,\ldots,s \tag{10.29}$$

We want to construct a NURBS surface, $\mathbf{S}(u,v)$, which interpolates the two sets of curves, that is

$$\mathbf{S}(u_\ell, v) = \mathbf{C}_\ell(v) \qquad \ell = 0,\ldots,s$$

$$\mathbf{S}(u, v_k) = \mathbf{C}_k(u) \qquad k = 0,\ldots,r \tag{10.30}$$

Notice that we have restricted the curves to be nonrational. Theoretically, the construction given later can be carried out in homogeneous space for rational curves; but it is generally not practical to do so, and the three-dimensional results can be unpredictable. If rational curves are involved, we recommend using the constrained approximation techniques of Chapter 9 to obtain nonrational approximations of the rational curves to within necessary tolerances. We refer the reader to Lin and Hewitt [Lin94] for more detail on the case of rational curves.

Gordon developed surfacing techniques satisfying Eq. (10.30) at General Motors Corporation in the late 1960s; hence they bear his name, *Gordon surfaces* [Gord69, 71, 93]. In particular, he showed that if $\{\phi_\ell(u)\}_{\ell=0}^{s}$ and $\{\psi_k(v)\}_{k=0}^{r}$ are any two sets of blending functions satisfying

$$\phi_\ell(u_i) = \begin{cases} 0 & \text{if } \ell \neq i \\ 1 & \text{if } \ell = i \end{cases}$$

$$\psi_k(v_i) = \begin{cases} 0 & \text{if } k \neq i \\ 1 & \text{if } k = i \end{cases} \tag{10.31}$$

then the surface given by

$$\begin{aligned} \mathbf{S}(u,v) &= \sum_{\ell=0}^{s} \mathbf{C}_\ell(v)\phi_\ell(u) + \sum_{k=0}^{r} \mathbf{C}_k(u)\psi_k(v) - \sum_{\ell=0}^{s}\sum_{k=0}^{r} \mathbf{Q}_{\ell,k}\,\phi_\ell(u)\,\psi_k(v) \\ &= \mathbf{L}_1(u,v) + \mathbf{L}_2(u,v) - \mathbf{T}(u,v) \end{aligned} \tag{10.32}$$

satisfies the interpolation conditions of Eq. (10.30). Hence, the desired surface is composed of three simpler surfaces, namely two lofted surfaces, $\mathbf{L}_1(u,v)$ and $\mathbf{L}_2(u,v)$, and the tensor product, $\mathbf{T}(u,v)$. Gordon experimented with various sets of blending functions, including simple step functions, Lagrange polynomials, and cubic splines.

Our task is to produce a NURBS representation of $\mathbf{S}(u,v)$. Clearly, if $\mathbf{L}_1(u,v)$, $\mathbf{L}_2(u,v)$, and $\mathbf{T}(u,v)$ are all compatible in the B-spline sense (defined on the same knot vectors), then they can be added and subtracted by applying the corresponding operations to their control points, that is, the control points $\mathbf{P}_{i,j}$ of $\mathbf{S}(u,v)$ are computed by

$$\mathbf{P}_{i,j} = \mathbf{P}_{i,j}^{L_1} + \mathbf{P}_{i,j}^{L_2} - \mathbf{P}_{i,j}^{T} \tag{10.33}$$

where $\mathbf{P}_{i,j}^{L_1}$, $\mathbf{P}_{i,j}^{L_2}$, and $\mathbf{P}_{i,j}^{T}$ are the control points of $\mathbf{L}_1(u,v)$, $\mathbf{L}_2(u,v)$, and $\mathbf{T}(u,v)$, respectively. Furthermore, it is easy to obtain NURBS representations of $\mathbf{L}_1(u,v)$, $\mathbf{L}_2(u,v)$, and $\mathbf{T}(u,v)$; the first two are skinned surfaces, and the latter is obtained by interpolating the points $\mathbf{Q}_{\ell,k}$ (see Section 9.3). The choice of parameters and knots for the skinning and point interpolation processes is determined by the given parameters, $\{u_\ell\}$ and $\{v_k\}$, and the knots U^C and V^C of the $\{\mathbf{C}_k(u)\}$ and $\{\mathbf{C}_\ell(v)\}$. We illustrate with a simple example.

Example

`Ex10.1` The data defining the network of curves in Figure 10.18 is

$$\mathbf{C}_k(u):\ n=5, p=3,\ \ U^C = \left\{0,0,0,0,\frac{3}{10},\frac{7}{10},1,1,1,1\right\}$$

$$\mathbf{C}_\ell(v):\ m=4, q=2,\ \ V^C = \left\{0,0,0,\frac{2}{5},\frac{3}{5},1,1,1\right\}$$

Figures 10.19a and 10.19b show the control points and the resulting surface of the u-directional lofting operation. The knot vectors are

$$U^{L_1} = \{0,0,0,0,1,1,1,1\}$$
$$V^{L_1} = \left\{0,0,0,\frac{2}{5},\frac{3}{5},1,1,1\right\}$$

The v-directional lofting is illustrated in Figures 10.20a and 10.20b. The knot vectors are

$$U^{L_2} = \left\{0,0,0,0,\frac{3}{10},\frac{7}{10},1,1,1,1\right\}$$
$$V^{L_2} = \{0,0,0,0.321,0.647,1,1,1\}$$

The tensor product surface is depicted in Figures 10.21a and 10.21b. The knots are

$$U^{T} = \{0,0,0,0,1,1,1,1\}$$
$$V^{T} = \{0,0,0,0.32,0.648,1,1,1\}$$

Notice the slight difference in the knot vectors V^{L_2} and V^T. This is because surface skinning and surface interpolation compute knot vectors differently (but meaningfully for their respective operations). The former uses the curve control points, while the latter utilizes the intersection points of the curve network. However, knots which are very close together are unnecessary and undesirable. A solution is to pass all previously computed knot vectors into the skinning and interpolation routines, allow them to compute new knots using their respective algorithms, compare these new knots with existing knots, and replace new knots with existing ones where the difference is small. Degree elevation is not required in this example, as lofting and interpolation use the curve degrees. However, knot refinement is required, and is depicted in Figures 10.22a–10.22c. The Gordon surface construction is shown in Figure 10.23a, and the surface is illustrated in Figure 10.23b. The final knots are

$$U = \left\{0,0,0,0,\frac{3}{10},\frac{7}{10},1,1,1,1\right\}$$
$$V = \{0,0,0,0.32,0.321,0.4,0.6,0.647,0.648,1,1,1\}$$

As alluded to earlier, the degrees of the input curves, those degrees used for lofting, and those used to construct $\mathbf{T}(u,v)$ can all be different. The final degree (p,q) of $\mathbf{S}(u,v)$ is simply the maximum of those used. The degrees of $\mathbf{L}_1(u,v)$, $\mathbf{L}_2(u,v)$, and $\mathbf{T}(u,v)$ must be raised to (p,q) before knot refinement. A sketch of the complete algorithm follows. `Ck[]` and `Cl[]` are arrays of input curves, and `ul[]` and `vk[]` are the parameters of the curve intersection points. To be

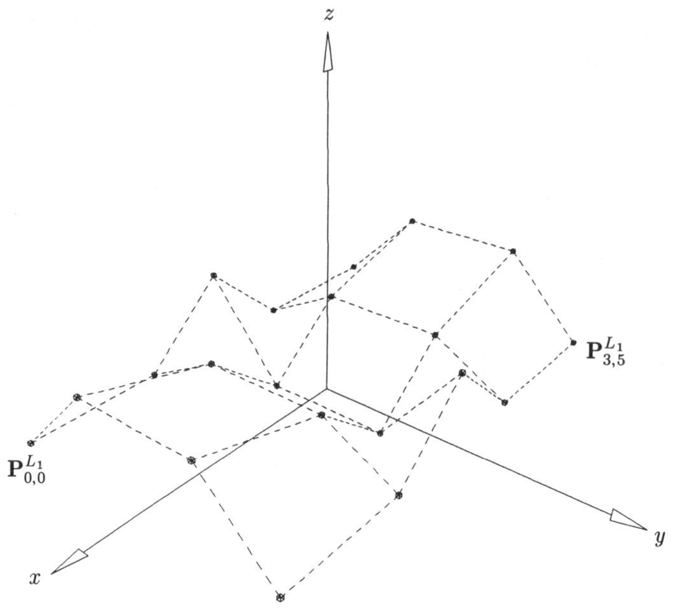

(a)

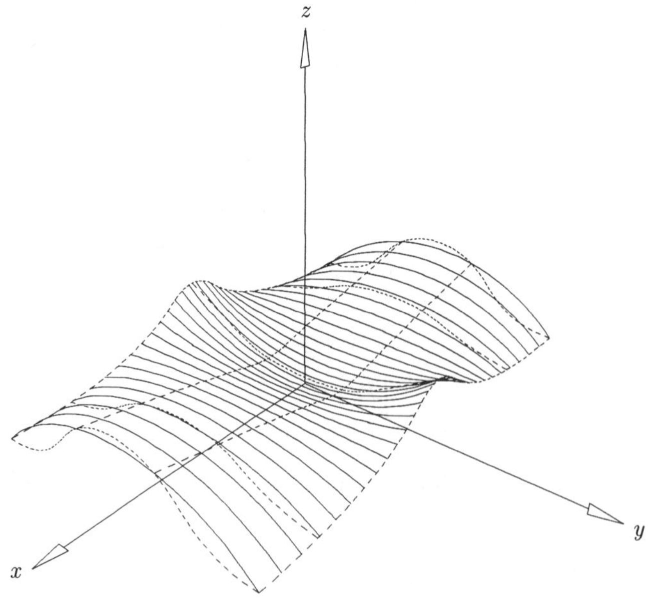

(b)

Figure 10.19. u-directional lofted surface. (a) Control net; (b) surface interpolating v curves.

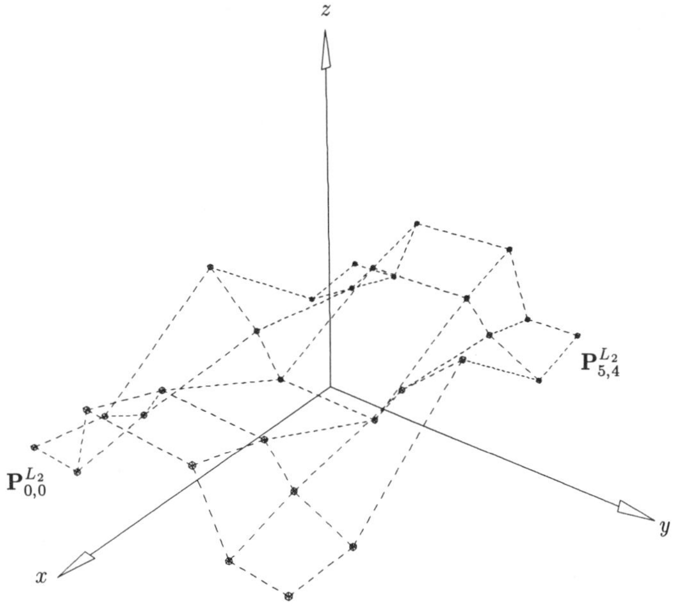

(a)

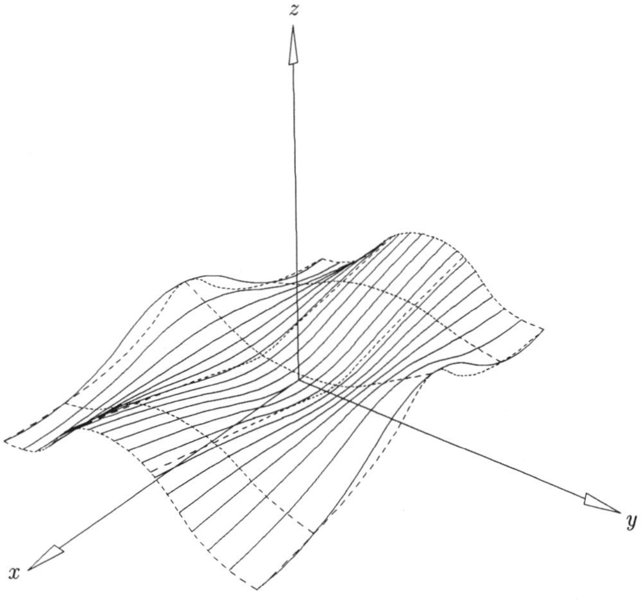

(b)

Figure 10.20. v-directional lofted surface. (a) Control net; (b) surface interpolating u curves.

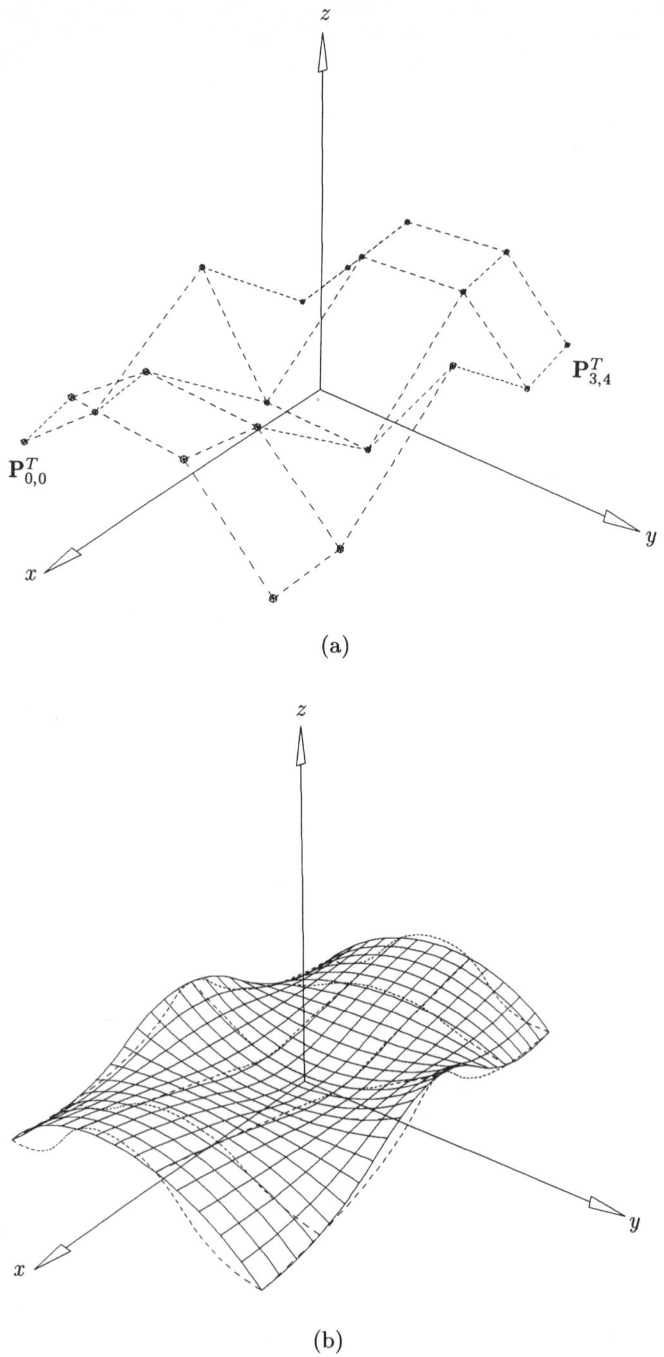

Figure 10.21. Tensor product surface. (a) Control net; (b) surface interpolating intersection points.

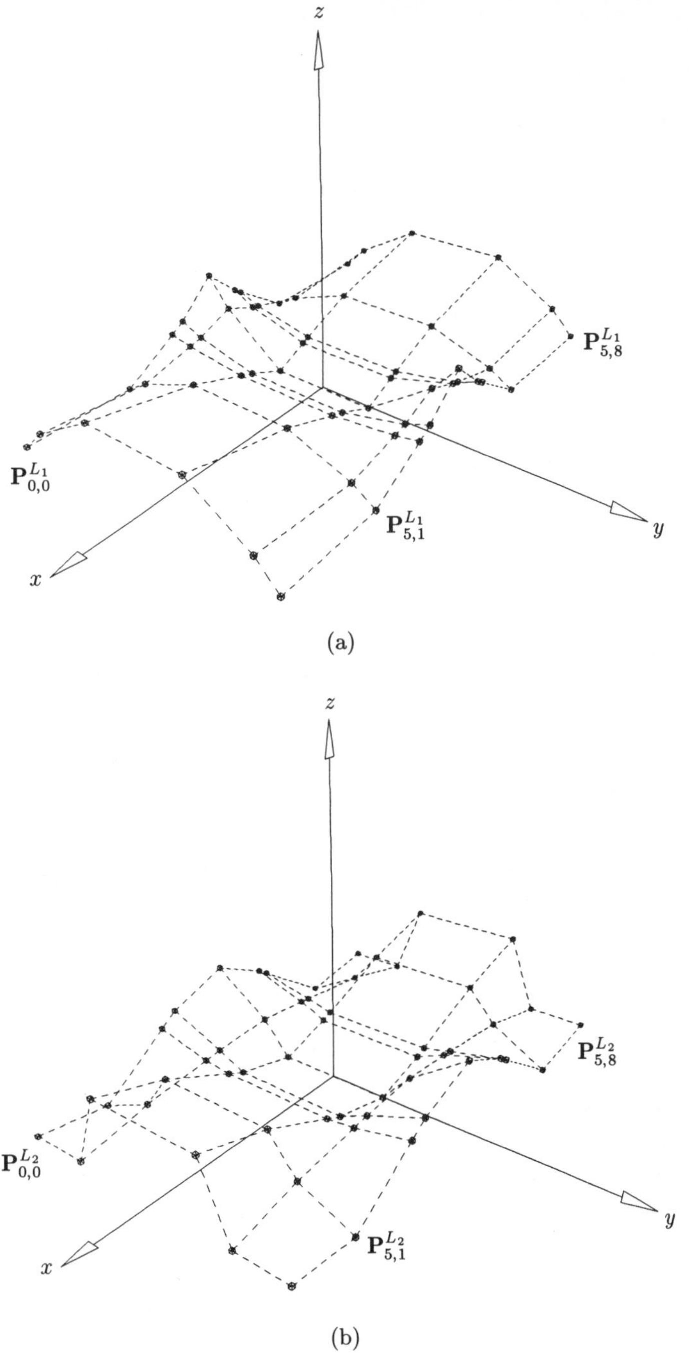

Figure 10.22. Knot refinement to construct a Gordon surface. (a) Ruled surface in the u direction refined; (b) ruled surface in the v direction refined.

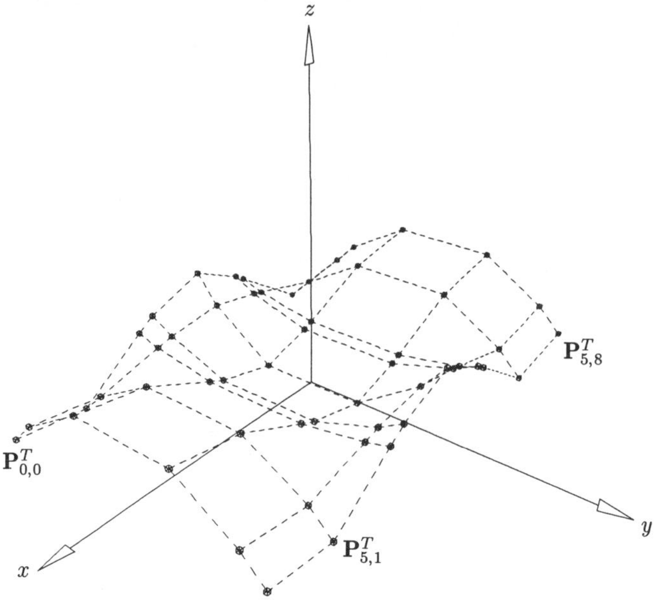

(c)

Figure 10.22. (*Continued.*) (c) tensor product in both directions refined.

completely general, the degrees pl,ql,pt,qt used for lofting and interpolation are also input. n,m,p,q,U,V,Pij define the output Gordon surface.

```
ALGORITHM A10.3
  GordonSurface(Ck,Cl,ul,vk,r,s,pl,ql,pt,qt,n,m,p,q,U,V,Pij)
    { /* Create Gordon surface. */
      /* Input:  Ck,Cl,ul,vk,r,s,pl,ql,pt,qt  */
      /* Output: n,m,p,q,U,V,Pij  */
    pc = degree of the Ck curves.
    qc = degree of the Cl curves.
    Choose a suitable U1 and loft to obtain L1(u,v)
      (degree (pl,qc)).
    Choose a suitable V2 and loft to obtain L2(u,v)
      (degree (pc,ql)).
    Choose suitable UT and VT, and interpolate to obtain T(u,v)
      (degree (pt,qt)).
    p = max(pc,pl,pt).
    q = max(qc,ql,qt).
    Degree elevate L1(u,v), L2(u,v) and T(u,v) to (p,q)
      as necessary.
    U = Merge(U1,U2,UT).
    V = Merge(V1,V2,VT).
```

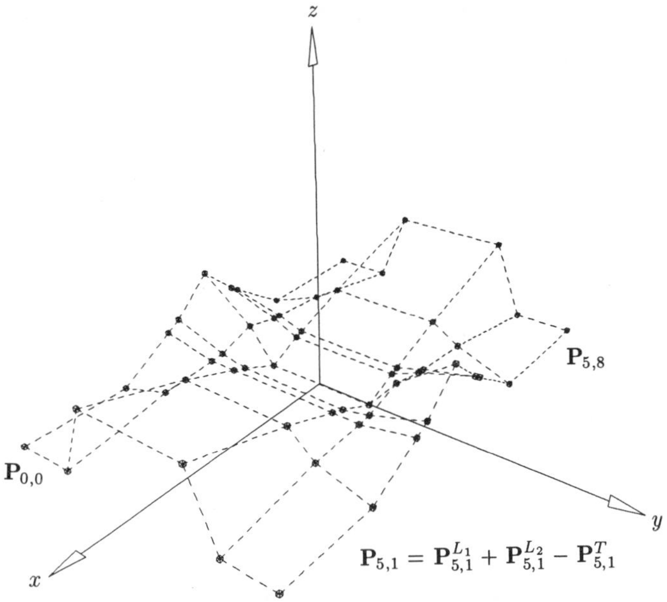

(a)

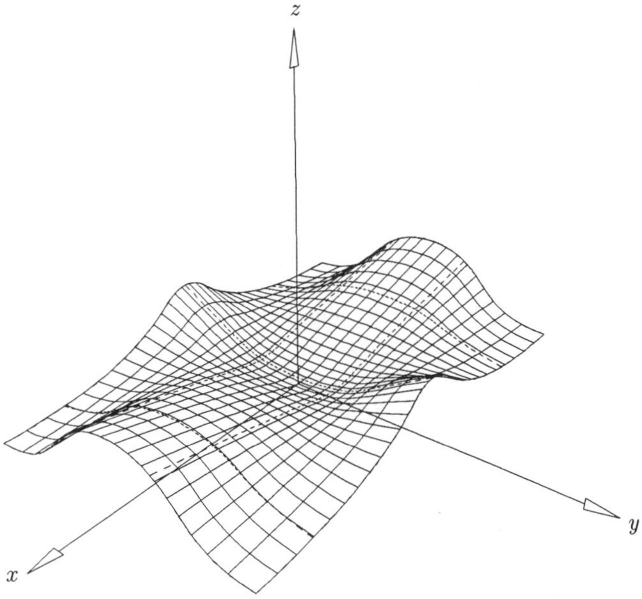

(b)

Figure 10.23. A Gordon surface. (a) Control net; (b) surface interpolating u- and v-directional curves.

```
Refine knot vectors of L1(u,v), L2(u,v) and T(u,v)
  as necessary.
n = (number of u-knots)-p-2.
m = (number of v-knots)-q-2.
Compute surface control points Pij by Eq.(10.33).
}
```

10.6 Coons Surfaces

Assume now that we have four curves

$$\mathbf{C}_k(u) = \sum_{i=0}^{n} N_{i,p}(u)\mathbf{P}_{k,i} \qquad k = 0,1 \quad u \in [0,1]$$

$$\mathbf{C}_\ell(v) = \sum_{j=0}^{m} N_{j,q}(v)\mathbf{P}_{\ell,j} \qquad \ell = 0,1 \quad v \in [0,1] \tag{10.34}$$

and that we want to construct a surface having these four curves as its boundaries. Furthermore, we assume that the curves satisfy the compatibility conditions

- as independent sets they are compatible in the B-spline sense, that is, the two $\mathbf{C}_k(u)$ are defined on a common knot vector, U, and the two $\mathbf{C}_\ell(v)$ are defined on a common knot vector, V;
-
$$\begin{aligned}
\mathbf{S}_{0,0} &= \mathbf{C}_{k=0}(u=0) = \mathbf{C}_{\ell=0}(v=0)\\
\mathbf{S}_{1,0} &= \mathbf{C}_{k=0}(u=1) = \mathbf{C}_{\ell=1}(v=0)\\
\mathbf{S}_{0,1} &= \mathbf{C}_{k=1}(u=0) = \mathbf{C}_{\ell=0}(v=1)\\
\mathbf{S}_{1,1} &= \mathbf{C}_{k=1}(u=1) = \mathbf{C}_{\ell=1}(v=1)
\end{aligned} \tag{10.35}$$

(see Figure 10.24). We do not restrict the curves to be nonrational in this section. The constructions given here usually yield satisfactory surfaces, even when carried out in homogeneous space. However, this complicates the algorithms. For example, Eq. (10.35) must hold in homogeneous space. This requires corner weight compatibility, which can require rational reparameterization of the curves (Section 6.4).

The *bilinearly blended Coons patch* is defined as

$$\mathbf{S}(u,v) = \mathbf{R}_1(u,v) + \mathbf{R}_2(u,v) - \mathbf{T}(u,v) \tag{10.36}$$

where $\mathbf{R}_1(u,v)$ and $\mathbf{R}_2(u,v)$ are ruled surfaces between $\mathbf{C}_{k=0}(u)$ and $\mathbf{C}_{k=1}(u)$, and $\mathbf{C}_{\ell=0}(v)$ and $\mathbf{C}_{\ell=1}(v)$, respectively, and $\mathbf{T}(u,v)$ is the bilinear tensor product surface

$$\mathbf{T}(u,v) = [1 \quad u] \begin{bmatrix} \mathbf{S}_{0,0} & \mathbf{S}_{0,1} \\ \mathbf{S}_{1,0} & \mathbf{S}_{1,1} \end{bmatrix} \begin{bmatrix} 1 \\ v \end{bmatrix}$$

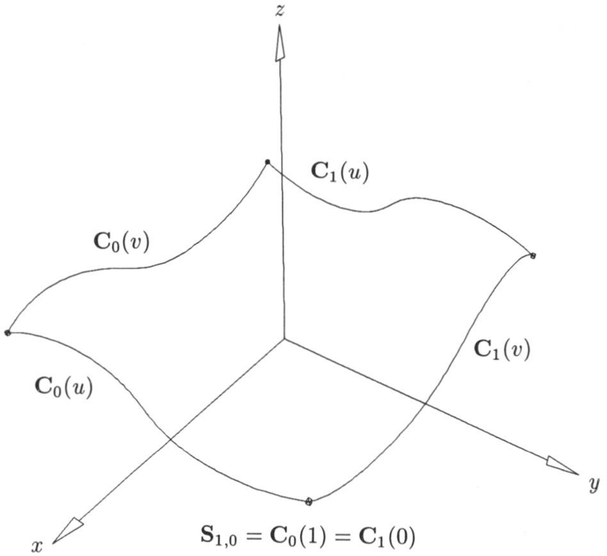

Figure 10.24. Compatible boundary curves to define a bilinearly blended Coons patch.

Clearly, this is a special case of the Gordon surface, and therefore Eq. (10.33) and Algorithm `A10.3` (simplified, and modified to handle rational curves) can be used to obtain a NURBS representation of the Coons surface given by Eq. (10.36). The input arguments `pl,ql,pt,qt` are set to 1 in this case. Figures 10.25a–10.25d show the construction of the bilinearly blended Coons patch defined by the curves in Figure 10.24. Figure 10.25a shows a ruled surface in the u direction, and Figure 10.25b illustrates the v-directional ruled surface. Figure 10.25c shows the bilinear surface defined by the four corner points. The bilinearly blended Coons patch is depicted in Figure 10.25d. It is important to note that the bilinearly blended Coons patch is, in general, not a bilinear surface.

Coons developed his patches in the mid 1960s [Coon67]. Although we present the bilinearly blended Coons patch as a special case of Gordon surfaces, we remark that Coons' work preceded and influenced the development of Gordon surfaces. Coons was interested in interpolation to position and tangent information in bidirectional networks of curves, as was Gordon later. Coons constructed a patch within each set of four curves, hence his was a local interpolation method. Gordon's method represents a global interpolation to a network of curves.

If two bilinearly blended Coons patches share a common boundary curve, they possess, in general, only C^0 continuity across that boundary; that is, the combined surface will have a crease along the common boundary. In order to obtain smooth, C^n continuous ($n > 0$) joins of his patches, Coons developed higher order patches using *cross-boundary derivative fields.* To illustrate, we present the *bicubically blended Coons patch.* Let $\mathbf{C}_k(u)$ and $\mathbf{C}_\ell(v)$ be four boundary

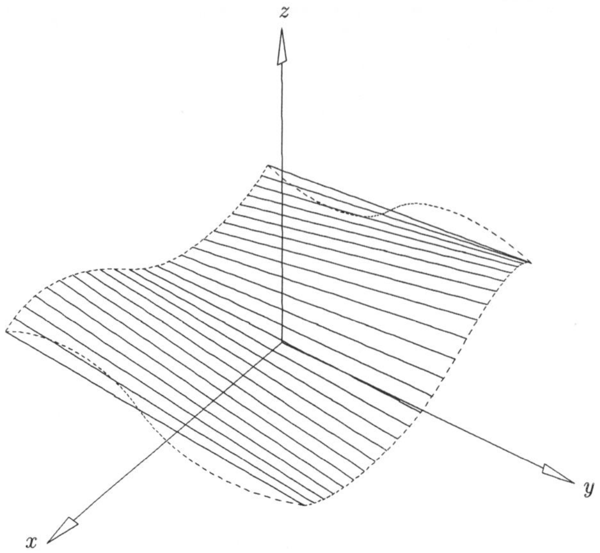

(a)

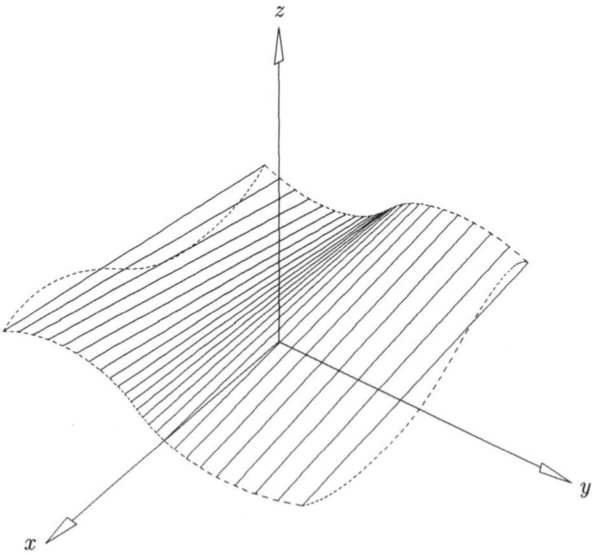

(b)

Figure 10.25. Bilinearly blended Coons patch. (a) A ruled surface in the u direction; (b) a ruled surface in the v direction; (c) a bilinear surface; (d) a bilinearly blended Coons patch.

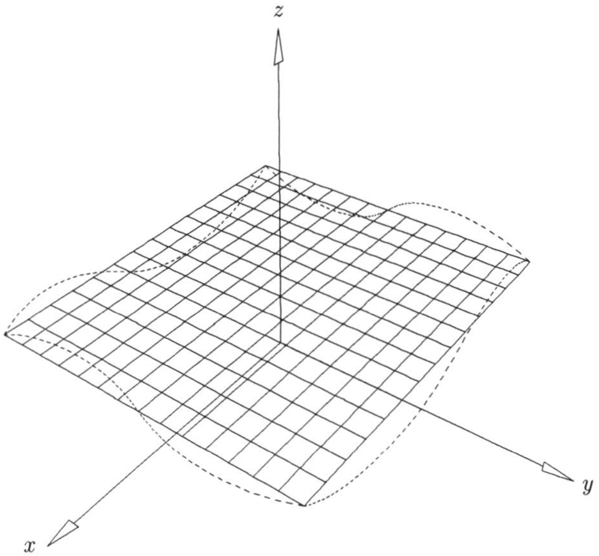

(c)

Figure 10.25. (*Continued.*)

curves as in Eq. (10.34), satisfying the two compatibility conditions given. We also assume four cross-boundary derivative fields (see Figure 10.26)

$$\mathbf{D}_k(u) = \sum_{i=0}^{n} N_{i,p}(u)\,\mathbf{Q}_{k,i} \qquad k = 0,1 \quad u \in [0,1]$$

$$\mathbf{D}_\ell(v) = \sum_{j=0}^{m} N_{j,q}(v)\,\mathbf{Q}_{\ell,j} \qquad \ell = 0,1 \quad v \in [0,1] \tag{10.37}$$

We want to construct a surface which has the $\mathbf{C}_k(u)$ and $\mathbf{C}_\ell(v)$ as its boundaries, and the $\mathbf{D}_k(u)$ and $\mathbf{D}_\ell(v)$ as its first partial derivatives along the boundaries, that is

$$\mathbf{D}_{k=0}(u) = \mathbf{S}_v(u,0) \qquad \mathbf{D}_{k=1}(u) = \mathbf{S}_v(u,1)$$

$$\mathbf{D}_{\ell=0}(v) = \mathbf{S}_u(0,v) \qquad \mathbf{D}_{\ell=1}(v) = \mathbf{S}_u(1,v)$$

The compatibility conditions

- the $\mathbf{C}_k(u)$ and the $\mathbf{D}_k(u)$ are compatible in the B-spline sense, as are the $\mathbf{C}_\ell(v)$ and $\mathbf{D}_\ell(v)$;
- $$\mathbf{T}_{0,0} = \frac{d\mathbf{D}_{k=0}(u=0)}{du} = \frac{d\mathbf{D}_{\ell=0}(v=0)}{dv}$$

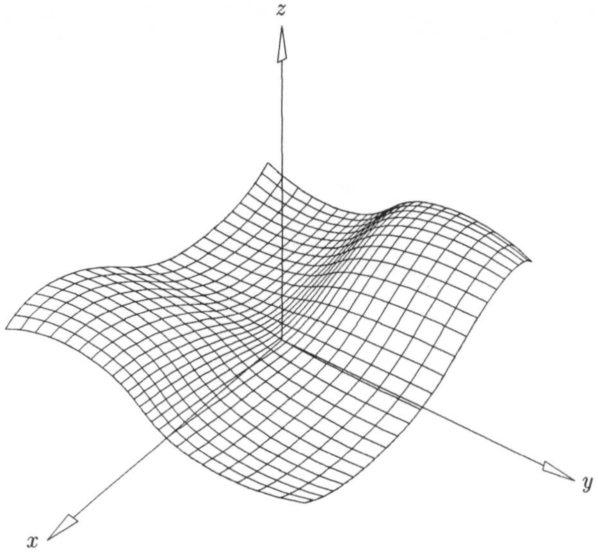

(d)

Figure 10.25. (*Continued.*)

$$\mathbf{T}_{1,0} = \frac{d\mathbf{D}_{k=0}(u=1)}{du} = \frac{d\mathbf{D}_{\ell=1}(v=0)}{dv}$$

$$\mathbf{T}_{0,1} = \frac{d\mathbf{D}_{k=1}(u=0)}{du} = \frac{d\mathbf{D}_{\ell=0}(v=1)}{dv}$$

$$\mathbf{T}_{1,1} = \frac{d\mathbf{D}_{k=1}(u=1)}{du} = \frac{d\mathbf{D}_{\ell=1}(v=1)}{dv} \qquad (10.38)$$

must hold. The $\mathbf{T}_{k,\ell}$ are the four *twist vectors.*

The bicubically blended Coons patch is defined by

$$\mathbf{S}(u,v) = \mathbf{S}_1(u,v) + \mathbf{S}_2(u,v) - \mathbf{T}(u,v) \qquad (10.39)$$

where $\mathbf{S}_1(u,v)$ is a cubic blend of the data $\mathbf{C}_k(u)$, $\mathbf{D}_k(u)$, $k=0,1$; $\mathbf{S}_2(u,v)$ is a cubic blend of the data $\mathbf{C}_\ell(v)$, $\mathbf{D}_\ell(v)$, $\ell = 0,1$; and $\mathbf{T}(u,v)$ is a bicubic tensor product surface (defined by 16 vector coefficients). Coons used cubic Hermite polynomials to blend the boundary data and to form $\mathbf{T}(u,v)$. Since our goal is to obtain a NURBS surface, we use cubic Bézier methods to blend and to form $\mathbf{T}(u,v)$. $\mathbf{S}_1(u,v)$ is a cubic Bézier in the v direction. Its four rows of control points are computed as $(i=0,\ldots,n)$

$$\mathbf{P}_{i,0}^{S_1} = \mathbf{P}_{k=0,i}$$

$$\mathbf{P}^{S_1}_{i,1} = \mathbf{P}_{k=0,i} + \frac{1}{3}\,\mathbf{Q}_{k=0,i}$$

$$\mathbf{P}^{S_1}_{i,2} = \mathbf{P}_{k=1,i} - \frac{1}{3}\,\mathbf{Q}_{k=1,i}$$

$$\mathbf{P}^{S_1}_{i,3} = \mathbf{P}_{k=1,i} \tag{10.40}$$

Note that the two interior rows are derived using the Bézier derivative formulas (Eq. [1.10]). The control points of $\mathbf{S}_2(u,v)$ are computed analogously, i.e.

$$\mathbf{P}^{S_2}_{0,j} = \mathbf{P}_{\ell=0,\,j}$$

$$\mathbf{P}^{S_2}_{1,j} = \mathbf{P}_{\ell=0,\,j} + \frac{1}{3}\,\mathbf{Q}_{\ell=0,j}$$

$$\mathbf{P}^{S_2}_{2,j} = \mathbf{P}_{\ell=1,\,j} - \frac{1}{3}\,\mathbf{Q}_{\ell=1,j}$$

$$\mathbf{P}^{S_2}_{3,j} = \mathbf{P}_{\ell=1,\,j} \tag{10.41}$$

$\mathbf{T}(u,v)$ is a bicubic Bézier surface. Equations (1.10) and (3.24) are used to derive the 16 control points, $\mathbf{P}^{T}_{i,j}$, $i,j = 0,1,2,3$. As an example, we show how

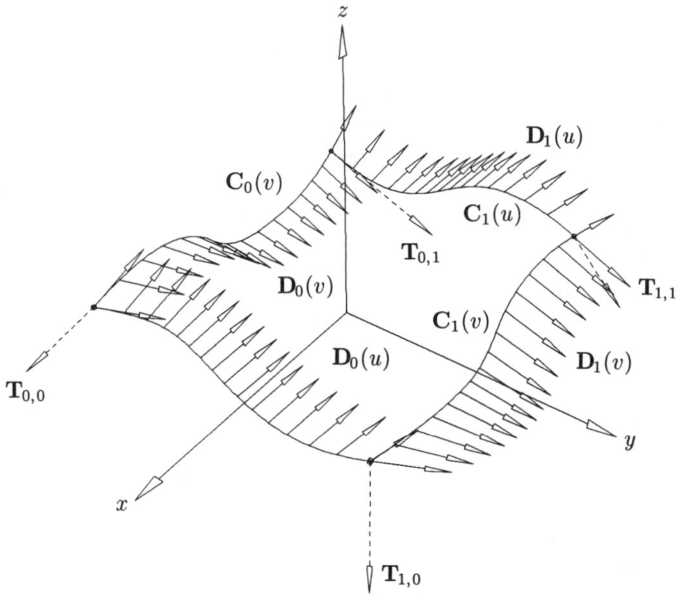

Figure 10.26. Compatible boundary curves along with cross-boundary tangent vector functions and twists.

to compute the four control points, $\mathbf{P}^T_{i,j}$, $i,j = 0,1$, adjacent to the corner $\mathbf{S}_{0,0}$. The other twelve are analogous.

$$\mathbf{P}^T_{0,0} = \mathbf{S}_{0,0} = \mathbf{C}_{k=0}(u=0) = \mathbf{C}_{\ell=0}(v=0)$$

$$\mathbf{P}^T_{1,0} = \frac{1}{3}\mathbf{D}_{\ell=0}(v=0) + \mathbf{P}^T_{0,0}$$

$$\mathbf{P}^T_{0,1} = \frac{1}{3}\mathbf{D}_{k=0}(u=0) + \mathbf{P}^T_{0,0}$$

$$\mathbf{P}^T_{1,1} = \frac{1}{9}\mathbf{T}_{0,0} + \mathbf{P}^T_{1,0} + \mathbf{P}^T_{0,1} - \mathbf{P}^T_{0,0} \tag{10.42}$$

The surfaces $\mathbf{S}_1(u,v)$, $\mathbf{S}_2(u,v)$, and $\mathbf{T}(u,v)$ must then be made compatible using degree elevation and knot refinement. Subsequently, the control points $\mathbf{P}_{i,j}$ of the Coons surface are computed by the formula

$$\mathbf{P}_{i,j} = \mathbf{P}^{S_1}_{i,j} + \mathbf{P}^{S_2}_{i,j} - \mathbf{P}^T_{i,j} \tag{10.43}$$

Figures 10.27–10.30 show the process of constructing a bicubically blended Coons patch. Figures 10.27a and 10.27b show a u-directional cubically blended surface, $\mathbf{S}_2(u,v)$, along with the defining control net. v-directional cubic blending is illustrated in Figures 10.28a and 10.28b $\big(\mathbf{S}_1(u,v)\big)$. A bicubic tensor product surface is depicted in Figures 10.29a and 10.29b. Finally, the Coons patch is illustrated in Figures 10.30a and 10.30b, after appropriate degree elevations and knot refinements are performed.

In Algorithm `A10.4`, `Ck[]`,`Cl[]` and `Dk[]`,`Dl[]` are arrays of boundary curves and cross-boundary derivatives, respectively. `n,m,p,q,U,V,Pij` define the output bicubically blended Coons surface.

```
ALGORITHM A10.4
  BicubicBlendCoons(Ck,Cl,Dk,Dl,n,m,p,q,U,V,Pij)
    { /*  Create bicubically blended Coons surface.  */
      /*  Input:  Ck,Cl,Dk,Dl  */
      /*  Output: n,m,p,q,U,V,Pij  */
    Compute the ctrl pts of S1(u,v) (Eq.10.40).
    Compute the ctrl pts of S2(u,v) (Eq.10.41).
    Compute the ctrl pts of T(u,v) (Eq.10.42).
    pcd = degree of the Ck curves and Dk derivatives.
    qcd = degree of the Cl curves and Dl derivatives.
    p = max(3,pcd);
    q = max(3,qcd);
    Degree elevate S1(u,v), S2(u,v) and T(u,v) to (p,q)
        if necessary.
    U = u-knot vector of S1(u,v).
    V = v-knot vector of S2(u,v).
```

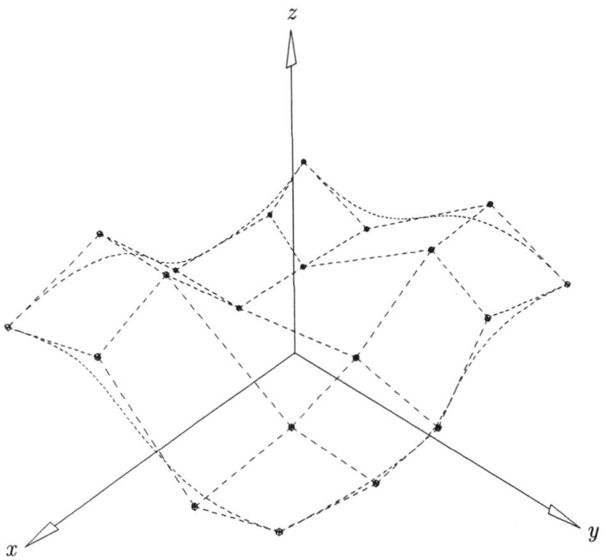

(a)

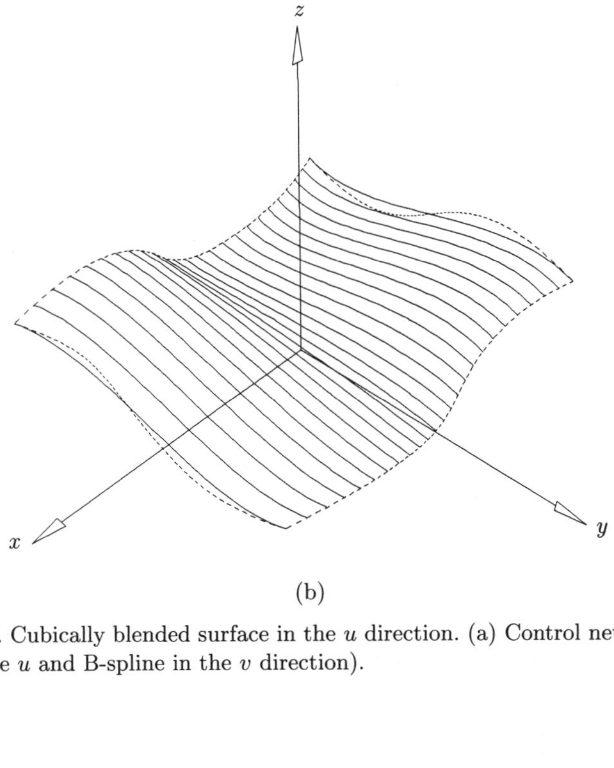

(b)

Figure 10.27. Cubically blended surface in the u direction. (a) Control net; (b) surface (Bézier in the u and B-spline in the v direction).

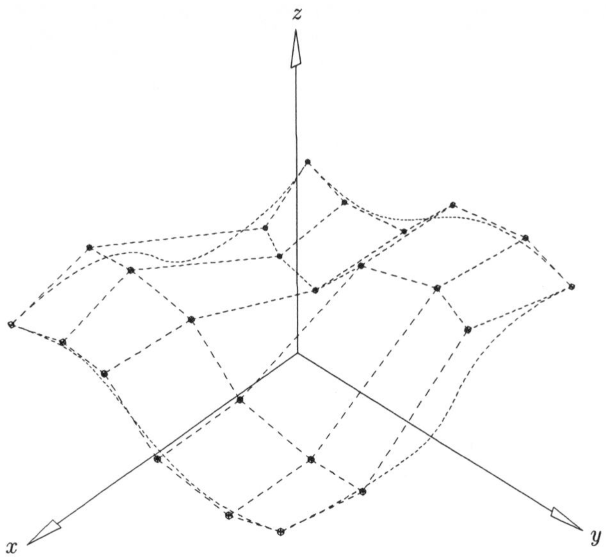

(a)

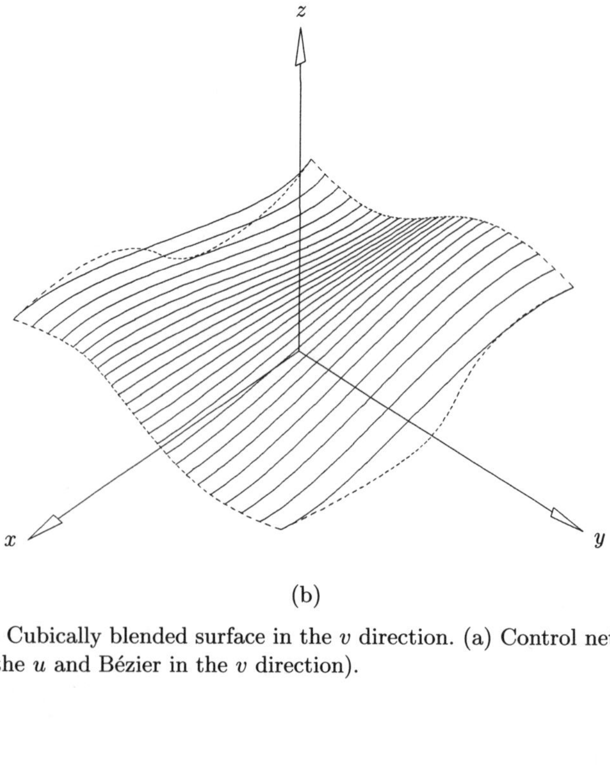

(b)

Figure 10.28. Cubically blended surface in the v direction. (a) Control net; (b) surface (B-spline in the u and Bézier in the v direction).

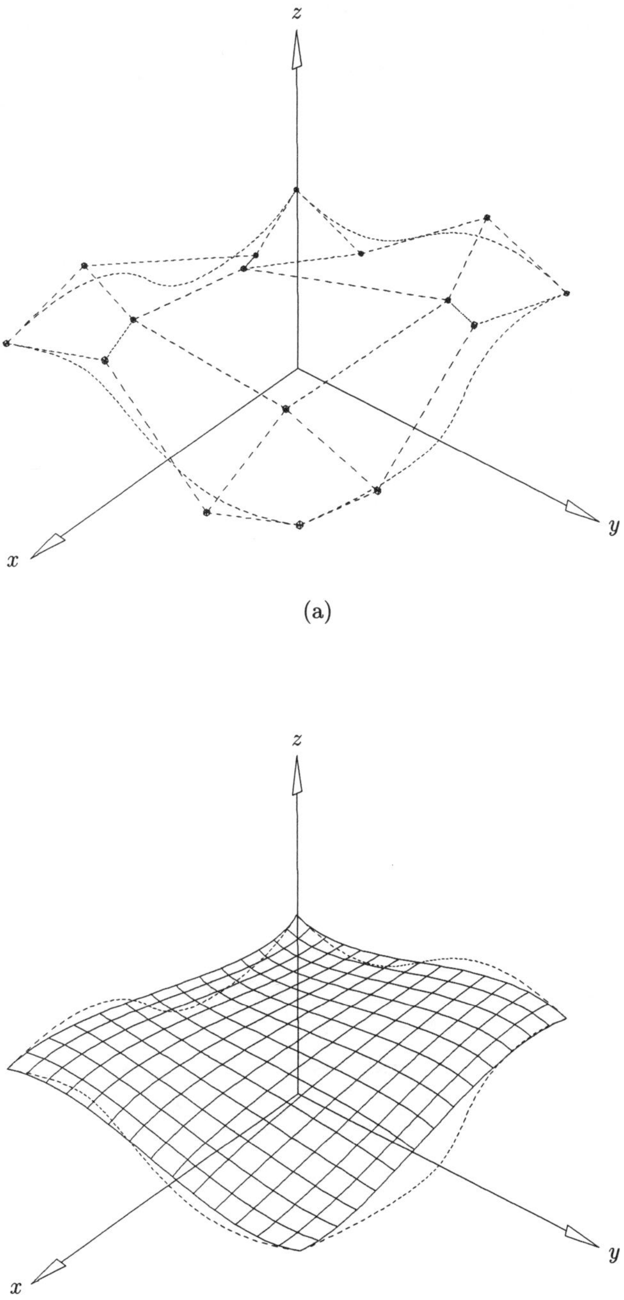

(a)

(b)

Figure 10.29. Bicubic tensor product surface. (a) Control net; (b) bicubic Bézier surface.

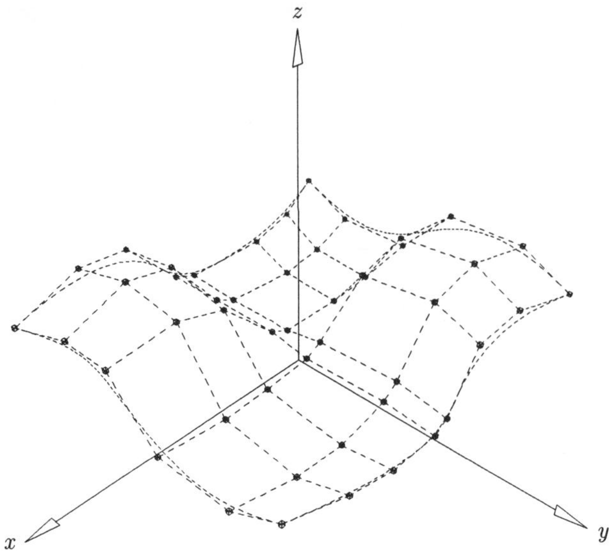

(a)

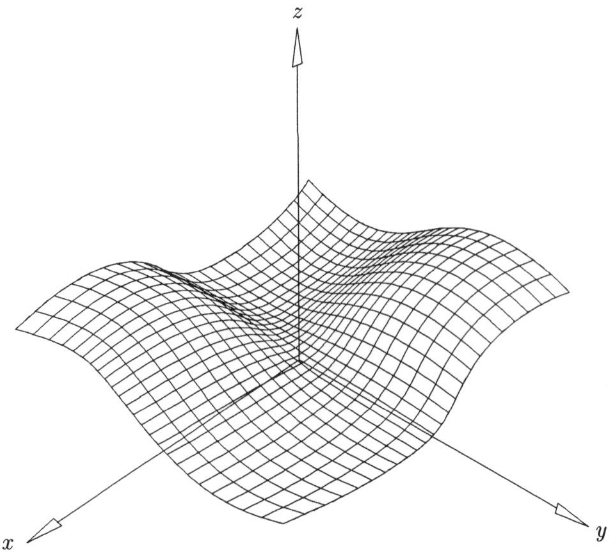

(b)

Figure 10.30. Bicubically blended Coons surface. (a) Control net after degree raising and knot refinement; (b) Coons surface.

```
Knot refine S_1(u,v), S_2(u,v) and T(u,v) to
    U and V if necessary.
n = (number of u-knots)-p-2.
m = (number of v-knots)-q-2.
Compute surface control points P_{i,j} by Eq.(10.43).
}
```

In practice, it is not easy to construct a bicubically blended Coons patch. First, the cross-boundary derivative fields are seldom available; even when they are available, the magnitudes of the derivatives may not be appropriate. Furthermore, one can almost never expect twist vector compatibility (Eq. [10.38]) to hold, that is, in general

$$\frac{d\mathbf{D}_{k=0}(u=0)}{du} \neq \frac{d\mathbf{D}_{\ell=0}(v=0)}{dv}$$

and likewise for the other three corners. The most common use of this patch is to attempt to fill a three- or four-sided hole in a patchwork of surfaces, smoothly in the G^1 sense. The boundary data is extracted from the neighboring surfaces. However, in this case derivative magnitudes are generally not meaningful, twist vectors are not compatible, and hence G^1 continuity between the patch and its neighboring surfaces is not possible. If the application can tolerate a small discontinuity in tangent direction across a boundary, then an angular tolerance can be specified and one of two approaches taken:

- use the iterative approximation techniques of Chapter 9 to obtain nonrational derivative fields which are twist compatible, and which approximate the vector directions of the original derivative fields to within the specified angular tolerance. If any one of the boundary curves is rational, then the problem becomes much more complex, as the twist vectors and derivative fields must be embedded in homogeneous space in such a way as to obtain four-dimensional compatibility while still maintaining the angular tolerance on the three-dimensional vector directions. Equations (4.7) and (4.26) are useful in this process;
- let
  $$\mathbf{T}^k_{0,0} = \frac{d\mathbf{D}_{k=0}(u=0)}{du} \qquad \mathbf{T}^\ell_{0,0} = \frac{d\mathbf{D}_{\ell=0}(v=0)}{dv}$$
  $\mathbf{T}^k_{0,0}$ and $\mathbf{T}^\ell_{0,0}$ are computed from the following control points of $\mathbf{D}_{k=0}(u)$ and $\mathbf{D}_{\ell=0}(v)$: $\mathbf{Q}_{k=0,0}$, $\mathbf{Q}_{k=0,1}$ and $\mathbf{Q}_{\ell=0,0}$, $\mathbf{Q}_{\ell=0,1}$. Set
  $$\mathbf{T}_{0,0} = \frac{1}{2}\left(\mathbf{T}^k_{0,0} + \mathbf{T}^\ell_{0,0}\right)$$
  Keeping $\mathbf{Q}_{k=0,0}$ and $\mathbf{Q}_{\ell=0,0}$ fixed, $\mathbf{Q}_{k=0,1}$ and $\mathbf{Q}_{\ell=0,1}$ can be modified to yield the common twist, $\mathbf{T}_{0,0}$. Knot insertion, applied prior to modifying $\mathbf{Q}_{k=0,1}$ and $\mathbf{Q}_{\ell=0,1}$, can be used to bound the angular error and restrict its domain of influence. The process is even more complicated if any of the curves or derivative fields are rational.

For a deeper and broader study of Coons patches, the reader should consult Barnhill's article [Barn93] and the references cited therein.

CHAPTER
ELEVEN

Shape Modification Tools

11.1 Introduction

The purpose of this chapter is to develop *tools* which allow a designer to *interactively* make *local* modifications to an *existing* NURBS curve or surface, in a way that is *natural* and *intuitive*. A NURBS curve or surface is defined by its control points, weights, and knots; modifying any of these changes the shape of the curve or surface. Generally designers do not want to work with such concepts; they prefer to specify constraints and shapes which apply directly to the curve or surface. In this chapter we develop tools which take such constraints and shape specifications and convert them into modifications in control point locations or weight values. Specifically, Sections 11.2 and 11.3 are based on specifying point constraints (i.e., the curve or surface is to change locally so that it passes through a given point); multiple point and derivative constraints are handled in Section 11.5, allowing control of tangent and curvature; and the methods of Section 11.4 allow a designer to specify the "shape" that a curve or surface is to assume in a selected region. These geometrically intuitive inputs are converted into control point relocations in Sections 11.2, 11.4, and 11.5, and into weight modifications in Section 11.3. The influence of control points and weights on shape is geometrically clear and intuitive. This was already shown, qualitatively, in previous figures, e.g., Figures 3.7, 3.23, 4.4, 4.6, 4.11, and 4.12; this chapter quantifies this influence. Although knot locations also affect shape, we know of no geometrically intuitive or mathematically simple interpretation of this effect, hence we present no techniques for moving knot locations.

The methods of this chapter are local, due to the local support property of B-splines. However, the extent of the curve or surface region which is to change can be made smaller by knot refinement, or larger by knot removal. Interactivity requires fast solutions, which in turn implies either simple equations, small linear systems, or a multistage solution in which the critical interactive stage is fast. The methods of Sections 11.2 and 11.3 are simple and very fast. The shape operators of Section 11.4 require knot refinement and knot removal as pre- and postprocessing steps, respectively. The technique in Section 11.5 requires inversion of a (usually small) matrix as a preprocessing step. We develop the mathematics of this chapter in detail, but we give only sketches of possible user interaction and algorithm organization. User interface and graphical interaction are beyond the scope of this book, and algorithm organization can depend on these as well as on the application area.

Many interesting topics which fall under the broad category of "shape control and modification" have been left out of this chapter – one has to draw the line somewhere. The body of literature is growing in the area known as "fairing" or "smoothing". There is no universal agreement on definitions for these concepts, but they generally involve properties such as geometric continuity, inflection points, convexity, and curvature. Many solution techniques in this area lead to constrained nonlinear minimization problems. Consequently, it is difficult to solve them at interactive speeds. We refer the reader to books by Su and Liu [Su89] and Hoschek and Lasser [Hosc93] and the many references therein. Welch and Witkin [Welc92] describe a method of surface design in which they minimize the integral of the weighted sum of the first and second fundamental forms over the surface. These forms measure how the surface is stretched and bent [DoCa76]. The designer can specify not only point and derivative, but also transfinite constraints (e.g., embedded curves). Their method leads to constrained minimization of a quadratic objective function with linear constraints.

A technique called Free-Form Deformation (FFD) can be useful for rough shaping, deforming, and sculpting of collections of curves and surfaces (which can form a closed object, for example). The geometry is considered to be embedded in a three-dimensional plastic environment, which in turn is defined by a trivariate, tensor product Bézier or B-spline function (mapping (u, v, w) parameters into (x, y, z) space). The surrounding plastic is deformed by moving its control points, $\mathbf{P}_{i,j,k}$, and the object geometry inherits this deformation. Further reading on FFDs can be found in [Sede86; Coqu90, 91; Hsu92].

B-spline surfaces (curves) can be superimposed to form a new surface (curve). In other words, if a collection of surfaces, $\mathbf{S}_1, \ldots, \mathbf{S}_n$, are all defined on the same u and v knot vectors, then a new surface is defined by the same knot vectors and the control points

$$\mathbf{P}_{i,j} = \alpha_1 \mathbf{P}^1_{i,j} + \cdots + \alpha_n \mathbf{P}^n_{i,j}$$

where $\{\alpha_k\}$ are scalars and $\{\mathbf{P}^k_{i,j}\}$ are the control points defining $\mathbf{S}_k$. The NURBS construction of Gordon and Coons surfaces are examples of this (see Eqs. [10.33] and [10.43]). This suggests the use of "additive" or "corrective" surfaces or surface patches. One can work with small, simple pieces and then superimpose them to form a new surface or to modify a region of an existing surface. Boundary conditions are easily controlled. Several authors have used such techniques for interactive surface design (see [Fors88; Mats92; Welc92]).

11.2 Control Point Repositioning

Let $\mathbf{C}(u) = \sum_{i=0}^{n} R_{i,p}(u)\mathbf{P}_i$ be a rational or nonrational B-spline curve. We want to reposition an arbitrary control point, $\mathbf{P}_k$, $0 \le k \le n$. Denote the new, translated control point by $\hat{\mathbf{P}}_k$, and the translation vector by $\mathbf{V} = \hat{\mathbf{P}}_k - \mathbf{P}_k$. Then the new curve, $\hat{\mathbf{C}}(u)$, is given by

$$\begin{aligned}\hat{\mathbf{C}}(u) &= R_{0,p}(u)\mathbf{P}_0 + \cdots + R_{k,p}(u)(\mathbf{P}_k + \mathbf{V}) + \cdots + R_{n,p}(u)\mathbf{P}_n \\ &= \mathbf{C}(u) + R_{k,p}(u)\mathbf{V} \end{aligned} \tag{11.1}$$

Equation (11.1) expresses a functional translation of all curve points, $\mathbf{C}(u)$, for which $u \in [u_k, u_{k+p+1})$; all curve points outside this interval are unaffected. The maximum translation occurs at the maximum of the function $R_{k,p}(u)$. This is illustrated in Figure 11.1.

Now suppose $\bar{u}$ is a fixed parameter value with $\bar{u} \in [u_k, u_{k+p+1})$, and $\mathbf{P} = \mathbf{C}(\bar{u})$. If we want to move $\mathbf{P}$ a distance d in the direction $\mathbf{V}$ by repositioning $\mathbf{P}_k$, then we must determine the α such that

$$\hat{\mathbf{P}}_k = \mathbf{P}_k + \alpha\mathbf{V} \tag{11.2}$$

effects the desired translation. Let $\hat{\mathbf{P}} = \hat{\mathbf{C}}(\bar{u})$. Clearly

$$|\hat{\mathbf{P}} - \mathbf{P}| = d = \alpha|\mathbf{V}|R_{k,p}(\bar{u})$$

which yields

$$\alpha = \frac{d}{|\mathbf{V}|R_{k,p}(\bar{u})} \tag{11.3}$$

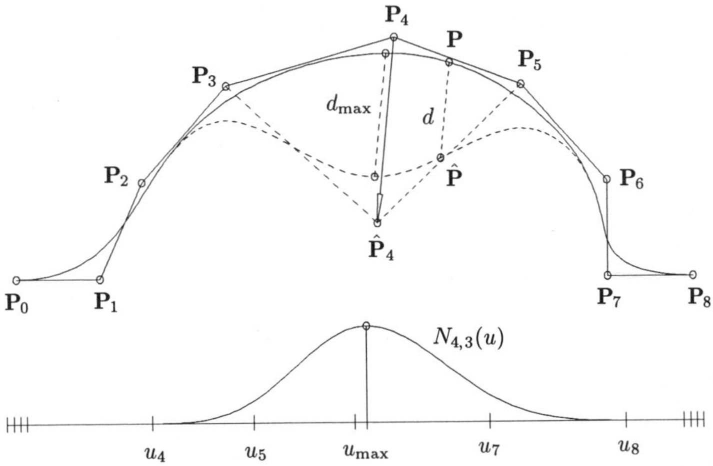

Figure 11.1. Moving $\mathbf{P} = \mathbf{C}(\bar{u} = 3/5)$ by repositioning $\mathbf{P}_4$; the corresponding node is $t_4 = 0.52$, and the curve degree is three.

From a user interface point of view, there are two broad approaches to control point repositioning, distinguished by whether the user picks on the control polygon or the curve. In the first scenario, the user might specify a vector direction and distance and then pick a point on the control polygon. If the picked point is an existing control point, the system simply translates it and redraws the curve. If not, then the system makes the point a control point through inverse knot insertion (see Chapter 5, Eqs. [5.19]–[5.21]), and it subsequently translates the new control point and redraws the curve. In the second scenario, the designer picks a curve point, $\mathbf{P}$ (from which the system computes $\bar{u}$), and then picks the point $\hat{\mathbf{P}}$ to which $\mathbf{P}$ is to be moved (from which the system computes d and $\mathbf{V}$). It remains for the system to choose a control point, $\mathbf{P}_k$, to be translated in order to produce the desired movement of $\mathbf{P}$. In general there are up to $p+1$ candidates, but it is usually desirable to choose $\mathbf{P}_k$ so that $R_{k,p}(u)$ is the basis function whose maximum lies closest to $\bar{u}$. A parameter value which generally lies quite close to (but not necessarily coincident with) the maximum of an arbitrary basis function, $R_{i,p}(u)$, is the so-called *node*, t_i, defined by (see [Ries73])

$$t_i = \frac{1}{p}\sum_{j=1}^{p} u_{i+j} \qquad i = 0, \ldots, n \tag{11.4}$$

Note that t_i is the average of the knots which are interior to the domain where $R_{i,p}(u)$ is nonzero. For interactive control point repositioning, we recommend choosing k based on the node values instead of actually computing the maximums of the $R_{i,p}(u)$; that is, k is chosen such that

$$|\bar{u} - t_k| = \min_i |\bar{u} - t_i| \tag{11.5}$$

Of course, the nodes can be used as start values to find the maximums using Newton iteration.

Figures 11.2 and 11.3 show two control point repositionings in which the index k was chosen based on the proximity of $\bar{u}$ to the nodes. Notice that Figure 11.2 is pleasing, while Figure 11.3 is asymmetric and not pleasing. The reason is that in Figure 11.2 $\bar{u}$ is very close to the node t_k (and to the maximum of $R_{k,p}(u)$), therefore the curve translation is rather symmetrical about $\mathbf{C}(\bar{u})$ and roughly maximum there. In Figure 11.3, $\bar{u}$ lies halfway between t_k and t_{k+1} (but t_k was chosen), therefore the maximum translation occurs to the left of $\mathbf{C}(\bar{u})$. There are two solutions to this dilemma:

- insert a knot in order to put a node at $\bar{u}$;
- reposition both $\mathbf{P}_k$ and $\mathbf{P}_{k+1}$.

Let us insert the knot $\hat{u}$ which forces t_{k+1} (the new $(k+1)$th node) to have the value $\bar{u}$. From Eq. (11.4) it is clear that $u_{k+1} < \hat{u} < u_{k+p+1}$, hence

$$\bar{u} = t_{k+1} = \frac{1}{p}\left(\hat{u} + \sum_{j=2}^{p} u_{k+j}\right)$$

and

$$\hat{u} = p\bar{u} - \sum_{j=2}^{p} u_{k+j} \tag{11.6}$$

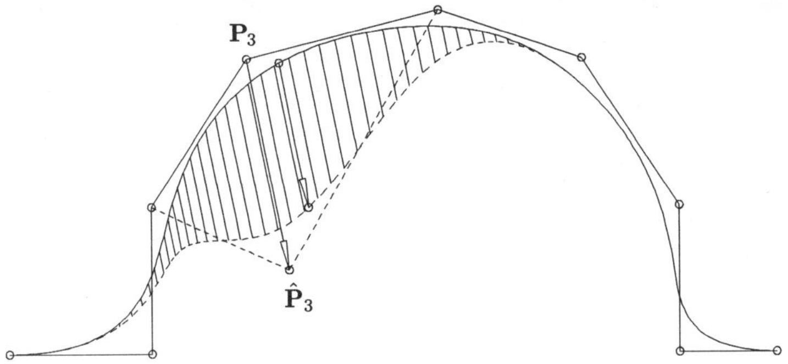

Figure 11.2. Moving $\mathbf{P} = \mathbf{C}(\bar{u} = 0.37)$ by repositioning $\mathbf{P}_3$; the corresponding node is $t_3 = 0.35$, and the curve degree is three. Notice the parallel translation of a segment of the curve.

Figure 11.4 shows the curve of Figure 11.3. The knot $\hat{u}$ from Eq. (11.6) was inserted to force $\bar{u}$ to be the $(k+1)$th node. The resulting $\mathbf{Q}_{k+1}$ was then moved to effect the desired curve modification. Notice the symmetry and the decreased domain of change. We caution the reader that $\hat{u}$ may already be a knot, and it may be undesirable to insert it. For example, let $\mathbf{C}(u)$ be a quadratic curve on $U = \{0, 0, 0, {}^1\!/_4, {}^1\!/_2, {}^3\!/_4, 1, 1, 1\}$ (see Figure 11.5). The nodes are $t_i = \{0, {}^1\!/_8, {}^3\!/_8, {}^5\!/_8, {}^7\!/_8, 1\}$. If the designer picks the point for which $\bar{u} = {}^1\!/_2$, then by Eq. (11.6) $\hat{u} = {}^1\!/_2$. If $\hat{u} = {}^1\!/_2$ is inserted then $\bar{u}$ becomes the node t_3, and if $\mathbf{Q}_3$ $\left(= \mathbf{C}({}^1\!/_2)\right)$ is moved, the resulting curve has a cusp at $u = {}^1\!/_2$, as shown in Figure 11.5.

Suppose we now want to move $\mathbf{P} = \mathbf{C}(\bar{u})$ along $\mathbf{V}$ a distance d by translating both $\mathbf{P}_k$ and $\mathbf{P}_{k+1}$ in the direction $\mathbf{V}$ $\left(\text{assuming } \bar{u} \in [u_{k+1}, u_{k+p+1})\right)$. Letting

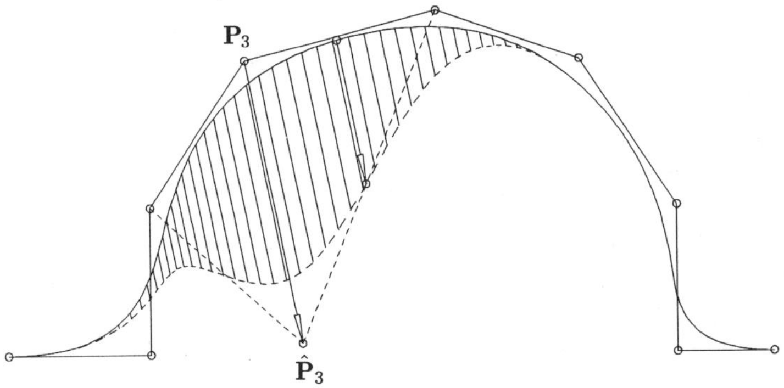

Figure 11.3. Moving $\mathbf{P} = \mathbf{C}(\bar{u})$ by repositioning $\mathbf{P}_3$. $\bar{u} = 0.43 = {}^1\!/_2(t_3 + t_4)$; the corresponding node is $t_3 = 0.35$, and the curve degree is three.

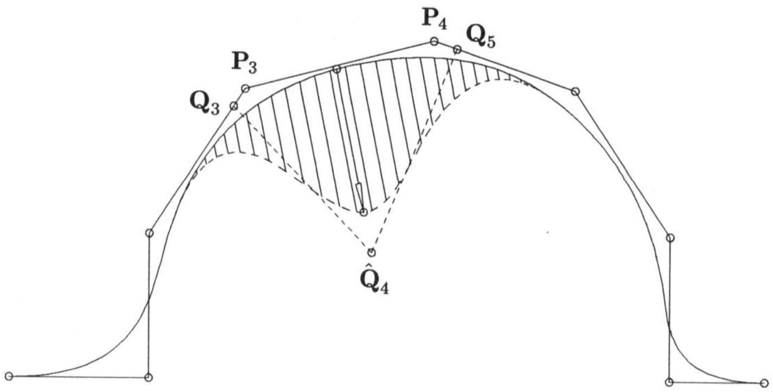

Figure 11.4. Repositioning a new control point obtained by knot insertion; the curve degree is three.

$0 \le \gamma \le 1$, we set

$$\hat{\mathbf{P}}_k = \mathbf{P}_k + (1-\gamma)\alpha\mathbf{V}$$

$$\hat{\mathbf{P}}_{k+1} = \mathbf{P}_{k+1} + \gamma\alpha\mathbf{V} \tag{11.7}$$

The parameter γ allows us to vary, on a linear scale, the movement of $\mathbf{P}_k$ and $\mathbf{P}_{k+1}$ relative to one another. The designer can set γ, or a good default is

$$\gamma = \frac{\bar{u} - t_k}{t_{k+1} - t_k} \tag{11.8}$$

where $t_k \le \bar{u} \le t_{k+1}$. From translational invariance (P4.9) we have

$$|\hat{\mathbf{P}} - \mathbf{P}| = d = |(1-\gamma)\alpha\mathbf{V}R_{k,p}(\bar{u}) + \gamma\alpha\mathbf{V}R_{k+1,p}(\bar{u})|$$

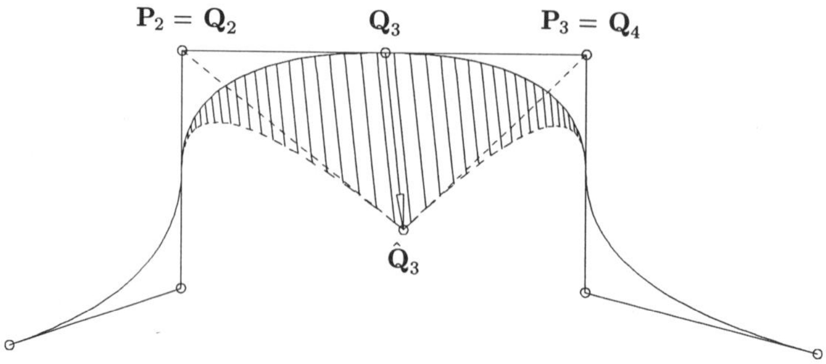

Figure 11.5. Repositioning a new control point obtained by knot insertion; the curve degree is two.

which implies that

$$\alpha = \frac{d}{|\mathbf{V}|\,[\,(1-\gamma)R_{k,p}(\bar{u}) + \gamma R_{k+1,p}(\bar{u})\,]} \tag{11.9}$$

Figure 11.6a shows the curve of Figure 11.3. Both $\mathbf{P}_3$ and $\mathbf{P}_4$ were moved, with $\gamma = 0.47$ (the default computed by Eq. [11.8]). Clearly, the disadvantage with this method is the broader domain of change, namely $[u_k, u_{k+p+2})$. In Figure 11.6b $\mathbf{P}_3$ and $\mathbf{P}_4$ were moved, with $\gamma = 4/5$.

Using these tools, it is easy to implement a user-friendly, interactive, graphical interface for control point repositioning. Notice that the value $R_{k,p}(\bar{u})$ in Eq. (11.3) does not change when $\mathbf{P}_k$ is repeatedly translated along the same vector direction (therefore neither does α). Furthermore, only that portion of the curve which is the image of $[u_k, u_{k+p+1})$ need be graphically updated for each

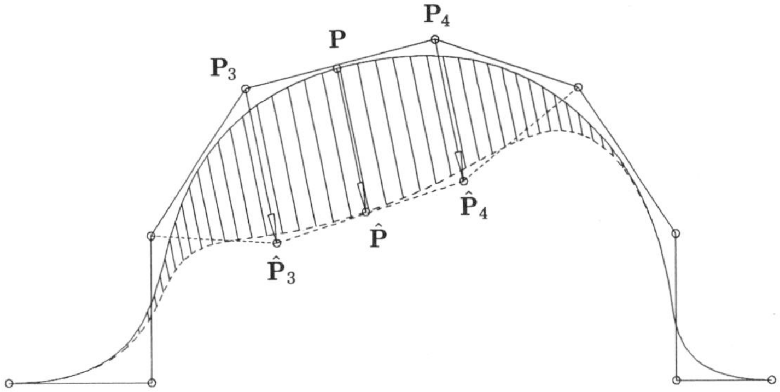

(a)

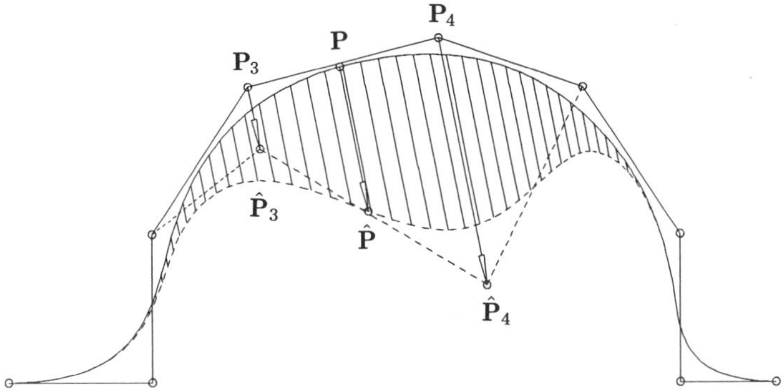

(b)

Figure 11.6. Simultaneous repositioning of $\mathbf{P}_3$ and $\mathbf{P}_4$; $\bar{u} = 0.43$. (a) $\gamma = 0.47$ (the default); (b) $\gamma = 4/5$.

repositioning. Figure 11.7 shows incremental repositioning of one control point. An increment, Δd, is specified, which fixes a $\Delta\alpha$. The relevant control point is then translated an increment $\Delta\alpha\mathbf{V}$, and the relevant curve segment is redrawn with each activation of a specified graphical input.

Finally, a designer can easily restrict the domain on which the curve should change by picking two more curve points, $\mathbf{Q}_1$ and $\mathbf{Q}_2$, which determine parameters $\bar{u}_1$ and $\bar{u}_2$, satisfying $\bar{u}_1 < \bar{u} < \bar{u}_2$. If $\bar{u}_1$ and $\bar{u}_2$ are not already knots, they are inserted one time each. Then, if necessary, additional knots are inserted on the intervals $[\bar{u}_1, \bar{u})$ and $[\bar{u}, \bar{u}_2)$ to guarantee that there is a suitable control point, $\mathbf{P}_k$, such that $\bar{u}$ is close to the node t_k and $\bar{u}_1 \le u_k$ and $u_{k+p+1} \le \bar{u}_2$. Knots should not be inserted with multiplicities greater than one, because this can cause unwanted discontinuities when control points are moved.

These techniques extend easily to surfaces. For completeness we state the relevant formulas. Let

$$\mathbf{S}(u,v) = \sum_{i=0}^{n}\sum_{j=0}^{m} R_{i,p;j,q}(u,v)\,\mathbf{P}_{i,j}$$

be a NURBS surface, and assume that $\mathbf{P} = \mathbf{S}(\bar{u},\bar{v})$ is to be translated along a vector, $\mathbf{V}$, a distance d by repositioning the control point, $\mathbf{P}_{k,\ell}$. Then

$$\hat{\mathbf{P}}_{k,\ell} = \mathbf{P}_{k,\ell} + \alpha\mathbf{V} \tag{11.10}$$

with

$$\alpha = \frac{d}{|\mathbf{V}|R_{k,\ell}(\bar{u},\bar{v})} \tag{11.11}$$

Either the designer selects k and ℓ, or the system chooses them based on the proximity of $\bar{u}$ and $\bar{v}$ to the u and v nodes, s_i and t_j, defined by

$$s_i = \frac{1}{p}\sum_{r=1}^{p} u_{i+r} \qquad i = 0,\ldots,n$$

$$t_j = \frac{1}{q}\sum_{r=1}^{q} v_{j+r} \qquad j = 0,\ldots,m \tag{11.12}$$

Using formulas analogous to Eq. (11.6), a u or v knot, or both, can be computed and inserted in order to decrease the domain of change and to bring $\bar{u}$ and/or $\bar{v}$ to nodal positions. If $0 \le \delta, \gamma \le 1$, then $\mathbf{P}_{k,\ell}$, $\mathbf{P}_{k+1,\ell}$, $\mathbf{P}_{k,\ell+1}$, and $\mathbf{P}_{k+1,\ell+1}$ can be translated simultaneously in the direction $\mathbf{V}$ by

$$\hat{\mathbf{P}}_{k,\ell} = \mathbf{P}_{k,\ell} + (1-\delta)(1-\gamma)\alpha\mathbf{V}$$

$$\hat{\mathbf{P}}_{k+1,\ell} = \mathbf{P}_{k+1,\ell} + \delta(1-\gamma)\alpha\mathbf{V}$$

$$\hat{\mathbf{P}}_{k,\ell+1} = \mathbf{P}_{k,\ell+1} + (1-\delta)\gamma\alpha\mathbf{V}$$

$$\hat{\mathbf{P}}_{k+1,\ell+1} = \mathbf{P}_{k+1,\ell+1} + \delta\gamma\alpha\mathbf{V} \tag{11.13}$$

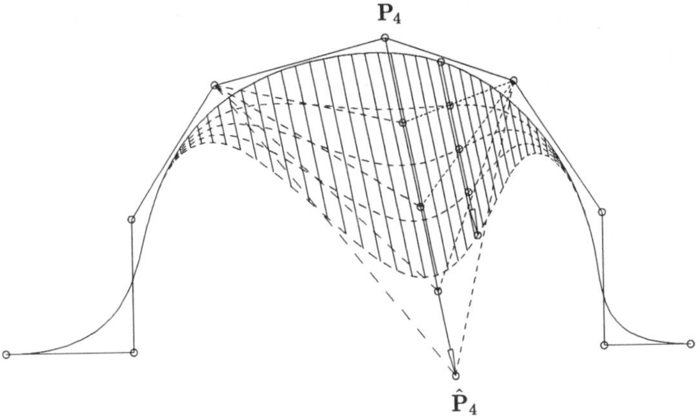

Figure 11.7. Pulling the curve with equal increments by repositioning $\mathbf{P}_4$; $\bar{u} = {}^3\!/_5$.

with $$\alpha = \frac{d}{|\mathbf{V}|\,[\,(1-\delta)(1-\gamma)R_{k,\ell}(\bar{u},\bar{v}) + \cdots + \delta\gamma R_{k+1,\ell+1}(\bar{u},\bar{v})\,]} \tag{11.14}$$

Figures 11.8a and 11.8b show translation of one control point, and Figures 11.9a and 11.9b illustrate simultaneous movement of four neighboring control points.

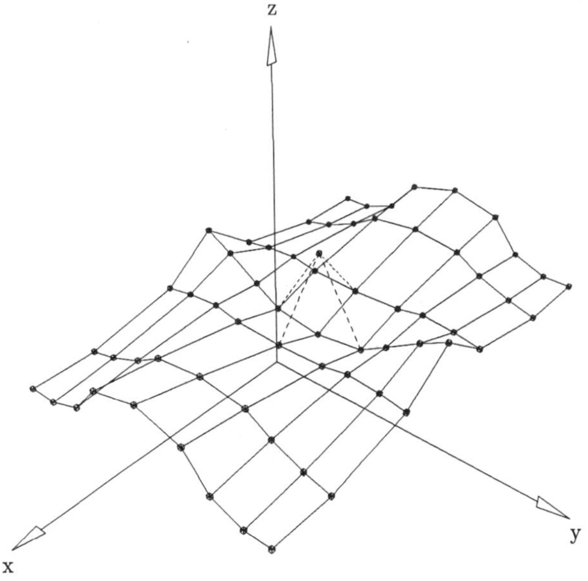

(a)

Figure 11.8. Repositioning $\mathbf{P}_{4,3}$, with $\bar{u} = \bar{v} = 0.55$. (a) Control net; (b) a surface with a local patch translated parallel to the direction of the control point movement.

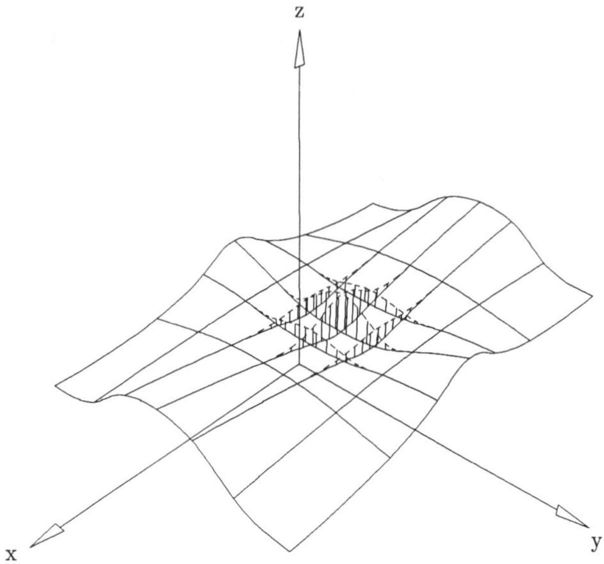

(b)

Figure 11.8. (*Continued.*)

Analogous to the curve case, knot insertion can be used to restrict the rectangular domain on which the surface is to change, and inverse knot insertion can be used to obtain additional control points at specified locations on the edges of the surface's control net. Point $\mathbf{Q}_u$, in the u direction, is inserted by the formula

$$\hat{u} = u_{k+1} + \alpha(u_{k+p+1} - u_{k+1}) \tag{11.15}$$

with
$$\alpha = \frac{w_{k,\ell}|\mathbf{Q}_u - \mathbf{P}_{k,\ell}|}{w_{k,\ell}|\mathbf{Q}_u - \mathbf{P}_{k,\ell}| + w_{k+1,\ell}|\mathbf{P}_{k+1,\ell} - \mathbf{Q}_u|}$$

(see [Pieg89d]). Similarly, $\mathbf{Q}_v$ is inserted by

$$\hat{v} = v_{\ell+1} + \beta(v_{\ell+q+1} - v_{\ell+1}) \tag{11.16}$$

with
$$\beta = \frac{w_{k,\ell}|\mathbf{Q}_v - \mathbf{P}_{k,\ell}|}{w_{k,\ell}|\mathbf{Q}_v - \mathbf{P}_{k,\ell}| + w_{k,\ell+1}|\mathbf{P}_{k,\ell+1} - \mathbf{Q}_v|}$$

11.3 Weight Modification

In this section we investigate the effect of modifying weights, in particular one or two neighboring weights for a curve, and one weight for a surface.

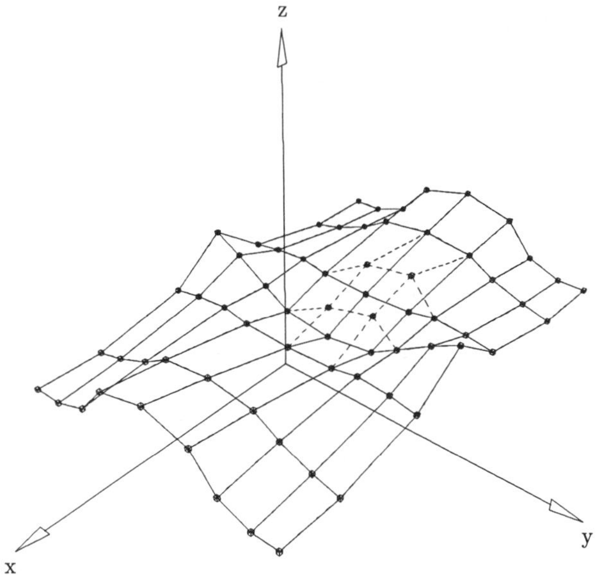

(a)

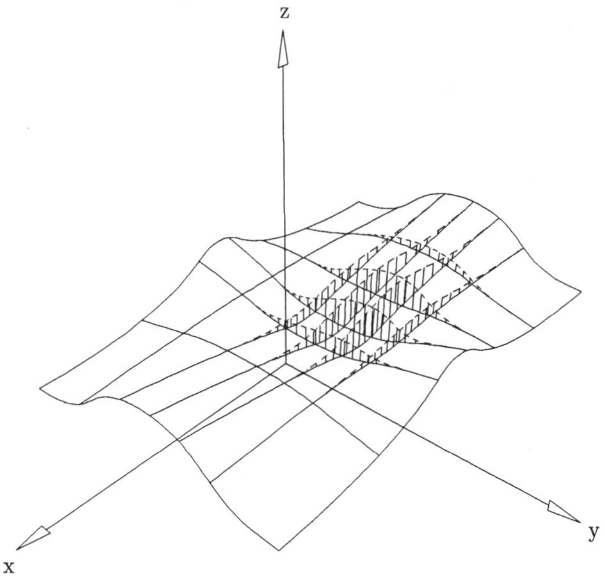

(b)

Figure 11.9. Repositioning four surface control points, $\mathbf{P}_{4,3}, \mathbf{P}_{5,3}, \mathbf{P}_{4,4}$, and $\mathbf{P}_{5,4}$, with $\bar{u} = \bar{v} = {}^3\!/_5$. (a) Control net; (b) a surface with a local patch translated parallel to the direction of the control point movement.

11.3.1 MODIFICATION OF ONE CURVE WEIGHT

Let

$$\mathbf{C}(u) = \sum_{i=0}^{n} R_{i,p}(u)\,\mathbf{P}_i \tag{11.17}$$

be a NURBS curve and $\bar{u}$ a fixed parameter value satisfying $\bar{u} \in [u_k, u_{k+p+1})$. We pointed out in Chapter 4 that the effect of modifying the value of the weight w_k is to move the point $\mathbf{C}(\bar{u})$ along a straight line defined by $\mathbf{P}_k$ and the original point, $\mathbf{C}(\bar{u})$ (see Figures 4.2, 4.4, and 4.6). Hence, whereas control point repositioning has a translational effect on a curve, weight modification has a perspective effect, where all curve points in the affected domain are pulled (or pushed) along straight lines which meet at the control point corresponding to the weight being modified. In this section we prove this statement, and we establish the precise geometric meaning of the weights.

The weight w_k can be considered a variable in Eq. (11.17), hence we can differentiate $\mathbf{C}(u)$ with respect to w_k. Using the identity

$$R_{k,p}(u) = \frac{N_{k,p}(u)w_k}{\displaystyle\sum_{r=0}^{n} N_{r,p}(u)w_r}$$

and the quotient rule for differentiation, we obtain

$$\begin{aligned}
\frac{\partial}{\partial w_k}\mathbf{C}(u; w_0,\ldots,w_n) &= \frac{\partial}{\partial w_k}\sum_{i=0}^{n} R_{i,p}(u)\,\mathbf{P}_i \\
&= \sum_{i\neq k} \frac{-N_{i,p}(u)w_i N_{k,p}(u)}{\left(\displaystyle\sum_{r=0}^{n} N_{r,p}(u)w_r\right)^2}\,\mathbf{P}_i \\
&\quad + \frac{N_{k,p}(u)\left(\displaystyle\sum_{r=0}^{n} N_{r,p}(u)w_r\right) - N_{k,p}(u)N_{k,p}(u)w_k}{\left(\displaystyle\sum_{r=0}^{n} N_{r,p}(u)w_r\right)^2}\,\mathbf{P}_k \\
&= \sum_{i\neq k} \frac{-N_{k,p}(u)}{\displaystyle\sum_{r=0}^{n} N_{r,p}(u)w_r}\,R_{i,p}(u)\,\mathbf{P}_i \\
&\quad + \frac{R_{k,p}}{w_k}\,\mathbf{P}_k - \frac{N_{k,p}(u)R_{k,p}(u)}{\displaystyle\sum_{r=0}^{n} N_{r,p}(u)w_r}\,\mathbf{P}_k
\end{aligned}$$

$$= \frac{R_{k,p}(u)}{w_k} \left(\mathbf{P}_k - \sum_{r=0}^{n} R_{r,p}(u) \mathbf{P}_r \right)$$

$$= \frac{R_{k,p}(u)}{w_k} \left(\mathbf{P}_k - \mathbf{C}(u) \right) = \alpha(k,u) \left(\mathbf{P}_k - \mathbf{C}(u) \right) \qquad (11.18)$$

Hence, the first derivative of $\mathbf{C}(u)$ with respect to w_k is a vector pointing in the direction from $\mathbf{C}(u)$ to $\mathbf{P}_k$. We now prove by induction that the derivatives of all orders have this form. Let $\alpha^{(1)} = \alpha(k,u)$, and assume the nth derivative has the form $\alpha^{(n)}(\mathbf{P}_k - \mathbf{C}(u))$. Then

$$\frac{\partial^{n+1}\mathbf{C}(u)}{\partial w_k^{n+1}} = \frac{\partial \left[\alpha^{(n)} (\mathbf{P}_k - \mathbf{C}(u)) \right]}{\partial w_k}$$

$$= \alpha^{(n)} \left(-\alpha^{(1)} \mathbf{P}_k + \alpha^{(1)} \mathbf{C}(u) \right) + \frac{\partial \alpha^{(n)}}{\partial w_k} \left(\mathbf{P}_k - \mathbf{C}(u) \right)$$

$$= \left(\frac{\partial \alpha^{(n)}}{\partial w_k} - \alpha^{(1)} \alpha^{(n)} \right) \left(\mathbf{P}_k - \mathbf{C}(u) \right) = \alpha^{(n+1)} \left(\mathbf{P}_k - \mathbf{C}(u) \right)$$

where

$$\alpha^{(n+1)} = \frac{\partial \alpha^{(n)}}{\partial w_k} - \alpha^{(1)} \alpha^{(n)}$$

This completes the proof.

It is easy to derive a recursive formula to compute the $\alpha^{(n+1)}$ and thereby obtain the formula for the higher derivatives

$$\frac{\partial^{n+1}\mathbf{C}(u)}{\partial w_k^{n+1}} = \alpha^{(n+1)} \left(\mathbf{P}_k - \mathbf{C}(u) \right) \qquad n = 1, 2, \ldots, \infty \qquad (11.19)$$

with

$$\alpha^{(n+1)} = (-1)(n+1) \alpha^{(n)} \alpha^{(1)} \qquad (11.20)$$

Equations (11.18)–(11.20) prove that an arbitrary curve point, $\mathbf{C}(u)$, moves along a straight line toward $\mathbf{P}_k$ as w_k increases in value.

We now take a more geometric approach. Starting with the curve of Eq. (11.17), let w_k vary, $0 \le w_k < \infty$. Denote the family of resulting curves by $\mathbf{C}(u; w_k)$ (see Figure 11.10). Assume $\bar{u} \in [u_k, u_{k+p+1})$, and define the points

$$\mathbf{R} = \mathbf{C}(\bar{u}; w_k = 0)$$

$$\mathbf{M} = \mathbf{C}(\bar{u}; w_k = 1)$$

$$\mathbf{P} = \mathbf{C}(\bar{u}; w_k \neq 0, 1) \qquad (11.21)$$

Notice that $\mathbf{R}$ and $\mathbf{M}$ are points on specific curves, but $\mathbf{P}$ can lie anywhere on the line between $\mathbf{R}$ and $\mathbf{P}_k$, for $w_k \ge 0$. Now $\mathbf{M}$ and $\mathbf{P}$ can be expressed as

$$\mathbf{M} = (1-s)\,\mathbf{R} + s\,\mathbf{P}_k$$

$$\mathbf{P} = (1-t)\,\mathbf{R} + t\,\mathbf{P}_k \qquad (11.22)$$

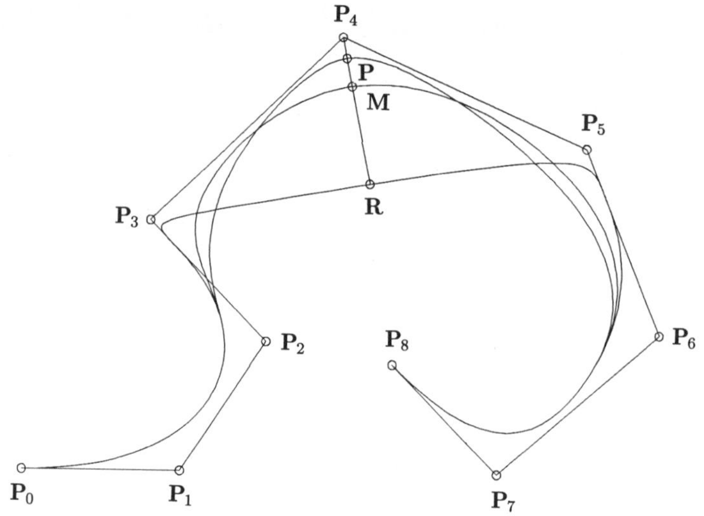

Figure 11.10. Geometric meaning of the weight.

where
$$s = \frac{N_{k,p}(\bar{u})}{\sum_{i \neq k} N_{i,p}(\bar{u})\, w_i + N_{k,p}(\bar{u})}$$

$$t = \frac{N_{k,p}(\bar{u})\, w_k}{\sum_{i=0}^{n} N_{i,p}(\bar{u})\, w_i} = R_{k,p}(\bar{u}) \tag{11.23}$$

To derive these equations note that

$$\mathbf{R} = \frac{\sum_{i \neq k} N_{i,p}(\bar{u})\, w_i\, \mathbf{P}_i}{\sum_{i \neq k} N_{i,p}(\bar{u})\, w_i} \qquad w_k = 0$$

and thus we have

$$\mathbf{P} = \sum_{i=0}^{n} R_{i,p}(\bar{u})\, \mathbf{P}_i = \sum_{i \neq k} R_{i,p}(\bar{u})\, \mathbf{P}_i + R_{k,p}(\bar{u})\, \mathbf{P}_k$$

$$= \frac{\sum_{i \neq k} N_{i,p}(\bar{u})\, w_i\, \mathbf{P}_i}{\sum_{i=0}^{n} N_{i,p}(\bar{u})\, w_i} + R_{k,p}(\bar{u})\, \mathbf{P}_k$$

$$= \frac{\sum_{i\neq k} N_{i,p}(\bar{u})\,w_i}{\sum_{i=0}^{n} N_{i,p}(\bar{u})\,w_i}\,\mathbf{R} + R_{k,p}(\bar{u})\,\mathbf{P}_k$$

$$= \left(\frac{\sum_{i=0}^{n} N_{i,p}(\bar{u})\,w_i}{\sum_{i=0}^{n} N_{i,p}(\bar{u})\,w_i} - \frac{N_{k,p}(\bar{u})\,w_k}{\sum_{i=0}^{n} N_{i,p}(\bar{u})\,w_i} \right) \mathbf{R} + R_{k,p}(\bar{u})\,\mathbf{P}_k$$

$$= \big(1 - R_{k,p}(\bar{u})\big)\,\mathbf{R} + R_{k,p}(\bar{u})\,\mathbf{P}_k = (1-t)\,\mathbf{R} + t\,\mathbf{P}_k$$

where $t = R_{k,p}(\bar{u})$. Finally, setting $w_k = 1$ yields

$$\mathbf{M} = \frac{\sum_{i\neq k} N_{i,p}(\bar{u})\,w_i\,\mathbf{P}_i}{\sum_{i\neq k} N_{i,p}(\bar{u})\,w_i + N_{k,p}(\bar{u})} + \frac{N_{k,p}(\bar{u})}{\sum_{i\neq k} N_{i,p}(\bar{u})\,w_i + N_{k,p}(\bar{u})}\,\mathbf{P}_k$$

$$= \frac{\sum_{i\neq k} N_{i,p}(\bar{u})\,w_i}{\sum_{i\neq k} N_{i,p}(\bar{u})\,w_i + N_{k,p}(\bar{u})}\,\mathbf{R} + \frac{N_{k,p}(\bar{u})}{\sum_{i\neq k} N_{i,p}(\bar{u})\,w_i + N_{k,p}(\bar{u})}\,\mathbf{P}_k$$

$$= \frac{\sum_{i\neq k} N_{i,p}(\bar{u})\,w_i + N_{k,p}(\bar{u}) - N_{k,p}(\bar{u})}{\sum_{i\neq k} N_{i,p}(\bar{u})\,w_i + N_{k,p}(\bar{u})}\,\mathbf{R} + \frac{N_{k,p}(\bar{u})}{\sum_{i\neq k} N_{i,p}(\bar{u})\,w_i + N_{k,p}(\bar{u})}\,\mathbf{P}_k$$

$$= (1-s)\,\mathbf{R} + s\,\mathbf{P}_k$$

where

$$s = \frac{N_{k,p}(\bar{u})}{\sum_{i\neq k} N_{i,p}(\bar{u})\,w_i + N_{k,p}(\bar{u})}$$

From Eqs. (11.22) and (11.23) we have

$$w_k = \frac{\sum_{i\neq k} N_{i,p}(\bar{u})\,w_i}{N_{k,p}(\bar{u})} \Bigg/ \frac{\sum_{i\neq k} N_{i,p}(\bar{u})\,w_i}{N_{k,p}(\bar{u})\,w_k}$$

$$= \frac{1-s}{\mathrm{s}} \Big/ \frac{1-t}{t} = \frac{\mathbf{P}_k\mathbf{M}}{\mathbf{RM}} \Big/ \frac{\mathbf{P}_k\mathbf{P}}{\mathbf{RP}} \tag{11.24}$$

Equation (11.24) says that w_k is the *cross ratio* of the four points, $\mathbf{P}_k$, $\mathbf{R}$, $\mathbf{M}$, and $\mathbf{P}$, denoted by $(\mathbf{P}_k, \mathbf{R}; \mathbf{M}, \mathbf{P})$ (see [Coxe74; Boeh94]). The cross ratio is a fundamental quantity of projective geometry. With respect to shape modifications of NURBS curves, we mention the following consequences of Eqs. (11.21)–(11.24):

- as w_k increases (decreases), t increases (decreases), thus the curve is pulled (pushed) toward (away from) $\mathbf{P}_k$;
- $\mathbf{P}$ moves along a straight line segment passing through $\mathbf{P}_k$; thus, a modification of w_k changes the curve in a predictable manner;
- as $\mathbf{P}$ approaches $\mathbf{P}_k$, t approaches 1 and w_k tends to infinity.

Now suppose the point $\mathbf{P} = \mathbf{C}(\bar{u})$ is to be pulled (pushed) toward (away from) $\mathbf{P}_k$ to a new location, $\hat{\mathbf{P}}$, by modifying w_k. Set $d = \mathbf{P}\hat{\mathbf{P}} = |\mathbf{P} - \hat{\mathbf{P}}|$. The required new weight, $\hat{w}_k$, is derived as

$$\hat{w}_k = \frac{\mathbf{P}_k\mathbf{M} \cdot (\mathbf{RP} \pm d)}{\mathbf{RM} \cdot (\mathbf{P}_k\mathbf{P} \mp d)}$$

$$= \frac{\mathbf{P}_k\mathbf{M} \cdot \mathbf{RP}}{\mathbf{RM} \cdot \mathbf{P}_k\mathbf{P} \mp d \cdot \mathbf{RM}} \pm \frac{d \cdot \mathbf{P}_k\mathbf{M}}{\mathbf{RM} \cdot (\mathbf{P}_k\mathbf{P} \mp d)}$$

Using
$$w_k = \frac{\mathbf{P}_k\mathbf{M} \cdot \mathbf{RP}}{\mathbf{RM} \cdot \mathbf{P}_k\mathbf{P}}$$

we have
$$\hat{w}_k = \frac{w_k \cdot \mathbf{P}_k\mathbf{P}}{\mathbf{P}_k\mathbf{P} \mp d} \pm \frac{d \cdot \mathbf{P}_k\mathbf{M}}{\mathbf{RM} \cdot (\mathbf{P}_k\mathbf{P} \mp d)}$$

$$= w_k \left(\frac{\mathbf{P}_k\mathbf{P}}{\mathbf{P}_k\mathbf{P} \mp d} \pm \frac{d \cdot \mathbf{P}_k\mathbf{P}}{\mathbf{RP} \cdot (\mathbf{P}_k\mathbf{P} \mp d)} \right)$$

$$= w_k \left(\frac{\mathbf{P}_k\mathbf{P} \cdot (\mathbf{RP} \pm d)}{\mathbf{RP} \cdot (\mathbf{P}_k\mathbf{P} \mp d)} \right) = w_k \left(\frac{(1-t)(\mathbf{RP} \pm d)}{t \cdot (\mathbf{P}_k\mathbf{P} \mp d)} \right)$$

$$= w_k \left(\frac{(1-t) \cdot \mathbf{RP} \mp td}{t \cdot \mathbf{P}_k\mathbf{P} \mp td} \pm \frac{d}{t \cdot (\mathbf{P}_k\mathbf{P} \mp d)} \right)$$

and from Eq. (11.24) we obtain

$$\hat{w}_k = w_k \left(1 \pm \frac{d}{R_{k,p}(\bar{u})(\mathbf{P}_k\mathbf{P} \mp d)} \right) \tag{11.25}$$

Where $\pm$ or $\mp$ appears, the top sign is to be taken in case of a pull operation, and the bottom sign in case of a push operation [Pieg89c].

To implement a user interface for modification of one curve weight, a designer picks a point $\mathbf{P}$ on the curve and a point on the control polygon. The system computes the parameter $\bar{u}$ such that $\mathbf{P} = \mathbf{C}(\bar{u})$. If the picked point on the control polygon is not already a control point, the system makes it a control point by using inverse knot insertion. Denote the control point by $\mathbf{P}_k$. The system then draws a line through $\mathbf{P}$ and $\mathbf{P}_k$. The designer picks the point $\hat{\mathbf{P}}$ on this line, allowing the system to then compute d, and finally $\hat{w}_k$ from Eq. (11.25). The reader should note that

- two user picks determine $\bar{u}$ and k. It is possible (but not likely) that $\bar{u} \notin [u_k, u_{k+p+1})$; the system should catch this and report it to the user as an invalid pick;
- in Eq. (11.25), the values $R_{k,p}(\bar{u})$ and $\mathbf{P}_k\mathbf{P}$ change with each modification of w_k, even when k and $\bar{u}$ remain constant; thus, if interactive incremental or continuous modification of the weight is desired, it is best to save the original $R_{k,p}(\bar{u})$, w_k, and $\mathbf{P}_k\mathbf{P}$ values and use them to compute new d and $\hat{w}_k$ values at each step;
- if we fix the weight change, Δw_k, and consider the distance $d(u) = |\mathbf{C}(u; w_k) - \mathbf{C}(u; \hat{w}_k)|$ as a function of u, it follows from Eq. (11.25) that $d(u)$ attains its maximum at the maximum of $R_{k,p}(u)$ (Figure 11.11);
- from a practical point of view, weight modification can/should only be used to effect small changes in a curve. For pull operations $\mathbf{P}_k$ is clearly a built-in bound on possible length of pull. This bound can be quite restrictive, particularly in cases where $\mathbf{P}_k$ was added through inverse knot insertion. Moreover, even moderate push/pulls often require substantial modifications in a weight; and widely varying weights can induce very poor

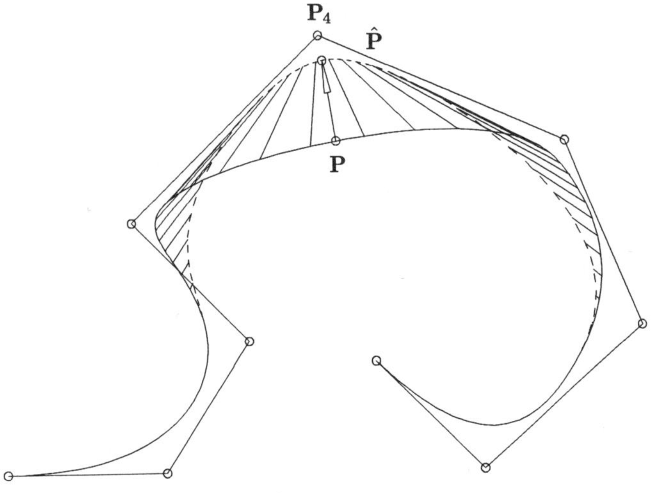

Figure 11.11. Pulling the curve at $t_4 = u = 0.52$ a distance $d = 0.075$ toward $\mathbf{P}_4$ by changing the weight $w_4 = 0.2$; the new weight computed is $\hat{w}_4 = 2.45$. Notice the perspective translation of the curve segment produced by the change of weight.

parameterizations, which often cause unexpected problems downstream. Figures 11.11 and 11.12 show such examples. For this reason, it may be advisable in a serious software implementation to restrict the range of allowable weight values;

- as was the case for control point repositioning, knot insertion can be used here to restrict the domain of curve change to lie between two user-specified curve points.

Figure 11.13 shows an example of incremental pulls. Note the exponential change of weights.

11.3.2 MODIFICATION OF TWO NEIGHBORING CURVE WEIGHTS

We consider now the simultaneous modification of two neighboring curve weights, w_k and w_{k+1}. Such a modification pulls (pushes) the curve toward (away from) the leg $\mathbf{P}_k\mathbf{P}_{k+1}$ of the control polygon. Fixing $\bar{u} \in [u_{k+1}, u_{k+p+1})$, let $\mathbf{P} = \mathbf{C}(\bar{u}; w_k, w_{k+1})$ and define

$$\mathbf{R} = \mathbf{C}(\bar{u}; w_k = w_{k+1} = 0) \tag{11.26}$$

(see Figure 11.14). Then $\mathbf{P}$ can be expressed as

$$\mathbf{P} = (1 - a_k - a_{k+1})\,\mathbf{R} + a_k\,\mathbf{P}_k + a_{k+1}\,\mathbf{P}_{k+1} \tag{11.27}$$

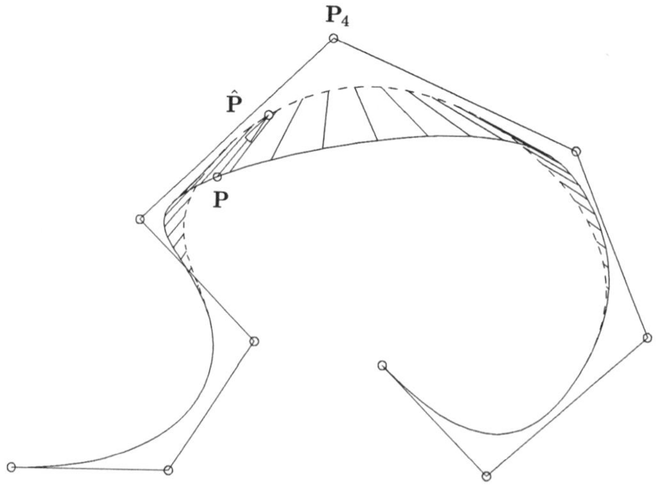

Figure 11.12. Pulling the curve at $u = 0.46$ a distance $d = 0.075$ toward $\mathbf{P}_4$ by changing the weight $w_4 = 0.2$; the new weight computed is $\hat{w}_4 = 0.97$.

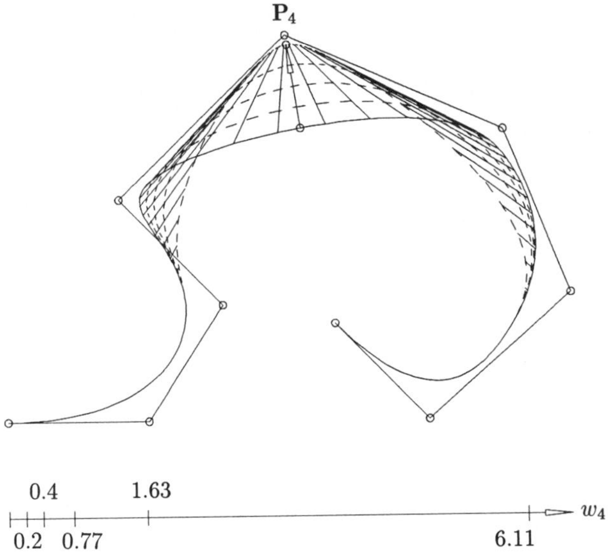

Figure 11.13. Pulling the curve at $t_4 = u = 0.52$ with equal increments $\Delta = 0.022$ toward $\mathbf{P}_4$ by changing the weight $w_4 = 0.2$; the new weights computed are $\hat{w}_4 = \{0.4, 0.77, 1.63, 6.11\}$.

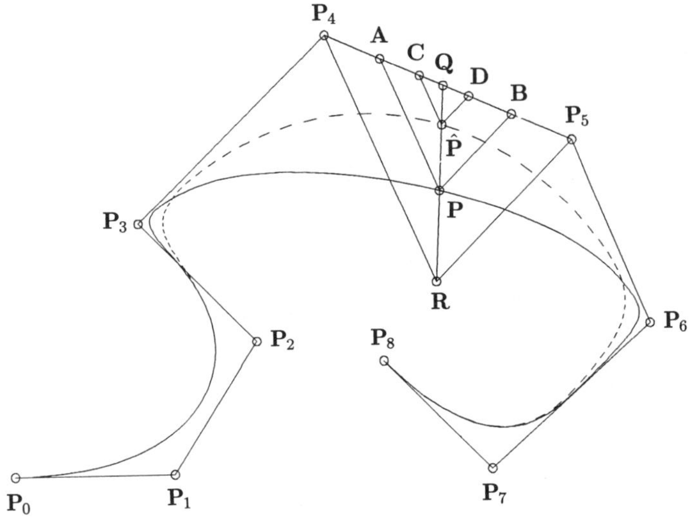

Figure 11.14. Simultaneous pull towards $\mathbf{P}_4$ and $\mathbf{P}_5$ by changing w_4 and w_5 at the same time.

with
$$a_k = \frac{N_{k,p}(\bar{u})\,w_k}{\sum_{i=0}^{n} N_{i,p}(\bar{u})\,w_i} \qquad a_{k+1} = \frac{N_{k+1,p}(\bar{u})\,w_{k+1}}{\sum_{i=0}^{n} N_{i,p}(\bar{u})\,w_i} \tag{11.28}$$

Equation (11.27) says that $\mathbf{P}$ lies on the plane of the barycentric coordinate system $(\mathbf{R}\mathbf{P}_k\mathbf{P}_{k+1})$ (readers not familiar with barycentric coordinates should consult Boehm and Prautzsch [Boeh94] or Farin [Fari93]). Assume now that $\mathbf{P}$ moves to a new position, $\hat{\mathbf{P}}$. We must determine the new weights, $\hat{w}_k$ and $\hat{w}_{k+1}$, which cause the desired movement. By Eq. (11.27) $\hat{\mathbf{P}}$ can be expressed as

$$\hat{\mathbf{P}} = (1 - \hat{a}_k - \hat{a}_{k+1})\,\mathbf{R} + \hat{a}_k\,\mathbf{P}_k + \hat{a}_{k+1}\,\mathbf{P}_{k+1} \tag{11.29}$$

with
$$\hat{a}_k = \frac{N_{k,p}(\bar{u})\,\hat{w}_k}{d} \qquad \hat{a}_{k+1} = \frac{N_{k+1,p}(\bar{u})\,\hat{w}_{k+1}}{d}$$

where
$$d = \sum_{i \neq k,k+1} N_{i,p}(\bar{u})\,w_i + N_{k,p}(\bar{u})\,\hat{w}_k + N_{k+1,p}(\bar{u})\,\hat{w}_{k+1}$$

If $\hat{w}_k$ and $\hat{w}_{k+1}$ are expressed in the form

$$\hat{w}_k = \beta_k w_k \qquad \hat{w}_{k+1} = \beta_{k+1} w_{k+1} \tag{11.30}$$

then after some manipulation one gets

$$\beta_k = \frac{1 - a_k - a_{k+1}}{a_k} \Big/ \frac{1 - \hat{a}_k - \hat{a}_{k+1}}{\hat{a}_k}$$
$$\beta_{k+1} = \frac{1 - a_k - a_{k+1}}{a_{k+1}} \Big/ \frac{1 - \hat{a}_k - \hat{a}_{k+1}}{\hat{a}_{k+1}} \tag{11.31}$$

Equations (11.27)–(11.31) result in a simple geometric method to solve for the unknowns, β_k and β_{k+1}, and thus to obtain $\hat{w}_k$ and $\hat{w}_{k+1}$ from w_k and w_{k+1}. Since a_k, a_{k+1}, $\hat{a}_k$, and $\hat{a}_{k+1}$ are barycentric coordinates with respect to $\mathbf{R}$, $\mathbf{P}_k$, and $\mathbf{P}_{k+1}$, they can be expressed by (see Figure 11.14)

$$a_k = \frac{|\mathbf{B} - \mathbf{P}_{k+1}|}{|\mathbf{P}_{k+1} - \mathbf{P}_k|} \qquad a_{k+1} = \frac{|\mathbf{A} - \mathbf{P}_k|}{|\mathbf{P}_{k+1} - \mathbf{P}_k|}$$
$$\hat{a}_k = \frac{|\mathbf{D} - \mathbf{P}_{k+1}|}{|\mathbf{P}_{k+1} - \mathbf{P}_k|} \qquad \hat{a}_{k+1} = \frac{|\mathbf{C} - \mathbf{P}_k|}{|\mathbf{P}_{k+1} - \mathbf{P}_k|} \tag{11.32}$$

where $\mathbf{A}$, $\mathbf{B}$, $\mathbf{C}$, and $\mathbf{D}$ are points along $\mathbf{P}_k\mathbf{P}_{k+1}$ such that $\mathbf{PA}$ and $\hat{\mathbf{P}}\mathbf{C}$ are parallel to $\mathbf{R}\mathbf{P}_k$, and $\mathbf{PB}$ and $\hat{\mathbf{P}}\mathbf{D}$ are parallel to $\mathbf{R}\mathbf{P}_{k+1}$. To have nonvanishing a_k, $\bar{u}$ must be within $[u_k, u_{k+p+1})$; similarly, for nonvanishing a_{k+1} $\bar{u}$ must be within $[u_{k+1}, u_{k+p+2})$. If $\mathbf{P}$ is chosen so that $\bar{u}$ is within the intersection of these intervals, neither a_k nor a_{k+1} vanishes, and consequently $\hat{\mathbf{P}}$ can be placed anywhere within the triangle $\mathbf{R}\mathbf{P}_k\mathbf{P}_{k+1}$. If, however, $\bar{u} \in [u_k, u_{k+1})$, then $a_{k+1} = 0$ and Eq. (11.27) degenerates to

$$\mathbf{P} = (1 - a_k)\,\mathbf{R} + a_k\,\mathbf{P}_k \tag{11.33}$$

i.e., the simultaneous modification degenerates to a single weight modification.

Figures 11.15 and 11.16 show simultaneous push/pulls. Notice that the curve change is pleasing and symmetric in Figure 11.15 but not in Figure 11.16. This is due to the fact that in Figure 11.15 the movement is along the line defined by $\mathbf{R}$ and the initial $\mathbf{P} = \mathbf{C}(\bar{u}; w_k)$. In this case we have

$$\frac{\hat{a}_k}{a_k} = \frac{\hat{a}_{k+1}}{a_{k+1}}$$

which implies that $\beta_k = \beta_{k+1}$ and

$$\frac{w_k}{w_{k+1}} = \frac{\hat{w}_k}{\hat{w}_{k+1}}$$

that is, the ratio of the weights is preserved.

A user interface for simultaneous weight modifications might be as follows. The designer picks a control polygon leg, $\mathbf{P}_k\mathbf{P}_{k+1}$. The system computes the corresponding nodes, t_k and t_{k+1}, and sets $\bar{u} = {}^1\!/_2(t_k + t_{k+1})$. The system then computes $\mathbf{R}$, $\mathbf{P} = \mathbf{C}(\bar{u})$, and $\mathbf{Q}$ (the intersection of $\mathbf{RP}$ with $\mathbf{P}_k\mathbf{P}_{k+1}$; see

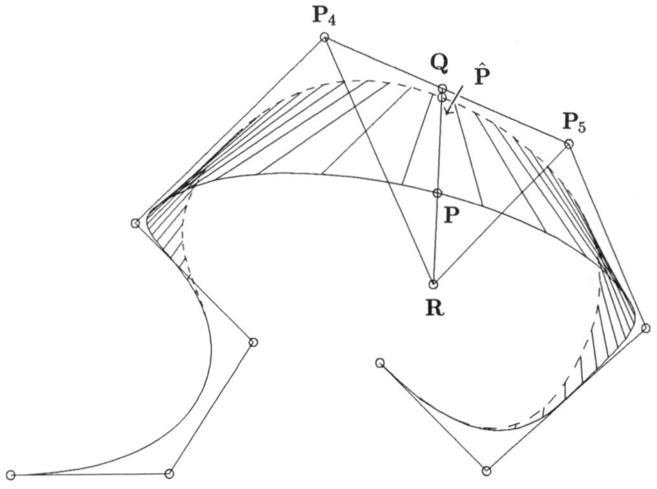

Figure 11.15. Simultaneous pull at $u = {}^1\!/_2(t_4 + t_5) = 0.608$ a distance $d = 0.088$ in the direction of $\mathbf{RQ}$ by changing $w_4 = w_5 = 0.05$; the new weights are $\hat{w}_4 = \hat{w}_5 = 1.23$. The curve change is neither perspective nor parallel.

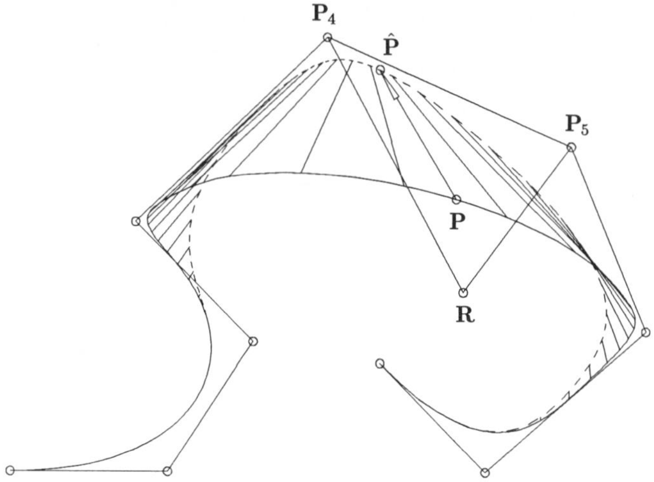

Figure 11.16. Simultaneous pull at $u = 0.612$ a distance $d = 0.088$ in a direction different from $\mathbf{RQ}$ by changing $w_4 = w_5 = 0.05$; the new weights are $\hat{w}_4 = 1.89$ and $\hat{w}_5 = 0.48$.

Figure 11.14). These components, including the line segment $\mathbf{RQ}$, are drawn on the screen. The designer can now interactively reposition $\mathbf{P}$ along the line $\mathbf{RQ}$ while the system computes new weights and redraws the affected curve segment. Of course, the designer should be able to override the default, $\bar{u}$, and the default line segment, $\mathbf{RQ}$.

Another scenario is to allow the designer to pick the curve point, $\mathbf{P}$ (and thereby $\bar{u}$), and the system subsequently chooses the polygon leg $\mathbf{P}_k\mathbf{P}_{k+1}$ by finding two nodes, t_k and t_{k+1}, such that $t_k < \bar{u} < t_{k+1}$. However, this is problematic if $\bar{u}$ is equal to or close to a node, as the push/pull effect is asymmetric if a polygon leg is arbitrarily chosen. In this case a knot, $\hat{u}$, can be inserted, which puts $\bar{u}$ halfway between two nodes. Specifically

$$\begin{aligned}\bar{u} &= \frac{1}{2}\left(\hat{t}_k + \hat{t}_{k+1}\right)\\ &= \frac{1}{2p}\left(u_{k+1} + \cdots + u_{k+p-1} + \hat{u} + u_{k+2} + \cdots + u_{k+p} + \hat{u}\right)\\ &= \frac{1}{2p}\left(u_{k+1} + u_{k+p} + 2\hat{u} + 2\sum_{j=k+2}^{k+p-1} u_j\right)\end{aligned}$$

which implies that

$$\hat{u} = p\bar{u} - \frac{1}{2}\left(u_{k+1} + u_{k+p}\right) - \sum_{j=2}^{p-1} u_{k+j}$$

However, we caution the reader that $\hat{u}$ may already be a knot; furthermore, the resulting new polygon leg, $\mathbf{P}_k\mathbf{P}_{k+1}$, may pass very close to $\mathbf{P} = \mathbf{C}(\bar{u})$, in which case the available pull length is very limited.

Finally, note that we assumed previously that the two control points whose weights we modified were neighbors. This was done because it yields pleasing results and is generally what is desired. However, the derivations of Eqs. (11.27)–(11.32) do not make use of this assumption. In fact, if $\mathbf{P}_r$ and $\mathbf{P}_s$ are chosen, then the only requirement is that $\bar{u} \in [u_r, u_{r+p+1})$ and $\bar{u} \in [u_s, u_{s+p+1})$, so that the barycentric coordinates, a_r and a_s, do not vanish. See [Pieg89c] for more details of this case.

11.3.3 MODIFICATION OF ONE SURFACE WEIGHT

Modification of a single surface weight, $w_{k,\ell}$, is similar to the curve case. Assume $\bar{u} \in [u_k, u_{k+p+1})$ and $\bar{v} \in [v_\ell, v_{\ell+q+1})$, and define

$$\begin{aligned}\mathbf{R} &= \mathbf{S}(\bar{u},\bar{v}; w_{k,\ell} = 0)\\ \mathbf{M} &= \mathbf{S}(\bar{u},\bar{v}; w_{k,\ell} = 1)\\ \mathbf{P} &= \mathbf{S}(\bar{u},\bar{v}; w_{k,\ell} \neq 0,1)\end{aligned} \tag{11.35}$$

Then $\mathbf{M}$ and $\mathbf{P}$ can be expressed as

$$\begin{aligned}\mathbf{M} &= (1-s)\,\mathbf{R} + s\,\mathbf{P}_{k,\ell}\\ \mathbf{P} &= (1-t)\,\mathbf{R} + t\,\mathbf{P}_{k,\ell}\end{aligned} \tag{11.36}$$

where

$$s = \frac{N_{k,p}(\bar{u})N_{\ell,q}(\bar{v})}{\displaystyle\sum_{i,j\neq k,\ell}\sum N_{i,p}(\bar{u})N_{j,q}(\bar{v})\,w_{i,j} + N_{k,p}(\bar{u})N_{\ell,q}(\bar{v})}$$

$$t = \frac{N_{k,p}(\bar{u})N_{\ell,q}(\bar{v})\,w_{k,\ell}}{\displaystyle\sum_{i=0}^{n}\sum_{j=0}^{m} N_{i,p}(\bar{u})N_{j,q}(\bar{v})\,w_{i,j}} = R_{k,\ell}(\bar{u},\bar{v}) \tag{11.37}$$

($i,j \neq k,\ell$ means exclude the (k,ℓ)th term.) Using Eqs. (11.36) and (11.37), one obtains the cross ratio

$$w_{k,\ell} = \frac{1-s}{s}\bigg/\frac{1-t}{t} = \frac{\mathbf{P}_{k,\ell}\mathbf{M}}{\mathbf{RM}}\bigg/\frac{\mathbf{P}_{k,\ell}\mathbf{P}}{\mathbf{RP}} \tag{11.38}$$

Equations (11.35)–(11.38) imply that

- as $w_{k,\ell}$ increases (decreases) t increases (decreases), and thus the surface is pulled (pushed) toward (away from) $\mathbf{P}_{k,\ell}$;

- **P** moves along a straight line segment passing through $\mathbf{P}_{k,\ell}$; thus, a modification of $w_{k,\ell}$ changes the surface in a predictable manner;
- as **P** approaches $\mathbf{P}_{k,\ell}$, t approaches 1 and $w_{k,\ell}$ tends to infinity.

Finally, if **P** is to move to the new location, $\hat{\mathbf{P}}$, and $d = |\mathbf{P} - \hat{\mathbf{P}}|$, then the required new weight value, $\hat{w}_{k,\ell}$, is

$$\hat{w}_{k,\ell} = w_{k,\ell}\left(1 \pm \frac{d}{R_{k,\ell}(\bar{u},\bar{v})(\mathbf{P}_{k,\ell}\mathbf{P} \mp d)}\right) \qquad (11.39)$$

Where $\pm$ or $\mp$ appears, the top sign is to be taken in case of a pull operation, and the bottom sign in case of a push operation [Pieg89d].

A user interface for modification of a single surface weight can be implemented in a manner analogous to that presented for curves. The designer can pick either an existing control point or one or two points lying on edges of the control net; if two, then they must lie on a quadrilateral of the control net, one on a u-directional side and one on a v-directional side. If an existing control point is not picked, then inverse knot insertion is used to obtain $\mathbf{P}_{k,\ell}$. From there, the process proceeds as for curve modification. Statements analogous to the five remarks mentioned previously in regard to curve weight modification also apply to surface weight modification. Figure 11.17 illustrates a surface push.

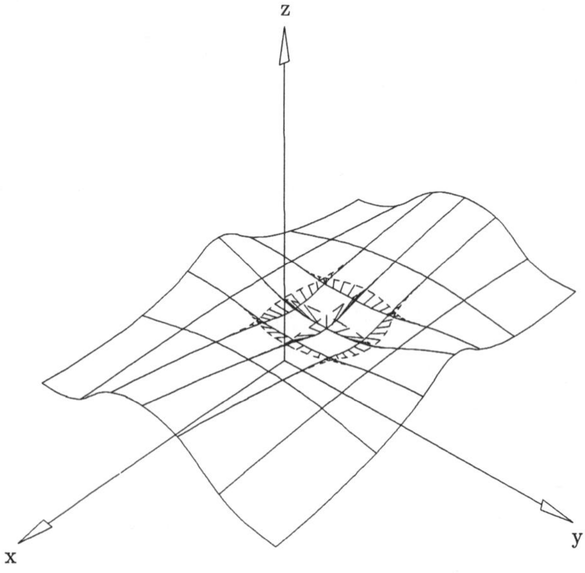

Figure 11.17. Surface push at $u = v = 0.55$ toward $\mathbf{P}_{4,3}$ a distance $d = 1$; notice the perspective change in surface shape.

11.4 Shape Operators

As defined here, shape operators are tools for rough sculpting of curves and surfaces. They operate as follows:

1. a local curve segment or surface region is specified, within which the shape modification is to occur; knot refinement is then used to introduce more control points locally;
2. control points whose influence is local to the specified segment or region are repositioned according to various parameters and/or functions;
3. knot removal to within a specified tolerance is applied to the local segment or region in order to reduce the number of defining control points.

We present three operators here: warp, flatten, and bend. Additional similar operators can be found in the literature, e.g., stretch, twist, and taper [Barr83; Cobb84]. We emphasize that our algorithms are based purely on geometry; they do not consider physical properties of materials or theories of elasticity and plasticity.

Before presenting the operators, we mention a few issues relating to the knot refinement and removal steps. The method and level of refinement affects the results of applying a shape operator. Hence, although the designer should be spared the details, he must be allowed to control the level of refinement. Assume that $[u_s, u_e]$ is a curve segment of interest. If u_s and u_e are not already knots, they are inserted. A good way to insert n additional knots into $[u_s, u_e]$ is to recursively insert a knot at the midpoint of the longest knot span in $[u_s, u_e]$. This tends to generate roughly evenly spaced knots, and hopefully (but not necessarily) the control points will also be roughly evenly spaced. Now if u_s and u_e are knots defining the limits of the final refined interval (note that e changes during refinement), then the following control points can be repositioned without modifying the curve outside of $[u_s, u_e]$

$$\mathbf{P}_s, \ldots, \mathbf{P}_{e-p-1} \tag{11.40}$$

where p is the degree of the curve. After the shaping operation, knot removal typically removes many of the inserted knots. If the curve is not to be modified outside $[u_s, u_e]$, then only the following knots are candidates for removal

$$\begin{array}{lll} u_i & i = s + \dfrac{p}{2}, \ldots, e - \dfrac{p}{2} - 1 & \text{if } p \text{ is even} \\[2ex] u_i & i = s + \dfrac{p+1}{2}, \ldots, e - \dfrac{p+1}{2} & \text{if } p \text{ is odd} \end{array} \tag{11.41}$$

11.4.1 WARPING

Warping is a tool which can be used to rather arbitrarily deform a local segment of a curve or region on a surface. First consider *curve warping*, which is implemented by means of control point repositioning based on the formula

$$\hat{\mathbf{P}}_i = \mathbf{P}_i + fd\,\mathbf{W} \tag{11.42}$$

Generally, f is a function, d a constant, and $\mathbf{W}$ can be either a function or a constant. f controls the warp shape, d is an upper bound on control point movement (and hence on warp distance), and $\mathbf{W}$ gives the direction of warp. The designer generally determines the extent of the warp by selecting curve points $\mathbf{C}(u_s)$ and $\mathbf{C}(u_e)$. The curve warp is restricted to this segment. A useful warping function is given by

$$f(t) = \frac{R_{3,3}(t)}{R_{\max}} \tag{11.43}$$

where $R_{\max} = R_{3,3}(1/2)$ and $R_{3,3}(t)$ is the rational cubic B-spline basis function

$$R_{3,3}(t) = \frac{N_{3,3}(t)w_3}{\sum_{i=0}^{6} N_{i,3}(t)w_i} \tag{11.44}$$

defined by the knot vector

$$T = \left\{0,0,0,0,\frac{1}{4},\frac{1}{2},\frac{3}{4},1,1,1,1\right\} \tag{11.45}$$

and weights

$$w_i = \{1,1,1,w_3,1,1,1\}$$

Figure 11.18 shows $f(t)$ for several different values of w_3. Clearly, functions of this form are appropriate for pulling out a bump or pushing in an indentation in a curve. Now suppose w_3 is fixed and the designer specifies a maximum

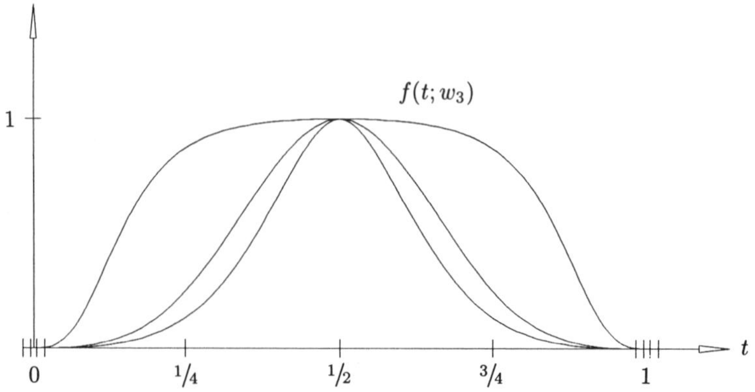

Figure 11.18. Warping functions using the rational basis function $R_{3,3}(t; w_3)$ with $w_3 = \{1/5, 1, 30\}$.

warp distance, d. The warp direction, $\mathbf{W}$, remains to be specified. Reasonable choices are:

- a variable direction given by

$$\mathbf{W}(t) = \pm\mathbf{N}\big(u(t)\big) \tag{11.46}$$

  where $\mathbf{N}(u)$ is the unit normal vector of $\mathbf{C}(u)$, and $u(t) = (u_e - u_s)t + u_s$;
- the constant direction given by

$$\mathbf{W} = \pm\mathbf{N}\Big(\frac{1}{2}(u_s + u_e)\Big) \tag{11.47}$$

The interval $[u_s, u_e]$ is now refined, yielding control points $\mathbf{P}_i$, $i = s, \ldots, e-p-1$ (Eq. [11.40]), which can be repositioned according to Eq. (11.42). In order to apply that equation, we must assign a parameter t_i to each $\mathbf{P}_i$, $i = s, \ldots, e-p-1$. Let δ denote the total accumulated chordal distance along the control polygon from $\mathbf{P}_{s-1}$ to $\mathbf{P}_{e-p}$. Denote by t_i the accumulated chordal distance from $\mathbf{P}_{s-1}$ to $\mathbf{P}_i$, normalized by δ. Notice that $0 \le t_i \le 1$ for $s \le i \le e-p-1$. Then $\mathbf{P}_i$ is repositioned by

$$\hat{\mathbf{P}}_i = \mathbf{P}_i + f(t_i)\,d\,\mathbf{W}(t_i) \qquad i = s, \ldots, e-p-1 \tag{11.48}$$

Finally, knot removal is applied to the interval as discussed previously.

Figures 11.19a–11.19d show the steps in curve warping. In Figure 11.19a the curve segment $[\mathbf{C}(u_s), \mathbf{C}(u_e)]$, the (constant) direction $\mathbf{W}$, and the distance d are selected. Figure 11.19b shows the knot refined curve. Local control points are repositioned, as shown in Figure 11.19c. Figure 11.19d depicts the final curve after knot removal is applied.

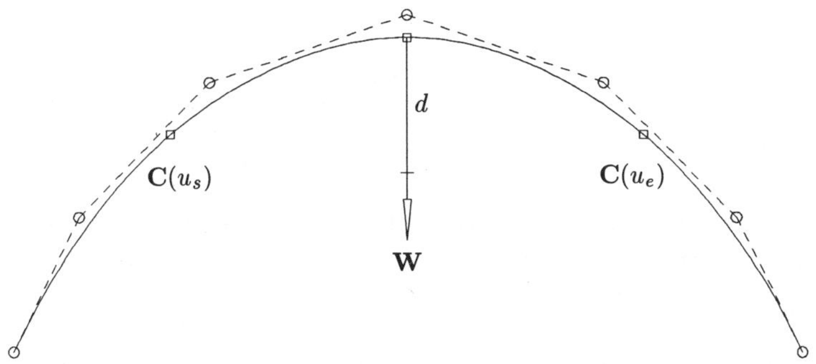

(a)

Figure 11.19. Curve warping. (a) The original curve with span $[\mathbf{C}(u_s), \mathbf{C}(u_e)]$ to be warped in the direction of $\mathbf{W}$ a distance d; (b) a curve span refined; (c) control points repositioned; (d) knots removed.

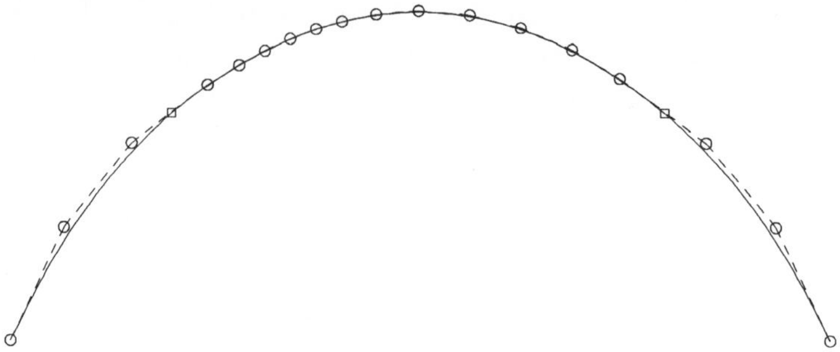

(b)

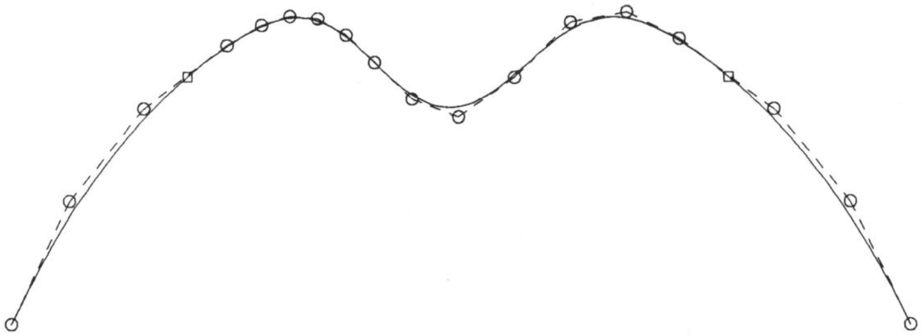

(c)

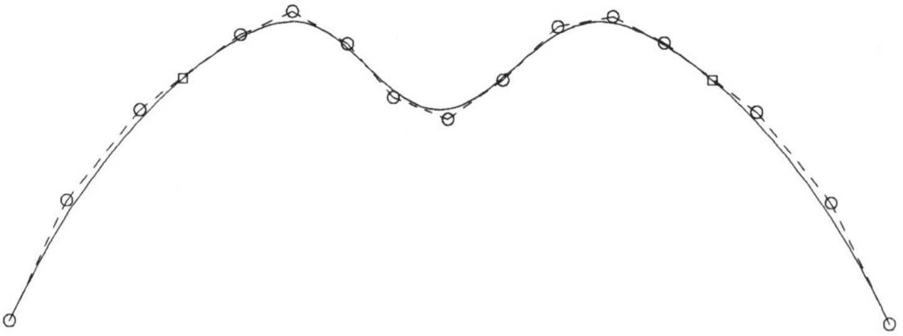

(d)

Figure 11.19. (*Continued.*)

The effects of changing the defining parameters are demonstrated in Figures 11.20a–11.20c. In Figure 11.20a different weights are used to "square" down the warped region. Figure 11.20b shows the effect of changing the warp direction while keeping both the weight and the distance constant. Finally, in Figure 11.20c different distances are applied to control the magnitude of the warp.

We conclude curve warping by noting that:

- clearly warps of almost any shape and magnitude are possible; one needs only to define the functions $f(t)$ and $\mathbf{W}(t)$ suitably. Two further examples are shown in Figures 11.21a and 11.21b;

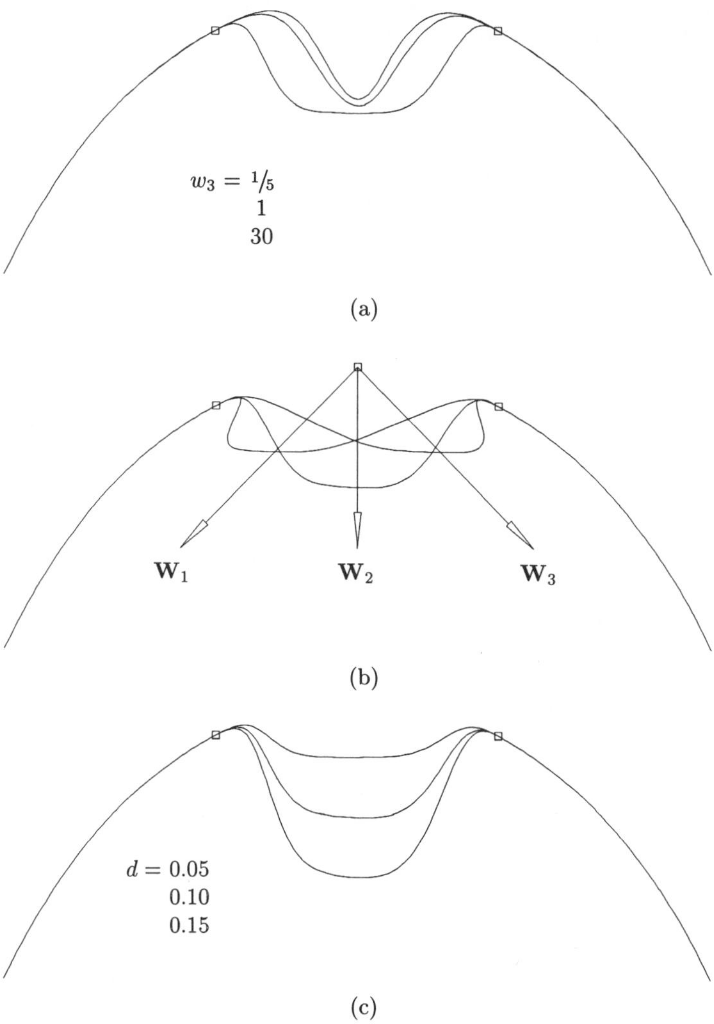

Figure 11.20. Curve warps (a) using different weights $w_3 = \{{}^1\!/_5, 1, 30\}$; (b) using different directions with $w_3 = 20$; (c) using different distances $d = \{0.05, 0.1, 0.15\}$.

- for interactive warping the designer may wish to select a curve point which is to be the center of the warp, and then to modify on a sliding scale the magnitude d, the weight w_3, and the extent of the warp segment. The segment is chosen to be as symmetric as possible about the warp center, measured in distance along the control polygon. Knot removal is done after completion of the interaction; knot refinement must be done either as a preprocessing step (either on the entire curve, or on a user-specified "maximum" segment), or the refinement must be updated (expanded) as the segment length is expanded;

- instead of computing the t_i as normalized distances, one can use the B-spline nodes computed by Eq. (11.4); in this case, the functions f and $\mathbf{W}$ must be parameterized on the interval $[u_s, u_e]$.

Surface warping is similar to curve warping. We distinguish two types, *region warping* and *surface curve warping.* In region warping we apply a warping function to a region of nonzero surface area; for surface curve warping we allow a univariate warping function to slide along a curve lying on the surface.

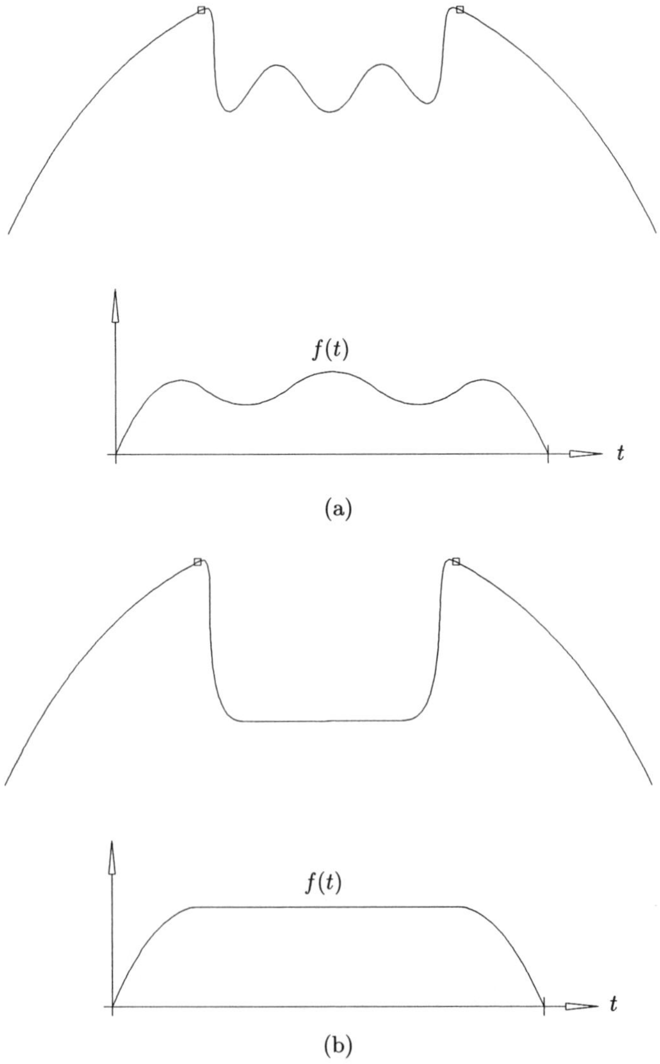

Figure 11.21. Curve warps with different shape functions.

Let $\mathcal{R}$ be a closed region in the parameter space of a surface, $\mathbf{S}(u,v)$. Examples are shown in Figures 11.22a and 11.23a. Region warping is produced by repositioning control points, based on the formula

$$\hat{\mathbf{P}}_{i,j} = \mathbf{P}_{i,j} + f d\,\mathbf{W} \tag{11.49}$$

Analogous to curve warping, knot refinement is applied to the area $[u_\alpha, u_\beta] \times [v_\gamma, v_\delta]$ (shown by dashed lines in Figures 11.22a and 11.23a) before using Eq. (11.49). Knot removal is applied in the appropriate region (see Eq. [11.41]) as a postprocessing step. A parameter pair (s_i, t_j) must be associated with each control point $\mathbf{P}_{i,j}$, $i = \alpha, \ldots, \beta - p - 1$, $j = \gamma, \ldots, \delta - q - 1$. These parameters are used to determine which $\mathbf{P}_{i,j}$ are to be repositioned and to evaluate the functions f and $\mathbf{W}$ of Eq. (11.49). Analogous to curve warping, we use normalized accumulated chord length. In particular, we apply Algorithm A9.3 to the set of points $\mathbf{P}_{i,j}$, $i = \alpha - 1, \ldots, \beta - p$ and $j = \gamma - 1, \ldots, \delta - q$. A $\mathbf{P}_{i,j}$ is repositioned by Eq. (11.49) only if (u_i, v_j) is in the warp region $\mathcal{R}$, where

$$u_i = (u_\beta - u_\alpha)s_i + u_\alpha \qquad v_j = (v_\delta - v_\gamma)t_j + v_\gamma$$

f can be any scalar-valued function defined on $[0,1] \times [0,1]$. As was the case for curves, B-spline basis functions are appropriate for pulls and pushes. For example, the normalized, bivariate, bicubic, rational B-spline basis function is suitable for rectangular regions

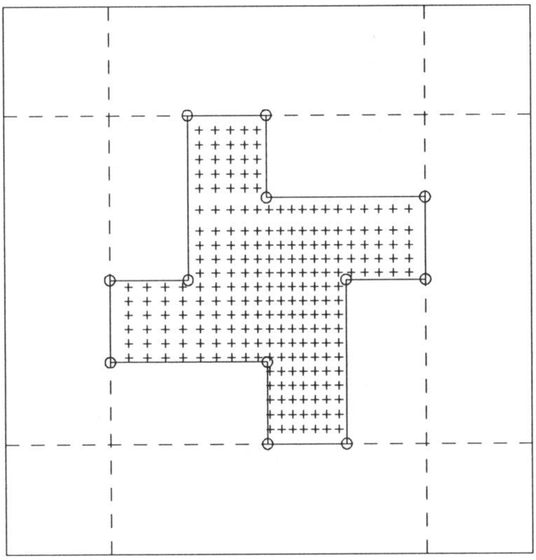

(a)

Figure 11.22. Surface region warping. (a) A region with bounding box and control points local to the region; (b) a surface warp after control point repositioning.

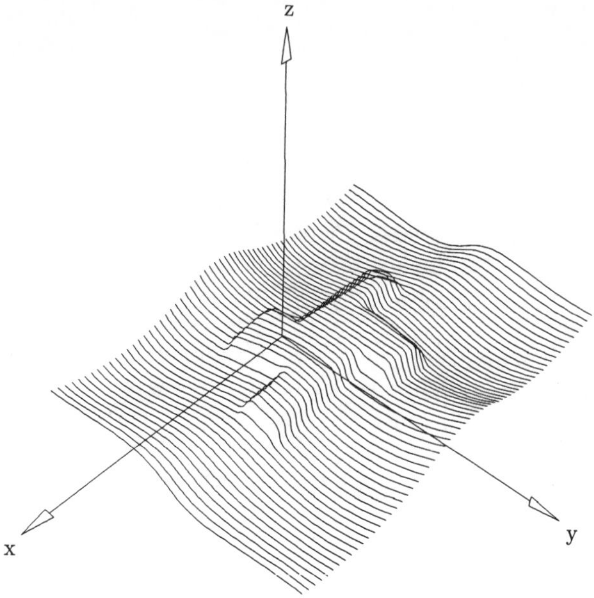

(b)

Figure 11.22. (*Continued.*)

$$f(s,t) = \frac{R_{3,3;3,3}(s,t)}{R_{\max}} \tag{11.50}$$

defined on the knot vectors

$$S = \left\{0,0,0,0,\frac{1}{4},\frac{1}{2},\frac{3}{4},1,1,1,1\right\}$$

and

$$T = \left\{0,0,0,0,\frac{1}{4},\frac{1}{2},\frac{3}{4},1,1,1,1\right\}$$

All weights are set to 1 except $w_{3,3}$, which is freely chosen. As another example, a rotated, univariate B-spline basis function can be used if the desired warp region exhibits circular symmetry.

Defining a warping function over arbitrary domains is difficult. The region warps of Figures 11.22 and 11.23 were created using the simple function

$$f(s,t) = \begin{cases} 1 & \text{if } \big(u(s), v(t)\big) \in \mathcal{R} \\ 0 & \text{otherwise} \end{cases} \tag{11.51}$$

where $\qquad u(s) = (u_\beta - u_\alpha)s + u_\alpha \qquad v(t) = (v_\delta - v_\gamma)t + v_\gamma$

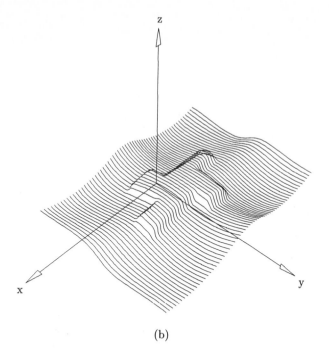

This warping function acts like a die punch, i.e., each control point for which

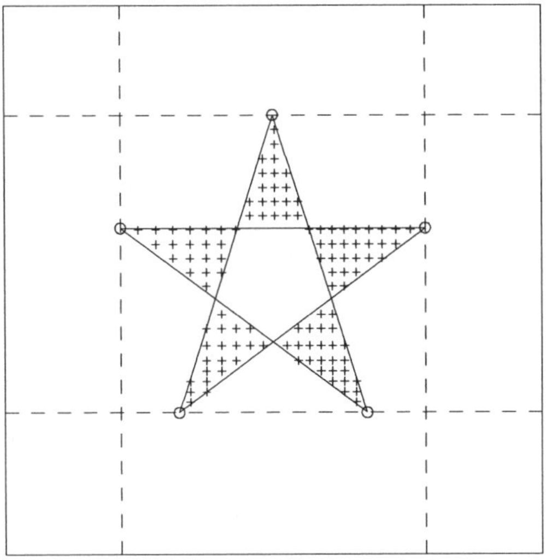

(a)

Figure 11.23. Surface region warping. (a) A region with bounding box and control points local to the region; (b) a surface warp after control point repositioning.

$\big(u(s_i), v(t_j)\big) \in \mathcal{R}$ is displaced a distance, d, in the direction of $\mathbf{W}$. The vector $\mathbf{W}$ can be the surface normal at each point, or any other user-defined vector. For Figures 11.22 and 11.23 a ray casting, point-in-polygon routine was used to determine point containment in the polygonal regions. Notice in Figure 11.23 that the routine handles self-intersecting polygons.

We now describe surface curve warping. Suppose

$$\mathbf{C}(\lambda) = \big(u(\lambda), v(\lambda)\big) \tag{11.52}$$

is a curve lying in the parameter space of $\mathbf{S}(u,v)$, and r is a distance measured to both sides of $\mathbf{C}(\lambda)$ along the line normal to $\mathbf{C}(\lambda)$ at each λ. Surface curve warping is applied by repositioning all those surface control points $\mathbf{P}_{i,j}$ whose parameters $(u(s_i), v(t_j))$ lie within distance r of $\mathbf{C}(\lambda)$ (the *field of gravity*). The relevant $\mathbf{P}_{i,j}$ are moved according to the formula

$$\hat{\mathbf{P}}_{i,j} = \mathbf{P}_{i,j} + f(d_{i,j})d\,\mathbf{W}(\lambda_{i,j}) \tag{11.53}$$

where $d_{i,j}$ is the distance of $\big(u(s_i), v(t_j)\big)$ to $\mathbf{C}(\lambda)$, and $\lambda_{i,j}$ corresponds to the projection of $(u(s_i), v(t_j))$ onto $\mathbf{C}(\lambda)$. A reasonable definition of the warp direction is

$$\mathbf{W}(\lambda) = \mathbf{N}\big(\mathbf{C}(\lambda)\big) \tag{11.54}$$

where $\mathbf{N}(u,v)$ is the surface normal vector.

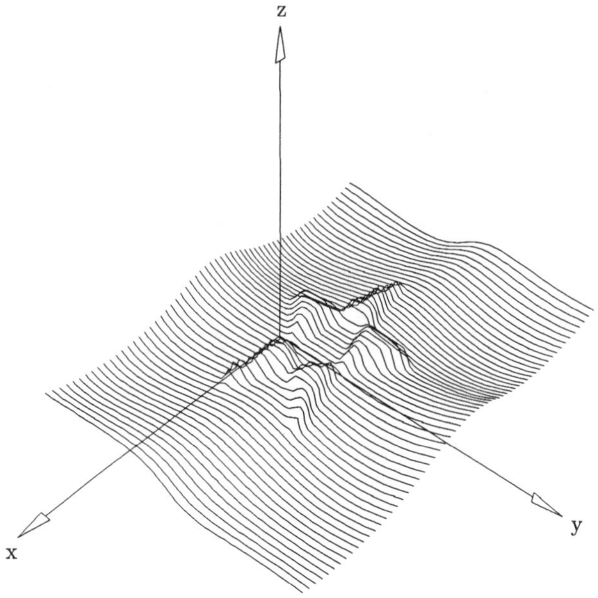

(b)

Figure 11.23. (*Continued.*)

Again, the definition of f can be delicate. We used the function

$$f(d_{i,j}) = \begin{cases} 1 & \text{if } d_{i,j} \le r \\ 0 & \text{otherwise} \end{cases} \tag{11.55}$$

The critical step in applying Eq. (11.53) is the computation of the $d_{i,j}$. This is simplified if $\mathbf{C}(\lambda)$ is a polyline. Figures 11.24 show an example of a *polyline warp*. Figure 11.24a depicts the acronym NURBS described as five polylines. Figure 11.24b shows the bounding box of the control points (marked with +s) that lie within the gravity fields of the five letters. The final polyline warped surface is illustrated in Figure 11.24c.

11.4.2 FLATTENING

The flatten operator allows a designer to easily introduce straight line segments into curves and planar regions into surfaces. No multiple knots are inserted, so the transition from the curved portions of the curve or surface into the flat portions possesses the smoothness inherent in the original geometry.

Consider curve flattening first, as shown in Figures 11.25 and 11.26; a curve, $\mathbf{C}(u)$, and a line, $\mathbf{L}$, are given. Curve flattening consists of three steps:

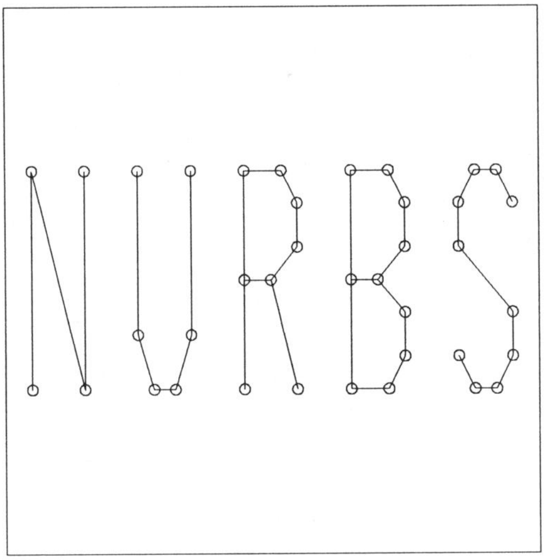

(a)

(b)

Figure 11.24. Surface polyline warping. (a) A polyline representing the acronym **NURBS**; (b) control points local to the gravity field of the polyline; (c) a surface polyline warp after control point repositioning.

1. refine the curve's knots to obtain more control points;
2. project some specified control points, $\mathbf{P}_i$, onto the line; denoting the projection of $\mathbf{P}_i$ by $\hat{\mathbf{P}}_i$, replace $\mathbf{P}_i$ by $\hat{\mathbf{P}}_i$;
3. remove unnecessary knots.

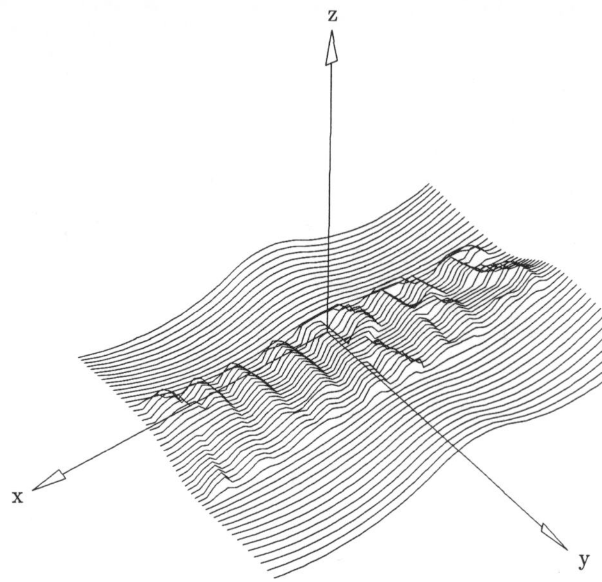

(c)

Figure 11.24. (*Continued.*)

In addition to $\mathbf{L}$ and $\mathbf{C}(u)$, the following items can be specified, either by the designer or defaulted by the system (Figure 11.25a):

- a vector, $\mathbf{W}$, defining the line of projection, i.e., $\hat{\mathbf{P}}_i = \mathbf{P}_i + \alpha\mathbf{W}$ (α can be negative or positive); this vector can be defaulted to be perpendicular to $\mathbf{L}$;
- parameters u_s and u_e: A control point, $\mathbf{P}_i$, is projected only if it is local to the interval $[u_s, u_e]$, i.e., $i = s, \ldots, e - p - 1$;
- two points, $\mathbf{Q}_1$ and $\mathbf{Q}_2$, on the line $\mathbf{L}$; a control point, $\mathbf{P}_i$, is replaced by its projection, $\hat{\mathbf{P}}_i$, only if $\hat{\mathbf{P}}_i$ lies within the segment $\mathbf{Q}_1\mathbf{Q}_2$.

Notice that the last two items are rules indicating which $\mathbf{P}_i$ to project and which $\hat{\mathbf{P}}_i$ to accept, respectively. For the situation shown in Figure 11.25a, setting $\mathbf{Q}_1 = \mathbf{C}(u_s)$ and $\mathbf{Q}_2 = \mathbf{C}(u_e)$ to be the points where $\mathbf{L}$ intersects $\mathbf{C}(u)$ is a reasonable system default. If the curve is xy planar and intersects $\mathbf{L}$, as in Figure 11.25a, another intuitive rule is to project only those $\mathbf{P}_i$ which lie to one side of $\mathbf{L}$, as shown in Figure 11.25b. If only those control points are projected which are local to $[u_s, u_e]$, unexpected results can occur if $\mathbf{L}$ intersects the curve (Figure 11.25c). If the curve does not intersect $\mathbf{L}$, projecting all control points local to $[u_s, u_e]$ flattens the segment $[\mathbf{C}(u_s), \mathbf{C}(u_e)]$, leaving the rest of the curve unaffected. This is illustrated in Figures 11.26a and 11.26b.

Finally, we caution that a flat segment is obtained only if the projection results in at least $p + 1$ consecutive points, $\hat{\mathbf{P}}_i$, where p is the degree of the curve. If

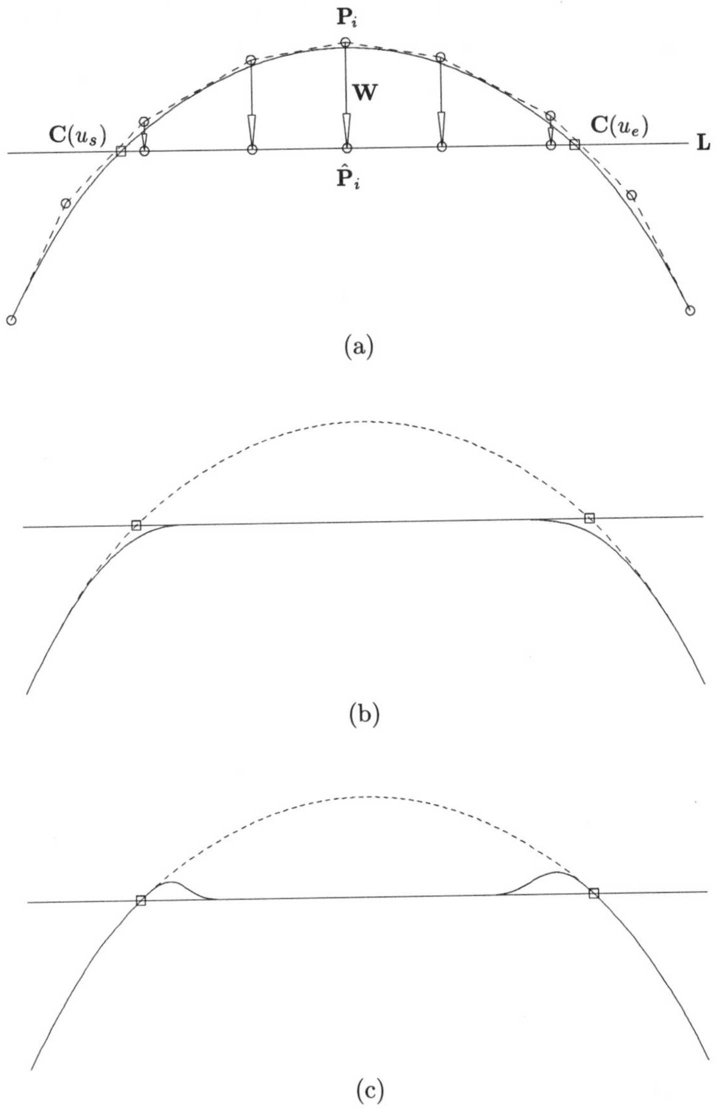

Figure 11.25. Curve flattening. (a) The original curve with span $[\mathbf{C}(u_s), \mathbf{C}(u_e)]$ to be flattened in the direction of $\mathbf{W}$ to the line $\mathbf{L}$ intersecting the curve; (b) a flattened curve obtained by projecting all control points lying on one side of $\mathbf{L}$; (c) a flattened curve obtained by projecting control points local to the span $[u_s, u_e]$.

this fails to be the case, then more knot refinement is required. If u_s and u_e are specified, then refinement is required only in the interval $[u_i, u_j]$, where u_i is the largest knot satisfying $u_i < u_s$, and u_j is the smallest knot such that $u_e < u_j$.

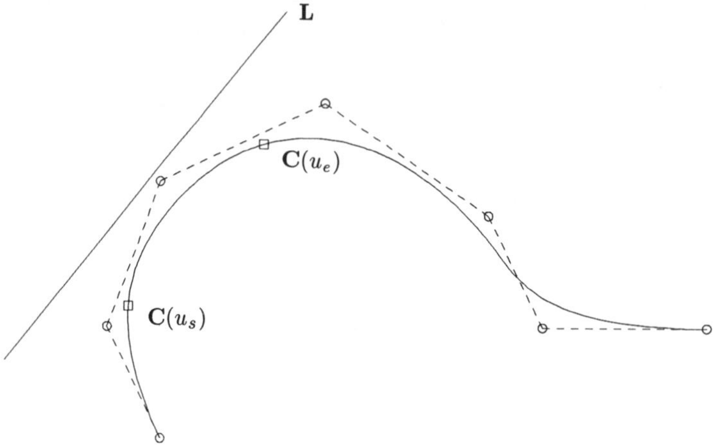

(a)

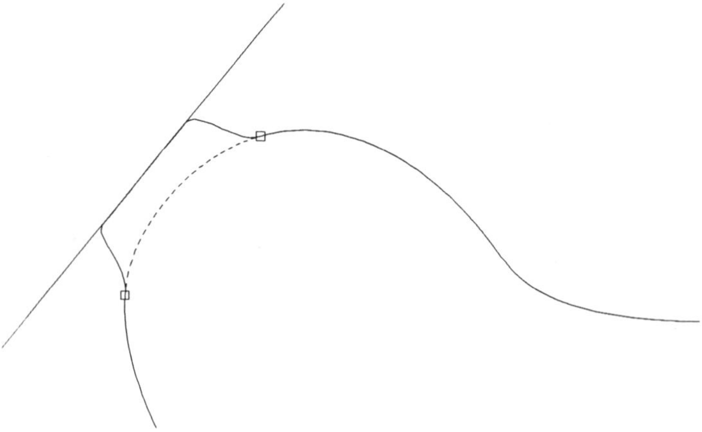

(b)

Figure 11.26. Curve flattening. (a) The original curve with span $[\mathbf{C}(u_s), \mathbf{C}(u_e)]$ to be flattened in the direction perpendicular to the line $\mathbf{L}$ not intersecting the curve; (b) a flattened curve obtained by projecting control points local to the span $[u_s, u_e]$.

A surface region is flattened by projecting control points $\mathbf{P}_{i,j}$ onto a plane, π. The $\mathbf{P}_{i,j}$ are replaced by their projections, $\hat{\mathbf{P}}_{i,j}$. In addition to π, one can specify (or default) the following:

- a vector $\mathbf{W}$ defining the line of projection, i.e., $\hat{\mathbf{P}}_{i,j} = \mathbf{P}_{i,j} + \alpha\mathbf{W}$ (α can be negative or positive); this vector can be defaulted to be perpendicular to π;

- a region, $\mathcal{R}_{uv}$, in the uv space of $\mathbf{S}(u,v)$ defined by a boundary curve, $\mathbf{C}_{uv}(w) = (u(w), v(w))$; $\mathbf{P}_{i,j}$ is projected only if its influence is local to the region $\mathcal{R}_{uv}$. If $[u_\alpha, u_\beta] \times [v_\gamma, v_\delta]$ is the minmax rectangle containing $\mathcal{R}_{uv}$, then knot refinement should be applied to the intervals $[u_i, u_j]$ and $[v_k, v_\ell]$, where u_i and v_k are the largest knots satisfying $u_i < u_\alpha$ and $v_k < v_\gamma$, and u_j and v_ℓ are the smallest knots satisfying $u_\beta < u_j$ and $v_\delta < v_\ell$;
- a region, $\mathcal{R}_\pi$, on the plane π, defined by a boundary curve, $\mathbf{C}_\pi(w)$; a control point, $\mathbf{P}_{i,j}$, is replaced by its projection, $\hat{\mathbf{P}}_{i,j}$, only if $\hat{\mathbf{P}}_{i,j}$ lies in the region $\mathcal{R}_\pi$.

Most often, $\mathbf{C}_{uv}(w)$ and $\mathbf{C}_\pi(w)$ are simple curves, such as polygons or circles, for which determination of point containment in the respective regions is easy and efficient. If the plane π intersects the surface, then instead of requiring a region $\mathcal{R}_{uv}$, a designer may want to specify that only those $\mathbf{P}_{i,j}$ lying on one side of π be projected. Cobb [Cobb84] suggests the use of additional planes to restrict the region of the control net to be projected. And finally, the projection must produce a connected grid of at least $(p+1) \times (q+1)$ $\hat{\mathbf{P}}_{i,j}$ in order to obtain a flat region in the surface. Figures 11.27a and 11.27b show an example of surface flattening.

11.4.3 BENDING

Several authors have investigated circular bending of curves and cylindrical bending of surfaces, e.g., see references [Barr83; Four83; Cobb84]. These authors develop equations based on trigonometry, which map points onto circles. Under these mappings a straight line segment maps onto a circle, and a general curve segment is bent in a circular fashion. Cobb [Cobb84] applies this technique, together with knot refinement, to map control points, thereby bending B-spline curves and surfaces.

We take a more general, geometric approach to bending. Analogous to the other shape operators, bending takes place in three steps:

1. refine the region of the curve or surface to be bent;
2. bend the region by repositioning control points;
3. remove unnecessary knots.

Only Step 2 requires elaboration. Consider curves first (see Figure 11.28). We bend the region of the curve $\mathbf{C}(u)$ between $\mathbf{C}(u_s)$ and $\mathbf{C}(u_e)$ about the *bend curve*, $\mathbf{B}(w)$, by mapping the relevant control points, $\mathbf{P}_i$ of $\mathbf{C}(u)$, "toward" $\mathbf{B}(w)$. Assuming u_s and u_e are knots, only $\mathbf{P}_s, \ldots, \mathbf{P}_{e-p-1}$ are mapped. Denote the image of $\mathbf{P}_i$ by $\hat{\mathbf{P}}_i$. We require one additional point, $\mathbf{O}$, called the *bend center*. Points $\mathbf{R}_i$ are obtained by intersecting each line segment, $\mathbf{O}\mathbf{P}_i$, with $\mathbf{B}(w)$. Finally, fixing a cross ratio, λ, the location of each $\hat{\mathbf{P}}_i$ is determined by λ, $\mathbf{O}$, $\mathbf{R}_i$, and $\mathbf{P}_i$ as follows. Analogous to Eq. (11.22), we have

$$\mathbf{R}_i = (1 - s_i)\mathbf{O} + s_i \mathbf{P}_i$$

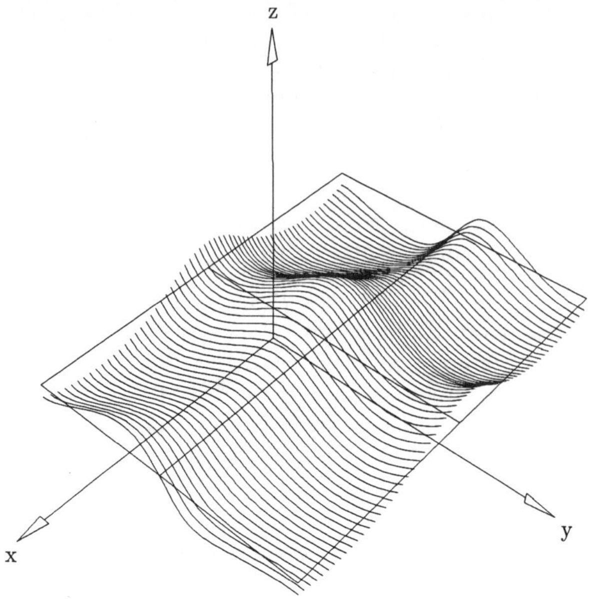

(a)

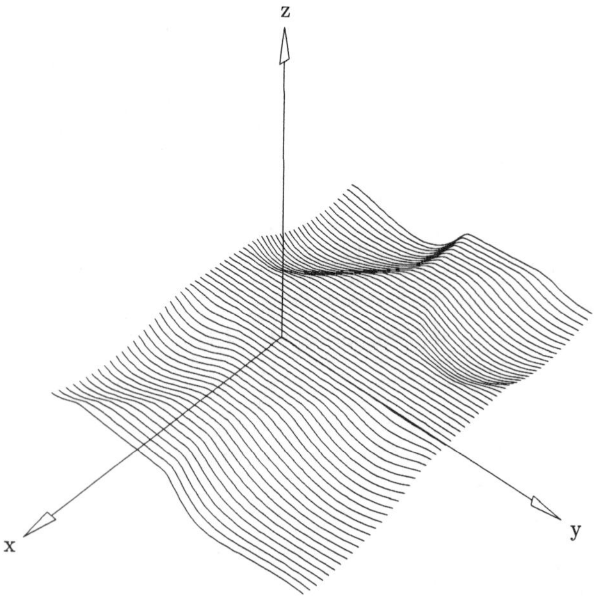

(b)

Figure 11.27. Surface flattening. (a) A surface and plane; (b) a flattened surface obtained by projecting all control points lying on one side of the plane.

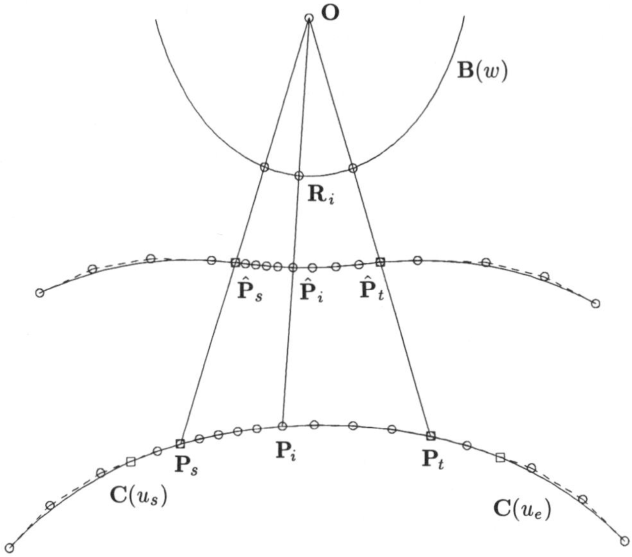

Figure 11.28. Curve bending.

$$\hat{\mathbf{P}}_i = (1 - t_i)\mathbf{O} + t_i \mathbf{P}_i \tag{11.56}$$

It follows that

$$s_i = \frac{\mathbf{OR}_i}{\mathbf{OP}_i} \tag{11.57}$$

Finally

$$\lambda = \frac{t_i(1 - s_i)}{s_i(1 - t_i)}$$

yields

$$t_i = \frac{\lambda s_i}{1 + (\lambda - 1)s_i} \tag{11.58}$$

Substituting t_i into Eq. (11.56) produces $\hat{\mathbf{P}}_i$.

Summarizing, u_s, u_e, $\mathbf{B}(w)$, $\mathbf{O}$, and λ are given, and the bend algorithm computes, in order: $\mathbf{R}_i$ (line/curve intersection), s_i, t_i, and $\hat{\mathbf{P}}_i$. The cross ratio λ can be modified interactively, in a range from $-\infty$ to ∞. Notice that $\lambda = 1$ implies $t_i = s_i$, hence $\hat{\mathbf{P}}_i = \mathbf{R}_i$; i.e., $\lambda = 1$ maps all $\mathbf{P}_i$ onto $\mathbf{B}(w)$, and thus $\mathbf{C}(u)$ assumes the (approximate) shape of $\mathbf{B}(w)$ in the region between $\mathbf{C}(u_s)$ and $\mathbf{C}(u_e)$. For $\lambda = 0$, all $\hat{\mathbf{P}}_i = \mathbf{O}$; and $\hat{\mathbf{P}}_i \to \mathbf{P}_i$ as $\lambda \to \infty$.

Let $t = e - p - 1$. After computing $\hat{\mathbf{P}}_s, \ldots, \hat{\mathbf{P}}_t$, the control points $\mathbf{P}_0, \ldots, \mathbf{P}_{s-1}$ and $\mathbf{P}_{t+1}, \ldots, \mathbf{P}_n$ must be rotated and translated into positions which yield natural transitions of the unchanged curve segments on $[u_{\min}, u_s]$ and $[u_e, u_{\max}]$ into the bent segment on $[u_s, u_e]$. Let θ denote the angle through which the bend mapping rotates the vector $\mathbf{P}_t - \mathbf{P}_{t-1}$. The new $\hat{\mathbf{P}}_{t+1}, \ldots, \hat{\mathbf{P}}_n$ are then obtained by rotating the $\mathbf{P}_{t+1}, \ldots, \mathbf{P}_n$ an angle, θ, about the point $\mathbf{P}_t$, and subsequently translating by the vector $\hat{\mathbf{P}}_t - \mathbf{P}_t$. An analogous rotation (defined by the rotation of $\mathbf{P}_{s+1} - \mathbf{P}_s$) and translation must be applied to $\mathbf{P}_0, \ldots, \mathbf{P}_{s-1}$.

Figures 11.29–11.31 show examples of circular and parabolic bends. In Figure 11.29 the effect of varying λ is illustrated. The bend region is symmetric about line $\mathbf{L}$ passing through the bend center, $\mathbf{O}$, and is perpendicular to $\mathbf{C}(u)$. Note that as λ approaches 1 the bend region gradually assumes the shape of the circle. The effect of positioning the center, $\mathbf{O}$, within the circle is shown in Figure 11.30. $\mathbf{O}_1$ is the circle center, $\mathbf{O}_2$ lies on the line $\mathbf{L}$, whereas $\mathbf{O}_3$ is an arbitrary point. Figure 11.31 illustrates the use of a parabolic bend curve to eliminate two unwanted inflection points in a curve.

Finally, we remark that for additional shape control the cross ratio can be a function, $\lambda(u)$, defined for $u \in [u_s, u_e]$. Then for $\mathbf{P}_i$, $\lambda_i = \lambda(t_i)$ is computed, where t_i is the ith node (not related to the t_i of Eq. [11.58]).

We now turn to surface bending. The natural extension of the curve bending technique to surfaces yields a very general and powerful surface modification capability. We start with a general definition of surface bending, but we then restrict our detailed discussion to a simple, but useful, special case.

A surface, $\mathbf{S}(u,v)$, is bent about a bend surface, $\mathbf{B}(s,t)$, either toward a central point, $\mathbf{O}$, or a central curve, $\mathbf{O}(w)$. Let the bend region, $\mathcal{R}$ in uv space, be bounded by the minmax rectangle, $\mathcal{M} = [u_\alpha, u_\beta] \times [v_\gamma, v_\delta]$. After knot refinement on $\mathcal{M}$ the subset of the control points, $\mathbf{P}_{i,j}$, $i = \alpha, \ldots, \beta-p-1$, $j = \gamma, \ldots, \delta-q-1$, whose influence is local to $\mathcal{R}$, are mapped to new locations, $\hat{\mathbf{P}}_{i,j}$, using a cross ratio, λ; a function $\lambda(u,v)$ can also be used. If a point $\mathbf{O}$ is used, then points $\mathbf{R}_{i,j}$

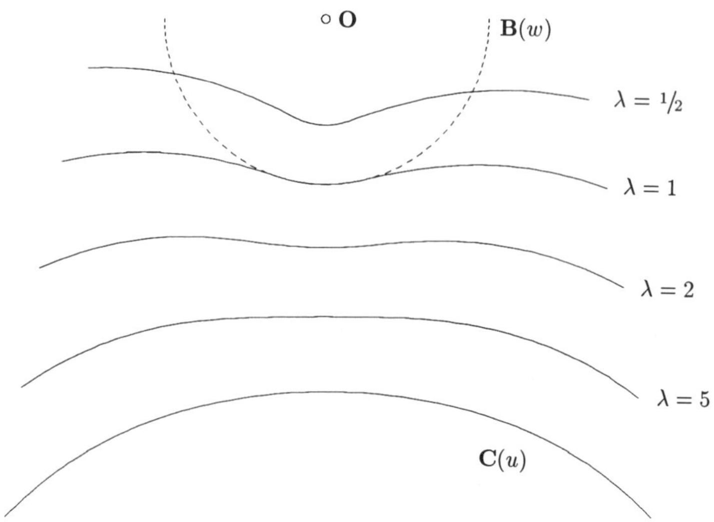

Figure 11.29. Curve bending examples using a circular arc as the bending curve $\mathbf{B}(w)$; the cross ratios are $\lambda = \{1/2, 1, 2, 5\}$.

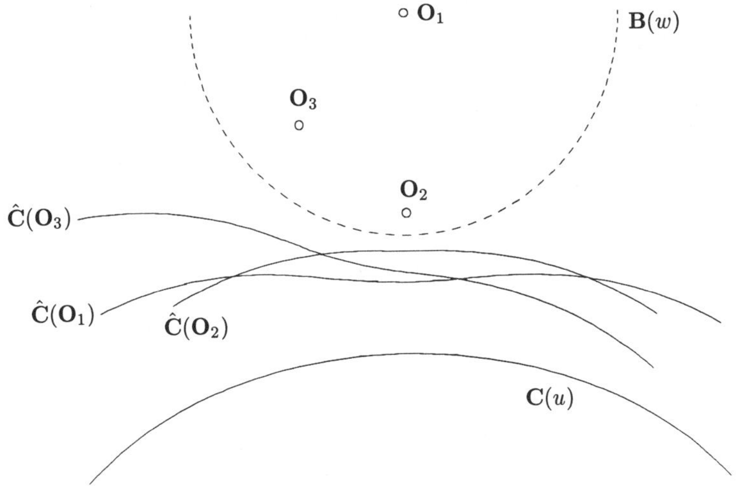

Figure 11.30. Curve bending examples obtained by using different positions of the bend center.

are obtained as the intersections of the line segments, $\mathbf{OP}_{i,j}$, with the surface, $\mathbf{B}(s,t)$. If a curve, $\mathbf{O}(w)$, is given, then parameters $w_{i,j}$ must be computed, and the $\mathbf{R}_{i,j}$ are obtained by intersecting $\mathbf{O}(w_{i,j})\mathbf{P}_{i,j}$ with $\mathbf{B}(s,t)$. The $\hat{\mathbf{P}}_{i,j}$ are then computed using

$$s_{i,j} = \frac{\mathbf{OR}_{i,j}}{\mathbf{OP}_{i,j}} \quad \text{or} \quad s_{i,j} = \frac{\mathbf{O}(w_{i,j})\mathbf{R}_{i,j}}{\mathbf{O}(w_{i,j})\mathbf{P}_{i,j}} \tag{11.59}$$

$$t_{i,j} = \frac{\lambda s_{i,j}}{1 + (\lambda - 1)s_{i,j}} \tag{11.60}$$

Finally

$$\hat{\mathbf{P}}_{i,j} = (1 - t_{i,j})\mathbf{O} + t_{i,j}\mathbf{P}_{i,j} \quad \text{or} \quad \hat{\mathbf{P}}_{i,j} = (1 - t_{i,j})\mathbf{O}(w_{i,j}) + t_{i,j}\mathbf{P}_{i,j} \tag{11.61}$$

Subsequently, the unmapped control points must be rotated and translated into positions which ensure a smooth and natural transition of the bent region into the unbent region. Knot removal is applied as a final step. For example, one obtains a spherical bend by letting $\mathbf{B}(s,t)$ be a sphere, with $\mathbf{O}$ its center. A cylindrical bend is produced if $\mathbf{B}(s,t)$ is a cylinder and $\mathbf{O}(w)$ is its axis.

In its full generality, surface bending is clearly complex. The computation of $\mathbf{R}_{i,j}$ requires line/surface intersections, obtaining suitable parameters $w_{i,j}$ can be difficult, and it is not obvious how to rotate and translate the unmapped control points. We detail here the special case of general cylindrical bends about the full length of an isocurve of a surface; that is, the bend region has one of the forms $[u_\alpha, u_\beta] \times [v_{\min}, v_{\max}]$ or $[u_{\min}, u_{\max}] \times [v_\gamma, v_\delta]$, and $\mathbf{B}(s,t)$ is a general circular cylinder obtained by sweeping a circle along the (possibly curved) axis,

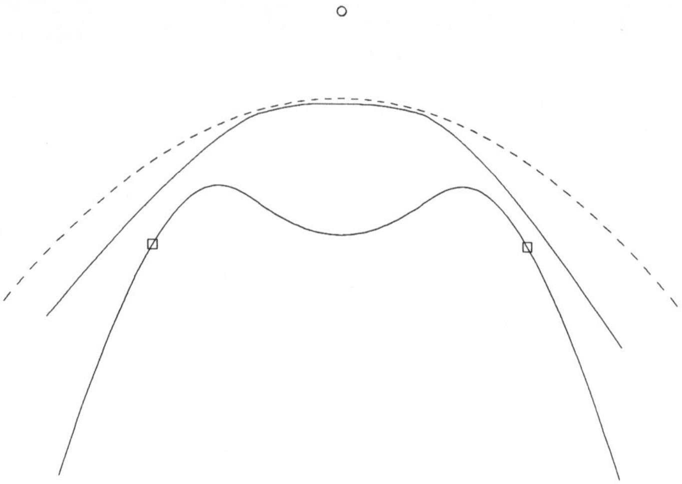

Figure 11.31. Parabolic bending used to eliminate inflexion points.

$\mathbf{O}(w)$. We present bending about an isocurve at fixed $u = u_c$; the case of fixed $v = v_c$ is analogous. Assume that u_c, u_α, and u_β satisfy $u_\alpha < u_c < u_\beta$. Let $\mathbf{C}_{u_c}(v)$ denote the isocurve on $\mathbf{S}(u,v)$ at $u = u_c$ (see Figure 11.32). The axis $\mathbf{O}(w)$ can be defined in either of two ways. It can be defined as the *offset* of

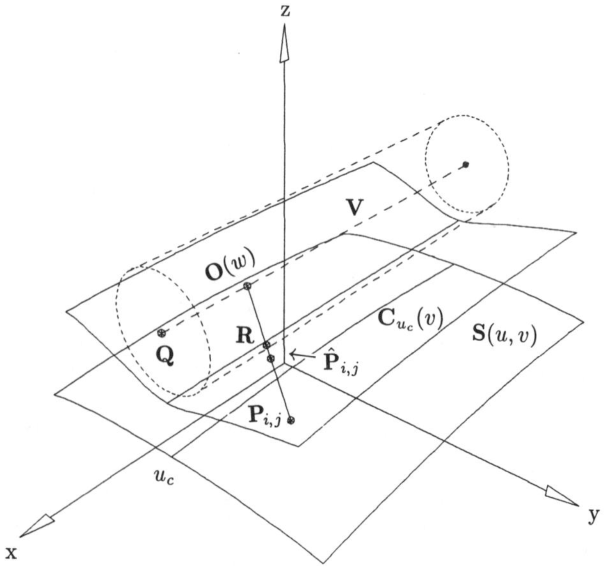

Figure 11.32. Surface bending using a cylinder.

$\mathbf{C}_{u_c}(v)$ along the surface normal, i.e.

$$\mathbf{O}(v) = \mathbf{C}_{u_c}(v) + d\mathbf{N}(u_c, v) \tag{11.62}$$

where $\mathbf{N}(u_c, v)$ is the unit length surface normal vector at (u_c, v) and d is a constant offset distance. We remark that, in general, the shape of $\mathbf{O}(v)$ can be radically different from that of $\mathbf{C}_{u_c}(v)$, and $\mathbf{O}(v)$ cannot be represented precisely as a NURBS curve (e.g., see [Till84; Coqu87b; Hosc88]). However, we assume here that $\mathbf{O}(v)$ is well-behaved and similar in shape to $\mathbf{C}_{u_c}(v)$; for surface bending this is a reasonable assumption. Moreover, we only need to compute selected points on $\mathbf{O}(v)$ (using Eq. [11.62]); we do not require an explicit NURBS representation of $\mathbf{O}(v)$. Finally, we note that in this case the parameter w corresponds to v.

The second method of defining $\mathbf{O}(w)$ is to let it be a straight line lying in the plane defined by $\mathbf{C}_{u_c}(v)$. In this case w does not correspond to v. By computing a least squares plane (defined by the control points of $\mathbf{C}_{u_c}(v)$), this method can be used even for nonplanar $\mathbf{C}_{u_c}(v)$.

$\mathbf{S}(u,v)$ is bent by applying the curve bending method to the $m+1$ rows of control points; i.e., for $j = 0, \ldots, m$, do the following:

1. for $i = s, \ldots, e-p-1$:
   1a. compute $w_{i,j}$ so that $\mathbf{O}(w_{i,j})$ is the point on $\mathbf{O}(w)$ closest to $\mathbf{P}_{i,j}$; if $\mathbf{O}(w) = \mathbf{Q} + w\mathbf{V}$ is a straight line, then $w_{i,j}$ is given by the formula

$$w_{i,j} = \frac{\mathbf{V} \cdot (\mathbf{P}_{i,j} - \mathbf{Q})}{|\mathbf{V}|^2} \tag{11.63}$$

   If $\mathbf{O}(w)$ is the offset of $\mathbf{C}_{u_c}(v)$, the point to curve projection technique of Section (6.1) can be used; the jth v node, t_j, is a good start point for the Newton iterations;

   1b. then set

$$\mathbf{R}_{i,j} = \mathbf{O}(w_{i,j}) + r\frac{\mathbf{P}_{i,j} - \mathbf{O}(w_{i,j})}{|\mathbf{P}_{i,j} - \mathbf{O}(w_{i,j})|} \tag{11.64}$$

   where r is the radius of the general circular cylinder $\mathbf{B}(s,t)$;

   1c. compute $\hat{\mathbf{P}}_{i,j}$ using Eqs. (11.59)–(11.61);

2. rotate and translate $\mathbf{P}_{0,j}, \ldots, \mathbf{P}_{s-1,j}$ and $\mathbf{P}_{e-p,j}, \ldots, \mathbf{P}_{n,j}$ into new positions, by a process similar to that used for curve bending.

Figures 11.33 and 11.34 show examples of cylindrical surface bending. In Figure 11.33 a planar surface is bent using $\lambda = \{1/2, 3/2, -3\}$. Note that a positive λ bends the surface toward the cylinder, whereas a negative one bends it away from the cylinder. Figure 11.34 shows cylindrical bends of the same planar surface using a cylinder touching the surface along the isoparametric curve $\mathbf{C}_{u_c}(v)$. Again, the sign of λ allows the surface to be bent in both directions. It is important to note that although the surface is planar, it is not degree (1×1); the surface in Figure 11.34 has degree (3×2). In general, the surface must have degree at least (2×2) in order to avoid discontinuities after control points are repositioned.

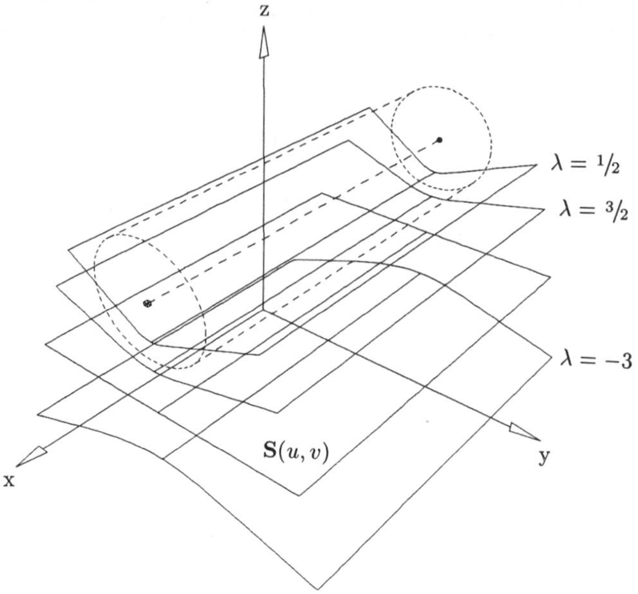

Figure 11.33. Surface bending examples with a nontouching cylinder, $\lambda = \{1/2, 3/2, -3\}$.

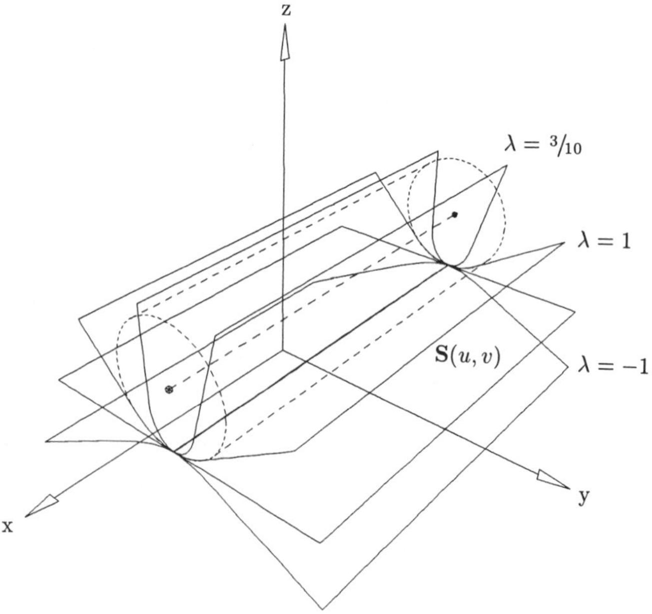

Figure 11.34. Surface bending examples with a touching cylinder, $\lambda = \{3/10, 1, -1\}$.

11.5 Constraint-based Curve and Surface Shaping

Next we present a method of forcing a curve or surface to assume specified derivatives at selected parameter values. The method allows for derivatives of arbitrary order, including zeroth order, hence point constraints are also included. By constraining first and second derivatives, curve/surface tangents and curvature can be controlled. The constraints are satisfied by repositioning control points in a way that minimizes the combined movement of all control points. Either a fully or an underdetermined system of linear equations is solved in a two-step process. This two-step solution allows the constraint-based modifications to be realized at interactive speeds. More material on this topic can be found in [Fowl92, 93].

11.5.1 CONSTRAINT-BASED CURVE MODIFICATION

Let $\mathbf{C}(u) = \sum_{i=0}^{n} R_{i,p}(u)\,\mathbf{P}_i$ be a NURBS curve. Suppose we are given parameter values $\{u_r\}$, $r = 1,\ldots,R$, and a set of derivative constraints, $\{\Delta\mathbf{D}_r^{(k)}\}$. $\Delta\mathbf{D}_r^{(k)}$ denotes the *change* in the kth derivative at $u = u_r$. k can have any nonnegative value, but typically $k = 0, 1, 2$, because these are the values which control the intuitive geometric properties of position, tangent, and curvature. Notice that we specify constraints in terms of *changes* in derivatives, not in terms of the target values.

Now fix k and r, and denote by $\mathbf{D}_r^{(k)}$ the kth derivative of $\mathbf{C}(u)$ at $u = u_r$. Then

$$\mathbf{D}_r^{(k)} = \sum_{i=0}^{n} R_{i,p}^{(k)}(u_r)\,\mathbf{P}_i \tag{11.65}$$

where $R_{i,p}^{(k)}$ denotes the kth derivative of the basis function. If the curve is nonrational, the derivatives of the basis functions are computed using Algorithm A2.3. Otherwise, the $R_{i,p}^{(k)}$ are computed utilizing the same technique that was used in Section 4.3 to obtain the derivatives of a rational curve, that is

$$R_{i,p}(u) = \frac{w(u)R_{i,p}(u)}{w(u)} = \frac{A_i(u)}{w(u)}$$

where

$$w(u) = \sum_{j=0}^{n} w_j N_{j,p}(u)$$

Using Leibnitz' Rule to differentiate $A_i(u)$ yields

$$R_{i,p}^{(k)}(u) = \frac{A_i^{(k)}(u) - \sum_{j=1}^{k}\binom{k}{j} w^{(j)}(u) R_{i,p}^{(k-j)}(u)}{w(u)} \tag{11.66}$$

with

$$A_i^{(k)}(u) = w_i N_{i,p}^{(k)}(u)$$

Applying the constraint $\Delta \mathbf{D}_r^{(k)}$ at $u = u_r$, we obtain the new kth derivative

$$\sum_{i=0}^{n} R_{i,p}^{(k)}(u_r)(\mathbf{P}_i + \Delta \mathbf{P}_i) = \mathbf{D}_r^{(k)} + \Delta \mathbf{D}_r^{(k)} \tag{11.67}$$

and it follows that

$$\sum_{i=0}^{n} R_{i,p}^{(k)}(u_r)\Delta \mathbf{P}_i = \Delta \mathbf{D}_r^{(k)} \tag{11.68}$$

Equation (11.68) is one linear equation in the $n+1$ unknowns $\{\Delta \mathbf{P}_i\}$ (actually $p+1$ unknowns, due to the local support property of B-splines). We remark that $\Delta \mathbf{D}_r^{(k)}$ can be the zero vector, in fact this is how one specifies that a point or derivative is not to change. If M is the total number of constraints, $M \geq R$, then applying Eq. (11.68) to each constraint yields a system of M linear equations in $n+1$ unknowns, that is

$$B\,[\Delta \mathbf{P}_i] = \left[\Delta \mathbf{D}_r^{(k)}\right] \tag{11.69}$$

Before we show how to solve Eq. (11.69), the following remarks are important:

- Equation (11.69) assumes some ordering of the constraints; the ordering can be arbitrary, but a natural method is to sort first on r, then on k. That is, suppose the $\Delta \mathbf{D}_r^{(k)}$ are ordered as $\Delta \mathbf{D}_1, \ldots, \Delta \mathbf{D}_M$, and write $\Delta \mathbf{D}_i = \Delta \mathbf{D}_{r_i}^{(k_i)}$. Then $i < j$ implies $r_i \leq r_j$, and additionally, either $r_i < r_j$ or $k_i < k_j$;

- due to the local support property of B-splines and the fact that constraints are usually applied only at a small number of parameter locations, many columns of B may be zero; that is, there are fewer than $n+1$ unknown $\Delta \mathbf{P}_i$. An efficient algorithm should set up the system Eq. (11.69) to contain only those $\Delta \mathbf{P}_i$ which change; denote by N the actual number of unknown $\Delta \mathbf{P}_i$;

- we require a precise solution to Eq. (11.69); however, the system may be under-, fully, or overdetermined, and it may not have a precise solution. For the solution method presented later, we require an under- ($M < N$) or fully ($M = N$) determined system, in which all rows of B are linearly independent. An overdetermined system ($M > N$) occurs when more constraints are specified than the degree p or the number N of affected control points supports. Clearly, no more than $p+1$ constraints may be specified on each knot span. If necessary, knot insertion and/or degree elevation can be used to ensure that a set of constraints produces an under- or fully determined system. If $M \leq N$, then linear dependence of the rows of B is rarely a problem – see [Scho66; Good81; Fowl93] for mathematical details – but a robust algorithm should check for this during the first step of the solution process;

- generally the designer is not expected to specify the parameters $\{u_r\}$ at which the constraints are applied; theoretically these can also be unknowns, but this gives rise to nonlinear equations. Thus, as usual the system should choose the parameters, based on curve points picked by the designer.

Considering these remarks, we now write Eq. (11.69) as

$$B\,[\,\Delta\mathbf{P}_{i_\ell}\,] = [\,\Delta\mathbf{D}_j\,] \qquad \ell = 1,\ldots,N \quad j = 1,\ldots,M \tag{11.70}$$

or for brevity

$$B\Delta\mathbf{P} = \Delta\mathbf{D} \tag{11.71}$$

For the moment, assume $M < N$. There exist infinitely many solutions to Eq. (11.70). We want the *minimum length solution*, i.e., the one which minimizes the combined movements of all control points (the one which minimizes the length of the N-dimensional vector, $\Delta\mathbf{P}$). From linear algebra, we can write the N vector, $\Delta\mathbf{P}$, in terms of two mutually orthogonal components, one in the row space of B and the other in the null space of B, that is

$$\Delta\mathbf{P} = B^T\lambda + \mathbf{z} \tag{11.72}$$

where λ is some M vector, $B\mathbf{z} = 0$, and $(\lambda^T B)\cdot\mathbf{z} = 0$. It follows that

$$\begin{aligned} |\Delta\mathbf{P}|^2 &= \left(B^T\lambda + \mathbf{z}\right)^T \cdot \left(B^T\lambda + \mathbf{z}\right) \\ &= \left(B^T\lambda\right)^T \cdot \left(B^T\lambda\right) + \mathbf{z}^T\cdot\mathbf{z} \\ &= \left|B^T\lambda\right|^2 + |\mathbf{z}|^2 \end{aligned} \tag{11.73}$$

From Eqs. (11.71) and (11.72) we obtain

$$\begin{aligned} \Delta\mathbf{D} &= B\Delta\mathbf{P} \\ &= B\left(B^T\lambda + \mathbf{z}\right) \\ &= BB^T\lambda + B\mathbf{z} \\ &= BB^T\lambda \end{aligned} \tag{11.74}$$

and therefore

$$\lambda = (BB^T)^{-1}\Delta\mathbf{D} \tag{11.75}$$

Since the components of $\mathbf{z}$ are irrelevant to the system, yet they contribute to the length of $\Delta\mathbf{P}$ (by Eq. [11.73]), we obtain the minimum-length solution to Eq. (11.70) by setting $\mathbf{z} = 0$. Substituting Eq. (11.75) into (11.72) leads to

$$\Delta\mathbf{P} = A\Delta\mathbf{D} \qquad \text{where } A = B^T(BB^T)^{-1} \tag{11.76}$$

The matrix BB^T is nonsingular if the rows of B are linearly independent. Finally, if $M = N$ there is a unique solution to Eq. (11.70) given by

$$\Delta\mathbf{P} = A\Delta\mathbf{D} \qquad \text{where } A = B^{-1} \tag{11.77}$$

We remark that it is also possible (and quite useful) to restrict certain control points from changing. This is accomplished (mathematically) simply by setting the corresponding column of B to zero. Algorithmically, this means that the corresponding $\Delta\mathbf{P}_{i_\ell}$ does not appear in Eq. (11.70), and N is reduced by 1. Normally, a constraint affects $p+1$ control points, and up to $p+1$ constraints can be specified in any span. If a control point is restricted not to move, then this reduces to p the number of constraints that can be specified in any span influenced by this control point. We give examples of this below.

Equation (11.76) (or Eq. [11.77]) represents the first step in the solution process. Before proceeding to the second step, we summarize the sequence of events which brought us to this point:

1. the designer picks points on the curve, yielding parameters $\{u_r\}$ (determined by the system) at which constraints are to be imposed; he simultaneously indicates what types of constraints are to be imposed at each parameter, but actual constraints need not be specified at this stage;
2. the system sets up Eq. (11.70); if it is overdetermined, the system either informs the designer so that he can modify his selections, or it adds control points by means of knot insertion and/or degree elevation in such a way that the resulting equation system is under- or fully determined;
3. the matrix A is then computed, either by Eq. (11.76) or (11.77).

The designer can now interactively specify constraints $[\Delta\mathbf{D}_j]$. With each change in constraints, the matrix A must be multiplied with the new vector $[\Delta\mathbf{D}_j]$ to yield the changes in control point locations, $[\Delta\mathbf{P}_{i_\ell}]$. The relevant control points are then updated by

$$\hat{\mathbf{P}}_{i_\ell} = \mathbf{P}_{i_\ell} + \Delta\mathbf{P}_{i_\ell} \qquad \ell = 1,\ldots,N \tag{11.78}$$

Example

Ex11.1 Figure 11.35a shows a cubic curve defined by $\mathbf{P}_0,\ldots,\mathbf{P}_7$, and $U = \{0,0,0,0,1/5,2/5,3/5,4/5,1,1,1,1\}$. We apply one point constraint at $u = 1/2$

$$\Delta\mathbf{D}_1 = \Delta\mathbf{D}_1^{(0)} = (0.04,-0.08,0)$$

Then

$$B\Delta\mathbf{P} = [\Delta\mathbf{D}_1]$$

where B is the 1×4 matrix

$$B = \left[R_{2,3}\left(\frac{1}{2}\right), R_{3,3}\left(\frac{1}{2}\right), R_{4,3}\left(\frac{1}{2}\right), R_{5,3}\left(\frac{1}{2}\right)\right]$$

and $\Delta\mathbf{P}$ is the 4×1 column vector with components

$$\Delta\mathbf{P}_2, \Delta\mathbf{P}_3, \Delta\mathbf{P}_4, \Delta\mathbf{P}_5$$

Hence, BB^T is a 1×1 matrix, and $A = B^T(BB^T)^{-1}$ is a 4×1 matrix

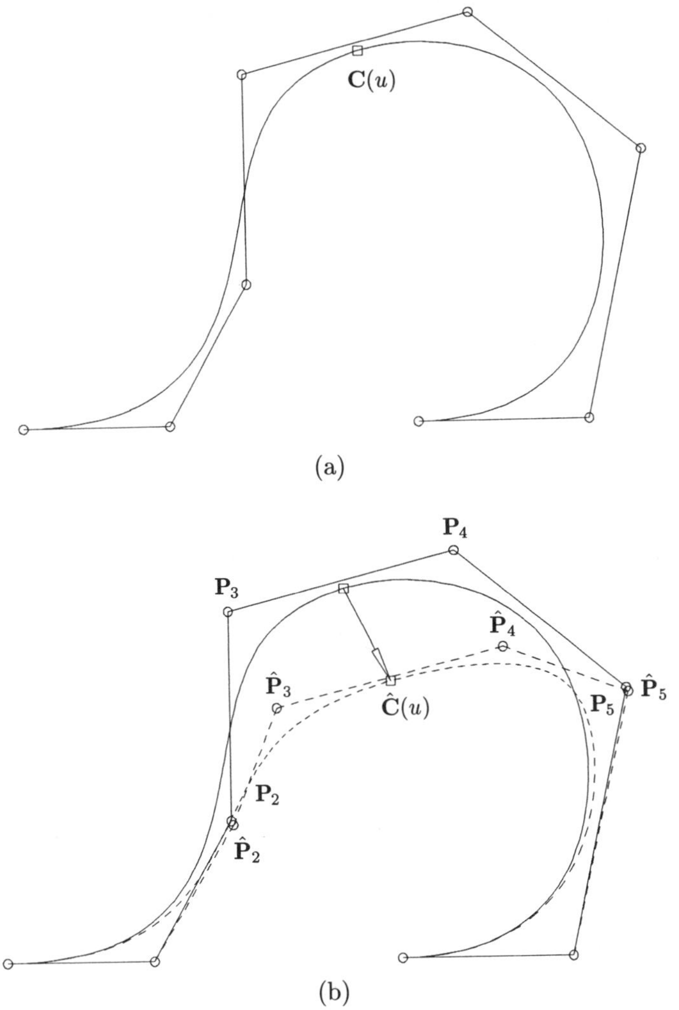

Figure 11.35. Constraint-based curve modification using positional constraints. (a) The original cubic curve with point to move; (b) all four local control points are allowed to move; (c) only $\mathbf{P}_3$ and $\mathbf{P}_4$ are allowed to move; (d) only $\mathbf{P}_3$ is allowed to move.

with components

$$a_0, a_1, a_2, a_3$$

It follows that

$$\Delta\mathbf{P}_i = a_{i-2}\,\Delta\mathbf{D}_1 \qquad i = 2,3,4,5$$

The result of applying the $\Delta\mathbf{P}_i$ is shown in Figure 11.35b. Note that $\mathbf{P}_3$ and $\mathbf{P}_4$ move the most, because these control points have the greatest

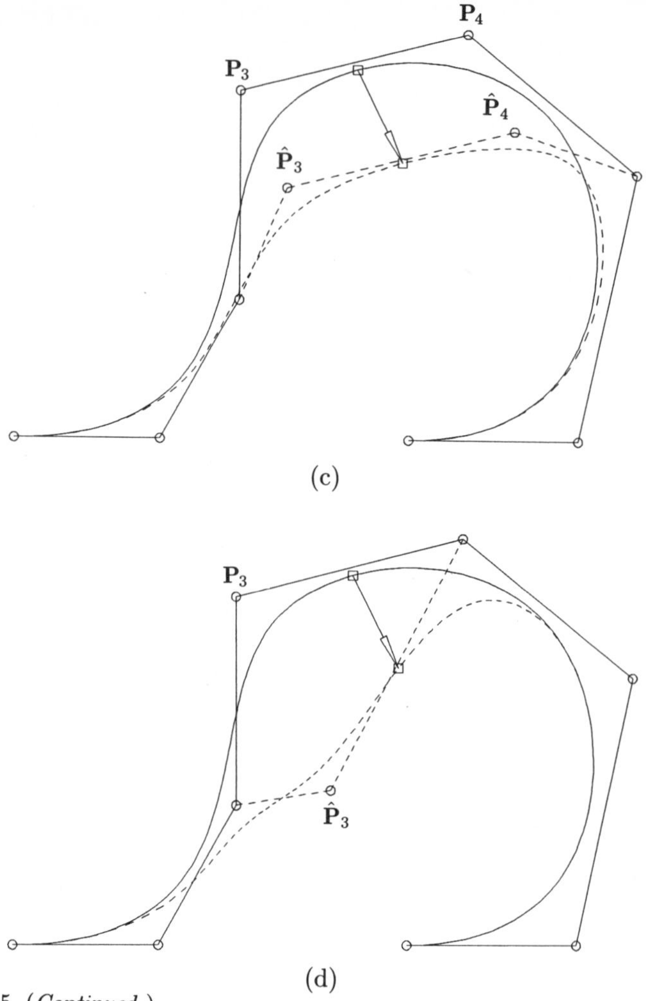

Figure 11.35. (*Continued.*)

effect on the curve at $u = 1/2$. We can restrict $\mathbf{P}_2$ and $\mathbf{P}_5$ from moving. Then B is the 1×2 matrix

$$B = \left[R_{3,3}\left(\frac{1}{2}\right), R_{4,3}\left(\frac{1}{2}\right) \right]$$

and $\Delta \mathbf{P}$ has components $\Delta \mathbf{P}_3$ and $\Delta \mathbf{P}_4$. A has components a_0 and a_1 (not the same as a_0, a_1 above), and

$$\Delta \mathbf{P}_i = a_{i-3} \Delta \mathbf{D}_1 \qquad i = 3, 4$$

Figure 11.35c shows the result of allowing only $\mathbf{P}_3$ and $\mathbf{P}_4$ to change, and Figure 11.35d illustrates the case in which only $\mathbf{P}_3$ is allowed to move.

This example clearly shows that for a given set of point and derivative constraints there is often flexibility in specifying how many and which control points should change, and this choice affects both the extent and the appearance (e.g., symmetry) of the corresponding curve change. However, dealing with control points can be less intuitive to a designer than imposing pure point and derivative constraints on a curve. A good user interface should package both a reasonable set of defaults and convenient handles for the more sophisticated designer to restrict control point movement. Finally, notice that any control point restrictions must be worked into Eq. (11.70) and into the first stage of the solution process.

In Figures 11.36a–11.36c point and derivative constraints are illustrated. Figure 11.36a shows the application of a derivative constraint only, while allowing $\mathbf{P}_3$, $\mathbf{P}_4$, and $\mathbf{P}_5$ to move. The magnitude of the first derivative vector is increased at $u = 0.556$, resulting in a local tension effect. It is interesting to observe what happens if only one control point is allowed to move, as shown in Figure 11.36b. The curve assumes the new derivative, but it suffers a positional displacement due to the absence of a positional constraint. In Figure 11.36c this problem is remedied by constraining the curve not to move at $u = 0.556$, and to assume a new derivative obtained by decreasing the magnitude of the old one. Two control points are allowed to move in order to obtain a system of equations which is not overdetermined.

In closing, we remark that Fowler and Bartels [Fowl93] give a different (but equivalent) method to represent matrix A in Eqs. (11.76) and (11.77). It is somewhat more complicated mathematically but is more efficient in some cases.

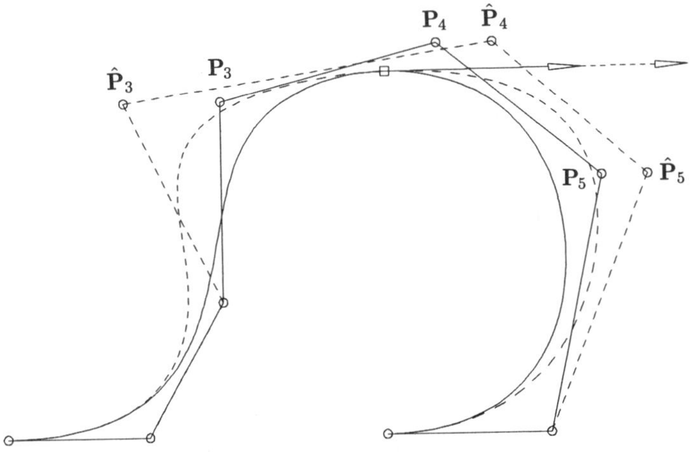

(a)

Figure 11.36. Constraint-based curve modification using positional and derivative constraints. (a) Derivative constraints are applied and $\mathbf{P}_3, \mathbf{P}_4$, and $\mathbf{P}_5$ are allowed to move; (b) derivative constraints are applied and only $\mathbf{P}_4$ is allowed to move; (c) derivative and positional constraints are applied, and $\mathbf{P}_3$ and $\mathbf{P}_4$ are allowed to move.

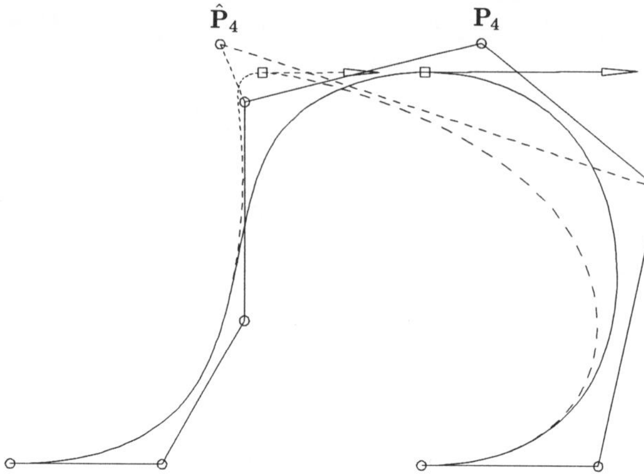

(b)

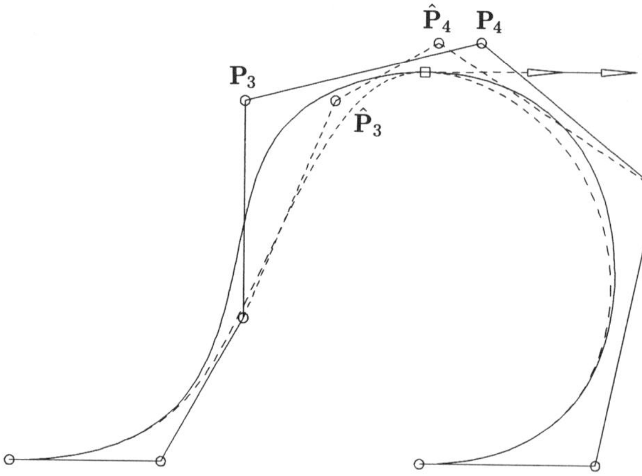

(c)

Figure 11.36. (*Continued.*)

11.5.2 CONSTRAINT-BASED SURFACE MODIFICATION

Let $\mathbf{S}(u,v) = \sum_{i=0}^{n} \sum_{j=0}^{m} R_{i,p;j,q}(u,v)\,\mathbf{P}_{i,j}$ be a (p,q)th degree NURBS surface. In this section we choose to write $\mathbf{S}(u,v)$ in the form

$$\mathbf{S}(u,v) = \sum_{s=0}^{(n+1)(m+1)-1} R_s(u,v)\,\mathbf{P}_s \tag{11.79}$$

where

$$s = j(n+1) + i \tag{11.80}$$

We call s the *absolute address* corresponding to (i,j). Notice that

$$\mathbf{P}_s = \mathbf{P}_{i,j} \qquad R_s(u,v) = R_{i,p;j,q}(u,v) \tag{11.81}$$

where

$$i = s \bmod n+1 \qquad j = \frac{s}{n+1} \tag{11.82}$$

If $\mathbf{S}(u,v)$ is nonrational, then $R_s(u,v) = N_{i,p}(u)N_{j,q}(v)$, where i and j are defined by Eq. (11.82). Now suppose we are given a set of point and partial derivative constraints, $\left\{\Delta\mathbf{D}_r^{(k,\ell)}\right\}$, $k,\ell \geq 0$, specified at the parameter locations $\{(u,v)_r\}$, $r = 1,\ldots,R$. Then for each r we have

$$\sum_{s=0}^{(n+1)(m+1)-1} R_s^{(k,\ell)}\big((u,v)_r\big)\Delta\mathbf{P}_s = \Delta\mathbf{D}_r^{(k,\ell)} \tag{11.83}$$

The partial derivatives $R_s^{(k,\ell)}\big((u,v)_r\big)$ can be computed in exactly the same way as the $\mathbf{S}^{(k,\ell)}(u,v)$ described in Section 4.5. Then, as was the case for curves, we can set up the $M \times N$ system of linear equations

$$B\left[\Delta\mathbf{P}_{s_\alpha}\right] = \left[\Delta\mathbf{D}_r^{(k,\ell)}\right] \qquad \alpha = 1,\ldots,N \tag{11.84}$$

M is the number of constraints ($M \geq R$), and N is the number of control points which are free to move. In general, a constraint involves $(p+1)\times(q+1)$ control points, but a control point can be held fixed simply by not including it in Eq. (11.84). Equation (11.84) can be under-, fully, or overdetermined. If overdetermined, then knot insertion and/or degree elevation can be used to obtain an under- or fully determined system.

Equation (11.84) is solved in precisely the same manner as for curves, i.e.

$$\left[\Delta\mathbf{P}_{s_\alpha}\right] = A\left[\Delta\mathbf{D}_r^{(k,\ell)}\right] \tag{11.85}$$

where

$$A = B^T(BB^T)^{-1} \tag{11.86}$$

(or $A = B^{-1}$ if Eq. [11.84] is fully determined). This yields a minimum combined movement of control points. The final step is

$$\hat{\mathbf{P}}_{s_\alpha} = \mathbf{P}_{s_\alpha} + \Delta\mathbf{P}_{s_\alpha} \qquad \alpha = 1,\ldots,N \tag{11.87}$$

Although the mathematics for curve and surface constraint-based modifications is virtually the same, the software required to set up the matrix A is more complicated for surfaces. Algorithm `A11.1` illustrates one possible solution. In addition to data defining the surface, a list (`CList`) of structures is input. The list contains R nodes; each node contains a parameter pair $(u,v)_r$ and a list of the types of constraints to be applied at that point (actual constraints are not input). Output consists of:

- `M` : the number of constraints (and columns of `A`);
- `N` : the number of control points which change (and rows of `A`);
- `A[][]` : the matrix A;
- `CpInd[]` : the absolute addresses, s_α, of the control points which change.

Furthermore, one of the following integer values is returned:

- 0 : no error;
- 1 : the system is overdetermined;
- 2 : the matrix is singular (rows of B are not linearly independent).

In order to build `A` and `CpInd`, three local two-dimensional arrays, `B[M][Nmax]`, `FreeCp[p+1][q+1]`, and `Map[n+1][m+1]`, and one four-dimensional array, `Funs`, and two new routines, `FreeCtrlPts(u,v,FreeCp)` and `RatDersBasisFuns(u,v,Funs)`, are used. `B` contains the matrix B of Eq. (11.84). `Map[i][j]`$= -1$ if $\mathbf{P}_{i,j}$ is not a part of the system defined by Eq. (11.84); otherwise, `Map[i][j]`$= \alpha \geq 0$ is an index for `CpInd`, and `CpInd[`α`]`$= s$ is the absolute address corresponding to (i, j). For a given (u, v), `FreeCtrlPts()` returns the Boolean array `FreeCp` that indicates which of the possible $(p + 1) \times (q + 1)$ control points influencing the surface at (u, v) are free to move. This routine can be implemented in a number of meaningful ways, thus we refrain from elaborating on it here. The routine `RatDersBasisFuns(u,v,Funs)` returns the basis functions and their partial derivatives. `Funs[k][l][i][j]` is the (k, ℓ)th partial derivative of the (i, j)th basis function.

```
ALGORITHM A11.1
ConstBasedSurfMod1(n,m,p,q,U,V,Pw,CList,R,M,N,A,CpInd)
  { /* Build the A matrix for surface constraints */
    /* Input: n,m,p,q,U,V,Pw,CList,R */
    /* Output: M,N,A,CpInd */
  Loop through the list CList and count constraints
    to obtain M.
  Nmax = Max((n+1)*(m+1),R*(p+1)*(q+1)); /* Max possible N */
  for (i=0; i<M; i++)
    for (j=0; j<Nmax; j++)    B[i][j] = 0.0;
  for (i=0; i<=n; i++)
    for (j=0; j<=m; j++)   Map[i][j] = -1;
  brow = 0;    N = 0;    /* N is computed in this loop */
  for (r=1; r<=R; r++)
    {
    Extract (u,v) value from the rth list node.
    FreeCtrlPts(u,v,FreeCp);
    uspan = FindSpan(n,p,u,U);
    vspan = FindSpan(m,q,v,V);
    for (i=0; i<=p; i++)
```

```
          for (j=0; j<=q; j++)
            if (FreeCp[i][j])
              { /* This ctrl pt is free to move */
              iup = i+uspan-p;    jvq = j+vspan-q;
              if (Map[iup][jvq] == -1)
                { /* Ctrl pt not yet in Eq. system */
                Map[iup][jvq] = N;
                CpInd[N] = jvq*(n+1)+iup;
                N = N+1;
                }
              }
        /* Compute required functions */
        RatDersBasisFuns(u,v,Funs);
        Loop through each type of constraint for this (u,v) and do:
          {
          Set k and ℓ indicating which derivative.
          for (i=0; i<=p; i++)
            for (j=0; j<=q; j++)
              {
              alf = Map[i+uspan-p][j+vspan-q];
              if (alf >= 0)  B[brow][alf] = Funs[k][l][i][j];
              }
          brow = brow+1;
          } /* End of loop through each type of constraint */
      } /* End of for-loop: r=1,...,R */
    if (M > N)  return(1);    /* system overdetermined */
    if (M == N)
      if (B singular)   return(2);
        else
          {
          A = B^-1;    return(0);
          }
    if (BB^T singular)   return(2);
      else
        {
        A = B^T(BB^T)^-1;    return(0);
        }
    }
```

Figures 11.37–11.39 show examples of applying surface constraints. In Figures 11.37a and 11.37b a point constraint is applied at $u = v = 1/2$, allowing all control points affecting the surface at this point to move. Figure 11.37a shows the new control net, and Figure 11.37b illustrates the change in surface shape. Note that the control points around the periphery of the local domain move very little. Figures 11.38a and 11.38b show what happens if only $\mathbf{P}_{1,2}$, $\mathbf{P}_{2,2}$, and $\mathbf{P}_{4,2}$ are

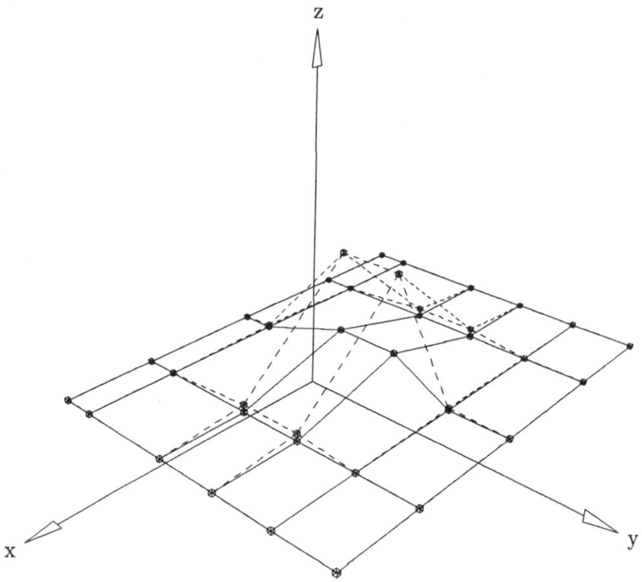

(a)

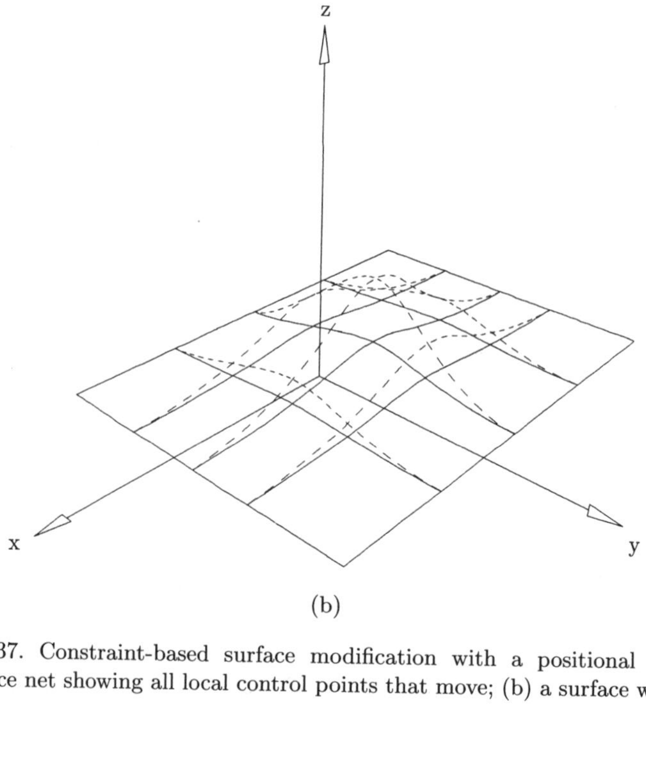

(b)

Figure 11.37. Constraint-based surface modification with a positional constraint. (a) A surface net showing all local control points that move; (b) a surface with change in shape.

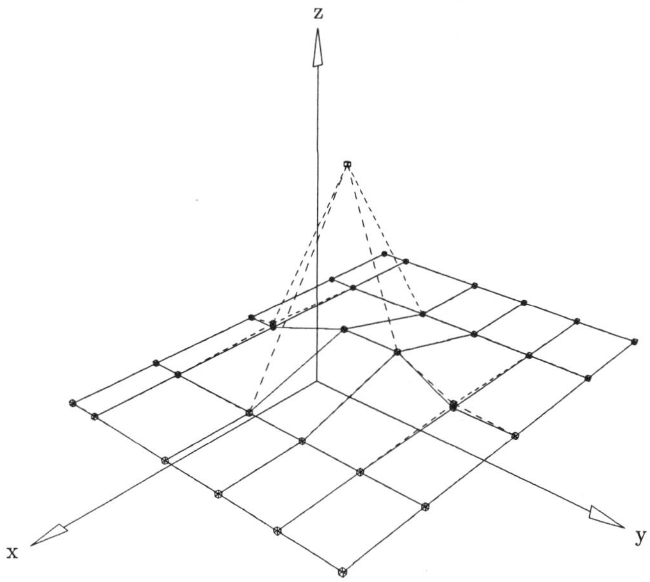

(a)

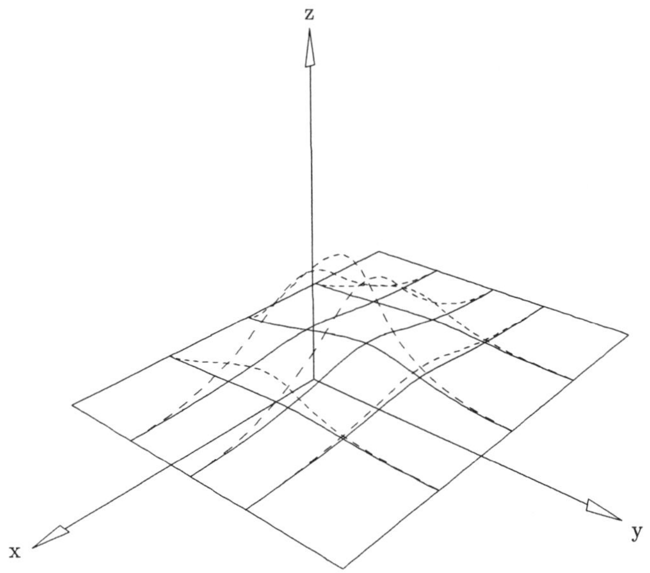

(b)

Figure 11.38. Constraint-based surface modification with a positional constraint. (a) A surface net showing that only $\mathbf{P}_{1,2}, \mathbf{P}_{2,2}$, and $\mathbf{P}_{4,2}$ are allowed to move; (b) a surface with change in shape.

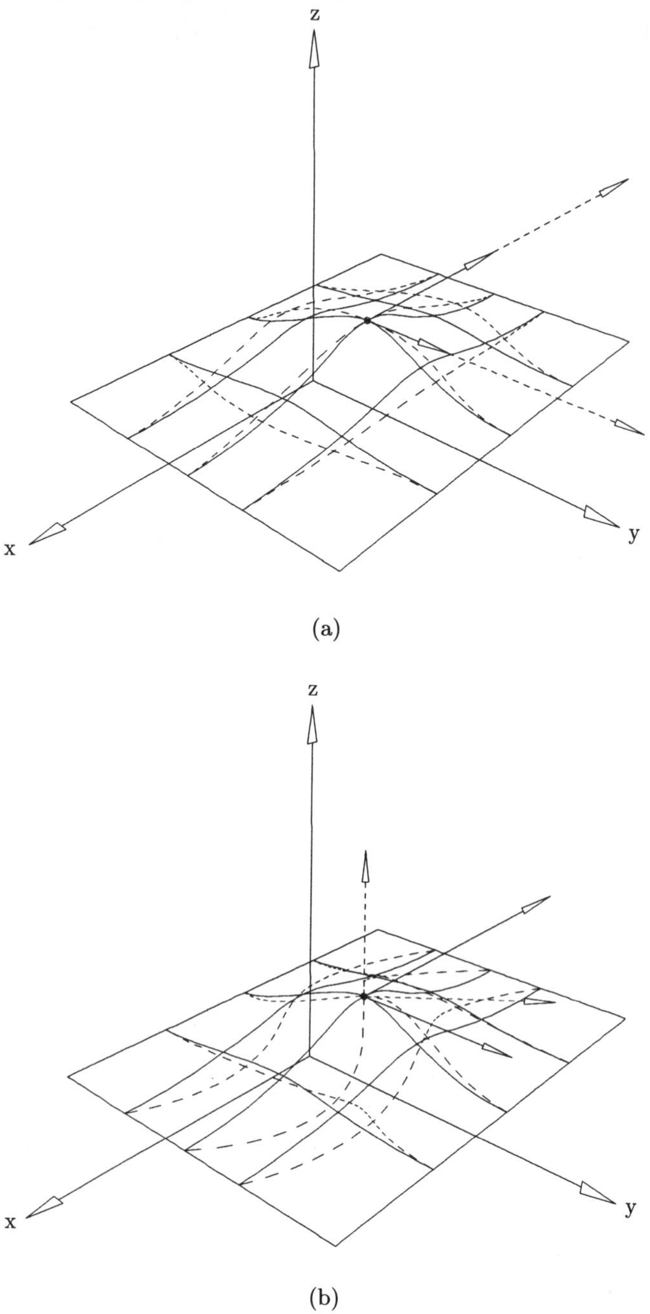

Figure 11.39. Constraint-based surface modification with positional and derivative constraints. (a) An increase in partial derivative magnitudes induces a local tension effect; (b) a change in partial derivative directions induces a local twist effect.

allowed to move. Finally, in Figures 11.39a and 11.39b partial derivative and positional constraints are applied. In Figure 11.39a the magnitudes of the partials are increased, resulting in a tension effect, whereas in Figure 11.39b the partials are rotated about the point $\mathbf{S}(1/2, 1/2)$, yielding a twist in the surface shape.

In closing, we remark that Fowler [Fowl92] gives an alternative (equivalent) solution for solving for the $\Delta\mathbf{P}_{i,j}$, which makes use of the tensor product structure of $\mathbf{S}(u,v)$. It is less general than this method, but in some cases it is more efficient.

CHAPTER

TWELVE

Standards and Data Exchange

12.1 Introduction

The central theme of this chapter is the relationship of NURBS geometry, as practiced in this book, to other methods of representing curves and surfaces, and to several important standard formats for the exchange of geometric data between two systems. We have used a specific form of knot vector throughout this book; Section 12.2 discusses another type of knot vector and the conversion between the two types. Section 12.3 describes how NURBS curves and surfaces are defined within the three standards: IGES, STEP, and PHIGS. We remark that our NURBS are compatible with the NURBS of these standards (with the exception that IGES and PHIGS allow discontinuous curves and surfaces). Finally, Section 12.4 gives some general guidelines for exchanging geometric data between a NURBS system and another system.

12.2 Knot Vectors

Knot vectors can be put into two groups, *clamped* and *unclamped*; and within each group there are *uniform* and *nonuniform* knot vectors. Some examples are:

clamped, uniform:

$$\{0,0,0,0,1,2,3,4,4,4,4\}$$

$$\{-0.5,-0.5,-0.5,1,2.5,4,4,4\}$$

clamped, nonuniform:

$$\{0,0,0,2,3,6,7,7,7\}$$

$$\{0,0,0,0,1,2,2,3,4,5,5,5,5\}$$

unclamped, uniform:

$$U_1 = \{-3, -2, -1, 0, 1, 2, 3, 4, 5\}$$

$$U_2 = \{0, 1, 2, 3, 4, 5, 6, 7, 8, 9, 10, 11\}$$

unclamped, nonuniform:

$$\{0, 0, 1, 2, 3, 4\}$$

$$\{-2, -1, 0, 4, 5, 6, 7\}$$

Hence clamped/unclamped refers to whether or not the first and last knot values are repeated with multiplicity equal to degree plus one, and uniform/nonuniform refers to the knot spacing. To be uniform and unclamped, all knot spans must be of equal length. To be uniform and clamped, only the "internal" knot spans must be of equal length. The reader has probably noticed that what we are now calling clamped, uniform and nonuniform, is exactly that which we have called *nonperiodic*, uniform and nonuniform, up to now. Following a brief study of unclamped knot vectors, we will offer a flimsy excuse for this changing of the terminology horse in the middle of the knot stream. Since clamped knot vectors are assumed throughout the book, they require no further elaboration here. However, before proceeding to a study of unclamped knot vectors we offer the following reminders relative to clamped knot vectors:

- if we are given a clamped knot vector with $m+1$ knots and end multiplicities of $p+1$, then we require $n+1$ $(= m-p)$ control points to define a pth degree curve; that is, the knot vector determines the degree, number of control points, and the valid parameter range;
- clamped curves can be open or closed, geometrically; if a curve is closed, then whether or not it is closed with C^k continuity depends on the first k and last k internal knot spans, and the first $k+1$ and last $k+1$ weights and control points.

Now consider the unclamped, uniform knot vector, U_1. Using the Cox-deBoor algorithm, Eq. (2.5), we can compute $8-p$ degree p basis functions, for $p = 0, \ldots, 7$. The degree 2 and 3 basis functions, along with a quadratic and cubic curve, are shown in Figures 12.1a and 12.1b. The knot locations are marked on the curves. Notice that the curves are not clamped at the ends, i.e., their start and end points do not coincide with control points. Furthermore, evaluation of the curves at $u \in [u_i, u_{i+1})$ requires the functions $N_{i-p,p}(u), \ldots, N_{i,p}(u)$; thus, the curves are defined only on the parameter range $u \in [u_p, u_{m-p}]$, as is the case for clamped curves. Thus, the quadratic curve of Figure 12.1a is defined on $u \in [-1, 3]$, and the cubic curve of Figure 12.1b is defined on $u \in [0, 2]$. Figure 12.2 shows how to define a closed, cubic curve using the unclamped, uniform knot vector, U_2. Since $m = 11$ and $p = 3$, we require eight control points $(n = 7)$. We wrap around p $(= 3)$ control points at the end; i.e., $\mathbf{P}_5 = \mathbf{P}_0$, $\mathbf{P}_6 = \mathbf{P}_1$ and $\mathbf{P}_7 = \mathbf{P}_2$. The valid parameter range is $u \in [3, 8]$. This yields curve closure, with C^2 continuity.

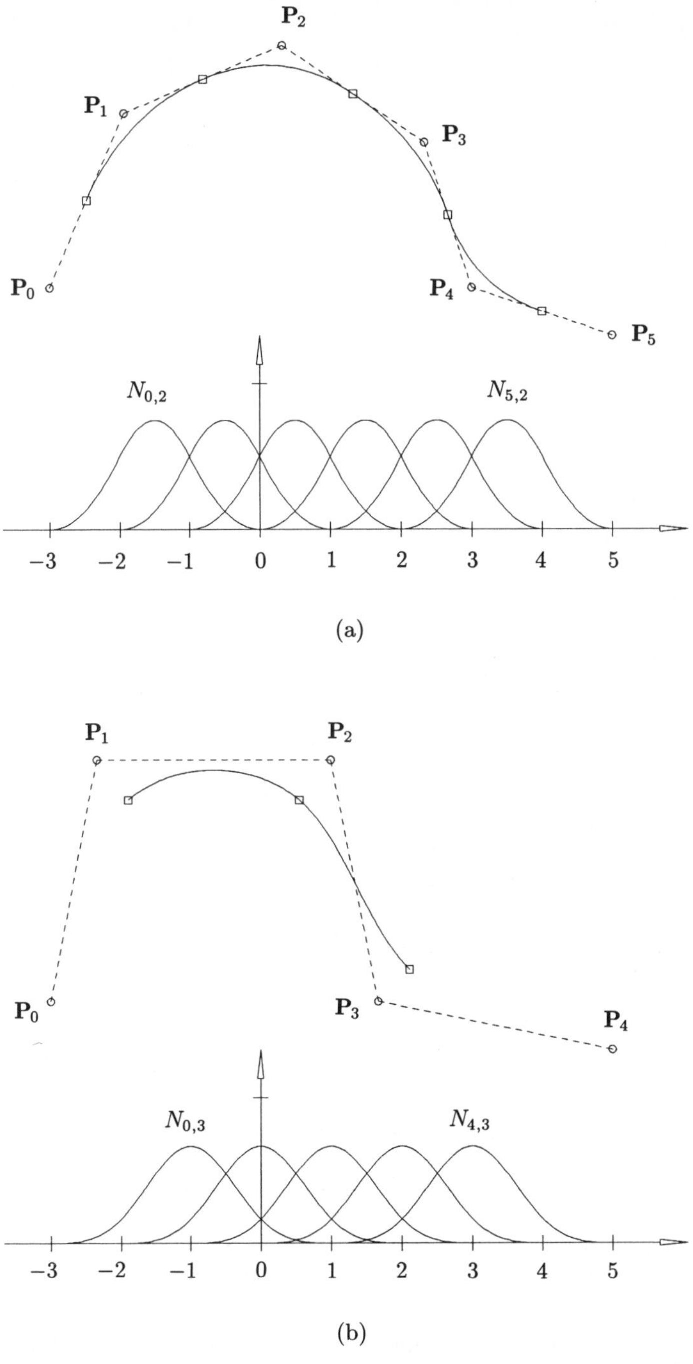

Figure 12.1. Unclamped NURBS curves. (a) Quadratic curve; (b) cubic curve.

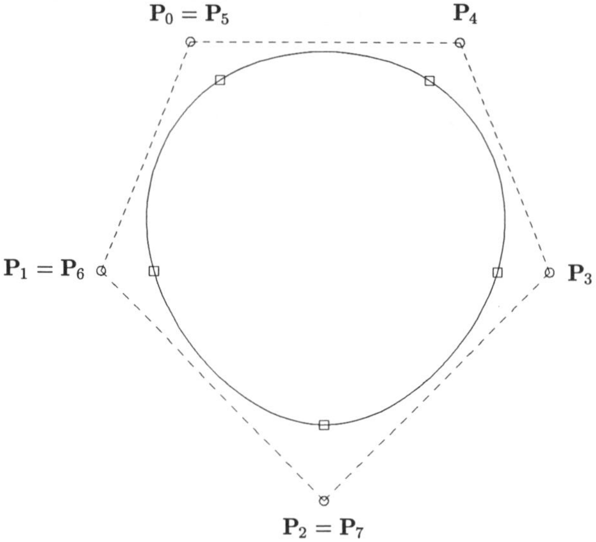

Figure 12.2. Closed C^2 continuous unclamped cubic curve.

Everything stated previously for unclamped, uniform curves also holds for unclamped, nonuniform curves, with the exception of C^{p-1} continuity at the start/end of a closed curve. Since continuity depends on knot values as well as on control point locations, C^{p-1} continuity of a closed, nonuniform curve does not necessarily imply precise wraparound of the control points. Figure 12.3a shows a closed, cubic curve defined on the clamped, uniform knot vector

$$U = \{3,3,3,3,4,5,6,7,8,8,8,8\}$$

The curve is C^2 continuous at the start/end point. Figures 12.3b and 12.3c show unclamped versions of (precisely) the same curve; the curve in Figure 12.3b uses the knots

$$U = \{0,0.5,2.3,3,4,5,6,7,8,8.7,10.5,11\}$$

and the curve in Figure 12.3c uses the knots

$$U = \{0,1,2,3,4,5,6,7,8,9,10,11\}$$

It is important to point out here that, algorithmically, there is little difference between clamped and unclamped curves. With only slight modifications, all the fundamental algorithms given in the first five chapters of this book can also be made to work for unclamped curves.

In the early days of B-splines in CAD/CAM (before the early 1980s), very little serious work was done using nonuniform knot vectors, clamped or unclamped. Although terminology has always been confusing in this area, early CAD/CAM workers commonly referred to B-splines as either *nonperiodic* or *periodic*;

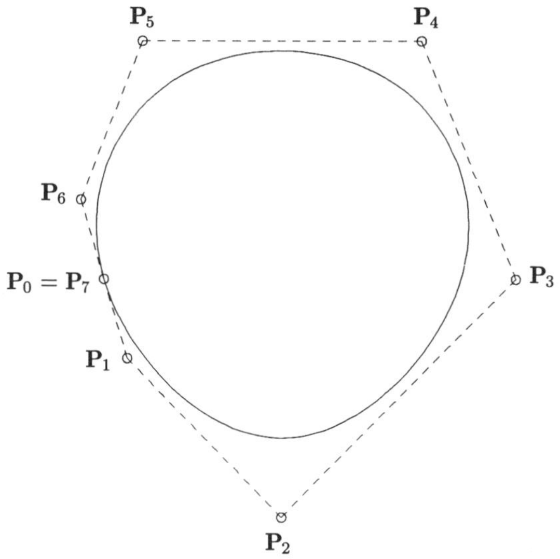

(a)

Figure 12.3. Examples of unclamping a closed curve with different knot vectors. (a) Closed clamped curve; (b) unclamping with no wraparound; (c) unclamping with wraparound.

nonperiodic was synonymous with clamped (as it is in this book), and these were used to define open curves and surfaces (uniform at first, and nonuniform later). Periodic was mathematically equivalent to unclamped, uniform, and these were used to construct C^{p-1} continuous closed curves and surfaces. Referring to Figures 12.1a and 12.1b, one sees that the unclamped, uniform basis functions are all translates of one another, hence they are often called periodic. For periodic B-splines there was no need to store a knot vector, the Cox-deBoor algorithm was not required, and control point wraparound was not necessary to obtain C^{p-1} continuous closed curves. A simple matrix formulation of the (one) basis function, together with a special control point indexing scheme, were sufficient to evaluate periodic B-spline curves (see [Mort85] for a detailed discussion). Although more efficient, this special treatment of periodic B-splines has all but disappeared from practice, probably due to the fact that the time required for software development and maintenance has become much more expensive than CPU time. Clamped and unclamped are newer terms which will probably grow in use, simply because they are more intuitive and accurate. Although one sees these terms rather infrequently in the literature, they seem to be quite prevalent in the CAD/CAM community. We use the term nonperiodic in this book simply because we have not yet managed to break the habit.

Many systems today use only clamped B-splines. However, both IGES and STEP provide for the exchange of unclamped B-splines. Precise conversions are

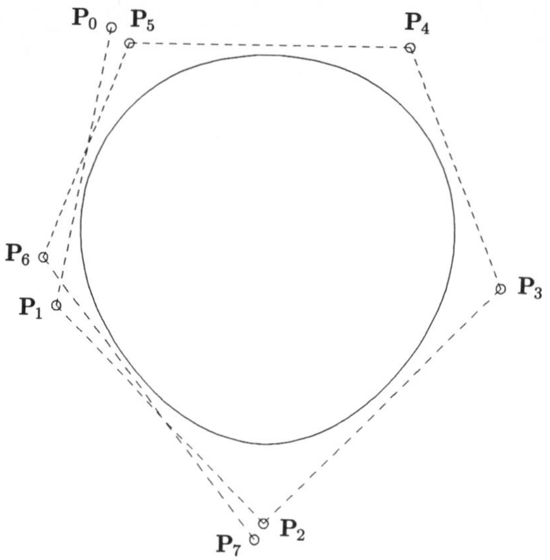

(b)

Figure 12.3. (*Continued.*)

possible both ways. Clamping a curve is nothing more than inserting the knots u_p and u_{m-p} until they have multiplicity p, and then discarding the knots and control points lying outside the clamped region. The knot insertion formula, Eq. (5.15), is also valid for unclamped curves, as long as one does not index knots outside the range 0 to m (which does not happen when clamping at u_p and u_{m-p}). We recommend (but leave as an exercise) that the reader write a routine to extract the subcurve between arbitrary parameters, u_1 and u_2, where $u_1 < u_2$. Such a routine not only handles clamping but also has many other uses, including one which we mention in the next section.

Unclamping is essentially knot removal. Although unclamping is rarely required (yes, there are systems which only handle unclamped B-splines), we present here Algorithm `A12.1`, which computes the $p-1$ new control points at each end and p new knots at each end, all in place. We remind the reader that the result is not unique (see Figures 12.3b and 12.3c). One is free to choose the $2p$ new end knots rather arbitrarily, and the new control point locations depend on the knots. We choose the new knots as follows

$$u_{p-i-1} = u_{p-i} - (u_{n-i+1} - u_{n-i}) \qquad i = 0, \ldots, p-1 \qquad (12.1)$$

and

$$u_{n+i+2} = u_{n+i+1} + (u_{p+i+1} - u_{p+i}) \qquad i = 0, \ldots, p-1 \qquad (12.2)$$

This choice of knots produces wraparound of the control points, as in Figures 12.2 and 12.3c, in case the clamped curve is closed with C^{p-1} continuity. The algorithm is:

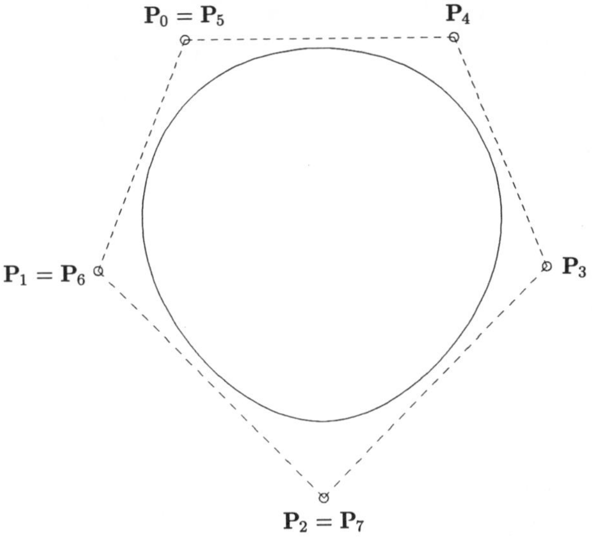

(c)

Figure 12.3. (*Continued.*)

```
ALGORITHM A12.1
  UnclampCurve(n,p,U,Pw)
    { /* Unclamp a clamped curve */
      /* Input:  n,p,U,Pw */
      /* Output: U,Pw */
    for (i=0; i<=p-2; i++)   /* Unclamp at left end */
      {
      U[p-i-1] = U[p-i] - (U[n-i+1]-U[n-i]);
      k = p-1;
      for (j=i; j>=0; j--)
        {
        alfa = (U[p]-U[k])/(U[p+j+1]-U[k]);
        Pw[j] = (Pw[j]-alfa*Pw[j+1])/(1.0-alfa);
        k = k-1;
        }
      }
    U[0] = U[1] - (U[n-p+2]-U[n-p+1]);   /* Set first knot */
    for (i=0; i<=p-2; i++)   /* Unclamp at right end */
      {
      U[n+i+2] = U[n+i+1] + (U[p+i+1]-U[p+i]);
      for (j=i; j>=0; j--)
        {
```

```
            alfa = (U[n+1]-U[n-j])/(U[n-j+i+2]-U[n-j]);
            Pw[n-j] = (Pw[n-j]-(1.0-alfa)*Pw[n-j-1])/alfa;
            }
        }
    U[n+p+1] = U[n+p] + (U[2*p]-U[2*p-1]);    /* Set last knot */
    }
```

Figures 12.4a–12.4d show the steps in unclamping the left end of a degree 4 curve. Figures 12.4b–12.4d correspond to the completion of the ith step, $i = 0, 1, 2$, respectively. Figure 12.5a shows the quadratic full circle, with knots

$$U = \left\{0, 0, 0, \frac{1}{4}, \frac{1}{4}, \frac{1}{2}, \frac{1}{2}, \frac{3}{4}, \frac{3}{4}, 1, 1, 1\right\}$$

(see Example Ex7.2). The nine control points are marked. Figure 12.5b illustrates the circle after unclamping by Algorithm A12.1. Notice that the control polygon does not wrap around, in the sense that none of the control points coincide. This is because the circle is only C^0 continuous in homogeneous space. The knot vector after unclamping is

$$U = \left\{-\frac{1}{4}, -\frac{1}{4}, 0, \frac{1}{4}, \frac{1}{4}, \frac{1}{2}, \frac{1}{2}, \frac{3}{4}, \frac{3}{4}, 1, \frac{5}{4}, \frac{5}{4}\right\}$$

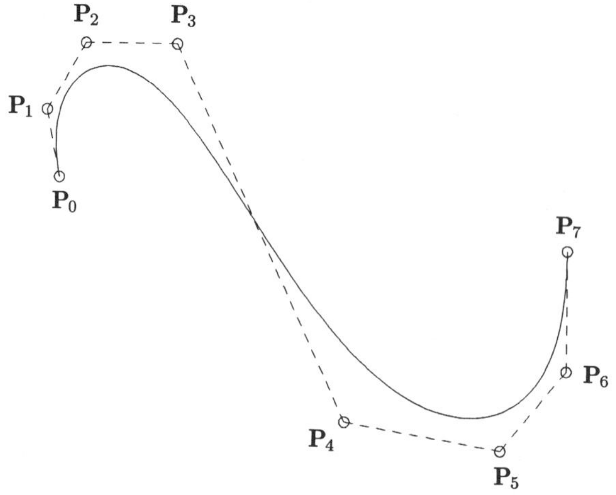

(a)

Figure 12.4. The process of unclamping a quartic curve at its left end. (a) Original clamped curve; (b) $i = 0; \rightarrow \mathbf{P}_0^0$ computed; (c) $i = 1; \rightarrow \mathbf{P}_0^1$ and $\mathbf{P}_1^1$ computed; (d) $i = 2; \rightarrow \mathbf{P}_0^2, \mathbf{P}_1^2$, and $\mathbf{P}_2^2$ computed.

Clearly, the extension of these results to surfaces is straightforward. A surface is unclamped in the u (v) direction by applying the computations of Algorithm A12.1 to the $m+1$ rows ($n+1$ columns) of control points. Figures 12.6a–12.6d show examples of surface unclamping. The original degree $(3,2)$ surface is shown in Figure 12.6a. Unclamping in the u direction is illustrated in Figure 12.6b, whereas unclamping in the v direction is pictured in Figure 12.6c. Figure 12.6d shows unclamping in both directions.

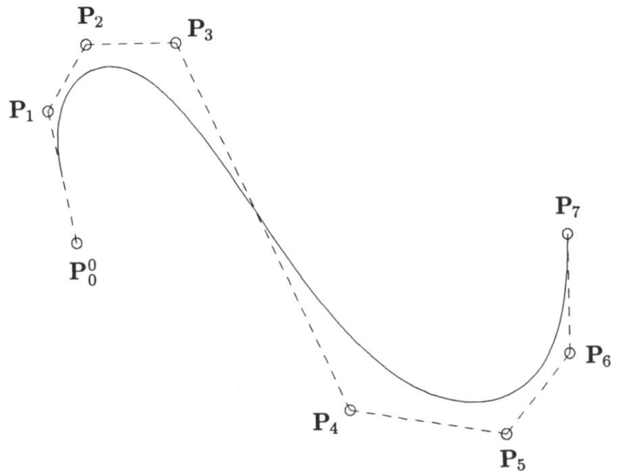

(b)

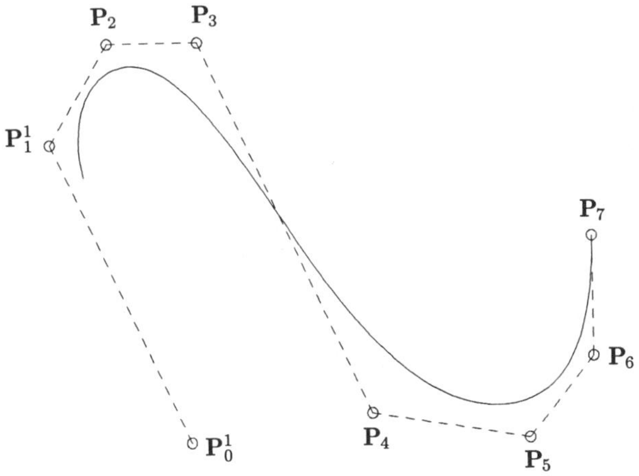

(c)

Figure 12.4. (*Continued.*)

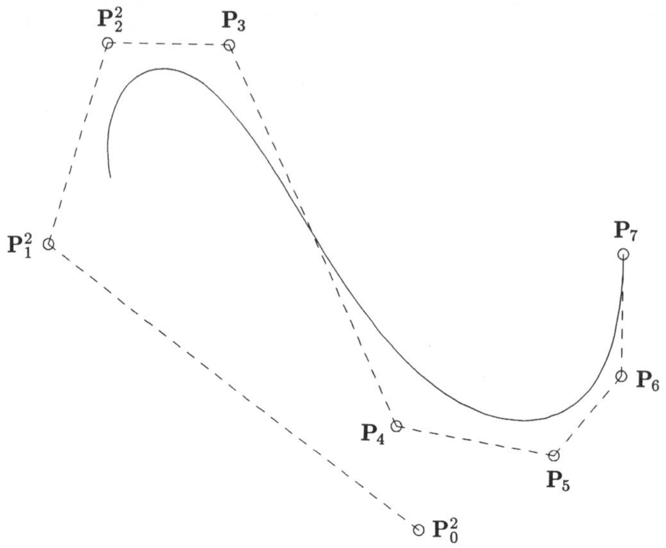

(d)

Figure 12.4. (*Continued.*)

12.3 NURBS Within the Standards

NURBS are not only a *de facto* standard throughout the CAD/CAM/CAE industry, but they are also incorporated into several international and American national standards:

- IGES : Initial Graphics Exchange Specification;
- STEP : Standard for the Exchange of Product Model Data;
- PHIGS : Programmer's Hierarchical Interactive Graphics System.

The definition of NURBS within these standards is the topic of this section. The purpose is to convey, conceptually, what defines a NURBS in each of the standards. To this end, we adopt an informal style and avoid the specific terminology of each standard. The reader should consult the relevant documents for a more rigorous study of these standards [PHIG92; IGE93; STEP94]. For additional reading see Bloor and Owen [Blor91] and Vergeest [Verg91] for STEP, and Howard [Howa91a] and Howard et al. [Howa91b] for PHIGS. Anyone designing a new NURBS system should ensure that it accommodates these standards as they relate to NURBS.

12.3.1 IGES

IGES, an American National Standard (ANS), is the most widely used format for exchanging product data among today's CAD/CAM/CAE systems. Developed

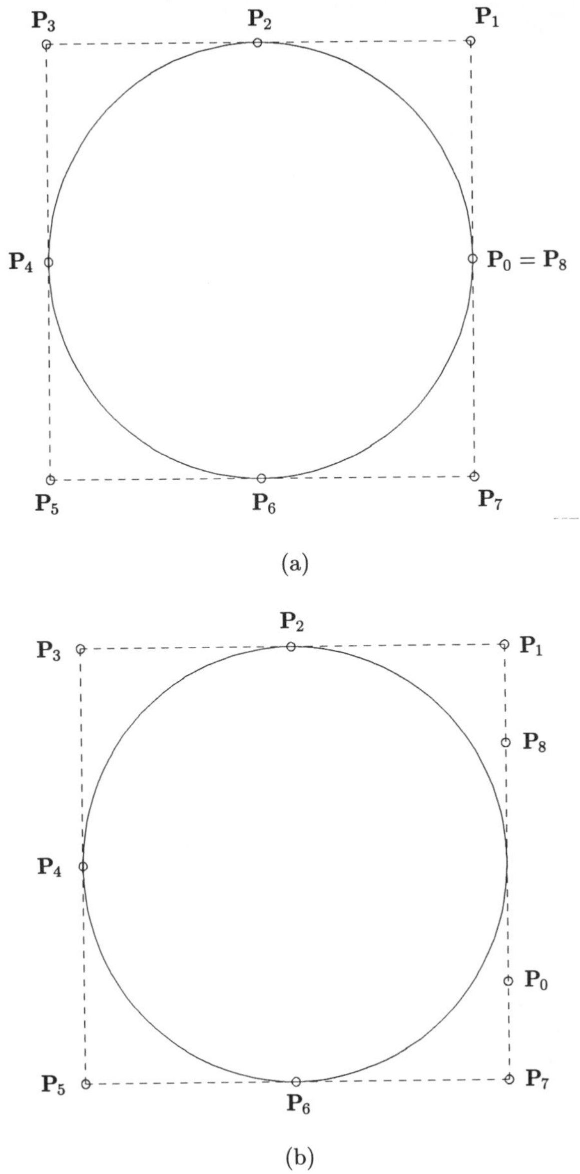

Figure 12.5. Unclamping the nine-point NURBS circle. (a) Original curve; (b) unclamped curve.

in the early 1980s, IGES specifies formats for exchanging graphics and geometry data, with support for various applications such as drafting, circuit design, finite elements, and piping. Curves, surfaces, and three-dimensional solids are supported. A NURBS curve is specified in IGES by:

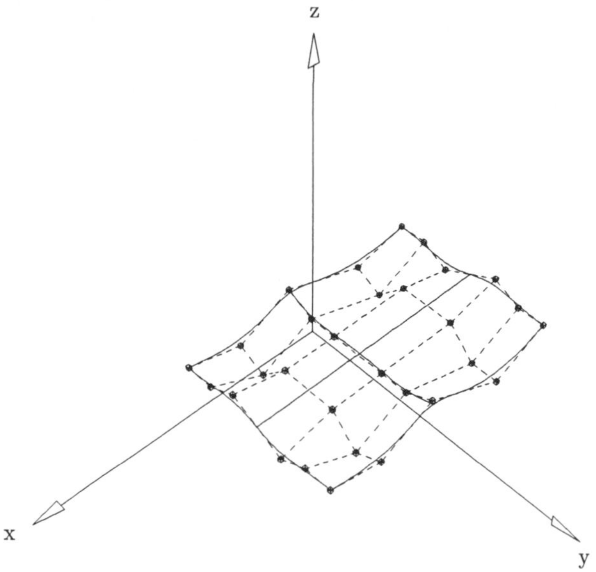

(a)

Figure 12.6. Unclamping a degree (3,2) surface. (a) Original surface; (b) unclamping in the u direction; (c) unclamping in the v direction; (d) unclamping in both directions.

- degree, p, and number of control points, $n+1$;
- Euclidean control points, $\mathbf{P}_i$, and weights, w_i;
- a knot vector, U, containing $m+1 = n+p+2$ knots;
- start and end parameter values, s_0 and s_1;
- other nonessential but useful information: whether the curve is planar or nonplanar, open or closed, truly rational (the w_i not all equal) or nonrational, periodic or nonperiodic; furthermore, a curve can be tagged as a special type, e.g., a line, or a circular or a conic arc.

Notice that control points and weights are separate items in IGES; there is no concept of homogeneous control points, $\mathbf{P}_i^w$. Only positive weights are allowed. The terms "periodic" and "nonperiodic" are not defined in the IGES manual, and therefore they are meaningless. Most often they are probably interpreted to mean unclamped and clamped, respectively, as defined in Section 12.2. The only constraints on the knots are $m = n+p+1$ and $u_{i-1} \leq u_i$ for $i = 1, \ldots, m$. Thus just about anything is allowed, including internal knots with multiplicity greater than p. The parameters s_0 and s_1 are an integral part of the definition, because they define the start and end points of the curve. The only restriction is that $u_0 \leq s_0 < s_1 \leq u_m$. That is, the intended curve can be a proper subcurve of the larger curve defined by the knots $u_0, \ldots, u_m$. A system which allows only clamped curves and no s_0 and s_1 values can accommodate IGES NURBS curves

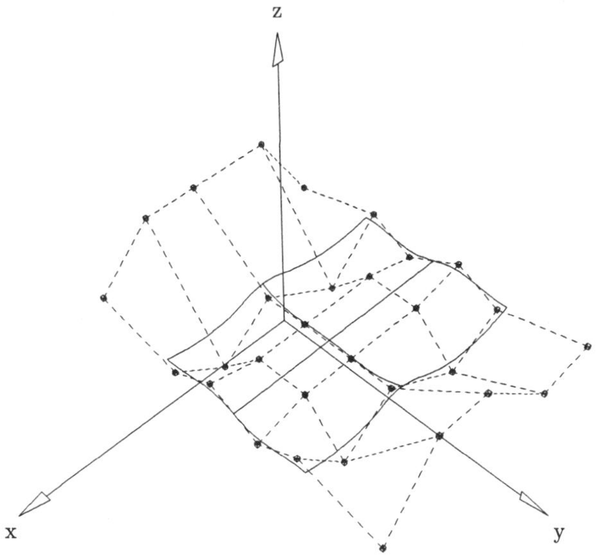

(b)

Figure 12.6. (*Continued.*)

(including unclamped curves) by applying subcurve extraction, which is simply knot insertion at s_0 and s_1, by using Algorithm A5.1.

IGES NURBS surfaces are defined analogously. Control points and weights are separate; weights must be positive. The only restrictions on the u and v knots are $r = n+p+1$, $s = m+q+1$, $u_{i-1} \leq u_i$ for $i = 1, \ldots, r$, and $v_{j-1} \leq v_j$ for $j = 1, \ldots, s$, where p and $n+1$, and q and $m+1$, are the degrees and the numbers of control points in the u and v directions, respectively. Parameters s_0, s_1 and t_0, t_1 define the intended surface, which can be a proper subsurface of the surface defined by the given knots, weights, and control points. If necessary, knot insertion is used to extract and clamp the intended surface. There are informational flags indicating whether the surface is open or closed, and periodic (?) or nonperiodic (?) in each direction, and whether the surface is truly rational (not all $w_{i,j}$ equal) or nonrational. An IGES NURBS surface can be tagged as one of nine special types: plane, circular cylinder, cone, sphere, torus, surface of revolution, general cylinder, ruled surface, or general quadric surface.

12.3.2 STEP

STEP is an emerging international standard for the exchange of product model data. It represents a major international effort, and the complexity, breadth, and depth of STEP dwarfs that of IGES. NURBS curves and surfaces are defined in the so-called Part 42, that part of STEP concerned with the basic geometry

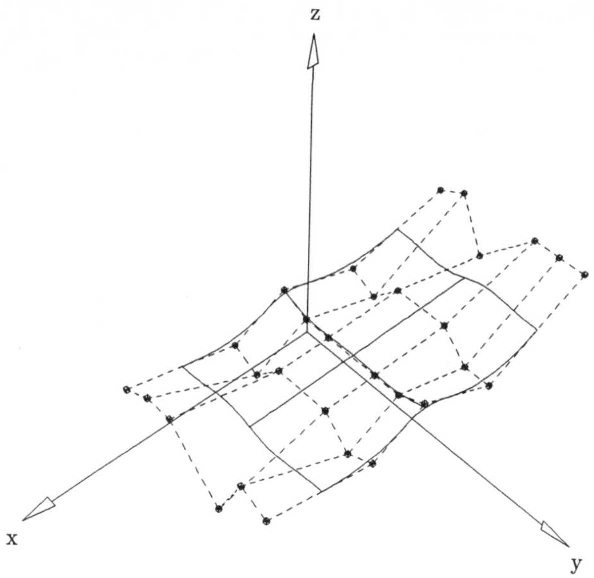

(c)

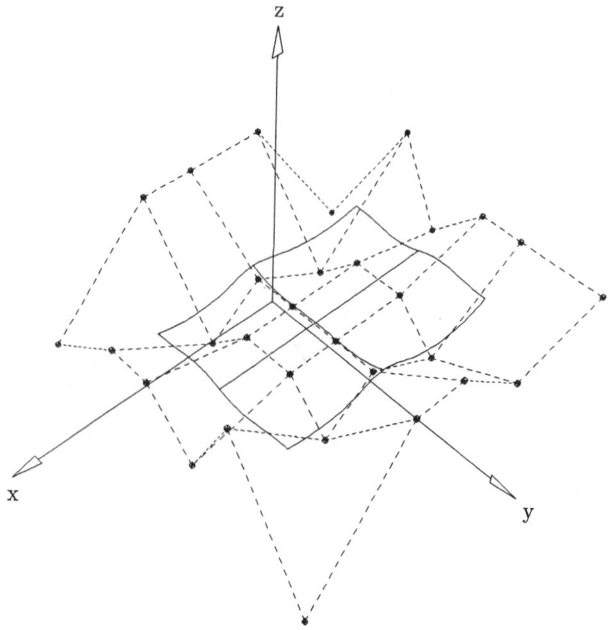

(d)

Figure 12.6. (*Continued.*)

and topology of a product model. In fact, because of the generality, numerical stability, and broad industrial acceptance of the NURBS representation, it was chosen as the *exclusive* method of exchanging general spline and single-span polynomial and rational curves and surfaces through STEP. Part 42 includes curves, surfaces, and three-dimensional solids. A NURBS curve is specified in STEP by:

- degree, p, and number of control points, $n+1$;
- Euclidean control points, $\mathbf{P}_i$, and weights, w_i (there is no concept of $\mathbf{P}_i^w$); only positive weights are allowed;
- a knot vector, U, containing $m+1 = n+p+2$ knots, and satisfying $u_{i-1} \le u_i$ for $i = 1, \ldots, m$; STEP bounds the multiplicity of knots – the first and last knot values can have multiplicity at most $p+1$, and the maximum multiplicity of all internal knot values is p;
- additional information such as the type of knot vector, whether the curve is open or closed, whether or not it is self-intersecting, and a type tag if applicable (polyline, circle, conic).

The concept of "trimming" a curve by parameters s_0 and s_1, $u_0 \le s_0 < s_1 \le u_m$, also exists in STEP, but at a higher level; it is not embedded in the definition of the curve. STEP distinguishes four types of NURBS curves, based on the form of their knot vectors: uniform, quasi-uniform, Bézier, and nonuniform. A knot vector is uniform if $u_i - u_{i-1} = d$ for $i = 1, \ldots, m$ and some positive constant d. This corresponds to unclamped and uniform in the terminology of Section 12.2. Quasi-uniform corresponds to clamped and uniform, i.e., $u_0 = \cdots = u_p$, $u_{m-p} = \cdots = u_m$, and $u_i - u_{i-1} = d$ for $i = p+1, \ldots, m-p$ and some positive constant, d. Bézier means that the *distinct* knot values are equally spaced, and that the first and last have multiplicity $p+1$ and all internal ones have multiplicity p, i.e., the curve is piecewise Bézier. Any knot vector not falling into one of these three categories is called nonuniform.

A STEP NURBS surface is defined analogously. Control points and weights are separate, and weights must be positive. A surface is uniform, quasi-uniform, or (piecewise) Bézier only if both its u and v knots are of the respective type; otherwise it is nonuniform. There is a self-intersection flag, an open/closed flag for both u and v directions, and, if applicable, a tag indicating a special type, such as plane, cylinder, ruled surface, etc.

12.3.3 PHIGS

Whereas IGES and STEP are data exchange standards, PHIGS is an international standard specifying a device-independent interactive graphics programming interface. PHIGS emerged in the mid 1980s, and NURBS were incorporated into the standard in 1992 as part of the PHIGS PLUS extension [Howa91b]. A PHIGS implementation supporting NURBS allows an application programmer to pass down NURBS curves and surfaces directly for display. A NURBS curve is defined in PHIGS by:

- order (= *degree* + 1), number of control points, and number of knots;
- the Euclidean control points, $\mathbf{P}_i$, if the curve is nonrational, otherwise the four-dimensional homogeneous control points, $\mathbf{P}_i^w$; a flag indicates rationality. Weights must be positive;
- the knots; only clamped knot vectors are allowed, either uniform or nonuniform. There is no bound on the multiplicity of knots;
- trimming parameters s_0 and s_1, defining the actual start and end of the intended curve.

NURBS surfaces are defined analogously, except there are no trimming parameters. More general trimming loops, consisting of NURBS curves in the surface's parameter domain, are allowed.

12.4 Data Exchange to and from a NURBS System

Throughout this section we assume two curve and surface systems, `A` and `B`, and we study the exchange of data between them. We assume that System `A` was designed and implemented based upon this book, i.e., it uses clamped NURBS curves and surfaces of arbitrary degree. For the sake of practicality and compatibility with most existing systems, we also require that all weights be positive, and that the multiplicity of internal knots not exceed the degree. For the moment we make no assumptions about how geometry is represented in System `B`.

When exchanging a curve or surface between two systems which represent geometry differently, there are three possible scenarios:

- a mathematically precise conversion is possible, which means that floating point roundoff is the only error incurred. The geometry is both geometrically and parametrically equivalent in the two systems; an example is the conversion between B-spline and piecewise power basis forms given in Section 6.6;
- the conversion is geometrically precise, but the parameterization is altered; an example is the circle, parameterized by trigonometric functions in System `B`. Notice that if the circle is used to form certain types of surfaces in Systems `A` and `B` (such as ruled, skinned, Gordon and Coons), the resulting surface geometry can be different;
- mathematically there exists no precise conversion between the two systems; in this case, an approximation to some specified tolerance is the best that can be done. For example, if System `B` allows only cubic curves, then higher degree curves from System `A` must be approximated.

For our purposes we distinguish two types of geometry:

- simple curves and surfaces of analytic geometry, such as lines, circles, conics, planes, circular or conic cylinders and cones, spheres, and tori;
- everything else.

Assuming that System B can represent the analytic types, the exchange of these between Systems A and B is geometrically precise in both directions. Consider the direction from B to A. Most systems represent the analytic types either in a rational form (e.g., rational power basis or Bézier), or in a form from which it is easy to derive the geometric characteristics such as center, axes, radii, vertices, etc. Section 6.6 shows how to convert from piecewise rational power basis or Bézier form to NURBS; going from other rational forms to NURBS is similar. Constructing the NURBS representations of the analytic types from their geometric characteristics is the topic of Chapters 7 and 8. Passing the analytic types from System A to B is more difficult. The problem is that the NURBS representation of a curve or surface is not unique. For example, there are infinitely many combinations of degree, knots, control points, and weights which produce the full unit circle centered at the origin. Hence it is not simple to determine if a NURBS curve is an analytic type and, if so, to compute its geometric characteristics. Section 7.6 presents a method to determine the geometric characteristics of a quadratic rational Bézier curve. However, degree reduction and knot insertion may be required to bring the NURBS curve into piecewise quadratic rational form (if possible). Moreover, the NURBS curve is a conic only if it yields the same geometric characteristics (to within a tolerance) on each Bézier segment. We emphasize that we make assumptions only about what constitutes a NURBS curve or surface in System A; we make no assumptions about how the specific analytic types are constructed as NURBS. Indeed, such geometry may be created in another system, in NURBS form, but using different combinations of knots, weights, and control points than presented in this book, and then passed into System A. Providing type-tags for NURBS geometry, as allowed in IGES and STEP (see Section 12.3), offers some help in this regard; but it does not eliminate the problem.

Now consider more complex geometry, ranging from general ruled and revolved surfaces to offsets, blends, fillets, and general free-form curves and surfaces. System B might use three methods to represent such geometry:

- implicit equations of the form $f(x,y) = 0$ or $f(x,y,z) = 0$;
- procedural definitions;
- one of the many forms of polynomial or rational splines.

Theoretically, a precise conversion of a NURBS to piecewise implicit form is possible, using techniques known as *implicitization* (e.g., see [deMo84; Sede84; Hoff89] and the references therein). However, it is not computationally practical; precise conversion from implicit to NURBS form is generally not possible, and thus approximation is required. In practice, implicit equations are rarely used to represent complex geometry, therefore we pursue the topic no further.

We say that a curve or surface is defined procedurally if it is not defined directly in terms of explicit coefficients or functions, but rather indirectly by means of other *base* curves or surfaces, together with a procedure or formula to compute points on the intended geometry from points on the base geometry.

Offset curves and *surfaces* are examples of procedurally defined geometry. An offset surface, $\mathbf{O}(u,v)$, is specified by

$$\mathbf{O}(u,v) = \mathbf{S}(u,v) + d\mathbf{N}(u,v) \tag{12.3}$$

where $\mathbf{S}(u,v)$ is the base surface, $d \neq 0$ is a constant scalar, and $\mathbf{N}(u,v)$ is the unit length normal vector of $\mathbf{S}(u,v)$ at (u,v). Offset curves and surfaces are mathematically complex and, in general, can rarely be represented precisely in NURBS form (see [Till84; Faro86; Coqu87b; Hosc88]). Blend and fillet surfaces are sometimes defined procedurally [Choi91], and Filip and Ball [Fili89] describe a procedural method of skinning. Such surfaces can seldom be passed into a NURBS (or any other) system without approximation.

Most CAD/CAM/CAE systems use piecewise polynomial or rational curves and surfaces to represent complex geometry. We refer to these, collectively, as splines. There are many different types of splines; but no matter what fancy name it has, a spline curve (surface) simply consists of a number of segments (patches), pieced together with some form of continuity. For brevity, we restrict our discussion to curves for the remainder of this section, but similar statements and algorithms hold for surfaces. In order to determine if a particular type of spline curve has an equivalent NURBS representation (and vice versa), one must consider three things:

- degree;
- rationality;
- continuity.

Degree and rationality are easy. Degree can be precisely raised, but not lowered; and a polynomial is a rational function, but the converse is not true. Since our System `A` allows rational curves of arbitrary degree, there are no problems in this regard in bringing geometry from System `B` into System `A`. However, if System `B` restricts degree or allows only nonrational geometry, then the corresponding curves must be approximated in going from System `A` to System `B`.

Continuity is more complicated. Let $\mathbf{C}(u)$ be a spline curve consisting of the segments $\mathbf{C}_i(u)$, $i = 1, \ldots, m$. $\mathbf{C}_i(u)$ is defined on the interval $[u_{i-1}, u_i]$, where $u_0 < u_1 < \cdots < u_{m-1} < u_m$. We call the values $\{u_i\}$ the *breakpoints*; if $\mathbf{C}(u)$ is in B-spline form, then the $\{u_i\}$ are the distinct knot values. Each pair of segments, $\mathbf{C}_i(u)$ and $\mathbf{C}_{i+1}(u)$, joins with some *type* and *order* of continuity, and the fundamental question in data exchange always boils down to whether or not the receiving system can represent the segments, connected with the appropriate continuity. By continuity type we mean parametric (C) versus geometric (G) continuity; see Section 9.3.1 and [Bars89, 90; Hosc93] and the references therein for more details on geometric continuity and various types of splines constructed to have G continuity. We remind the reader that:

- G^1 continuity at u_i means that the first derivative vectors, $\mathbf{C}'_i(u_i)$ and $\mathbf{C}'_{i+1}(u_i)$, point in the same direction but can have different magnitudes;

- for B-splines, knot multiplicity indicates continuity of the basis functions, which is generally the parametric continuity of the curve in homogeneous space;
- reparameterization of a curve segment changes its parametric continuity with its neighbors, but not its geometric continuity.

Since System `A` allows arbitrary knot spacing and multiplicity, it is capable of representing precisely, geometrically and parametrically, virtually all polynomial and rational spline curves which are at least C^0 continuous. However, going from `A` to `B` can require either an approximation or reparameterization of the segments (which does not change the overall curve geometry). For example, if System `B` uses rational B-splines but does not allow multiple internal knots, then a C^{p-2} continuous B-spline curve with double internal knots must be approximated. If System `B` allows multiple knots but requires distinct knots (breakpoints) to be equally spaced, then all curves of System `A` can be passed geometrically precisely into System `B`; however, reparameterization is required, and parametric continuity is lost in the process. The algorithm is:

1. insert all internal knots until they have multiplicity p, thus obtaining a piecewise Bézier curve; this yields the control points for the curve in System `B`;
2. let
$$d = \frac{u_m - u_0}{m}$$
and define the knot vector for System `B` to be
$$U = \{\underbrace{u_0, \ldots, u_0}_{p+1}, \underbrace{u_1, \ldots, u_1}_{p}, \ldots, \underbrace{u_{m-1}, \ldots, u_{m-1}}_{p}, \underbrace{u_m, \ldots, u_m}_{p+1}\}$$
where $$u_i = u_0 + i \cdot d \qquad i = 1, \ldots, m-1$$
3. apply knot removal (to a zero tolerance), but all breakpoints must remain with multiplicity at least one so that they are equally spaced.

Note that if this algorithm is used to pass a curve from `A` to `B` and then back to `A`, the original and the returned curves in `A` differ parametrically and in their number of knots. Notice also that, even though the curves are geometrically equivalent, if they are used in System `A` to construct ruled surfaces (for example) then the resulting surfaces may not be geometrically equivalent.

Regardless of the type of spline used in System `B`, the continuity issue is comprised of two parts:

- does the representation allow for nonuniformly spaced breakpoints;
- what types and orders of continuity are possible?

We remark that the first part can be answered even for systems in which there is no concept of global breakpoints. For example, many geometrically continuous splines are constructed by local methods using a local parameter t, $t \in [0, 1]$, for each segment. Such systems may allow for a global parameterization, in which case global breakpoints, u_i, are available, and nonuniform spacing is most probably allowed. In systems with no concept of a global parameterization, equally spaced global breakpoints are implied. As seen previously, reparameterization can be used to transform nonuniformly spaced breakpoints into uniformly spaced ones; however, parametric continuity is altered in the process. Conversely, reparameterization which transforms uniformly spaced breakpoints to nonuniformly spaced ones is useful in converting (geometrically precisely) a G^k continuous spline to a C^k continuous B-spline (e.g., this was done in Section 9.3.2, Eqs. [9.37]–[9.39]). With regard to the second part, one must determine the minimum order of continuity allowed. For example, a system based on fifth-degree G^2 continuous splines can represent all quintic G^k continuous splines, for $k \geq 2$; however, a quintic G^k continuous spline with $k < 2$ must be approximated. As another example, curves of a B-spline system allowing only single internal knots are C^{p-1} continuous. Hence all orders of continuity are possible, but the degree must be at least one greater than the minimum desired continuity (i.e., the minimum order of continuity may depend on the degree).

We now summarize the exchange of spline curves between Systems `A` and `B`. All spline curves which are at least C^0 continuous can be passed precisely (geometrically and parametrically) from System `B` to `A`. Multiple knots are necessary for G continuous curves, but, if desired, reparameterization can be used to achieve C continuity and lower the multiplicity of internal knots. The use of reparameterized curves in certain types of surface constructions (e.g., ruled surfaces) can change surface geometry. A typical algorithm to effect the conversion first computes either the power basis or Bézier coefficients for each segment, and it then applies the techniques of Section 6.6 to build the NURBS representation.

The conversion from System `A` to System `B` can be more complicated. Algorithm `A12.2` gives the logical thought process necessary to determine how such a conversion should proceed. Denote the pth degree NURBS curve by $\mathbf{C}$, and assume System `B` can represent splines of degree k, where $p_{\min} \leq k \leq p_{\max}$.

```
ALGORITHM A12.2
  if (C is rational and System B only represents polynomials)
    {
    Approximate C;
    return;
    }
  if (p > p_max)
    {
    Approximate C;
    return;
    }
  if (p < p_min)
    {
    DegreeElevateCurve(C);    /* to degree p_min */
    return;
```

```
  }
Let m be the minimum order continuity allowed in System B
  for a degree p curve.
Determine the minimum order, k, of continuity at any
  breakpoint of C.
if (k < m)
  {
  Approximate C;
  return;
  }
Extract the segments of C (knot insertion), and convert them
  to the segment coefficients required by System B
  (reparameterization may be necessary).
If applicable, load the global breakpoints into System B.
```

Determining the minimum continuity values, m and k, requires elaboration. There is C continuity and G continuity, and for rational curves there is continuity in homogeneous space versus continuity in Euclidean space. The values m and k must refer to the type of continuity on which System B's splines are based. For example, suppose System B uses a rational G^2 continuous spline. This spline is based on tangent and curvature continuity in Euclidean space, hence the value k must be based on the G continuity of System A's NURBS curve in Euclidean space. Notice that the quadratic full circle of Example Ex7.2 is precisely representable as a G^2 spline in System B, even though, as a NURBS curve, it is only C^1 continuous in Euclidean space and even has cusps in homogeneous space.

We close this chapter with the observation that the NURBS form is not only a powerful and flexible method for curve and surface design, but it is also clearly today's most suitable representation for the exchange of complex curve and surface data.

CHAPTER

THIRTEEN

B-spline Programming Concepts

13.1 Introduction

In the previous twelve chapters we introduced different aspects of modeling with NURBS. These chapters covered basically two things: (1) the underlying mathematics, and (2) algorithms illustrating how the tools can be turned into computer code. Although the pseudocodes presented in each chapter are fairly detailed, containing all the necessary information to turn them into workable routines, it is a long way from the algorithmic sketch to a useful system. How to design a useful system is a very difficult question (contrary to many researchers who consider it as a minor "implementation issue"). A NURBS system has to satisfy many requirements in order to be useful in a complex surface or solid modeler. In this chapter we introduce a number of programming concepts that, we believe, contribute to good programming practices. We are fully aware of the diversity of programming styles and conventions. Consequently, we do not attempt to present the *best* or the *ultimate* solution simply because there is none.

During the course of writing this book we developed a comprehensive library, *Nlib V2.0*, implemented in ANSI C. This library contains numerous routines necessary to implement every tool discussed in the book. In this chapter we present the philosophy, architecture, and organization of that library. While developing *Nlib V2.0* we required our routines to adhere to the following general standards [see Stra92]:

- *toolability*: available tools should be used to build new routines;
- *portability*: it should be easy to port the software to different software and hardware platforms;
- *reusability*: the program should be written in such a way as to be able to reuse sections of the code;
- *testability*: the code should be made consistent and simple so that testing and debugging become easy;
- *reliability*: errors should be handled consistently and gracefully;

- *enhanceability*: the code must be easily understood so that new features can be added without significant effort;
- *fixability*: it must be reasonably easy to locate bugs;
- *consistency*: programming conventions should be consistent throughout the library;
- *communicability*: it must be easy to read and to understand the program.

We believe that these standards are necessary to minimize what is commonly referred to as "the nightmare of software maintenance". A common disease in the software industry is "software trashing", i.e., when one employee leaves the company his code gets trashed because nobody understands it, hence maintenance becomes impossible.

In addition to these general standards, we followed some specific standards:

- *style of programming*: we wanted the code to look very much like the mathematics in the book so that the reader has little trouble following the various steps; in addition, we followed a "user friendly" programming style as suggested in [Baly94];
- *usability*: since NURBS are very popular in many application areas, it should be easy for nonexperts to use the library to build higher level applications of various types;
- *numerical efficiency*: one of the reasons why NURBS were chosen in many standards is because of their excellent numerical properties; NURBS evaluations are mixed with other numerical code which we carefully wrote so as not to destroy the overall numerical efficiency;
- *object based programming*: programming curves and surfaces requires dealing with large amounts of data; to avoid carrying this data around and to enhance understanding the code, we grouped various entities into objects.

A word on Object Based Programming (OBP): When dealing with OBP, many people automatically think of languages such as C++. We did not implement *Nlib V2.0* in C++ simply because plain C does just fine, allowing both the C and the C++ programmer to use the library routines.

In the sections that follow we deal with issues of (1) data types and portability, (2) data structures, (3) memory allocation, (4) error handling, (5) utility routines, (6) arithmetic operations, (7) example programs, (8) some additional structures, and (9) system structure. These issues are often more complicated than the mathematics of NURBS. The mathematics is basically right or wrong; software is a large gray area with no boundaries.

13.2 Data Types and Portability

In this section we deal with the following portability problems:

- data type portability, e.g., one system represents integers as 32 bit numbers whereas the other uses only 16 bits;

- operations portability, e.g., arithmetic operations yield different results on different machines;
- domain portability, e.g., one system is a drafting system performing operations mainly in two-dimensional space, whereas the other is a design system requiring computations in three-dimensional space.

We deal with these issues in three ways: (1) using predefined data types and avoiding the explicit use of compiler defined data types, (2) introducing special arithmetic functions that take care of all arithmetic operations in all of the two-dimensional, three-dimensional, or four-dimensional domains (rational or nonrational, two-dimensional or three-dimensional), and (3) defining objects that are dimensionless. To fix portability problems one has to change only a few lines of code in one of the include files, or fix a few arithmetic routines, or redefine some of the objects. The rest of the system, which can contain millions of lines of code, remains intact.

In *Nlib V2.0* we use several predefined data types. Some examples are:

```
typedef int INDEX;
typedef short FLAG;
typedef int INTEGER;
typedef double REAL;
typedef char * STRING;
typedef short DEGREE;
typedef double PARAMETER;
```

The `INDEX` data type is used to declare variables that are used as the highest indexes of arrays of different dimensions. For example, if the highest index never exceeds 32,767 (16 bit), then the current definition is adequate. However, if arrays of larger dimensions are required, then the definition

```
typedef long INDEX;
```

must be used. Similar arguments hold for the `FLAG` data type (for example, used to "flag" or select different cases in a switch statement) and for the `INTEGER` data type. If a system uses only 8 bit integers, then the only change required is to make `INTEGER` `short` as opposed to `int`. The `REAL` data type is defined by default as `double`, which can be changed to `float` if single precision is satisfactory or the rest of the system uses single precision. The `STRING` data type is introduced for convenience and for conceptual reasons.

The explanation behind the `DEGREE` and the `PARAMETER` data types is similar to the `INDEX` data type, that is, the degree of a curve or surface is much lower than the integers used as variables. Consequently, a `short` integer is quite adequate. Defining `DEGREE` as a new data type also signals the fact that it is *different* from ordinary integers; it belongs to the parameters that collectively define a curve or a surface. The same holds for the `PARAMETER` type, which can be either `double` or `float`, depending on the application or on the current system's floating point computation.

One of the most difficult tasks in floating point calculations is to deal with numerical imprecision. It is almost impossible not to use tolerances for point coincidence or to measure the equality of two floating point numbers. In *Nlib V2.0* we use the following constants defined by the compiler:

```
#define BIGD DBL_MAX
#define SMAD DBL_MIN
#define BIGI INT_MAX
#define SMAI INT_MIN
#define DEPS DBL_EPSILON
```

`BIGD` and `SMAD` are the largest and the smallest double precision numbers, respectively. The ANSI C standard specifies that they must be defined in `float.h`. It also requires `BIGD` to be at least 10^{37} or greater and `SMAD` to be at least 10^{-37} or smaller. The requirement for the double precision epsilon `DEPS` is at least 10^{-9} or smaller.

Limits for integer variables are stored in `limits.h`. Some typical ranges are $-32,768$ to $32,767$ for `int`, and $-2,147,483,648$ to $2,147,483,647$ for `long`. The range for the `unsigned long` is up to 4,294,967,295. Working with these constants ensures the consistency of computations no matter which hardware platform one uses.

Operations and domain portabilities are ensured through special arithmetic functions operating on objects. Examples are given in subsequent sections.

13.3 Data Structures

As mentioned in Section 13.1, we intend to use object based concepts and to follow the mathematical notation and concepts of previous chapters. As an example, in the curve evaluation routine we write

```
FLAG N_evncur( CURVE *cur, PARAMETER u, POINT *C )
```

or, given a `CURVE` and a `PARAMETER`, compute a `POINT` on the `CURVE` at the given `PARAMETER` value. The nice thing about this type of programming is that the user need not know anything about how the different entities (curve, parameter, and point) are represented internally. They are considered as objects built from smaller components. To define a curve (or shall we say, to define a curve *object*), we need to store these entities:

- n: the highest index of control points;
- $\mathbf{P}_0^w, ..., \mathbf{P}_n^w$: the control points;
- p: the degree;
- m: the highest index of knots;
- $u_0, ..., u_m$: the knots.

Although this data can be passed directly to every NURBS routine, it is fairly inconvenient and unnatural to the programmer, who thinks at different levels of abstraction. For example, when dealing with curves for interactive design, he works with them without regard to the number of control points and knots. Or, for example, when dealing with curve/curve intersection, he might descend his thinking to the level of the control polygon if the overlapping of bounding boxes is what needs to be examined. For these and many other similar reasons, *Nlib V2.0* considers every geometric entity as an object built from simpler components.

In the design of a huge structure, simple building blocks are created first from basic data types. One of the basic elements of a curve object is the control point. It can be rational or nonrational, two-dimensional or three-dimensional, that is, it needs to hold two, three, or four coordinates. In addition, it plays a dual role as a control point for B-spline computations and as a Euclidean point used for simple geometric manipulations, such as computing distances, bounding boxes, and so on. A third requirement is to be able to refer to this entity as `P[i]`, just as its mathematical abstraction is referred to in the book. To simplify matters and to satisfy object based concepts, we separated control points from "regular" Euclidean points just as we did in the book, by writing $\mathbf{P}$ for a Euclidean point and $\mathbf{P}^w$ for a control point that can be weighted. Hence the definitions of points are (see Figure 13.1):

```
typedef struct point
{
  REAL x,
       y,
       z;
} POINT;

typedef struct cpoint
{
  REAL x,
       y,
       z,
       w;
} CPOINT;
```

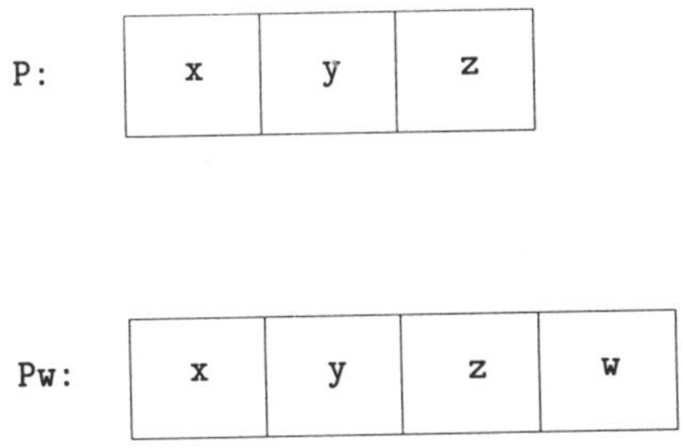

Figure 13.1. Point and control point data structures.

The attractive feature of these definitions is that they make programming fairly clean. The price one pays for this is waste of memory, e.g., if the curve is a two-dimensional nonrational curve, then half of the memory used to store the control points is wasted. While this certainly was an issue in the past, code understanding and maintenance have become more important then speed and memory. There is one thing, however, that one can do to restrict arithmetic operations to two-dimensional or three-dimensional in case the curve is nonrational or planar. The third and/or the fourth component can be set to a special value. *Nlib V2.0* uses the following:

```
#define _NOZ +BIGD
#define _NOW -BIGD
```

If the third component is set to _NOZ (no z), then no operation is performed on the z component, and similarly in case of _NOW, the w component is ignored.

Having defined points and control points, let us now build more complex objects. The next level of abstraction contains the control polygon and knot vector objects defined as (see Figures 13.2 and 13.3):

```
typedef struct cpolygon
{
  INDEX n;
  CPOINT *Pw;
} CPOLYGON;

typedef struct knotvector
{
  INDEX m;
  REAL *U;
} KNOTVECTOR;
```

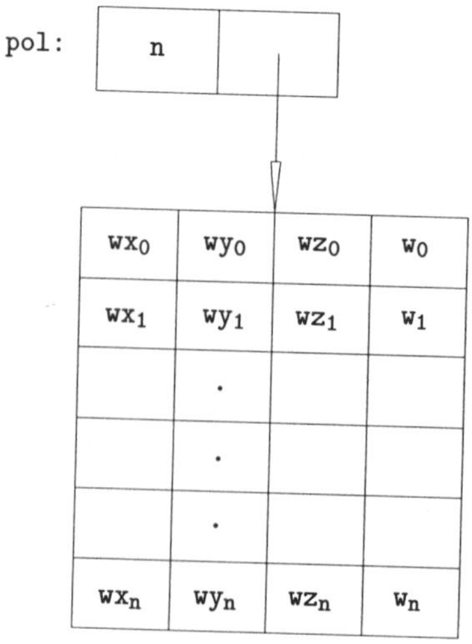

Figure 13.2. Control polygon data structure.

In other words, the control polygon object is simply a structure containing the highest index and a pointer to an array of control points. The knot vector also has a highest index field and a pointer to the array of knots. These structures contain the bare minimum of data. One can extend them according to special needs, e.g., the control polygon structure can store information on the bounding box, or the knot vector structure can store a flag as to whether it is uniform or nonuniform. Now, given a control polygon, a knot vector, and a specified degree, one can build a curve from these constituents as follows (see Figure 13.4):

```
typedef struct curve
{
  CPOLYGON *pol;
  DEGREE p;
  KNOTVECTOR *knt;
} CURVE;
```

that is, a curve object consists of a polygon pointer, the degree, and a knot vector pointer. The beauty of this definition is that the various constituents are easily extracted for further processing. For example, if one needs to compute the bounding box of a curve, in that routine the polygon subobject is extracted and passed on to another routine that deals with bounding box computation. Similarly, if a knot span is sought in which a parameter lies, the knot vector object is detached from the curve and passed on to a routine. Assuming that the current routine receives a curve pointer, the programming is fairly simple.

```
...

CPOLYGON *pol;
KNOTVECTOR *knt;
```

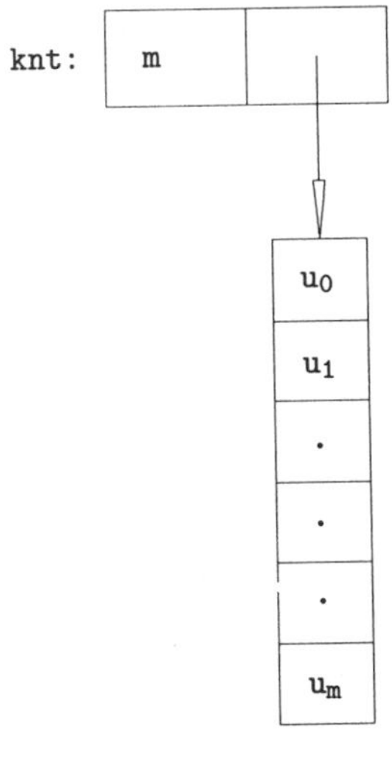

Figure 13.3. Knot vector data structure.

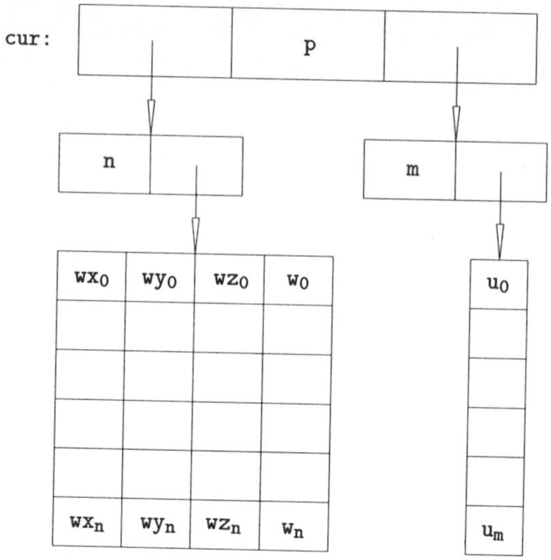

Figure 13.4. Curve data structure.

```
...
pol = cur->pol;
knt = cur->knt;
...
N_polbox(pol,...);
N_findsp(knt,...);
```

In other words, simple pointer assignments allow the program to descend to a lower level of abstraction, perform the necessary operations, and return the result to the calling routine's level.

The definition of a surface object is quite similar. It needs a control net, two degrees, and two knot vectors. The control net is defined as (see Figure 13.5):

```
typedef struct cnet
{
  INDEX n,
        m;
  CPOINT **Pw;
} CNET;
```

It contains the highest indexes in both directions and a pointer to a pointer, that is, a pointer to an array of pointers pointing to the first element in each column of control points. When one writes `P[i][j]`, then `P[i]` refers to the ith pointer in the pointer array pointing to the beginning of the ith column. The index `[j]`

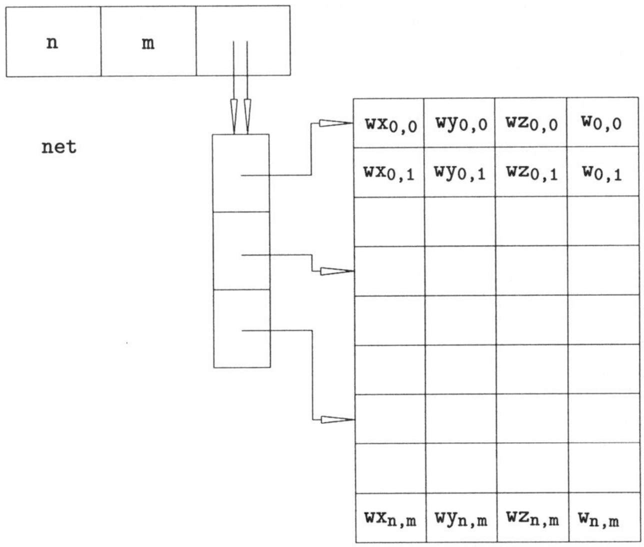

Figure 13.5. Control net data structure.

is the jth offset in this column. Putting the control net, the degrees, and two knot vectors together results in a surface defined as (see Figure 13.6):

```
typedef struct surface
{
  CNET *net;
  DEGREE p,
         q;
  KNOTVECTOR *knu,
             *knv;
} SURFACE;
```

Again, the control net and the knot vectors are extracted easily to perform various operations. If one has to perform many operations on the same curve or surface, these definitions become fairly natural to use and very economical; only pointers to different structures need to be passed around.

13.4 Memory Allocation

One of the most powerful tools of the C language is its ability to allocate and deallocate memory dynamically. This power, however, has its price: improperly allocating, using, or deallocating memory can cause fatal errors. Hence *Nlib V2.0* has very strict rules regarding memory allocation and deallocation. The most

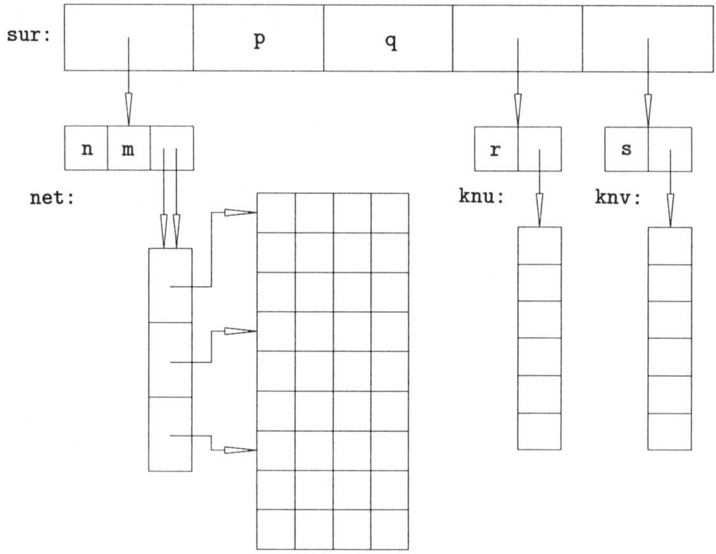

Figure 13.6. Surface data structure.

important one is that no routine is allowed to allocate and to deallocate memory other than the specially written memory handlers.

All memory allocated in a routine and not being passed back to the calling routine must be deallocated before returning. This fact, together with proper error handling, can lead to rather messy code, as this code segment illustrates.

```
x = (double *) malloc ( n1*sizeof(double) );
if ( x == NULL ) return( error );

y = (double *) malloc ( n2*sizeof(double) );
if ( y == NULL )
{
  free( x );
  return( error );
}

z = (double *) malloc ( n3*sizeof(double) );
if ( z == NULL )
{
  free( x );
  free( y );
  return( error );
}
```

This process can quickly become fairly complex if several allocations are required.

One can easily see that $n+1$ memory allocations require $n(n+1)/2$ lines of code for deallocation to handle the possible error, e.g., a code requiring 21 arrays contains 210 lines of **free** statements just to deal with the possible failure of dynamic memory allocation.

To make matters more manageable, *Nlib V2.0* has a three-step process to handle memory allocation and deallocation:

- on entering a new program, a memory stack is initialized to the empty stack;
- if memory is needed, special routines are called that allocate the required memory and save the memory pointers on appropriate stacks (see Figure 13.7);
- upon leaving the program the memory stacks are traversed, and memory, pointed to by the saved pointers, is deallocated.

As the programming examples in a later section show, this type of memory management is fairly clean, hides all unnecessary detail, and makes sure that all allocated memory is deallocated properly. Let us now examine the three steps in more detail.

The structure of every NURBS routine is sketched using this simple example:

```
...

FLAG error = 0;
INDEX n, m;
CPOINT **Pw;
```

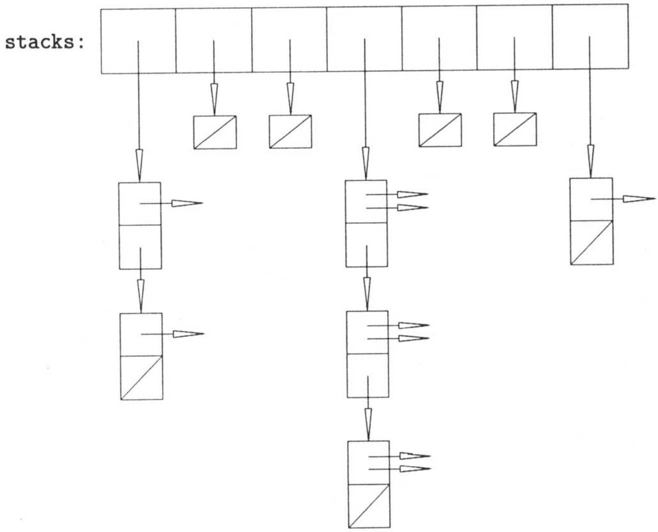

Figure 13.7. Memory stacks.

```
STACKS S;
...
N_inurbs(&S);
...
Pw = S_getc2d(n,m,&S);
if ( Pw == NULL ) { error = 1; goto EXIT; }
...
Pw[i][j] = ...;
...
EXIT:

N_enurbs(&S);
return( error );
```

Each routine has its own memory stack defined in `nurbs.h` as follows (see Figure 13.7):

```
typedef struct stacks
{
  I1DNODE *i1d;
  I2DNODE *i2d;
  R1DNODE *r1d;
  R2DNODE *r2d;
  ...

  KNTNODE *knt;
} STACKS;
```

In other words, it is a structure of pointers pointing to linked lists of nodes that store the different types of memory pointers – one- or two-dimensional `INTEGER` and `REAL` arrays, `POINT` arrays, and so on. When a routine is entered, memory for this structure is allocated and the pointers are set to `NULL` by the `N_inurbs()` routine. In order to allocate memory, the program (1) declares the appropriate memory pointer (`**Pw` in the previous example), and (2) calls a memory routine (`S_getc2d()`). The memory routine then allocates the required memory and saves the pointer(s) on the stack. As an example, let us see how `S_getc2d()` allocates memory for a two-dimensional array of control points (error handling, used in this routine, is discussed in Section 3.5).

```
#include "nurbs.h"
static STRING rname = "S_GETC2D";

CPOINT **S_getc2d( INDEX n, INDEX m, STACKS *S )
{
  INDEX k, l;
  CPOINT **Pw, *Qw;
```

```
C1DNODE *c1d;
C2DNODE *c2d;

/* Allocate memory */

Pw = (CPOINT **) malloc ( (n+1)*sizeof(CPOINT *) );
if ( Pw == NULL )
{
  E_seterr(MEM_ERR,rname);
  return NULL;
}

Qw = (CPOINT *) malloc ( (n+1)*(m+1)*sizeof(CPOINT) );
if ( Qw == NULL )
{
  E_seterr(MEM_ERR,rname);
  free( Pw );
  return NULL;
}

/* Make pointer assignments */

l = 0;
for ( k=0; k<=n; k++ )
{
  Pw[k] = &Qw[l];
  l = l+m+1;
}

/* Put pointers on memory stacks */

c1d = (C1DNODE *) malloc ( sizeof(C1DNODE) );
if ( c1d == NULL )
{
  E_seterr(MEM_ERR,rname);
  free( Pw ); free( Qw );
  return NULL;
}
c1d->ptr = Qw;
c1d->next = S->c1d;
S->c1d = c1d;

c2d = (C2DNODE *) malloc ( sizeof(C2DNODE) );
if ( c2d == NULL )
{
  E_seterr(MEM_ERR,rname);
  free( Pw );
```

```
      return NULL;
    }
    c2d->ptr = Pw;
    c2d->next = S->c2d;
    S->c2d = c2d;

    /* Exit */

    return Pw;
  }
```

The nodes C1DNODE and C2DNODE are defined in geometry.h as

```
  typedef struct c1dnode
  {
    CPOINT *ptr;
    struct c1dnode *next;
  } C1DNODE;

  typedef struct c2dnode
  {
    CPOINT **ptr;
    struct c2dnode *next;
  } C2DNODE;
```

Similar nodes are used for other types of memory pointers.

Once the memory is allocated it can be used as needed throughout the program. At the end, all allocated memory is freed by the N_enurbs() routine that traverses the different memory stacks, frees the allocated memory, and kills the linked lists. It is sketched as follows:

```
  #include "nurbs.h"

  VOID N_enurbs( STACKS *S )
  {
    I1DNODE *i1p;
    ...

    KNTNODE *knp;

    /* Free integer arrays */

    while ( S->i1d != NULL )
    {
      i1p = S->i1d;
      S->i1d = i1p->next;
      free( i1p->ptr );
      free( i1p );
    }
```

```
    ...

    /* Free knot vectors */

    while ( S->knt != NULL )
    {
      knp = S->knt;
      S->knt = knp->next;
      free( knp->ptr );
      free( knp );
    }
  }
```

This style of memory management provides a fairly clean way of dealing with the difficult task of memory allocation and deallocation. It frees the programmer from the burden of handling distracting details and remembering to deallocate all dynamically allocated memory. In its present form the method does not allow deallocation in the middle of a running program. If this creates a problem in a particular application, simple free routines can be written to deallocate memory and to eliminate nodes from the memory stack.

A note on the `N_inurbs()` and `N_enurbs()` routines: In the previous discussions these routines initialized and killed memory stacks. However, these routines can also be used to initialize and de-initialize other global parameters the programmer wants to use throughout a NURBS routine. This is one of the many reasons why *every* NURBS routine starts with `N_inurbs()` and ends with `N_enurbs()` even if no dynamic memory allocation is required. The concept is similar to building cars prewired for a car phone. The driver may never want a phone, but if he does the installation becomes a five-minute (clean) job. NURBS routines in *Nlib V2.0* are "prewired" for dynamic memory allocation and for initialization so that adding new features is easy and requires no change in the overall structure of the program.

13.5 Error Control

Error handling is one of the most crucial issues in designing a system. Each routine can have errors, and the calling routine has to deal with these errors in a sensible manner. There are basically two types of error processing:

- *direct control*: in case of an error a message is printed; if the error is fatal the process is killed;
- *indirect control*: each routine returns an error flag to the calling routine, and that determines how to handle the error and how to pass this information to a higher level routine.

Direct control is appropriate in a system like a compiler but is not acceptable in a NURBS system. For example, a geometry routine can return an error flag indicating that the given lines cannot be intersected because the input data, representing the lines, has corrupt information (e.g., a line of zero length). Since this error can possibly be corrected from the calling routine and hence the process completed with success, it is totally unacceptable to kill the entire session and print an error message.

NURBS routines need to handle errors in the background by passing error flags back to each calling routine. This can be done in a number of different ways. One sophisticated method is to use an *error stack*. If a routine locates an error it is put on the stack and control is returned to the calling routine. This routine either deals with the error or puts its own error onto the stack and returns control to a higher level routine. At each higher level, the calling routine receives a stack of errors (see Figure 13.8) that show the *error history*, and at each level the routine can correct the error, if possible, or pass the stack (with its own error on top) one level higher. Ultimately, a routine at a level higher than the NURBS library deals with the error. Let us consider a simple example. The data reduction algorithm discussed in Chapter 9 uses the following simple calling hierarchy:

```
Data reduction;
    Interpolate with given knot vector;
    Remove knots;
    Compute degree elevated knot vector;
    Least-squares approximation with given knot vector;
        LU decomposition;
```

If LU decomposition fails at the deepest level, least-squares approximation cannot be performed. Instead of killing the entire process, the data reduction routine can elect to restart the entire process with a higher degree interpolatory curve (which is exactly what the actual implementation does).

Although error stacking is a sophisticated technique, it requires some programming to respond to the different errors at each level. In *Nlib V2.0* this technique is not employed, mainly for two reasons: (1) each NURBS routine calls only a few other routines, i.e., the call stack is fairly small, and (2) the calling routine

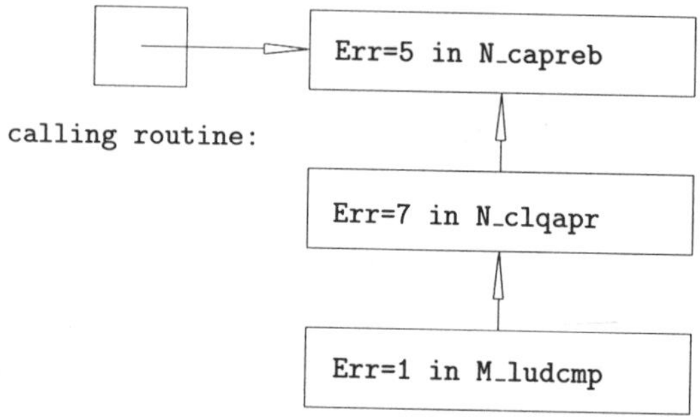

Figure 13.8. Error stack.

checks for most errors, hence only a few errors remain to be detected in lower level routines. Thus it seems reasonable for *Nlib V2.0* to pass around only one error flag, and to make each routine responsible for dealing with this error. The error flag is a simple structure defined in `datastr.h` as:

```
typedef struct enode
{
  INTEGER eno;
  STRING fna;
} ENODE;
```

that is, the structure contains an error number and the name of the routine where the error was detected. The most frequently occurring errors are numbered and defined in `datastr.h`. Some examples are:

```
#define CUR_ERR 1
#define SUR_ERR 2
#define DEG_ERR 3
#define KNT_ERR 4
#define WEI_ERR 5

...

#define MEM_ERR 15
...
```

where `CUR_ERR` is curve definition error; `KNT_ERR` is knot vector error, for example decreasing knots; `MEM_ERR` is memory allocation error, and so on; as a convenience, an error file can be created where all these errors are explained in more detail. Using these error numbers, a global error variable is required. *Nlib V2.0* defines and initializes the error variable `NERR` in `globals.h` as

```
extern volatile ENODE NERR = { 0, " " };
```

As soon as an error is detected, `NERR` receives a new value by means of the error routine `E_seterr()`:

```
#include "nurbs.h"
extern volatile ENODE NERR;

VOID E_seterr( INTEGER err, STRING name )
{
  NERR.eno = err;
  NERR.fna = name;
}
```

Nlib V2.0 has a set of error routines that check every conceivable error and set `NERR` to the appropriate value. We present two examples here; the first checks whether knots are nondecreasing, whereas the second performs a complete curve check, i.e., it checks curve definition consistency, weights, and the knot vector.

```
#include "nurbs.h"

FLAG E_kntdef( KNOTVECTOR *knt, STRING rname )
{
  FLAG error = 0;
  INDEX i, m;
  REAL *U;

  /* Convert to local notation */

  m = knt->m;
  U = knt->U;

  /* Check knots */

  for ( i=0; i<m; i++ )
  {
    if ( U[i] > U[i+1] )
    {
      E_seterr(KNT_ERR,rname);
      error = 1;
      break;
    }
  }

  /* Exit */

  return( error );
}
```

In other words, if no error is found the routine returns 0, otherwise it returns 1 and sets NERR to the appropriate value.

In many applications curve data is read from a file, for example from an IGES file. Before calling any NURBS routine it is prudent to make sure that the file contains correct information, i.e., it is useful (and necessary) to perform a complete curve (surface) check. An additional positive feature of this check is that further curve (surface) error checking is not required when curves and surfaces are passed to a NURBS routine. Before the complete curve check routine is considered, two more error routines are discussed: (1) check curve definition consistency, and (2) check weights. First consider the curve definition check routine.

```
#include "nurbs.h"

FLAG E_curdef( CURVE *cur, STRING rname )
{
  FLAG olddim, oldrat, newdim, newrat, error = 0;
  INDEX i, n, m;
```

```
  DEGREE p;
  CPOINT *Pw;

  /* Convert to local notation */

  n = cur->pol->n;
  Pw = cur->pol->Pw;
  p = cur->p;
  m = cur->knt->m;

  /* Check definition */

  if ( (n+p+1) != m )
  {
    E_seterr(CUR_ERR,rname);
    error = 1;
    goto EXIT;
  }

  /* Check for consistency */

  if ( Pw[0].z == _NOZ ) olddim = 2; else olddim = 3;
  if ( Pw[0].w == _NOW ) oldrat = 0; else oldrat = 1;
  for ( i=1; i<=n; i++ )
  {
    if ( Pw[i].z == _NOZ ) newdim = 2; else newdim = 3;
    if ( newdim != olddim )
    {
      E_seterr(CUR_ERR,rname);
      error = 1;
      break;
    }
    if ( Pw[i].w == _NOW ) newrat = 0; else newrat = 1;
    if ( newrat != oldrat )
    {
      E_seterr(CUR_ERR,rname);
      error = 1;
      break;
    }
  }

  /* Exit */

  EXIT:

  return( error );
}
```

The weight check routine is:

```
#include "nurbs.h"

FLAG E_curwei( CURVE *cur, STRING rname )
{
  FLAG error = 0;
  INDEX i, n;
  CPOINT *Pw;

  /* Convert to local notation */

  n = cur->pol->n;
  Pw = cur->pol->Pw;

  /* Check if curve is rational */

  if ( Pw[0].w == _NOW ) return( 0 );

  /* Now check the weights */

  for ( i=0; i<=n; i++ )
  {
    if ( Pw[i].w <= 0.0 )
    {
      E_seterr(WEI_ERR,rname);
      error = 1;
      break;
    }
  }

  /* Exit */

  return( error );
}
```

As a practical matter, application programmers might want to set a limit to the largest permissible weight and check for it in this routine. Large weights create very bad parametrizations, which in turn can result in unacceptable surfaces constructed from curves.

The input checking routine is:

```
#include "nurbs.h"

FLAG E_curinp( CURVE *cur, STRING rname )
{
```

```
  FLAG error;
  KNOTVECTOR *knt;

  /* Convert to local notation */

  knt = cur->knt;

  /* Check curve definition */

  error = E_curdef(cur,rname);
  if ( error > 0 ) return(1);

  /* Check curve weights */

  error = E_curwei(cur,rname);
  if ( error > 0 ) return(1);

  /* Check knot vector */

  error = E_kntdef(knt,rname);
  if ( error > 0 ) return(1);

  /* Exit */

  return(0);
}
```

Each NURBS routine can, in principle, handle error checking individually. However, with error routines programming becomes a lot cleaner. The programmer can focus on the task at hand, e.g., curve refinement, and miscellaneous tasks such as error checking and memory allocation are handled at a conceptual level.

13.6 Utility Routines

Utility routines aid the programmer in creating special structures or in converting one type of input to another. There is an infinite variety of such utility programs, but one must draw the line somewhere. In *Nlib V2.0* a few dozen such routines exist that support special structure constructions.

Creating a curve structure can be done in a number of different ways, depending on what type of information is available at which level. A simple example is:

```
#include "nurbs.h"

VOID U_makcu1( CURVE *cur, CPOLYGON *pol, DEGREE p,
               KNOTVECTOR *knt )
{
```

```
    cur->pol = pol;
    cur->p = p;
    cur->knt = knt;
  }
```

This is probably the simplest type of utility responsible for assigning pointers of existing structures to the elements of the curve structure. Polygons and knot vectors can also be created by utility routines. A simple example is:

```
#include "nurbs.h"

FLAG U_makpl2( CPOLYGON *pol, REAL *wx, REAL *wy, REAL *wz,
               REAL *w, INDEX n, STACKS *S )
{
  INDEX i;
  CPOINT *Pw;

  /* Allocate memory for point array */

  Pw = S_getc1d(n,S);
  if ( Pw == NULL ) return (1);

  /* Fill in point array */

  for ( i=0; i<=n; i++ )
  {
    Pw[i].x = wx[i];
    Pw[i].y = wy[i];
    if ( wz != NULL )
      Pw[i].z = wz[i];
    else
      Pw[i].z = _NOZ;
    if ( w != NULL )
      Pw[i].w = w[i];
    else
      Pw[i].w = _NOW;
  }

  /* Make pointer assignments */

  pol->n = n;
  pol->Pw = Pw;

  /* Exit */

  return (0);
}
```

This routine not only creates a polygon structure (memory to store the structure is allocated in the calling routine), it also converts the traditional (wx, wy, wz, w) type input to the more object based point input. And it also takes care of the proper setting of the z and w components for nonrational or planar curves. We present a similar routine that creates a curve from the smallest bits and pieces:

```
#include "nurbs.h"

FLAG U_makcu3( CURVE *cur, REAL *wx, REAL *wy, REAL *wz,
               REAL *w, INDEX n, DEGREE p, REAL *U, INDEX m,
               STACKS *S )
{
  CPOINT *Pw;
  CPOLYGON *pol;
  KNOTVECTOR *knt;

  /* Allocate memory */

  Pw = S_getcpa(wx,wy,wz,w,n,S);
  if ( Pw == NULL ) return (1);
  pol = S_getpol(S);
  if ( pol == NULL ) return (1);
  knt = S_getknt(S);
  if ( knt == NULL ) return (1);

  /* Make pointer assignments */

  pol->n = n;
  pol->Pw = Pw;
  knt->m = m;
  knt->U = U;
  cur->pol = pol;
  cur->p = p;
  cur->knt = knt;

  /* Exit */

  return (0);
}
```

Notice how well the memory routines `S_getcpa()`, `S_getpol()`, and `S_getknt()` are integrated with this utility. No explicit allocation and deallocation is taking place, yet there is proper error handling through the global error flag `NERR`. This routine is also a good example illustrating how errors are handled in a higher level routine. If an error is detected in any of the three previous memory routines, `NERR` is set and control is returned. `U_makcu3` handles the error by returning the control one level higher. Since memory allocation is the problem in both the memory routines and in the utility routine, no new setting of the global `NERR` is required.

As a final example, let us consider a surface utility routine which creates a surface from control point and knot vector information.

```
#include "nurbs.h"

FLAG U_maksu2( SURFACE *sur, CPOINT **Pw, INDEX n, INDEX m,
               DEGREE p, DEGREE q, REAL *U, REAL *V, INDEX r,
               INDEX s, STACKS *S )
{
  CNET *net;
  KNOTVECTOR *knu, *knv;

  /* Allocate memory for control net */
  /* and knot vector structures */

  net = S_getnet(S);
  if ( net == NULL ) return(1);
  knu = S_getknt(S);
  if ( knu == NULL ) return(1);
  knv = S_getknt(S);
  if ( knv == NULL ) return(1);

  /* Make pointer assignments */

  net->n = n;
  net->m = m;
  net->Pw = Pw;
  knu->m = r;
  knu->U = U;
  knv->m = s;
  knv->U = V;
  sur->net = net;
  sur->p = p;
  sur->q = q;
  sur->knu = knu;
  sur->knv = knv;

  /* Exit */

  return (0);
}
```

13.7 Arithmetic Routines

Performing operations on NURBS curves and surfaces, e.g., evaluation or knot insertion, requires arithmetic operations on the control points. Since control points are considered as objects, special arithmetic routines are needed to perform such tasks as convex combination (corner cutting), summation, or projection to Euclidean space. Besides performing arithmetic on objects, these routines help to understand the programs and make it possible to port NURBS routines to different environments. For example, assume that a three-dimensional design system, based on rational curves and surfaces, is to be used as a two-dimensional drafting system employing only nonrational curves. Since the control point object is dimensionless, only its definition needs to be changed and a few arithmetic routines need to be modified. The rest of the system, which could contain millions of lines of code, remains unchanged.

We show a few examples of arithmetic routines used in *Nlib V2.0*. The first example is an initialization routine. Computing a point on a curve or surface calls for summation, which requires that the sum be initialized to zero.

```
#include "nurbs.h"

VOID A_initcp( CPOINT Aw, CPOINT *Bw )
{
  Bw->x = Aw.x;
  Bw->y = Aw.y;
  Bw->z = Aw.z;
  Bw->w = Aw.w;
}
```

This routine takes proper care of the different types of control points, rational or nonrational, two-dimensional or three-dimensional, through `Aw`'s third and fourth coordinates.

The next example is a routine that updates a given control point used again to compute a sum of blended control points.

```
#include "nurbs.h"

VOID A_updcpt( REAL alpha, CPOINT Aw, CPOINT *Bw )
{
  Bw->x = Bw->x + alpha*Aw.x;
  Bw->y = Bw->y + alpha*Aw.y;
  if ( Aw.z != _NOZ )
    Bw->z = Bw->z + alpha*Aw.z;
  else
    Bw->z = _NOZ;
  if ( Aw.w != _NOW )
    Bw->w = Bw->w + alpha*Aw.w;
  else
    Bw->w = _NOW;
}
```

As a final example we consider the projection routine, which maps a rational point to the Euclidean space.

```
#include "nurbs.h"

VOID A_euclid( CPOINT Pw, POINT *P )
{
  if ( Pw.w != _NOW )
  {
    P->x = Pw.x/Pw.w;
    P->y = Pw.y/Pw.w;
    if ( Pw.z != _NOZ )
      P->z = Pw.z/Pw.w;
    else
      P->z = 0.0;
  }
  else
  {
    P->x = Pw.x;
    P->y = Pw.y;
    if ( Pw.z != _NOZ )
      P->z = Pw.z;
  else
      P->z = 0.0;
  }
}
```

These routines are used in the next section to illustrate two NURBS routines, curve and surface evaluations.

13.8 Example Programs

In this section we present two complete programs, one for curve evaluation and the other for surface evaluation. These routines show the structure of NURBS programs and how the different utility routines are integrated with higher level NURBS routines. First consider the curve evaluator.

```
#include "nurbs.h"
static STRING rname = "N_EVNCUR";
extern CPOINT CZERO;

FLAG N_evncur( CURVE *cur, PARAMETER u, POINT *C )
{
  FLAG error = 0;
  INDEX i, j, k;
  DEGREE p;
  REAL *N;
  KNOTVECTOR *knt;
  CPOINT *Pw, Cw;
```

```
    STACKS S;

    /* Start NURBS environment */

    N_inurbs(&S);

    /* Get local notation */

    Pw = cur->pol->Pw;
    p = cur->p;
    knt = cur->knt;

    /* Check parameter */

    error = E_parval(knt,u,rname);
    if ( error == 1 ) goto EXIT;

    /* Compute non-vanishing B-splines */

    N = S_getr1d(p,&S);
    if ( N == NULL ) { error = 1; goto EXIT; }
    error = N_allbas(knt,p,u,LEFT,N,&j);
    if( error == 1 ) goto EXIT;

    /* Compute the point on the curve */

    A_initcp(CZERO,&Cw);
    for ( i=0; i<=p; i++ )
    {
      k = j-p+i;
      A_updcpt(N[i],Pw[k],&Cw);
    }
    A_euclid(Cw,C);

    /* End NURBS and exit */

    EXIT:

    N_enurbs(&S);
    return(error);
}
```

As mentioned earlier, each NURBS routine starts with `N_inurbs()`, which initializes the memory stacks to `NULL`. After initialization, local notations are normally introduced to help follow the computational details. The notation `Pw[k]` is visually more pleasing than `cur->pol->Pw[k]` and much closer to the customary notation, $\mathbf{P}_k^w$. The next step in almost every NURBS routine is to check the incoming parameters for possible error. `E_parval()` checks if the given parameter u is outside of the range $[u_0, u_m]$. The rest of the code deals with the actual computation of a curve point. To do so, the nonvanishing basis functions are computed first after the proper amount of memory is allocated to store them (since there is no limit on the degree, the memory must be dynamically allocated). Arithmetic routines, discussed in the previous section, are then used to compute the sum

$$\mathbf{C}^w(u) = \sum_{k=j-p}^{j} N_{k,p}(u)\mathbf{P}_k^w$$

and to locate the point in the Euclidean space; note the index transformation to use the proper basis functions. Finally, `N_enurbs()` deallocates all allocated memory, and control is returned to the calling routine by returning either zero (no error) or one (error saved in NERR).

This next test program shows how easy it is to compute a point on the curve.

```
#include "nurbs.h"
#include "globals.h"

REAL wx[6]  = { 0.2, 0.8, 0.4, 1.2, 1.2, 0.8 };
REAL wy[6]  = { 0.2, 0.4, 0.4, 0.8, 0.4, 0.2 };
REAL wz[6]  = { 0.2, 0.4, 0.2, 0.4, 0.4, 0.2 };
REAL w[6]  = { 1.0, 2.0, 1.0, 2.0, 2.0, 1.0 };
REAL U[10]  = { 0.0, 0.0, 0.0, 0.0, 0.3, 0.7, 1.0, 1.0, 1.0,
                1.0 };

main( )
{
  FLAG error;
  CURVE cur;
  PARAMETER u;
  POINT C;
  STACKS S;

  /* Start processing */

  N_inurbs(&S);

  /* Create the curve */

  U_makcu3(&cur,wx,wy,wz,w,5,3,U,9,&S);

  /* Compute a point on the curve */

  printf( "Enter parameter u = " ); scanf( "%lf", &u );
  error = N_evncur(&cur,u,&C);
  if ( error > 0 )
  {
    printf( "error = %d %s", NERR.eno, NERR.fna );
    goto EXIT;
```

```
  }
  printf( "C = %lf %lf %lf", C.x, C.y, C.z );

  /* End NURBS session */

  EXIT:

  N_enurbs(&S);
}
```

The many utility routines allow the programmer to define a curve in a number of different ways, e.g., reading in a curve file, receiving the (wx, wy, wz, w) coordinates from a curve sketching interface, and so on.

The structure of surface programs is very similar to the curve programs. This next surface evaluator shows an example.

```
#include "nurbs.h"
static STRING rname = "N_EVNSUR";
extern CPOINT CZERO;

FLAG N_evnsur( SURFACE *sur, PARAMETER u, PARAMETER v,
               POINT *S )
{
  FLAG error = 0;
  INDEX i, j, k, l, ju, jv;
  DEGREE p, q;
  REAL *NU, *NV;
  KNOTVECTOR *knu, *knv;
  CPOINT **Pw, *Tw, Sw;
  STACKS ST;

  /* Start NURBS environment */

  N_inurbs(&ST);

  /* Get local notation */

  Pw = sur->net->Pw;
  p = sur->p;
  q = sur->q;
  knu = sur->knu;
  knv = sur->knv;

  /* Check parameters */

  error = E_parval(knu,u,rname);
  if ( error == 1 ) goto EXIT;
  error = E_parval(knv,v,rname);
```

```
    if ( error == 1 ) goto EXIT;

    /* Compute nonvanishing B-splines */

    NU = S_getr1d(p,&ST);
    if ( NU == NULL ) { error = 1; goto EXIT; }
    NV = S_getr1d(q,&ST);
    if ( NV == NULL ) { error = 1; goto EXIT; }
    error = N_allbas(knu,p,u,LEFT,NU,&ju);
    if ( error == 1 ) goto EXIT;
    error = N_allbas(knv,q,v,LEFT,NV,&jv);
    if ( error == 1 ) goto EXIT;

    /* Compute the point on the surface */

    Tw = S_getc1d(p,&ST);
    if ( Tw == NULL ) { error = 1; goto EXIT; }
    for ( i=0; i<=p; i++ )
    {
      A_initcp(CZERO,&Tw[i]);
      k = ju-p+i;
      for ( j=0; j<=q; j++ )
      {
        l = jv-q+j;
        A_updcpt(NV[j],Pw[k][l],&Tw[i]);
      }
    }

    A_initcp(CZERO,&Sw);
    for ( i=0; i<=p; i++ )
    {
      A_updcpt(NU[i],Tw[i],&Sw);
    }
    A_euclid(Sw,S);

    /* End NURBS and exit */

    EXIT:

    N_enurbs(&ST);
    return(error);
  }
```

The next test program shows another way to create a surface and to evaluate a point on it. The routine `U_inpsur()` reads in a data file, named `SURFACE.DAT`, containing the control polygon and knot vector information. `U_inisur()` is a routine that initializes the surface object to the `NULL` object to let `U_inpsur()` know that memory allocation is required.

```
#include "nurbs.h"
#include "globals.h"

main( )
{
  FLAG error;
  SURFACE sur;
  PARAMETER u, v;
  POINT S;
  STACKS ST;

  /* Start processing */

  N_inurbs(&ST);

  /* Read in surface data */

  U_inisur(&sur);
  error = U_inpsur(&sur,"SURFACE.DAT",&ST);
  if ( error > 0 )
  {
    printf( "error = %d %s", NERR.eno, NERR.fna );
    goto EXIT;
  }

  /* Compute surface point */

  printf( "Enter parameters <u,v> = " ); scanf( "%lf%lf", &u, &v );
  error = N_evnsur(&sur,u,v,&S);
  if ( error > 0 )
  {
    printf( "error = %d %s", NERR.eno, NERR.fna );
    goto EXIT;
  }
  printf( "S = %lf %lf %lf", S.x, S.y, S.z );

  /* End NURBS session */

  EXIT:

  N_enurbs(&ST);
}
```

13.9 Additional Structures

In order for the NURBS library to be useful for a large variety of purposes, some additional structures (objects) are required. These structures are mostly used to convert from the NURBS form to other forms, to reparametrize a NURBS entity, and so on.

A simple modification of the NURBS curve and surface objects results in scalar-valued univariate and bivariate B-spline functions. The only change one has to make is to replace the control polygon and control net objects with curve values and surface values defined as:

```
typedef struct cvalue
{
  INDEX n;
  REAL *fu;
} CVALUE;

typedef struct svalue
{
  INDEX n,
        m;
  REAL **fuv;
} SVALUE;
```

Special routines, for example function evaluation and knot insertion, can be written that deal with functions that are used mostly for functional compositions (see Section 6.4).

Vector valued polynomials play an important role in data exchange and in form conversion. *Nlib V2.0* has curve and surface polynomial entities to be able to convert from the NURBS form to piecewise polynomial form, and back. These are defined as:

```
typedef struct cpoly
{
  CVECTOR *cve;
  DEGREE p;
  INTERVAL I;
} CPOLY;

typedef struct spoly
{
  SVECTOR *sve;
  DEGREE p,
         q;
  RECTANGLE R;
} SPOLY;
```

where the curve vector `CVECTOR` and surface vector `SVECTOR` entities are defined just as the control polygon and control net objects. The interval and rectangle objects are simply

```
typedef struct interval
{
  PARAMETER ul,
            ur;
} INTERVAL;
```

```
typedef struct rectangle
{
  PARAMETER ul,
            ur,
            vb,
            vt,
} RECTANGLE;
```

That is, polynomials are defined by their vector coefficients and the one- and two-dimensional interval/rectangle to which the polynomial is restricted.

Bézier curves and surfaces play an important role in any NURBS-based system, not because they are special cases of NURBS but rather because many operations can be performed very efficiently on the individual Bézier components. For this reason, two special structures are introduced, one for curves and one for surfaces.

```
typedef struct bcurve
{
  CPOLYGON *pol;
  INTERVAL I;
} BCURVE;

typedef struct bsurface
{
  CNET *net;
  RECTANGLE R;
} BSURFACE;
```

Thus the control polygon/net and the parameter interval/rectangle uniquely define a Bézier curve/surface.

In closing, we present a few additional objects used mainly in simple geometric computations and in some mathematical routines. *Nlib V2.0* has extensive geometry and mathematics libraries used to support various NURBS operations. First we consider some geometric objects.

```
typedef struct vector
{
  REAL x,
       y,
       z;
} VECTOR;

typedef struct line
{
  POINT P;
  VECTOR V;
  FLAG bounded;
} LINE;
```

```
typedef struct plane
{
  POINT P;
  VECTOR N;
} PLANE;

typedef struct circle
{
  POINT C;
  REAL r;
  VECTOR N;
} CIRCLE;
```

Although the POINT and the VECTOR structures contain the same structure elements they are conceptually different, hence their introductions. A last example is the matrix object that represents real matrices.

```
typedef struct rmatrix
{
  INDEX n,
        m;
  REAL **RM;
  MATRIXTYPE mtp;
  INDEX bandwidth;
} RMATRIX;
```

where MATRIXTYPE is defined as follows:

```
typedef enum
{
  full,
  lowerleft,
  upperright,
  banded
} MATRIXTYPE;
```

Similar structures are available for integer (IMATRIX), point (PMATRIX), and control point (CMATRIX) matrices. Row and column *vectors* are considered as $(1 \times m)$ and $(n \times 1)$ matrices, respectively. No special vector structure is introduced.

13.10 System Structure

Nlib V2.0 has the following routines as parts of a complex structure:

- NURBS routines (N_*.c);
- Bézier routines (B_*.c);
- geometry routines (G_*.c);

- mathematics routines (`M_*.c`);
- utility routines (`U_*.c`);
- memory allocation routines (`S_*.c`);
- error handling routines (`E_*.c`);
- arithmetic routines (`A_*.c`).

These routines must be integrated into a complex system that satisfies all the requirements mentioned in the previous sections. The dependence relationship of each module is shown in Figure 13.9. The different layers represent individual modules, and the arrows illustrate their dependence on lower level routines, i.e., they make calls to these routines. In the center there are three modules, memory allocation, error handling, and arithmetic routines. Although these are somewhat dependent on one another, e.g., error routines might need some memory, and memory routines have to report errors, their dependence is not as substantial as those in the upper layers. As we go to the second and higher layers, routines become dependent on all the lower layer programs. For example, mathematics routines need utility programs to create matrices; they need memory, error checking, and special arithmetic to perform matrix operations with matrices having control points as matrix elements. At the top there are the NURBS programs that make calls to every other program in the system. For instance, it is very

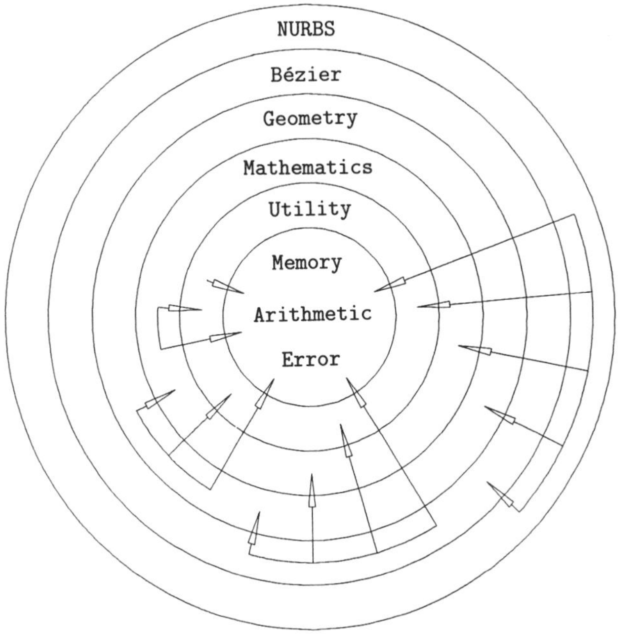

Figure 13.9. *Nlib V2.0*'s system structure.

rare that a geometry routine has to make a call to an existing NURBS program. If this happens to be the case, a special lower level routine can be written so that the correspondence among the layers remains unidirectional. This isolation of the different layers becomes important if parts of the system are to be used for purposes other than NURBS geometry. For example, the mathematics and geometry libraries should be stand-alone libraries so that they can be used for simple geometric and mathematical computations without worrying about the much larger Bézier and NURBS libraries.

We close this section by restating our opinion on system design: it is very difficult, it is not unique, and it is changing as computer technology advances. However, designing and implementing a system is enlightening and essential in obtaining a broad and deep knowledge of NURBS technology. As Herbert B. Voelcker puts it [Pieg93]

> "It is important to do both theoretical research and experimental system building. They are synergistic, and the exclusive pursuit of either can lead to sterile theory or quirky, opaque systems."

This book is intended to provide both the theory and the implementation of NURBS. Let the reader judge whether this goal has been successfully met.

REFERENCES

[Ahuj68] Ahuja, D.V., and Coons, S.A., Geometry for construction and display, *IBM Syst. Jour.*, Nos. 3–4, pp. 188–205, 1968.

[Akim70] Akima, H., A new method of interpolation and smooth curve fitting based on local procedures, *Jour. ACM*, Vol. 17, pp. 589–602, 1970.

[Akma92] Akman, V., and Arslan, A., Sweeping with all graphical ingredients in a topological picturebook, *Comput. and Graph.*, Vol. 16, No. 3, pp. 273–281, 1992.

[Ball74] Ball, A., CONSURF. Part 1: Introduction to the conic lofting tile, *CAD*, Vol. 6, No. 4, pp. 243–249, 1974.

[Ball75] Ball, A., CONSURF. Part 2: Description of the algorithms, *CAD*, Vol. 7, No. 4, pp. 237–242, 1975.

[Ball77] Ball, A., CONSURF. Part 3: How the program is used, *CAD*, Vol. 9, No. 1, pp. 9–12, 1977.

[Baly94] Ballay, H., and Storn, R., A tool for checking C coding conventions, *C/C++ Users Journal*, Vol. 12, No. 27, pp. 41–50, 1994.

[Barn93] Barnhill, R., Coons' patches and convex combinations, in [Pieg93].

[Barr83] Barr, A.H., *Global and local deformations of solid primitives*, SIGGRAPH 83 Tutorial Notes, Detroit, 1983.

[Bars89] Barsky, B.A., and DeRose, T.D., Geometric continuity of parametric curves: Three equivalent characterizations, *IEEE Comput. Graph. and Appl.*, Vol. 9, No. 6, pp. 60–68, 1989.

[Bars90] Barsky, B.A., and DeRose, T.D., Geometric continuity of parametric curves: Construction of geometrically continuous splines, *IEEE Comput. Graph. and Appl.*, Vol. 10, No. 1, pp. 60–68, 1990.

[Bart87] Bartels, R.H., Beatty, J.C., and Barsky, B.A., *An Introduction to Splines for Use in Computer Graphics and Geometric Modeling*, San Mateo, CA: Morgan Kaufmann, 1987.

[Beac91] Beach, R.C., *An Introduction to the Curves and Surfaces of Computer-Aided Design*, New York: Van Nostrand Reinhold, 1991.

[Bern12] Bernstein, S.N., Démonstration du théorème de Weierstrass fondée sûr le calcul dès probabilités, *Commun. Soc. Math. Khrakow*, Vol. 12, No. 2, pp. 1–2, 1912.

[Bezi72] Bézier, P.E., *Numerical Control: Mathematics and Applications*, New York: John Wiley, 1972.

[Bezi86] Bézier, P.E., *The Mathematical Basis of the UNISURF CAD System*, London: Butterworth, 1986.

[Blom91] Bloomenthal, M., and Riesenfeld, R.F., Approximation of sweep surfaces by tensor product NURBS, *Curves and Surfaces in Computer Vision and Graphics II*, *SPIE Proc.* (Society of Photo-Optical Instrumentation Engineers), Vol. 1610, pp. 132–144, 1991.

[Blor91] Bloor, M., and Owen, J., CAD/CAM product-data exchange: The next step, *CAD*, Vol. 23, No. 4, pp. 237–243, 1991.

[Boeh80] Boehm, W., Inserting new knots into B-spline curves, *CAD*, Vol. 12, No. 4, pp. 199–201, 1980.

[Boeh84] Boehm, W., Farin, G., and Kahmann, J., A survey of curve and surface methods in CAGD, *Comput. Aid. Geom. Des.*, Vol. 1, No. 1, pp. 1–60, 1984.

[Boeh85a] Boehm, W., and Prautzsch, H., The insertion algorithm, *CAD*, Vol. 17, No. 2, pp. 58–59, 1985.

[Boeh85b] Boehm, W., On the efficiency of knot insertion algorithms, *Comput. Aid. Geom. Des.*, Vol. 2, Nos. 1–3, pp. 141–143, 1985.

[Boeh91] Boehm, W., and Hansford, D., Bézier patches on quadrics, in *NURBS for Curve and Surface Design*, Farin, G., Ed., Philadelphia: SIAM, pp. 1–14, 1991.

[Boeh94] Boehm, W., and Prautzsch, H., *Geometric Concepts for Geometric Design*, Wellesley, MA: A.K. Peters, 1994.

[Bron92] Bronsvoort, W., and Waarts, J., A method for converting the surface of a generalized cylinder into a B-spline surface, *Comput. and Graph.*, Vol. 16, No. 2, pp. 175–178, 1992.

[Butt76] Butterfield, K.R., The computation of all the derivatives of a B-spline basis, *Jour. Inst. Math. Applic.*, Vol. 17, pp. 15–25, 1976.

[Chan81] Chang, G., and Wu, J., Mathematical foundations of Bézier's technique, *CAD*, Vol. 13, No. 3, pp. 133–136, 1981.

[Choi90] Choi, B.K., and Lee, C., Sweep surfaces modelling via coordinate transformations and blending, *CAD*, Vol. 22, No. 2, pp. 87–96, 1990.

[Choi91] Choi, B.K., *Surface Modeling for CAD/CAM*, New York: Elsevier, 1991.

[Chou92] Chou, J., and Piegl, L., Data reduction using cubic rational B-splines, *IEEE Comput. Graph. and Appl.*, Vol. 12, No. 3, pp. 60–68, 1992.

[Chou95] Chou, J.J., Higher order Bézier circles, *CAD*, to be published, 1995.

[Cobb84] Cobb, E.S., "Design of Sculptured Surfaces Using the B-spline Representation," Ph.D. dissertation, University of Utah, 1984.

[Cohe80] Cohen, E., Lyche, T., and Riesenfeld, R.F., Discrete B-splines and subdivision techniques in Computer-Aided Geometric Design and Computer Graphics, *Comput. Graph. and Image Process.*, Vol. 14, pp. 87–111, 1980.

[Cohe85] Cohen, E., Lyche, T., and Schumaker, L.L., Algorithms for degree-raising of splines, *ACM TOG*, Vol. 4, No. 3, pp. 171–181, 1985.

[Coon67] Coons, S.A., Surfaces for computer-aided design of space forms, MAC-TR-41, MIT, June 1967.

[Coqu87a] Coquillart, S., A control-point-based sweeping technique, *IEEE Comput. Graph. and Appl.*, Vol. 7, No. 11, pp. 36–45, 1987.

[Coqu87b] Coquillart, S., Computing offsets of B-spline curves, *CAD*, Vol. 19, No. 6, pp. 305–309, 1987.

[Coqu90] Coquillart, S., Extended free-form deformation: A sculpturing tool for 3D geometric modeling, *Comput. Graph.*, Vol. 24, No. 4, pp. 187–193, 1990.

[Coqu91] Coquillart, S., and Jancene, P., Animated free-form deformation: An interactive animation technique, *Comput. Graph.*, Vol. 25, No. 4, pp. 23–26, 1991.

[Cox72] Cox, M.G., The numerical evaluation of B-splines, *Jour. Inst. Math. Applic.*, Vol. 10, pp. 134–149, 1972.

[Coxe67] Coxeter, H.S.M., and Greitzer, S.L., *Geometry Revisited*, Washington, DC: Mathematical Association of America, 1967.

[Coxe74] Coxeter, H.S.M., *Projective Geometry*, Toronto, Canada: Univ. of Toronto Press, 1974.

[Coxe80] Coxeter, H.S.M., *Introduction to Geometry*, New York: John Wiley, 1980.

[Curr47] Curry, H.B., and Schoenberg, I.J., On spline distributions and their limits: the Pólya distribution functions, Abstract 380t, *Bull. Amer. Math. Soc.*, Vol. 53, p. 109, 1947.

[Dani89] Daniel, M., and Daubisse, J.C., The numerical problem of using Bézier curves and surfaces in the power basis, *Comput. Aid. Geom. Des.*, Vol. 6, pp. 121–128, 1989.

[Dann85] Dannenberg, L., and Nowacki, H., Approximate conversion of surface representations with polynomial bases, *Comput. Aid. Geom. Des.*, Vol. 2, pp. 123–132, 1985.

[DeBo72] De Boor, C., On calculating with B-splines, *Jour. Approx. Theory*, Vol. 6, pp. 50–62, 1972.

[DeBo78] De Boor, C., *A Practical Guide to Splines*, New York: Springer-Verlag, 1978.

[DeBo87] De Boor, C., Cutting corners always works, *Comput. Aid. Geom. Des.*, Vol. 4, Nos.1–2, pp. 125–131, 1987.

[DeBo93] De Boor, C., B(asic)-spline basics, in [Pieg93].

[deCa86] de Casteljau, P., *Shape Mathematics and CAD*, London: Kogan Page, 1986.

[deCa93] de Casteljau, P., Polar forms for curve and surface modeling as used at Citroën, in [Pieg93].

[deMo84] de Montaudouin, Y., and Tiller, W., The Cayley method in computer-aided geometric design, *Comput. Aid. Geom. Des.*, Vol. 1, No. 4, pp. 309-326, 1984.

[DoCa76] Do Carmo, M.P., *Differential Geometry of Curves and Surfaces*, Englewood Cliffs, NJ: Prentice-Hall, 1976.

[Eck93] Eck, M., Degree reduction of Bézier curves, *Comput. Aid. Geom. Des.*, Vol. 10, pp. 237–251, 1993.

[Fari83] Farin, G.E., Algorithms for rational Bézier curves, *CAD*, Vol. 15, No. 2, pp. 73–77, 1983.

[Fari89] Farin, G.E., Rational curves and surfaces, in *Mathematical Aspects in Computer Aided Geometric Design*, Lyche, T., and Schumaker, L.L., Eds., New York: Academic Press, 1989.

[Fari93] Farin, G.E., *Curves and Surfaces for Computer Aided Geometric Design – A Practical Guide*, 3rd ed., Boston: Academic Press, 1993.

[Faro86] Farouki, R., The approximation of non-degenerate offset surfaces, *Comput. Aid. Geom. Des.*, Vol. 3, pp. 15–43, 1986.

[Faro87] Farouki, R.T., and Rajan, V.T., On the numerical condition of polynomials in Bernstein form, *Comput. Aid. Geom. Des.*, Vol. 4, pp. 191–216, 1987.

[Faro88] Farouki, R.T., and Rajan, V.T., Algorithms for polynomials in Bernstein form, *Comput. Aid. Geom. Des.*, Vol. 5, pp. 1–26, 1988.

[Faux81] Faux, I.D., and Pratt, M.J., *Computational Geometry for Design and Manufacture*, Chichester, UK: Ellis Horwood Ltd., 1981.

[Ferg66] Ferguson, J.C., Form, characterized in a special class of parametrized curves, Report 3122-31, TRW Corporation, Redondo Beach, CA, 1966.

[Ferg67] Ferguson, J.C., Form, characterized in a special class of parametrized curves – II, Report 3122-3-237, TRW Corporation, Redondo Beach, CA, 1967.

[Ferg69] Ferguson, J.C., and Miller, K.L., Characterization of shape in a class of third degree algebraic curves, Report 5322-3-5, TRW Corporation, Redondo Beach, CA, 1969.

[Ferg93] Ferguson, J.C., F-methods for free-form curve and hypersurface definition, in [Pieg93].

[Fili89] Filip, D., and Ball, T., Procedurally representing lofted surfaces, *IEEE Comput. Graph. and Appl.*, Vol. 9, No. 6, pp. 27–33, 1989.

[Fole90] Foley, J., van Dam, A., Feiner, S., and Hughes, J., *Computer Graphics: Principles and Practice*, Reading, MA: Addison-Wesley, 1990.

[Forr68] Forrest, A.R., "Curves and Surfaces for Computer-Aided Design," Ph.D. dissertation, Cambridge University, Cambridge, UK, 1968.

[Forr70] Forrest, A.R., Shape classification of the non-rational twisted cubic curve in terms of Bézier polygons, CAD Group Document No. 52, Cambridge Univ., Cambridge, UK, 1970.

[Forr72] Forrest, A.R., Interactive interpolation and approximation by Bézier polynomials, *The Comput. Jour.*, Vol. 15, No. 1, pp. 71–79, 1972. Corrected and updated version in *CAD*, Vol. 22, No. 9, pp. 527–537, 1990.

[Forr80] Forrest, A.R., The twisted cubic curve: A computer-aided geometric design approach, *CAD*, Vol. 12, No. 2, pp. 165–172, 1980.

[Fors88] Forsey, D., and Bartels, R., Hierarchical B-spline refinement, *Comput. Graph.*, Vol. 22, No. 4, pp. 205–212, 1988.

[Four83] Fournier, A., and Wesley, M., Bending polyhedral objects, *CAD*, Vol.15, No. 2, pp. 79–87, 1983.

[Fowl92] Fowler, B., Geometric manipulation of tensor product surfaces, Special Issue of *Comput. Graph.*, Symposium on Interactive 3D Graphics, pp. 101–108, 1992.

[Fowl93] Fowler, B., and Bartels, R., Constraint-based curve manipulation, *IEEE Comput. Graph. and Appl.*, Vol. 13, No. 5, pp. 43–49, 1993.

[Fuhr92] Fuhr, R.D., and Kallay, M., Monotone linear rational spline interpolation, *Comput. Aid. Geom. Des.*, Vol. 9, No. 4, pp. 313–319, 1992.

[Geis90] Geise, G., and Langbecker, U., Finite quadratic segments with four conic boundary curves, *Comput. Aid. Geom. Des.*, Vol. 7, pp. 141–150, 1990.

[Good81] Goodman, T., Hermite-Birkhoff interpolation by Hermite-Birkhoff splines, *Proc. Roy. Soc. Edinburgh*, Vol. 88(A), Parts 3/4, pp. 195–201, 1981.

[Gord69] Gordon, W., Spline-blended surface interpolation through curve networks, *Jour. Math. Mech.*, Vol. 18, No. 10, pp. 931–952, 1969.

[Gord71] Gordon, W., Blending-function methods of bivariate and multivariate interpolation and approximation, *SIAM Jour. Numer. Anal.*, Vol. 8, pp. 158–177, 1971.

[Gord74a] Gordon, W.J., and Riesenfeld, R.F., Bernstein-Bézier methods for the computer-aided design of free-form curves and surfaces, *Jour. Assoc. Computing Mach.*, Vol. 21, No. 2, pp. 293–310, 1974.

[Gord74b] Gordon, W.J., and Riesenfeld, R.F., B-spline curves and surfaces, in *Computer Aided Geometric Design*, Barnhill, R.E., and Riesenfeld, R.F., Eds., New York: Academic Press, 1974.

[Gord93] Gordon, W., Sculptured surface definition via blending function methods, in [Pieg93].

[Gugg89] Guggenheimer, H., Computing frames along a trajectory, *Comput. Aid. Geom. Des.*, Vol. 6, pp. 77–78, 1989.

[Hoff89] Hoffmann, C.M., *Geometric & Solid Modeling*, San Mateo, CA: Morgan Kaufmann, 1989.

[Hohm91] Hohmeyer, M. and Barsky, B., Skinning rational B-spline curves to construct an interpolatory surface, *Comput. Vis., Graph. and Image Processing: Graphical Models and Image Processing*, Vol. 53, No. 6, pp. 511–521, 1991.

[Hosc88] Hoschek, J., Spline approximation of offset curves, *Comput. Aid. Geom. Des.*, Vol. 5, pp. 33–40, 1988.

[Hosc92a] Hoschek, J., Bézier curves and surface patches on quadrics, in *Mathematical Methods in Computer Aided Geometric Design II*, Lyche, T., and Schumaker, L., Eds., New York: Academic Press, pp. 331–342, 1992.

[Hosc92b] Hoschek, J., Circular splines, *CAD*, Vol. 24, No. 11, pp. 611-618, 1992.

[Hosc93] Hoschek, J., and Lasser, D., *Fundamentals of Computer Aided Geometric Design*, Wellesley, MA: A.K. Peters, Ltd., 1993.

[Howa91a] Howard, T., Evaluating PHIGS for CAD and general graphics applications, *CAD*, Vol. 23, No. 4, pp. 244–251, 1991.

[Howa91b] Howard, T.L.J., Hewitt, W.T., Hubbold, R.J., and Wyrwas, K.M., *A Practical Introduction to PHIGS and PHIGS PLUS*, Reading, MA: Addison-Wesley, 1991.

[Hsu92] Hsu, W., Hughes, J., and Kaufman, H., Direct manipulation of free-form deformations, *Comput. Graph.*, Vol. 26, No. 2, pp. 177–184, 1992.

[IGE93] The Initial Graphics Exchange Specification (IGES) Version 5.2, ANSI Y14.26M, available from U.S. Product Data Association (US PRO), Fairfax, VA, USA, 1993.

[Ilyi84] Ilyin, V.A., and Poznyak, E.G., *Analytic Geometry*, Moscow: Mir Publishers, 1984.

[Kapl52] Kaplan, W., *Advanced Calculus*, Reading, MA: Addison Wesley, 1952.

[Klok86] Klok, F., Two moving coordinate frames for sweeping along a 3D trajectory, *Comput. Aid. Geom. Des.*, Vol. 3, pp. 217–229, 1986.

[Knut73] Knuth, D.E., *The Art of Computer Programming.* Vol. 1, *Fundamental Algorithms*, Reading, MA: Addison-Wesley, 1973.

[Lach88] Lachance, M.A., Chebyshev economization for parametric surfaces, *Comput. Aid. Geom. Des.*, Vol. 5, pp. 195–208, 1988.

[Lanc86] Lancaster, P., and Salkauskas, K., *Curve and Surface Fitting*, New York: Academic Press, 1986.

[Lane80] Lane, J.M., and Riesenfeld, R.F., A theoretical development for the computer generation and display of piecewise polynomial surfaces, *IEEE Trans. Patt. Anal. Mach. Intell.*, Vol. PAMI-2, No. 1, pp. 35–46, 1980.

[Lane83] Lane, J.M., and Riesenfeld, R.F., A geometric proof for the variation diminishing property of B-spline approximation, *Jour. Approx. Theory*, Vol. 37, pp. 1–4, 1983.

[Laur93] Laurent-Gengoux, P., and Mekhilef, M., Optimization of a NURBS representation, *CAD*, Vol. 25, No. 11, pp. 699–710, 1993.

[Lawr72] Lawrence, J.D., *A Catalog of Special Plane Curves*, New York: Dover, 1972.

[Lee83] Lee, E.T.Y., *B-spline Primer*, Boeing Document, 1983.

[Lee87] Lee, E.T.Y., Rational quadratic Bézier representation for conics, in *Geometric Modeling: Algorithms and New Trends*, Farin, G.E., Ed., Philadelphia: SIAM, pp. 3–19, 1987.

[Lee89] Lee, E.T.Y., Choosing nodes in parametric curve interpolation, *CAD*, Vol. 21, pp. 363–370, 1989.

[Lee91] Lee, E.T.Y., and Lucian, M.L., Möbius reparametrization of rational B-splines, *Comput. Aid. Geom. Des.*, Vol. 8, pp. 213–215, 1991.

[Limi44] Liming, R.A., *Practical Analytic Geometry with Applications to Aircraft*, New York: Macmillan, 1944.

[Limi79] Liming, R.A., *Mathematics for Computer Graphics*, Fallbrook, CA: Aero Publishers Inc., 1979.

[Lin94] Lin, F., and Hewitt, W., Expressing Coons-Gordon surfaces as NURBS, *CAD*, Vol. 26, No. 2, pp. 145–155, 1994.

[Lore86] Lorentz, G.G., *Berntein Polynomials*, New York: Chelsea Publishing Co., 1986.

[Lych85] Lyche, T., Cohen, E., and Morken, K., Knot line refinement algorithms for tensor product splines, *Comput. Aid. Geom. Des.*, Vol. 2, Nos.1–3, pp. 133–139, 1985.

[Lych87] Lyche, T., and Morken, K., Knot removal for parametric B-spline curves and surfaces, *Comput. Aid. Geom. Des.*, Vol. 4, pp. 217–230, 1987.

[Lych88] Lyche, T., and Morken, K., A data reduction strategy for splines with applications to the approximation of functions and data, *IMA Jour. Num. Anal.*, Vol. 8, pp. 185-208, 1988.

[Mats92] Matsuki, N., An interactive shape modification method for B-spline surfaces, in *Human Aspects in Computer Integrated Manufacturing*, Olling, G., and Kimura, F., Eds., Amsterdam: Elsevier Science Publishers B.V. (North-Holland) (IFIP), pp. 385–397, 1992.

[Mort85] Mortenson, M.E., *Geometric Modeling*, New York: John Wiley, 1985.

[Patt85] Patterson, R.R., Projective transformations of the parameter of a Bernstein-Bézier curve, *ACM TOG*, Vol. 4, No. 4, pp. 276–290, 1985.

[Pieg86] Piegl, L., A geometric investigation of the rational Bézier scheme of Computer Aided Design, *Comput. in Industry*, Vol. 7, pp. 401–410, 1986.

[Pieg87a] Piegl, L., and Tiller, W., Curve and surface constructions using rational B-splines, *CAD*, Vol. 19, No. 9, pp. 485–498, 1987.

[Pieg87b] Piegl, L., A technique for smoothing scattered data with conic sections, *Comput. in Industry*, Vol. 9, pp. 223–237, 1987.

[Pieg87c] Piegl, L., On the use of infinite control points in CAGD, *Comput. Aid. Geom. Des.*, Vol. 4, pp. 155–166, 1987.

[Pieg87d] Piegl, L., Interactive data interpolation by rational Bézier curves, *IEEE Comput. Graph. and Appl.*, Vol. 7, No. 4, pp. 45–58, 1987.

[Pieg88a] Piegl, L., Hermite- and Coons-like interpolants using rational Bézier approximation form with infinite control points, *CAD*, Vol. 20, No. 1, pp. 2–10, 1988.

[Pieg88b] Piegl, L., Coons-type patches, *Comput. and Graph.*, Vol. 12, No. 2, pp. 221–228, 1988.

[Pieg89a] Piegl, L., Key developments in computer-aided geometric design, *CAD*, Vol. 21, No. 5, pp. 262–273, 1989.

[Pieg89b] Piegl, L., and Tiller, W., A menagerie of rational B-spline circles, *IEEE Comput. Graph. and Appl.*, Vol. 9, No. 5, pp. 48–56, 1989.

[Pieg89c] Piegl, L., Modifying the shape of rational B-splines. Part 1: curves, *CAD*, Vol. 21, No. 8, pp. 509–518, 1989.

[Pieg89d] Piegl, L., Modifying the shape of rational B-splines. Part 2: surfaces, *CAD*, Vol. 21, No. 9, pp. 538–546, 1989.

[Pieg90] Piegl, L., Algorithms for computing conic splines, *Jour. Comput. in Civil Engrng.*, Vol. 4, No. 3, pp. 180–197, 1990.

[Pieg91a] Piegl, L., On NURBS: A Survey, *IEEE Comput. Graph. and Appl.*, Vol. 10, No. 1, pp. 55–71, 1991.

[Pieg91b] Piegl, L., and Tiller, W., Storage efficient decomposition of B-spline curves, CSE 91-01, Department of Computer Science and Engineering, Univ. of South Florida, Tampa, FL, 1991.

[Pieg93] Piegl, L., Ed., *Fundamental Developments of Computer Aided Geometric Modeling*, London: Academic Press, 1993.

[Pieg94] Piegl, L., and Tiller, W., Software engineering approach to degree elevation of B-spline curves, *CAD*, Vol. 26, No. 1, pp. 17–28, 1994.

[Pieg95] Piegl, L., and Tiller, W., Algorithm for degree reduction of B-spline curves, *CAD*, Vol. 27, No. 2, 1995.

[Prau84] Prautzsch, H., Degree elevation of B-spline curves, *Comput. Aid. Geom. Des.*, Vol. 1, No. 1, pp. 193–198, 1984.

[Prau91] Prautzsch, H., and Piper, B., A fast algorithm to raise the degree of spline curves, *Comput. Aid. Geom. Des.*, Vol. 8, pp. 253–265, 1991.

[Prau92] Prautzsch, H., and Gallagher, T., Is there a geometric variation diminishing property for B-spline or Bézier surfaces?, *Comput. Aid. Geom. Des.*, Vol. 9, No. 2, pp. 119–124, 1992.

[Pres88] Press, W., Flannery, B., Teukolsky, S., and Vetterling, W., *Numerical Recipes in C*, Cambridge, UK: Cambridge University Press, 1988.

[PHIG92] Programmer's Hierarchical Interactive Graphics System (PHIGS), ISO/IEC 9592-4: (1992), available from National Institute of Standards and Technology (NIST), Gaithersburg, MD, USA.

[Rams87] Ramshaw, L., Blossoming: A connect-the-dots approach to splines, Report 19, Digital, Systems Research Center, Palo Alto, CA, 1987.

[Renn82] Renner, G., A method of shape description for mechanical engineering practice, *Comput. in Ind.*, Vol. 3, pp. 137–142, 1982.

[Ries73] Riesenfeld, R.F., "Applications of B-spline Approximation to Geometric Problems of Computer-Aided Design," Ph.D. dissertation, Syracuse Univ., 1973.

[Ries81] Riesenfeld, R.F., Homogeneous coordinates and projective planes in computer graphics, *IEEE Comput. Graph. and Appl.*, Vol. 1, No. 1, pp. 50–55, 1981.

[Robe65] Roberts, L.G., Homogeneous matrix representation and manipulation of n-dimensional constructs, Technical Report MS-1405, Lincoln Laboratory, MIT, Cambridge, MA, 1965.

[Roge90] Rogers, D.F., and Adams, J.A., *Mathematical Elements for Computer Graphics*, 2nd ed., New York: McGraw-Hill, 1990.

[Salm79] Salmon, G., *A Treatise on Conic Sections*, Longman, Green & Co., 6th Edition, London, 1879, Reprinted by Dover Pub., New York.

[Scho46] Schoenberg, I.J., Contributions to the problem of approximation of equidistant data by analytic functions, *Quart. Appl. Math.*, Vol. 4, pp. 45–99, 1946.

[Scho66] Schoenberg, I.J., On Hermite-Birkhoff interpolation, *Jour. Math. Analysis and Applic.*, Vol. 16, No. 3, pp. 538–543, 1966.

[Sede84] Sederberg, T., Anderson, D., and Goldman, R., Implicit representation of parametric curves and surfaces, *Comput. Vis., Graph. and Image Process.*, Vol. 28, pp. 72–84, 1984.

[Sede86] Sederberg, T., and Parry, S., Free-form deformation of solid geometric objects, *Comput. Graph.*, Vol. 20, No. 4, pp. 151–160, 1986.

[Silt92] Siltanen, P., and Woodward, C., Normal orientation methods for 3D offset curves, sweep surfaces and skinning, *Proc. Eurographics 92*, Vol. 11, No. 3, pp. C-449–C-457, 1992.

[Smit71] Smith, L.B., Drawing ellipses, hyperbolas or parabolas with a fixed number of points and maximum inscribed area, *The Comput. Jour.*, Vol. 14, No. 1, pp. 81–86, 1971.

[Smit74] Smith, R., Price, J., and Howser, L., A smoothing algorithm using cubic spline functions, NASA Technical Note, TN D-7397, NASA Langley Research Center, Hampton, VA, 1974.

[STEP94] Standard for the Exchange of Product Model Data (STEP), ISO 10303, A series of documents. Part 42: *Geometric and Topological Representation*, ISO 10303-42, Available from ISO Secretariat, National Institute of Standards and Technology (NIST), Gaithersburg, MD, 1994.

[Ston89] Stone, M.C., and DeRose, T.C., A geometric characterization of parametric cubic curves, *ACM TOG*, Vol. 8, No. 3, pp. 147–163, 1989.

[Stra92] Straker, D., *C-style Standards and Guidelines*, New York: Prentice Hall, 1992.

[Stro91] Strotman, T., Private communication, 1991.

[Su89] Su, B., and Liu, D., *Computational Geometry – Curves and Surface Modeling*, Boston: Academic Press, 1989.

[Till83] Tiller, W., Rational B-splines for curve and surface representation, *IEEE Comput. Graph. and Appl.*, Vol. 3, No. 6, pp. 61–69, 1983.

[Till84] Tiller, W., and Hanson, E., Offsets of two-dimensional profiles, *IEEE Comput. Graph. and Appl.*, Vol. 4, No. 9, pp. 36–46, 1984.

[Till92] Tiller, W., Knot-removal algorithms for NURBS curves and surfaces, *CAD*, Vol. 24, No. 8, pp. 445–453, 1992.

[Vand83] Vandergraft, J., *Introduction to Numerical Computations*, New York: Academic Press, 1983.

[Verg91] Vergeest, J., CAD surface data exchange using STEP, *CAD*, Vol. 23, No. 4, pp. 269–281, 1991.

[Vers75] Versprille, K.J., "Computer-Aided Design Applications of the Rational B-spline Approximation Form," Ph.D. dissertation, Syracuse Univ., 1975.

[Wang81] Wang, C.Y., Shape classification of the parametric cubic curve and the parametric B-spline cubic curve, *CAD*, Vol. 13, No. 4, pp. 199–206, 1981.

[Watk88] Watkins, M.A., and Worsey, A.J., Degree reduction of Bézier curves, *CAD*, Vol. 20, No.7, pp. 398–405, 1988.

[Wein92] Weinstein, S.E., and Xu, Y., Degree reduction of Bézier curves by approximation and interpolation, in *Approximation Theory*, Anastassiou, G. A., Ed., New York: Dekker, 1992, pp. 503–512.

[Welc92] Welch, W., and Witkin, A., Variational surface modeling, *Comput. Graph.*, Vol. 26, No. 2, pp. 157–166, 1992.

[Wood87] Woodward, C., Cross-sectional design of B-spline surfaces, *Comput. and Graph.*, Vol. 11, No. 2, pp. 193–201, 1987.

[Wood88] Woodward, C., Skinning techniques for interactive B-spline surface interpolation, *CAD*, Vol. 20, No. 8, pp. 441–451, 1988.

[Yama88] Yamaguchi, F., *Curves and Surfaces in Computer Aided Geometric Design*, New York: Springer-Verlag, 1988.

Nlib Ordering Information

To purchase a copy of the latest version of *Nlib*, send your name, address, affiliation, telephone number, Fax number and/or e-mail address (as appropriate) to:

Dr. Wayne Tiller
GeomWare, Inc.
3036 Ridgetop Road
Tyler, TX 75703
Phone: (903) 839-5042
Fax: (903) 839-5042
E-mail: 76504.3045@CompuServe.com

Indicate your special need:

- Current price
- Software licensing
- Software maintenance
- Software enhancement

INDEX

Printing: Mercedesdruck, Berlin
Binding: Buchbinderei Lüderitz & Bauer, Berlin